CW01022966

The War in the North Sea

The Royal Navy and the Imperial German Navy 1914-1918

Quintin Barry

Helion & Company Limited

Helion & Company Limited
26 Willow Road
Solihull
West Midlands
B91 1UE
England
Tel. 0121 705 3393
Fax 0121 711 4075
Email: info@helion.co.uk
Website: www.helion.co.uk
Twitter: @helionbooks
Visit our blog http://blog.helion.co.uk/

Published by Helion & Company 2016
Designed and typeset by Mach 3 Solutions Ltd (www.mach3solutions.co.uk)
Cover designed by Paul Hewitt, Battlefield Design (www.battlefield-design.co.uk)
Printed by Gutenberg Press Limited, Tarxien, Malta

Front cover: Battleships at Target Practice in the Atlantic (William Wyllie).
Rear cover: HMS *Renown* (William Wyllie).

ISBN 978-1-911096-38-2

British Library Cataloguing-in-Publication Data.
A catalogue record for this book is available from the British Library.

For details of other military history titles published by Helion & Company Limited contact the above address, or visit our website: http://www.helion.co.uk.

We always welcome receiving book proposals from prospective authors.

Contents

List of Illustrations

Illustrations appear in plate sections

Personalities

Paintings

Other aspects

List of Maps

Acknowledgements

I should begin by recording the immense debt I owe to the work of the many historians that I have consulted in the writing of this book. In particular I must acknowledge my obligation to the work of the late Professor Arthur J Marder, the outstanding naval historian of the period. His monumental history of the Royal Navy before and during the First World War will never be surpassed for its insight and grasp of detail, even though the field seems likely to be a fertile ground for a long time to come, not least for the many controversies which it has generated. Even as I write these lines I am aware of a number of important works on the subject that are on the point of publication.

As always, I have been greatly encouraged and assisted by my publisher Duncan Rogers; I would like in particular to record my thanks for all his work in selecting the illustrations and also to Laurence Townsend for his help with these. I wish also to thank George Anderson for the charts and maps, specially commissioned for this book. I am very grateful to Tim Readman and Martin Allen, both of whom read the book in draft and made valuable suggestions. I should like to thank in particular, as always, Jean Hawkes and Liz Haywood, who typed the book from my execrable handwriting. I should also record my appreciation of Kim McSweeney's work on the typesetting. My thanks go also to the staff at the National Archives and the Caird Library at the National Maritime Museum for their help in locating texts.

- The quotation on page is reprinted by permission of Boydell and Brewer Ltd from *The British Naval Staff in the First World War by* Nicholas Black (Boydell Press, 2009) p 238.
- The quotations on pages are reprinted by permission of Mrs Judith Evans and Mrs Caroline Gay from *Room 40* by their father Patrick Beesly (Hamish Hamilton, 1982) pp 57, 161, 165, 285, 287 and 295.
- The quotations on pages are reprinted by permission of Oxford University Press from *From the Dreadnought to Scapa Flow* by Arthur J Marder (Oxford University Press, 1961-1970) volume 1 (pp 328-339, 405 and 427) Volume II (pp 14 and 425-426) volume III (pp 47, 149 and 204) volume IV (p 330) and volume V (pp, 79-80, 314 and 333n)
- The quotation on page is reprinted from *Captains and Cabinets,* by David F Trask, by permission of the University of Missouri Press. Copyright © 1972 by the Curators of the University of Missouri.

Part I

Before Jutland

1

British Strategic Planning

Of all the decisions which shaped the conduct of the naval war in the North Sea, by far the most important was that taken by the British Admiralty only a month before the outbreak of war. On July 3 1914 the war plans issued to the Grand Fleet restated the general policy on which they were based, but also introduced a fundamental change to the strategy to be pursued.

The basic policy was stated in terms which reflected its gradual evolution over a number of years:

> The general idea is primarily to ensure the destruction of the enemy's naval forces and obtain command of the North Sea and Channel with the object of preventing the enemy from making any serious attack upon British territory or trade or interfering with the transport of British troops to France should the situation necessitate their despatch. Until the primary object is attained, the continual movement in the North Sea of a fleet superior in all classes of vessels to that of the enemy will cut off German shipping from direct oceanic trade, and will as time passes inflict a steadily increasing degree of injury on German interests and credit sufficient to cause serious economic and social consequences. To prevent or counter this Germany may send a force into the North Sea sufficient not only to break up the Squadrons actually employed in watching the entrances, but also to offer a general action. Germany may also in combination with the above attempt raids upon our coasts by military disembarkations.[1]

What was significant about the new plans was that they finally gave up the notion of an observational blockade, which had been gradually introduced into Admiralty thinking between 1888 and 1904 in substitution for the policy of close blockade on which strategy had previously been loosely based. An observational blockade had involved the principle of patrolling a line from South West Norway to a point midway between Britain and Germany roughly level with Newcastle on Tyne, and then south to the Dutch coast. The Grand Fleet was to remain to the west of this line. Following the incorporation of this idea into the war plans, there arose serious misgivings about its efficacy. The line was nearly 300 miles long, and it was doubtful if it could really be watched effectively day and night, or that it could be properly supported if the Germans launched an attack, while it would require the employment of very many cruisers and destroyers required elsewhere.[2]

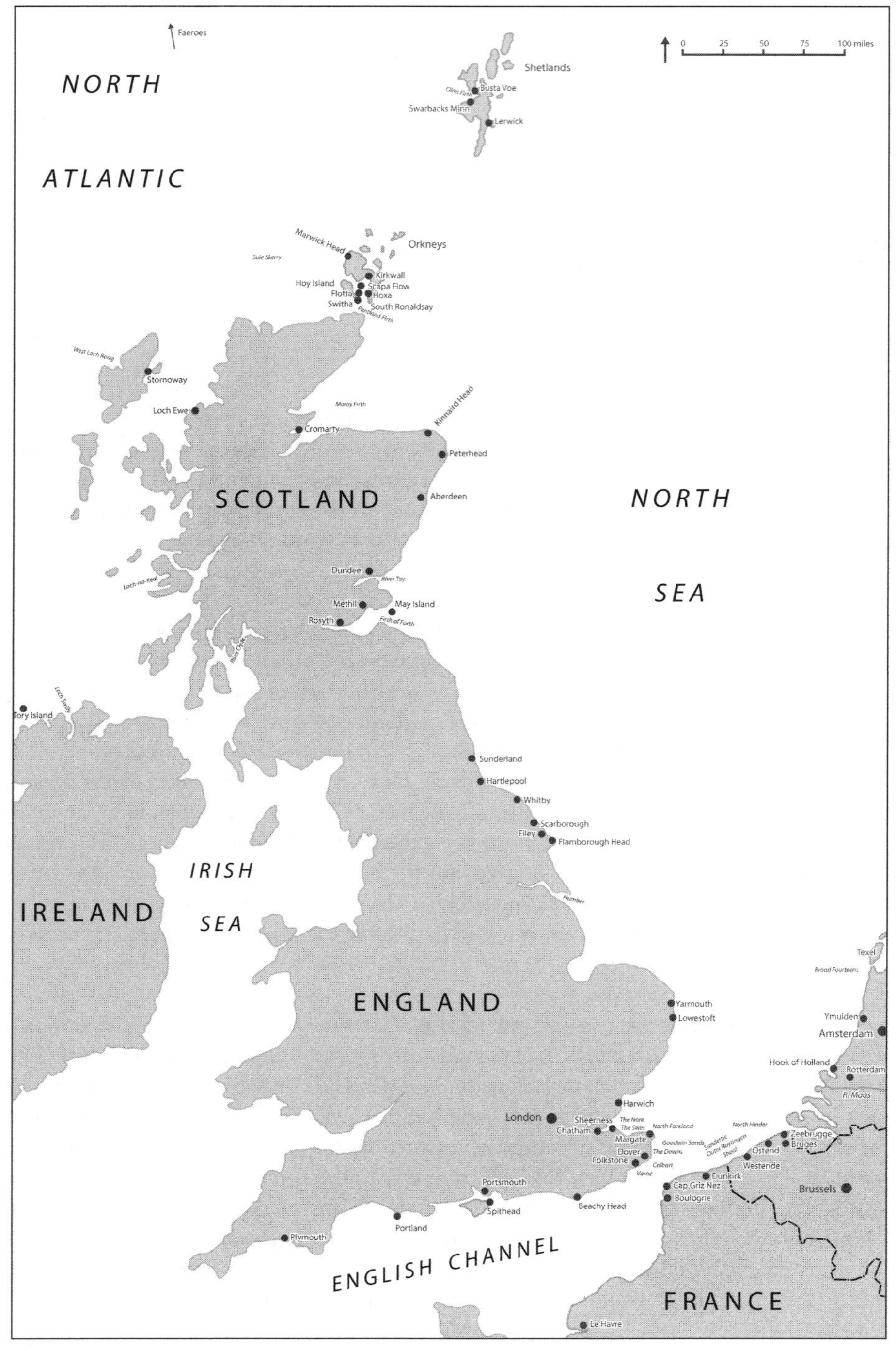

Map 1 North Sea (west).

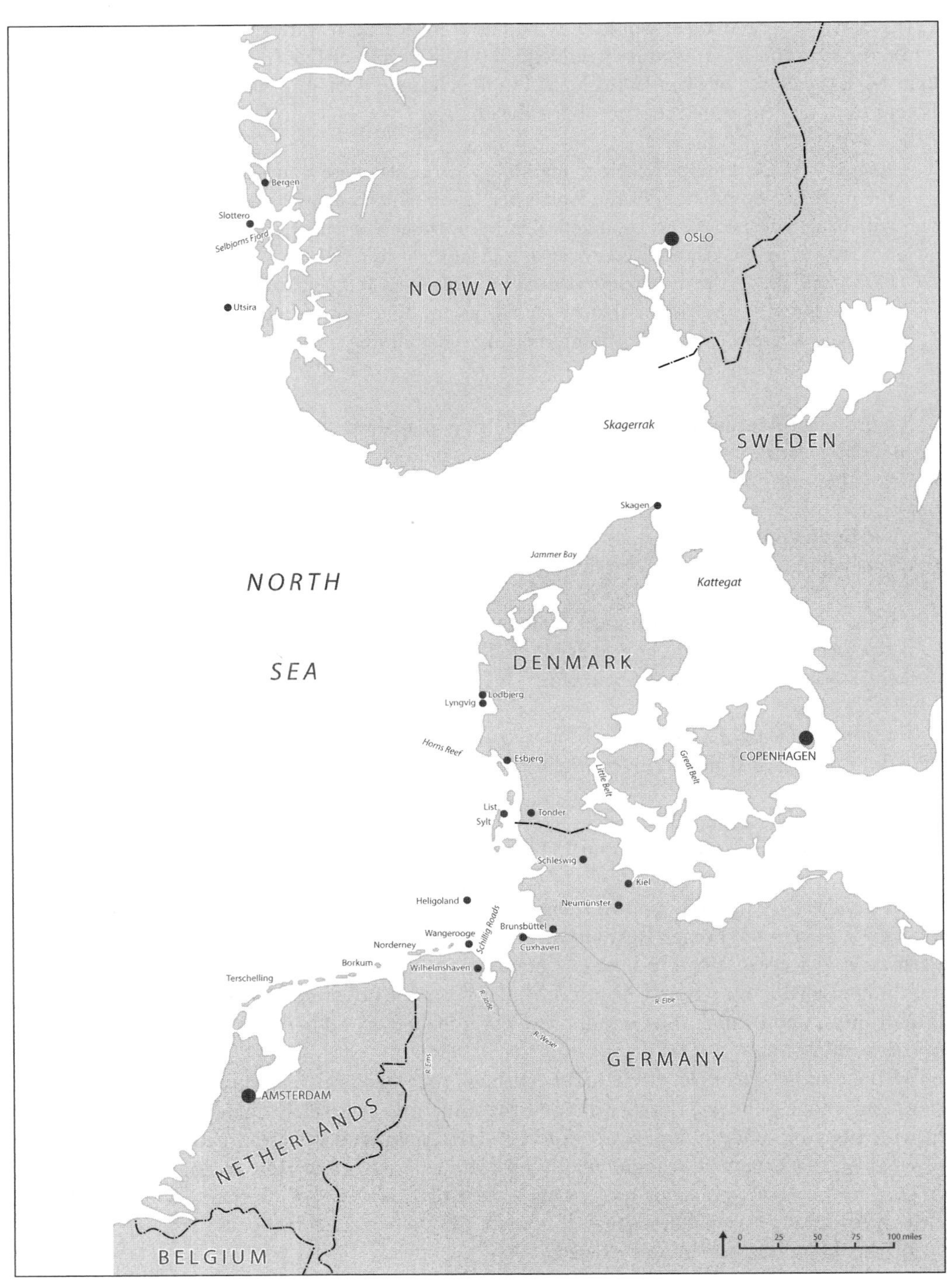

Map 2 North Sea (east).

Instead, the Grand Fleet would now be based in northern waters, probably at Scapa Flow, while the Channel Fleet would effectively close the Straits of Dover. In this way the only two exits from the North Sea would be blocked to the German fleet. The war plans set out the Grand Fleet's task, and explained the reason for the change:

> As it is at present impracticable to maintain a perpetual close watch off the enemy's ports, the maritime domination of the North Sea, upon which our whole policy must be based, will be established as far as practicable by occasional driving or sweeping movements carried out by the Grand Fleet traversing in superior force the area between the 54th and 58th parallels … The movements should be sufficiently frequent and sufficiently advanced to impress upon the enemy that he cannot at any time venture far from his home ports without such serious risk of encountering an overwhelming force that no enterprise is likely to reach its destination.[3]

As Professor Marder has pointed out, the new plans removed at a stroke one of the most significant means available to the Germans of gradually reducing British superiority by the attritional opportunities afforded by a blockade. The German Naval Staff had certainly worked out that the British would move away from the principle of a close blockade; but they still counted on the probability that a distant blockade and close blockade 'would alternate or merge frequently into one another as the situation changes':

> It is very probable that during the first days of the war, when attacks on our part may be expected, our waters will be closely blockaded … also when it is intended to transport the Expeditionary Force to the Continent.[4]

The consequences of a British decision to conduct only a distant blockade was remarked upon by Admiral August von Heeringen, the Chief of Admiralty Staff, when he observed in 1912:

> If the English have really adopted a wide blockade, then the role of our beautiful High Seas Fleet could be a very sad one. Our U-boats will have to do the job then![5]

The policy of trying to shut up an enemy in his ports went back a long way. In the Seven Years War, and again in the French Revolutionary and Napoleonic Wars, the British fleet maintained, with varying success, a blockade of key French naval bases. It was these operations more than anything else which prompted Admiral Mahan's famous observation: 'Those far distant, storm beaten ships, upon which the Grand Army never looked, stood between it and the domination of the world.'[6]

By the 1880s, of course, there had been huge technological developments. Steam propulsion, long range gunnery, the torpedo and the mine had completely changed the environment in which any blockade of any kind could be maintained, and it was argued by many that the concept of blockade had become wholly obsolete as a means of neutralising an enemy fleet. In fact, however, the policy of conducting a close blockade was not entirely abandoned by the British Admiralty as a viable strategy even after 1887, when naval manoeuvres began to demonstrate the difficulties which now existed.

In his brilliant and detailed analysis of the development of British strategy in the three decades before the outbreak of the First World War, Shawn T Grimes has pointed out that the evidence that close blockade was no longer considered feasible 'is not that definitive'.[7] The problems of maintaining a blockade were still being constantly examined in annual naval manoeuvres. In fact, what the Naval Intelligence Department, founded in 1887 and effectively for many years the centre of naval war planning, evolved was the principle of maintaining an observational blockade. This was to be based on the establishment of advanced flotilla bases, and would fulfil the Admiralty's primary objectives of defeating the enemy's fleet, preventing invasion and defending the trade routes. By 1896 this policy was seen as the primary means of meeting the threat posed by the French 'Jeune École' strategy of commerce raiding; later it was to be applied to the case of war against Germany, as that possibility gradually became the more likely contingency.[8]

This policy naturally required an emphasis on the effectiveness of torpedo craft. A war plan produced by the Naval Intelligence Department in July 1904, assuming a war with France provided for three formations consisting of the new *Scout* class cruisers, torpedo gunboats and destroyer flotillas to be based at Falmouth, Portland and Dover, serving as inshore squadrons keeping watch on Brest, Cherbourg and Dunkirk. Manoeuvres in August 1904 tested the plan; although these were too short to produce a definitive conclusion, it was argued by many of the senior officers involved that these manoeuvres had demonstrated 'that the close blockade and observation of an enemy's ports were extinct.'[9]

Although historians have disputed the precise point of the Admiralty's recognition that it was Germany and not France that was the more likely adversary, the 1904 manoeuvres showed that France was still perceived as a most serious threat. Thereafter, the focus shifted. The NID had, by 1902, already started looking at the conditions that would exist in the case of war with Germany. Early planning for this contingency was based around an offensive, inshore, observational blockade, together with combined operations against the German North Sea and Baltic coasts.

The continuous review by the Admiralty of the correct strategy to be followed in the event of war against Germany took place, during the decade before it broke out, against a background of vigorous intellectual dispute. This, fundamentally, resolved itself into the question of whether to adopt an offensive or a defensive strategy. The former view was based to some extent on the influential teachings of Admiral Mahan, who drew from his studies of the influence of sea power the conclusion that attack was the best form of defence. He laid down the principle on which naval strategy should be based in the first of his great books on the influence of sea power:

> It is not the taking of individual ships or convoys, be they few or many, that strikes down the money power of a nation, it is the possession of that overbearing power on the sea which drives the enemy's flag from it, or allows it to appear only as a fugitive; and which by controlling the great common, closes the highways by which commerce moves to and from the enemy's shores. This overbearing power can only be exercised by great navies.[10]

It was, he argued, the decisive command of the sea that was of prime importance; the attainment of this meant that the purpose for which a navy existed was above all an offensive purpose. This being so, it was a key feature of his philosophy that the fleet was never to be divided or dispersed, but must be concentrated where it could best strike a decisive blow at the enemy. Its first duty was always to seek out and destroy the enemy; the corollary of this was that in respect of blockading operations these must be conducted as close as possible to the enemy's coast.

A different view was put forward by Julian Corbett. Unlike Mahan, he was not a naval officer; his civilian background meant that his views did not always carry conviction to the minds of traditionalist naval officers. Nevertheless, Corbett had become a very talented and authoritative naval historian. He was recruited by the Admiralty to teach at the War Course, where he was able to develop his conclusions as to the principles of naval strategy. His audience, consisting largely of captains, appears to have been not altogether receptive. Donald M Schurman, in a paper written for a conference held in 1992, has observed that 'when Corbett showed that the real significance of a historical event might be more appreciated by someone other than a naval officer, they felt threatened or patronised.'[11]

However, Corbett enjoyed the support and respect of Sir John Fisher, and by 1906 he was serving as a member of an ad hoc sub committee under Captain George Ballard, the task of which was to draft the Naval War Plans. Five years later, Corbett set out his fundamental principle in *Some Principles of Maritime Strategy*:

> The object of naval warfare must always be directly or indirectly either to secure the command of the sea or to prevent the enemy from securing it.

He went on to emphasise the alternative:

> The second part of the proposition should be noted with special care in order to exclude a habit of thought, which is one of the commonest sources of error in naval speculation. That error is the very general assumption that if one belligerent loses the command of the sea it passes at once to the other belligerent. The most cursory study of naval history is enough to reveal the falseness of such an assumption.[12]

The alternative objective which Corbett thus put forward at once marked out his departure from Mahan's position. This defensive option was at odds with the views of many naval officers, who saw the next naval war in terms of major battlefleet confrontation. This, indeed, was hardly surprising; their entire professional upbringing, steeped in the tradition of past victories, was heavily reinforced by the building of bigger and better battleships, the function of which was to destroy an enemy. When, in the United States, naval war planners quoted in 1911 with approval a passage from Corbett's *England in the Seven Years War*, Mahan was quick after reading it to express his disagreement with views which suggested that taking the offensive at all times was 'not to show vigour but to play stupidly into the enemy's hands.' Anything which qualified the importance of an offensive strategy was anathema to Mahan and to those who accepted his basic propositions.

The fact that Corbett was to a certain extent a protegé of Fisher did not mean that he approved of Fisher's approach to strategic planning. The First Sea Lord was very much given to grandiose statements about the first duty of the Royal Navy in wartime, and Corbett sought in the introduction which he wrote to the report of the Ballard Committee to apply a corrective:

> For the purpose of forming war plans it must always be remembered that when we state the maxim that command [of the sea] depends on the battle fleet, we are stating the conclusion

> of a logical argument, the initial steps of which are highly important and cannot be ignored. The habitual oblivion of them frequently leads to false strategical conclusions ... Again when we say that the function of the battle fleet is to seek out and destroy the enemy's battle fleet, although we are stating what is usually true, we are not helping ourselves to a logical grasp of naval strategy.[13]

In the plans which they produced, the Ballard Committee contemplated the possibility of both a distant and a close blockade. It has been written of the Committee's approach that it showed clearly 'the lack of an agreed basis for strategic planning within the navy, and how little notice had been taken of the revolutionary developments in sea warfare.'[14] When the plans were circulated to senior commanders, they did not show much greater understanding, although Sir Arthur Wilson, at that time Commander in Chief of the Channel Fleet, had recognised the problems of maintaining a close blockade:

> A continuous watch off all the German ports, in sufficient strength to prevent anything coming out, would be very difficult and costly to maintain and if effective, would bring us no nearer the end.[15]

However, during the Fisher era attempts to evolve a clear strategy were doomed to failure, because his approach to such planning was that it was ultimately the sole responsibility of the First Sea Lord, and he was not going to disclose his plans to anybody.

Of all the revolutionary developments in naval warfare which had latterly taken place, that which most affected both strategy and tactics was the torpedo, which, whether delivered by surface vessels or submarines, was perceived as the greatest threat to the battle fleet. This was in spite of the fact that in the Russo-Japanese War of 1904-1905 the employment by the Japanese of torpedo boats had not been particularly successful. They had fired a total of 370 torpedoes of which only 17 had hit their target. However, the efficiency of the torpedo had greatly advanced in the following ten years, its effective range more than doubling to 11,000 yards, while its speed had been substantially increased, reaching 45 knots if set for 7000 yards. The torpedo had also considerably increased in size, from a 14 inch diameter to 21 inches. The surface vessels delivering the torpedo had also changed; instead of relatively small torpedo boats and destroyers, much larger destroyers, capable of operating at a longer range, had been developed, and peacetime trials suggested that an attack by destroyers in a fleet action in misty weather would probably succeed unless steps were taken to meet the threat.[16]

However, the increased power of the torpedo brought sharply into focus the danger from submarines. In 1912 the Admiralty War Staff found 'the great development of the submarine as the outstanding lesson.' This conclusion impressed Churchill, as First Lord, but not the rest of the Board of Admiralty. Fisher, in 1904, had written that it had not been even faintly recognised that the submarine would effect an 'immense impending revolution'; in the years that followed some observers began to agree with him, Lord Esher for instance commenting on the effect on the power of the battleship as being like 'the old knight in armour after the discovery of powder.' One of the most outspoken of the revolutionaries was Admiral Sir Percy Scott. Retired since 1909, Scott had been in the forefront of those seeking to improve the Navy's gunnery. Now, in June 1914, he wrote a long letter to *The Times* in which he argued that the battleship had had its day. He set out in pungent terms the reason for his conclusion, the gist of which he summarised as follows:

> That as we had sufficient battleships, but not sufficient submarines and aircraft, we should stop building battleships and spend the money voted for their construction on the submarines and aircraft that we urgently needed.
>
> That submarines and aircraft had entirely revolutionised naval warfare.
>
> That if we were at war with a country within striking distance of submarines, battleships on the high seas would be in great danger; that even in harbour they would not be immune from attack unless the harbour was quite a safe one.
>
> That probably if we went to war, we should at once lock our battleships up in a safe harbour, and that the enemy would do the same.[17]

This letter provoked a storm of indignant comment in the British Press in the days that followed. Among those denouncing Scott's conclusions was Lord Charles Beresford; the two men had quarrelled bitterly during the latter's command of the Channel Fleet. The *Pall Mall Gazette* was typical of many commentators in dismissing Scott's ideas as approaching 'the boundaries of midsummer madness.' While much of the criticism came from the pens of uninformed journalists, they were supported by a number of other senior admirals, including Admirals Cleveland, Fremantle, Bridge, Bacon and Bridgeman as well as Lord Sydenham.

However, the threat from the torpedo had already set in motion the process of evolving a strategy to cope with it, and which led ultimately to the abandonment of the close blockade. An Admiralty study of December 1912 reached a conclusion that made this inevitable:

> The enemy's submarine, in conjunction with the destroyer, has made an efficient blockade impossible. They have increased the difficulty of getting intelligence of the movements of the battle squadron of the enemy, since the light cruisers which would have to be employed to watch the enemy's harbours have now to be thrown out so far from the main body that their support becomes difficult, and they can be driven off from their watching station by superior force before they can be sufficiently supported.[18]

This paper was probably produced by the newly created Admiralty War Staff which came into existence in January 1912. Fisher, whose successor Wilson also believed that war planning was solely the province of the First Sea Lord, had effectively evaded the establishment of a proper Naval Staff; what he wanted was merely an informal advisory body to assist him in developing strategy. When Wilson put up an inadequate performance at the famous meeting of the Committee of Imperial Defence of August 23 1911, the external pressure on the Admiralty to set up a Naval Staff became irresistible. Although its role was to be purely advisory, it was given specific functions which gave it the chance to be a major influence on the deliberations of the Board of Admiralty.[19]

In addition to the threat from the torpedo carried both by the longer range destroyers and by submarines, the battle fleet faced the danger from a weapon which *had* proved very effective during the Russo-Japanese War. During the war both sides made extensive use of mines; the Russians laid a total of 4,275 mines which had resulted in the sinking of two Japanese battleships, two cruisers, five gunboats, six destroyers and a dispatch vessel. For their part, the Japanese laid minefields which sank one Russian battleship, one cruiser, two destroyers, a torpedo boat and a gunboat.[20] This record had considerably impressed Fisher for a time; but his subsequent enthusiasm for the potential offered by the submarine apparently led him to underrate their importance. Professor Marder summarised the Admiralty's position:

> Down to 1914 mines were not regarded in the Navy as formidable weapons whether for offence or defence. They were looked upon as rather expensive luxuries in an unimportant branch of naval warfare. When the War Staff in 1913 drew up a scheme for mining the Heligoland Bight and Straits of Dover, which was rather similar in its main features to the scheme adopted late in the war, Churchill alone was interested in the scheme – until he got the figure for the cost of 50,000 mines. When war came, Britain had no mining policy and consequently very few mines. In the appreciation and use of the mine Germany and Russia were far ahead of England at the beginning of the war.[21]

The use of minefields, therefore, was not a factor in pre war British strategic planning, but as soon as the war commenced it was seen that there were important tactical considerations that must be taken into account. Nicholas Black had pointed out that any consideration of the work, tactics and manoeuvrability of the Grand Fleet must take place in the context of the zone of its operations. If the Grand Fleet was to carry out its sweeps in the North Sea, the area could not be used as a significant minefield: 'In many respects the two weapons were incompatible.'[22]

Apart from the questions raised by these technological advances, strategic consideration in the decade before the war was heavily influenced by other factors. Foremost among these was the perceived risk of a German invasion, a threat that had been much worked up in the popular press, which inspired, and was inspired by a number of works of popular fiction. To this the CID had been obliged to respond; in 1913 H H Asquith, the Prime Minister, constituted a powerful Sub Committee on Invasion to look again at the invasion threat. It confirmed the primary conclusion reached five years earlier that so long as naval supremacy was maintained, invasion was impracticable, but that if permanent command of the sea was lost, 'whatever may be the strength and organisation of the Home Force, the position of the country would be desperate.'[23] It was the Admiralty's position, expressed by Churchill in the House of Commons in March 1914, that there must be sufficient military forces in the country to require an invader to come in such large numbers that would offer the Navy a target; for the Navy to have to guard the country without such a force 'would be like playing an international football match without a goalkeeper.' In practice, therefore, the invasion threat did not impact on the strategic distribution of the fleet.

Another factor that influenced strategic thinking was the real danger of the enemy following a *guerre de course*. Mahan largely dismissed this as a fundamental threat, considering it probably to be a delusion that it could be decisive. Others took a different view, pointing out that the Hague Conference of 1907 did not forbid the arming of merchant ships at sea to serve as commerce raiders. Two years later the Declaration of London, endorsed by eight great naval nations, did not outlaw the practice, and this was seen as allowing the reintroduction of privateering, which had been rendered unlawful by the Treaty of Paris of 1856. The Admiralty, however, more or less adopted Mahan's position, principally relying for the protection of trade on an immediate attack on the enemy's fleet, and the dispersion of trade routes. In 1914 the official policy was based on the provision of sufficient armed merchantmen to deal with those of the enemy, the introduction of a war risks insurance scheme, the dispersion of trade and the stationing of older cruisers at key points.[24] No one, however, foresaw the extent to which the submarines would impact on commerce destroying.

When Corbett came to write the earlier volumes of the *Official History of Naval Operations*, he opened his account with an Introduction which did not disguise his satisfaction that the principles for which he argued had been so firmly adopted:

> The dominant problem had been to fix the disposition of the main fleet. The reversal of the old geographical considerations which was the outstanding difficulty of a war with Germany, overrode all the considerations, which had determined the key position of the fleet in former wars, and a new one had to be found from which it could best discharge its primary function. What those functions had always been must be clearly apprehended, for of recent years, by a strange misreading of history, an idea had grown up that its primary function is to seek out and destroy the enemy's main fleet.

Corbett went on to describe the real duty of the Grand Fleet:

> Its paramount duty was to secure the command of Home Waters for the safety of our coasts and trade. There was no question of seeking out the enemy, for normally his fleet lay behind his base defences where it was inaccessible. All our own fleet could do was to take the most suitable position for confining him to port or bringing him to action if he put to sea. There was always the hope that the pressure so exercised would sooner or later force him to offer battle. But until an opportunity for decisive action arose, it was by patient and alert vigil it sought to attain its ultimate object.[25]

With a defensive strategy having been thus adopted, it was not difficult to decide the right position for the Ground Fleet. This was to be in Scottish waters, from which it could control the approach to the North Sea, just as the Western Squadron had historically controlled the Channel and its approaches. As will be seen, however, the very serious problem which this presented was the lack of prepared bases.

2

The Development of the High Seas Fleet

As the nineteenth century was drawing to a close, and in spite of the huge expansion of German overseas trade and its recent acquisition of colonies, there seemed to be little likelihood of any proportionate increases in the size of the German Navy. There were of course those who argued for this, most prominently Kaiser William II, a passionate naval enthusiast from childhood. In November 1895, however, there was what proved to be a decisive change in the situation, when Admiral Eduard von Knorr, the Chief of the Naval High Command, produced a paper which foreshadowed the subsequent Naval Laws which were to lead to the expansion of the Navy to the point at which it was capable of challenging the Royal Navy. In this paper Knorr noted that 'all states which recognise the importance of a fleet for their world positions and economic interests have been making great efforts to develop and expand their navies.' Germany's probable enemies were, it was suggested, France and Russia. Against them, her basic naval strategy must be defensive, but this required that the fleet be at least thirty per cent stronger than either of the northern fleets of these two Great Powers. Within two years this was considered insufficient; the target became fifty per cent of the combined fleets of France and Russia.[1]

Although these targets meant huge increases in the naval budget, the way in which the policy was framed was, as has been pointed out, less aggressive than the 'risk theory' later adopted, because it 'left the initiative to Germany's opponents; if they built no ships, Germany built none.'[2] The fundamental strategy behind the building plan was based on the principle that a decisive battle should be fought in home waters, and thereafter German battleships were designed to operate within a limited range.

With the arrival of Alfred von Tirpitz as State Secretary of the Imperial Naval Office, the perception of the probable opponent significantly changed. The development of the 'risk theory', first outlined by Tirpitz in a memorandum for the Kaiser before he took office, demanded a significantly more powerful battlefleet:

> Even the greatest sea state of Europe would be more conciliatory towards us if we were able to throw two or three highly trained squadrons into the political scales and correspondingly into the balance of conflict. We shall never achieve that using overseas cruisers.[3]

By the time he took up his duties in June 1897, Tirpitz was more explicit. Germany should, he believed, build ships to meet the greatest threat to its sea power; he was already clear that that threat was Great Britain, and that in consequence 'the fleet must be so constructed that it can unfold its greatest military potential between Heligoland and the Thames.' This meant building battleships in as great a number as possible; and this meant a potentially bruising encounter in the Reichstag, where there would be vociferous opposition to such a naval expansion.

In 1897, when Tirpitz introduced his first Navy Bill, Germany ranked far behind Britain in the number of her battleships, with twelve against sixty two. What was more, since the passing of Britain's Naval Defence Act of 1889, she had built 24 battleships to Germany's six, a statistic which, with many other telling arguments, Tirpitz used to good effect in the stormy debates in the Reichstag. By March 1898 the Navy Bill had completed its Committee stage; on March 26 Tirpitz was able to telegraph the news to the Kaiser that it had been passed. During this lengthy struggle Tirpitz had shown himself a master of political manoeuvre; it was a skill which he used to good effect in the following years.

For Tirpitz, it was only the start of a long term programme to create a world class battlefleet. This first Navy Law (Novelle) provided for the construction of 19 battleships, 8 armoured cruisers, 12 large and 30 light cruisers by April 1 1904. The heavy units were to be replaced every twenty five years and the light cruisers every fifteen years. Little more than two years passed before the second Navy Bill effectively doubled the size of the fleet, providing for 38 battleships, 20 armoured cruisers and 38 light cruisers.[4] The battleships were to be organised in four squadrons of 8 ships, with two fleet flagships and four in reserve. Whereas the first law had set a limit on expenditure, the new bill did not. Even now, however, Tirpitz regarded this as merely an interim stage.[5] He was already contemplating further additions, his target being to strengthen the fleet to the point where a ratio of 2:3 in battleships between Germany and Britain was reached.

In the first years of the twentieth century, warship designers around the world were working on plans for larger battleships with a main armament consisting of all big guns of one calibre; this process had been accelerated by an article by the Italian designer Vittorio Cuniberti on the subject in *Jane's Fighting Ships* of 1903. In March 1904 German designers came up with a plan for a vessel of 14,000 tons armed solely with heavy guns. A later design in October 1905 was for a 17,000 ton vessel with eight heavy guns.

In Britain, Fisher had embarked on a similar course, establishing a 'Committee on Designs', which by January 1905 had produced a design for a 17,000 ton battleship with twelve 12 inch guns and a speed of 24 knots. Fisher wasted no time; the keel of such a battleship was laid on October 2 1905. She was launched on February 10 1906 and her sea trials took place on October 3 of that year. Named *Dreadnought*, she had immediately rendered obsolete all the world's battleships, and if Tirpitz took up the challenge of building similar ships, an extraordinary arms race would begin. Later, Tirpitz would be profoundly critical of Fisher's decision, claiming that it was a serious mistake; but in fact the First Sea Lord could hardly allow other nations to be ahead in the building of all big gun vessels. As it was, shocked by this development, Tirpitz accepted the challenge. In the meantime, after assessing the inevitable increases in building costs, he introduced a Supplementary Navy Law in 1906 providing for the necessary funds for the building of Dreadnoughts, and for the construction of six additional cruisers. Three battleships and one battle cruiser were to be laid down annually. Two years later another Supplementary Navy Law was passed by the Reichstag; this shortened the life span of heavy units from twenty five to twenty years, thereby enabling the faster replacement of obsolete units. By 1914 it was planned for the German fleet to consist of 16 battleships and 5 battlecruisers, and by 1920 to 38 battleships, 20 battlecruisers, 38 light cruisers and 144 torpedo boats.[6]

The ensuing race between Britain and Germany to outbuild each other imposed enormous stress on national budgets. In spite of this, the British Cabinet decided that in order to maintain the nation's naval supremacy it must lay down eight ships in 1909 – 1910, double the rate of Germany's annual dreadnought programme of four ships. This followed intense pressure from Fisher and the Sea Lords, in which they were supported by Reginald McKenna, the First Lord. After the first of the Cabinet discussions on the subject in February 1909 Fisher wrote to Garvin, the editor of the *Observer*, in characteristically extravagant terms:

> Well you want me to tell you, 'May I assume that the SIX are secured?' YES YOU MAY! I have had to hunt for the red ink so as to emphasise that! I nearly wrote it in my own blood! … (NB The beauty of it is that though SIX are sufficient I am going for *eight*!!! and if the Germans … should have made the progress that is possible though not probable *we shall have the eight*! but don't allude to this). Really McKenna's conversion is almost up to Saul of Tarsus! … now he's all with me for the eight though only to ask for the six at first … rely on me my dear friend and believe in the line of absolute trust in Asquith, Grey and McKenna is the one that will pay.[7]

The British acceleration was such that even Tirpitz at once realised he could not match it, and his reaction was to propose a naval agreement based on a ratio of 3:4 in dreadnoughts. It was not a proposal that Britain could accept, and the new Chancellor, Theobald von Bethmann-Hollweg, would not allow it to be put forward.[8] The difference between Britain's political leaders and those in Germany was that the former saw this issue as utterly crucial, while the latter, ultimately seeing the army rather than the navy as their first priority, did not. By 1909 Bülow was by no means alone in believing that Tirpitz's policy was wrong. Thus it was that the British Admiralty was able to prevail over the fiercest resistance of the economy-minded members of the Cabinet, while Tirpitz struggled to overcome similar opposition in Germany.

In creating a navy virtually from scratch, the Germans had the opportunity to devise an ideal organisational structure unhampered by traditional practice or longstanding vested interests. This proved not to be the case. The distinguished German historian Walter Hubatsch observed, in something of an understatement, that 'the organisation of the Naval High Command in Germany was changed more often than was good for the navy's successful development.'This was certainly true. The structure of naval administration was subjected to a number of changes arising to a considerable extent from a clash of the leading naval personalities, and the desire of William II to exercise the supreme authority over the navy. In March 1889 it was decreed that the Admiralty should be abolished and that there should henceforth be three centres of administration. These were the *Marine-Kabinett*, responsible for all questions of personnel; the Supreme Command, responsible for military decisions; and the Department of the Navy, concerned with administration and technical development.[9] Ten years later, it was recognised that this decision had been a mistake, and the Supreme Command was abolished, and replaced by five new boards, directly subordinate to the Emperor and working in coordination with the Chief of the *Marine-Kabinett* and the State Secretary for the Navy. Theoretically increasing the Emperor's authority by making the new board subordinate to and with direct access to him, it in fact fatally weakened his authority. The five centres of authority were now to be the fleet commander, the chiefs of the North Sea and Baltic naval bases, the Inspector of the Training Corps and the Chief of the Naval Staff.[10]

These changes did, however, give the Naval Staff a chance of achieving real reform, particularly when the able Vice Admiral Otto von Diederichs was appointed to lead it in December 1899. His aim was to increase the influence of the Naval Staff over the affairs of the navy. To achieve this, he hoped to recruit the ablest officers to serve on the staff, much as was the case with the General Staff, with which he sought close cooperation. However, he came up against the burning ambition of Alfred von Tirpitz, who had no intention of allowing the Chief of the Naval Staff to gain authority at the expense of that of the State Secretary; in 1901 he wrote a personal report to William II resisting the strengthening of the Naval Staff. This achieved its object, and William decreed on June 24 that Tirpitz and the *Reichsmarineamt* must be the principal authority for the implementation of the navy laws.[11]

Although Diederichs continued to struggle to assert the independence of the Naval Staff, arguing that the tripartite authority of General Staff, War Ministry and Military Cabinet had served the army well in 1870-1871, Tirpitz continued to oppose him at every turn. By May 1902 Diederichs had had enough, and formally applied for imperial permission to retire. With him went the last hope of those who were opposed to Tirpitz's complete domination of the navy. Diederichs, alone of the navy's most senior officers, was not prepared to be subservient to the imperial will when he could see that William's judgment was at fault. His adjutant at the Naval Staff, Gustav von Bachmann, who during the war would succeed to his office, wrote of Diederichs: 'He simply had no patience for courtly etiquette and alienated the emperor with his stubborn attitude.'[12]

As the naval race went on, international relations took a sharp turn for the worse with the Agadir crisis. In the Leipzigerplatz in Berlin Tirpitz was watching developments with great anxiety, when there came like a thunderclap the famous Mansion House speech of David Lloyd George on July 21 1911. Lloyd George, who had fought hard as Chancellor of the Exchequer against increases in naval spending, was a spokesman for those who sought an understanding with Germany, and as such his words carried particular weight. Saying that he would make great sacrifices to preserve peace, he added a momentous warning:

> But if a situation were forced upon us in which peace could only be preserved by the surrender of the great and beneficent position Britain has won by centuries of heroism and achievement, by allowing Britain to be treated, where her interests were vitally affected, as if she were of no account in the Cabinet of nations, then I say emphatically that peace at that price would be a humiliation intolerable for a great country like ours to endure.[13]

Although gloomy about the relative position of the two fleets, Tirpitz was quick to see that the Agadir crisis, although in the end peaceably resolved, had given him plenty of ammunition to strengthen his arguments for increased expenditures under a further Novelle to be introduced in 1912. In August 1911 the Kaiser had called for more naval increases 'so that we can be sure that nobody will dispute our rightful place in the sun,' and public hostility in Germany to Great Britain continued unabated. It was against this background that Lord Haldane, the Secretary of State for War, came to Berlin on February 8 1912, to talk about the naval race. Although at first Haldane thought his meeting with William had gone very well, in fact Tirpitz was determined to scupper the talks, fearing that they would impede his progress to his target of 60 battleships. Next day in Glasgow Churchill, who had the previous year succeeded McKenna as First Lord of the Admiralty, set the cat among the pigeons by making a speech in which he observed that 'from some points of view the German Navy is to them more in the nature of a luxury.'[14] Predictably, this caused enormous resentment in Germany, and was a further reinforcement of Tirpitz's case for a new Novelle, which was duly passed in April providing for 41 battleships, 12 large and 30 light cruisers. Meanwhile Churchill and the British Admiralty were committed to a superiority in battleships of 60% by laying down two capital ships for every one laid down by Germany. So the arms race rolled on. The Kaiser, who also had not wished to see the Haldane mission succeed, was delighted, saying of the Britisth that 'we have them up against the wall.'

By treating the planned large cruisers as battlecruisers Tirpitz planned to have a total of 20 of these vessels by 1920. But his fleet for the moment was decisively behind Britain in terms of ships built and buildings, and the announcement in 1912 of the plan for 5 British 'super dreadnoughts' of the *Queen Elizabeth* class, with eight 38cm guns and a speed of twenty five knots, further underlined the gap. Throughout the period of the naval race there had been a constant anxiety in Germany that so threatening was their naval expansion that Britain might attempt to 'Copenhagen' their fleet by a surprise attack. While such a course was never contemplated, the fear was not unreasonable; Fisher, for one, would have relished such a step. When, in 1914, Churchill publicly suggested an Anglo German 'naval holiday', the Kaiser's reaction reflected the anxiety felt: 'The British surprise attack is here.'[15]

The way in which the naval race had been launched, and the way in which it developed, virtually determined what must be Germany's strategy in the event of war with Britain. Although, as Jan Breemer has pointed out, naval officers on both sides of the North Sea expected and longed for a decisive battle such as Trafalgar to decide the outcome of the naval war at one blow, the disparity of force, and basically the British choice of a distant blockade, precluded this unless the Grand Fleet sought it.[16] This was the paradox which Tirpitz's creation of a powerful but inferior fleet had produced. Tirpitz recognised this, asking Admiral Friedrich von Ingenohl, the commander of the High Seas Fleet in May 1914: 'What will you do if they do not come?'[17] Ingenohl did not reply. Thus it was that the German strategy was based on the hope that the Grand Fleet would come out, or rather parts of it would, which could be overwhelmed and defeated in detail, until with the reduction of the British numerical superiority the High Seas Fleet had a real chance of winning a major confrontation with the Grand Fleet.

Tirpitz, although recognising in 1914 that the disparity would at first be too great for this, began the consideration of other strategic ideas. His options were limited by geography, as Michael Epkenhans has pointed out.[18] He apparently contemplated at one point the development of a flying squadron of fast battlecruisers to wage cruiser warfare in the Atlantic Ocean, but in the event war broke out before he could put the plan forward. Tirpitz was, in 1914, neither ready for war with Britain or, even after the assassination of the Archduke Franz Ferdinand, expecting it. He set out the position as he saw it in his Memoirs:

> England did not fear an attack from us. She had a guarantee against this in our unfavourable strategical situation in the 'wet triangle,' which did not increase, but limited, the effectiveness of our fleet, and together with our lack of any strong naval allies could not produce

> a desire for war in any responsible German. There was another guarantee in the proportion of five German to eight English squadrons, with which we had declared our ultimate aim satisfied.[19]

Tirpitz was outspoken in his memoirs about the failures of the civilian politicians who could and should, he argued, have prevented war breaking out. He denied the suggestion that Germany had systematically worked for the war:

> If the Chancellor had consulted me, as was his duty – he ought to have reconnoitred the military possibilities in every direction before taking such a course – then I should have had to tell him that from the standpoint of the navy, the danger of war, which was undesirable in itself, would not offer any favourable strategic moments. The building of Dreadnoughts, by the introduction of which England automatically doubled the fighting force of our navy, had only been going on for four years. The Kiel Canal was not ready. The fleet would not reach its maximum until 1920 … Although our alliances did not guarantee us any important or certain support at sea, I reckoned that from about 1916 onwards an English attack would no longer be probable from a naval point of view. Every year of peace was therefore an inestimable gain for us.[20]

Vice Admiral Reinhard Scheer, later to lead the High Seas Fleet, was in 1914 in command of the II Squadron of eight predreadnoughts. He commented in his memoirs on the pre war strategic considerations and their effect on the design of the German dreadnoughts:

> Only in one material point were our strategical views based on an assumption which proved unfounded, the assumption that the English Fleet, which had kept ahead of ours in its construction at every stage, would seek battle in the German Bight in the North Sea, or would force its way to wherever it hoped to find the German Fleet. On that account we had attached particular importance to the greatest offensive and defensive powers, and considered we might regard speed and radius of action as secondary matters. The difference between our type of ships and that of the English shows that in both Fleets strategic ideas governed the method of construction. The English were content with less armour, but attached importance to higher speed and the largest possible calibre of gun so that they could impose on their opponent their own choice of battle area.[21]

History and geography had combined to circumscribe Germany's strategic options. History, which had delivered a powerful German fleet that was nonetheless significantly inferior to its opponent, had unfolded to bring about a war long before Tirpitz and the creators of the modern German navy were ready for it. And geography gave the fleet little choice in its concentration area. Only in the North Sea could it threaten the coasts of England, and it was there that it must engage the Grand Fleet. Its fundamental strategy had to be to do what it could to reduce the superiority of its opponent. It must follow one of Mahan's precepts, which was a statement of the extremely obvious; a weaker fleet 'could be used offensively only by great care, and through meeting the enemy in detail.'[22]

Herbert Rosinski, born and educated in Germany, was serving on the faculty of the German Naval Staff College until he fled to England in 1936 to escape Nazi persecution. He went to the

United States in the 1940s. He became an influential and highly regarded writer on military and naval subjects. A collection of his essays on 'The Development of Naval Thought' included a review of German theories of sea warfare, in which he contended that 'the German Navy's ideas on strategy were not only thrown into a hopeless confusion but almost completely stunted.' He was in no doubt of the reason for this:

> The fundamental reason for the atrophy of strategic thought in the German Navy before the war was the state of permanent inferiority in which the Tirpitz 'risk policy' placed the German Navy vis a vis its British opponent, making all reasonable strategic considerations out of the question.[23]

Since it was, Rosinski argued, doomed to a hopeless defensive, the idea of a decisive battle became for the German Navy practically an end in itself; although theoretically aiming at the command of the sea, that was seen as purely the attainment of military supremacy rather than the means to attain the proper objective of war at sea, which was the control of communications.

In terms of the ability to launch any offensive sorties, Scheer noted the difficulty faced by the High Seas Fleet:

> Our position in the North Sea suffered from the fact that for any enterprise we had only one point of exit: in that far corner which faces the mouths of the Elbe and the Weser. From it alone could the Fleet emerge for an attack, and to it must return again to seek the shelter of our bases in the estuaries of the Jade and Elbe. The route round Skagen and the Belt was closed to us, as the Danes had laid minefields in these waters. The sides of the 'Wet Triangle', the apex of which can be imagined at Heligoland, ended at Sylt in the north and the mouth of the Ems in the west. The left bank of the Ems is in Dutch, and therefore neutral, territory. All movements of ships there could accordingly be observed and the observation brought to the knowledge of the enemy in the shortest time. The channel at Sylt is navigable solely for destroyers and light cruisers, and then only in favourable conditions of wind and tide.[24]

Scheer does not, in this passage, mention one real advantage which the German Navy possessed, which was to be found in the bases to which he referred. The principal German naval bases were at Kiel, Wilhelmshaven and Cuxhaven, protected by the heavily fortified island of Heligoland and themselves well appointed and strongly defended against attack. From Wilhelmshaven the fleet could enter the North Sea through the River Jade; Hamburg was linked to the North Sea through the Elbe, and Bremen through the Weser. Kiel, protected by minefields laid in the Great and Little Belts at the Baltic end of the Kiel Canal, was readily accessible to the fleet, and wholly inaccessible to the British. The island of Borkum covered the Ems estuary. The anti submarine defences of these harbours were, however not completed until 1915. They did possess one serious defect; two tides were required for the whole of the High Seas Fleet to pass over the bars of the Elbe and Weser rivers.[25] Professor Marder noted the further advantages of the German network of bases and their communications:

> The Ems was connected with Wilhelmshaven by the Ems – Jade Canal, which was navigable for destroyers. From the great naval port of Kiel warships could reach the North Sea

> and the oceans of the world by the Kaiser Wilhelm Canal or by way of Danish waters: through the three international channels, the Sound, the Great Belt, and the Little Belt (large ships had to use the Great Belt), and on through the Kattegat and Skagerrak. The strength of the German position was in the shoals off the coast, the first class fortress of Heligoland, which partly covered the entrance to the Elbe and Jade, and the torpedo bases, forts and guns placed at all suitable positions along the coast. These were among the conditions that made the German coast difficult to approach.[26]

Writing in 1925, Rear Admiral Wolfgang Wegener, as he then was, looked back at the strategic situation at the outbreak of the war and in the years that followed it. He was one of the outstanding thinkers among Germany's naval leaders. His analysis was penetrating:

> The general principle that the stronger must seize the strategical offensive is not at all applicable in naval warfare. England found herself simply in a brilliant strategic position at the outbreak of the war. The arteries of her commerce lay in the Atlantic, unreachable by the German fleet from the Elbe. The German trade routes, on the other hand, could easily be severed in the Channel and off Scotland. The North Sea, through which no trade route any longer went, became a dead sea. The strategic position was so perfect that England never once felt the need to improve her position throughout the course of the war. From the very start, England was 'saturated' with command of the sea and remained so after the danger of losing Cherbourg and Brest to us had been removed by the Battle of the Marne .... It becomes evident that the English operations plan had nothing to do with the material superiority of the British fleet; rather, England's plan was dependent solely upon the existing strategic position at the outbreak of the war.[27]

Thus the absolute and inescapable fact of Britain's strategic advantage in geographical terms could only be overcome by Germany by the construction of a fleet at least as powerful as the Royal Navy. This was a necessity, as Mahan had pointed out in 1902, because geographical facts influenced the odds in any naval war:

> Distance is a factor equivalent to a certain number of ships. Sea-defence for Germany, in case of war with France or England, means established naval predominance at least in the North Sea; nor can it be considered complete unless extended through the Channel and as far as Great Britain will have to project hers into the Atlantic. This is Germany's initial disadvantage of position, to be overcome by adequate security of numbers; and it receives little compensation from the security of her Baltic trade, and the facility for closing that sea to her enemies ... For all the communities west of the Straits of Dover it remains true that in war commerce is paralysed, and all the resultant consequences of impaired national strength entailed, unless decisive control of the North Sea is established.[28]

It could be argued, however, that the building of a fleet of a size credibly to challenge the British control of the North Sea was probably always going to be a political and financial impossibility, even if Tirpitz's plans were not aimed at reaching maturity until 1920 at the earliest. The implementation of such a programme could never have been contemplated by any British government

British Ships

Iron Duke.

Agincourt with *Erin.*

Warspite.

Benbow.

Centurion.

Lion.

New Zealand.

Indefatigable.

Invincible.

Indomitable.

Princess Royal.

Queen Mary.

Tiger.

Defence.

Southampton.

Centaur.

Nottingham.

Calypso.

Fearless.

Arethusa.

Shark.

Nicator.

without responding in kind, with a consequent further acceleration of the arms race and all its political, economic and social implications.

Paul Kennedy has shown how the absolute fact of Britain's strategic advantage in geographical terms could, in the end, only be overcome by Germany if it was able to build a fleet at least as powerful as the Royal Navy.[29] It was an ineluctable necessity, as Mahan had pointed out before the naval race began further to accelerate. But the building of such a fleet was probably always going to be a political and financial impossibility, even if Tirpitz's plans were not intended to reach maturity until 1920 at the earliest, since no British government could have contemplated such a programme without responding in kind.

3

Ships

In August 1914 the British navy already enjoyed a pronounced numerical superiority in all classes of ships. Including the two battleships built for Turkey which were seized on the outbreak of war, Britain had twenty two dreadnoughts. Although losing one when *Audacious* was mined and sunk off Lough Swilly on October 28 1914, the British margin of superiority substantially increased during the war, eleven new dreadnoughts joining the fleet before the battle of Jutland on May 31 1916; two more were added before the end of the war. Germany began the war with thirteen dreadnoughts; three were added in October 1914, and another in July 1915, with the last two additions coming in July 1916 and March 1917. The gap was at its narrowest during the late autumn of 1914, at which point the British had twenty three dreadnoughts in commission, while the High Seas Fleet had sixteen. All the dreadnoughts on both sides were concentrated in the North Sea.

The same was not true of the battlecruisers. Of the nine which Britain possessed, three were on the outbreak of war in the Mediterranean. Another joined the Grand Fleet in October 1914, while two more joined in the late summer of 1916. There were also the three so called light battlecruisers which were added later that year and in 1917. Germany had four battlecruisers in commission in August 1914, one of which was in the Mediterranean. Two more joined the fleet before Jutland, but only one more after this, in May 1917.

There were, however, considerable differences between the various classes of ships constructed on each side. *Dreadnought*, of course, had led the way as the first all big gun battleship. Completed in December 1906, she had a normal displacement of 17,900 tons and carried ten 12 inch guns as her main armament; her armoured belt was 11 inches thick, while the turrets had 8 inch armour. Her design speed was 21 knots. It was more than two years before the next dreadnoughts joined the fleet. These were the three battleships of the *Bellerophon* class, completed in 1909. They marked no significant advance on their predecessor, having the same dimensions as *Dreadnought*, but had a normal displacement of 18,600 tons. They carried the same main armament, but their secondary armament was increased to 16 four inch guns, as became the norm in subsequent designs. They carried the same armour protection. This class was followed in 1910 by the slightly larger *St Vincent* class, of 19,250 tons. The armoured belt was reduced to ten inches, but the turret armour was increased to eleven inches. Their 12 inch guns had a longer barrel of 50 cal. These first seven dreadnoughts had the capacity to fire an eight gun broadside, two of the turrets being mounted amidships.[1]

The next battleship, *Neptune*, completed in January 1911, had the theoretical ability to fire a broadside of all twelve guns, the wing turrets being mounted en echelon; in practice, however, this proved not to be feasible. The after turrets were superimposed. There was a further increase in size (546 feet × 85 feet) and displacement (19,900 tons). She was capable of 21 knots. She was followed by the two ships of the *Colossus* class, slightly larger again and with an eleven inch armour belt and twelve inches of armour on the turrets. Their speed was much the same as their predecessors. These were the last battleships built for the Royal Navy to be armed with 12 inch guns, but in August 1914 the decision to take over the Turkish *Sultan Osman I* added a further, and very remarkable, 12 inch gun battleship to the Grand Fleet. *Agincourt*, as she was renamed, was 671½ feet long with a beam of 89 feet. She carried no less than fourteen 12 inch guns, in seven turrets in the centre line. Her armoured belt was 9 inches; the turret armour was 12 inches. She displaced 30,250 tons, and exceeded 22 knots on her trials.

The *Orion* class, displacing 22,500 tons, was the first to be equipped with 13.5inch guns, of which she carried ten. The four ships of the class were popularly known as 'super dreadnoughts'; 584ft long, with a beam of 85 feet, they had increased armour protection. There was, however, no planned increase in speed. All four entered service during 1912. Close behind them came the four ships of the *King George V* class, the name ship of which was commissioned in November 1912, with the other three following during 1913. A further slight increase in size (to 598 × 89 feet) resulted in a normal displacement of 23,000 tons. In one respect in particular they differed from their predecessors in not at first being fitted with tripod masts, although these were added later. *Centurion* of this class was the first to be fitted with director controlled secondary armament and with searchlights. *Audacious* had been one of this class.[2]

The *Iron Duke* class of four ships was the first to have a secondary armament of twelve 6 inch guns. There was a further increase in dimensions (to 620 × 89½ feet) and a corresponding increase in displacement, to 26,400 tons. *Iron Duke* (fitted as the fleet flagship) and *Marlborough* entered service before the outbreak of war; *Emperor of India*, previously to have been named *Delhi*, and *Benbow* joined the fleet in the autumn of 1914. All four ships were capable of between 21 and 22 knots. So was the last battleship to join the Grand Fleet carrying ten 13.5 inch guns. This was *Erin*, ordered for Turkey as *Reshadieh*, and taken over by the Admiralty on the outbreak of war. She was commissioned on August 22. Somewhat smaller than the *Iron Duke*, she was 560 feet long and 92 feet in the beam, with a displacement of 25,250 tons, and capable of the usual speed of 21 knots.[3] There was an obvious continuity down the line from the original *Dreadnought*, but the next design marked a significant improvement.

The *Queen Elizabeth* class of five ships which joined the fleet between January 1915 and February 1916, was larger, faster, more heavily armoured and with a heavier main armament than any battleship that had gone before. With a length of 640 feet and a beam of 90½ feet, all these vessels greatly exceeded their design displacement of just under 28,000 tons; when completed their normal displacement was 31,000 tons. Nor did they attain their design speed of 25 knots; the fastest was *Warspite*, which reached a little better than 24½ knots.[4] These ships have been described as the 'most perfect example of the naval constructor's art as yet put afloat', and in shipbuilding terms had decidedly raised the stakes.[5] They were armed with eight 15 inch guns in four super firing turrets. They were oil fired, coal being used only for auxiliary purposes, and for the first time geared cruising turbines were fitted.

The final battleship class to join the Grand Fleet during the war was the *Royal Sovereign* class of five ships. Originally seven were ordered, but *Repulse* and *Renown* were redesigned as battlecruisers. The five battleships were laid down at the end of 1913 and the beginning of 1914, and came into service between May 1916 and October 1917. They were slightly smaller than the

Queen Elizabeths but had heavier turret protection, and displaced 31,250 tons. They were also markedly slower, attaining slightly less than 22 knots on their trials; they, like their immediate predecessors, were oil fired. Their eight 15 inch guns were supported by a secondary armament of fourteen 6 inch guns.

One further battleship remains to be mentioned. In September 1914, instead of highhandedly requisitioning the vessel, the Admiralty negotiated with the Chilean government for the purchase of *Almirante Latorre*, a 32,000 ton battleship being built on the Tyne by Armstrong Whitworth. She entered service as *Canada* with the Grand Fleet in September 1915. Alone among British ships she was armed with ten 14 inch guns. She was less heavily armoured than the rest of the Grand Fleet, with a 9 inch belt. She was, however, faster than all save the *Queen Elizabeth* at 24 knots.[6]

In ten years the British dreadnought battleship had grown enormously in size and its armament had correspondingly increased; the weight of broadside of *Queen Elizabeth* was 15,600lb. It was also the case that the complement of the later vessels was greater; the crew of *Dreadnought* comprised 862 men, while that of *Queen Elizabeth* amounted to 1,016 men. As they came into service, the *Queen Elizabeth* class formed a squadron of fast battleships intended to operate as a link between the main body of the Grand Fleet and the battle cruiser force, and it was in this capacity that (with the exception of the name ship) they took part in the battle of Jutland.

The notion of the all big gun ship had been accepted in Germany before the launch of *Dreadnought*. A design for a 15,700 ton battleship carrying eight 11 inch guns was completed in 1905; it was not, however, accepted because the displacement would have unduly limited the vessel's armour protection. It was necessary to build to a heavier tonnage and, in October 1905 Tirpitz recommended that the displacement limit for battleships be increased to 19,000 tons.[7] The design for the first class of German dreadnoughts evolved into four ships of 18,900 tons, carrying twelve eleven inch guns and twelve 5.9 inch. The main armament was in six turrets, with two on either side; this configuration limited the broadside to eight guns. Bürkner, the designer, placed particular emphasis on an extensive system of underwater protection, dividing the hull into a series of narrow watertight compartments. The *Nassau* class were only 478 feet long, but had a beam of 89 feet, considerably improving their stability. They were powered by triple expansion machinery with three screws, because German constructors did not yet have sufficient experience of turbines. They were capable of a speed of 20 knots. *Nassau* and *Westfalen* joined the fleet in October 1909, *Posen* and *Rheinland* following in March 1910.[8]

The next battleships comprised the *Helgoland* class; much larger, they displaced 22,800 tons, being 546 feet long and 93½ in the beam. The main armament was twelve 12 inch guns, but the previous layout of turrets was retained. Secondary armament was fourteen 5.9 inch guns and fourteen 4.1 inch; the armoured belt was 11¾ inch, slightly thicker than in the *Nassaus*. Their speed was slightly greater, at 21 knots. They had the same system of subdivision into watertight compartments. German battleship design was based, as previously noted, on the strategic plans that envisaged that any engagement would take place in the North Sea, close to home bases and requiring, therefore, less provision to be made for long range operations. This particular point may perhaps have been somewhat overstated by historians; *Helgoland* had an effective range of 5,500 nautical miles at 10 knots; *Orion*, completed at much the same time, had a range of 6200 miles at the same speed.[9]

The next class of battleships were fitted with turbines, which proved entirely successful. The *Kaiser* class, of 24,380 tons with a length of 564 feet and a beam of 95½ feet, were armed with ten 12 inch guns, one turret firing forwards and two after with one each side diagonally located. The secondary armament consisted of fourteen 5.9 inch and twelve 4.1 inch guns. The main belt was 13¼ inches; the turret armour was 11¾ inches. This class consisted of five ships, the fifth being *Friedrich der Grosse*, fitted as the fleet flagship. *Kaiser* and *Friedrich der Grasse* joined the fleet in October 1912; the three remaining ships in August of the following year. One ship of the class, *Prinzregent Luitpold*, had only two turbines together with an experimental two stroke diesel engine driving the centre shaft; the experiment was not regarded as altogether successful and the diesel was omitted.[10]

König, the name ship of the following class, was launched on March 1 1913. The four ships of this class were 580 feet long and 97 feet in the beam, displacing 25,390 tons. The armament was the same as that in the *Kaisers*, but the five 12 inch turrets were all on the centre line, even though the *Reichsmarineant* apparently favoured the diagonal layout. There was a secondary armament of fourteen 5.9 inch, twelve 4.1 inch and four 3.4 inch anti aircraft guns. Rene Greger has observed that these architecturally demanding and very reliable ships were also fast (up to 24 knots in service), but they were weakly armed for their size at the time of commissioning.[11] Like their immediate predecessors, they were very good sea boats, with easy motion but with severe weather helm. Like all the German dreadnoughts they carried a larger crew than their British equivalents, with 1,136 aboard. The greater size of these vessels did not, apparently increase the cost; at 45 million marks they cost much about the same as the *Kaisers* but almost twice the cost of the last German pre dreadnoughts.[12]

In his penetrating analysis of German capital ship design, Norman Friedman has described the various influences that bore heavily on Tirpitz during the period before the First World War. Perhaps most important of these were the budget restraints within which Tirpitz had to operate, and the need to take account of the effect on the Reichstag of the mounting cost of each class in its turn. Another not inconsiderable influence was that of the Kaiser, who took a deep and well informed interest in ship design. He had a strong preference for speed, and was constantly pressing for the introduction of fast battleships. Tirpitz had all the time to keep in mind William's sensitivity to information about advances in warship design in other navies.[13]

The last of the German dreadnoughts represented a direct response to the *Queen Elizabeth*s. Four ships of the *Bayern* class were ordered in April 1913. First to be completed was *Bayern*, which entered service in July 1916, followed by *Baden* in October of that year. Displacing 28,500 tons, they were 623⅓ feet long and 99 feet in the beam, and were extremely stable gun platforms. Armour protection was 13¾ inches in the belt and the same for the turrets. Their speed was slightly less than the *Königs*. Their complement was 1,300 men. Their designed range was 5,000 miles at 12 knots. What particularly distinguished these vessels, however, was their main armament of eight 15 inch guns in four superfiring turrets. They carried a secondary armament of sixteen 5.9 inch and four 3.4 inch anti aircraft guns. The two remaining ships of this class, *Sachsen* and *Württemberg*, were not completed, their construction being suspended in 1917.[14]

So substantially did the power of the modern battleships exceed that of the pre-dreadnoughts on each side that there is little to be gained by a comparison of the relative merits of the latter. At the outbreak of war Britain had forty one pre-dreadnoughts in commission, ranging from the elderly *Redoubtable* to the so called 'semi-dreadnoughts' of the *Lord Nelson* class, completed in 1907 – 1908. These two vessels, displacing 16,500 tons, had four 12 inch and ten 9.2 inch as a main armament. Germany possessed twenty pre-dreadnoughts, although only the five ships of the *Braunschweig* class and the five of the *Deutschland* class had any pretensions to being able to take part in main fleet actions. These vessels, all armed with four 11 inch guns, displacing from 13,000–14,000 tons, had a maximum speed of about 19 knots.[15] The huge numerical superiority in such vessels which Britain possessed was not without its advantages; pre-dreadnoughts were used extensively in coastal and subsidiary operations including, for instance, at the Dardanelles. German pre-dreadnoughts would largely operate in the Baltic, although a squadron of these vessels would take part in the battle of Jutland.

The concept of the all big gun battleship, on which was based the design of *Dreadnought*, was one which, once he had adopted it, Fisher pushed through with all the exceptional energy and enthusiasm that characterised him. It had not been introduced without great controversy. Many observers considered that its introduction was a serious error, and adverse comment continued to be heard well after *Dreadnought* had joined the fleet. Among the critics was the famous designer Sir William White, whose comments were neatly demolished by a leading article in *The Observer*:

> When Sir William White suggests that both the United States and Germany are foolish and deluded powers slavishly copying the errors of a blind Board in Whitehall, he surely takes up the position of the dissenting juryman who had never met eleven such obstinate fellows in his life.[16]

The dreadnought controversy had rumbled on, being intensified by disputes as to the appropriateness of the battlecruiser design which Fisher introduced with the *Invincible* class of three ships, the name ship of which was completed in March 1908 but which due to electrical faults was not commissioned until March of the following year. In the meantime her sisters *Indomitable* and *Inflexible* had joined the fleet in June and October 1908 respectively. Designed as ships able to destroy inferior vessels but with the speed to keep away from more powerful vessels capable of inflicting damage, the battlecruiser design sacrificed protection for speed and gun power. The *Invincible*, 567 feet in length with a beam of 79 feet, displaced 17,250 tons. Armed with eight 12 inch guns and sixteen 4 inch she had an armoured belt six inches thick and her turrets had seven inches of armour plate. Their speed was 25 knots.[17] The next class of battlecruisers adopted the same configuration of main armament, but the wing turrets were more widely spaced, making an eight gun broadside possible. This was the *Indefatigable* class of 18,750 tons, also with eight 12 inch and sixteen 4 inch, 590 feet long, with a beam of 80 feet; these vessels were capable of 26 knots. The armoured protection was similar to that of the *Invincibles*.[18]

Battlecruiser design moved up a gear with the *Lion* class of 26,820 tons. The largest warships thus far built, they were 700 feet long with a beam of 88½ feet. Matching the so called 'super dreadnoughts', they were armed with eight 13.5 guns in four superfiring turrets, with a secondary armament of sixteen 4 inch. Protection was 9 inches in the armoured belt and on the turrets. What was really remarkable about these vessels, however, was their speed. As with the earlier battle cruisers, they were powered by turbines with four screws and achieved in excess of 27 knots. *Lion* joined the fleet in June 1912, *Princess Royal* in November 1912 and *Queen Mary* in September of the following year.

The fourth ship of the class was modified in the light of the design of the Japanese battlecruiser *Kongo*. This was *Tiger*, of 29,200 tons. Slightly larger than the *Lion* class, she was the heaviest ship in the fleet when she was commissioned in October 1914. It is recorded that she was the first to develop over 100,000 horsepower, which could drive her over 29 knots.

Protection was the same as the *Lion* class, as was her main armament; her secondary armament was twelve 6 inch. Her complement was nearly 1,200 men.[19]

Renown and *Repulse*, originally ordered as part of the *Royal Sovereign* class of battleships, and redesigned as battle cruisers, displaced 28,400 tons and 27,770 tons. They were no less than 794 feet long with a beam of 90 feet. Armed with six 15 inch and seventeen 4 inch guns, they were designed to be extremely fast. This they certainly were, attaining 32 knots. Originally the armoured belt was 6 inches, with the turrets 11 inches, but after Jutland additional protection was built into them. *Repulse* was commissioned in September 1916 and *Renown* in January 1917.

The remaining British battlecruisers were the product of further extravagant enthusiasm on the part of Fisher, when he returned as First Sea Lord in 1914. The *Glorious* class was designed to support amphibious operations against the Frisian Islands or in the Baltic. With a draught of 25-26 feet compared to 30-34 feet of the regular battlecruisers, these 'light battlecruisers' were armed with four 15 inch guns (*Furious* was fitted instead with two 18 inch guns) and eighteen 4 inch guns. Their speed was 31 knots; their protection limited to an armoured belt of 3 inches with 9 inches on the turrets. *Glorious* and *Courageous* joined the fleet at the end of 1916, and *Furious* in July of the following year.[20]

As with their battleships, the German battlecruisers proved a good deal more robust than their opponents. The first such vessel, however, was something of a hybrid. *Blücher* was designed to carry twelve 8.2 inch, 8 5.9 inch and 16 4.1 inch guns. Displacing 15,500 tons she was in effect a heavy armoured cruiser, and as such was a fine ship, capable of attaining a speed of 26 knots. Both armoured belt and turrets were of 6 inch plate. As Rene Greger noted, however, 'she should never have been ordered, for six months before her keel was laid it was learned that the armoured cruisers ordered for the Royal Navy under the 1905 estimates were to be equipped with eight 12 inch guns.'[21] *Blücher* joined the fleet in September 1909, but experience was to demonstrate that she had no place in the line of battle.

The first German battle cruiser proper was *Von der Tann*. Laid down in 1908, she was completed in September 1910, but not commissioned until February 1911. Displacing 19,100 tons, she was 562 feet long and 87 feet in the beam. She was armed with eight 11 inch, ten 5.9 inch, and 16 4.1 inch. Fitted with turbines and four screws, she was capable of 25 knots. Her armoured belt was 9¼ inches; the turrets had 9 inch plate. She was a good sea boat, with slight weather helm. Like most of the German battlecruisers she was built by Blohm and Voss. When she attended the Coronation Naval Review in 1911, she apparently created a great impression. All in all, hers was a most satisfactory design.[22]

The *Moltke* class of two ships came next. Displacing 22,980 tons, they were 610 feet long with a beam of 96½ feet. They were armed with ten 11 inch guns with the same configuration as the *Kaiser* class battleships, together with twelve 5.9 inch and twelve 4.1 inch. They were capable of 28 knots. *Moltke* joined the fleet in September 1911 and *Goeben* in July 1912. Like all the German capital ships, they were to prove able to absorb a great deal of punishment, with armour plate of 11 inches for both belt and turrets. These vessels were followed by *Seydlitz*, which entered service in August 1913. She was somewhat larger, at a displacement of 24.610 tons, being 656 feet long and with a beam of 93½ feet. She exceeded 28 knots on her trials. Armour was 11 inches on the belt and 8 inches on the turrets. Armament was the same as the *Moltke* class, with a similar complement of just over 1100 men. She was another good sea boat; she had a raised forecastle, which assisted greatly in this respect.[23]

The next class had some claim to being the outstanding battlecruiser design of the First World War. The three ships of the *Derfflinger* class displaced 26,180 tons and were 689 feet long and 95¼ in the beam. They were capable of 26.5 knots, which was slightly less that their immediate predecessors. For armament they carried eight 12 inch guns in four superfiring turrets, with twelve 5.9 inch and eight 3.4 inch anti aircraft guns. The armoured belt was 12 inches thick and the armour on the turrets 11 inches. There was a slight increase in complement at 1,125 men. *Derfflinger* and *Lützow* were commissioned in time to take part in the battle of Jutland, in September 1914 and August 1915 respectively. *Hindenburg* joined the fleet in May 1917. Her main armament was fitted on new mountings which gave an elevation of 16 degrees. This class was designed to operate at a longer range than the earlier German battlecruisers, *Derfflinger* and *Lützow* at 5600 nautical miles at 14 knots and *Hindenburg* at 6100 nautical miles. The comparative range of British battlecruisers is hard to assess, since the recorded data is measured against higher speeds.[24]

The *Derfflingers* were the last completed German battlecruisers. *Mackensen,* the first of a class intended to comprise seven ships, was laid down in January 1915 and launched in April 1917. Designed for an even longer range, she and the next three of the class were to carry eight 14 inch guns; the last three were redesigned for eight 15 inch guns. *Mackensen* was to displace 31,000 tons, and be 730 feet long and 99 feet in the beam, and to have a speed of 28 knots. Work on her was continuing at the end of the war but she was not completed. The only other vessel of the class to be launched was *Graf Spee*, launched in September 1917, and she too was ultimately broken up incomplete.[25]

Battlecruisers were sometimes designated as large armoured cruisers, but this was certainly a misnomer, since their size and combat effectiveness distinguished them completely from the armoured cruisers that had gone before. The fate of *Blücher* at the battle of Dogger Bank and of Sir Robert Arbuthnot's armoured cruisers at the battle of Jutland showed clearly that they had no place in a combat with modern capital ships.

At the outbreak of war Britain had 34 vessels rated as armoured cruisers, eight of which were stationed outside home waters. The last to be completed formed the *Minotaur* class, of 14,600 tons. These had a speed of 23 knots and a mixed main armament of four 9.2 inch and ten 7.5 inch, with sixteen 12 pounder guns; they were protected by a 6 inch armoured belt. Apart from *Blücher,* described above, Germany possessed six armoured cruisers, of which the two most modern were *Scharnhorst* and *Gneisenau*. Displacing 11,600 tons, they had a speed of 22.5 knots, and were armed with eight 8.2 inch, six 5.9 inch and twenty 3.4 inch guns. They had an armoured belt of 6 inches. These two vessels formed part of the East Asia Squadron of Vice Admiral Maximilian von Spee, based in Tsingtao.

Britain possessed 53 protected cruisers, a category of warship that had effectively become obsolete by 1914, although remaining useful for escort and blockading duties. Protected cruisers lacked an armoured belt, but their vital underwater parts were shielded by steel decks of varying thickness, and by the location of coal bunkers at the sides of the ship. Many of the older protected cruisers had been discarded when Fisher embarked on his clear out of vessels too slow to run and too weak to fight. Some classes of protected cruisers were quite large vessels; the *Crescents* and *Edgars,* for instance, were of 7,700 tons. These carried one or two 9.2 inch and ten or twelve 6 inch guns. Seven of the *Apollo* class were converted as minelayers. Twelve protected cruisers were stationed abroad in 1914. The last protected cruisers to be completed had joined the fleet in 1905.

There were 17 German protected cruisers. Of these, five were as large as 5,600 tons, carrying two 8.2 inch guns as a main armament; the rest were significantly smaller. The last of these to be built, the *Gazelle, Nymphe* and *Frauenlob* classes joined the fleet between 1899 and 1903. These were of 2,645 tons, carrying ten 4.1 inch guns and capable of 21.5 knots. One of these, *Frauenlob*, was to take part in and be sunk at the battle of Jutland, while *Ariadne* was sunk at the battle of Heligoland Bight on August 28 1914. The remainder played only a modest part in the World War.

A much more important category was that of light cruiser. This was a design first introduced in the Royal Navy as 'Scouts'; four classes of these, totalling fifteen ships, joined the fleet between 1905 and 1913. In size, they ranged from 2,900 tons to 3,440 tons, and were armed with between six and ten 4 inch guns and one 3 inch anti aircraft gun. Their designed speed was between 25 and 26 knots, and they were intended to operate with the new seagoing destroyers. These were followed by the 'Town' classes, which comprised a total of seventeen ships, plus three Australian vessels. They ranged in size from 4,800 to 5,200 tons. The *Bristol* class carried two 6 inch and ten 4 inch guns, with one 3 inch anti aircraft gun; the *Weymouth* and *Chatham* classes were armed with eight 6 inch and one 3 inch anti aircraft gun; the *Birmingham* class with nine 6 inch and one 3 inch anti aircraft gun; and *Birkenhead* and *Chester*, building for Greece and taken over by the Admiralty, were armed with ten 5.5 inch and one 3 inch anti aircraft gun. Apart from the last two ships, all joined the fleet before the outbreak of war. They proved valuable work horses for a variety of tasks, all being able to achieve about 26 knots. At the start of the war, eight of them, together with the three Australian ships, were serving outside home waters.

These light cruisers were quite closely modelled on the German light cruisers. Their speed, however, was not really adequate to work with the newest destroyers, and a compromise design eventually of forty two vessels, somewhat between the 'Town' and 'Scout' classes, was evolved specifically for North Sea operations. The first class, five of which joined the fleet before the outbreak of war, consisted of eight *Arethusas.* Somewhat smaller, at 3,512 tons, armed with three 6 inch and four 4 inch, plus anti aircraft guns, they could steam at nearly 30 knots. Like the 'Town' classes they had a three inch armoured belt. The *Caroline* class of six ships came into service soon after the start of the war; slightly larger, they carried four 6 inch guns, as did the succeeding *Cambrian* class, also of six ships. Further vessels joined the fleet throughout the war; the *Centaur, Caledon, Ceres* and *Carlisle* classes (sixteen ships) carried five 6 inch guns. With each succeeding class the size of the vessels increased; the *Carlisle* class displaced 4,290 tons. The last six such vessels were the *Danae* class of three ships, of 4,650 tons and with six 6 inch, which joined the fleet in 1918, and the *Delhi* class, which were not completed until after the end of the war.[26]

When war broke out, the German fleet possessed a total of twenty three light cruisers of which six were serving outside home waters. All were named after German towns. The oldest class of these ships was the *Bremen* class of five vessels. Displacing 3,250 tons, they mounted ten 4.1 inch guns; they were not particularly fast however, with a speed of 23 knots. They were followed by the very similar *Leipzig* and *Danzig*, which joined the fleet in 1906 and 1907. Next came *Königsberg,* of 3,400 tons, with a slightly higher speed. In 1908 the three ships of the *Stettin* class were completed, slightly larger and with a speed of up to 25.5 knots. There followed in 1908 and 1909 the two ships of the *Dresden* class, of 3,650 tons. With the *Kolberg* class of four ships (1909-1910) there was a pronounced increase in size and armament; they displaced 4,350 tons and carried twelve 4.1 inch guns (later altered for *Kolberg* and *Augsburg* to six 5.9

inch guns), and could attain a speed in excess of 27 knots. None of the foregoing classes of light cruiser carried an armoured belt, although they all had an armoured deck of 2 inches.[27]

With the first four ships of the *Magdeburg* class, which arrived in 1912, there was introduced for the first time an armoured belt of 2½ inches. The largest light cruisers yet built for the German navy, they displaced 4,550 tons; they were 455 feet long with a beam of 43½ feet and mounted twelve 4.1 inch guns (*Stralsund* and *Strassburg* were later fitted with seven 5.9 inch). Their speed was up to 30 knots. Thereafter the light cruisers were designed in pairs. The last two ships to join before the outbreak of war constituted the *Karlsruhe* class. Slightly larger than the *Magdeburgs*, they were generally very similar to that class. The cost of each vessel had naturally increased with each progression in size; the *Bremens* had cost on average a little under 5m marks each; by the time the two *Karlsruhe* ships were added the cost was a little over 8.1m marks, and the figure continued to rise.[28]

During the war there were added the two ships of the *Graudenz* class, which closely resembled the *Karlsruhe*, although converted later to carry seven 5.9 inch, and two 3.4 inch anti aircraft guns and 120 mines. They were both completed in 1914. Next came the *Frankfurt* class, larger again at 5,120 tons; fitted from the outset with eight 5.9 inch guns and two 3.4 inch anti aircraft guns, they could steam at 28 knots. They also carried 120 mines. Two vessels originally building for Russia were requisitioned in August 1914, and became the *Pillau* class; slightly smaller than *Frankfurt*, they were similarly armed. They had no armoured belt, however. *Pillau* joined the fleet in December 1914, and *Elbing* nine months later.[29]

Brummer and *Bremse* were laid down as fast minelayers. When completed in 1916, they displaced 4,000 tons and were armed with four 5.9 inch and two 3.4 inch anti aircraft guns. They were protected with an armoured belt of 1½ inches. They were equipped to carry 360 mines. They were fitted with two sets of turbines, originally intended for the Russian battlecruiser *Navarin*, as a result of which they could attain a high speed, according to Le Fleming as much as 34 knots, although Gröner puts it much lower.[30]

The *Königsberg* class of four ships all bore the names of light cruisers that had been lost during the war; three joined the fleet during 1916 and one, *Nürnberg*, in February 1917. Larger again, at 5440 tons, they carried the same armament as *Frankfurt*. They had a speed of a little under 28 knots. They were followed in early 1918 by the last two light cruisers to join the Imperial Navy; these were two ships of the *Köln* class which, apart from slight changes in appearance, were similar to the *Königsberg* class. Five more ships of this class were launched, but construction was halted at the end of the war, and they were broken up. *Köln*, of this class, appears to have been able to steam at 29 knots.[31]

The destroyers of the First World War had evolved from the much smaller torpedo boats. Since the threat of the torpedo was perceived by the British Admiralty as demanding an effective response, it ordered 42 'Torpedo Boat Destroyers' from fourteen different shipbuilders, which were given great latitude in the design of the vessels. They were all however to have turtleback forecastles, to displace between 220 and 300 tons, to be armed with a 12 pounder gun and three or five 6 pounders, to be powered by triple expansion engines and have a contract speed of 27 knots. They were delivered in 1893-1894. They were followed by 60 more in the next seven years; as the design evolved it was seen that too much had been sacrificed to speed, and by 1903 design changes had improved seaworthiness at the expense of lower speeds. Until 1907, however, destroyers remained very small, and the lower speeds had been considered to be acceptable. In that year the first of the 'Tribal' class destroyers joined the fleet. These represented a revolution in destroyer design, intended as they were to be ocean going vessels. Size was almost double, speeds were increased to as much as 36 knots and in the later and larger ships of the class two 4 inch guns were mounted. All the destroyer classes were fitted with two torpedo tubes – it was not until the 'L' class of 1913-1915 that four tubes were fitted to each vessel.

After the later 'Tribals', which had a displacement for the first time in excess of 1,000 tons, evolution continued, but for the moment the essential pattern remained. By the outbreak of war, including so called 'destroyer leaders', and vessels acquired from abroad, the Admiralty had commissioned a total of 271 destroyers. During the course of the war a further 290 joined the fleet. The largest group was the 'M' class, of which there were a number of variants. Importantly, this class, armed with three 4 inch guns, could generally attain a speed of 34 knots, while some could achieve as much as 39 knots. The vessel that was most particularly an outlier was *Swift*; completed in 1907, she was designed as a Special Flotilla Leader, and displaced 1825 tons. She was regarded as the fastest ship in the fleet, having been able to exceed 40 knots.[32]

In Germany destroyers were officially termed 'Large Torpedo Boats'. They bore numbers, not names, and in this respect continued the practice of numbering torpedo boats. They were designed with seaworthiness in mind, with a high forecastle, and with a break before the bridge. Most of the German destroyers were built by three shipyards, a policy which assisted uniformity of design. The earliest classes were between 300 and 400 tons, with speeds of up to 28 knots; armament was three 4 pounders and three torpedo tubes. As in Britain, the gradual evolution of the destroyer produced a steady increase in size. The vessels joining the fleet in 1907 (the *T138* class) were over 500 tons, with a speed of 30 knots and an armament of one 3.5 inch gun, with three 4 pounders and the standard three torpedo tubes. Three years later, with the arrival of the *T186* class, size had increased to 650 tons, and speed to over 35 knots. Main armament was two 3.5 inch guns. The vessels joining the fleet in 1914 (the *V25* and *S31* classes) were over 800 tons, armed with three 3.5 guns, and were fitted with six torpedo tubes. They could attain a speed of up to 36 knots. Before the start of the war, a total of 143 destroyers had been commissioned into the German fleet; during the course of the war a further 93 destroyers were completed. By 1916 the vessels of the *G85* class, for instance, were of 960 tons; their speed was 34 knots and their armament was three 4.1 inch guns. Somewhat larger vessels joined the fleet towards the end of the war; the ships of the *B97* class were 1374 tons, with a speed of 37.5 knots and an armament of four 4.1 inch guns. The fitting of six torpedo tubes was by now standard. The largest German destroyers were *S113* and *V116*, of 2060 tons; they were fitted with four 5.9 inch guns and were designed to achieve 37 knots. These were designed as destroyer leaders but proved disappointing, being top heavy and inclined to roll badly, while not being able to reach their design speed.[33]

4

Men

In 1914 the German navy could look back on half a century of development; the Royal Navy, on the other hand, had behind it centuries of history in which it had almost invariably demonstrated its superiority over all its enemies. Although, with the exception of the one sided battle of Navarino, the Royal Navy had had no fleet to fleet encounters since the end of the Napoleonic wars, it had continued to establish itself as a central pillar of the British Empire's expansion and consolidation. It appeared to have been able steadily to adapt itself during a century of huge technological change, and it enjoyed the confident support of the British people. For most of the century, the enemy against which the navy had had to prepare was France, which, if it was generally beaten in combat, had a considerable tradition of its own. The German navy, on the other hand, had the look of an upstart that, in the popular mind, must surely give best when it came to it.

The rapid process of change, both in industrial and social terms, found the naval establishment reluctant to abandon systems that had served the navy well during its glorious past. For a long time it continued to rely on an entirely haphazard recruiting system and a primitive system of training. Even after steam had effectively replaced sail as the method of propulsion of its ships, sail training continued to be at the heart of practical seamanship. As the years went by, however, the importance of gunnery was more clearly perceived, and better training was essential for the proper working of the new types of guns.

One of the Royal Navy's major problems in the years before 1914 had been the need to recruit stokers. These, rather than seamen, represented the largest part of the increase in the naval establishment. Seamen as such were less in demand as increasing mechanisation took over, and the need for sails to be handled and trimmed disappeared. Overall, the workforce increased markedly, but the specialist fighting skills required were now for gunners and torpedomen. In 1889 the navy consisted of 64,405 men; by 1914 the total was 151,000. Stokers were paid a third more than seamen; by 1910 they outnumbered the seamen. In addition to their work in the stokehold they could be employed on damage control or to assist with working the guns.[1] Fisher would have liked to merge the two categories, but although seamen were taught how to work in the stokehold, this did not happen. The requirement for gunners continued to increase with the size and armament of the new warships coming into service. A 12 inch gun turret, housing two guns, required an officer, two midshipmen and a total of 67 other men. Other specialist seamen were required, particularly for signalling and telegraphy.

Life aboard ship was not easy; Winston Churchill wrote a paper illustrating some of the problems as war approached:

> The sailor's life is one of exceptional hardship. Service in a ship of war is not only strenuous but more uncomfortable than twelve or fourteen years ago. Instead of seeing something of the world, the young sailor knows nothing but the North Sea and a few war anchorages around the coast. The construction of a modern warship renders it extremely uncomfortable and even unhealthy as a living place. Nothing is possible in the nature of a recreation room on board, nor are there facilities for any kind of rest privacy or amusement … the life of the bluejacket and stoker in our finest ships of war around the British Coasts and in the North Sea is one of pitiable discomfort, which cannot, while the present competition in armaments continues and the present types of warship construction prevail, be effectively alleviated.[2]

Churchill, partly in response to the campaign for reform of the lower deck movement led by Lionel Yexley, campaigned for better pay and conditions for the men; in this he was partly successful. It is not, however, surprising that there was a constant undercurrent of discontent among the lower deck. There were no less than 24 recorded incidents of mutiny between 1900 and 1914, although none could be classed as a major breakdown in discipline, being of a local nature and a reaction to the conduct of particular officers. With the outbreak of war, the Admiralty found itself competing with the army for volunteers, and made a number of further improvements in conditions, including opportunities for promotion, allowances and leave.[3]

Former seamen came forward to rejoin the navy; they were taken on 'for the period of hostilities only', although otherwise on the same terms as the continuous servicemen. However, the intake of new seamen was qualitatively unsatisfactory; Jellicoe in April 1915 was asking for ordinary seamen 'of better physique and improved development'. He suggested a minimum height of five feet four inches, with a chest measurement of thirty five inches. However, recruitment in one category was less of a problem; by now the need for stokers had begun to lessen, with the introduction of more oil fired ships. This of course meant that the burden of coaling ship, which involved the whole of the crew, was removed for those fortunate enough to serve on such vessels.

The navy was a mirror of the society which it served, which meant that the social gulf between officers and men was enormous. For the best part of a century after the Napoleonic wars no one from the lower deck was commissioned as an officer. Lionel Yexley commented on the continuing gap:

> At one end of service life we have the officer recruited from that comparatively small class that is wealthy enough to spend £700 on a boy; at the other end we have the men recruited from the poor artisan and labouring class. In between lies the pick of the nation. It will not send its sons on to the lower deck because of the great limitation in the facilities for advancing; it cannot send its sons in as officers through lack of money.[4]

In Imperial Germany the class system was even more rigidly defined, although in some important respects the social origins of naval officers differed from their British counterparts. In Germany, the army had been pre-eminent; it was into the army that the sons of the aristocracy had always gone, and the military successes of the Wars of Unification had confirmed this. On the other hand, as the navy expanded it attracted a large number of middle class officers and Tirpitz claimed that the navy had become the 'melting pot' of Germany, drawing 'hundreds of thousands from a provincial way of looking at things to a common horizon':

> No navy in the world had such an excellent personnel as we had in our coastal population, in the merchant seamen who, owing to their service in the navy, cast off more and more their former international character, and in the fishermen who, particularly indispensable for the manning of our small ships, returned to their villages, after serving in the navy, with a widened mental horizon and professional ambition.[5]

Tirpitz went on to argue that when the seafaring population of Germany's northern coast line proved inadequate to provide the required number of recruits, 'we went inland for recruits; service on modern ships did not make the same demands on seamanship as in the old days of sailing vessels.' South Germans, he noted, had distinguished themselves in the navy.[6]

Holger Herwig, in his study of the German naval officer corps, has cast doubt on the proposition widely accepted by historians, that naval officers tended to have cosmopolitan and even liberal views, at least in comparison with the army. Among the historians who have subscribed to this view was Jonathan Steinberg, who wrote that the navy 'was a symbol of national unity in a nation which, even after unification, had a very fragile sense of nationhood.' Wahrhold Drascher suggested that executive officers had become a 'special social type in the empire.' Herwig, on the other hand, argues that 'by the turn of the century the executive officers abandoned much of their "liberal" and "cosmopolitan" middle class heritage and adopted instead the social standards, manners and attitude of the Prussian army officer corps.'[7]

Whatever may be the truth of this, there was not a great deal of difference between the German navy and the British navy in terms of the social gulf between the officer class and their men. One British officer at least was sure that this was all to the good, claiming that 'the general wish of the lower deck is to be officered by gentlemen of the upper and middle classes. Not that they wish to close the door to the "ranker"; but they prefer that, other things being equal, their officers should be men trained in the traditions of the "gentry".'[8]

There was little to choose between the human material at the disposal of the two navies. As between the two sets of officers, Marder noted that the British had the great advantage of confidence, born of the centuries old tradition of success of the Royal Navy. However, the British Naval Attaché in Berlin noted that the German flag officers and senior captains were 'in no way inferior' to their opposite numbers, and that they were 'hardworking, keen and zealous' and came from a better class and were better educated. He thought, though, that they seemed rather to be soldiers at sea than seamen.[9]

A further advantage which Marder identified was the much greater amount of time that the British spent at sea, which he thought helped to explain 'the magnificent seamanship and navigation of the officers in the war.' By comparison, the German fleet spent much more time in harbour, while much of its training was in sheltered waters. The British fleet also benefited from the voluntary recruitment policy, which gave a minimum service term of twelve years, while the German navy had a short service term of only three years. This, the British Naval Attaché observed, meant that every year the officers had to 'make trained men out of a fresh lot of conscripts totally strange to sea life.' The men were, nonetheless, well drilled and trained.[10]

There is no evidence that the men of the Royal Navy went about their duty with more loyalty and patriotism than their opponents, at least until the end of the war when it was clear that Germany was losing. Then it was the German sailors who mutinied on a large scale, and who by doing so put paid to the plans for a last offensive of the High Seas Fleet, and went on to become the most potent symbol of the revolution in Germany; but by then their situation was very different from their British counterparts. The projected operation was seen as effectively a suicide mission which could destroy the hopes of an armistice for which the German sailors, like the rest of the population, desperately craved. Seaman Richard Stumpf, a loyal and patriotic seaman who kept a diary throughout the war, was far from unique in becoming transformed in the last days of October 1918 into an anti-militarist and a republican; he wrote of the burgeoning mutiny in the High Seas Fleet:

> It is sad, tragic that it could go so far as this. But somehow even with the best of intentions I cannot suppress a certain sense of frantic joy ... As late as a few months ago I would have laughed at anyone who suggested that our people would simply throw up their hands at the approach of our enemy.[11]

It was Stumpf's duty, like that of all the men serving with the Grand Fleet and the High Seas Fleet, to carry out his orders and, of course, neither he and the rest of the seamen, nor even most of the officers, had any say in the matter. It is, therefore, with the decisions of the admirals which affected the course of events that historians must be principally concerned; and perhaps it must be concluded that there were few on either side who deserved any considerable praise for their performance. That was certainly the view of Professor Marder:

> There were few really top-notch admirals in 1914 – men who were exceptional tacticians and fleet commanders in the Hawke-Nelson tradition or war thinkers in the Anson–Barham tradition. One reason was that the pre-1914 generation of admirals had not had the opportunity to be trained in the hard school of war. Another reason was that ... the '*matériel*' school was in the ascendant. A third reason was that all senior officers had been brought up in sail and many of them never shook off the sailing-ship mentality.[12]

Marder was writing about the British admirals, but his criticism would apply equally to their German opponents. The lack of an enduring naval tradition may have limited their confidence; this was perhaps compensated for by a somewhat less conservative approach to their profession.

Marder's view merely confirmed a number of contemporary opinions, Churchill thought that there was a 'frightful dearth of first-class men in the Vice Admirals' and Rear Admirals' lists'; Commander Stephen King-Hall was even more trenchant in his observations:

> There were a number of shockingly bad admirals afloat in 1914. They were pleasant, bluff old seadogs, with no scientific training; endowed with a certain amount of commonsense, they had no conception of the practice and theory of strategy or tactics.[13]

As First Lord of the Admiralty, the flamboyant Winston Churchill inspired in the Royal Navy a mixture of wonder and dismay. Full of energy, he was prepared to ride roughshod over accepted professional opinion. Beatty, serving as his Naval Secretary from January 1912 until

February 1913, had a better opportunity than most of seeing Churchill at close quarters. His opinion of the First Lord may of course have been enhanced by the fact that Churchill generally accepted Beatty's advice, but in general it was favourable. On a trip on the Admiralty yacht *Enchantress,* Beatty wrote to his wife on May 27 1912 that 'Winston talks about nothing but the sea and the Navy and the wonderful things he is going to do.' He found the trip very boring, but gave a warm assessment of Churchill:

> Of all the lot on board I like Winston the best. He is sincere, he does enthuse, he is keen and he is appreciative of the Navy so shall not like to hurt his feelings and it will have to be managed skilfully.[14]

His letters to his wife on the subject of the First Lord were not always so complimentary. After a debate in the House of Commons on July 22 he wrote:

> I have not yet seen in the paper what Winston said yesterday in the House, but whatever it was I know it will raise a storm. I cannot think what has come over him. When I left him last everything was satisfactorily arranged, both for ship construction and increasing the personnel, and I suppose his confrères in the Cabinet have got at him and overcome his arguments. I fear he is not a strong man when it concerns a really big thing, only about the little things which don't really count is he strong. It is most disappointing and I fear he'll drag the Board into the ignominy of it all with him.[15]

Herbert Richmond, whose diary contained outspoken comments about just about all his colleagues, was not impressed with Churchill's grasp of what he called the 'elementary lessons' of war at sea:

> Winston does not understand sea-strategy. He has never read a word about it, and imagines that he can apply a few rules of thumb derived from military handbooks, all untranslated into sea-terms. Of course the main principles are the same, but there is a wide difference in their application.[16]

Churchill's First Sea Lord was Admiral Prince Louis of Battenberg, who enjoyed an enormously high professional reputation among most officers of the Royal Navy. Typically, Richmond, after a meeting of senior officers to discuss the tactical exercise of the Home Fleet in 1910, wrote of Battenberg that he was 'the only one who appears to think his reasons out: he is worth 100 of the others.'[17] Described as having an orderly mind, Battenberg had worked with Churchill for nearly two years before the war and hoped that he would be able to provide some effective guidance for the First Lord. It was widely believed, however, that he was rarely able to restrain his political master, who described their working relationship in these terms:

> We met every day and sometimes twice a day, read the whole position and arrived at a united decision on every matter of consequence … Besides our regular meetings, the First Sea Lord and I consulted together constantly at all hours.[18]

There were those however, such as Lord Charles Beresford, who displayed what Fisher described as 'malignant rancour and jealousy' against Battenberg, and the popular press frequently expressed mistrust of him due to his German origins.

When Battenberg replaced his predecessor, Admiral Sir Francis Bridgeman, Churchill's first thought had been to recall Fisher, of whom he held the highest opinion and with whom he had kept in constant touch. Fisher, however, had been a supporter of Battenberg's appointment and during the latter's tenure of office he was not critical of him; after his resignation, however, he felt able to write (to Jellicoe) that 'Battenberg was a cypher and Winston's facile dupe.'[15] By then Fisher had returned to office as First Sea Lord, bringing with him the enormous reputation he had acquired while in the post from 1904 to 1910, when his reforms effectively created a modern navy fit to fight a major war.

John Rushworth Jellicoe had been earmarked by Fisher as a future leader of Britain's fleet, when he wrote presciently in 1911: 'Jellicoe to be Admiralissimo on October 21, 1914, when the battle of Armageddon comes along.'[20] Born to a middle class family in 1859, Jellicoe had worked closely with Fisher since 1884. He had enjoyed a remarkably successful career, as well as a fortunate one; among other adventures, in 1893 he survived the sinking of the battleship *Victoria*, and in 1900 survived a bullet in his lung when serving as Chief of Staff of the Allied relief column marching on the besieged Western legations during the Boxer rebellion. A small man, five feet six inches tall, he inspired trust and affection in the officers and men who served under him. Typical of these was Captain WW Fisher, who wrote of 'our beloved Commander-in-Chief, the finest character that ever was.'[21] His steady progress up through the ranks of the Royal Navy was due to his absolute integrity and thorough professional ability, his remarkable self control and his ability swiftly and coolly to analyse any situation with accuracy and confidence. By 1908 he was serving with Fisher again as Third Sea Lord and Controller, intimately involved in the design and constructions of the ships which he would in due course command in battle. In 1910 he took command of the Atlantic Fleet; he was back at the Admiralty in 1912 as Second Sea Lord. The German Naval Attaché wrote to Tirpitz that year:

> If one asks English naval officers which admiral would have the best chances for a brilliant career on the basis of his capability, one almost always receives the same answer: besides Prince Louis of Battenberg, unquestionably Sir John Jellicoe. Sir John possesses the absolute confidence of his superiors as well as his subordinates.[22]

Next year, visiting Berlin, where he had many friends in the German navy, Jellicoe asked a similar question when attending a dinner for those who had been in China at the time of the Boxer rebellion, as he recorded in his autobiographical notes:

> I recollect that in the course of conversation, when I asked who were expected to be coming leaders afloat of the German Navy, I was told that Admiral Scheer was certainly one of the future leaders and von Trotha another.[23]

Churchill had been impressed by all that he saw of Jellicoe; on July 28, 1914 he appointed him as second in command of the First Fleet. Jellicoe had already been designated to succeed the Commander-in-Chief, the 62 year old Admiral Sir George Callaghan, in December. Churchill was, however, convinced that the appointment must be brought forward to take effect immediately. Jellicoe was horrified; although he was in no doubt he could do the job, he shrank from supplanting the popular Callaghan, and did all he could to persuade Churchill not to make the change. In spite of the series of telegrams which Jellicoe sent as he made his way north, and which pleaded with him to this effect, the First Lord was adamant, giving Jellicoe only 48 hours after joining before he must be ready to take over.[24]

The charismatic David Beatty was in very many ways the polar opposite of Jellicoe. Born in 1871, he too had an adventurous career as a young officer, serving with the Nile river flotilla during the operations in the Sudan in 1896-1898, and then in China during the Boxer rebellion, where he was wounded in the fighting around Tientsin. At the young age of 29 he was promoted to captain. In the following year he married the recently divorced Ethel Tree, only daughter of the fabulously wealthy American store magnate Marshall Field; with her he came to have a decidedly turbulent relationship. Beatty was a well known figure in London society, and in hunting circles, so much so that, as Professor Marder put it, only those who knew him intimately before the war knew that he was thinking a great deal about the conduct of war. One officer who served under him throughout the war suggested that what made Beatty so preeminent was his spirit, and 'the gift of distinguishing between essentials and not wasting time on non-essentials.'[25] He had a decided propensity for self advertisement, and was at all times a great favourite with the press.

In 1905 Beatty took up the post of Naval Adviser to the Army Council; three years later he was appointed to command the battleship *Queen* in the Atlantic Fleet. He did not form a very favourable view of his superiors there:

> We have a very fine Fleet and the best materials … But we have eight Admirals, and there is not one among them unless it be Prince Louis, who impresses me that he is capable of a great effort, and 34 Captains among whom there is really fine material, which seems wasted for the want of a guide or leader.[26]

Soon, however, Beatty was himself to join the ranks of the admirals, being promoted to Rear Admiral on January 1, 1910, the youngest to reach flag rank since the late eighteenth century. It was after a spell of unemployment, during which he declined the offer of the post of second in command of the Atlantic Fleet, that he became Naval Secretary to Winston Churchill, after which his continued progress was assured.

The commanders of Jellicoe's four battle squadrons at the outbreak of war were not especially able. The 1st Battle Squadron was led by Vice Admiral Sir Lewis Bayly, described by Marder as 'a hard, tough, independent man, a stern disciplinarian, and a most redoubtable autocrat. He certainly did not suffer fools or weaklings gladly.'[27] Vice Admiral Sir George Warrender, commanding the 2nd Battle Squadron, was regarded as a very able man, although events would show that this was an overestimate of his abilities. The 3rd and 4th Battle Squadrons were led by Vice Admirals Edward Bradford and Douglas Gamble, who were 'good seamen who lacked the gift of magnetic leadership and had never revealed any creative powers or willingness to use the brains of their subordinates.'[28] Among Jellicoe's cruiser squadron commanders were the eccentric Rear Admiral William Pakenham and the very capable Commodore Goodenough.

The commander of the Channel Fleet (who in December was to become second in command of the Grand Fleet) was Vice Admiral Sir Cecil Burney. The best that Marder could find to say about him, apart from noting his reputation as a fine seaman, was that he had a powerful physique; regrettably, he had little imagination. Jellicoe was served as his Chief of Staff by Rear Admiral Charles Madden, his brother-in-law, another admiral without much imagination but a sound and knowledgeable tactician.

Although junior in rank, there were two other post holders who would play a key part in the naval war. Commodore Reginald Tyrwhitt commanded the Harwich Force, which turned out to be crucially important throughout the war. He had a somewhat erratic early career, one of the low points being his conviction by a court martial of hazarding his ship after a night time collision in heavy weather between the *Arun*, the destroyer which he commanded, and the *Decoy*. He was widely held to have been harshly treated, and the *St James's Gazette* quoted approvingly his appeal to the court martial which was put forward,

> not only on his own behalf, but also on behalf of the large number of officers who were ever willing and able to incur the great risks and responsibilities inseparable from and necessary to the good and efficient development of the torpedo boat service.[29]

Tyrwhitt reached the rank of Captain in 1908, and after leading a flotilla of destroyers with the Home Fleet was promoted to Commodore (Second Class) in command of all the destroyers with the Fleet. With the outbreak of war he took command of the Harwich Force, consisting of three light cruisers and thirty nine destroyers. Marder wrote admiringly of Tyrwhitt that he 'was a magnificent man of more than middle height, with a sharp-featured, bronzed face, a strong nose above a determined chin, and bright eyes shielded by black eyebrows.'[30] He, in the same way as Jellicoe, was regarded with immense trust and affection by all those who served with him.

Commodore Roger Keyes, commanding the submarines at Harwich, worked closely with Tyrwhitt, with whom he had a very good working relationship. Tyrwhitt wrote on August 1 to his wife:

> Roger and I get on well and he is a great comfort to me, as he approves of my arrangements and I of his. Perhaps we are a mutual admiration society, which is just as well, as we have much in common just now.[31]

Keyes was popular, enthusiastic and a great leader of men, although generally felt to be lacking in intellectual capacity. He had displayed his fearlessness in China where, like Jellicoe and Beatty, he had served with the relief force; Marder records that he squeezed through a hole in the legation wall with a white ensign wrapped round him to be the first to announce the arrival of the relief.[32]

At the Admiralty, Vice Admiral Sir Henry Jackson had been serving as Chief of the War Staff since 1913. In 1914 he was earmarked for the command in the Mediterranean, but in the event was retained at the Admiralty for special services, and he remained there until May 1915 when he was appointed First Sea Lord. He was succeeded as Chief of Staff by Vice Admiral Sir Doveton Sturdee, who was one of the officers within the group around Beresford, who described him as 'one of the most brilliant, if not the most brilliant, officers of my acquaintance.' Whatever his qualities, this would have been sufficient to damn him in Fisher's eyes, and in fact his abilities fell far short of his own assessment of them. The rationale for his appointment appears to have been his reputation as a student of history. Under him, as the Director of the

Operations Division, was Rear Admiral Arthur Leveson, not a popular man; and the latter's assistant was the acerbic Captain Herbert Richmond, whose comments on life at the Admiralty and its inhabitants were invariably pungent, if sometimes hasty. Rear Admiral Henry Oliver, who would in due course come to exercise a huge influence on the naval war, was serving as Naval Secretary to the First Lord.

In Germany, the apparently dominant figure in naval circles was of course Grand Admiral Alfred von Tirpitz. Ever since he was appointed as State Secretary of the Imperial Naval Office in 1897, he had had the ear of the Kaiser, and he thereafter had steadily increased his power and influence. Born in 1849, he entered the German navy at the age of 16. In 1877, when he held the rank of lieutenant commander, he joined the Torpedo Research and Development Section of the Admiralty, where he remained until 1886 when he became Inspector of the Torpedo Boat Division, a post he held for three years. Reaching the rank of captain, he had two seagoing appointments before becoming Chief of Staff of the Baltic Naval Station in 1890. Five years later, with the rank of Rear Admiral, he became Chief of Staff of the High Command; then, in 1896, he took command of the East Asiatic Cruiser Squadron for a year. By now he was marked as the coming man with clear ideas as to the future development of the German Navy; they attracted the enthusiastic support of the Kaiser and he was appointed as State Secretary on June 15 1897, with the opportunity to put into practice his far reaching policies for the navy. Promotions duly followed to the rank of Vice Admiral in 1899, Admiral in 1903 and Grand Admiral in 1911.[33]

His contribution to the development of the High Seas Fleet has already been explored, as has been his conviction that war could and should have been avoided. On its outbreak he was soon at odds with the other senior figures in the naval establishment. He intrigued ceaselessly to gain a position in which he could actively control naval policy, not least through the network of his supporters that he had built up over the years. However, even the great power and influence that he had amassed was not enough for his campaigns to prevail. Although he had proved himself an extremely skilful politician during the years of the navy's expansion, again and again cajoling and persuading the Reichstag into giving him the budgetary support which he needed for his construction programme, his political skills were not enough to overcome the naval establishment.

Tirpitz was, by 1914, in substantial conflict with Admiral Georg von Müller, who as Chief of the Naval Cabinet was probably the strongest influence over the Kaiser's thinking. Müller had not supported Tirpitz as he would have wished during the introduction of the Supplemental Naval Law of 1912, and it was becoming apparent that his influence over the Kaiser had waned considerably. And, with the outbreak of war, the limitations on the power that Tirpitz could wield as State Secretary rapidly became apparent. The division of responsibility in the naval command structure seriously inhibited his effort to control policy. Officially, the Chief of the Admiralty Staff, Admiral Hugo von Pohl, was the Kaiser's primary naval adviser, while Müller's position continued to strengthen. There was no appetite for the appointment of Tirpitz as Supreme Commander of the navy, which was what above all he craved.[34]

Admiral Hugo von Pohl was appointed Chief of the Admiralty Staff in 1913. Born in Silesia in 1855, he entered the navy at the age of twenty one. In 1900, after a stint working in the Imperial Naval Office under Tirpitz, he reached the rank of captain; he had previously been one of a number of Admiralty Staff officers who had been associated with Tirpitz and the Torpedo Boat Division. Many of these remained closely in touch with the State Secretary, and were a group which somewhat resembled the 'Fishpond', the term used to describe the group of officers similarly assembled by Jacky Fisher. As time went by, however, Pohl ceased to be one of Tirpitz's closer confidants. He was promoted to commodore in 1905; by 1909 he reached the rank of vice admiral, commanding a battle squadron with the High Seas Fleet.

Pohl succeeded Heeringen as Chief of the Admiralty Staff in 1913. He was, apparently, very sensitive to the fact that he was born into a modest middleclass family, being recorded as remarking to Bogislav von Selchow:

> But, my dear Selchow, you do not even know far ahead of the others you are by belonging to an old noble family; for what to you seems to be a matter of course, others need unlimited amounts of sweat. And that is something that is very ugly; one has constantly to wipe it off.[35]

Pohl was not a particularly effective leader, and was generally disliked on account of his arrogance. Captain Hugh Watson, who had been serving as British Naval Attaché at the outbreak of war, gave Jellicoe a pen picture of the man:

> Short and square built, but slim. Has the reputation of being a good seaman. Gives impression of ability, quickness of decision and force of character ... a very taciturn fellow who looks as if he had lost half a crown and found sixpence ... He won't enthuse people at all [but] ... a man of some character, and with a good knowledge of his profession. He does not look very healthy.[36]

The third member of the triumvirate that presided over the German Navy was Admiral Georg Alexander von Müller. Born in 1854, he entered the navy in 1871. In 1879 he encountered Tirpitz when he was transferred to the torpedo service. Thereafter he served in the Admiralty Staff in the Intelligence Section before a seagoing appointment with the East Asiatic Squadron. In 1889, when William II established a Naval Cabinet for the first time, Müller was appointed to serve in the office under its first Chief, Gustav von Senden-Bibran. The latter held that post until 1909. Müller thus became closely acquainted with the Kaiser. He went on to hold a number of appointments, rising steadily before returning to become departmental chief in the Naval Cabinet with the rank of captain. Two seagoing appointments followed before he became an aide to the Kaiser in 1904. In 1905, Senden-Bibran told him, when Müller applied for another overseas commission, that he had been chosen as his successor. It was a post for which Müller seriously doubted his suitability but in 1906 he took over from Senden-Bibran whose health had given way. He was formally appointed to the post in April 1908.[37]

The duties of the Chief of the Naval Cabinet, as with his military opposite number, brought a good deal of influence to the holder of the post; he was responsible for personnel issues and, crucially, for promotions, and thereby exerted a considerable effect on the policies of the navy and the way it both prepared for, and in due course conducted, the war. By the time of its outbreak he was seriously concerned about the ceaseless manoeuvring of Tirpitz and his allies. He was supportive of the Chancellor, Theobald von Bethmann-Hollweg, although aware of his limitations as a statesman. Müller tried to hold the balance between the warring factions of the navy, but not always successfully, as his diary shows.

Commanding the High Seas Fleet was Admiral Friedrich von Ingenohl. Born in 1857, he joined the navy in 1874. In 1888 he came under the influence of Tirpitz for the first time, when serving in a torpedo boat. He rose steadily, with the rank of captain coming in 1902 and Rear Admiral in 1907, when he commanded the Imperial yacht *Hohenzollern*. From 1910 to 1913 he commanded the II Battle Squadron, and was then appointed to the High Seas Fleet. Hugh Watson thought him 'a more cheerful personality' than Pohl, although with less experience.[38]

It was made clear to Ingenohl that, from the outset, a cautious strategy must be adopted, and he published an Order of the Day on August 14 to explain this:

> All the information we have received about the English naval forces points to the fact that the English Battle Fleet avoids the North Sea entirely and keeps far beyond the range of our own forces ... This behaviour on the part of the enemy forces us to the conclusion that he himself intends to avoid the losses he fears he may suffer at our hands and to compel us to come with our battleships to his coast and there fall a victim to his mines and submarines. We are not going to oblige our enemy thus ... But they must, and will, come to us some day or other. Our immediate task is therefore to cause our enemy losses by all the methods of guerrilla warfare and at every point where we can find him ... the duty of those of us in the battleships of the Fleet, meanwhile, is to keep this, our main weapon, sharp and bright for the decisive battle which we shall have to fight.[39]

Among Ingenohl's Squadron Commanders was the highly regarded Vice Admiral Reinhard Scheer. Like many of his senior colleagues, he came from a middle class background. He was born in 1863 and entered the navy at the age of sixteen. As a sea cadet he received the second highest grade in his class. After graduating, he served in the armoured cruiser *Hertha* on a world tour, and subsequently in two tours of duty with the East Asiatic Squadron. After the first of these, when he struck up a friendship with the future Admiral Henning von Holtzendorff, he spent four years acquiring expertise in torpedo technology, in which he soon became known as a specialist. Thus he too became part of the coterie of promising officers around Tirpitz. In 1897 he followed Tirpitz into the Imperial Naval Office, to work in the Torpedo Section.[40] Returning to a seagoing appointment, he took command of the light cruiser *Gazelle* where he had the reputation of being a strict disciplinarian, known as 'the man in the iron mask'. Thereafter, in 1903 he returned to the Imperial Naval Office as Chief of its Central Division. In 1905 he reached the rank of captain, and in 1907 was posted to command the pre-dreadnought battleship *Elsass*. His fitness reports at the Imperial Naval Office had spoken of his high sense of duty, selflessness and technical competence, while as captain of *Elsass* he was reported 'as filling the position well and very accomplished in gunnery; should be suited for a high staff position'.[41] In 1909 his old friend Holtzendorff, commanding the High Seas Fleet, offered him the post of Chief of Staff, in which he served until the autumn on 1911. In 1910 he was promoted to Rear Admiral.

He next went back to the Imperial Naval Office as Chief of the General Department for a year before returning to the High Seas Fleet as commander of the II Battle Squadron, and was promoted to vice admiral in December 1913. He was still in this post at the outbreak of war. He was an intuitive leader, as his flag lieutenant at Jutland, Ernst von Weizsäcker, wrote many years later.

> Scheer had no use for rigid schemes. He was always ready to look at a problem from a new angle. Someone on his staff once called him the *primesautier*, which is a person who reacts

> on the first stimulus. He surrounded himself with men he knew and could trust, such as Trotha and Levetzow.[42]

Scheer himself wrote in his account of the Battle of Jutland:

> In judging the proceedings it must be borne in mind that at sea a leader adapts his action to the events taking place around him. It may possibly reveal errors which can only be accounted for by reports from his own ships or valuable information from enemy statements. The art of leadership consists in securing an approximately correct picture from the impression of the moment, and then acting in accordance with it.[43]

Destined to be Beatty's opponent, Rear Admiral Franz Hipper was born in Bavaria in 1863. Like many of his contemporaries he came from the middle class, growing up in Southern Germany. His career began, as was usual, in the sail training ship *Niobe*. He soon passed into the Torpedo Division, and was appointed as torpedo officer in various ships until serving as senior watch officer in the battleship *Wörth*, commanded by Prince Henry of Prussia, in 1894-1895. His next posting was as commander of the Second Torpedo Boat Reserve Division, where he particularly distinguished himself. This was followed by two postings as navigator, first in *Kurfürst Friedrich Wilhelm* and then in the Imperial yacht *Hohenzollern*. This latter posting brought him into contact with the highest military and naval circles which, with the good opinion Prince Henry had formed of him, stood him in good stead. In 1902 he was appointed to the command of the Second Torpedo Flotilla, after which he joined in 1905 the staff of the North Sea Naval Station for six months, followed by the command of the light cruiser *Leipzig* in 1906 for a further six months, and then the armoured cruiser *Friedrich Karl*, with the rank of captain. Pohl, at that time commanding the reconnaissance forces, reported on Hipper's command of *Friedrich Karl:*

> He has brought the ship to a higher degree of combat effectiveness, and the ship has won the Kaiser Prize for good shooting. One of the best captains we have in the Cruisers. A good example for his officers. Recommended for battleship command and for higher independent commands.[44]

Hipper's next posting in 1908 was to commission the new armoured cruiser *Gneisenau*, after which he returned to the command of torpedo boats for the next three years. His biographer has noted that his total service in the torpedo branch was 10.3 years, more experience than in any other branch of the navy.[45] In October 1911 he was appointed to command the armoured cruiser *Yorck*, serving also as Chief of Staff to Rear Admiral Gustav von Bachmann, the deputy commander of the reconnaissance forces. When Bachmann in January 1912 became commander, Hipper followed as his deputy, becoming a rear admiral at the age of 49.

Bachmann was in October 1913 made Chief of the Baltic Station, and Hipper again moved into his post as commander of the reconnaissance forces. In this position Hipper inherited as Chief of Staff the future Grand Admiral Erich Raeder, who wrote of the change in leadership:

> But if we had to lose Admiral Bachmann, we could not have had a replacement more to our liking than Rear Admiral Hipper … Our new commander was an energetic and impulsive

> individual, with quick perception and a keen 'seaman's eye', but unlike his predecessor, he had risen exclusively through performance in the fleet, having distinguished himself successively with the torpedo boats, then as captain of the armoured cruiser *Gneisenau*, and then as commander of the light cruiser and torpedo boat forces. Sheer theory was not his forte; he hated paperwork, and up to this time had never had a staff larger than a Chief of Staff and a flag lieutenant. Now, as commander of all the scouting forces, he had to put up with the reports and suggestions of a large staff.[46]

At the outbreak of war the most powerful squadron of the High Seas Fleet was the I Battle Squadron of eight dreadnoughts (four of the *Nassau* class and four of the *Ostfriesland* class, commanded by Vice Admiral Wilhelm von Lans. He was born in 1861, entering the navy in 1878. Between spells of seagoing duty he had served on the Admiralty Staff. In 1899 he took command of the new gunboat *Iltis* on the East Asiatic station, and in this capacity took part in the Allied operations during the Boxer Rebellion in China; he was present in the capture of the Taku forts. By 1907 he was serving as Chief of Staff of the High Seas Fleet, and was involved in acrimonious disputes with the Admiralty Staff. From this post he moved on to the Inspectorate of the Torpedo Forces, where he became involved in the disputes between Holtzendorff, as Commander-in-Chief, and Tirpitz, strongly supporting the former in his belief that the State Secretary was 'disastrous for the navy.'[47] He was one of the senior officers most strongly urging a defensive strategy, explaining to Tirpitz his view that preserving the High Seas Fleet was important to the guaranteeing of Denmark's neutrality.

The III Battle Squadron was commanded by Rear Admiral Felix Funke. It consisted of the four newest dreadnoughts available in August 1914, the *Kaiser* class. Funke was born in 1865, joining the navy in 1882, and rising steadily through the ranks. In 1904 he was posted to Tsingtao, and was an observer of much of the Russo–Japanese War at Sea. In due course in December 1914 he was to change places with Scheer. The remaining three squadrons were not deployed as part of the High Seas Fleet; they were composed of the older pre-dreadnoughts that were certainly not fit to fight in the line of battle. The IV, V and VI Squadrons were commanded respectively by Vice Admiral Erhard Schmidt, Vice Admiral Grepow and Rear Admiral Richard Eckermann; the latter was, shortly after the outbreak of war, appointed as Ingenohl's Chief of Staff.

5

The First Battle of Heligoland Bight

The outbreak of the First World War occurred at a moment of extreme good fortune for the Royal Navy. Instead of the normal summer manoeuvres in 1914, there was held a test mobilisation of the Third Fleet – the reserve units that would be brought to operational readiness in case of war. This began on July 15, 20,000 reservists having been called up, and on July 17-18 a grand review of the entire fleet took place at Spithead. On the days following, the fleet put to sea for tactical exercises; after this, on July 23, the units of the Third Fleet began to return to their home ports. On July 26, with the diplomatic situation having sharply deteriorated, Battenberg, as First Sea Lord, suspended the demobilisation. It thus came about that the First Fleet, soon to be called the Grand Fleet, was effectively on a war footing and on the night of July 29/30 it sailed through the Dover Straits en route for its battle stations at Scapa Flow, Cromarty and Rosyth.[1]

The Grand Fleet, at the outbreak of war, consisted of the 1st, 2nd, 3rd and 4th Battle Squadrons and the 1st Battle Cruiser Squadron, a total of twenty one dreadnoughts, four battle cruisers and eight predreadnoughts. In addition there were the 2nd and 3rd Cruiser Squadrons, comprising eight armoured cruisers; and the 1st Light Cruiser Squadron of four ships, with nine other cruisers and forty two destroyers. It left behind the Channel Fleet, based on Portland, consisting of the 5th, 7th and 8th Battle Squadrons, with a total of nineteen predreadnoughts. At Harwich, under Commodore Tyrwhitt, who reported to Jellicoe, was a force of light cruisers and destroyers, together with a force of the newer submarines under Commodore Keyes. In addition, there were a series of Patrol Flotillas based on Dover, the Humber, the Tyne and the Forth. The 12th Cruiser Squadron patrolled the western end of the Channel.[2]

The bases to which it was steaming were not, however, by any means in an ideal state. The navy's traditional bases at Portsmouth and Plymouth were too far from the North Sea to be useful and Chatham, on the east coast, was also too far to the south. It had been resolved, therefore, as early as 1903 to establish a first class base at Rosyth, on the Firth of Forth, where the excellent anchorage was roughly equidistant from Heligoland and the Skagerrak. The extensive works required, however, were frequently postponed for economic reasons; in addition, as Professor Marder observed, the Firth of Forth did have a number of disadvantages, which contributed to the delay, such as its exposure to danger from minelaying, the limited area of deep water above the line of defence, and the tidal stream above what Fisher, who disliked Rosyth, called 'that beastly bridge'.[3] Since Rosyth would not be fully ready until 1915, it was resolved to look about for what were termed 'advanced bases of a temporary and auxiliary character', and these were found at Cromarty Firth and Scapa Flow in the Orkneys.

Scapa Flow and its strategic significance was succinctly described by one of its historians:

> A large area of water, some 120 square miles of it, almost totally enclosed by a ring of islands, the South Isles of Orkney, and this whole mosaic of land and sea, poised strategically just off the north coast of Scotland, divides the long grey surges of the Atlantic Ocean from the equally inhospitable waters of the North Sea. It is this combination of geographical location and natural formation which has given Scapa Flow its unique character and its potential as a naval base; a potential it has held throughout the centuries, for whoever controls it commands the North Sea with easy access to either side of the British Isles and the wide oceans of the world beyond.[4]

Originally there were nine major entrances to Scapa Flow, but four of these were later blocked during the Second World War by massive causeways. The principal entrance used by the larger units of the fleet was Hoxa Sound, between the islands of Flotta and South Ronaldsay; smaller vessels such as destroyers tended to used Switha Sound, between Flotta and Switha. The actual appearance of Scapa Flow was lyrically described by the Orkney author Eric Linklater, who wrote:

> On calm days the islands floated on a deep-blue sea in a charm of shadowed cliffs and reddish moors, the harvest was ripe, and the fields were bearded with bright gold or gay in a lovely green. The forehead of the hills rose in smooth lines against a lucent sky, and rippled lakes provoked a passion for mere water.[5]

Thus Scapa Flow in the golden days of summer; but during less clement weather it was a grim place to be. Linklater also wrote of the experience of a south easterly gale as enduring 'such a hurly burly, so rude and ponderous a buffeting, that one could hardly deny a sense of outrage, a suspicion that the wind's violence was a personal enmity.'

In the Napoleonic wars a battery was built, to defend Longhope Bay together with two Martello towers; but during the following century little more was done to make Scapa Flow a secure naval base, and it was virtually defenceless when the Grand Fleet arrived. Nonetheless, it had its advocates, most prominent of whom was Fisher who, after the war, wrote in characteristically boastful terms, to *The Times*, to claim to have discovered it:

> Once looking at a chart in my secluded room at the Admiralty, in 1905, I saw a large landlocked sheet of water unsurveyed and nameless. It was Scapa Flow. One hour after this an Admiralty survey ship was en route there. Secretly she went for none but myself and my most excellent friend the Hydrographer knew.[6]

It was to Fisher that Jellicoe wrote as late as January 1915 to express his concern at the complete defencelessness of Scapa Flow as a base for the Grand Fleet:

> If you would only just compare the orders for the protection of the High Seas Fleet ... with the arrangements here you would be horrified. *I wonder if I ever slept at all.* Thank goodness

> the Germans imagine we have proper defences. At least so I imagine – otherwise there would be no Grand Fleet left now.[7]

Churchill was particularly concerned about the seriousness of the submarine threat to Scapa Flow. Prompted by a letter from Beatty complaining that 'we are gradually being pushed out of the North Sea and off our own particular perch,' he demanded action, addressing a note to the First Sea Lord, the Third Sea Lord, the Fourth Sea Lord and the Naval Secretary on October 24:

> Every nerve must be strained to reconcile the fleet to Scapa. Successive lines of submarine defences should be prepared, reinforced by electric-contact mines as proposed by the Commander-in-Chief. Nothing should stand in the way of the equipment of this anchorage with every possible means of security. The First Lord and the First Sea Lord will receive a report of progress every third day until the work is completed and the Commander-in-Chief satisfied.[8]

Nevertheless, in the years before the war, in spite of Fisher's enthusiasm for Scapa Flow, he and Churchill had supported the Admiralty's view in 1912 that Cromarty Firth would be a better choice as the advanced base for the main fleet. The conclusive reason for this appears to have been the Admiralty's finding that the sea could run so high inside Scapa Flow as to make the use of a floating dock and repairing facilities at times impracticable. The recommendation went on to note that Cromarty was connected to the rail network of the UK. In addition:

> Apart from its primary value as a second class naval base Cromarty has a secondary and slightly less important value as a War Anchorage. Under the protection of the defences provided for the security of the floating repairing facilities, vessels containing fuel and stores of all kinds may be accumulated for the use of the fleet, forming a source of supply alternative and supplementary to Rosyth. Owing to the vast size of modern fleets, which makes their accommodation at a single anchorage almost impossible, the provision of supplementary war anchorage is a matter of great importance.[9]

Cromarty, the Admiralty recommended, should be heavily fortified, whilst Scapa Flow should not be provided with fixed defences. This, it appears, was due solely to the cost involved. Cromarty, unlike Scapa Flow, could easily be made impregnable to attack from submarines; the multitude of entrances to Scapa Flow made the cost greater than, it was thought, justifiable. Thus it was that the Grand Fleet's principal base at the outbreak of war was undefended. By comparison, as described in Chapter 2, the defences of the bases of the High Seas Fleet were, as Professor Marder put it, 'simply terrific.'

The High Seas Fleet, which had been cruising off the Norwegian coast, was not immediately recalled because it was feared that this step would escalate the diplomatic crisis. By July 26, however, William was prepared to wait no longer and ordered the recall of the fleet. It returned to its bases to prepare to execute the War Orders issued to it. These were summarised by Scheer:

> The order underlying this plan of campaign was this: The Fleet must strike when circumstances are favourable; it must therefore seek battle with the English Fleet only when a

> state of equality has been achieved by the methods of guerrilla warfare. It thus left the Commander-in-Chief of the High Seas Fleet freedom of action to exploit any favourable opportunity and put no obstacles in his way, but it required of him that he should not risk the whole Fleet in battle until there was a probability of victory. Moreover, it started from the assumption that opportunities would arise of doing the enemy damage when, as was to be expected, he initiated a blockade of the German Bight which was in accordance with the rules of International Law.[10]

This assumption, that the British would penetrate at once into the Heligoland Bight, underpinned German thinking to the point that if it simply did not happen, Germany might in the words of Ivo Nicolai Lambi, be in the position of approaching the war 'with no definite plans for naval operations against Britain and the Triple Entente.'[11] This assumption was held, as has been pointed out, after a series of war games to test the likely outcome of a British imposition of a blockade. In readiness for the imminent attack, the High Seas Fleet began on July 31 to move through the Kiel Canal to its bases on the North Sea. By the outbreak of war on August 4 the two dreadnought squadrons of the battle fleet, the I and II, were respectively stationed at the mouth of the Jade River and behind the Jade Bar, while Scheer's II Squadron of eight predreadnoughts was assigned to the mouth of the Elbe between Cuxhaven and Brunsbüttel. Hipper's I Scouting Group of four battle cruisers was at the mouth of the Jade. The other Scouting Groups, consisting of light cruisers and destroyers, were deployed around the entrances to the Jade, Elbe and Weser rivers.

On both sides, the taut expectation of immediate action was disappointed, and within two weeks this was already being strongly felt. Tyrwhitt wrote from Harwich on August 15 that he was starting to feel 'rather bored at looking for nothing' and that he was 'beginning to give up hope of getting at the Germans for some time.'[12] Beatty was similarly disillusioned, writing to his wife on August 24:

> We are still wandering about the face of the ocean and apparently get no nearer to the end. In fact we have not begun yet. This waiting is the deuce and, as far as we can see, has no limit. We are entirely in the hands of our friends the Germans as to when he [sic] will come out and be whacked.[13]

The Germans shared the British feeling of surprise, but for Scheer the postponement of any immediate confrontation was all to the good:

> The fact that an English offensive did not materialise in the first weeks of the war gave cause for reflection, for with every day's grace the enemy gave us he was abandoning some of the advantage of his earlier mobilisation, while our coast defences were improved. The sweep of light cruisers and destroyers which, starting out star-wise from Heligoland, had scoured the seas over a circumference of about 100 sea miles had produced nothing.[14]

Roger Keyes, as commodore commanding the submarines, based at Harwich, was even more discontented than his friend Tyrwhitt, especially following an incident in the southern part of the North Sea on August 18. That day, two German light cruisers, *Stralsund* and *Strassburg*, covered by a screen of submarines, came out in search of British patrols. They met the light cruiser *Fearless*, commanded by Captain Wilfred Blunt, which was leading sixteen destroyers of the Harwich 1st Flotilla. *Fearless* was a 3,440 ton cruiser of the *Active* class, armed with 10 – 4 inch guns; *Stralsund* and *Strassburg* were both 4,550 tons of the *Breslau* class, carrying 12 – 4.1inch guns. Blunt, however, after having gone in pursuit of *Stralsund*, wrongly identified her as the armoured cruiser *Yorck*, of 9,350 tons, mounting 4 – 8.2 inch guns and 10 5.9 inch guns. Fearing that the armoured cruiser's guns would outrange those of his force, Blunt turned away and called for support from Tyrwhitt. Had *Stralsund* continued steaming southwest in pursuit of *Fearless*, she would have sailed into a trap; but her captain being warned of this, she turned away.

This prompted an anguished letter from Keyes to Leveson, the Director of Operations of the Naval War Staff, on August 21:

> When are we going to make war and make the Germans realise that wherever they come out – destroyers, cruisers, battleships or all three – they will be fallen on and attacked? I feel sick and sore ... a light cruiser equal in offensive power to the *Fearless*, has put 16 destroyers and the *Fearless* to flight. However one glosses it over, those are the facts. Don't think I am blaming Blunt or his captains ... But it is not by such incidents we will get the right atmosphere.[15]

Burning to take the offensive, Tyrwhitt and Keyes conceived a plan for a raid into the Heligoland Bight. Strictly speaking, both of them were under the command of Rear Admiral Christian, the overall commander of the Southern Force, but they were resolved themselves to take the initiative. The plan was based on information gathered by Keyes's submarines about the German patrols in the Bight. It was noted that their practice was for light cruisers to lead out a flotilla of destroyers each evening; the destroyers then fanned out during the night, returning the following morning to rejoin the light cruisers 20 miles NW of Heligoland. Keyes 'was of opinion that a well organised drive, commencing inshore before dawn, should inflict considerable loss on the returning night patrols'.[16] The plan was revised to provide that the advance was not to be made until 8.00am, so that the target would now be the enemy's daytime destroyer patrols. Two lines of submarines were to be posted to attack any German cruisers that came out to support their destroyers. The strike force was to be Tyrwhitt's new flagship, the light cruiser *Arethusa*, and *Fearless*, leading the 1st and 3rd Flotillas respectively. Support would be provided by the battlecruisers *Invincible* and *New Zealand*, based in the Humber.[17]

Keyes, who at first had received little attention from the Naval War Staff when he first took his plan to the Admiralty on August 23, obtained an interview with Churchill who was immediately taken with the scheme. Next day a meeting with the First and Second Sea Lords was convened, to which Keyes and Tyrwhitt were invited, and the plan was approved with some variations. These in part were due to the fact that the operation was intended as a cover for the proposal to land three Royal Marine battalions to hold Ostend.[18]

The intention was for Keyes to sail on August 26 and the remaining forces next day, so that the sweep could begin on August 28. Extraordinarily, the Naval War Staff did not tell Jellicoe of what was planned until two days after the meeting, and then he was only informed that a sweep by the 1st and 3rd Flotillas was planned for August 28 from east to west, commencing between Horns Reef and Heligoland with battlecruisers in support. Two hours later, at 4.35pm, Jellicoe replied that he proposed to cooperate in the operation and asking for full details of the plan; he would leave at 6.00am on August 27. He got no immediate reply, and his next signal, at 5.54pm illustrated his perplexity:

> Until I know the plan of operations I am unable to suggest the best method of cooperation, but the breadth of sweep appears to be very great for two flotillas. I could send a third flotilla, holding a fourth in reserve, and can support by light cruisers. What officers will be in command of operations, and in what ships, so that I can communicate with them? What is the direction of the sweep and [the] northern limits, and what ships take part?[19]

Sturdee's indifference to Jellicoe's concern may be judged by the tone of his eventual reply, sent just after midnight on August 27: 'Cooperation by battle fleet not required. Battlecruisers can support if convenient.'[20] Jellicoe ordered Beatty and Goodenough to sail at 5.00am on August 27, and himself put to sea with the 2nd and 4th Battle Squadrons at 5.45 pm that day; the 1st and 3rd Battle Squadrons were already at sea. Beatty aimed to rendezvous with Moore's two battlecruisers 90 miles NW of Heligoland. As Goldrick remarks, Jellicoe's 'sane measures had restored some chance of success to what had become a dubious venture indeed.' Meanwhile nobody told Tyrwhitt and Keyes of the support they were to receive. When the Admiralty finally sent a message to Harwich for them they were by then out of range for a wireless message from the port.

Deficient though the Admiralty's management of the operation was, the German dispositions in the Bight were such as to give the British plan every chance of success. Responsibility for the patrols belonged to Hipper as commander of the scouting forces, but Ingenohl, characteristically, issued instructions as to how the patrols should operate. Erich Raeder, Hipper's Chief of Staff, was extremely critical in his memoirs:

> According to these instructions, the light forces, during daylight, were stationed in patrol sectors centred on the outermost Elbe lightship and covering the entire Bight. Upon approach of darkness they would steam to sea to form an advanced picket line against any approach, and then return to their inshore stations at daylight. Naturally, as the patrolling ships ranged farther and farther from Heligoland, the circles widened and the gaps between the respective patrol craft increased. Consequently the ships had to patrol singly, instead of in pairs or groups as prudence would have dictated in the presence of a strong enemy… using the light cruisers for routine picket line work not only exposed them to enemy submarine attacks, but likewise took them, as it also did the torpedo boat squadrons, away from their correct tactical employment – which was to conduct long range night reconnaissance.[21]

The consequence of these fundamentally defective dispositions was soon to be dramatically demonstrated.

Keyes, with the destroyer leader *Lurcher* and *Firedrake*, and eight submarines, put to sea at midnight on August 26. He was followed five hours later by Tyrwhitt with the Harwich Force, while at the same time Moore sortied from the Humber, his two battlecruisers accompanied by four destroyers. Finally the five elderly armoured cruisers that constituted Cruiser Force C, under the overall command of Rear Admiral Christian, sailed on the night of August 27 to patrol off Terschelling. What followed was an extremely confused affair indeed.

At about 3.30 am Tyrwhitt's lookouts sighted dark shapes approaching from astern, which to his great surprise turned out to be Goodenough's squadron. Tyrwhitt, puzzled by this, signalled: 'Are you taking part in the operation?' To this Goodenough replied: 'Yes, I know your course and will support you. Beatty is behind us.'[22] It was as well that Tyrwhitt now knew the true position; the silhouette of Goodenough's light cruisers, having two masts and four funnels, would have led them to be taken to be enemy ships. Keyes, still in ignorance of Goodenough's arrival, was soon to do just that.

The situation was further complicated by the weather; as the British forces steamed eastward, a thickening fog reduced visibility. First contact came just before 7.00 am, when the 1st Flotilla sighted the German destroyer *G 194*, which made off southeast, pursued by *Laurel* and three others of the 4th Division. Hipper, on receiving the news, issued an order to the light cruisers *Stettin* and *Frauenlob* to 'hunt destroyers'; the other light cruisers were ordered to raise steam. Tyrwhitt turned to follow *Laurel* and the others; meanwhile other German destroyers were steering parallel with *Arethusa*. The German destroyers, the V Flotilla, were soon suffering from engineering problems as they were unprepared for high speed operations; their speed dropping, they called for cruiser support, of which the first elements, in the form of *Stettin* and *Frauenlob*, arrived at 7.57 am.

Fearless engaged *Stettin*, scoring one hit before the German light cruiser turned away, principally to raise steam in all her boilers; *Fearless* turned SSW to follow *Arethusa*. Tyrwhitt's flagship was engaging *Frauenlob*, and having rather the worst of it, suffering 15 direct hits on the side and waterline and many inboard. However she hit *Frauenlob* 10 times before turning away to the west; her adversary did not follow, retiring south eastward. While this was occurring Keyes, to the north west, had sighted two four funnelled cruisers which he supposed to be hostile, being still unaware of Goodenough's presence.

At 8.20 am *Fearless* and her destroyers sighted the isolated German destroyer *V187*. Attempting to outrun the 5th Division of destroyers sent by Blunt to pursue her, *V187* found herself steaming directly towards *Lowestoft* and *Nottingham*, detached by Goodenough to support Tyrwhitt. *V187* executed a 180 degree turn, but now encountered the rest of Blunt's flotilla. Within a few moments she was fatally damaged; her remaining gun fired at and hit *Goshawk*. At 9.10 am *V187* went down. As several boats from the British destroyers moved towards the survivors in the water *Stettin* reappeared; Captain Nerger was unaware that rescue operations were in progress, as he later reported:

> At 9.06 am eight destroyers were sighted bunched together. I at once signalled the Admiral commanding the Scouting Forces, 'Am in action with flotilla in square 133,' turned to port and opened fire at 7200 metres. The first salvo straddled and thereafter many hits were observed. While most of the destroyers scattered, two remained on the spot, apparently badly damaged, but were soon lost to sight in the mist.[23]

In addition to *Stettin* and *Frauenlob*, Hipper had also ordered *Köln* and *Strassburg* from Wilhelmshaven and *Mainz* from Ems to put to sea, while the elderly *Hela* and *Ariadne*, which had been on patrol, were also at sea. *Köln* was the flagship of Rear Admiral Leberecht Maass, the commander of the II Scouting Group. In addition, Hipper put three further light cruisers on standby, being *Stralsund, Danzig* and *München*. At this time Hipper was unaware of the presence at sea of Beatty's battlecruisers, but at 8.50am he asked Ingenohl: 'Will you permit *Moltke* and *Von der Tann* to leave in support as soon as it is clear?' Pondering this. Ingenohl replied at 9.08 that the battlecruisers would be released only when the full strength of the British was known, subsequently authorising the sortie.[24] As Eric Osborne points out, however, the exchange was academic. That day, the tide was particularly low, and the depth of water over the Jade Bar was at 9.33 only twenty six feet. Both battlecruisers drew over twenty six feet, and would in any case not be able to pass the bar before noon.[25] Two battleships, *Heligoland* and *Thüringen* were outside the bar; but Ingenohl refused to allow them to weigh anchor.

Meanwhile at 8.55am *Fearless* had come up with the badly damaged *Arethusa*, and with her steamed slowly west south west, while the flagship's crew worked desperately to repair some of the damage. Hearing from Keyes at 9.45 that he was being chased by enemy cruisers (in fact Goodenough's light cruisers) Tyrwhitt turned back towards Heligoland. His speed, however, was down to ten knots and he soon realised that Keyes had in fact seen Goodenough's ships, so he turned again and then, at 10.20, stopped to continue the repair work, *Fearless* and the 1st Flotilla remaining with him while the 3rd Flotilla continued to the westward.[26]

Anxious to get to grips with the enemy, Maass did not wait to concentrate what would, united, have been a powerful force of light cruisers. His failure to do so was his undoing. He was unaware of Beatty's presence at sea, or even that of Goodenough. When he left Wilhelmshaven he did so in clear weather with good visibility; in the Bight, however, there was a thick fog, which also delayed *Mainz* as it left the Ems estuary. None of the German units involved had warned Maass of this. In *Köln* he steamed northwest, which so far as he knew was the direction in which to find the British, while *Strassburg* steamed west north west aiming at what was taken to be the flank of the British fores. *Mainz* was ordered to pursue a course NNE to aim at Tyrwhitt's rear.

At 10.55 *Strassburg* sighted *Arethusa* and *Fearless* through the mist, and opened fire. Tyrwhitt considered his force outgunned and turned away southwest, launching a destroyer attack on the German light cruiser. As it turned away, to avoid the torpedoes, all of which missed, it lost contact with Tyrwhitt's ships; Captain Retzmann decided not to renew the action because of the risk of further torpedo attacks. Next on the scene was *Köln*: the brief engagement that resulted followed the pattern of that involving *Strassburg*. Significantly, however, Tyrwhitt identified *Köln* as an armoured cruiser of the *Reon* class, and radioed Beatty for support. The latter's immediate reaction was to order Goodenough to detach two more light cruisers; but Goodenough decided to head for Tyrwhitt with all four remaining ships of his squadron.

Strassburg now reappeared, and brought *Arethusa* and *Fearless* under such heavy fire that Blunt followed up Tyrwhitt's previous appeals with another message to Beatty: 'Assistance urgently required.'[27] It was about 11.30am. Beatty was at this time about forty miles north west of Tyrwhitt's force, and he had an immediate and difficult decision to take, which he discussed with Chatfield, his Flag Captain:

> The Bight was not a pleasant spot into which to take great ships; it was unknown whether mines had been laid there, submarines were sure to be on patrol, and to move into this area so near to the great German base at Wilhelmshaven was risky. Visibility was low, and to be surprised by a superior force of capital ships was not unlikely. They would have had plenty of time to leave harbour since Tyrwhitt's presence had been first known. Beatty was not

German Ships

Friedrich der Grosse.

Kronprinz Wilhelm.

Posen.

Kaiser.

Helgoland.

Prinzregent Luitpold.

Lützow.

Seydlitz.

Hindenburg.

Moltke.

Von der Tann.

Pommern.

Derfflinger.

Brummer.

Frauenlob.

Pillau.

Wiesbaden.

Ariadne.

Elbing.

Frankfurt.

Mainz.

B 97.

B 98.

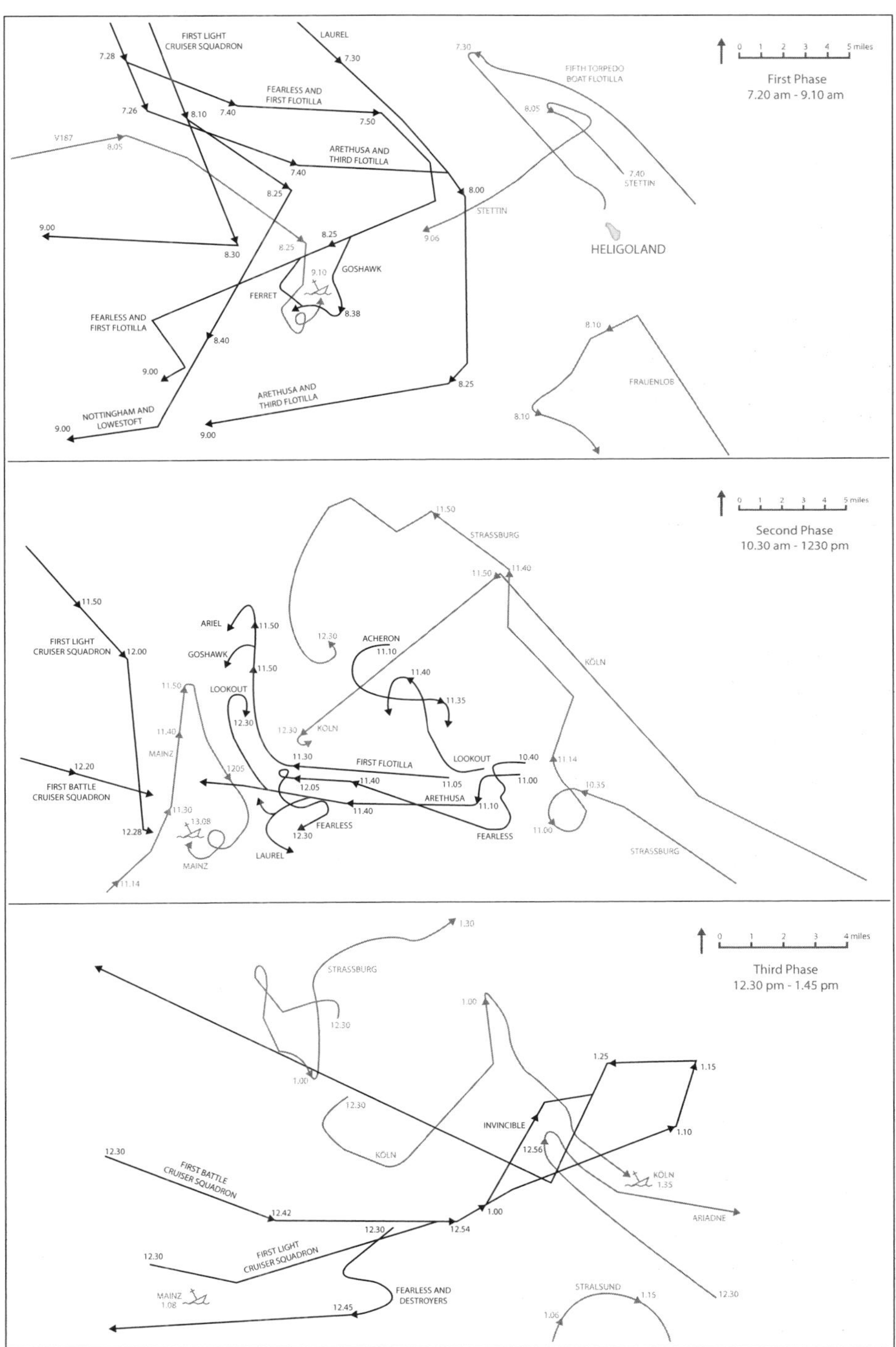

Map 3 First Battle of Heligoland Bight (3 phases).

> long making up his mind. He said to me, 'What do you think we should do? I ought to go and support Tyrwhitt, but if I lose one of these valuable ships the country will not forgive me.' Unburdened by responsibility, and eager for excitement, I said, 'Surely we must go.' It was all he needed but whatever I had said would have made little difference.[28]

Beatty turned his squadron to the south east, at a speed of 26 knots. At 11.45 he altered course to ESE, increasing speed to 27 knots, signalling to Blunt that he was coming to his support.

Meanwhile *Mainz* had arrived, and had begun engaging the destroyers of the 1st Flotilla. Just as she threatened to inflict serious damage, however, Goodenough appeared. *Mainz* at once turned away, as her first lieutenant later described:

> Immediately on identifying three cruisers of the 'Town' class ahead of us the helm of the *Mainz* was put hard over to starboard, but even in the act of turning the enemy's first salvos were falling close to us and very soon afterwards we were hit in the battery and the waist.[29]

As she headed south at her maximum speed, *Mainz* sighted *Fearless* with six destroyers. Opening an accurate fire, she disabled *Laurel*, and then concentrated on *Liberty*, hitting her twice, and wrecking her bridge and killing her captain. Transferring her fire to *Lysander* and *Laertes*, she hit the latter with a salvo of six shells, hitting her boilers and bringing her to a standstill. It was an impressive demonstration of what would have been the vulnerability of Tyrwhitt's force had it not been so heavily supported.

By now, however, Goodenough's cruisers had again caught up with *Mainz*, and subjected her to a furious cannonade. Briefly, *Mainz* disappeared into the mist, and was almost at once torpedoed by the destroyer *Lydiard*; when she became visible to Goodenough's cruisers, she was lying nearly stopped. Lieutenant Stephen King-Hall, in *Southampton*, described *Mainz*'s fate:

> We closed down on her, hitting with every salvo. She was a mass of yellow flame and smoke as the lyddite detonated along her length. Her two after funnels melted away and collapsed. Red glows, indicating internal fires, showed through gaping wounds in her sides. At irregular intervals one of her after guns fired a solitary shot, which passed miles overhead. In ten minutes she was silenced and lay a smoking, battered wreck, her foremost anchor flush with the water. Ant-like figures could be seen jumping into the water as we approached. The sun dispersed the mist, and we steamed slowly to within 300 yards of her, flying as we did so the signal 'Do you surrender?' in International Code. As we stopped the mainmast slowly leant forward, and, like a great tree, quite gradually lay down along the deck. As it reached the deck a man got out of the main control top and walked aft – it was Tirpitz junior.[30]

At 12.25pm Goodenough ordered 'cease fire' and *Lurcher* went alongside the stricken cruiser to rescue survivors. Keyes, seeing one young officer remaining on the poop after superintending the removal of the wounded, called to him and held out his hand to help him:

> But the boy scorned to leave his ship as long as she remained afloat, or to accept the slightest favour from his adversary. Drawing himself up stiffly, he stepped back, saluted, and answered: 'Thank you, no.'[31]

At 13.10 *Mainz* went down, the survivors in the water being picked up by *Firedrake* and *Liverpool*. Among them were the young officer and also Lieutenant Wolf von Tirpitz. When the latter came aboard *Liverpool*, he was grateful for his courteous reception:

> They offered us clothes while our own were drying in the engine room. We were given port wine and allowed to use the wardroom. Only the sentries before the door reminded us that we were prisoners. Shortly after I came on board the captain sent for me and read me a wireless signal from his admiral: 'I am proud to be able to welcome such gallant officers on board my Squadron.' I repeated this message to my comrades. It cheered us up, for it showed that *Mainz* had made an honourable end.'[32]

By now, Beatty's battlecruisers were arriving on the scene. Almost at once, *Strassburg* turned away; but *Köln* turned too late, and for seven minutes presented an unmissable target for the main armament of the battle cruisers, which inflicted terrible damage on her. She was given a reprieve when *Ariadne*, steaming for the sound of the guns, appeared. *Lion* shifted her fire to the elderly cruiser, and her consorts joined in; *Ariadne* lurched away, a mass of flame and smoke. Beatty, anxious to keep his ships concentrated, and fearful of reported mines in the vicinity, also turned away and went to finish off *Köln*. *Ariadne* stayed afloat until 3.10pm by which time *Danzig* had arrived to take off survivors.

Beatty soon found *Köln* again, sighting her at 1.25pm. *Lion's* first salvo smashed the armoured conning tower, the steering gear, and the engine rooms. Chatfield watched her destruction:

> She bravely returned our fire with her little four-inch guns aiming at our conning tower. One felt the tiny four-inch shell spatter against the conning tower armour, and the pieces 'sizz' over it. In a few minutes the *Köln* was also a hulk.[33]

Köln sank within ten minutes; of her crew of five hundred men only one, a stoker, survived. Beatty now ordered all the British forces to withdraw, particularly keen to get the damaged vessels away as quickly as possible.

At 2.25 *Moltke* and *Von der Tann*, under Rear Admiral Tapken, belatedly arrived on the scene; Ingenohl had ordered them 'not to become engaged with the enemy armoured cruiser squadron,' and Hipper had instructed Tapken in any case to wait until he himself arrived in *Seydlitz*, an hour behind. When he arrived, the three battle cruisers, with *Kolberg, Stralsund* and *Strassburg*, began a search for the missing cruisers, but it was soon evident to Hipper that they must have gone down, and at 4.00pm he turned for home.

Tyrwhitt, in the crippled *Arethusa*, limped homeward until 7.00pm when her engines failed, and he had to radio for assistance, which arrived in the form of the armoured cruiser *Hogue* at about 9.00pm, and which took her in tow. As she entered the Nore, *Arethusa* was cheered all the way. At Sheerness, Churchill came aboard and, as Tyrwhitt described, 'fairly slobbered' over him. The victory, such as it was, had come at just the right moment to confirm the public belief in the supremacy of the Royal Navy. Beatty wrote to his wife to tell her of the victory:

> Just a line to say all is well. I sent *Liverpool* in to Rosyth today with some prisoners and wounded. We got at them yesterday and got three of their cruisers under the nose of Heligoland, which will have given them a bit of a shock. The ones in the *Liverpool* were all

> that were saved out of one ship and, alas, none were saved from the others that sank. The 3rd disappeared in fog in a sinking condition and I doubt if she ever got back. I could not pursue her further, we were too close already and the sea was full of mines and submarines, and a large force might have popped out on us at any moment. Poor devils, they fought their ships like men and went down with colours flying like seamen, against overwhelming odds.[34]

Beatty's euphoria did not last long; by September 2 he was complaining bitterly to his wife at the lack of any commendation from the Admiralty:

> I had thought I should have received an expression of their appreciation from Their Lordships, but have been disappointed, or rather not so much disappointed as disgusted, and my real opinion has been confirmed that they would have hung me if there had been a disaster, as there very nearly was, owing to the most extraordinary neglect of the most ordinary precautions on their part. However, all's well that end's well, and they haven't had an opportunity of hanging me yet and they won't get it.[35]

In fact, Beatty did subsequently get his commendation in the form of a letter from the Admiralty on October 22, expressly referring to 'the risks he had to face from submarines and floating mines' in bringing his force into action.

The defeat imposed even greater caution on the German high command, and the Kaiser issued a personal order that no operations involving the heavy units of the fleet were to be carried out without his express permission. Admiral von Müller laconically noted in his diary for August 29:

> Tirpitz is beside himself. The Kaiser was swift with his reproaches: carelessness on the part of the Fleet, inadequate armour of the cruisers and destroyers. Pohl was shrewd and championed the Fleet.[36]

Immediate precautions were taken to strengthen the German defences. Two large minefields were laid to the west of Heligoland, which Scheer recorded as being effective, and in conjunction with improved weaponry such as aircraft and anti submarine equipment 'kept the inner area so clear that the danger from submarines came at last to be quite a rare and exceptional possibility.'[37] He was, however, concerned that the Heligoland Bight raid was merely a precursor to a more ambitious offensive move; the defensive posture imposed on the High Seas Fleet must make such a British move much more dangerous:

> To anticipate it it was therefore obvious that our High Command would desire greater freedom of movement in order to have a chance of locating parts of the enemy forces. This could only be done if the light forces sent out ahead could count on timely intervention by the whole High Seas Fleet. On the other hand, it was not the Fleet's intention to seek battle with the English Fleet off the enemy's coasts. The relative strength (as appeared from a comparison of the two battle lines) made chances of success much too improbable.[38]

Keyes and Goodenough put the outcome of the battle in perspective, both regarding it as having been a missed opportunity. The former wrote that 'an absurd fuss was made over the whole affair … It makes me sick and disgusted to think what a complete success it might have been but for, I won't say dual – but multiple control.'[39] At the Admiralty Captain Herbert Richmond was even more scathing:

> Anything worse worded than the order for the operations of last Friday [August 28] I have never seen. A mass of latitudes and longitudes, no expression to show the object of the sweep, and one grievous error in actual position, which was over 20 minutes out of place. Besides this, the hasty manner in which, all unknown to the submarines, the 1st Light Cruiser Squadron suddenly turned up in a wholly unexpected direction, thereby running the gravest dangers from our own submarines. The weather was fairly foggy, ships came up on one another unexpectedly, and with such omissions and errors in the plan it was truly fortunate that we had no accidents.[40]

Richmond was thoroughly discontented with the Admiralty's general policy at this time, writing in his diary on September 4:

> If we go on like this the North Sea deserves its other name of German Ocean. It *is* the German Ocean at this moment. Only those fatuous and self-satisfied creatures, Sturdee and Co, with their sprinkling of undigested knowledge, can think it a sea in which we retain or have any command.[41]

6

Intelligence

Within a month, a disaster off the Dutch coast compensated the Germans for their losses at Heligoland Bight. Prior to the action on August 28, *Invincible* and *Inflexible*, under Rear Admiral Moore, constituted as Cruiser Force K, had been organised as a support to the light forces operating out of Harwich. The torpedoing of the light cruiser *Pathfinder* on September 5 in the Firth of Forth led Jellicoe to the conclusion that Rosyth was no longer a safe place for capital ships, and he ordered Moore to rejoin Beatty and the remaining battle cruisers with the Grand Fleet. This left Cruiser Force C, the five elderly armoured cruisers of the *Bacchante* class, as the only support for the Harwich Force. They had been widely regarded as extremely vulnerable in any case, especially by Tyrwhitt and Keyes; on August 21 the latter had written to Rear Admiral Leveson, the Director of Operations, to plead for their removal:

> Think of the tale two or three well-trained German cruisers will tell if they fall in with those *Bacchantes*. How can they be expected to shoot straight or have any confidence in themselves, when they know that they are untrained and can't shoot, and may meet a highly trained enemy? Why give the Germans the smallest chance of a cheap victory and an improved morale? … For Heaven's sake, take those *Bacchantes* away! … I don't say those cruisers will be attacked, but the Germans must know they are about, and if they send out a sensible force, God help them.[1]

In fact, the Germans were not aware of the patrols being conducted by these elderly vessels on the Broad Fourteens.

They formed part of the Southern Force, commanded by Rear Admiral Henry Christian, whose flagship was *Euryalus*. Cruiser Force C was commanded by Rear Admiral Henry Campbell, who flew his flag in *Bacchante*. On September 17 Churchill went with Sturdee and Oliver for a conference with Jellicoe aboard *Iron Duke* at Loch Ewe; they took with them Tyrwhitt and Keyes. Both Jellicoe and Churchill were readily convinced of the danger to the 'live bait' squadron, as the *Bacchantes* were known. Sturdee, on the other hand, arrogantly dismissed the concerns raised by Keyes: 'My dear fellow, you don't know your history. We've always maintained a squadron on the Broad Fourteens.'[2] Next day Churchill instructed Battenberg that the *Bacchantes* should go to the western end of the Channel to relieve other ships there; the First Sea Lord agreed. However, Sturdee persuaded him that in the heavy weather being experienced in the southern part of the North Sea, which prevented destroyers from patrolling, the

Bacchantes should continue their patrols until light cruisers were available. On September 19 Sturdee ordered Christian to patrol the Broad Fourteens, and *Euryalus*, *Aboukir*, *Hogue* and *Cressy* assembled off the Maass Light Vessel early on September 20. *Bacchante*, with Campbell, was to return to Chatham Dockyard.

The weather continued foul, and *Euryalus* suffered damage to her wireless aerial; added to which, she needed coaling, and Christian returned to Harwich, handing over command to Captain Drummond of *Aboukir*. *Euryalus* was not part of Cruiser Force C, and was only there to keep the numbers up; it has been pointed out that if *Euryalus* had to go to Harwich, Christian should not have allowed Campbell to remain with *Bacchante* in the dockyard.[3] Throughout September 21 the three remaining cruisers patrolled the Broad Fourteens, rolling in the heavy weather. At nightfall the seas began to moderate and by midnight the wind had dropped; this was not the case at Harwich, however, where it still seemed too rough to send the destroyers out. Tyrwhitt, with *Lowestoft* and eight destroyers, finally put to sea at 5.00am on September 22.

U-9 (Lieutenant Commander Otto Weddigen) sighted the three cruisers at about 5.00 am steering abreast on a front of three miles north north east, making about ten knots. *Aboukir* was in the middle of the line; Weddigen approached on her port bow and fired one torpedo, which struck the cruiser amidships. Within minutes she was listing heavily. Drummond at first supposed her to have struck a mine; then, realising that she had been torpedoed, ordered the others to keep away. Nicholson, the captain of *Hogue*, thought he would be safe enough if he remained on *Aboukir*'s starboard side; but Weddigen had circled round, and at 6.55am he put two torpedoes into *Hogue*, just as *Aboukir* went down. *Hogue* sank in ten minutes. *Cressy*, in spite of the obvious danger, lingered to pick up survivors. At 7.20am Weddigen fired two torpedoes; one hit her on her starboard side, but the damage appeared not serious. Weddigen was not finished, however, firing another torpedo, which hit just below the bridge. Turning on to her beam ends, *Cressy* lay awash for a quarter of an hour before sinking.[4]

Tyrwhitt arrived at 10.45am in time to rescue a number of survivors; others had been picked up by British and Dutch trawlers. The loss of life, however, was very great indeed. 60 officers and 777 men were saved; 62 officers and 1,397 men died. Many of the latter were reservists, while forty five Dartmouth cadets were distributed among the three cruisers. Keyes, bitterly angry, persuaded Captain Blunt of *Fearless* to go out under his command in an attempt to avenge the cruisers; but Keyes was forbidden by Sturdee to carry out the operation and was ordered to return, subsequently receiving a severe rebuke for his pains.[5]

A Board of Inquiry was convened into the loss of the three cruisers. Its findings seriously annoyed Battenberg, who considered them a reflection on the Admiralty, although Churchill thought that the critical comments were just. The board found it not possible to measure the degree of blame, although adding that it rested with the Admiralty's telegram of September 19, which had ordered the patrol of the Broad Fourteens. It also concluded that the patrol was certain to be attacked, being so close to the German base, and was critical of all three captains for their handling of the incident. The board, composed of relatively junior officers, stopped short of a direct criticism of Christian and Campbell, stating only that it was not satisfied with the excuses put forward for their absence.[6]

Not surprisingly Richmond, whose opinion of Sturdee had not improved, had been outraged by the incident, writing in his diary on September 23:

> It is utterly sickening that such carelessness should be the cause of this waste of life. To my mind it is simply criminal. We had a lesson when *Pathfinder* was sunk for want of look-outs, but our wiseacres cannot take a lesson to heart, and send three lumbering cruisers to patrol in an area full of fishing vessels, where every movement can be reported, without any precautions whatever. The attitude of the Chief of Staff seemed to be that it was hard luck on *him*.[7]

The British hit back on October 17, when the light cruiser *Undaunted* and four destroyers of the Harwich force intercepted four German torpedo boats off the Texel en route to lay mines in the mouth of the Thames, and sank them all. Subsequently, crucially important intelligence was gathered from one of the wrecks. Later in the month, however, the Grand Fleet suffered its most serious setback so far. From the outbreak of war Jellicoe had been anxious about the security of the Grand Fleet's possible bases, and in particular was concerned that Scapa Flow might become untenable in the event of a submarine attack.[8] He had accordingly arranged for coaling and storing facilities at Loch Ewe, to be used as an alternative base if necessary. There had been a number of reported sightings of submarines, although many of these were false alarms. On September 1, while the Grand Fleet was at Scapa Flow, there were a number of alarms; so seriously was the threat perceived that Jellicoe took the fleet to sea. In spite of a dense fog, the fleet cleared the Pentland Firth successfully by 11.00pm. No trace of a submarine was discovered; but the obvious vulnerability of the anchorage at Scapa Flow made it necessary to take immediate steps to block all the entrances apart from the Hoxa and Hoy channels.

Meanwhile the fleet remained at sea until September 5, when it arrived at Loch Ewe to coal. The battle cruisers remained at Rosyth as their base. On September 10 the battle fleet again carried out a sweep into the North Sea, returning to Loch Ewe on September 13, where it stayed until September 17, while the battle cruisers, minus *Inflexible* and *Invincible* which were supporting the Southern Cruiser Force from the Humber, remained at Scapa Flow. On September 17 Churchill paid his visit to Jellicoe, where the latter hoped he had scotched the idea of an attack on Heligoland, and the withdrawal of the *Bacchantes* from the Broad Fourteens was agreed upon; and that evening the Grand Fleet put to sea again. Jellicoe felt much more comfortable when his ships were at sea than when they lay at anchor in poorly defended bases. The news of the loss of *Aboukir, Cressy* and *Hogue,* with the indication of increased U-boat activity, heightened his concern.

A partial submarine obstruction of the Hoxa entrance to Scapa Flow gave some reassurance when Jellicoe brought the battle fleet there on October 12 after a series of operations. On October 15, however, his anxieties were sharpened when the redoubtable Weddigen in *U-9* succeeded in sinking the cruiser *Hawke*, hitting her amidships which caused her to capsize and sink within ten minutes. There were also reports of submarine sightings in Loch Ewe and Scapa Flow; a good deal of ammunition was expended in firing at objects taken to be periscopes. Jellicoe was certain that immediate action must be taken:

> The reports signalled to me convinced me that, until the matter was cleared up with certainty, and until some more absolute security against submarine attack on the Fleet at anchor could be provided, it was courting disaster to have battleships or battle cruisers at Scapa Flow. We had seen in the loss of the *Hawke* that enemy submarines could quite well operate in northern waters, and it was thought to be only a matter of time before they would

> attempt an attack on the Fleet in Scapa Flow, if indeed the attempt had not already been made. I decided, therefore, that it was necessary to seek for a temporary base which could be used with safety while the submarine obstructions at Scapa were being perfected. The incident that had already occurred at Loch Ewe cast doubt on the safety of that base, since it was unprovided with any obstructions at all and the depth of water made it impossible to improvise them with Fleet resources.[9]

Thus the Grand Fleet was again rendered homeless; seeking about for temporary shelter, Jellicoe decided on Lough Swilly on the North coast of Ulster for the bulk of the fleet, and Loch-na-Keal on the Island of Mull for those for whom space was not available at Lough Swilly. By October 23 the 1st and 4th Battle Squadrons were tucked up safely at Lough Swilly behind the anti submarine obstructions which had been put in place. The 2nd Battle Squadron had gone to Loch-na-Keal, and on the evening of October 2 put to sea for target practice next day off the north of Ireland. The Grand Fleet, however, had merely exchanged one danger for another. While *U-9* operated to the east of the Orkneys, *U-20* was off the west coast of Ireland, moving northwards.[10]

There was, however, an even graver threat. On October 16 three minelayers, the light cruiser *Kolberg*, *Nautilus* and *Berlin* put to sea. The first two were directed towards the Firth of Forth, but aborted their mission in the face of British activity in the area; *Berlin* was to mine the southern approaches to the Clyde. Here, too, wireless traffic indicated that the chances of reaching the target area undetected were not great, and Captain Pfundheller decided instead to lay his mines off Tory Island, north west of Lough Swilly. This he did on the night of October 22/23, laying two hundred mines before heading out into the Atlantic. Rounding Iceland, he turned eastward for home, narrowly escaping a series of British patrols. Pfundheller next operated off the Norwegian coast with a view to interrupting British traffic. On November 16 he took *Berlin* into Trondheim, where she was interned. It is unclear whether his decision was prompted by inexperienced monitoring of enemy wireless traffic, as Paul Schmalenbach notes, or by the fact that fuel was running low and her machinery was giving trouble.[11]

Berlin's minefield claimed its first victim on October 26, when the British merchantman *Manchester Commerce* struck a mine and sank instantly. However, her loss was not reported until October 28, when her survivors were landed at Fleetwood. Meanwhile, at 9.00am on October 27 Vice Admiral Warrender was leading his squadron towards the location of the intended firing practice, when, 20 miles to the north east of Tory Island, *Audacious*, the third ship in his line, struck a mine on her port side. *Audacious* was a 13.5 inch gun battleship of the *King George V* class, completed in October 1913. This was the second class of the so called 'super dreadnoughts,' and as such she was one of the most powerful units of the Grand Fleet.

It was not immediately clear whether it was a mine or a torpedo. It was not a location in which a minefield was to be expected, so in accordance with the recent general order Warrender led the rest of the squadron away, and called for assistance for the stricken battleship. The port engine room of *Audacious* had been flooded almost immediately, and at first she began to settle by the stern. There was a heavy sea running at the time. The light cruiser *Liverpool* stood by, circling the battleship at high speed, while the target towing tugs closed in. After a while *Audacious* ceased to settle, and Captain Dampier turned her south towards Loch Swilly, steaming at 9 knots. At about noon the White Star liner *Olympic* arrived on the scene, and offered to tow *Audacious*. She was now again settling by the stern and was almost unmanageable; when a towline was passed at 2.00pm, it parted almost at once. Dampier had by now sent all but 250 of his crew away, the remainder staying aboard as a working party.[12]

Jellicoe, once satisfied that the damage was caused by a mine, sent the predreadnought *Exmouth* to the scene; but before she arrived it was evident that the battleship was doomed. At 9.00pm, after a twelve hour struggle, at the end of which all her crew had been taken off, *Audacious* blew up and sank. The ships around her returned to Lough Swilly, including *Olympic*, which was detained there for several days for security reasons. Jellicoe was desperately anxious to conceal the fact of the dreadnought's loss; the Admiralty was not unsympathetic, but it was obvious that, *Olympic* having been at the scene, the news could only be suppressed for a week or ten days. However, because of the sensitive situation with regard to Turkey, at that time under pressure from the Central Powers to come into the war, it was decided not to make the loss public, and Jellicoe was instructed to keep the secret locally as best he could:

> So the departure from the time-honoured British practice, which proved so distasteful to public opinion, was sanctioned for high reasons of state. That the Turkish crisis, at least, was sharp enough to justify exceptional measures was soon made only too clear.[13]

By November 19, however, the Germans were perfectly aware of the sinking of *Audacious*, a fact that was generally known in neutral countries, and the silence of the Admiralty contributed to a widespread view that its announcements were unreliable. As Goldrick observes, it was 'a state of mind that was to have disastrous repercussions after the Battle of Jutland in 1916.'[14]

It was more than a general policy of keeping significant information from the enemy that had prompted Jellicoe's anxiety. His margin of superiority over the High Seas Fleet was, in late October, becoming dangerously narrow. Apart from the loss of *Audacious,* both *Ajax* and *Iron Duke* had condenser trouble; *Orion* had turbine trouble; *Conqueror* was refitting. The two battleships hijacked from Turkey, *Erin* and *Agincourt*, had only just been commissioned; the battlecruiser *New Zealand* was in dry dock.[15] Goldrick observes that at this time 'Jellicoe was not willing to accept battle with the High Seas Fleet,' considering that his own forces were only half trained, and that the Germans were superior in the use of mines and torpedoes. The loss of a valuable unit of his battle line, the heavier guns of which were the Grand Fleet's principal advantage, was a heavy blow.[16] At its lowest, Jellicoe's numerical superiority in dreadnoughts sank to the ratio 17 : 15.

German naval intelligence was evidently not up to much, since this narrowing of the gap, if known to the high command, should have been seen as an excellent opportunity to meet the Grand Fleet with odds not much worse than even. It was the best chance that the High Seas Fleet would have; thereafter, the arrival of new ships for the Grand Fleet and the discharge from the dockyards of others steadily widened the gap again.[17]

Scheer recorded the response of the High Seas Fleet to the lack of action:

> Strategical reasons had made it necessary to keep our Fleet back, and this looked like a want of confidence and affected the morale of the men, and gradually lowered their belief in their own efficiency to a regrettable degree. An impressive recital of these facts with the request that the Commander-in-Chief of the Fleet should be allowed greater latitude was met with a decided rebuff.[18]

This response from the Admiralty Staff did, however, contain one observation that would give Ingenohl an opportunity for action: 'There is nothing to be said against an attempt of the big cruisers in the North Sea to damage the enemy.'[19] The policy of pursuing a *Kleinkrieg*, and avoiding a major action, was supported not only by Pohl, as Chief of the Admiralty Staff, but also by Bethmann-Hollweg, the Chancellor, and by Müller. It was, of course, fiercely opposed by Tirpitz and those around him, and would be the subject of continued dispute within German naval circles.[20]

Both sides, of course, were very much aware of the risks which a major fleet action would bring. A cautious attitude was, nonetheless, at odds with the public expectation of an early confrontation. Jellicoe, for one, was very much aware of this. On October 30 he sent a memorandum to the Admiralty reviewing what conclusions might be drawn from German methods since the start of the war, and the tactical responses that would be appropriate to deal with them. In it, he dwelt on the risks from mines and submarines, and in a frequently quoted passage set out firmly the way he would act in response to the enemy's tactics:

> If, for instance, the enemy battlefleet were to turn away from an advancing Fleet, I should assume that the intention was to lead us over mines and submarines, and should decline to be so drawn … I desire particularly to draw the attention of their Lordships to this point, since it may be deemed a refusal of battle, and, indeed, might possibly result in failure to bring the enemy to action as soon as is expected and hoped … I feel that such tactics, if not understood, may bring odium upon me, but so long as I have the confidence of their Lordships, I intend to pursue what is, in my considered opinion, the proper course to defeat and annihilate the enemy's battlefleet, without regard to uninstructed opinion or criticism.[21]

He could not have spelled out his position more clearly.

On August 25 there had occurred an incident which was to confer on the Royal Navy a priceless advantage for the early years of the war. Two German light cruisers, with accompanying destroyers, were engaged on a reconnaissance mission at the entrance to the Gulf of Finland when one of them, *Magdeburg*, became separated in thick fog and ran aground on the island of Odersholm off Russian Estonia. A destroyer came to her assistance, but before her crew and confidential papers could be transferred and the ship blown up, two Russian cruisers appeared and opened fire. In the confusion only part of the crew escaped; the captain and 57 of his crew were captured together with the secret SKM codebook, the current key and other confidential papers. The Russians, 'with uncommon good sense and in a spirit of cooperation which was not repeated in World War II,' as Patrick Beesly puts it, arranged for the delivery of the codebook to the Admiralty. It arrived on October 13.[22]

Worse was to come for the German navy; on October 17, after the action in which four old destroyers were sunk off the Texel, the senior commander had properly jettisoned all his secret papers in a lead lined chest. That might have been the end of it, had not a British trawler fishing off the Dutch coast on November 30 chanced to drag up the chest. When it reached the Admiralty it was found to contain the VB codebook, the third German naval codebook, which completed the information required to decode any intercepted German wireless signal, and was passed to Room 40. This had been set up by Rear Admiral Oliver, the Director of Naval Intelligence, in 1914, who had invited Sir Alfred Ewing, the Director of Naval Education, to take charge of a unit to study intercepted signals:

> After lunch Oliver saw Churchill who agreed to give Ewing a free hand to erect intercepting stations and engage staff. The first members of the staff, which was to grow into a department of nearly a hundred men and women inside the Admiralty and eight hundred wireless operators at the Intercepting and Direction finding Stations, were four masters from Osborne and Dartmouth, and Fleet Paymaster Rotter.[23]

Aware of the crucial importance of the German code book, Churchill prudently insisted on keeping the secret of its discovery to only a few senior officers, including Jellicoe and Tyrwhitt.

Astonishingly, the German Naval Staff did not react to the possibility that key documents had been lost with *Magdeburg*, even though it was apparent that this might have happened. On February 19 1915, Prince Henry, the Commander in Chief in the Baltic, wrote to Pohl, the newly appointed Commander in Chief of the High Seas Fleet:

> The very searching legal enquiry into this matter has shown that at least certain naval charts in use … were lost. It must be assumed with virtual certainty that these charts were fished up by the Russians who came on the scene immediately afterwards. It is probable that an SKM key similarly fell into the hands of the Russians; finally the possibility must be envisaged that the Russians recovered one of the signal books from the clear and not deep water by diving. The War Diary was probably captured by the Russians.[24]

In spite of this, with an irresponsibility that is hard to understand, no effective action was taken to revise the reciphering system until 1917. As Room 40 subsequently reported, 'even after four years of war, the German Admiralty got no further than to devise a key which could be solved in three or four days.'[25] It should be noted, however, that the British codes were by no means satisfactory, either. The scope for intelligence gathering from wireless traffic took both sides by surprise.

7

Churchill and Fisher

At this moment there was a major change in the leadership of the British navy. Due, to a considerable extent, to a grotesque and ill natured press campaign against him based on his German origins, Prince Louis of Battenberg on October 28 tendered his resignation as First Sea Lord. His loyalty and professionalism had never for a moment been in doubt, and it has been suggested that his resignation was readily accepted because he had failed to keep Churchill sufficiently in order. Professor Marder goes further; basing his opinion on what he was told many years later by Oliver, who at the material time was serving as Churchill's Naval Secretary, and hence close to the centre of events at the Admiralty and in government, Marder concludes that 'the initiative for Battenberg's resignation definitely came from the Cabinet.' He points out that the idea that Fisher should be recalled to replace Battenberg had already surfaced and been the subject of discussion.[1]

Certainly Churchill wanted Fisher, confident that notwithstanding his 74 years the old admiral was still up to the job. Oliver was doubtful that these two particularly strong willed men would be able to work together; but Churchill was insistent, firmly rejecting all the alternative names put forward, and letting it be known that if he did not get his way he would himself resign. On October 29, not without misgivings as to how it would be received in the navy as a whole, the King signed Fisher's appointment. Beatty, at first at any rate, was enthusiastic, telling his wife that it was the best that could have been, and that the old admiral still had 'fire, zeal, energy, and determination, coupled with low cunning, which is eminently desirable just now. He also has courage and will take any responsibility.' He added that the new First Sea Lord would 'rule the Admiralty and Winston with a heavy hand.'[2]

It was never likely that Sturdee would survive long in his position as Chief of Staff once Fisher had returned, and on November 4 he was dismissed and replaced by Oliver. In the meantime the shocking news of von Spee's defeat of Cradock at Coronel had arrived, and it was convenient, if rather hard on their commander Rear Admiral Moore, to send Sturdee with the battlecruisers *Invincible* and *Inflexible* to deal with Spee's Squadron. There was an obvious irony in this, since it was Sturdee's strategic decisions that had largely exposed Cradock to defeat in the first place. Richmond was in no doubt about this:

> Sturdee is primarily responsible; Leveson shares the blame, but how much Leveson has tried to get a real concentration of strength I don't know. Sturdee is an obstinate creature, and Leveson has either given way to his mulishness, or has agreed with his views, or has

> had no proper opportunity of putting forward his own. Sturdee deserves all he gets. If he was put ashore out [of] a job, it would do him no injustice. He has now a heavy load of losses directly attributable to him.[3]

Beatty was of a similar view, writing to his wife on November 16:

> Sturdee has been one of the curses of the Navy since he went to the Admiralty as Chief of the War Staff. He was principally responsible for all our disasters afloat and Fisher showed his acumen by turning him out. All I regret is that he gave him employment at all.[4]

In the meantime, taking advantage of the permission granted to him to make use of the battlecruisers, Ingenohl launched Hipper's squadron on a raid against the East Coast. Hipper, with *Seydlitz, Moltke, Von der Tann* and *Blücher* and four light cruisers, sailed on the afternoon of November 2, reaching Yarmouth at dawn the following morning. After a brief bombardment of the port, Hipper turned for home, while the cruiser *Stralsund* laid a line of mines. Notwithstanding a tremendous amount of activity on the part of the British Admiralty, which issued a stream of orders to various units in an effort to bring him to action, Hipper was able to return unscathed to the Jade. Unfortunately, thick mist in the Heligoland Bight and a navigational error on the part of the armoured cruiser *Yorck* led the latter into one of the German minefields, and she sank with heavy loss of life.

One of the movements ordered by the Admiralty had been to despatch the 3rd Battle Squadron to Portland. On reflection it was felt that these ships would be best employed in the North Sea, but further south than Scapa Flow, and the Squadron was ordered to Rosyth on November 18. The Admiralty also cranked up the legal basis of the blockade by publishing a declaration on November 5 to the effect that henceforth the whole of the North Sea would be considered to be a war area.

A fortnight after the Yarmouth raid Ingenohl resolved to try again, his hope being that British public opinion would force the Admiralty to divide the Grand Fleet into squadrons located to protect the East Coast against further raids. For this operation Hipper had five battlecruisers, the excellent *Derfflinger* having recently joined his squadron, four light cruisers (*Kolberg, Strassburg, Stralsund* and *Graudenz*) and two flotillas of torpedo boats. The plan was to tempt a part of the Grand Fleet to come southwards and hopefully into a minefield laid by *Kolberg* off Filey. Hipper sailed at 3.20am on December 15, followed by the main body of the High Seas Fleet twelve hours later. However, the British Admiralty's intelligence division was, with the aid of the German cypher signals books captured in the Baltic by the Russians, now able to decode wireless messages sufficiently to work out the German plan. The British aim was to employ Beatty's battlecruisers from Cromarty, with the 3rd Cruiser Squadron from Rosyth and Goodenough's 1st Light Cruiser Squadron, supported by the six dreadnoughts of the 2nd Battle Squadron (Warrender) to trap the German battlecruisers. In the course of the operations that followed, the British forces found themselves entangled with the cruiser and destroyer screen of the High Seas Fleet, and at one point were less than ten miles from Ingenohl's main body. Ingenohl, afraid of exposing his battleships to a torpedo attack, and convinced that the whole of the Grand Fleet was at hand, turned away before finally setting a course for his bases.

Meanwhile Warrender, blissfully unaware of the danger that he had escaped, continued to the rendezvous with Beatty's battlecruisers; a report from a destroyer to Warrender of the presence of the armoured cruiser *Roon* and five destroyers steering east led Beatty, not realising that his quarry was the entire High Seas Fleet, to set off in pursuit, which he maintained for an hour and a half until news came from Scarborough of Hipper's activities. At 9.00am *Derfflinger* and *Von der Tann* arrived off Scarborough and began to shell the town while *Kolberg* laid her minefield. Further north, *Seydlitz, Moltke* and *Blücher* began the bombardment of Hartlepool. Both forces then withdrew, reappearing off Whitby to shell that port. By 10.15am the rapidly worsening weather obliged Hipper to withdraw, sending away his light cruisers (except *Kolberg*) and destroyers as the northwesterly gale intensified, intending them to rejoin Ingenohl. At 12.25 they began to pass through the gap which had opened between Beatty and Warrender, where they were sighted by the British light cruisers. A badly worded signal led Goodenough to assume that an order to the two light cruisers ahead of Beatty to resume their position screening the battlecruisers applied also to the rest of his squadron:

> Not only did this allow Hipper's light forces to pass between the gap in the British forces unmolested, but it saved Hipper's skin as well; if he had held his easterly course after turning away from Whitby, he would have run headlong into Beatty's squadron. But his luck was in. The chance encounter of the opposing light forces warned him of the position of the enemy approaching from the mists ahead, and, shrouded in the thick weather, he wheeled sharply away.[5]

On each side the feeling of disappointment at the lost opportunities was intense. Tirpitz was livid with rage at the knowledge that *his* fleet had wasted such a chance, writing on January 9:

> My, in my opinion, successful life-work to be made use of in this way is hard to bear. There were chances from the first, but only *chances*. On December 16 Ingenohl had the fate of Germany in the palm of his hand. I boil with inward emotion when I think of it.[6]

The German Official History was equally severe, criticising Ingenohl's decision to turn away before checking the equal strength of the enemy before him. Scheer, with his Second Battle Squadron now with the rest of the High Seas Fleet a long way to the east of Warrender, heard the reports from *Stralsund* of the location of the British forces with dismay:

> If our big cruisers had got into difficulties between the enemy battle squadron and other cruisers already reported and still in the vicinity, our help would be too late. There was no longer any possibility while it was still day of coming up with the enemy battle squadron, which at one o'clock was 130 nautical miles distant from us. Our premature turning on to a ESE course had robbed us of the opportunity of meeting certain divisions of the enemy according to the prearranged plan, which was now seen to have been correct. At all events the restrictions imposed on the Commander in Chief of the Fleet brought about the failure of the bold and promising plan, owing to its not having been carried out in the proper manner.[7]

Corbett took the view that it was not Ingenohl's orders which caused him to turn back, but the fear of an attack by destroyers in the dark; having done so, he must have lost four hours but could have regained contact early in the afternoon when the Rosyth force would have been

150 miles to the north and the rest of the Grand Fleet only just leaving Scapa Flow. Corbett conceded, though, that 'the situation is therefore too full of vague possibilities and indeterminate factors to allow of a final judgment.'[8]

It was clear that Goodenough's misunderstanding had contributed substantially to Hipper's escape, and both Beatty and Jellicoe reproved him for it, the latter observing that he should most certainly have kept in touch with the three German light cruisers and reported their presence to Beatty.[9] Jellicoe was reacting to the particularly severe criticism of Goodenough in Beatty's report of December 19, in which he somewhat unfairly suggested that Goodenough should have doubted the meaning of the signal from *Lion*, adding that Goodenough was in breach of the 'elementary duty of cruiser officers.' It would not be the last time that Beatty would be quick to blame others for a setback. For the British admirals, the missed opportunity was immense; Beatty wrote to his wife: 'If we had got them Wednesday, as we ought to have done, we should have finished the war from a naval point of view.'[10] And Fisher, cursing the weather which had saved the enemy 'in the very jaws of death' was scarcely less upset than Tirpitz about the events of December 16.

Before this there had come the news of the battle of the Falklands on December 8, where Sturdee's battlecruisers and cruisers had destroyed Spee's squadron, only the light cruiser *Dresden* escaping. Richmond was profoundly unimpressed with this success, achieved in spite of what he categorised as a series of mistakes:

> It is indeed an irony that Sturdee, the man who more than anyone else is responsible for the loss of Cradock's Squadron, should be the person who profits principally by it, and should be made a national hero! … I confess it makes me sick that this consequential blunderer should get the credit, when the keels of 5 good ships and some 3500 men lie to his account.[11]

The day after the Scarborough raid there was a change of senior commander, Vice Admiral Sir Lewis Bayly, hitherto commanding the 1st Battle Squadron changing places with Vice Admiral Sir Cecil Burney, the commander of the Channel Fleet. This included the 5th and 6th Battle Squadrons, the former at Sheerness and the latter at Portland. The 5th Battle Squadron, consisting of *Lord Nelson* and *Agamemnon* and seven predreadnoughts of the 'Formidable' class, had suffered a serious loss when the battleship *Bulwark* blew up on November 26 when taking in ammunition with the loss of her entire crew of 750 save for twelve survivors. The two squadrons changed bases when Vice Admiral Bayly decided that the 5th Battle Squadron required to undertake firing exercises; these had been carried out by the 6th Battle Squadron off Portland, which was a more suitable location for the necessary manoeuvres. Bayly notified the Admiralty that he would sail from Sheerness at 10.00am on December 30, and on December 31 began carrying out steaming and firing exercises, which he decided to continue until the following morning. Bayly was apparently sceptical of the threat from submarines, which was why his only escort consisted of the old cruisers *Topaze* and *Diamond*. The squadron, however, had been tracked all day by *U-24*, commanded by Kapitanleutnant Rudolph Schneider, and at 2.12am he fired a torpedo at *Formidable*, at the end of the line, hitting abreast of the fore funnel. At 3.07 he fired a second torpedo, this time hitting her abreast of the after funnel. *Topaze* and *Diamond* did what they could to rescue survivors, but at about 4.45am the battleship sank; out of a total crew of 780 only 233 were saved.[12]

At the Admiralty, Richmond was scathing when he heard the news: 'It looks like some lunacy of Bayly's. So I should expect it to be. The man has no judgment, is as obstinate as a mule, and is too stupid to convince.'[13] Richmond's comments reflected opinion at the Admiralty; Bayly's explanation was not accepted, and it was concluded that his handling of the squadron 'was marked by a want of prudence and good seamanship in the avoidance of unnecessary risks inexplicable in an officer holding high and responsible command.'[14] Bayly was accordingly on January 16 relieved of his command; he was refused the court martial for which he asked in an endeavour to clear his name.

Fisher, who on December 28 had written of Bayly that 'he is certainly full of ginger and a welcome change to the dismal Burney,' swiftly changed his opinion, minuting Oliver and Churchill on January 6 that Bayly should remain at Portland pending further orders:

> His letter indicates no sense on his part of the dangers of submarine attack and of necessary precautions, and unless this telegram is sent we may have another calamity put upon us by a pig-headed officer, for it must have been patent to every officer and man in his squadron that to steam at slow speed in close order on a moonlight night on a steady course in the vicinity of the Start Light was to make his squadron an easy target to the hostile submarines which all the precautions taken by the Admiralty to escort his Squadron from Sheerness must have convinced him was a very present danger.[15]

Fisher was convinced of the immensity of the submarine danger, and took every opportunity to impress on Jellicoe the need for caution. Here, of course, he was pushing at an open door; Jellicoe was in no mood to take risks, but his concerns can only have been sharpened by the kind of letters he was getting from the First Lord, as for instance that of December 26:

> I am in entire accord with you as to bearing in mind ALWAYS *the big thing of the War*! Which is to keep our Big Fleet in big preponderance, intact and ever ready to cope with the German Big Fleet! *In my decided opinion your Fleet and no big ship of your Fleet should EVER be in the North Sea.* NEVER. I have said so constantly since I came and I think I must *now* make a formal written statement. I have written it informally, over and over again.[16]

Fisher had not been impressed by what he found of strategic thinking at the Admiralty, telling Beatty on November 28:

> I'm in the position of a chess player coming into a game after some d----d bad moves have been made in the opening of the game by a pedantic ass, which Sturdee is, has been, and always will be! It's very difficult to retrieve a game badly begun.[17]

8

The Dogger Bank

A sortie in force by Beatty to a point 60 miles west of the Heligoland Bight was spotted by a German reconnaissance seaplane on January 19, and an attempt to set up a barrier line of U-boats was made. This proved abortive when Beatty turned away. It came at a time when the High Seas Fleet in general, and Hipper and the First Scouting Group in particular, were champing at the bit to see some action. Ingenohl, of course, was still bound by the Kaiser's diktat that the battle fleet should not be risked, and his first reaction to an offensive proposal from Eckermann, his Chief of Staff, was negative. Indeed, he seems to have told Hipper that there would be no action for the battle cruisers in the near future.[1] It was in any case not a propitious moment for an offensive, since *Von der Tann* was in dock being refitted.

Eckermann's plan involved an advance to the Dogger Bank, where there were, it was believed, to be found a large number of apparently neutral trawlers, ostensibly fishing but in reality collecting intelligence for the British Admiralty. It was considered that these might be equipped with wireless. Furthermore, it was possible that British light forces might also be present, unsupported by heavy units of the Grand Fleet. The idea of such an operation had been around for some time, but could not have been executed due to bad weather in the North Sea, even if Ingenohl had sanctioned it.

On January 22, however, the weather markedly improved, and Eckermann again put forward his plan to Ingenohl, with the enthusiastic support of Hipper. The Commander-in-Chief was doubtful. He certainly did not want to take the battle fleet to sea; but in the face of Eckermann's persuasion, and recognising that the objective appeared to be a valid one, he finally gave way. Hipper was able to reassure him about the risk of his battlecruisers being cut off by saying that he intended to turn if there was any suggestion that British heavy ships might be in the vicinity.[2] It was, though, a venture that was very much riskier than Eckermann and Hipper supposed; and to embark on it without the support of the battle fleet significantly increased the risk. It is very doubtful, therefore, that it was sensible to launch the operation for such modest potential rewards, which could almost certainly have been as easily obtained by employing light cruisers for the sortie.

Hipper proposed to take his three available battle cruisers, *Seydlitz, Derfflinger* and *Moltke*, and the armoured cruiser *Blücher*. For the addition of the latter vessel he has been severely criticised, the general view being that her slower speed held back the faster battle cruisers. Tobias Philbin, one of Hipper's biographers, takes a different view. Noting that *Blücher* had advanced reciprocating engines and was officially capable of 24.5 knots, and during the battle was estimated by the British to be doing 25 knots, he points out that the average speed of the battle cruisers was only 23 knots, which was the highest continuous speed they had attained off Yarmouth and Scarborough as well. Philbin argues that the real problem in involving *Blücher* in an action with battle cruisers was the inadequacy of her armour protection against the heavy shells of the enemy, being 'weaker in protection on the water line and on armament than the three battle cruisers'.[3]

However, in his later book on the Dogger Bank battle he does suggest that taking *Blücher* along 'was probably a good idea', as she was essentially an armoured cruiser version of the *Nassau* class dreadnoughts, while her exposure at the end of Hipper's line was the same as it would have been to any vessel in that position.[4]

Fatally, however, for Hipper's prospects of carrying out the operation and returning unscathed, the oral order given by Ingenohl to Hipper to 'reconnoitre the Dogger Bank' was confirmed by a wireless message in cipher at 10.00am on January 23:

> To *Seydlitz*, for Senior Officer of the Scouting Vessels: First and Second Scouting Groups, Senior officer of torpedo boats and two flotillas chosen by Senior Officer of Scouting Vessels to reconnoitre the Dogger Bank. Proceed to sea this evening after dark, return after dark the following evening.[5]

It was a needless gift to Room 40, as Raeder pointed out; the flagship *Seydlitz* was anchored in Wilhelmshaven Roads, where she could easily have been reached by visual signal.[6]

Hipper duly sailed with his four big ships, the light cruisers *Graudenz, Rostock, Stralsund* and *Kolberg* and nineteen destroyers at 5.45pm on January 23, entirely unaware that the wireless message had been picked up and promptly decoded by Room 40:

> On this occasion there could be no doubt about the scale, timing, objective and area of the German operation. The ordering of coastal lights for the night departure, the warning to German U-boats that their own forces would be at sea, the choice, left to Hipper, of the two destroyer flotillas which were to accompany him, all signalled, one would suppose, in different codes (SKM and HVB), were now as simple for Room 40 to unbutton as for their official recipients.[7]

At the Admiralty, Churchill had just returned from a visit to Fisher, who was laid up in bed too ill to work. Churchill described what followed:

> It was nearly noon when I regained my room in the Admiralty. I had hardly sat down when the door opened quickly and in marched Sir Arthur Wilson unannounced. He looked at me intently and there was a glow in his eyes. Behind him came Oliver with charts and compasses. 'First Lord, those fellows are coming out again.' 'When?' 'Tonight. We have just got time to get Beatty there.'[8]

Tyrwhitt and Keyes had been engaged in the early stages of an operation to attack the Zeppelin sheds at Cuxhaven, and Keyes sailed with *Lurcher* and *Firedrake* and eight submarines at 1.00pm. He was at once recalled, while Tyrwhitt was told of the cancellation of the operation, and that all his destroyers and light cruisers would be wanted that night. To Beatty went an order to prepare at once to sail with all his battle cruisers, light cruisers and seagoing destroyers. Beatty had the 1st Battle Cruiser Squadron of *Lion, Tiger* and *Princess Royal*, and the 2nd Battle Cruiser Squadron, under Rear Admiral Moore, consisting of *New Zealand* and *Indomitable.* He also had Goodenough's 1st Light Cruiser Squadron, and with these forces was to rendezvous with Tyrwhitt next morning at 8.00am 30 miles north of the Dogger Bank and 180 miles west of Heligoland. Just after, therefore, Hipper's force had weighed anchor, Beatty left Rosyth.

Keyes was ordered to take his two destroyers with four submarines towards Borkum, and Vice Admiral Bradford, commanding the 3rd Battle Squadron of seven pre-dreadnoughts, was to head north to meet Rear Admiral Pakenham's three armoured cruisers of the 3rd Cruiser Squadron; his task would be to cut off the German ships if they attempted to escape to the north. Three sides of the trap were therefore set. From Scapa Flow Jellicoe sailed with the 1st, 2nd and 4th Battle Squadrons, between 6.30 and 8.30pm, intending to concentrate next morning at 9.30am, 150 miles NNW of the rendezvous of the battle cruisers with the Harwich Force. The latter sailed at 5.30pm on January 23 in two parts; fog came down before *Aurora, Undaunted* and two destroyer flotillas could get out of harbour, and Tyrwhitt went on with *Arethusa* and the 'M' class destroyers, leaving the rest to catch up as quickly as they could.

On both sides, spirits were high. In Beatty's ships there was a general anticipation that they would meet the enemy next day. Hipper's men were also confident, although he was very mindful of the risk of running into a British trap. Without the support of the battle fleet, it was essential to avoid action with major British forces. Hipper, although advised by the signal station at Neumünster of the British call sign for the day, did not have benefit of decodes of the British wireless traffic, and sailed on in ignorance of the fact that not only Beatty but also the whole Grand Fleet was at sea and knew of his operation.[9] The weather looked likely to be fine and clear for the day, which would mean that he could not slip into the mists as had been the case during the Scarborough raid. As the night wore on, noting that what lay ahead would be the first engagement between capital ships of the dreadnought era, another of Hipper's biographers described the scene in florid terms:

> During the night powerful forces were steaming silently towards one another with lights screened, ghostly bands of steel-shrouded warrior giants filled with a fighting force such as had never yet given tongue at sea. The God of War himself may well have felt a tremor. What was to be the outcome when steel hammered steel with unprecedented fury, when the whole strength of a war technique raised to the highest peak of efficiency was loosed from either side in a blaze of battle fury.[10]

Beatty was steaming SSE towards the rendezvous with Tyrwhitt; the latter was heading north. At 6.30am Beatty signalled to Tyrwhitt that when they met he should take up a position to the west of the battle cruisers; Goodenough's 1st Light Cruiser Squadron was to the west. Hipper's force was preceded by *Kolberg* and *Rostock,* about ten miles ahead of his main body, which was led by *Graudenz* and *Stralsund.*

As dawn was breaking, *Aurora* sighted *Kolberg* and four destroyers about four miles to the east. Captain Nicholson was momentarily uncertain whether these vessels were *Arethusa* and accompanying destroyers, and flashed the recognition signal. *Kolberg,* noting down the code, replied with a single letter before opening fire and reporting the sighting to Hipper. Hits were exchanged before *Kolberg* turned away NE. Hipper, far from sure what the encounter portended, turned his battle cruisers towards *Kolberg*; Beatty, seeing the gunflashes to the south, turned his force in their direction. At 7.30 Goodenough sighted cruisers to the south and to the east. The cruiser to the south was from the Harwich force, and he swung south east in pursuit of *Graudenz* and *Stralsund*. *Aurora* now reported sighting Hipper's heavy units, apparently heading north, and Goodenough signalled this to Beatty, who continued to head south while working up to full speed.

Hipper's anxiety was greatly increased when *Stralsund* reported smoke from a number of large ships bearing NNW. Hipper turned away to the south east at about 7.35am, and in his official despatch, described the situation which he faced. The first reports indicated the presence of eight heavy ships, which was exceedingly worrying:

> The presence of such a large force indicated the proximity of further sections of the British Fleet, especially as wireless intercepts revealed the approach of the 2nd Battle Cruiser Squadron. We therefore communicated to the Fleet our intention to retire towards the German Bight ... Meanwhile to the WNW, abaft the starboard beam of the battle cruisers, five heavy smoke clouds were sighted, which were soon recognised as the 1st Battle Cruiser Squadron. They were also reported by *Blücher*, which had opened fire on a light cruiser and several destroyers coming up from astern. The pace at which the enemy was closing in was entirely unexpected. The enemy battle cruisers must have been doing 26 knots. They were emitting extraordinarily dense smoke clouds.[11]

At the maximum speed of which his squadron was capable, about 23 knots, Hipper steamed to the south east, his ships also emitting dense clouds of black smoke. The fastest of Beatty's battle cruisers, *Lion*, *Tiger* and *Princess Royal*, steaming at 27 knots, began rapidly to close the gap. Relieved of the anxiety that there might be other capital ships close at hand, Hipper now knew that it was for the moment Beatty's five battle cruisers with which he had to deal. It would, though, be madness to stand and fight it out; other units of the Grand Fleet might be at sea in support, and although on receiving Hipper's reports Ingenohl had ordered the units of the High Seas Fleet to begin raising steam, there was no great sense of urgency, so Hipper could expect no help from that quarter.[12]

At 8.07 Hipper turned briefly to port to give his light forces the chance to take up their positions around his main force, and then resumed his course, SSE at first and then, as the range closed, SE. Beatty was being kept well informed; at 8.17 Tyrwhitt reported that Hipper's destroyers were on his starboard bow, and at 8.23 Goodenough reported to Jellicoe, in a general signal, the composition and course of Hipper's ships. At 8.34 Beatty ordered speed to be increased to 27 knots, greater than *New Zealand*'s designed speed; *Indomitable* began to drop further back. Meanwhile, *Aurora* and the 'M' class destroyers were by some way the closest British ships to Hipper's line – so close, in fact, that *Blücher* opened fire on them at a range of 7000 yards, and although she scored no hits, it was clearly too dangerous for them to remain there. Accordingly Beatty ordered them to take stations astern of *Lion*.

As the two squadrons raced across the North Sea, the range continually came down. At 8.52 *Lion*'s gunnery officer reported to Chatfield that it was now 22,000 yards, the maximum range of her 13.5inch guns. Chatfield referred to the Vice Admiral:

> I proposed to Beatty that we should open fire slowly. He assented. Off went the two foremost turrets; the time of flight at such ranges is about fifty seconds. It seemed an age for the shells to fall, but when they did, they were short. We waited and then tried again. This time the salvo fell over; we were in action. I swung the *Lion* two points to starboard to bring the full broadside of the squadron to bear. Almost at the same time the *Tiger* opened and shortly after the *Princess Royal*.[13]

At first, firing slow, deliberate salvoes from their forward turrets, all three battle cruisers concentrated their fire on *Blücher*, at first without scoring any hits. The first shell to strike her was fired at 9.09am. Two minutes later, with the range down to 18,000 yards, the German ships began to reply, concentrating on *Lion*, which was hit for the first time at 9.28, when a shell burst on her waterline. In the rear, *New Zealand* and *Indomitable* pounded along at their best speed, but their 12 inch guns were well out of range. At 9.20 Beatty ordered the Harwich Force to take up a position ahead of his battle cruisers, to cover any torpedo attack which Hipper might order.

At 9.35, shortly after altering course to ESE, Beatty, at Chatfield's suggestion, signalled: 'Engage the corresponding ship in the enemy's line.' By now *New Zealand* had got in range of *Blücher*, so the intention was that *Lion* should engage *Seydlitz*, *Tiger* should engage *Moltke* and *Princess Royal* should engage *Derfflinger*. *New Zealand* would concentrate on *Blücher*. At this point things went wrong. Captain Pelly, of *Tiger*, concentrated his fire on *Seydlitz* rather than *Motlke;* his decision was based on the Grand Fleet Battle Orders, which provided that where there were more British ships, the two leading ships were to engage the first German ship and so on down the line until the numbers were equalised. His mistake was to include *Indomitable*, but she was not yet in action. In addition, *Tiger*'s gunnery officer mistook the shell splashes from *Lion*'s salvoes as being those from *Tiger*. *Moltke*, accordingly, was left to concentrate her fire uninterruptedly on *Lion* and *Tiger*.

The first, and as it turned out, most serious blow to *Seydlitz* came at about 9.40am, when she suffered a heavy direct hit aft, which caused a serious fire in her aft turrets, both of which were put out of action, and their crews killed. The after engine room had to be abandoned for a time, and the magazines were flooded by the prompt order of the executive officer.[14] This fearful blow cost the lives of 159 men. The experience, however, brought with it a realisation of the need for improved anti flash precautions to prevent a fire reaching the magazines, the introduction of which were to prove their worth at Jutland.[15]

As the action continued, Hipper's battle cruisers had the range of *Lion* and were hitting her repeatedly. At 10.01 *Seydlitz* knocked out two of *Lion's* dynamos, and at 10.18 two shells from *Derfflinger* pierced her waterline armoured belt. As a result seawater got into her port feed tank, and after half an hour her engine had to be stopped. At the rear of the German line, however, *Blücher* was beginning to suffer heavily, and was beginning to fall behind. At 10.25 she was seen to be on fire and at 10.48 *Indomitable* came within range of her and opened fire. By now *Tiger* had shifted her fire to *Blücher* as well, having realised the difficulty of spotting the fall of shot around *Seydlitz*.

Concerned about the damage to *Seydlitz* and the plight of *Blücher*, Hipper turned away briefly ENE in an effort to throw out the British gunners. This brought him within range of Goodenough's light cruisers, and the latter wisely swung around to the north to get out of range, just in time, since *Blücher's* 5.9 inch secondary armament was coming into action with considerable effect. The amount of smoke around the German ships was by now considerable,

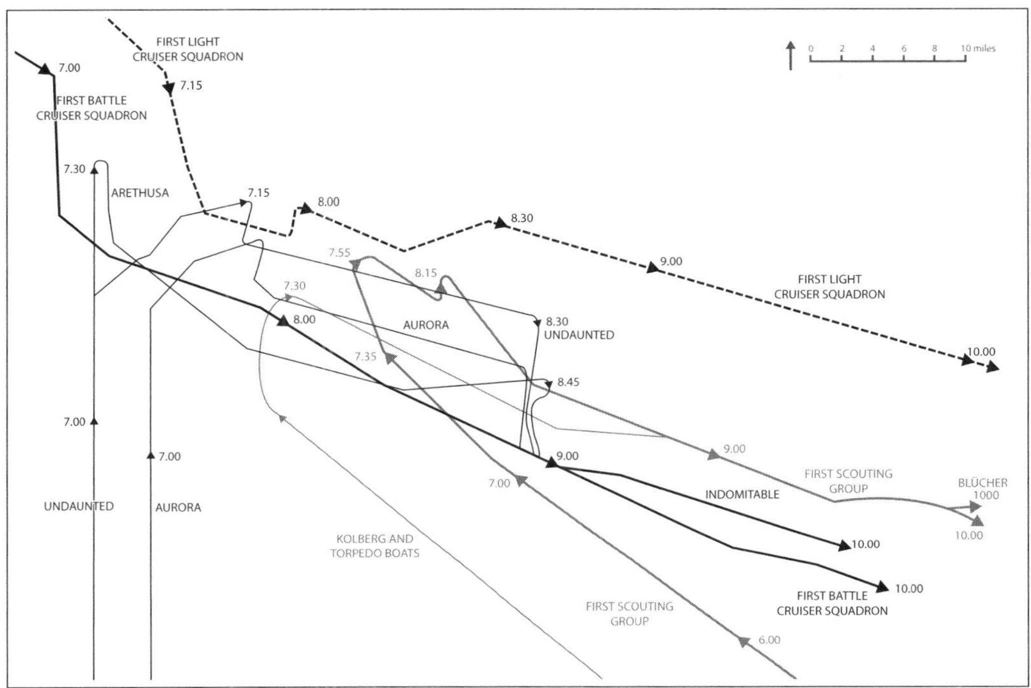

Map 4 Battle of Dogger Bank: 6.00 am to 10.00 pm.

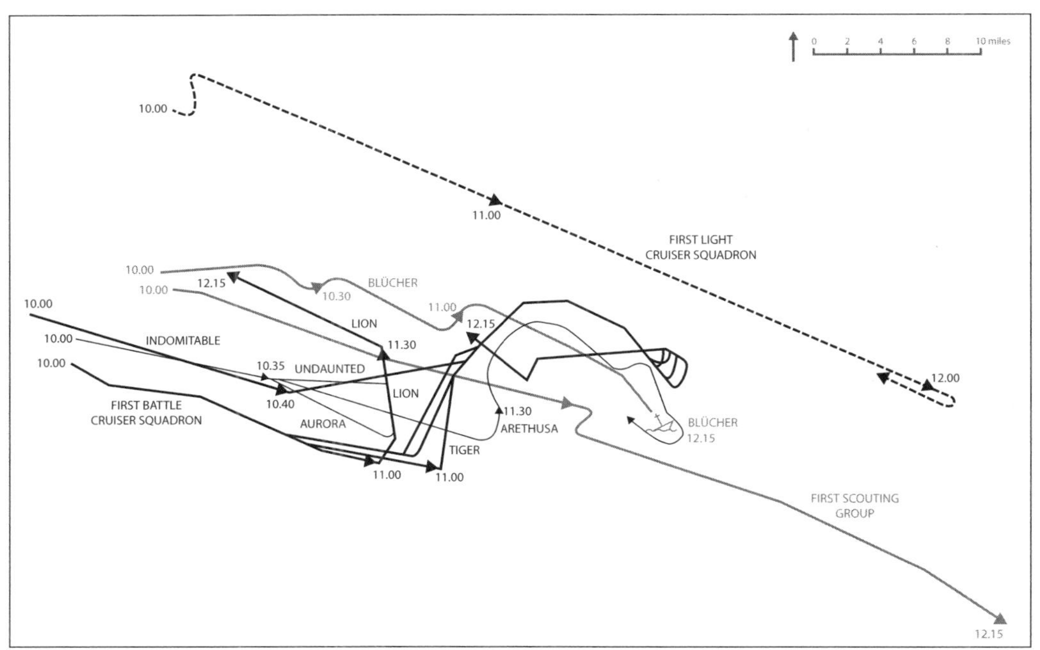

Map 5 Battle of Dogger Bank: 10.00 am to 12.15 pm.

hampering their own gunners but also those of *Lion* and *Princess Royal*, who were at times unable to make out their targets.[16] These had become well spread out, a situation with which Hipper was content, since their frequent changes of course were also confusing to the British gunners.

Hipper had not yet employed his destroyers but now was coming to the conclusion that their time had come:

> The launching of a destroyer attack had been kept in view from the start, but there could be no question of it during the first phases of the action, for one reason owing to the great distance, and further because our intention was to draw the enemy on into the German Bight until his or our losses imposed a different tactical conduct of the situation. Only when the *Blücher* began to lag seriously did the question become urgent, and the order was given 'flotillas stand by to attack.' It is very difficult to give accurate views of the behaviour of the enemy in this running fight, owing to the visibility conditions. Sharp turns at times would cause two enemy ships to be taken for one, so that there was occasional doubt as to the number of ships actually engaged.[17]

The poor visibility made signalling difficult. Even more so did the high speed at which the ships were steaming, causing signal flags to stream out dead astern. At 10.27 a signal from *Lion* to form on a compass line of bearing NNW at maximum speed had caused confusion, when *New Zealand* and *Indomitable* misread it. At 10.45 a signal 'close the enemy as rapidly as possible consistent with keeping all guns bearing' was seen only by *Tiger*, and she only saw the instruction to close the enemy. As Goldrick points out, if Moore had seen it he would have been in a better position, shortly after, to understand what Beatty was trying to achieve.

As it was, *Lion* was suffering badly; as a result of the hits already received, and of further hits between 1049 and 1051, she had 3000 tons of water on board, had lost the use of 'A' turret, and all but two of her signal halliards had been shot away.[18]

As Hipper prepared to launch his destroyers, submarines were reported to Beatty on the starboard bow, and he saw what he took to be the wash of a periscope. At once he signalled: 'Turn eight points together.' The signal was hoisted without the submarine warning, and caused great confusion, not least on the bridge of *Tiger* whose captain later wrote:

> Whilst this signal was still flying I observed the flagship developing a big list. She was evidently badly damaged. She began to drop back and from then onward took no further part in the action. *Tiger* steered to pass between her and the enemy, and the Germans' fire was concentrated on her. For nearly five minutes this alter course signal remained flying and giving us all plenty of time to comment on it. I remember asking my navigating officer if he could explain the meaning of it, for to my mind it seemed to mean breaking off the action. He replied: 'I have no idea, unless the *Lion* has better knowledge of minefields about than we have.'[19]

With his battle cruisers beginning to draw away from him, Beatty ordered 'course NE' to bring them back in pursuit of the enemy. Meanwhile Hipper, who had seen *Lion* beginning to haul out of line, altered course at 10.58 to south south east and two minutes later ordered his destroyers to attack. Almost at once, however, he observed the British turn away, and at 12.07 ordered the recall of the destroyers, and instead considered what else he could do to help *Blücher*.

Beatty's signal caused further confusion among his subordinates. In addition to prescribing course north east, he added 'Attack the rear of the enemy,' this being the nearest that the signal book came to his wish that the enemy main body be engaged. Unfortunately the two signals were hoisted nearly simultaneously on the two remaining halliards, so that taken together they became 'Attack the rear of the enemy bearing north east.' Taken also with the eight point turn away, they left his captains uncertain of what was intended. Moore, in *New Zealand*, was the man on whom decision now rested, with *Lion* out of the action. Since *Blücher* represented the German rear, and bore north east, that must be the target. Ahead of Moore, *Tiger* was facing considerable difficulties as a result of a hit from *Moltke* that had destroyed her communication system; as a result of this Pelly decided to complete the turn he was making, which seemed to conform to the movements of the rest. Behind her, inside the line, *Princess Royal* had to follow suit.[20]

Hoping to correct the disastrous misunderstanding of his signals, Beatty took up Flag Commander Plunkett's suggestion that he used Nelson's signal 'Engage the enemy more closely;' but once again the signal book let him down, the nearest contemporary equivalent being 'Keep closer to the enemy.' In any case, it seems not to have been taken in by the battle cruisers as Moore prepared to close in on *Blücher*.[21]

Hipper was still keen to do what he could do to assist her:

> In order to help the *Blücher* it was decided to try for a flanking move. With this in view the line ahead was restored and the course altered to SW. But as I was informed that in my flagship turrets 'C' and 'D' were finally out of action, we were full of water aft, and the *Seydlitz* had only 200 rounds of heavy shell left, I dismissed any further thought of supporting the *Blücher*. Any such course, now that no intervention from our Main Fleet was to be counted on, was likely to lead to further heavy losses. The support of the *Blücher* by the flanking move would have brought my formation between the British battle cruisers and the battle squadrons which were probably behind.[22]

It was a profoundly painful decision that Hipper was now obliged to take, as Raeder recorded:

> With a heavy heart Admiral Hipper countermanded his order and directed a resumption of the withdrawal south easterly towards Heligoland. Eyes blurred as the sinking *Blücher* disappeared in the haze astern. The enemy did not pursue.[23]

Behind them, Moore's four battle cruisers, *Arethusa*, and Goodenough's light cruisers circled the crippled *Blücher*, although she continued to fight back with the only two turrets remaining. At 11.20am *Meteor*, with three other 'M' class destroyers closed on her to attack with torpedoes; *Blücher* hit *Meteor* with an 8.2 inch shell which struck the forward boiler room, disabling her and killing four stokers. It was estimated that five torpedoes hit *Blücher*, but notwithstanding this she was able to launch a torpedo herself at *Arethusa*, which missed; the light cruiser had closed in to a range of 2,500 yards.

At 11.45, it seemed to Tyrwhitt that *Blücher* had struck, and he closed in to rescue survivors. He wrote later: 'She was in a pitiable condition – all her upper decks wrecked and fires could be seen raging between decks through enormous shot holes in her sides.'[24] Corbett paid a moving tribute to the stricken cruiser and her brave crew:

> For three hours, during which she had been the focus of an overwhelming concentration of fire, she had never ceased to reply. Twice our light cruisers had approached to complete her destruction and twice she had forced them to withdraw. As an example of discipline, courage and fighting spirit her last hours have seldom been surpassed.[25]

She had taken over seventy hits from the British fire, but had continued to fight back to the bitter end. At 12.10 she suddenly rolled over and sank quickly; of her crew of 792 only 237 were saved. The rescue operations were hampered when a seaplane from Borkum attempted to bomb the destroyers, evidently supposing the sinking ship to be British, compelling Tyrwhitt to break off the rescue operations. The suggestion that the Zeppelin *L5* also bombed the British destroyers is apparently incorrect.[26]

Moore now had to consider what to do. Hipper was by now some 30,000 yards away, and it would take nearly three hours at maximum speed to get back within range, by which time the battle cruisers would be some 70 miles nearer to Heligoland. A signal from the Admiralty to Keyes, picked up in *New Zealand*, informing him that the High Seas Fleet was coming out, made up Moore's mind, and at 11.52 he ordered his force to turn west. Beatty had in the meantime called up the destroyer *Attack*, which he boarded at 11.50, coming up with the battle cruisers at about noon. He immediately ordered the course to be reversed, to the south east, and at 12.27 went on board *Princess Royal*. It did not take long for him to realise that to continue the pursuit was hopeless, as he wrote much later:

> I was always expecting to meet the High Seas Fleet during the chase of the enemy battle cruisers into the Heligoland Bight and was filled with anxiety as to the possibilities that might ensue, when the *Lion* was reduced to 12 knots, before the Grand Fleet, distant over 100 miles, could arrive to our support.[27]

Accordingly he returned to *Lion* in order to screen her return to port. By 3.30pm it was clear that she could not do so unaided. Chatfield was told that the engines were unlikely to remain operational during the night, and *Indomitable* took her in tow. The two ships had an anxious journey homewards, during which there was a constant fear of torpedo attacks from German destroyers and submarines. None of these materialised, however, and they finally made port in Rosyth before dawn on January 26.

Neither the British nor German naval leaders could, at the best of times, be described as a band of brothers, having a decided tendency to *ad hominem* criticism of each other and a very considerable readiness to apportion blame after every perceived set back. The aftermath of the Dogger Bank was no exception to this. Beatty, as usual, was quickly off the mark. He had never liked Moore and had not at all wanted him as part of the Battle Cruiser Fleet. Although not publicly blaming Moore, in his official report, he wrote privately to Jellicoe: 'Frankly between you and I he is not of the right sort of temperament for a B.C.S ... Moore had a chance which most fellows wd have given [the] eyes in their head for and did nothing'.[28] Accordingly, he made sure that Moore was replaced in command of the 2nd Battlecruiser Squadron by Rear Admiral William Pakenham, of whom he had a high opinion. Captain Geoffrey Bennett remarked that Beatty had himself contributed to Moore's conduct:

> His signal, 'Attack the enemy's rear', was as unnecessary as it was open to misinterpretation. For this reason he refrained from condemning Moore, leaving the Admiralty to remove him quietly from the Grand Fleet. But a court martial would have done more to drive home the lesson that, for the second time in two months, the Grand Fleet had lost the chance of inflicting a decisive defeat through a flag officer complying too rigidly with superior orders instead of using his own judgment and initiative.[29]

Pelly, the captain of *Tiger*, was blamed for his interpretation of the signal to engage the corresponding enemy ships; he did, however, put up a stout defence that he believed that by disabling the leading ship of the enemy the British would have a better chance of catching them all. Beatty was unimpressed; but Andrew Gordon has pointed out that in any case the Battlecruiser Fleet Orders did expressly refer to the case where the rear ships of an enemy fleet might be damaged and reduced in speed, in which case fire should be concentrated on them.[30]

At the Admiralty, Fisher was furious, condemning Moore's actions as 'despicable.' He added that 'no signals (often unintentionally ambiguous in the heat of action) can ever justify the abandonment of a certain victory such as offered itself here.'[31] He was even more severe on Pelly, whom he described as a poltroon: 'He was a long way ahead, he ought to have gone on, had he the slightest Nelsonic temperament in him, regardless of signals! Like Nelson at Copenhagen and St Vincent! In war the first principle is to disobey orders. *Any fool can obey orders!*'[32] Jellicoe, mulling over the reports of all those concerned, agreed with the criticisms of both Moore and Pelly, as did many others in the navy.

Beatty had convinced himself that had things been differently handled, the whole of the First Scouting Group would have been destroyed. In a private letter to Keyes of February 10, he wrote:

> The disappointment of that day is more than I can bear to think of, everybody thinks it was a great success, when in reality it was a terrible failure. I had made up my mind that we were going to get four, the lot, and *four* we ought to have got.[33]

Not only had Beatty succeeded in convincing himself of this; he seems to have convinced others, including Jellicoe. It was, perhaps, something of an overstatement; having regard to the superior gunnery of Hipper's squadron, had Moore caught up with it at odds of 4 : 3 it might not have been any kind of victory. Certainly, with the benefit of hindsight afforded by the first phase of Jutland, Beatty's battle cruisers might not have fared as well as he expected.

Tobias R Philbin, in his account of the battle, reckons that the British enjoyed a tactical supremacy for a number of unrelated reasons. The first of these was the British battlecruiser construction programme. Next was the setting up of an integrated signals in the intelligence system. Third was the huge advantage gained by the recovery of the code and signals books of *Magdeburg*. This was reinforced by the recovery of the *Handelsschiffsverkehrsbuch* from the German merchant ship *Hobart* by the Royal Australian navy. Finally, there was the lucky finding of the *Verkehrsbuch* from one of the three old German destroyers sunk on October 18 1914.[34]

Throughout the action the German gunnery had been outstanding, and emphatically superior to that of the British battle cruisers. The standard of the latter's gunnery was, au fond, the responsibility of their commander, but Beatty attracted little direct criticism at the time for this. Jellicoe however did take to heart the superior accuracy of the German gunfire which he much later regarded as 'confirming my suspicion that the gunnery of our Battle Cruiser Squadron was in great need of improvement, a fact which I very frequently urged upon Sir David Beatty'.[35] Chatfield, in his report of the battle, did concede that firing slowly in the early stages of the battle was an error;' the mistake made was in not at once going into rapid independent and putting forth our whole volume of fire, regardless of ammunition expenditure.'[36]

On the other hand, the Germans could be justifiably proud of their gunnery. While, apart from *Blücher*, Hipper's ships had suffered only three hits, one on *Derfflinger* and two on *Seydlitz*, they scored sixteen hits on *Lion* and six on *Tiger*. There was, therefore, some encouragement to be drawn from the experience of the action, even if the strategy which prompted the operation was seriously flawed. Scheer, in his memoirs, looked at the credit side:

> This first serious fight with large ships which the Fleet had had the opportunity of participating in proved that the fighting preparedness of the ships as regards the training of all on board was on a very high level, that the ships were handled in a correct and reliable manner and that the serving of the guns, the signalling, and the transmission of orders from ship to ship during the fight, as well as the measures necessitated by leakages, had all worked admirably. Everywhere the behaviour of the crews was exemplary. The case of the *Seydlitz* (Captain von Egidy), from which ship, in spite of the fierce fire raging on board, the command of the whole unit was calmly maintained, deserves special emphasis.[37]

In the long term these aspects of the action could well be regarded as a source of comfort to the leaders of the High Seas Fleet, as could in particular be the courage and dedication of *Blücher*'s crew. Many in Germany took heart from the fact that, notwithstanding the pronounced enemy superiority, the German battlecruisers had put up a good fight, and their performance offered some reason to hope for success in the future. The Kaiser, addressing officers and men in Wilhelmshaven on February 4, pointed with pride to the heroism of the crew of *Blücher*:

> It is not important that we have victory every time: it is important that your deeds show your *spirit*. And this spirit, this death-defying, joyful attitude at the moment when the ship goes down, it is that which has won the greatest respect from the enemy and all nations of the world. For that I express my thanks to you. Our task now as before remains, when and where possible, to do harm to the enemy. And if your own ship goes down, he must go down *with it*.[38]

There was nevertheless a sense on the German side that things could have gone very much better. Tobias R Philbin, in his account of the battle, quotes from the war diary of *Seydlitz* and Captain Maurice von Egidy:

> The plan of the attack did not foresee the probability of encountering important British ships in the North Sea. The actuality of the 24th has on the other hand shown into what an awkward position even fast battlecruisers may get when they are forced to give battle without support from the main fleet. If we had known our main force to be in the rear of us, the commander of the Scouting Forces would not have found himself in the desperate position where he had to deide to leave *Blücher* to its fate. We would have carried the ship

> away in much the same manner as the British did with *Lion*, which probably was not any worse damaged than *Blücher* was originally.[39]

It is not surprising that the German naval heart searching was, therefore, even more profound than that on the opposite side of the North Sea. From the outbreak of the war there had been serious dissension among German naval leaders on both a professional and personal basis. Much of this centred around Tirpitz, who had as early as July 29 1914 had proposed that the role of State Secretary of the Imperial Navy Office and of the Chief of the Admiralty Staff should be combined in his person. The Kaiser had not adopted the suggestion, but had ordered that the Chief of the Admiralty Staff should consult with Tirpitz before referring any question to the Kaiser.[40]

Tirpitz, violently at odds with Pohl and Müller about the defensive strategy of the *Kleinkrieg*, soon began to campaign assiduously for appointment in Pohl's place, in order thereby to be able to influence operational policy. The order that Tirpitz join the Imperial Headquarters came as very bad news to Pohl, who gloomily observed that 'Tirpitz will not avoid interfering in my affairs.' He was certainly right about this, and the result was that Pohl increasingly took up a position closer to Müller and Bethmann-Hollweg. On October 3 1914 Tirpitz noted angrily:

> Just now Admiral von Müller came to call on me here. He was not in agreement with me about our naval war policy. The Foreign Office is behind this question. Müller is evidently now completely in their hands.[41]

Three days later Tirpitz was even crosser:

> Pohl has just come back from Wilhelmshaven, having got Ingenohl's consent to nothing being done. The submarine danger, and especially the idea to preserve the fleet, outweigh everything else. Pohl has got hold of the childish notion that the fleet must be doubled after the war, and Bethmann shares this opinion, while the highest probability points to the reverse, politically, financially, and also with regard to the submarines.[42]

Müller, noting the report made by Pohl to the Kaiser of his visit, thought it 'not very skilful'; in addition to Ingenohl, Pohl had spoken to Lans and Scheer who, he noted in his diary, 'were entirely in accord with his ideas on the use of the Fleet'.[43]

Meanwhile Eckermann, who had initially been supportive of Pohl's position as to the *Kleinkrieg*, had had a visit from Tirpitz, following which he came round to the idea that Tirpitz should take over as Chief of the Admiralty Staff. On learning that the intention was that in that case Pohl should replace Ingenohl, Eckermann sharply reversed course; at all costs he wished to avoid that. He wrote to Captain Hopman, one of Tirpitz's closest confidants, on November 25; 'If a replacement proves to be unavoidable, because of events in the future, I cannot mention anybody else but Scheer.' Scheer's elevation, thought Eckermann, would give him the opportunity to lead a battle squadron.[44] Eckermann, who seems to have spent a good deal of time in these intrigues, wrote again to Hopman on January 22 1915 to propose that Scheer replace Ingenohl, that Ingenohl should replace Pohl, and that he, Eckermann, should succeed Scheer as a battle squadron commander. After the Dogger Bank action, Hopman took his letter on January 26 to Müller. Next day Hopman followed it up, telling Müller that 'Ingenohl could not inspire anyone, lacked imagination, intuition and strategic instincts, was too petty and pedantic, and in general lacked the qualities of a great leader.'[45] Reporting on his discussion to Eckermann, Hopman made it clear that he was acting with the full knowledge of Tirpitz; he was, however pessimistic about the outcome.

On January 31 Müller thought the matter over, recording his conclusion in his diary:

> Sunday. A heavy day for me … Studied the report on the cruiser action off the Dogger Bank and to my chagrin came to the conclusion that a change in the command of the High Seas Fleet striking forces was necessary; that Admiral von Ingenohl must be replaced by Admiral von Pohl and the latter by Admiral Bachmann. A very difficult decision to make.[46]

In fact, of course, there was nothing in the Dogger Bank action that pointed to Ingenohl's removal; rather, it was his lack of success and also lack of charisma that brought about his removal. He was, for the next six months, transferred to the command in the Baltic, before he was retired. It appears that Tirpitz also wanted Hipper removed, but Müller would not have this. Tirpitz went along with Bachmann's appointment, presumably because he was likely to be more malleable: Müller observed that he was not regarded as a strong personality. Although Tirpitz had grudgingly accepted the command changes, he was at heart still dissatisfied, as was shown by his account of a discussion with Müller on February 6:

> I have moreover told Müller that my duty to the Fatherland alone keeps me from tendering my resignation now; I shall certainly do so after the war … The real contention between the Kaiser and myself is that I thought it essential to send out the Fleet and the Kaiser refuses. Now other reasons are being found and a scapegoat sought.[47]

Tirpitz was no doubt correct when he wrote to Captain Adolf von Trotha in March that nobody wanted to give him the Admiralty Staff or the High Seas Fleet, mainly because they did not wish to give him more power.[48] It is interesting to speculate as to what, given the chance, he would have done with it.

The last word on the conclusions to be drawn from the Dogger Bank action may fairly be left to Hipper and Beatty. Hipper drew a number of mainly strategic conclusions from the events of January 24 in his report to Ingenohl of January 27:

> I The experiences of January 24 have shown that the North Sea can in no way be considered clear of the English Fleet. The bombardment of the East Coast has apparently resulted in their taking up positions from which they can be committed to an immediate defence of the East Coast. At least light forces will be stationed in such positions and possibly battle cruisers are stationed on the North Sea. Battleships must be kept in neighbouring bases ready for action (Humber, Firth of Forth). Therefore it appears to me:
>
> (1) It is again possible for us to damage the English fleet by U-boats in the North Sea
>
> (2) All operations have to be planned so that a reserve formation is available for timely support of advanced forces. Hence the decisive battle could be developed on any occasion; in the future the fleet will [have to] stand to with its full strength of modern warships in a state of readiness to support such operations.

II The superiority of the English fleet must cause us to conduct the battle under the most favourable circumstances possible, as soon as [such a battle] is generally desired politically. That is:

(1) The battle should not be fought in an easterly wind.

(2) The plan must include a U-boat line which can attack before or after the battle.

(3) The battle must be within our waters, not farther than 50 sea miles from Heligoland. A venture farther than 70 sea miles from Heligoland should not be allowed …

(4) Only completely battleworthy ships should be committed to the battle; every old ship is easy prey for the enemy because of the enormous power of modern artillery; the enemy themselves will bring only first class materiel. All flotillas must be brought to their places. The older squadrons could be utilised only as floating batteries. We should not avoid the necessity of decommissioning old ships in favour of modern battleworthy (*Lützow*) type ships which are the best possible weapons.[49]

Additionally, Hipper warned that the British would utilise superior speed and firepower to develop an action at the longest possible range; made a suggestion that the after funnels of German destroyers be painted red; complained that it was difficult to conduct a battle from the armoured conning tower due to the amount of smoke; and suggested that the succession to the command of the Scouting Groups should be settled in the event of his death or disability.

As the events of May 1916 showed, not all the suggestions put forward by Hipper as valuable lessons to be learned from the Dogger Bank had been adopted for the High Seas Fleet. Some were, however, adopted by Pohl when he assumed command.

Beatty also set down a substantial number of lessons to be learned from the Dogger Bank, in a report to the Admiralty of February 9. His conclusions were tactical in nature. He observed that ' as the Germans also will have learnt valuable lessons, we can only hope to gain advantage from the battle if we can apply our lessons in a practical manner without delay.' Some of his principal recommendations were:

Zigzags

3 As the enemy zigzag whenever they are being hit, it is most important to practise this at spotting tables or when doing target practice. Rates and Dumaresqs become almost useless under these conditions. Range-finders may help, but spotting must be the primary aid for keeping on the target

4 There can be no doubt we should make a turn, in or out, when enemy begins to hit; 2 points would be ample, or at high speed 1 point. Small helm should be used. This has often been practised, and will in no way interfere with our gunnery …

Lee Position

6 This is usually much superior to the weather position, but there are many pros and cons to be carefully considered:-

Against lee position: spray will come on board from enemy's shots; but this will happen almost equally in weather position. Spray is bad when steaming fast and when firing before the beam, particularly so if wind is fresh.

Against weather position: Smoke is the only hindrance, but this is very serious when steaming fast. The after guns will rarely get a clear view, and if smoke is blowing towards enemy the whole armament and the Control Officers may be masked.

Vide reports from *Invincible* and *Blücher*, smoke difficulty may be got over by opening out the ships and using director, but the Germans did both of these on January 24 and their shooting was usually much worse than ours. We have, therefore, to balance smoke *versus* spray, taking into consideration the special circumstances of each case. On most occasions, as we have proved so often at battle practice, the lee position is the best …

Fighting Range
8 The Falkland Islands Fight and January 24 have proved that hits can be made without difficulty at 19,000 or 20,000 yards, but this range is not decisive, and the percentage of hits is too small. An hour's fighting may find guns disabled and ammunition running short with no decisive results obtained; therefore there is no harm in slow firing at long range, but we *must* try to get in closer without delay. Probably 12,000 to 14,000 yards would suit us well, this being outside the effective range of enemy's torpedoes and 6 inch guns. We must try to combine early hits with *decisive hitting* soon afterwards …

Tactics
11 The tactics of pursuit are certainly difficult owing to the inevitable concentration on leading ship and the menace from mines and torpedoes. Some advantage can be gained, however, by getting on enemy's lee quarter and thus causing him serious smoke interference. The presence of enemy torpedo-craft on our engaged bow was most inconvenient. Our 4-inch guns could never prevent torpedo firing at long range, and manning the guns means exposing a large number of men.[50]

Apart from his remarkable and quite unjustified complacency about the superiority of his gunnery, there is a striking difference of opinion with Chatfield about slow firing in the early stages of the action. As with Hipper's recommendations, by no means all of Beatty's suggestions were to be acted upon.

Personalities

Sir Henry Oliver as C-in-C Atlantic Fleet.

Jellicoe with Halsey and Lieutenant Fitzherbert.

Commodore Reginald Tyrwhitt.

Admiral Sir Roslyn Wester Wemyss.

Admiral Sir Herbert Richmond.

Admiral Sir William Pakenham.

Admiral Sir Roger Keyes.

Jellicoe aboard *Iron Duke*.

Commodore William Goodenough.

Lord Northcliffe.

Admiral Sir Reginald Bacon.

Sir Edward Carson.

Arthur Balfour.

Sir Eric Geddes.

David Lloyd George.

Vice Admiral Sir Trevelyan Napier.

Admiral of the Fleet Lord Fisher.

Winston Churchill.

Rear Admiral Horace Hood.

Admiral Sir Frederick Doveton Sturdee.

Admiral Sir John Jellicoe.

Admiral Sir Charles Madden.

Admiral Sir David Beatty.

King George with Beatty.

Admiral Ludwig von Schröder.

Grand Admiral von Tirpitz.

Admiral von Ingenohl.

Vice Admiral Franz Hipper.

Admiral Reinhard Scheer.

Admiral Ludwig von Reuter.

Admiral Georg von Müller.

Kaiser Wilhelm with Admiral von Holtzendorff II and von Tirpitz.

9

Balfour and Jackson

While the German High Command was adjusting itself to the consequences of its reshuffle, the British Admiralty was deeply involved in a projected operation that would in due course also result in a crisis of leadership. The idea of an attack on the Dardanelles had been floated in 1906, when there appeared to be a possibility of war with Turkey over the Sinai boundary dispute. That had blown over, but when on October 31 1914 war did break out, the operation seemed a very possible option, so that on November 3 an Anglo-French Squadron carried out a very brief bombardment of the the outer forts. It may have disclosed some possibility of damaging the forts by naval gunfire, but what it certainly did do was to ensure that the Turks and their German advisers would thereafter be on their guard.

The suggestion of a joint military and naval attack on the Dardanelles, made by Churchill on November 25, was disposed of by Kitchener, whose immediate response was that no troops were available. It reappeared at the beginning of January in a scheme sponsored by Fisher, and Hankey as Secretary to the War Council. It was a plan which, as Marder noted, disregarded realities; but it contained a reference to forcing the Dardanelles with old battleships, which intrigued Churchill, and he telegraphed Admiral Carden, who was on the spot, whether the Dardanelles could be forced by ships alone. Carden replied that they could not be rushed but might be forced by a large number of ships in extended operations. Here was the genesis of a steadily evolving Greek tragedy in which the interaction of the personalities of those involved, particularly Churchill and Fisher, inexorably drove events forward.

Fisher, at first, was keen, proposing to add the newly commissioned *Queen Elizabeth* to the squadron of old battleships to be employed, since she had to complete her gunnery exercises and her 15 inch guns might be decisive in destroying the forts.

The War Council adopted the idea, and planning proceeded at the Admiralty. Fisher, however, was already having second thoughts about going without the army, writing to Jellicoe on January 19 to say that for him there was 'only one way out and that is to resign.' but in deference to Jellicoe's wishes he would not, even though he didn't 'agree with one single step taken'.[1]

Fisher's anxieties deepened; he tried to avoid attending a War Council meeting on January 28, but was left with no option when Asquith, at the end of a private meeting with Churchill and Fisher, announced that the operation would proceed. At the meeting, Fisher tried to walk out, but Kitchener dissuaded him. He continued to work on the project, justifying this to himself by believing that if all did not go well, the ships involved could be withdrawn at any time.[2]

The fundamental problem, which Churchill and the War Staff brushed aside, was that ships traditionally were at a severe disadvantage when attacking forts. Within the Admiralty Jackson was increasingly stressing the need for a military force to be available at least to follow up a successful naval operation. Tempers were becoming frayed, as Richmond observed:

> Oliver told me a few days ago that Fisher does nothing, Winston proposes mad things and hangs grimly onto his silly Naval Division, whom he will not allow to be used anywhere, Wilson opposes all suggestions, and cannot get it out of his head that anyone younger than himself can possibly know anything ... It is hopeless trying to make war with men like these.[3]

Planning for the naval operation continued, although by February 9 Kitchener had moderated his stance; military forces would be available at a later stage. Carden was reinforced off the Dardanelles by two more admirals: Rear Admiral Rosslyn Wemyss and Rear Admiral John de Robeck. The build up of battleships under Carden's command continued with the arrival of the French Admiral Guépratte, with four old battleships. All told there were now 18 predreadnoughts available, and two semi dreadnoughts (*Lord Nelson* and *Agamemnon*) together with the battle cruiser *Inflexible*, and *Queen Elizabeth*. The bombardment began on February 19, and was sufficiently successful to suggest that although it might take longer to complete, it would ultimately achieve its object. Bad weather delayed the resumption of the bombardment until February 25 when de Robeck in *Vengeance* led the fleet up to the mouth of the straits, and the German and Turkish gunners in the ante-most forts withdrew, enabling landing parties to go ashore to complete the destruction caused by the bombardment. By March 2 Carden was predicting that he hoped, if given fine weather, to reach Constantinople in about two weeks. In the next few days, the attack began to lose its impetus; the gunners returned, and the battleships could not go forward for fear of mines, which the minesweepers could not deal with due to the fire of the forts. A full scale attack on the Narrows was planned for March 18; three days before this, Carden's health broke down, and de Robeck took command.

In fine weather, the fleet moved forward, led by the French squadron; when battle was joined, both ships and forts suffered serious damage, but on the whole the ships were getting the better of it. De Robeck brought up his next line, ordering the French to retire, but as they did so a huge explosion rocked *Bouvet*, which capsized and sank in two minutes. Just over two hours later *Inflexible* stuck a mine, and listing heavily, made her way with great difficulty to the island of Tenedos. Next, *Irresistible* struck a mine, and was abandoned by all save a skeleton crew. Commodore Roger Keyes, now serving as de Robeck's Chief of Staff, went aboard the destroyer *Wear* to see if she could be salvaged, supported by the battleships *Ocean* and *Swiftsure*. He found *Irresistible* still afloat and ordered *Ocean* to tow her clear, a task which her captain protested was not feasible. Next *Ocean* struck a mine and then a shell from one of the forts destroyed her steering gear, and she too was abandoned. After nightfall, Keyes went back in the destroyer *Jed* to look for the two lost battleships, where he found that all was silent in the straits. For four hours he searched for the ships, without success; but he was sure that the battle was as good as won, as he wrote later:

> I had a most indelible impression that we were in the presence of a beaten foe. I thought he was beaten at 2.00pm. I knew he was beaten at 4.00pm – and at midnight I knew with still greater certainty that he was absolutely beaten.[4]

But de Robeck did not share his view, on March 23 telegraphing Churchill that he would not renew the attack without military assistance, which would be available in mid April. Churchill was dismayed; he drafted an immediate order for the renewal of the attack, but the War Group at the Admiralty refused to endorse it. Asquith, when consulted, supported Churchill, but declined to act against the advice of the admirals. As Alan Moorehead wrote: 'A silence now settled on the Gallipoli peninsula: no ship entered the straits, no gun was fired. The Fleet lay at anchor in the islands. The first part of the great adventure was over.'[5]

And so began on April 25 the ill fated military operations on the Gallipoli peninsula. By May 8 it was clear that the invading army needed reinforcements; at a stormy War Council meeting on May 14 nothing was settled, though it appeared to Fisher that more ships might be sent to the Dardanelles. Later, Fisher and Churchill had what appeared to be a satisfactory meeting as to the ships to be sent; but in the early hours of the following morning Fisher received four minutes from Churchill which convinced him that the First Lord would not stick to any agreement. Before breakfast his resignation was en route to Asquith and Churchill; attempts to persuade him to withdraw it failed, and by May 17 a full scale Government crisis erupted. The press was united in its belief that Fisher should stay, and Churchill go. Jellicoe, like most of the navy, was appalled, writing to Hamilton, the Second Sea Lord, on May 19:

> Lord Fisher had many enemies, more enemies than friends, in the service, but even his enemies have been saying that his presence at the Admiralty was essential, as he was the only person who could tackle the First Lord ... Winston Churchill is a public danger to the Empire.[6]

For a few days the situation hung in the balance, as Fisher scented an opportunity to return to the Admiralty on his own terms, with Churchill having been turned out, but his demands were too much for Asquith and, indeed, the King. On May 22 Asquith finally accepted Fisher's resignation. By then Churchill's fate was sealed. In the new coalition government which Asquith formed, he was relegated to the Duchy of Lancaster, a sinecure which Lloyd George described as for beginners or for those who 'had reached the first stages of unmistakable decrepitude.' The Navy, generally, was glad to see the back of a First Lord who had caused constant alarm during his term of office. Jellicoe later wrote that he had long 'thoroughly distrusted Mr Churchill because he consistently arrogated to himself technical knowledge which, with all his brilliant qualities, I knew he did not possess,' while Beatty told his wife that 'the Navy breathes freer now it is rid of the succubus Churchill.'[7]

The key to Churchill's public character and motivation, at this point in his career at any rate, is to be found in the closing words of his letter to Asquith of May 17, when he said that he would only take the War Office or the Admiralty in any new government. If not, he looked for 'employment in the field.' What he wanted above all things was to exercise command in war, and he was in no doubt of his capacity to do so. Therein lay the origin of the many bold schemes which he put forward, and which caught his imagination.

The question of who should succeed Churchill was a complex one for Asquith to decide. Having consented to a coalition, he was obliged to consider the views of the Conservative Party, the leaders of which had insisted that Churchill must go. Churchill, in his efforts to hang on to his job, had suggested that Arthur Balfour should be appointed to the War Office; but to remove Kitchener was impossible. Balfour, alone of the Tory leaders, had been an active member of the

Committee of Imperial Defence and the War Council, and by May 19 had emerged as the likely replacement for Churchill. He was reluctantly prepared to accept the post, writing to a previous First Lord in Lord Selborne, who had urged that Fisher remain as First Sea Lord, next day:

> I do not the least know, as yet, what place Asquith desires me to occupy. I have told him that personally I would rather occupy *none*; but after what Bonar Law said to me on Monday, this, I take it, is impossible. I saw Asquith on Tuesday evening, and wrote to him yesterday to say that the only administrative office I thought I could usefully fill would be the Admiralty; but that I was prepared to join the new Government with or without a portfolio ... I am afraid that Jacky is a little mad. He has been using, I hear, the most violent language about me, whom I believe at one time he used to 'butter up to the skies.' I am not sure that even if Asquith consented to his remaining at the Admiralty, he would consent to serve under me. There would be no use our attempting to work together unless he really was prepared to go cordially with me.[8]

Fisher's demands having made his retention impossible, consideration must next be given to a suitable replacement. This was not easy. Admiral of the Fleet Sir Arthur Wilson was, according to Selborne, a very bad administrator', refusing to recognise how things had changed, and had become a dangerous adviser; in any case, he had said he would serve under nobody but Churchill.[9] Admiral Sir George Callaghan was apparently thought not up to the task of becoming First Sea Lord; there was no logical successor to Jellicoe as Commander-in-Chief of the Grand Fleet, so he could not be spared. Everyone's second choice was Admiral Sir Henry Jackson; since none of the other candidates was appointable, it was he who was appointed. Balfour's biographer describes him as 'the scientific, dismal, desk-bound Jackson', which seems a little harsh; Marder, observing that he was almost unknown to the nation, remarks that his appointment 'elicited a lukewarm reception', but it was apparently well received in the Fleet.

Arthur Balfour accordingly joined the coalition government as First Lord of the Admiralty, with Jackson as First Sea Lord. Asquith's Private Secretary, reviewing the candidates, wrote of the latter:

> He has been in the machine from the beginning of the war, his paperwork is admirable, and he would have the confidence of the Admiralty and I think of the fleet. On the other hand, according to his opinion, he is not at present really sufficiently acquainted with the North Sea position, as the nature of his work has not admitted of this.[10]

Beatty feared that Jackson was 'not man enough for the job'; Jellicoe, considering that 'the naval policy will now be sound,' was concerned that his health would not stand the strain.[11] However else Balfour and Jackson might be judged, they certainly headed a regime entirely different from that which it replaced. Hankey wrote later that the Admiralty had jumped form one extreme to the other: 'In place of two men of driving power, initiative and resource, but occasionally lacking in judgment, there were now in charge two men of philosophic temperament and first rate judgment but less dynamic than their predecessors.'[12]

Jackson, born in 1855, had enjoyed a successful but not high profile career. He reached the rank of captain at the age of 41, by which time he was already becoming known for his scientific interests. In June 1901 he received the distinction of being elected a Fellow of the Royal

Society. Fisher wrote of him in 1902 in his service record that he could not speak too highly of him; he was a thorough master of every branch of his profession, and equally excelled as a practical as well as a scientific officer. That year Jackson presented a paper on wireless telegraphy to the Royal Society, entitled *On Some Phenomena Affecting the Transmission of Electric Waves over the Surface of the Sea and Earth.* He served as Third Sea Lord from 1905 to 1908, and then commanded a cruiser squadron in the Mediterranean for two years before returning to administrative functions. He was promoted admiral in 1914, and was intended to succeed Sir Berkeley Milne as Commander-in-Chief in the Mediterranean; however, when war broke out he was retained for special service at the Admiralty. Churchill had come to have a considerable respect for him but his opinion was evidently not shared by everyone; Hamilton, the Second Sea Lord, noted in his diary in February 1916: 'It is a pity Jackson is so taciturn before the politicians as he does not do justice to himself.'[13] Jackson was also given to irritability with his naval colleagues and even, on occasion, with Balfour himself.

One casualty of the change in leadership was the concept of establishing command of the Baltic. Although the possibility of operations there was considered later in 1915 and again in 1916, Jackson regarded it as a 'trap'; without the advocacy and energy of Churchill and Fisher, the various schemes lacked the impetus to be adopted. Marder, observing 'near unanimity among both Fisher's congenital critics and his supports that his Baltic Scheme was a hare-brained one that offered no chance of success,' swims against the tide with only Admiral Bacon on which to rely. He thought that the scheme's critics overlooked the possibility that the operation might have brought about the full scale encounter with the High Seas Fleet that everyone craved.[14] The question which arose was whether the new Board would put any similarly bold strategy in place, and it was soon clear that they would not. Sir Percy Scott thought the new Board was 'extraordinarily gentlemanly', but wondered if a touch of devilment ought not to be introduced.[15]

The changes in leadership on the other side of the North Sea did not bring about any change in the policy to be followed. Scheer summarised Pohl's intentions:

> The action of the Fleet under Pohl's leadership coincided with the views held by him when Chief of the Naval Staff – that the maintenance of the Fleet intact at that stage of the war was a necessity. His plan was by frequent and constant advances of the entire High Seas Fleet to induce the enemy to operate in the North Sea, thus either assuring incidental results of leading to a decisive battle under favourable conditions to ourselves, that is to say, so close to our own waters that, even if the actual battles were undecided, the enemy's total losses, owing to the longer route home with his damaged ships, would be much greater than ours.[16]

In choosing a successor for Pohl as Chief of the Admiralty Staff, Müller had encountered difficulties. Admiral Friedrich von Baudissin, who had retired six months earlier on health grounds, would have been popular within the navy, but apart from his health, the personal hostility felt for him by the Kaiser made his appointment impossible. Müller settled, therefore, for Bachmann, setting out in his diary his reasons for doing so:

> Admiral Bachmann ranked as a calm, experienced man, equally at home on the Staff or at sea. Although unsuited to Commander-in-Chief he would certainly get on better with Tirpitz than Pohl had done. He did not have a reputation of being a strong man and had

> never been, with regard to the Kaiser. He was acceptable to the State Secretary, who knew him well from earlier posts in the Navy Office.[17]

Bachmann did his level best to avoid the appointment, writing in his diary on February 2:

> The Chief of the Cabinet informed me that I was to take the place of Admiral von Pohl. I begged that, if it were still possible, I should be passed over for the post, as I regarded the position of Chief of the Naval Staff as an absurdity. The war at sea could not in my firm conviction be controlled from GHQ, lying as it did far inland, nor should its conduct be hampered by the need for obtaining the decision of His Majesty on every occasion.[18]

Bachmann argued for the appointment of a supreme naval commander; when Müller asked him who that should be, he unhesitatingly replied that the only possible person was Tirpitz. To this, Müller's response was that 'Tirpitz had been out of active naval service for eighteen years,' and was accordingly 'no longer capable of leading the large forces which were now at our disposal.' They debated the question for some time, with Müller adamant that it was not possible, ending the discussion by saying that Bachmann had been duly appointed as Chief of Naval Staff.

It was certainly true that Tirpitz was favourably disposed towards Bachmann; the Grand Admiral felt considerable satisfaction that, as he thought, Müller, whom he described as 'that curious and somewhat incomprehensible person,' had erred:

> In connection with the appointment of Pohl as Commander in Chief of the Fleet, which was received with the greatest astonishment by the navy, the Chief of the Cabinet attributed great importance to finding a successor to him at GHQ who would fall in with Bethmann's naval policy. If, however, he regarded Admiral Bachmann as suitable from this point of view, then as was so often the case, his judgment of men was at fault. Far from falling in with the Chancellor's policy, Bachmann was such a frank supporter of the views prevailing in the navy that his position as Chief of the Naval Staff was soon rendered difficult and he was succeeded by Admiral von Holtzendorff in September 1915.[19]

Pohl's strategy therefore called for the High Seas Fleet to come out whenever it could in order to tempt the Grand Fleet into danger. With Jellicoe as his opponent, this was always going to be an unlikely outcome, as Pohl well understood. He wrote to Bachmann on April 7 bluntly stating the position as he saw it:

> No one can desire our fleet to achieve such partial results more than I do. But I know of no method by which they can be obtained without at the same time risking the whole Fleet. An advance to the enemy's coast involves the great danger of being forced to fight off the enemy's coast. To assume that the enemy would send inferior portions of his Battle Fleet right into the German Bight, is to credit him with quite exceptional stupidity. In war such underestimation of the enemy always has its revenge.[20]

However, in the four months following his appointment the High Seas Fleet made six sorties, never going further than about 120 nautical miles from Heligoland. On every occasion a careful search was made for mines, and precautions taken against submarine attacks, while the scouting undertaken by the limited number of cruisers available was supplemented by aerial reconnaissance. The range of these operations meant that the distance to be covered was such that could be achieved in a night or in a day.

In practice, therefore, these sweeps by the High Seas Fleet were not very likely to bring on a major fleet action, as Scheer noted:

> Whenever the news of our putting to sea reached the enemy, as we gathered from his wireless messages and certain other means, he began to make a move, but he never left the northern part of the North Sea. The enemy thus left to us that area of the sea in which our movements took place, and we observed a similar method of procedure with regard to him, so that a meeting between the two Fleets seemed very improbable. If it was the enemy's object to entice us nearer to his coasts, he failed to achieve it; we did not favour him by adapting our course of action to suit his pleasure. Admiral von Pohl considered that a big surplus of forces was necessary for an offensive of that kind, and if it was available for the enemy it certainly was not for us.[21]

With not a great deal happening in the North Sea, the attention of the German Admiralty staff turned, like their opposite numbers in London, to the question of the Baltic, where a genuine threat was perceived from the Russian navy. In June, the IV Squadron, consisting of the old battleships of the *Wittelsbach* class, under Vice Admiral Erhard Schmidt, was transferred to Kiel, together with the IV Scouting Group and a flotilla of torpedo boats. In August Hipper was ordered to take his I and II Scouting Groups into the Baltic to reinforce the operations there. However, the threat to his big ships from submarines and mines seriously hampered his effectiveness. On August 19 *Moltke* was hit by a torpedo, and although the damage was not very serious she had to go into dry dock for repairs. To Hipper's great relief, the participation of his squadrons ended on August 22, and he returned to the North Sea. His comments on the operation were succinct:

> To keep valuable ships for a considerable time in a limited area in which enemy submarines were increasingly active, with the corresponding risk of damage and loss, was to indulge in a gamble out of all proportion to the advantage to be gained from the occupation of the Gulf *before* the capture of Riga from the land side. I therefore regard a repetition of the operation as justified only if the army can co-operate. Until that time arrives the Pütziger Wik must be made safe as a base for big ships – by a minefield at least and, if possible, by nets.[22]

One of Pohl's last acts before leaving the Admiralty Staff for the High Seas Fleet had been to issue an order giving effect to the policy finally approved by Bethmann-Hollweg and the Kaiser of an out and out submarine war on commerce. Hitherto, the German Naval Prize Regulations had, more or less, been followed, providing that only if it was impossible or impracticable to bring a prize into port could it be destroyed there and then, and this must not be done 'until after all persons on board are placed in safety, with their goods and chattels if possible.'[23] The operations of submarines were not, however, compatible with the traditional law and custom of the sea. Men could not be spared for a prize crew, there was insufficient room to take on board the crew of a sunken ship, and above all by surfacing and acting in accordance with custom, the submarine compromised its safety.

The possibility that submarines would be used by the Germans in an unrestricted war against commerce had been raised in 1913 by Fisher. He pointed out that 'an enemy can lay mines without outraging propriety! After all, submarines can exercise discretion – mines can't!' It was impossible, he added, for a submarine to deal with commerce in accordance with existing international law.[24] Corbett referred to the response of the Admiralty to this suggestion:

> The more general belief was that they were too sound strategists to risk raising fresh enemies against them by so flagrant a violation of the ancient customs of the sea. Though this saner view seems certainly to have been weightily held in Germany, it was now becoming apparent that under the provocation of our blockade it had to give way to the more reckless policy.[25]

The potential difference that the adoption of such a policy could make was enormous. From the start of the war until the end of January 1915, submarines sank a total of only ten British merchant ships, representing 7 per cent of the 273,000 tons of British shipping lost.[26] The ineffectiveness of the submarines while following the existing restrictions caused a steady hardening of opinion in Germany, and Bethmann-Hollweg's conversion, after prolonged hesitation, was decisive. On February 4 1915 Germany proclaimed that the waters around Great Britain and Ireland were, from February 18 to be treated as a war zone in which all merchant vessels would be sunk 'without it always being possible to avoid danger to the crews and passengers.' Furthermore, neutral merchantmen were put on notice that if they entered the war zone they would be at grave risk.[27]

When the campaign began, there were 22 U-boats available. By the end of April 39 merchant vessels of 105,000 tons had been sunk. On May 7 the British liner *Lusitania* was sunk, with the loss of 1198 lives, including 128 Americans, prompting strong protests from the United States. Sinkings continued to increase; in the month of August 49 ships were lost. One of these was the liner *Arabic*, sunk off the coast of Ireland with the loss of 40 lives, three of them American. Further outraged protest from the United States led to a ban on August 30 on the sinking of any passenger liner without giving warning and saving the passengers and crews. This was followed on September 18 by the withdrawal of U-boats from the Channel and the Western Approaches, while activity in the North Sea more or less ended in October. Thereafter the emphasis, so far as the U-boat operations from the Flanders bases was concerned, was on minelaying activity. During 1915, U-boats had accounted for the destruction of 748,000 tons of British merchant shipping, at a cost of 20 submarines. New vessels more than replaced those lost; and the Germans completed 61 new U-boats, having a total of 58 in service by the end of the year.[28]

In 1915 Lieutenant Commander Wolfgang Wegener was serving as First Admiralty Staff Officer to Vice Admiral Wilhelm von Lans, commanding the First Squadron. Wegener had come to this appointment in 1913 after a series of highly flattering fitness reports from previous postings. He had already made a name for himself by important work for the Naval Academy. In January 1915 he wrote to a fellow graduate, Siegfried Westerkamp, to express his disappointment at the outcome of the Dogger Bank, and he mentioned his thoughts on the matter to Lans, who asked him to produce a memorandum for the squadron. This he did, and Lans endorsed it with his signature. Entitled 'Reflections on our Maritime Situation', it stated firmly:

> We must avoid a decisive or even major naval engagement in the North Sea because such an engagement would probably so weaken our fighting forces that the political significance of our fleet would disappear. Given the tremendous superiority of the English fleet, even a brilliant German victory would leave total sea control of the North Sea and Baltic Sea in the hands of that part of the English fleet not engaged in the battle, [and would also leave a relatively] strengthened Russian Baltic Fleet.[29]

The Baltic, he argued, was decisive for a victory in the war; the North Sea was not, and operations there must reflect that reality. Wegener went on to review the lessons of the war so far, concluding that in the North Sea operations should be based on submarine warfare, mine warfare and, if possible 'preparation of the Heligoland Bight for the exploitation of a partial success against the enemy.' This, he thought, could only come about by chance. Far ranging advances must be avoided. In the Baltic, Germany should in the spring concentrate its good squadrons to deal with the Russian fleet.

Later in February, Lans was retired as the commander of the I Squadron. He was very much on Tirpitz's black list as having been an outspoken critic of a forward policy in the North Sea, so his endorsement of Wegener's paper probably did not materially affect his fate. Müller appears to have accepted Tirpitz's description of Lans as being completely burnt out, also suggesting that he was still suffering from the effect of the serious wound which he had sustained during the Boxer rebellion; when reviewing the changes in the high command Müller seems to have it firmly in his mind that Lans was 'close to a nervous collapse.'[30] Lans was extremely bitter about his dismissal, which he believed was down not only to Müller, but also to Holtzendorff. It is worth noting that his health cannot have been too bad; he long outlived most of his colleagues, dying in 1947 at the age of 86. The outcome of his removal was the promotion to command the I Battle Squadron of Rear Admiral Eckermann, who thus secured the prize for which he had been lobbying.

As the months passed, Wegener found time to develop his ideas, which he put in the form of a trilogy written between June and August 1915. The first part entitled 'Thoughts about our Maritime Situation' argued that 'war at sea exerts itself only by indirect means,' and that meeting the Grand Fleet head on was not the military object of the war.[31] This was followed by 'Can we Improve our Situation' in July, in which Wegener considered how the German fleet could break out of its imprisonment. Examining the flanking positions on either side of the German bases, he considered that there was little point in moving to occupy the Dutch coastline; its importance was 'minimal because we are in possession of Flanders'. However, a different situation arose in relation to Denmark:

> All principles of naval warfare direct us to the Kattegat and the Skagerrak, whose value is so great that this flanking position, [once] endowed with bases, probably can become the primary theatre. The Belts and the waters of the Skagerrak and Kattegat possess a significance for the navy similar to Belgium's for the army. With [free] passage of the Belts, we get the chance to exercise sea control and, by fighting for this measure of sea control, to accrue advantages under favourable conditions, without exposing ourselves to a decisive battle against our will.[32]

The subject of Denmark was one which would recur.

In his third paper, 'Naval Bases, Policy and Fleet' of August 1915, Wegener began by reiterating that ' we are currently locked in the North Sea as in a cage, and the English fleet guards the exit.' Examining the suggestion that the training and strength of the German fleet were sufficient to seek out the enemy off Scotland, he observed that this 'would not be commensurate with the purpose of the war.' Although a victory there would be of a great psychological significance, the gain in prestige would not offset the loss of the greater part of the fleet. The principle on which he proceeded was that ' a total, even if modest success is better than no battle at all, but no battle at all is better than a battle against one's will.'[33] He went on, however, to propound an extremely adventurous strategy that could only have been relevant had Germany won the war and even then was probably quite unrealistic, as he more or less conceded, at the end of his paper: 'Even if much of what has previously been stated amounts to futuristic dreams and goes beyond the immediate actions of our fleet, the discussion is still valuable.'[34]

Wegener's three papers got a wide circulation, and a number of leading naval personalities commented on them. Not surprisingly, Pohl approved; equally unsurprisingly Tirpitz was furious, denouncing Wegener's arguments as 'poison for the fleet.' Trotha, following Tirpitz's line, was not impressed, finding that Wegener's work lacked 'aggressive spirit,' although he later adopted Wegener's case for bases in Scandinavia. The new commander of the I Battle Squadron, Eckermann, was also unconvinced of Wegener's argument against a major battle in the North Sea.[35] Wegener was clearly seen as an influential voice in naval circles; Captain Magnus von Levetzow, who joined Scheer's staff in early 1916, recorded after the war that in company with Scheer and Schmidt he had a meeting with Wegener at which the latter was ordered to lay down his pen for the rest of the war.[36]

Meanwhile at the end of August 1915 there was a major clash between Tirpitz and Bethmann-Hollweg. The latter had obtained the Kaiser's approval to a public statement of the policy to spare passenger vessels without consultation with either Tirpitz or Bachmann, both of whom were outraged by being kept out of the loop. On August 27, Tirpitz tendered his resignation. Next day the Kaiser summoned Müller in a towering rage. The admiral 'recommended careful consideration before replying,' and two days later the resignation was refused. After noting the impossibility of effective cooperation between the Chancellor and Tirpitz on naval matters, the order, drafted by Müller, went on:

> We refuse, however, most decidedly to release you from your position as Secretary of State for naval affairs. You cannot but know that a change in this office during the war – especially in the present position of the personnel at the Admiralty – would have serious disadvantages for the work of the whole navy.[37]

Tirpitz was mollified by the Kaiser's assurance that he would be consulted on important questions of naval policy, and agreed to stay on. Bachmann, however, who had strongly protested about Bethmann-Hollweg's proceedings, was relieved as Chief of the Admiralty Staff, and replaced by Admiral von Holtzendorff. Bachmann returned to his previous post of Chief of the Baltic Station, and was no doubt rather glad to do so. Holtzendorff, who had retired in 1912, was gloomily noted by Tirpitz as having expressed views in accordance with those of the Chancellor, and was accordingly 'as a red rag to a bull' to the Grand Admiral.[38] It did not make for a very happy team going forward.

Henning von Holtzendorff, who was born in 1853, had risen to the top of the German navy, commanding the High Seas Fleet from 1909 to 1913. Earlier in his career he had commanded the battleship *Friedrich Wilhelm* from 1899 to 1900; he had then headed the naval shipyard in Danzig before being second in command of the Cruiser Squadron from 1903 – 1904. Following this, he was second in command of the II Battle Squadron, and then in 1906 was appointed to the command of the I Battle Squadron. As Commander in Chief he was soon at odds with the Admiralty Staff over their plans for war in the North Sea, advocating a move of the High Seas Fleet to Skagen on the outbreak of war, there to await opportunities as they arose; alternatively, if the battleships were not immediately ready for combat, he thought they should await the enemy in the Baltic.[39] In the following years disputes as to the strategy to be adopted continued; in the end the views of the Admiralty Chief of Staff (by then Admiral August von Heeringen), which coincided with those of Tirpitz, prevailed over those of Holtzendorff and Lans. In a conflict in which Tirpitz was involved, it was always likely that this would be the outcome, but Holtzendorff had gone down fighting, writing to Levetzow, at that time in the Operations Department of the High Seas Fleet staff, to record the support he was hoping to gather:

> If Ingenohl and Bachmann follow the same line as Lans, I will not hesitate to suggest a radical onslaught. This would mean, however, a full scale attack on the *Reichsmarineamt* and, if this succeeds, the resignation of Tirpitz. I see this man still as disastrous for the navy, though there is no personal prejudice on my part.[40]

As a result, Holtzendorff was retired in the Spring of 1913, although he remained in the background, with frequent rumours of his return to service.

In January 1916, Pohl was taken seriously ill; he had been unwell for some time, but had tried to keep this secret. Scheer was at once appointed to deputise for him, being formally appointed as Commander-in-Chief of the High Seas Fleet on January 18. It was an appointment which Hipper learned of with relief; he had been particularly concerned that Holtzendorff might be appointed.[41] Scheer at once set about reorganising the staff, appointing Trotha, at that time commanding the battleship *Kaiser*, as Chief of Staff and Levetzow, commanding the battlecruiser *Moltke*, as Chief of the Operations Department. Both men were close to Scheer, and he had absolute confidence in them, writing in his memoirs:

> My very special gratitude is due to Rear Admiral von Trotha, on whose prudent and circumspect judgment I invariably relied. He supplemented in the happiest manner the keen and eager leader of the Operating Division, Captain von Levetzow. They were both upright men with independent views based on much learning, who stood by their opinions, were closely linked in faithful comradeship, and formed a circle to which I look back with pride and gratitude.[42]

10

Scheer Takes Over

The key subordinate to the commander of the High Seas Fleet would of course be Franz Hipper, who was not, however entirely secure in his job. He faced in particular the sustained hostility of Tirpitz and his supporters. This went back at least as far as the battle of Heligoland Bight. On the following day, believing incorrectly that his son had not survived the engagement, Tirpitz wrote angrily:

> The small cruisers were too reckless, and, apart from that, I feel very bitterly that my advice did not appear to be properly followed. One doesn't send them forward against armoured ships unless one has his battleships and torpedo-craft close behind. But I won't protest, as I can't review the events that preceded it.[1]

His restraint evidently did not last long; later that day he complained to the Kaiser that the battlecruisers and the main fleet should have come out in support, and repeated this to Pohl; on September 4 he told the Kaiser that Hipper was to blame for the outcome of the battle. He also took up the matter with Lans (apparently because he believed himself not entitled to write direct to Ingenohl). Lans, however, rejected the criticism of Hipper, while Ingenohl also defended him to the Kaiser. On the other hand, both Pohl and Prince Henry were apparently critical of both Hipper and his subordinate captains.[2]

Tirpitz's disapproval of Hipper was sharpened both by the latter's support for the continuation of a defensive strategy and his criticism of some of the design aspects of warships built by Tirpitz. After the Dogger Bank he had pressed Müller to relieve Hipper; with Pohl's departure, another opportunity arose, and, through Levetzow, newly appointed to Scheer's staff, he again lobbied for Hipper's removal. Levetzow had begun a campaign for Hipper to be retired on the grounds of ill health in January 1915, with a letter to Holtzendorff, not at that time in office; Holtzendorff was unimpressed. He was no more sympathetic when, as Chief of the Admiralty Staff, he received a letter from Scheer to be forwarded to Müller, dated April 15 1916. In that letter, Scheer reiterated that that the need for Hipper's retirement was on the grounds of ill health.[3]

Scheer was apparently sufficiently anxious about the state of Hipper's health to telephone Holtzendorff, as a note of the call in the Admiralty records shows:

> Vice Admiral Scheer feels that he has come to the conclusion that Vice Admiral Hipper no longer possesses the qualities of robustness and elasticity which the assignment of Flag Officer, Reconnaissance Forces demands and that it is also his view that the end of leave will not effect a complete restoration of his abilities. Besides, a change has been in order because the burdens of the *Bda* have increased tremendously since the beginning of the war. The man acting in the assignment of *Bda* Rear Admiral Boedicker, has shown himself to be the most suitable replacement since assuming his duties.[4]

As an alternative, Scheer suggested reducing Hipper's burden by assigning responsibility for torpedo boats and airships elsewhere.

Müller, to whom Holtzendorff had recommended that no action be taken on the letter, agreed that Hipper should remain. It was evidently not something that he felt was important enough to refer to in his diary. Hipper had, in fact, not been very well with sciatica, complaining of terrible pain and exhaustion, and towards the end of March went on sick leave. He does not seem to have been very concerned about the possibility of not returning to duty; the principal subject of his farewell meeting with Raeder, his Chief of Staff, was his anxiety that Boedicker, his deputy, might change his band, of which he was very proud, for the worse. Boedicker, he thought, liked 'Prussian marches, treacly waltzes and bits out of Fledermaus.'[5] Hipper's doctor, however, was able to pronounce that there was nothing to worry about, and he returned to his command towards the end of May with his health fully restored. Levetzow, who had apparently addressed a direct enquiry to his doctor, (so much for medical confidentiality) received a similar assurance.[6]

It was Hipper, of course, who commanded the only units which had had the opportunity to draw practical conclusions from combat experience in the North Sea. He was asked by Pohl on February 20, following his recommendations arising from following the battle of the Dogger Bank, for his opinion on the type of capital ships to be built in the future. He replied:

> In order to answer this properly, I should have to know what was the situation, what were the government's political objectives, and what role the armed forces of the country were to have in attaining these objectives.[7]

It was his view that large capital ships would be required, particularly if Atlantic operations were to be undertaken. For the moment, he suggested among other things that construction should be concentrated on battle cruisers, carrying at least four turrets of heavy calibre weapons on the centre line, with increased armour for both decks and turrets, if necessary at the expense of the side armour. He also looked to the improvement of machinery to result in a substantial increase of speed, as well as a longer operational range.

Hipper had also explored with his battle cruiser captains some of the technical issues which arose from the Dogger Bank. Captain von Egidy, based on the experiences of *Seydlitz* during the battle, argued for the removal of ventilation ducts between magazines to prevent the spread of fire. Levetzow, commanding *Moltke*, advocated that the range of the main armament of the battle cruisers be increased by modifying them to allow them to be elevated to attain a range of 25,000 metres. Steps were taken to introduce these improvements, at least partially; the benefits would be seen at the next major encounter with the British.

As soon as he took command Scheer set about revising a number of the operational policies of the High Seas Fleet. He looked first at the safety of the German Bight:

> Fresh rules were laid down dealing with the action of the Fleet when in the Bight, and instructions issued concerning protection and outpost duty. Arrangements were also made as to action under an enemy attack which would save waiting for lengthy orders in an urgent emergency, and would render it possible for all subordinate officers to play the part expected of them in such an event. The aim of the organisation was to keep the Bight clear by means of aeroplanes, outpost flotillas, minesweeping formations, and barrier breakers, and [a] regular reconnaissance, guard and mine-searching service was established.[8]

The outpost flotillas, consisting of some eighty fishing steamers, had as their prinicipal task the searching of the Inner Bight for enemy submarines. The torpedo boats were responsible for hunting any submarines that were discovered.

Scheer also addressed the question of the readiness of the High Seas Fleet to act as a whole:

> In order not to keep the entire Fleet constantly under steam and thus overtire both men and machinery and use up material to no purpose, and yet provide that they should be ready with considerable fores for any enemy enterprises, an outpost service was organised. In the Jade there lay always in readiness a squadron of battleships, two battle cruisers, a cruiser-leader of torpedo boats, and a torpedo boat flotilla; a scouting division of light cruisers were in the Jade and the Weser, a torpedo boat flotilla in Heligoland harbour; half the ships of Squadron II in the Cuxhaven Roads, at Altenbruch; and, if sufficient torpedo boats were available, another torpedo boat half-flotilla was stationed on the Ems or in List Deep (at Sylt) – constituting approximately half the total forces of the High Seas Fleet.[9]

Apart from the Heligoland flotilla, which was to be kept ready for sea immediately, these forces were to be ready to sail threequarters of an hour after orders reached them. The rest of the fleet was divided more or less equally between the inner roads of Wilhelmshaven or Brünsbuttel, or in harbour, to be ready on three hours notice.

Scheer also strengthened the defences of the Bight by additional minelaying, while establishing a safe area for assembling the fleet inside the line Horns Reef – Terschelling. The fleet, both as a whole and in separate units, was put on a regime of frequent navigation and firing exercises; it was no longer found necessary to move units into the Baltic for this purpose. Even more significantly, however, Scheer immediately instituted a programme of increased offensive activity. Light forces advanced at night to the edge of the Bight to attack any forces found there, suspicious vessels were stopped, and support given to Zeppelins on bombing raids. These activities were supported by a division of light cruisers, while the battle cruisers were located in the Schillig Roads, or deployed at sea. When the night advances were prolonged until daybreak, the entire High Seas Fleet put to sea. Scheer also planned a further series of coastal bombardments in the hope that the British fleet would be obliged to intervene.

Corbett, in the British Official History, summarised Sheer's objectives:

> By some means or other the British sea power must be broken. In battle there lay no hope, for it was only under exceptionally advantageous conditions in their own prepared waters

> that it was possible to meet the Grand Fleet with success, and that was a chance it was vain to expect. The British people, he was sure, knew too well the security Admiral Jellicoe was giving them as he sat immovably on the ocean communications ever to throw it away by clamouring for a hazardous advance into German waters. But short of that he believed that with his increased forces much might be done to make them weary of the war, and he lost no time in bracing the fleet for the schemes that were teeming in his mind.[10]

The first direct result of Scheer's more aggressive policy came on February 10, when a force of German destroyers sortied beyond the Dogger Bank. A flotilla of *Flower* class sloops of 1250 tons had been engaged in sweeping one of the channels kept clear for the passage of the fleet during the day; at night three of the four ships withdrew, leaving *Arabis* at sea to stand by the marker buoy showing the swept channel, while the others steamed on and off. At midnight *Arabis* was encountered by the German destroyers, and although putting up a stout resistance was soon sunk, the Germans rescuing some of the survivors. Tyrwhitt's force had put to sea since a major operation was suspected, but was recalled when it was realised that this was not the case. Unluckily, as he returned, his flagship *Arethusa* struck a mine and although a towline was twice got aboard her, both parted, and she went aground, breaking in two.

During February, having completed his review of the situation and prepared an outline of his strategic ideas, Scheer went to Berlin to confer with Holtzendorff, who endorsed his proposals. The next step was to run these past the Kaiser, who on February 23 visited Wilhelmshaven in a blinding snowstorm. Müller, who accompanied him, recorded his account of Scheer's presentation:

> The Kaiser crossed the coaling bridge past the *U98* to the flagship *Friedrich der Grosse*, and in the wardroom listened to an incisive report by the C-in-C Vice Admiral Scheer on the conduct of naval war in the North Sea and the increased U-boat warfare. His Majesty, out of regard for America, counselled the sparing of passenger liners, the result of his conversation yesterday with the Chancellor. Among other things he said: 'Were I the Captain of a U-boat I would never torpedo a ship if I knew that women and children were aboard.'[11]

Scheer's presentation was based on his paper 'Guiding Principles for Sea Warfare in the North Sea.' The central thrust of his proposals was based on a recognition that the High Seas Fleet could not simply seek a decisive battle with the Grand Fleet, but pressure must be applied on the British fleet to force it to give up its waiting attitude and send out part of its forces. The German pressure should be through U-boat warfare, minelaying, attacks on the Scandinavian trade route, aerial warfare and sorties by the High Seas Fleet.[12]

Scheer's presentation was persuasive, and he obtained the approval which he sought for a more adventurous policy. He wasted little time in putting his ideas into practice, on March 5 taking the High Seas Fleet, with the exception of the 2nd Battle Squadron, into the Hoofden with the object of intercepting any British light forces that might be operating in that area. The intention was for the battlecruisers to be off Terschelling at dawn and to move to the limit of the British minefields, with the battleships some thirty miles behind. When it was learned that the High Seas Fleet was out, the Grand Fleet sailed southward to try to intercept it, while Tyrwhitt went to reconnoitre. A heavy easterly gale developed; there was no contact with the British light forces and Scheer returned home, as did the Grand Fleet when it was clear that there was no possibility of contact.[13]

Three weeks later a British move to attack the Zeppelin hangars in Schleswig created an opportunity that might have led to the kind of encounter that Scheer was after. The plan was to launch five seaplanes from the seaplane carrier *Vindex*; Tyrwhitt was to cover the operation while Beatty sailed to a point some forty five miles west of Horns Reef in support. In the event the raid was a failure, and in the course of a counter attack by German aircraft on Tyrwhitt's force the destroyer *Laverock* rammed *Medusa,* another of his destroyers. Tyrwhitt endeavoured to save the seriously damaged vessel, but had to abandon her; meanwhile German torpedo boats from their outpost line arrived on the scene, and an action began in a night of gales and snowstorms. The light cruiser *Cleopatra* rammed and sank a German torpedo boat before herself being rammed by her consort *Undaunted*. In the confusion, Tyrwhitt's forces were widely scattered; at the time Beatty's battlecruisers were some fifty miles to the north. Tyrwhitt ordered all his force to make for home.

Meanwhile Scheer had ordered the High Seas Fleet to sea, led by Hipper's I Scouting Group, since the fact of Beatty's presence had become known as a result of wireless intercepts. By 6.30am however, Hipper was obliged to report that weather conditions were now so bad that an engagement would be impossible, and Scheer reluctantly ordered a return to base. The Grand Fleet, meanwhile, had at 1.00am been ordered to put to sea in the suspicion that the High Seas Fleet was out, but it would necessarily have been unable to arrive on the scene of the action that would, but for the weather, have ensued, until after it had taken place.[14]

The morale of the Commander-in-Chief of the Grand Fleet was not very high in the early part of 1916. This was particularly noticeable to Beatty when he visited him at the beginning of February, so much so that he was moved to write direct to the Prime Minister to set out the reasons for Jellicoe's gloom:

> I have just left the Commander-in-Chief, whom I have not seen for five months, and left him so perturbed and despondent about the delays in new construction that I felt impelled to write to you privately on matters which I feel to be of the greatest importance. The Admiralty I understand are powerless to prevent the depletion of the ship building yards of labour which goes away daily to supplementing the making of munitions, with the result that the programme of completing destroyers and light cruisers and battle cruisers has been thrown back four to eight months. No doubt you are aware of this, and have been duly informed by the Admiralty. But what you cannot be aware of is the very serious view of the situation taken by the Commander-in-Chief, which I feel is of national importance and so take the liberty of calling your attention to it.[15]

Scheer's appointment, and the signs of increased German activity which followed, prompted further consideration of the deployment of the Grand Fleet, which at Scapa Flow was too far off for any emergency intervention. The obvious alternative was Rosyth, but the base was inadequate for so many ships. The Admiralty decided, rather irresolutely, to move the fleet to the Forth but not until sufficient outer defences had been completed. The uncertainty of the Admiralty would have come as no surprise to Richmond, whose opinion of its leaders continued to be extremely low:

> We are content to sit like a tar-baby, taking the punches of the enemy and hoping that his fists will stick somewhere – feeble, wretched policy, but natural to people whose upbringing

> does not put them in contact with military thought. Sir H Jackson is an electrician and engineer, Oliver is a navigator – and he is the best of the lot – T Jackson is a mathematician, Sir F Hamilton is a social success, Tudor is a gunnery expert, Lambert is nothing in particular; and upon my soul the only man who has any military education is the civilian, Balfour, as his predecessor Churchill was.[16]

Although he was deeply concerned about the Grand Fleet's margin of superiority over its opponent, Jellicoe did have the very considerable reinforcement of the *Queen Elizabeth* class of five battleships, the last of which had joined the fleet during February. Jellicoe's original hope that they would attain a speed of 28 knots was, however, to be disappointed, when he was told that *Warspite* could at best do 23½ knots. This, he thought, put paid to the idea that the five ships (forming the 5th Battle Squadron) should be attached to Beatty's Battle Cruiser Fleet.[17] Beatty, on the other hand, continued to argue for their assignment to him. He submitted papers written by two of his subordinates, Brock and Pakenham, which asserted the relative weakness of the Battle Cruiser Fleet.[18] There was at this time a mistaken belief that the new German battlecruisers were armed with 15 inch guns or even 17 inch guns. Jellicoe, who rejected the arguments, nonetheless forwarded them to the Admiralty with his own comments.

There, the general opinion was to concur in in Jellicoe's reasoning. Oliver, however, thought that the assignment of the *Queen Elizabeths* to Beatty would be justified by the distance of the Grand Fleet at Scapa Flow from the scene of any likely German coastal raids. He reckoned that steps should be taken to prolong the chance of a decisive engagement with all or part of the German battle fleet; if Beatty encountered the High Seas Fleet, and had the 5th Battle Squadron on which to fall back, he would be reinforced within the hour, and the opportunity would exist to lure the enemy northwards in a trap.[19]

Jackson agreed; he was not pleased with Beatty's approach, as he recorded in a testy minute of February 27:

> This correspondence arose through letting the Flag Officers know what we are building and what we think the Germans are building and the possible 15" guns in the *Lützow* and *Hindenburg* has had more effect than was anticipated. The spirit of asking for all one can get seems to have gone down from the top, and it is to be hoped that it will not descend lower, as it might affect the old spirit of our seamen to do their best with what they have got.[20]

Reviewing Oliver's proposal to use the Battle Cruiser Fleet and the 5th Battle Squadron as the bait for the trap into which the High Seas Fleet was to be lured, Nicholas Black has noted that Jackson and Oliver had devised a bold strategy, 'rather than feebly putting out feelers for ideas that any old sea dog had for a way to attack Germans.'[21] The policy was certainly risky; and Scheer and his staff were no doubt perfectly capable of realising the possibility that the pursuit of a part of the British fleet might lead to an encounter with its main body.

In his analysis of the debate about the deployment of the Grand Fleet, Black sets out to defend the Admiralty from criticisms from such as Marder that it was capable only of reacting to events rather than making its own policy. He points out that the proposal to shift the centre of gravity of the battleships of the Grand Fleet southwards had been on the table for several months, and that the Admiralty was not guilty of Beatty's charge that it was pursuing a 'wait and see' policy. Looking at the response of Jackson and Oliver, it would seem that the Admiralty can be acquitted of this offence at least.

While the British Admiralty wrestled with the issues of Grand Fleet deployment and Scheer prepared the next move in his campaign, the German Admiralty was heavily involved in a politico-military dispute that was at the centre of German foreign policy and naval strategy. This was the future of submarine warfare, which was an issue with which all the naval leaders had been actively concerned since the previous autumn. At that time, soon after his appointment as Chief of the Admiralty Staff, Holtzendorff had concluded that the U-boat campaign had failed as a result of the restrictions placed on submarine commanders, and ordered that for the next few weeks there should be no U-boat activity to the west of Great Britain or in the Channel. In the North Sea the prize rules would be followed. This effectively brought to an end the submarine war on trade, which in fact was a considerable relief to the owners of the British merchant fleet, for whom the U-boat successes during August had been a serious warning of what might be to come.[22]

Later in the autumn U-boat warfare was resumed, which began the so called 'twilight phase' or restricted submarine war on trade. On November 21 Holtzendorff ordered the Flanders Flotilla to sink enemy freighters without warning in the Channel between Dunkirk and Le Havre, although as Professor Halpern has pointed out this did not mean a great deal until the following February, when the improved UB II type was available. In January the Kaiser was persuaded to agree to the sinking of armed enemy freighters and then on March 13 to the sinking without warning of all enemy freighters within the war zone.[23] The varying restrictions placed on U-boat commanders were complex and, in the course of operations, difficult to interpret.

As the months went by Holtzendorff was coming round to the idea of an unrestricted U-boat campaign. He received advice from shipping experts to the effect that the reduction in the number of new merchant vessels being built in Britain, and the employment of a large part of the existing merchant tonnage for military purposes meant that increases in the size of the U-boat fleet would provide the chance to knock Britain out of the war in six to eight months.[24] General Erich von Falkenhayn, the Chief of the Great General Staff, found Holtzendorff's arguments persuasive. At this point the intervention of Robert Lansing, the American Secretary of State, gave the proponents in Germany of increased submarine activity an opportunity to counter the objections of Chancellor Bethmann-Hollweg. Lansing proposed that German submarines should follow international law by stopping and searching vessels, and ensuring the safety of passengers and crew before sinking, while Britain and France should stop arming merchant ships which would otherwise be treated as auxiliary cruisers.

Scheer was thoroughly in favour of the enhanced U-boat war, but the Kaiser, as his reported remarks at the February 23 briefing indicated, was still anxious, and Holtzendorff banned attacks on passenger vessels. A Crown Council meeting followed on March 4 attended by the Kaiser, Bethmann-Hollweg, Falkenhayn, Holtzendorff, Colonel General Hans von Plessen, the Kaiser's Adjutant General, General Moritz von Lyncker, the Chief of the Military Cabinet, and Müller. The latter, who noted that the Kaiser had conducted the meeting 'with great tact', recorded the rather fudged decision reached:

> The Kaiser wishes to wait one month to see the results of the unrestricted U-boat warfare which has now been launched against armed merchantmen In the meantime the Foreign

> Office and the Press are to work on an unrestricted campaign against England alone. His Majesty will give the signal to start when he thinks fit.[25]

Müller thought that the meeting 'was on a consistently higher plane than usual.' There remained, however, a considerable gulf between the Chancellor, whose anxieties were of course about the United States, and the soldiers and sailors, who were much more gung-ho in their approach.

Notably, the meeting had not been attended by Tirpitz, who had become convinced that an all out U-boat war was essential, writing to Falkenhayn in February:

> Immediate and relentless recourse to the submarine weapon is absolutely necessary. Any further delay ... will give England time for further naval and economic defensive measures, cause us greater losses in the end, and endanger quick success ... If we defeat England, we break the backbone of the hostile coalition.[26]

A few days later Bethmann-Hollweg, who had long wanted to see the back of Tirpitz, had his chance, when one of the Grand Admiral's staff was found to have produced misleading figures as to the number of U-boats available. The Chancellor at once sought Tirpitz's resignation which, grudgingly, on March 9 in the form of a request to hand over his duties on health grounds, Tirpitz provided. To the Kaiser he wrote: 'The grave anxiety at seeing the life work of Your Majesty and the national future on the path to ruin makes me realise that my services can be of no further use to Your Majesty'.[27] His successor was to be Admiral Eduard von Capelle, of whom Tirpitz had a very high opinion.

While Scheer was getting ready for the next sortie of the High Seas Fleet, and a British cruiser force was sent on a raid into the Kattegat on April 20, the British Admiralty became aware next day that something was in the wind, and ordered the Grand Fleet to sea. The bulk of the fleet was to concentrate in the Long Forties, about 100 miles east of Aberdeen, with the battle cruisers about 40 miles ahead. The Admiralty's information was that the High Seas Fleet was at sea, but next morning it was learned that it had returned to port. It was proposed however that the Grand Fleet remain at sea to support the cruiser operation and by 6.00pm Beatty was 75 miles northwest of Horns Reef. Now, however, a thick fog descended, in which *Australia* and *New Zealand* collided; the damage to the former required that she go into dry dock for repairs. The fog claimed other victims; three destroyers collided, *Ardent* being seriously damaged, while a neutral merchant vessel rammed and damaged the battleship *Neptune*.[28]

Scheer's plan involved a raid on Lowestoft and Yarmouth, both minor ports but which were seen as important bases for minelaying and submarine operations respectively. If the raid was to bring out substantial British forces, it was in any case desirable that its targets be as far south as possible. The intention was for the I Scouting Group, supported by light cruisers and destroyers, to carry out the bombardment, supported by the main body of the High Seas Fleet which would follow some hundred miles or so behind the battlecruisers. On this occasion the latter were commanded by Rear Admiral Friedrich Boedicker, in Hipper's absence on sick leave. The date for the raid was chosen to coincide with the Irish nationalist rising in Dublin on Easter Sunday.

Boedicker sailed from the outer Jade Roads at 9.55am on April 24 with five battlecruisers (*Seydlitz, Derfflinger, Moltke, Lützow* and *Von der Tann*) accompanied by six light cruisers and two flotillas of destroyers. Scheer, with the main body of the High Seas Fleet, put to sea at 12.40pm, heading for a point west of Terschelling, about 70 miles from the English coast.

Room 40 picked up the orders issued by Scheer, and was apparently able to detect not only that the High Seas Fleet was to sail, but also its direction.[29] Oliver, at the Admiralty, at 3.50pm merely put the Grand Fleet on two hours notice, and waited until 7.05pm before ordering it to put to sea. Since he warned all local commands at 6.15pm of the possibility of a demonstration, his delay seems surprising. Picking up this point, Jellicoe suggested a month or so later to Jackson that in future, when an enemy movement appeared likely, the Grand Fleet should be ordered to raise steam at once instead of going to two hours notice, thereby giving the chance of getting out earlier.[30]

As it was, Boedicker had soon encountered a problem, when *Seydlitz*, his flagship, struck a mine at 2.48pm. The explosion damaged her hull plating on the starboard side, and she took on board 1,400 tons of water. Her speed reduced to 15 knots, she turned back to the west to limp home covered by the light cruisers. The other battlecruisers turned south to join the High Seas Fleet; Scheer decided against steaming to the northward, as had been his intention, and kept closer to the Dutch coast. Boedicker, meanwhile, had transhipped to the destroyer *V28*, and set off to rejoin his squadron, hoisting his flag on *Lützow*, while *Seydlitz* made her way home. He steamed on towards his target at Lowestoft, and at 3.50am next morning sighted Tyrwhitt with three light cruisers (*Conquest, Cleopatra* and *Penelope*) and twelve destroyers. Tyrwhitt, seeing the battlecruisers beyond the light cruiser screen, turned sharply to the south, in order to tempt Boedicker to pursue. The German commander was not so easily seduced from his objective, and he held on his course, opening fire on Lowestoft at 4.11am.[31]

The bombardment lasted only about 53 minutes, during which the shore batteries were silenced and some 200 houses destroyed. The squadron then turned south for Yarmouth. Captain Zenker, of *Von der Tann* reported on the operation:

> Mist over the sea and the smoke from the ships ahead made it difficult for us to make out our targets as we steered for Lowestoft. But after we turned, the Empire Hotel offered us an ample landmark for effective bombardment. At 4.14 we opened fire with our heavy and medium calibres on the harbour works and swing bridges. After a few 'shorts' the shooting was good. From the after-bridge a fire in the town, and from another vantage point a great explosion at the entry and the bridges were reported. On the way to Yarmouth the outlying seamarks could easily be seen. The coast on the other hand was swathed in a thick mist. Nelson's column could only be made out for a short time. We therefore refrained from firing ourselves – also for the reason that we did not want to hinder the fire of the ships ahead.[32]

The bombardment of Yarmouth was very brief, thanks to the poor visibility.

Tyrwhitt, disappointed that he had failed to entice Boedicker into following him, turned back to the north and almost at once ran into the German light cruiser screen, and he opened fire at a range of 13,000 yards. The German cruisers turned away towards Boedicker, who came in sight of Tyrwhitt at 4.47, opening fire at long range. In the next few minutes Tyrwhitt's force began to pay for his temerity, *Conquest* being heavily damaged by a 12 inch salvo, and the destroyer *Laertes* being hit and a boiler disabled. Tyrwhitt's light forces were clearly no match for Boedicker's battle cruisers, and he made off to the south. Boedicker pursued briefly, but in the light of reports of submarines and torpedo tracks broke off the action and steamed eastward to rejoin the High Seas Fleet. Tarrant observes that 'here was a splendid German opportunity to cut off and destroy a much weaker force, but Boedicker failed to grasp it'; while Corbett noted that 'there was no waiting to engage forces their raid might have brought out, yet had they really sought them they were not far away'. Halpern thought that 'Boedicker apparently lacked the killer instinct'.[33] These criticisms are, however, a little unfair. The object of the exercise, such as it was, had been achieved; the deteriorating weather deprived Scheer of his airship reconnaissance, and he ordered the High Seas Fleet to return home. He reported subsequently:

> There was no point in hanging about further. As a counter attack by the enemy could not in any event develop before the following day, our main concern was that the cruisers and destroyers should refuel as quickly as possible.[34]

That was how it appeared to Scheer at the time. What he did not know, however, when he decided to turn back, was that Beatty was heading south at full speed and was well ahead of the main body of the Grand Fleet, over four hours steaming to the north. If Scheer had hung around, he would have had an opportunity to encounter Beatty's force; although, being confronted by overwhelming odds, the latter would no doubt have speedily fallen back on Jellicoe. Marder is inclined to jeer also at the German commander for his caution:

> His strategy was no bolder than Boedicker's tactics. The condition of the February memorandum had been met: he had drawn an important detachment of the Grand Fleet into waters favourable for action; but his movements in the Lowestoft raid were not framed on those lines.[35]

In a letter to Jackson on April 26, Jellicoe reflected on the reality of the situation in which the bulk of the Grand Fleet was as far away as Scapa Flow:

> I hope the coast towns did not suffer much. The wonder is that the Germans did not do it before. I hoped the submarines would have got them, as those at both Yarmouth, Harwich and the Humber could be there in time … A raid near the Firth of Forth is unthinkable with our strong force there. I can *never* be south in time, even when based on Rosyth, for a locality as far down as Yarmouth. I had to leave my destroyers behind. The sea was too much for them and [I] came down with only three attached cruisers to screen the whole Battle Fleet, but at 19 knots I felt safe against anything but a browning shot. It would have been awkward to join action without a single destroyer however.[36]

The Lowestoft raid concentrated attention on the question of the possible reassignment of the 5th Battle Squadron to Beatty's command, and further correspondence and discussions took place. Jellicoe, perfectly aware that Beatty's headstrong leadership could create serious problems for him, was still extremely reluctant to let him have the 5th Battle Squadron; as he wrote to Jackson: 'The stronger I make Beatty, the greater is the temptation for him to get involved in an independent action.'[37] The Admiralty was decidedly uneasy about the vulnerability of the southern section of the East Coast to further German raids, as Corbett noted:

> The expected blow had fallen; nothing had been near enough to prevent it or to retaliate; the chance of an action had been missed. It was now imperative that something must be

> done at once, and the Admiralty hastened to ask the Commander-in-Chief what he would propose. 'The enemy,' they said, 'have practically tested our weakness in southern waters and will probably act on the offensive in those waters shortly.'[38]

Furthermore, Tyrwhitt's effectiveness had been markedly reduced by the events of April 25, when two of his light cruisers had been damaged; this followed the previous loss of *Arethusa*. Jellicoe was told that, for the moment, the Grand Fleet would have to provide protection for this area.

Jellicoe's immediate response was to propose that the 3rd Battle Squadron, consisting of the seven surviving members of the *King Edward VII* class, should be transferred from Rosyth together with the 3rd Cruiser Squadron, and be based in the Swin, or at Sheerness or Dover, and that the submarines at Rosyth should move to Yarmouth. This, he considered, would be a 'sufficiently strong covering force to encounter enemy battle cruisers at present strength.' *Dreadnought*, currently refitting, would be added to the squadron when available. Jellicoe's proposal was accepted, and the 3rd Battle Squadron (Bradford) and the 3rd Cruiser Squadron arrived at Sheerness on May 2. Richmond, now commanding the battleship *Commonwealth*, recorded the reaction of some of his colleagues:

> Great sadness on the part of some of the captains, who look upon us as a sacrifice if the battle cruisers come over. But, provided we are made strong and numerous enough, are properly provided with fleet minesweepers to work ahead of us, and an adequate flotilla got together when warning is given, and followed by the monitors from Dover, we shall be all right.[39]

It was Richmond's belief that all the forces between the Humber and Portsmouth should be placed under a single command, to provide a force capable of damaging the enemy and hampering his return. He passed this suggestion to Hankey, only to be told that 'it probably won't be done.'

Public concern in Britain about the ease with which the Germans had been able to carry out the raid on Lowestoft and Yarmouth prompted Balfour to write a reassuring letter to the Mayors of the two towns. In this, he explained that the naval forces were to be redistributed in a way that would make a repetition of such a raid extremely dangerous to the enemy. This was possible because the new ships joining the Grand Fleet enabled important forces to be brought south without endangering its superiority.[40] Balfour's endeavour to reassure public opinion was not a success, several newspapers being extremely critical both of the redistribution of force and the terms in which he had described it. On May 10 *The Globe* observed: 'The prudent cat does not indulge in vociferation when she is watching the rathole. She restrains herself until the quarry is actually under her claws.' Next day *The Times* offered a weightier critique of the Admiralty's decision:

> The First Lord appears to adumbrate a reversal of that policy of offensive defence which has been followed by our fathers with success since King Edward III fought the battle of Sluys in 1340, and Drake singed the beard of the King of Spain nearly 250 years later. 'The frontiers of England are the coasts of the enemy.' Only once did our rulers voluntarily adopt an attitude of passive resistance as an exchange for one of active, resolute opposition, and then the Hollander came up the Medway and destroyed the ships off Chatham.[41]

The Grand Fleet had in the meantime embarked on a raid of its own. On May 4 the seaplane carriers *Vindex* and *Engadine*, escorted by the 1st Light Cruiser Squadron from Rosyth, under Commodore Alexander-Sinclair, arrived off Sylt with a view to launching an air raid on the Zeppelin sheds at Tondern. It was intended by this operation to oblige the High Seas Fleet to come out, and the Grand Fleet sailed to take up a position off the Skagerrak, with Beatty's battle cruisers further south. The weather again intervened; sea conditions were so bad that only one of the eleven seaplanes could take off and bomb the objective, and the conditions discouraged Scheer from coming out. Jellicoe had waited off the Heligoland Bight for nearly seven hours, and at 2.00pm he turned back, Beatty following to the southward. Jellicoe was anxious about his fuel, writing in his report:

> No purpose would be served by our forces returning to the vicinity of the Horn Reefs at daylight on May 5. In view of the possibility of a movement on the part of the enemy on the night of the 5th … I deemed it advisable to replenish as quickly as possible.[42]

In fact the High Seas Fleet did come out, but not until 3.00pm, by which time Jellicoe and Beatty were on their way home. Scheer remained at sea off Sylt until 2.30am on May 5, and then himself returned to base.

Beatty was particularly disappointed by the failure of the operation, writing to Jellicoe on May 7:

> You can understand my disappointment when we were ordered to return to base. Why cannot the Admiralty leave the situation to those on the spot? As you have pointed out, under any circumstances they could not get to Horn Reef until late in the day, and in the special circumstances obtaining they had evidently started late and would not get up until later still; therefore at day light the *next* day there were infinite possibilities of striking him a very severe blow.[43]

On this occasion Beatty, who told his wife that he was 'heartbroken' over the missed opportunity, misjudged the Admiralty; it was Jellicoe's decision to withdraw.

On May 12 a conference was held at Rosyth between Jackson, Jellicoe and Beatty with their Chiefs of Staff to review the strategic distribution of the fleet, and to consider the work to be done to make the anchorage below the Forth bridge safe for the Grand Fleet. It was concluded that as a priority the necessary work should be done to enable the Firth of Forth to become the Grand Fleet's primary base. Scapa was considered too valuable to be disestablished even when the Grand Fleet moved, and was to remain as an alternative base. The Humber was also to be an alternative base: there would be a reorganisation of the Grand Fleet, by which all the 12 inch gun dreadnoughts (except for *Dreadnought* herself) were to be formed into the 4th Battle Squadron, which could be detached there if required.[44] Jellicoe, however, was most reluctant to see it used as a base, although recognising the necessity. In a paper written for the conference he observed: 'The Humber is of course a most objectionable base for a squadron, and any means that can be devised to avoid placing a squadron there would be most beneficial.[45] As to the 5th Battle Squadron, Jellicoe remained opposed to its permanent attachment to the Battle Cruiser Fleet, but since the 3rd Battle Cruiser Squadron under Hood was shortly to move to Scapa for exercises, it was agreed that the four *Queen Elizabeth* class battleships should temporarily take its place. Evan-Thomas had *Barham, Malaya, Valiant* and *Warspite*; *Queen Elizabeth* herself was in dock for the moment. Thus Beatty got his way, at least for the time being. The reinforcement more than outweighed the additions which it was believed had been made to Hipper's 1st Scouting Group, consisting of *Lützow* and *Hindenburg*. The latter, however, was not in fact completed until May 1917.

11

Eve of Battle

Following the Crown Council meeting on March 4, and the provisional decision to commence an all out U-boat campaign on April 4, the matter continued to be the subject of debate at the highest level. When Admiral von Capelle, the successor to Tirpitz as State Secretary, came to see the Kaiser for the first time on March 15, Müller offered his own opinion of the situation: 'I would use the toughest methods against England. What's holding me back at the moment is the belief that for the moment the political damage caused by unrestricted U-boat warfare would outweigh the military gains.' Three days later Holtzendorff presented a report to the Kaiser brushing aside the latter's misgivings about German unpreparedness for unrestricted U-boat warfare.[1] It was in this climate of hesitant ruthlessness that there came an incident which had explosive consequences.

On March 24 *UB29* torpedoed the French cross-Channel steamer *Sussex*, which was carrying 380 civilian passengers, many of whom were American. Some of the latter were among those killed or injured. The U-boat commander had assumed that the vessel was carrying troops and that she was therefore a permissible target. Although she was saved and towed into port, the American reaction to the attack on the *Sussex* was predictably furious, and there was a storm of protest culminating in an ultimatum from Washington on April 20:

> Unless the Imperial Government should now immediately declare and effect an abandonment of its present methods of submarine warfare against passenger and freight carrying vessels, the Government of the United States can have no choice but to sever diplomatic relations with the German Empire altogether.[2]

This was greeted with alarm amounting almost to panic among the civilian members of the German government. Müller, too, was despondent:

> I ask myself whether I should not have been even more vehement in my demands for moderation in the U-boat warfare or at least have protested against unarmed vessels also being torpedoed without warning, which our declaration to sink armed merchantmen without warning undoubtedly implies.[3]

Holtzendorff, however, was unrepentant, arguing strongly against making further concessions to the United States, a position strongly endorsed by Falkenhayn; the latter contended that the

Verdun offensive had been launched on the assurance of a ruthless U-boat campaign to interdict the flow of supplies to the French armies. When Bethmann-Hollweg prepared and sent a Note in reply to the American demand, without having cleared it with Falkenhayn, the Chief of the General Staff attempted to resign. The decision on April 24 that the High Seas Fleet submarines and the Flanders Flotilla should thereafter 'only act against commerce in accordance with prize regulations' gravely disappointed the admirals. Scheer, who believed that such a campaign could not succeed and that in any case it exposed submarines to unacceptable risk, immediately recalled all his U-boats, as did Schröder, the commander of the Flanders Flotilla.

Holtzendorff continued to keep the issue alive, writing on May 16 to Müller to stress the importance of tightening the blockade:

> To speak the truth I am more convinced than ever that England's shortage of shipping space in the event of continued submarine warfare will bring us nearer to peace sooner from a purely military standpoint. If, as Scheer and I concede, America's siding with our opponents can lead in quite another way to a prolongation of the war, methods and means must be found to make the U-boat blockade effective within the present defined limits.[4]

To this Müller replied that for the moment the principal objective for the U-boats must be to attack British warships. Holtzendorff replied to the effect that there was a particular reason for holding back the U-boats temporarily; Müller noted on May 17 that this was 'the incorporation of U-boats in our intended increased aggression by the Fleet.'

Scheer's insistence on recalling his U-boats rather than operate under prize rules was not unanimously endorsed within the German navy. Capelle apparently believed that the U-boat campaign conducted under prize rules could still have been almost as effective. Halpern suggests that Scheer's position may have been taken to prompt such a strong reaction that Bethmann-Hollweg might be forced from office.[5] Scheer's Chief of Staff, Adolf von Trotha, wrote to Müller on May 21 to convey 'his anxiety at the failure of a grand-style leadership, at the gradual decline in the morale of the nation and the catastrophic submission to America.' Müller replied to argue that there was no national weakening, and that it would have been 'a crime against the German nation to have encouraged a break with America at this point.' He defended Holtzendorff for having complied with the political decision that was taken; there was no case for his abandoning his duty and stepping aside.[6] Müller was obviously being kept informed of Scheer's intentions, referring on May 27 to 'naval plans in the North Sea.'

Beatty had had a meeting with Tyrwhitt, and what he was told about the way in which the Admiralty had handled the Harwich Force prompted him to write a letter to Jellioe on May 18 which was violently critical of the War Staff. He poured out all his frustrations at the opportunities that had been missed:

> The system of water-tight compartments has reached its climax. The Chief of the War Staff has priceless information given to him which he sits on until it is too late for the Sea Forces to take action with any possibility of achieving a decisive result. What it amounts to is that the War Staff has developed into a One Man Show. The man is not born yet who can run it by himself. There is no general plan laid down on which movements of the various units are governed. Every case that occurs is considered at the time, and orders are then issued. It is the Wait and See policy carried into Naval Strategy!! It is perfectly ridiculous and must be

> changed, if we are to achieve any success. The 24th April was an object lesson which makes me weep when I think of it. There was absolutely no reason why every unit should not have been on the move 3½ hours before it was!! … It amounts to this, that we were without general principles and had no plan, no combination and no decision. The opportunities of inflicting damage were priceless; they were thrown away and may never occur again.[7]

Neither Nicholas Black, in his careful analysis of the War Staff during the war, nor Admiral Sir William James, in his hagiography of Oliver, address Beatty's criticisms, which although expressed in such shrill terms do appear to have some justification. Marder, however, points out that Jellicoe 'thought it best for the Admiralty to give the Harwich Force its orders, since any attempt by himself to do this must cause delay.'

Jellicoe and his staff had meanwhile been working out plans for an operation intended to tempt Scheer into moving further north than he had previously attempted. Described by Marder as a 'juicy bait', the intention was for two light cruiser squadrons to sweep down the Kattegat as far as the Great Belt and the Sound, with a battle squadron in the Skagerrak in support. The rest of the Grand Fleet and the Battle Cruiser Fleet would be in position to the northwest, ready to intervene if a major German force put to sea. Submarines would be deployed off Horns Reef and the Dogger Bank to lie in wait for the High Seas Fleet; a minefield would be laid to the south of Horns Reef, while the seaplane carrier *Engadine* would be employed to look out for and hopefully to intercept Zeppelins. The operation was planned to take place on June 2.

Meanwhile Scheer had been planning his next operation. As a result of the damage to *Seydlitz* sustained on April 24, which it was estimated would take until the middle of May to repair, Scheer proposed that the operation commence on May 17. It was to be based on a further attack on the East Coast. This time Sunderland was to be the target, significantly further north than previous objectives. Fundamentally it was very similar to the scheme on which Jellicoe had been working, being intended to draw out the Grand Fleet as a target for all the U-boats available to Scheer as a result of the cessation of the campaign of commerce warfare. The plan was described in the German Official History:

> [It] contemplated the appearance off Sunderland at dawn … [of] Hipper's battlecruisers supported by light cruisers and the three fastest torpedo boat flotillas, where they were to bombard establishments of military importance with the object of compelling the enemy to send out his forces. In order to attack the latter, I & III Battle Squadrons, supported by light cruisers and the remainder of the torpedo boat flotillas, were to assemble between Flamborough Head and the South West Patch of the Dogger Bank, about 50 miles east of the former point, while the U-boats of the High Seas Fleet were to take up positions off Scapa Flow, the Moray Firth, the Firth of Forth and the Humber, and north of Terschelling. The U-boats of the Flanders Flotilla were to be posted off the entrance channels to some of the enemy's ports. All available airships were to take part. Some of them [were] to scout in the direction of the Firth of Forth, the Humber, the Hoofden and toward the Skagerrak, whilst others were to act as scouts for the battlecruisers. The original intention was to detail II Squadron for the protection of the German Bight during the absence of the Fleet, but, owing to the pressing representations of Rear Admiral Mauve, the Squadron Commander, it was finally decided to let it take part, in spite of the inferior fighting qualities, slow speed and low powers of resistance of the obsolete ships comprising it.[8]

The inclusion of Mauve's squadron was explained by Scheer in his own account, in a passage in which he sought to justify a decision which has generally been regarded as unwise. It followed a meeting which he had with Mauve early in May. There were, he wrote, military considerations as well as the question of the honour and feelings of the crews of the squadron who would not hear of being reduced, themselves and their ships, to the second class. He added:

> For battleships to have their activity limited absolutely to guarding the German Bight without any prospect of getting into touch with the enemy – to which they had been looking forward for a year and a half – would have caused bitter disappointment; on the other hand, however, was the responsibility of sending the ships into an unequal fight where the enemy would make use of his very best material. I cannot deny that in addition to the eloquent intercession of Rear Admiral Mauve, the Squadron Commander, my own former connection with Squadron II also induced me not to disappoint it by leaving it behind. And thus it happened that the Squadron played its part on May 31, and in so helpful a manner that I never had cause to regret my decision.[9]

Nonetheless, it was a sentimental decision that could have grave consequences. Mauve's predreadnoughts were at least two knots slower than the dreadnoughts of Squadrons I and III, and were caustically known as 'five minute ships', since that was how long they were expected to survive in battle against dreadnoughts.[10]

Work on repairing *Seydlitz* took longer than expected, obliging Scheer to postpone the operation until May 23. A further reason for this was that a number of the most modern battleships of III Squadron had developed condenser trouble, which had to be rectified. So serious were these problems that they prevented *König Albert* from taking part in the operation at all. As a result of the delay Scheer agreed with Captain Bauer, commanding his submarines, that all those available should move into the centre of the North Sea between May 17 and 22 to reconnoitre for British warships, and to attack them if found. Thereafter they would take station off Scapa Flow and the Firth of Forth, ready to intercept the Grand Fleet and Battle Cruiser Fleet as they emerged. Three large minelaying U-boats were to lay new minefields in the Firth of Forth and the Moray Firth, and also to the west of the Orkneys. Meanwhile the surface vessels of the High Seas Fleet had been concentrated by May 22 in the Jade. Next day, however, Scheer learned that *Seydlitz* was still not ready for action, and the operation was further postponed, this time until May 29.

By then, however, the weather had turned against Scheer. Strong easterly and northerly winds made it impossible for the Zeppelins to conduct reconnaissance. Further postponement meant in effect aborting the operation altogether since the U-boats would have to return on June 1 to avoid running out of fuel. As a result Scheer opted for an alternative plan, this time based on sending Hipper's force up the Danish coast and into the Skagerrak as if threatening British naval and commercial activity there. The lack of Zeppelin cover was no problem, since the western flank of the advance would be covered by light forces.[11]

In preparing for his next operation against the High Sea Fleet Jellicoe intended to follow the principles of a paper which he had written for the benefit of the Admiralty and his senior commanders on April 12:

> The first axiom appears to me to be that it is the business of the Grand Fleet to nullify any hostile action on the part of the High Sea Fleet; secondly, to cover all surface vessels that are employed, either in protecting our own trade, or in stopping trade with the enemy; thirdly, to stop invasion, or landing raids, in so far as the strategical position of the Grand Fleet permits of this ... it is not, in my opinion, wise to risk unduly the heavy ships of the Grand Fleet in an attempt to hasten the end of the High Seas Fleet, particularly if the risks come, not from the High Seas Fleet itself, but from such attributes as mines and submarines.

He went on to reiterate his intention to run no risks unless there was a reasonably substantial chance of destroying the enemy's heavy ships. 'Any real disaster to our heavy ships lays the country open to invasion, and also gives the enemy the opportunity of passing commerce destroyers out of the North Sea.'[12] His cautious policy having been spelled out in such specific terms, it would have been open to the Admiralty, or indeed, Beatty, to express disagreement; but none came.

Admiral Bacon, in his biography of Jellicoe, summarised Jellicoe's opinion:

> He knew his strength, he also knew the difficulties attending a modern fleet action. He had no doubt of the outcome of a gunnery duel in daytime. He and his predecessors had trained the fleet; he knew what his ships could do in this respect. He had great confidence in his admirals, captains, and other officers, and as to the men, he knew the spirit that inspired them; but there remained a great doubt as to what would be the practical outcome of the successful use of the new and hitherto untried weapons with which the modern battlefleets had been equipped. Surprises might well be in store – as indeed was shown by the blowing up of some of our ships by flash to the magazines, but there was no reason why one side should be favoured more than the other. He was fully determined that oneoutstanding principle had to be conserved; the fleet should not be risked merely for spectacular effect.[13]

Bacon went on to compare the realism of Jellicoe's conclusion with the expectations of the British public, 'brought up in the belief that our Navy was not only invulnerable but, as in the olden days, would sink and destroy any enemy's fleet that might be encountered on the High Seas.'

In preparing for the operation, Scheer had issued detailed written orders to Hipper and his other senior commanders outlining the latest information available about the Grand Fleet, the objectives for the High Seas Fleet and the procedure and order of battle to be followed. At 11.02 pm on May 28, Scheer ordered the High Seas Fleet to assume a state of special readiness, the intention being to confine the order for the start of the operation to a short coded message by radio. At 4.10 pm next day a signal was sent to one of the U-boats asking for a report on how far penetration into the Firth of Forth was possible. At 9.52 am on May 30 the High Seas Fleet was instructed to move into the outer Jade Roads, and at 10.08 am the Flanders Flotilla was notified that enemy forces could be at sea on May 31 and June 1. All these signals were picked up and decoded by Room 40 at the Admiralty, although the last was interpreted as referring to German forces rather than British. These indications confirmed the view that a major German operation was about to take place, and at 12 noon the Admiralty warned Jellicoe and Beatty that the High Seas Fleet would probably be at sea on May 31.[14]

At 3.30 pm Scheer issued to the High Seas Fleet the coded signal to begin the operation: '31 gg 2490.' Then, at 5.00 pm, he signalled:

> Head of Squadron III will pass Jade war lightship at 3.30 am. Squadron II will take part in the operation from the beginning and will join up astern of Squadron I. Wilhelmshaven 3rd Entrance will control W/T in German Bight.[15]

This indicated that the Wilhelmshaven W/T station was to start using the C-in-C's normal call sign DK. This particular signal, however, was not decoded by Room 40 until the afternoon of May 31, having apparently been enciphered in a new code. A separate signal to Mauve informed him that prize crews were not to be embarked, a further indication that a fleet action was contemplated. There was apparently another signal announcing that the C-in-C was taking over W/T control; Room 40 was aware that this was a standard procedure intended to mislead British direction finding stations. There had previously been unusual activity by minesweepers and barrier breakers on the northern route out of the German Bight up to the Horns Reef, and taken all in all it seemed clear that the High Seas Fleet was intending to sail up the Danish coast.[16]

Oliver was duly informed; he, however, was mesmerised by the possibility that the Germans might intend to force the Dover Straits. To deal with such a threat, of course, there was the 3rd Battle Squadron in the Swin, but since this squadron had no destroyer escort, Oliver prohibited Tyrwhitt's Harwich Force from sailing to reinforce the Grand Fleet, although Jellicoe had been promised this as far back as November 1914. For some reason, Sir Henry Jackson, the First Sea Lord, was not made aware of this promise until much later. Oliver explained his anxieties:

> Thomas Jackson, the DOD, and Brand, his assistant, and I were always expecting the Huns to make some attempt to block the Channel ports and destroy our line of communications with the Army in France, such as rushing Dover Straits with predreadnought type ships and using them as blockships, and all we had to counter such an attack was the old battlefleet in the netted anchorage in the Swin, without destroyers; if they had to sail, the Harwich Force had to go with them, I determined to keep the Harwich Force until we could be sure the old German battleships were with the High Seas Fleet in case the High Seas Fleet went north to decoy our Grand Fleet while the old German ships attacked on the Thames or tried to disable or block the French Channel ports, and Sir Henry Jackson, the 1st SL agreed. We did not get evidence that the old ships were with the High Sea Fleet till very late on the night after the battle, and the Harwich Force were then sent to clear up the mess and look for disabled ships.[17]

In fact, the information was available during the afternoon. Admiral James, however, defends the decision, saying that in retrospect Oliver's decision was the wisest one, dismissing criticisms on the basis that 'senior Grand Fleet officers gave no thought to the consequences of leaving the Channel open for a major attack by the German pre-dreadnought ships and the probability of such an attack taking place.'[18]

At 5.40pm the Admiralty ordered Jellicoe to put to sea and to concentrate the Grand Fleet 100 miles east of Aberdeen, there to await further developments. Jellicoe would sail with a total of 24 dreadnoughts, 3 battle cruisers (Hood's 3rd Battle Cruiser Squadron, at the time at

Scapa Flow for gunnery practice), 8 armoured cruisers, 12 light cruisers. 5 destroyer leaders, 46 destroyers and one minelayer. The seaplane carrier *Campania* did not get the signal to leave port, and set off two hours after the fleet only, at 4.37am, to be sent back to base by Jellicoe, who feared the risk posed to her by submarines. Beatty, from the Firth of Forth, had with him a force of 4 dreadnoughts (the 5th Battle Squadron), 6 battlecruisers, 14 light cruisers, 27 destroyers and one seaplane carrier. A total of 155 ships, manned by 60,000 men, would depart to contest the greatest sea battle that the world had yet seen.

Admiral Bacon observed that Jellicoe 'had great confidence in his admirals', but in fact his squadron commanders were not an outstanding group. His second in command, who led the 1st Battle Squadron, was Vice Admiral Sir Cecil Burney, an unimaginative officer apparently described by one officer as 'a piece of solid wood.'[19]

The 2nd Battle Squadron was commanded by Vice Admiral Sir Martyn Jerram, assessed by Marder as colourless and lacking in initiative and dash, though reasonably competent. Vice Admiral Sir Doveton Sturdee, commanding the 4th Battle Squadron, the *bête noir* of both Lord Fisher and Captain Richmond, was vain and obstinate. Rear Admiral Hugh Evan-Thomas, who led the 5th Battle Squadron, was on the other hand highly regarded.

A rather less sympathetic analysis of the battle squadron commanders of the Grand Fleet was provided by Andrew Gordon. Conceding that good seamanship was not necessarily incompatible with competent leadership, he noted that many great admirals were not great seamen, citing Nelson, Fisher, Beatty and Mountbatten, whose success was due to other attributes. It was noteworthy, Gordon considered, that Jellicoe 'sheltered many of his subordinates – men like George Warrender, Cecil Burney, Martin Jerram, Edward Bradford, Douglas Gamble, Dudley de Chair – on the vague unhappy grounds of their seamanship.'[20]

Jellicoe himself corresponded with Jackson about command changes in which he offered some outspoken comments, dismissing a number of candidates as a successor to Burney. He was 'of a very decided opinion that the two officers who are really fitted for the command of the 1st Battle Squadron are Colville and Madden.' The latter was his Chief of Staff, and he did not want to lose him. He also wrote:

> In regard to Sturdee, I should never feel safe with him in command of the most important squadron and leading the van … I am sorry to say that I do not trust his judgement in tactical questions. *I feel very strongly about this* and I know that the other flag officers hold the same views.[21]

John Horsfield has written that Jellicoe and Sturdee 'detested each other,' although Gordon thought that was rather extreme for the mild mannered C-in-C.[22] Sturdee had indeed gone quite a long way to annoy Jellicoe by the assertive way in which he had put forward his ideas as to the way in which the Grand Fleet should be handled. He later wrote of what he considered Jellicoe's rigid and formal tactics: 'I took every opportunity as tactfully as I could to persuade the C-in-C to modify them but broadly without success.' Jellicoe does not seem to have considered Sturdee's ideas, as set out in his 'Seven Tactical Principles' which he circulated to him and the other admirals, as having been especially tactfully expressed, and he did not convene the meeting to discuss them for which Sturdee asked. Instead, firmly restating the tactical principles which he had enshrined in the Grand Fleet Battle Orders, Jellicoe wrote to Sturdee on November 17 1915:

> I am afraid that the controversy that has arisen over this matter is doing harm in the Fleet. I know that this is quite unintentional on your part, but I hope you will take my word for it, that it *is* doing harm, and is causing unrest and possibly criticism of the manner in which I intend to handle the Fleet, which is bound to be injurious. I know this because I am being told so by senior officers. Therefore I am writing to ask you to accept my Battle Orders as they stand, or at any rate if you have any suggestions to make for alterations, that you should make them to me, and should not let them become the subject of controversy in the Fleet by discussion with others.[23]

Marder regarded the commanders of the battle cruiser squadrons as 'all first rate'; these were Rear Admiral Osmond Brock (1st Battle Cruiser Squadron), Rear Admiral Sir William Pakenham (2nd Battle Cruiser Squadron) and Rear Admiral Horace Hood (3rd Battle Cruiser Squadron). The commanders of the four light cruiser squadrons were also highly rated. On the other hand, the two squadrons of armoured cruisers were led by Rear Admiral Heath, 'quite undistinguished' according to Marder, and the harsh and oddly violent disciplinarian Rear Admiral Sir Robert Arbuthnot.

Scheer would take to sea with him a total of 16 dreadnoughts, 6 predreadnoughts, 6 light cruisers and 32 destroyers, while the force under Hipper would consist of 5 battle cruisers, 5 light cruisers and 30 destroyers, 100 ships in all with a total complement of 45,000 men. The commander of I Squadron, consisting of the eight dreadnoughts of the *Nassau* and *Helgoland* classes, was the entirely competent Vice Admiral Erhard Schmidt, who had succeeded Eckermann during 1915. The lead squadron of the High Seas Fleet, the III Squadron composed of the most modern dreadnoughts of the *Kaiser* and *König* classes, was commanded by Rear Admiral Paul Behncke, who had previously served as Deputy Chief of the Admiralty Staff; in that position he had supported Tirpitz's arguments for a more forward policy. After the war he was to rise to the post of Commander-in-Chief of the navy. Scheer's light cruisers were commanded by Commodore Ludwig von Reuter. In the early months of the war he had been captain of *Derfflinger*; at the end of the war he was saddled with the disagreeable and burdensome responsibility of commanding the High Seas Fleet as it lay interned at Scapa Flow. Hipper's second in command was Rear Admiral Friedrich Boedicker, who had led the battle-cruisers during the Lowestoft raid. He was a sound if unimaginative commander, who had done enough to convince Scheer that he would be a suitable successor to Hipper. Overall, the leading German admirals were at least the equal of their opponents, as they were about to demonstrate.

In addition to its substantial numerical advantage in ships, the Grand Fleet was superior in other ways; four of Beatty's battlecruisers were three knots faster than any of Hipper's; Jellicoe's battlefleet was a knot faster than the High Seas Fleet or four knots faster if the latter had Mauve in company; the battleships of the 5th Battle Squadron were more heavily armed than any German battleship; and Scheer was desperately short of cruisers. As Geoffrey Bennett put it: 'In a sentence, Jellicoe had a fleet double the size of Scheer's, able to fire more than twice the weight of shell.'[24]

Part II

Jutland

12

Enemy In Sight

Historians from time to time casually refer to a fleet putting to sea; but for the Grand Fleet it must be borne in mind that this was a task calling for great seamanship. The very large number of ships that must leave the anchorage in the least possible time involved the most careful attention to the procedures laid down. The long period during which the Grand Fleet had been based at Scapa Flow, from which it had sailed so many times, had however enabled an efficient system to be devised, as Jellicoe explained:

> As the Grand Fleet increased in size, and the danger from mine and submarine grew, so the problem of leaving Scapa Flow and re-entering that base with safety became more complicated. The necessity for the Fleet leaving harbour in the shortest possible time and with the fewest number of signals was obvious. Similarly on returning, the various squadrons had to enter the base with the least practical delay in order to avoid giving submarines engaged in watching the approaches an opportunity for getting into positions for attacking the squadrons in rear, after having sighted those in the van. The operations, both of departure and entry, were rendered the more difficult owing to the very strong and erratic tides experienced in the Pentland Firth, while all ships navigating at night had to be navigated without showing lights.[1]

The first thing that must be done was to raise steam; a preparatory signal ordering all ships to raise steam for 18 knots at two hours notice would start the process, during which time a further signal would be made advising the time at which the first squadron to leave was to move out of the anchorage, and the speed to be maintained. Standing orders prescribed the order of sailing and interval between squadrons or divisions, usually one mile in daylight and two miles at night. If sailing eastwards, successive squadrons or divisions would alternately pass north or south of the Pentland Skerries. Thereafter, the squadrons would each take one of three defined routes, some seven miles apart, and arrive at a concentration point shortly after daylight.[2]

At 7.30pm Jellicoe ordered Jerram, whose squadron was based for the moment at Cromarty, to proceed to sea, aiming to rendezvous with the rest of the Grand Fleet at 2.00pm next day. At 7.37pm he sent orders to Beatty:

> Available vessels, Battle Cruiser Fleet, 5th Battle Squadron and tbds, including Harwich tbds, proceed to approximate position Lat. 56° – 40'N, Long. 5° – 00'E. Desire to economise

> tbds fuel. Presume you will be there about 2.00pm thirty first. I shall be in about Lat. 57° – 45'N, Long. 4° – 15'E, by 2.00pm unless delayed by fog. 3rd Battle Cruiser Squadron, *Chester* and *Canterbury* will leave with me. I will send them on to your rendezvous. If no news by 2.00pm, stand toward me to get in visual touch. I will steer for Horns Reef from position in Lat.57° – 45, Long. 4° – 15'E. Repeat back rendezvous.[3]

These orders, sent by wire and hence not capable of interception, would put Beatty about 69 miles to the south of the Grand Fleet's rendezvous. The need for the gap was explained by Marder:

> The battle fleet had to be far enough to the northward to cover the Northern Patrol against a German effort to crush it and raise the blockade, and the Battle Cruiser Fleet had to be sufficiently to the southward to intercept any raiders. These two conditions could be met only if the distance between Jellicoe and Beatty was at least 50 miles.[4]

Later, Jellicoe blamed himself for the distance between his principal forces, writing to Jackson that next time he must keep Beatty nearer, so that they could start with a knowledge of each other's position. Marder observed that the solution was to concentrate the entire Grand Fleet at Rosyth, a conclusion that was not altogether consistent with the explanation for the gap quoted above. At 9.30 pm the Grand Fleet began leaving the anchorage and headed out from Scapa Flow into the darkening North Sea, finally clearing the harbour an hour later. From Cromarty at 10.15 pm Jerram's squadron followed suit, steaming at 19 knots rather than the 17 knots of the Grand Fleet as it had further to travel. To the south the Battle Cruiser Fleet began leaving Rosyth at 10.00 pm, followed 40 minutes later by the 5th Battle Squadron. Receiving reports of a U-boat attack on the destroyer *Trident* earlier in the evening, Beatty ordered all squadrons to pass north of May Island and to steer 66° at 18 knots for 20 miles before setting course for the position ordered by Jellicoe for 2.00 pm.[5]

Not many of the officers and men aboard the British ships that night supposed that the movement meant anything special; there had been too many fruitless sorties into the North Sea to have any expectation that this one would be any different. Commodore von Schoultz, the Russian attaché to the Grand Fleet, who had been advised by Jellicoe on May 29 to stay with the fleet rather than attend a conference in London over the next few days, had some sense of what might be to come:

> I have not made up my mind whether I had a premonition of coming events, or whether my conversation with Admiral Jellicoe and the reading of his operation orders had made a special impression on me. Be that as it may, my thoughts busied themselves for a long time with these impressions, and I spent nearly the whole of the first night on the bridge of the *Hercules*, filled with a vague expectation of coming events. I was myself not clear as to what I actually expected, but I remember very clearly that every signal during that evening interested me more than any had ever done before.[6]

While Jellicoe's forces were leaving their respective harbours, the High Seas Fleet still lay peacefully at anchor in the Outer Jade Roads. Its crews were better informed of what was likely to happen than their opposite numbers in the Grand Fleet. Seaman Richard Stumpf recalled that Captain von Kameke of *Helgoland* called all hands on deck after breakfast on May 30:

What was going on? I was soon to learn. The Captain stood on deck with two sheets of paper in his hand. Aha! Something is brewing! 'Close ranks; pay attention,' he began. 'We can look forward to something very special … The first [objective] will be war against enemy shipping. However recently many warships have been sighted in that area and we would also like to give them a little tickle … Our bait, the light cruisers, will draw the stupid fools out to sea with their wireless messages …' He said this in such a droll Berliner accent that everyone laughed out loud. The expression on the Captain's face while he said this was interesting. He appeared to be completely serious but his small gray eyes shone and blinked with such great delight that we found it impossible to suppress our laughter and chuckles.[7]

In fact, of course, neither the wireless messages to which Kameke referred, nor the orders to Hipper to show himself off the coast of Norway, were required to draw out the British. Long before *Helgoland* and the rest of the High Seas Fleet weighed anchor, the Grand Fleet was already on its way.

The strength of the High Seas Fleet was somewhat less than the British were expecting; *König Albert* would not be sailing, her condenser problems not yet resolved, and the battleship *Bayern* (still undergoing trials) had not yet joined the fleet, and nor had the battlecruiser *Hindenburg*. British intelligence credited Scheer with all these vessels, together with the predreadnought *Preussen*, three light cruisers, a minelayer and 15 destroyers, which were also absent. At the same time Jellicoe was missing four battleships (*Royal Sovereign, Emperor of India, Queen Elizabeth* and *Dreadnought*) which might have been expected to take part, and the battlecruiser *Australia* and two armoured cruisers. He was also 11 destroyers short. Jellicoe, even after the war, was under the impression that Scheer had with him 88 destroyers rather than the 61 that actually took part. Looking at the relative strength of the fleets during the battle, Commander Frost considers that Jellicoe could afford to be reasonably bold:

It is our conclusion that the British Commander-in-Chief should have been prepared to run reasonable risks in an earnest endeavor to gain the great advantages that a decisive victory over the High Seas Fleet would have won for the allied cause. Specifically, he should have been prepared to follow a retiring enemy, with reasonable precautions against the torpedo fire of large units of German destroyers, until he had received some appreciable losses.[8]

Hipper left the Jade at 4.00 am on May 31, followed half an hour later by the rest of the High Seas Fleet. Commander Georg von Hase, the Gunnery Officer of the *Derfflinger*, described the scene:

We had spent the night at anchor in the Schillig Roads, off the entrance to the Jadebusen. Ahead of us stretched the small cruisers and some flotillas of destroyers. It was a beautiful clear night which soon gave place to a splendid morning. The sun rose magnificently, covered the sea with its golden rays, and soon showed us the picture of the whole High Seas Fleet proceeding to meet the enemy, always a wonderful sight and one never to be forgotten. Far ahead of us steamed the small cruisers in line ahead, surrounded by a cordon of destroyers steaming ceaselessly round the cruisers, on the look out for enemy submarines, like dogs round a flock of sheep.[9]

As the I Scouting Group sailed north there was a widespread optimism that on this occasion there would be action:

> At midday dinner, at which the officers of the watch were not present, there was great excitement and enthusiasm. Nearly everyone was agreed that this time there would be an action, but no one spoke of anything more important than an action involving the lighter fighting forces or the older armoured cruisers. No one thought of the possibility that the whole English fleet could be only a few hours away from us. Some few were pessimistic, and said we should soon turn about again without having accomplished anything.[10]

The first report from Scheer's U-boat screen came at 7.30 am, when *U32* reported sighting 70 miles east of the Firth of Forth a force of two battleships, two cruisers and several destroyers steering south east. An hour later she reported the interception of a W/T message referring to two large battleships with groups of destoyers leaving Scapa Flow. At 8.48 am *U66* reported 8 battleships with light cruisers and destroyers 60 miles east of Kinnaird Head, steering north east. The U-boat screen had however, entirely failed in its offensive object, being unable to launch any effective torpedo attacks on the units of the Grand Fleet as they left harbour. For what they were worth, the sighting reports that Scheer received encouraged him to believe that he might encounter separated portions of the Grand Fleet.

Weizsäcker, however, aboard *Friedrich der Grosse* with Scheer's staff, did not expect to see action:

> When we left port on May 31 we did not believe we should encounter the enemy. Scheer's attention was fully occupied with a trivial matter – namely, how to stop a sliding door on the quarter deck from rattling, since it had disturbed his sleep the previous night and he did not want this to happen again.[11]

Hipper, on the other hand, was of a different view. As Scouting Group 1, preceded by Boedicker's Scouting Group II, steamed north beyond the Amrum Bank, he talked to his staff about the prospects for the day.

> That morning he had been saying that he was certain the enemy would be encountered. They would be 'at it hammer and tongs' by the afternoon. His staff was astounded. Their barometer of hope was not so high. Hipper stuck to his prophecy and even went on to express the view that there would be heavy losses of human life when they really got down to grips with the British – he always had a warm corner for the bluejacket – and then consoled himself with the reflection that 'it was all in God's hands.'[12]

As the Grand Fleet, in its separate formations, made its way that morning across the North Sea, there was little to disturb shipboard routine. With the coming of dawn, Beatty's forces began zig-zagging, altering course 22° to port and then starboard every ten minutes on a signal from *Lion*. *Tiger*, nearest to the 5th Battle Squadron, was ordered to repeat flag signals to Evan-Thomas by searchlight. Aboard *St Vincent* Captain Fisher, like Kameke aboard *Helgoland*, assembled part of the crew on deck and told them what he knew; Major Wallace, visiting the Fleet on leave from the trenches of the Western Front, where he had dreamed of a great naval battle taking place, recorded the incident:

> 'We have tried to do this so often [he said] without bringing the Germans to book; but today it is a little different. We have a staff officer who has come direct from the trenches. Please God, may the shells follow him here; he may bring us luck.' His words sent a cold shiver down my spine, for they were almost exactly the words which had been heard by me in just such a scene as this in my premonition of the battle. This made me even more certain that what I had been dreaming about for months was about to come true.[13]

While Beatty and Jelliocoe placidly steamed on and Hipper and Scheer sailed past the Horns Reef, a critical incident occurred at the Admiralty. The Director of the Operations Division was Captain Thomas Jackson (soon to be promoted to Rear Admiral), and about noon he visited Room 40 to ask the location of the DK call sign of *Friedrich der Grosse*, and was correctly told that it was in Wilhelmshaven. According to one observer 'without further ado and without asking for an explanation or comment, the insufferable Jackson turned on his heel and left the room.'[14] Most historians have followed this account, given by Lieutenant William Clarke, RNVR; Gordon described Jackson as a 'ridiculous angry blundering officer.' It has been only recently that a defender has come forward; Nicholas Black has described Jackson as 'perhaps the most vilified staff officer of the First World War,' and makes a number of telling points that indicate that he may not have been by any means as stupid as has been suggested.[15] Corbett, in the Official History, makes no adverse comment on the incident, merely remarking that 'our directional wireless up till noon could only indicate that the battle fleet was still in the Jade.'[16] But then he rarely descended to individual criticism.

However, the information that Jackson gathered led Oliver to despatch a signal to Jellicoe and Beatty at 12.30:

> No definite news of the enemy. They made all preparations for sailing early this morning. It was thought fleet had sailed but directionals place the flagship in the Jade at 11.10 am GMT. Apparently they have been unable to carry out air reconnaissance which has delayed them.[17]

Marder reckons that the mistake was to have far reaching consequences, suggesting that since as a result Jellicoe reduced speed to conserve the fuel of his destroyers, an hour or two of daylight had been lost. Furthermore, he says, Jellicoe and Beatty had had their confidence in intelligence reports from the Admiralty badly shaken, and thereafter they tended to put more faith in information given by the ships under their command. In his report, Jellicoe cited a signal which he made to the Grand Fleet at 1.55 pm, enquiring the rate at which battleships could refuel destroyers, as showing that as a result of Oliver's message he expected to remain at sea awaiting events.[18] Gordon, however, discounts the alleged loss of daylight, calculating that if instead Jellicoe had received a signal correctly reporting the High Seas Fleet to be at sea and had at once ordered full steam, some 107 minutes earlier than he did, he would have arrived at the point where he actually met the enemy 35 minutes sooner; but the Germans would not have got there yet, so he would have to steam on, meeting them some 16 minutes earlier.[19]

An even more controversial tactical decision was Beatty's handling of the 5th Battle Squadron. Beatty stationed this squadron five miles to the north west of the Battle Cruiser Fleet, rather than deploying it as part of his fleet. It was a decision that had been pored over by historians with the greatest care, and at the end of their deliberations there remains a profound disagreement as to whether, in the words of Langhorne Gibson and Admiral Harper, it was a 'fatal error' on Beatty's part, or whether it was an entirely sensible disposition.[20] The reasons put forward for the latter view are first, that the speed of the 5th Battle Squadron not being equal to that of the Battle Cruiser Fleet, it should not be put in a position from which it could only extricate itself with more difficulty than the battle cruisers. Secondly, putting Evan-Thomas where Beatty did assisted in fitting the squadron into its place at the head of the Grand Fleet when he turned north for his rendezvous with Jellicoe. Marder concluded that as a result of the Admiralty telegram both Jellicoe and Beatty, no longer expecting to meet the enemy, were thinking more about their junction. On balance, he felt that the separation of five miles was reasonable.[21] Gordon has taken a diametrically opposite view; Beatty's positioning of the four battleships of the 5th Battle Squadron was unsound, ensuring that he would have to go into action without them or 'hang around for them to catch up while the enemy got away'.[22] At a meeting on June 26, attended by Sir Henry Jackson, his Naval Secretary and Jellicoe, in which Beatty criticised Evan-Thomas's ship handling, he claimed that if he had worked with him before, he would have stationed him at two miles: Gordon, not unreasonably, calls this 'fairly outrageous'.[23] Looking at this and at the other excuses subsequently put forward by Beatty's adherents, Gordon's view of the matter is much to be preferred. A failure to concentrate was really not forgivable, and in any case Beatty made his dispositions before sunrise; the Admiralty telegram did not come until 12.30 pm.

The three light cruiser squadrons with Beatty were disposed about eight miles ahead of his battle cruisers, with *Yarmouth* as the linking ship and the seaplane carrier *Engadine* in the centre of the cruiser screen. The destroyer screens were on either side of the big ships. At 1.30 pm, in preparation for his turn to the north to the rendezvous with Jellicoe, Beatty changed the line of bearing of his cruiser screen to ENE and WSW, with the centre bearing SSE from the *Lion*. At the same time he changed the position of the 2nd Battle Cruiser Squadron and the 5th Battle Squadron by two points; Evan-Thomas was now five miles NNW of Beatty, and when the turn was made would be on *Lion's* port bow. The light cruisers would be covering the rear. At 2.00 pm, wrongly believing himself ten miles short of his assigned position (the actual distance was fifteen miles) Beatty made a general signal for all units to turn north at 2.15 pm.[24]

At this moment chance intervened. The light cruiser *Elbing*, with three destroyers of the IV Half-Flotilla, formed part of the port side screen of the 1 Scouting Group which by 2.00 pm was some 65 miles west of Lodbjerg on the Danish coast; at that moment, if Beatty's easterly course had continued, it would have taken him to a point 40 miles astern of Hipper's force and 20 miles ahead of the main body of the High Seas Fleet about 4.30 pm. Beatty and Hipper were 45 miles apart when at 2.00 pm *Elbing* sighted to the west smoke from the small Danish tramp steamer *N J Fjord*, and ordered *B109* and *B110* to investigate. Almost at the same time, the light cruisers *Galatea* (flagship of Commodore Alexander-Sinclair's 1st Light Cruiser Squadron) and *Phaeton* also sighted the smoke, and turned east to close the Danish steamer, followed by *Inconstant* and *Cordelia*. By 2.20 pm the two German destroyers were sighted by *Galatea*, which hoisted the signal 'Enemy in sight' and reported by wireless: 'Urgent. Two cruisers, probably hostile, bearing ESE, course unknown'. *Galatea* had mistaken the destroyers for cruisers; but soon *Elbing* came in sight, followed by *Pillau* and *Frankfurt*.[25]

Even as 'Action Stations' was sounded aboard *Galatea*, it was still at first thought to be a drill, as one of her officers recorded:

> I was aft on the quarter deck quietly basking in the sun, and on hearing the bugle was in little hurry as I had heard that we were going to action stations for drill purposes sometime during the afternoon. So I strolled forward to my station – a little home-made Wireless Office on the foc'sle, more like a rabbit hutch than a W/T office, where I coded and decoded signals in action. But just as I went up to the ladder on to the foc'sle I was deafened by the report of the foc'sle 6-inch firing, and was almost blown down the ladder again by its blast; it was so unexpected.[26]

Galatea had at 2.28 pm just fired the first shot in the battle of Jutland.

At 2.25 Beatty ordered his destroyers to form a submarine screen on a SSE course and at 2.32 made a general signal to alter course in succession and increase to full steam. Jellicoe was later critical of the delay in altering course; on this occasion Gordon is prepared to give Beatty some benefit of the doubt. A more serious problem, however, immediately arose. Although the rest of his own squadron, and Pakenham's 2nd Battle Cruiser Squadron both executed the order to alter course, the signals yeoman aboard *Barham*, Evan-Thomas's flagship, was unable to read it, and at first it was assumed that the battlecruisers had resumed a zig-zag course following the turn to the north. *Tiger*, hitherto repeating signals by searchlight to the 5th Battle Squadron, assumed that with the change of course this responsibility had ended. The result was that Evan-Thomas zig-zagging, turned to north by west as Beatty turned in the opposite direction. For several minutes, gazing at the rapidly disappearing battlecruisers, Evan-Thomas waited for a clear order; not getting one, he turned on his own initiative at 2.40 pm. What had happened is far from clear; an analysis by Gordon of the consequent increase in the gap between Evan-Thomas and Beatty as a result of the former's delay in turning SSE suggests that it had increased to ten miles. Evan-Thomas, during the next hour or so, succeeded in reducing the gap to a certain extent, but the incident delayed the participation of his powerful battleships for at least half an hour.[27] The blame for what occurred has been laid at his door, for his slow response; at the door of those responsible for signalling aboard *Lion*; and at Beatty's door, for his tactical error in positioning the 5th Battle Squadron. All were, in fact, elements that contributed to the mishap. Before leaving the issue, it is worth noting that Evan-Thomas, in explanation for his response time, suggested after the war that having had no clear signal, it at first seemed to him that Beatty intended him to go north to catch the enemy between two fires.[28] Reviewing Beatty's outraged feelings at Hipper's previous escapes from his clutches, Roskill concludes that he regarded Hipper as his particular quarry, and was this time determined to 'bag the lot'. He finds a clue in a remark by Beatty's particular friend Walter Cowan of the *Princess Royal*, who wrote that during the approach to the battle he had feared that the 'damned 5th Battle Squadron is going to take the bread out of our mouths.' Roskill finds it 'much more reasonable to extend Cowan's thinking to the Admiral he so fervently admires than to accept Marder's justification for Beatty's handling of Evan-Thomas's ships.' He goes on to record a sense of unease in his mind that Beatty on this occasion ignored Nelson's dictum that 'only numbers can annihilate,' although on other occasions he quoted Nelson when it suited him.[29] And certainly a feeling that he wanted this time to make sure of Hipper for himself and his battlecruisers would go a long way to explaining why he rushed off after his opponent without waiting to concentrate.

Jellicoe, in his note on 'Errors made in Jutland Battle', criticised Beatty for his failure to concentrate his force, since the 5th Battle Squadron was both the strongest portion of his force and was 3 – 4 knots slower. Since Beatty's signal to his destroyers showed his intention to turn

SSE at 2.25, there was no reason not to warn Evan-Thomas at that time; and 'the signal should of course have been made by searchlight or wireless or both,' since the flag signal would not have been distinguishable at five miles.[30]

Beatty and Hipper were now approaching each other at a combined speed of over 40 knots. At 2.39 pm *Galatea* sent a further signal: 'Have sighted a large amount of smoke as though from a fleet, bearing ENE.' This was followed shortly after by: 'Smoke seems to be seven vessels besides cruisers and destroyers.' Beatty, at 2.47 pm, ordered *Engadine* to launch a seaplane to reconnoitre; by 3.08 pm a Short seaplane was airborne and ten minutes later the pilot, Lieutenant Frederick Rutland, was in sight of the light cruisers *Elbing, Frankfurt* and *Pillau.* At 3.31 pm his observer began to send a series of observation reports which *Engadine* passed on to *Galatea*; the seaplane carrier also tried but failed to pass these on to *Iron Duke* and *Barham.* The important information that the German vessels had turned and were steering south east was reported by *Galatea* to Beatty at 3.44. At 3.47 pm, however, Rutland was forced by a broken fuel pipe to land and wait recovery.

Jellicoe, picking up the signals from *Galatea*, ordered the Grand Fleet to be ready for full speed. At 2.43 pm, hearing that *Galatea* had sighted a large amount of smoke, he ceased zig-zagging, and at 2.55 pm increased speed to 18 knots. At 3.10 pm he ordered Heath and Arbuthnot, whose squadrons were steaming as a look out line ahead of the fleet, to increase their distance to 16 miles; these armoured cruisers, however, had little margin of speed over the Grand Fleet's battleships. At the same time Hood's 3rd Battle Cruiser Squadron with its attendant light cruisers and destroyers increased speed to 22 knots. Jellicoe was still doubtful that there were more substantial German units at sea:

> The earliest reports from the *Galatea* had indicated the presence of light cruisers and destroyers only, and my first impression was that these vessels, on sighting the British force, would endeavour to escape via the Skagerrak, as they were to the eastward of our vessels and were consequently not in so much danger of being cut off as if they turned to the southward. The 3rd Battle Cruiser Squadron, which was well placed for cutting the enemy off, had the anticipated move taken place, was ordered to frustrate any such intention; but at 4.00 pm, on the receipt of the information of the presence of enemy battle cruisers, it was directed to reinforce Sir David Beatty. At about 3.40 pm I received a report from Sir David Beatty that he had sighted five battle cruisers and a number of destroyers, and he also gave his position.[31]

With characteristic attention to detail, Jellicoe signalled one of his battleships at 3.45: 'You must steer a steadier course in action or your shooting will be bad.'[32]

13

'Something Wrong with Our Bloody Ships Today'

Hipper had sighted his opponent first, at 3.20 pm, columns of large dark grey vessels with tripod masts silhouetted against the bright blue of the afternoon sky. He could be in no doubt what they were. At 3.28 he called back his light cruisers from their engagement with Alexander-Sinclair, and altered course to the south. He was perfectly aware that Beatty would endeavour to get between his forces and their base, and acted at once:

> His unruffled calm communicated itself to his staff and all those on the bridge of the flagship. Work was carried on exactly as it had been on manoeuvres in peacetime. Commander Prentzel had no superior in everything connected with navigation and had also always proved himself a rapid and reliable worker on charts. At this moment, however, he took a back seat. Hipper led his division in a tactical sense with a positively remarkable sense of self reliance.[1]

Erich Raeder, his Chief of Staff, watched as Hipper calmly issued his orders:

> There was a moment of supreme tension as the great turrets rotated and the gray gun muzzles elevated. The imminence of a great naval engagement was unmistakable, and on the *Lützow's* bridge we felt a sense of elation at the orderliness with which decisions were being made and signals sent and executed. Our second staff officer, Commander Hansen, who had only recently joined, exclaimed enthusiastically, 'Why, it's as calm as if it were nothing but a drill.'[2]

At first, based on an incorrectly transcribed searchlight message from *Elbing*, Hipper thought that the whole of the Grand Fleet was before him, and so informed Scheer; almost at once he corrected his error and, steaming south at 18 knots, aimed to lure Beatty into the path of the oncoming High Seas Fleet.

Aboard *Derfflinger*, Hase, hearing that enemy battle cruisers had been reported, had trained his guns on what he expected would be their position:

> I adjusted my periscope to its extreme power – fifteen diameters, the adjustment for perfect visibility. But there was no sign of the enemy. Nevertheless, we could see a change in the situation: the light cruisers and destroyers had turned about and were taking shelter behind

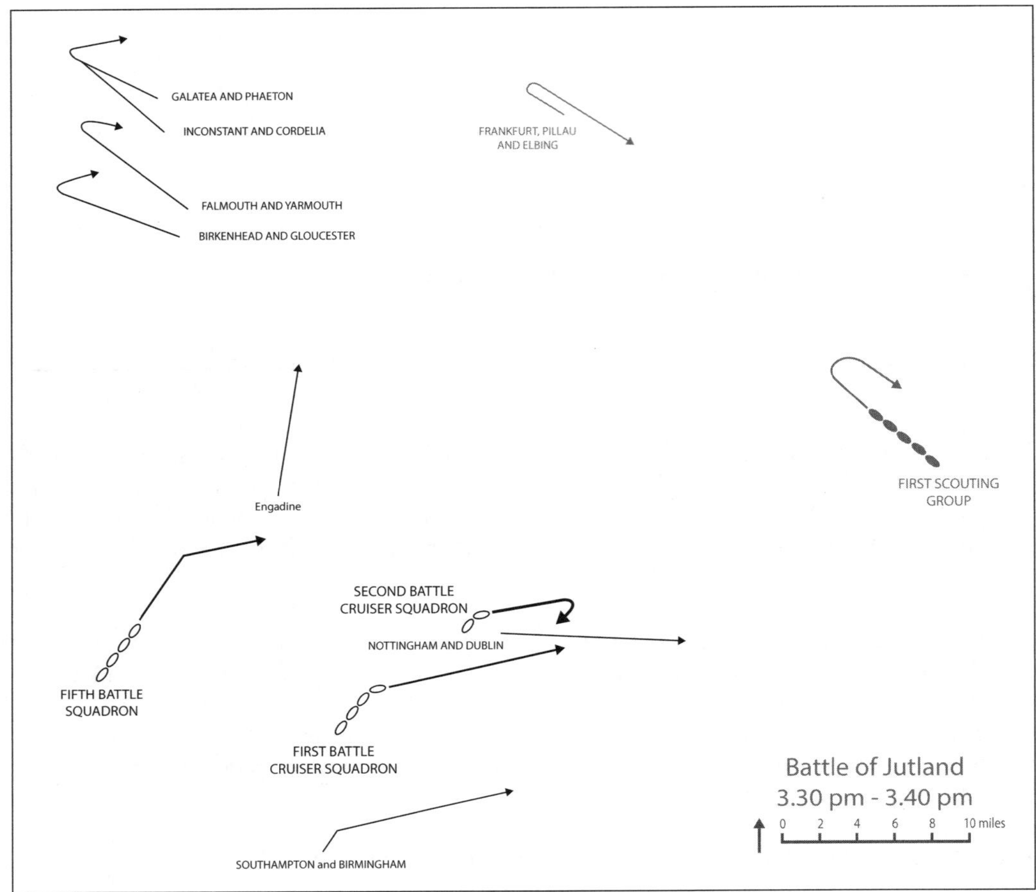

Map 6 Battle of Jutland: 3.30 pm to 3.40 pm.

> the battle cruisers. Thus we were at the head of the line. The horizon ahead of us grew clear of smoke, and we could now make out some English light cruisers which had also turned about. Suddenly my periscope revealed some big ships. Black monsters; six tall broad-beamed giants steaming in two columns. They were still a long way off, but they showed up clearly on the horizon, and even at this great distance they looked powerful, massive … I could now recognise them as the six most modern enemy battlecruisers. Six battlecruisers were opposed to our five; we went into battle with nearly equal forces. It was a stimulating, majestic spectacle as the dark grey giants approached like fate itself.[3]

Beatty sighted Hipper's battlecruisers some twelve minutes after his own ships had first come into his opponent's view; as Hipper turned south, Beatty ordered *New Zealand* and *Indefatigable* into line astern, signalling to Evan Thomas to turn east, speed 25 knots.

In his subsequent report Beatty wrote as follows:

> At 3.30 pm I increased speed to 25 knots and formed the Line of Battle, the 2nd Battle Cruiser Squadron forming astern of the 1st Battle Cruiser Squadron, with destroyers of the 13th and 9th Flotillas taking station ahead. I turned to ESE, slightly converging on the enemy, who were now at a range of 23,000 yards, and formed the ships on a line of bearing to clear the smoke. The 5th Battle Squadron, who had conformed to our movements, were now bearing NNW, 10,000 yards. The visibility at this time was good, the sun behind us and the wind SE. Being between the enemy and his base, our situation was both tactically and strategically good.[4]

John Brooks has pointed out that the times 'are very different from those in the 'Narrative' still to be found in his personal records,' and concludes that Beatty 'appears to have deliberately misrepresented his conduct of the approach, probably to forestall anticipated criticism of his tactics.'[5] He goes on to point out that all other sources describe the wind as a light westerly breeze. And, of course, by no means was Beatty 'between the enemy and his base;' regrettably, statements of this kind do not encourage confidence in the reader of Beatty's truthfulness. Hipper's battlecruisers were hull down, some 11 miles away and indistinct on the horizon, and Beatty held on at 25 knots to close the enemy.

Beatty's change of course to the east was soon apparent to Hipper; it would put the Battle Cruiser Fleet between his battlecruisers and the High Seas Fleet, and at about 3.33 he altered course to the south east. At this point Hipper seems not yet to have spotted the 5th Battle Squadron, although *Seydlitz* recorded its presence. Evan-Thomas had now worked up to a squadron speed of 24½ knots. Commander Frost is extremely critical of Beatty's instruction:

> It is hardly utilising the talents of an officer of flag rank, commanding an independent squadron, to direct his course and speed. In fact, we contend that Beatty's signal was against every principle of effective leadership. He should have told Evan-Thomas of his intentions and given him general instructions. It would have been simple to have signalled his intention to deploy for decisive action on course SE (122°) and to have directed the 5th Battle Squadron to support the battlecruisers. Similar instructions and information should have been sent to the other subordinate commanders.[6]

And, as Frost points out, the order to steam east 'was the last order Evan-Thomas was to receive from his superior for a long, long time;' on that course he would never close with the battle cruisers.

Pakenham had carried out the order to take station behind the 1st Battle Cruiser Squadron promptly, and Beatty ordered the six battle cruisers to turn ESE. At 3.46 pm he directed *Lion* and *Princess Royal* to concentrate their fire on the leading enemy ship. Hipper, knowing that the British ships could outrange his, was anxious to close the range as soon as possible. He had ordered fire distribution from the left, ship against ship, at 3.39 pm, and he turned sharply towards Beatty, though baffled by the fact that the British had not yet opened fire, as Otto Groos records in the German Official History:

> Owing to the decisive importance of obtaining early hits, Hipper had to stake everything on passing as quickly as possible through the danger area in which only the British ships could fire. At 3.45 he therefore turned the battle cruisers two points to starboard together

> to the south-south-east so as to close the enemy more rapidly. But, much to everyone's surprise, the enemy's guns remained silent. The hostile vessels were, however, still in the process of deploying.[7]

The explanation for this was simple; Beatty did not realise that the enemy was in range. Range finding conditions were poor due to the smoke and haze, and when Beatty opened fire at 3.47 at what he believed was 18000 yards, the range was probably about 15000 yards. As a result, the first British salvoes landed about a mile beyond the German line, causing more danger to the light cruiser *Regensburg* and her destroyers, 2000 yards beyond Hipper's line, than to his battle cruisers.[8] Hipper had opened fire at the same moment; his gunlayers also overestimated the range, and the first German salvoes were also over. Chatfield recorded the problems faced by Beatty's gunners:

> Whereas we had behind us to the westward a clear sky and a horizon which silhouetted our ships clearly, the enemy ships were difficult to discern. Behind them to the eastward there was a dull grey sky and a misty horizon; spotting for us was therefore difficut and for him much easier.[9]

Hase started badly; it took four minutes before *Derfflinger*, firing at *Princess Royal*, straddled his target:

> That wasn't a very cheering result. Our first rounds had been well over. This was due to inaccurate estimation of the opening range and a delay in the first reports of the measured range. I explain the serious error of calculation as follows: The Bg. men were completely overwhelmed by the first view of the enemy monsters. Each one saw the enemy ship magnified twenty three times in his instrument! Their minds were at first concentrated on the appearance of the enemy.[10]

Once he had found the range of his target, after each salvo from *Derfflinger's* 12 inch guns, the secondary armament fired two salvoes in quick succession:

> While the firing was going on any observation was out of the question. Dense masses of smoke accumulated round the muzzles of the guns, growing into clouds as high as houses, which stood for seconds in front of us like an impenetrable wall and were then driven by the wind and the weigh over the ship. In this way we often could see nothing of the enemy for seconds at a time as our fire control was completely enveloped in thick smoke.[11]

Hase soon realised that, for the moment, he was being assisted by a mistake on the part of *Queen Mary*, which had apparently missed Beatty's signal for *Princess Royal*, like *Lion*, to concentrate on Hipper's leading ship, his flagship *Lützow*,. *Queen Mary*, instead of aiming at *Derfflinger*, second in the line, took *Seydlitz*, the third ship as her target, so for ten minutes at least Hase was able to concentrate on his gunnery undisturbed.[12] It was an advantage shared by *New Zealand*, fifth in Beatty's line, as *Von der Tann*, the last of the German ships, concentrated her fire on *Indefatigable*, the last in the British line. The Germans were making good use of their leeward position, which meant that funnel smoke and gunsmoke cleared more quickly than for their opponents, which suffered from the smoke being blown in front of them by the west-north-westerly wind.

Aboard *Lion* Beatty, who had been below on his own bridge with his staff, now came up to the compass platform to join Chatfield. His flag captain was supremely confident, reflecting that they had sunk *Blücher* and badly damaged *Seydlitz* at the Dogger Bank:

> We now had better instruments, better gunnery, as efficient at least as any other capital ships in the Fleet; our gunnery control officers were all specially selected and of the highest ability; we had to a large extent standardised our methods and profited by our experiences; why should we not now sink more of our old opponents?[13]

Events were soon to show that Chatfield's faith was somewhat misplaced.

Hipper was equally confident, as he stood in the control tower of his flagship:

> He could not be separated from the telescope. There was nothing which escaped him, nothing he forgot, and he personally issued the vital orders even on matters of detail. Just before fire opened the First Staff Officer and the Gunnery Officer were discussing the favourable fire distribution. Hipper intervened with the remark that this was *his* business. No one need worry about it.[14]

A little later, in similar vein, he interrupted another conversation:

> The question was being discussed whether a signal should not be given which would draw the attention of our own line to certain British destroyers which were attacking. Hipper left his telescope for a second or two, turned round and said somewhat sharply: 'I've seen everything, gentlemen, and will give the order when the signal is to be given.'[15]

By 3.54 the range between the two battle lines was down to 13,000 yards. It was at this point that the German battlecruisers began using their secondary armament, as described by Hase. Hipper now ordered his ships to take station directly astern, which made station keeping easier. By now the German gunnery was proving highly effective. In particular, *Moltke* was hitting *Tiger*, putting two of her turrets out of action for a considerable time, while *Lützow* scored several hits on *Lion* and *Derfflinger* was hammering *Princess Royal*. Beatty had no option but to turn away one point to the south, making a total of six points since the action began.[16]

As the two lines of battlecruisers, guns blazing, drove southwards through the calm sea, smoke belching from the funnels, they passed on either side a Norwegian barque, lying becalmed, a mute witness to the savage battle; for her crew the experience was the stuff of nightmares as the shells shrieked relentlessly overhead.

At 4.00 *Lützow* scored its fourth hit on *Lion*, which might easily have been fatal. It burst through the armour of 'Q' turret amidships, killing all but Marine Major Harvey and his sergeant. Harvey, mortally wounded, sent the sergeant to Chatfield to report before himself giving the order to flood the magazines; but for his courage, posthumously marked with the award of the Victoria Cross, *Lion* would have been destroyed.[17] As the flagship reeled from this blow, worse was to come. At the end of the battle cruiser line, *Indefatigable* had been engaged in a fierce duel with *Von der Tann*. An officer aboard *New Zealand* watched as *Indefatigable* lurched out of line:

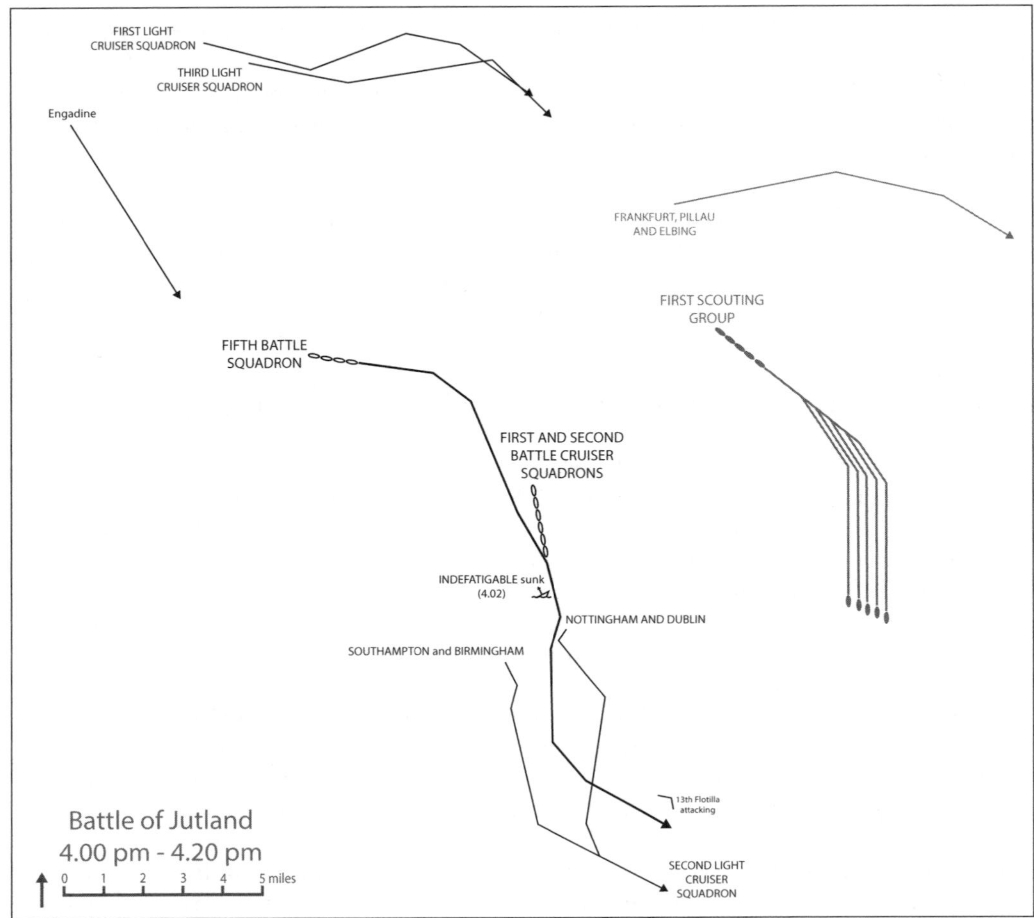

Map 7 Battle of Jutland: 4.00 pm to 4.20 pm.

We were altering course at the time, and apparently her steering gear was damaged, as she did not follow round in our wake, but held on until she was about 500 yards on our starboard quarter, in full view from the conning tower. Whilst he was still looking at her through his glasses she was hit by two shells, one on the foc'sle and one on the fore turret. Both shells appeared to explode on impact. Then there was an interval of about 30 seconds, during which there was absolutely no sign of fire or flame or smoke, except the little actually formed by the burst of the two shells, which was not considerable. At the end of the interval of about 30 seconds the ship completely blew up, commencing apparently from for'ard. The main explosion started with sheets of flame, followed immediately after by a dense, dark smoke, which obscured the ship from view. All sorts of stuff was blown high into the air, a 50 foot steam picket boat, for example, being blown up about 200 feet, apparently intact, though upside down.[18]

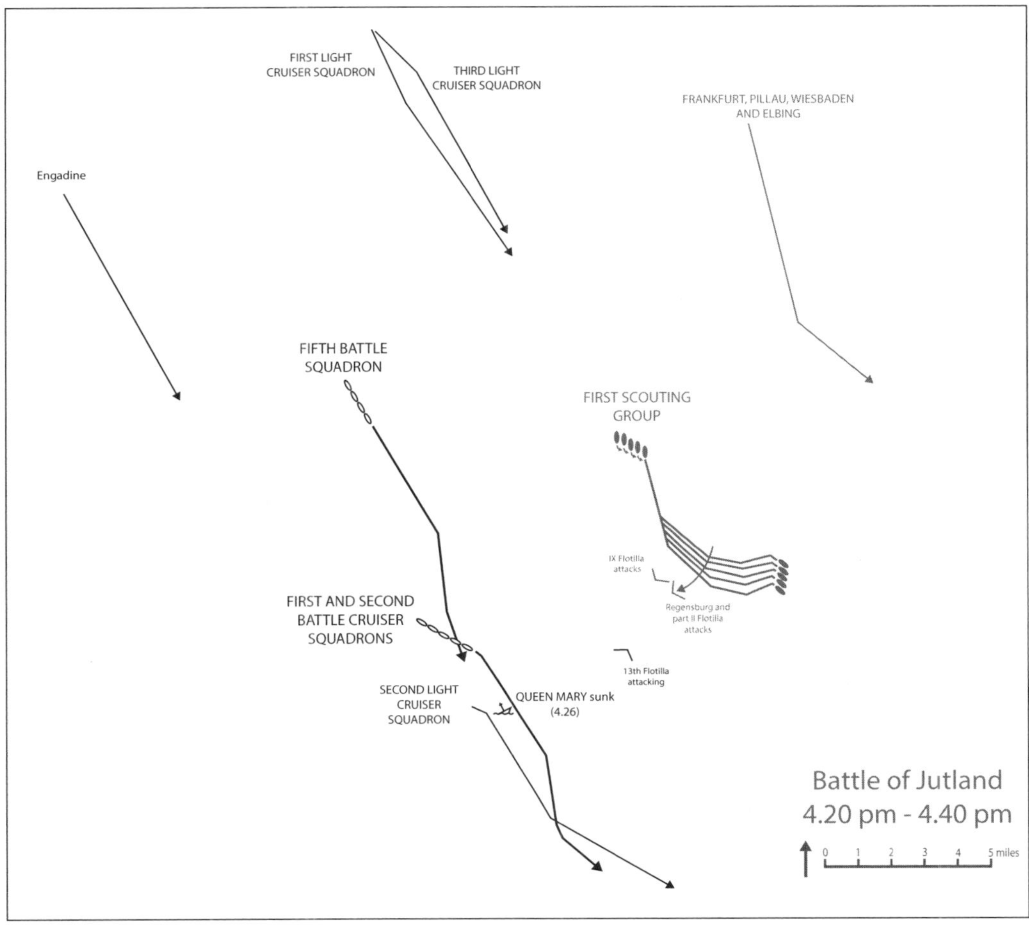

Map 8 Battle of Jutland: 4.20 pm to 4.40 pm.

There were only two survivors, rescued later by the German destroyer *S68*; 57 officers and 960 men went down with the ship.

Beatty's course alteration, to which Hipper conformed, had given Evan-Thomas a chance to close the gap by cutting the corner, and his four battleships now came into action, first against Hipper's light cruisers, which were forced to turn away to the eastward, and then, at about 4.08, against *Von der Tann* at the end of the battlecruiser line. Their shooting, unlike that of the Battle Cruiser Fleet, impressed the Germans, Hipper observing that 'the salvoes arrived absolutely dense (with no spread). The fall, in both elevation and direction, covered almost the same 'spot."[19] It was also notable that the 5th Battle Squadron opened fire at very long range; Gordon shows that this was more likely to have been at 23,000 yards rather that the 19,000 yards reported by Evan-Thomas.

The arrival on the scene of Evan-Thomas and his four *Queen Elizabeths* coincided with a reduction in the ferocity of the engagement between the battle cruisers, as the German Official History noted:

> In spite of all Admiral Hipper's attempts to engage the enemy closely, the violence of the artillery action between the two opposing lines of battle cruisers had meanwhile abated considerably owing to the increase in range from 4.06pm onwards. Observation of the fall of shot became increasingly difficult for both sides, particularly when the moment of impact coincided with the flash of the opponents' guns. According to British observations, many of the German shells were at this time falling short. Enemy salvoes falling short also threw up tremendous quantities of water in front of the German ships, thus further obscuring the field of vision in the direction of the enemy.[20]

From the start of the action Hipper had kept the speed of his battlecruisers down to 21 knots, a voluntary restraint which Gordon describes as 'potentially suicidal'; his reason appears to have been to ensure that the Battle Cruiser Fleet stayed closely in touch as he led it towards Scheer, but with the arrival on the scene of the 5th Battle Squadron he ordered an increase in speed to 23 knots. At 4.09 Beatty ordered his destroyers to attack the enemy, although it was several minutes before this got under way; by the time it did the German destroyers had themselves dashed forward to the attack.

While this was developing, *Derfflinger* and *Queen Mary* were engaged in a fierce gunnery duel; Hase had shifted his fire to *Queen Mary* when *Lion* turned sharply out of line for a few moments leaving *Princess Royal* as apparently the lead ship ahead of *Queen Mary*. The latter was also being engaged by *Seydlitz*. Hase described what happened next:

> Since 4.24 pm every one of our savoes had straddled the enemy. When the salvo fired at 6.26 fell, heavy explosions had already begun in the *Queen Mary*. First of all a vivid red flame shot up from her fore part. Then came an explosion forward which was followed by a much heavier explosion amidships, black debris of the ship flew into the air, and immediately afterwards the whole ship blew up with a terrific explosion. A gigantic cloud of smoke rose, the masts collapsed inwards, the smoke-cloud rose higher and higher. Finally nothing but a thick black cloud of smoke remained where the ship had been. At its base the smoke column only covered a small area, but it widened towards the summit and looked like a monstrous black pine. I estimated the height of the column at from 300 to 400m.[21]

From the conning tower of *Tiger*, the next ship in line, her torpedo officer was watching *Queen Mary* and was able to see the effect of hits at close quarters. At first it seemed that her armour was standing up to the hits she received:

> The next salvo that I saw straddled her, and two more shells hit her. As they hit, I saw a dull red glow amidships, and then the ship seemed to open out like a puffball, or one of those toadstool things when one squeezes it. Then there was another dull red glow somewhere forward, and the whole ship seems to collapse inwards. The funnels and masts fell into the middle, and the hull was blown 100 feet high, then everything was smoke, and a bit of the

stern was the only part of the ship left above water. The *Tiger* put her helm hard – a – starboard, and we just cleared the remains of the *Queen Mary's* stern by a few feet.[22]

Beatty and Chatfield turned in time to see the explosion. Chatfield thought both of the friends he had lost, and how lucky *Lion* had been; Beatty, displaying characteristic sang-froid, turned to him and said: 'There seems to be something wrong with our bloody ships today.'[23] Later, some writers, led by Churchill, embellished the story by adding the words 'Steer two points nearer the enemy.' but there is no evidence to suggest this, and Chatfield explicitly confirmed Beatty's actual words in a letter to Marder. Actually, at this point Beatty turned away two points. Over a period of a few minutes Hipper did the same, turning away a total of five points, due both to the developing destroyer action and the damage which his ships were sustaining, particularly at the hands of the 5th Battle Squadron.

Queen Mary took down with her 1266 officers and men; there were only nine survivors, two of whom were picked up by German destroyers. It was a stunning blow, and Hipper's ships had now achieved a remarkable result during the engagement. They themselves were by no means unscathed; the excellent gunnery of Evan-Thomas's ships was beginning to tell and both *Von der Tann* and *Moltke* sustained several 15 inch hits. *Moltke* listed about three degrees to starboard as a result of suffering a total of five hits (four from 15 inch shells), which was corrected by counter-flooding; she took on board about 1000 tons of water, but in spite of this was still able to steam at 25 knots. *Von der Tann* had sustained three hits since the start of the action, two from 13.5 inch shells and one from a 15 inch shell. *Seydlitz* was hit five times, and *Lützow* four times, in the period up to 4.54. *Derfflinger* at this point had suffered no hits from heavy shells at all.[24] During the same period Beatty's battlecruisers sustained a total of 42 hits from 11 inch and 12 inch shells; in addition *Barham* was hit twice.

The British destroyers formed up to deliver their attack; almost simultaneously Heinrich ordered his destroyers to launch a torpedo attack to relieve the pressure on Hipper's battle cruisers. It was the moment for which the destroyer captains had been waiting:

> At 4.15 the port division, led by Commander the Hon. Barry Bingham in the *Nestor*, swerved out of the line at full speed to attack. Other divisions followed, until, steaming at speeds of nearly 34 knots, as fast as they could be driven, a dozen destroyers were tearing for the area of 'no man's sea' between the opposing squadrons. It was a chance vouchsafed to few destroyer officers, and then only once in a lifetime. They had started on the most exciting race in the world, a race towards the enemy, a race which had as its prizes honour and glory – possibly death.[25]

Corbett graphically described the confused conflict:

> It was a wild scene of groups of long low forms vomiting heavy trails of smoke and dashing hither and thither at thirty knots or more in the smother and splashes, and all in a rain of shell from the secondary armament of the German battlecruisers, as well as from the *Regensburg* and the destroyers, with the heavy shell of the contending squadrons screaming overhead. Gradually a pall of gun and funnel smoke almost hid the shell-tormented sea.[26]

The German destroyers had themselves surged forward so that by 4.30 the fierce close range action was raging between the lines of capital ships. The British destroyers comprised the 13th

Flotilla (minus *Onslow* and *Moresby* which were with *Engadine*) and four ships of the 10th Flotilla, a total of 12 vessels. Neither *Nottingham* nor *Dublin* were able to offer much in the way of support. For the Germans, the eleven destroyers of the IX Flotilla, supported by the light cruiser *Regensburg* and four destroyers of the *G101* class took part. During this violent struggle, which lasted for a period of about fifteen minutes, the Germans lost *V27* and *V29*, while the British *Nomad* and *Nestor* were lost.

The destroyer flotillas on both sides carried out their attacks with the utmost courage, as the circumstances of these four losses demonstrated. When *V27* had her steam line cut, *V26* turned back at once to assist her. Shortly after, *S35* also turned back to the aid of *V29*, which had been hit by a torpedo from *Petard*. Frost described what followed:

> The rescue work of the *V26* and *S35* was one of the finest exploits of the this great battle, so replete with deeds of extraordinary heroism. The *V26*, skilfully handled by Lieutenant Commander Hans Köhler, came alongside the *V27* and rescued her entire crew, including two badly wounded men. Then at about 4.38 she sank the *V27* by gunfire, proceeded alongside the *V29* and took off part of the crew of that vessel. The *S25*, Lieutenant Commander Ihm, rescued the remainder in an equally gallant manner at about 4.48. This rescue work was performed under a heavy fire from the British destroyer, in particular from the *Obdurate, Morris, Nerissa* and *Termagant*.[27]

During these rescue operations, Köhler and Ihm had the benefit of support from *Regensburg* and the 2nd Flotilla, hitting *Obdurate* twice.

Meanwhile *Nomad* and *Nestor*, both seriously damaged during the attack on Hipper's battlecruisers, now found themselves stopped in the path of Scheer's oncoming battleships:

> The *Nicator* was ordered to save herself. The *Petard's* offer of a tow was refused. Bingham feared that it would cause the loss of two ships instead of one. However, there was probably time for the crews of both the *Nomad* and *Nestor* to be rescued by other destroyers after their sea valves had been opened. Unfortunately this was not the British doctrine. With Spartan heroism they prepared to fight their ships to the end. There was always a chance that they might hit the oncoming battleships with their remaining torpedoes. Hats off to those brave destroyer sailors.[28]

Both the British destroyers succeeded in firing their remaining torpedoes at the oncoming battleships, albeit without success. Under heavy fire, both were soon reduced to a sinking condition, and their crews were rescued by the German destroyers.

By 4.36 Hipper, who had turned away to avoid the torpedoes launched by the British destroyers, had for the moment broken off the action and was heading east. In fact neither group of destroyers had much success with their torpedoes; the British hit one destroyer and also *Seydlitz*, although not inflicting serious damage, while their opponents hit one destroyer. At 4.43, however, *Lion* suddenly signalled the recall to the destroyers.

What had happened was that Goodenough, in *Southampton*, had worked himself into a position some two or three miles ahead of Beatty, and had to his great surprise sighted the battleships of the High Seas Fleet to the south eastward. His signal officer expressed in terms the drama of the moment, as Goodenough recorded:

> About 4.30pm we saw ahead of us, first smoke, then masts, then ships. 'Look, Sir,' said Arthur Peters, 'this is the day of a light cruiser's lifetime. The whole of the High Seas Fleet is before you.' It was: sixteen battleships with destroyers disposed around them on each bow. That was reported. We hung on for a few minutes to make sure before confirming the message. My Commander, efficient and cool, said: 'If you're going to make that signal, you'd better make it now, Sir. You may never make another' .... The signal made, we turned and received the attention of the enemy at a range of about 12,000 to 13,000 yards.[29]

Goodenough's full signal, sent by wireless to Beatty and Jellicoe at 4.38 read: 'Have sighted enemy battlefleet bearing approximately SE, course of enemy NE'.[30] The signal was immediately confirmed by *Champion*. Beatty acted at once, turning to port in the direction in which Goodenough had reported the High Seas Fleet, while the 5th Battle Squadron held on its course, firing on the retreating German battlecruisers:

> Wholly unexpected as Admiral Scheer's arrival was, all doubt was quickly at an end. Two minutes after the *Lion* altered course she could see the leading German battleship less than twelve miles away to the south-eastward, and then an apparently interminable line of battleships came into view, attended by light cruisers and a swarm of destroyers. There could be no question as to what it meant, and at 4.40 Admiral Beatty swung back sixteen points in succession to northwest and then northward to join the Commander-in-Chief by the shortest possible course.[31]

Beatty's general signal to turn had been taken in by Goodenough, but he did not immediately obey the instruction, pressing on towards Scheer's battleships in order to verify his information. At 4.48 he signalled by wireless:

> Urgent. Priority. Course of enemy's battlefleet N single line ahead. Composition of van *Kaiser* class. Bearing of centre E. Destroyers on both wings and ahead. Enemy's battlecruisers joining battlefleet from northward.[32]

With this signal sent, it was time to go. Goodenough only escaped serious injury by turning and steaming at full tilt into the shell splashes of the heavy salvoes opened on *Southampton* by Scheer's battleships.

Meanwhile Evan-Thomas was still heading south in action against Hipper's battlecruisers and facing torpedo attacks by Heinrich's destroyers. At the time of Beatty's general signal he was eight miles astern of *Lion*, a distance which was far too great to read flag signals, particularly in the prevailing visibility. Once again a serious mistake had been made by *Lion's* signalling staff, since the signal was not repeated by searchlight – if, that is to say, Beatty intended the signal to apply to Evan-Thomas. This has generally been assumed by historians to be the case but Gordon disagrees, pointing out first that if the 5th Battle Squadron had turned when *Lion* did, the gap of eight miles would have been maintained, which would have been undesirable; secondly, Evan-Thomas was still in action against Hipper, and keeping him occupied; and thirdly if, as will be seen, Beatty intended Evan-Thomas to comply he would have reiterated the signal so that the question of passing up his exposed side did not arise.[33]

As it was, by the time Beatty had completed his turn to the northwest he could see Evan-Thomas approaching almost head on; one of Beatty's staff asked which side he wanted the 5th Battle Squadron to pass and he replied to port. *Lion* accordingly turned four points to starboard; almost at once, *Barham* also turned to starboard, so that the two lines of ships would pass port to port at a distance of two miles. Gordon, although noting that Beatty's decision 'was no doubt the product of traditional warrior qualities – courage, aggression, bravado etc,' concludes that it was wrong. It caused Hipper to transfer his attention back to the battered ships of the Battle Cruiser Fleet; it meant that Beatty and his staff were denied a brief respite of calm in which to get their act together; it meant Beatty having to change course; and it created a manoeuvring problem for Evan-Thomas.[34]

What followed has also been the subject of controversy. It seems clear that, as the flagships of Beatty and Evan-Thomas approached each other, *Lion* signalled by flag an order to the 5th Battle Squadron to alter course in succession 16 points to starboard, and this was hoisted at 4.48. The *Official Despatches* record that Evan-Thomas did not obey the signal until 4.57; Gordon, with a painstaking reconstruction of the sequence of events shows conclusively that this could not be right, and concludes that the signal was not hauled down (upon which the order should be executed) before 4.51 and probably not until 4.54. The errors, if errors were there, could easily have been caused by the hectic time which Beatty's staff were having. At all events, he finds that *Barham* turned at 4.54, by which time Scheer's leading ships were no more than 20,000 yards away.[35]

When Hipper first reported that he had sighted strong enemy forces, Scheer received the news with aplomb, as Weizsäcker recorded:

> When I brought him the first reports from the reconnaissance ships that English men-of-war had been sighted, he went up to the captain's bridge in a calm and almost nonchalant manner. And this calmness he maintained throughout the whole battle. Very soon he left his steel conning-tower for the open deck, and remained there, in order to get a better view of the field of battle. In this greatest naval battle in history the action-drill we had learned in peacetime proved its value.[36]

The cruising formation of the High Seas Fleet put Rear Admiral Paul Behncke's Squadron III at the head of the line, led by his flagship *König,* followed by *Grosser Kurfürst, Kronprinz* and *Markgraf,* comprising Division V, and then *Kaiser* (Rear Admiral Nordmann), *Kaiserin, Prinzregent Luitpold* and *Friedrich der Grosse,* comprising Division VI. Next came Vice Admiral Erhard Schmidt's Squadron I: his flagship *Ostfriesland. Thüringen, Helgoland* and *Oldenburg* (Division I) followed by *Posen* (Rear Admiral Engelhardt), *Rheinland, Nassau* and *Westfalen* (Division II). Mauve, with Squadron II, was in the rear. His flagship was *Deutschland;* his remaining ships were *Hessen* and *Pommern* (Division III) and Division IV consisting of *Schlesien, Schleswig Holstein* and *Hannover* (Rear Admiral von Dalwigk zu Lichtenfels). The latter was ordered to take station at the end of the line so that there should be a flagship posted there.[37] *Kronprinz* and *Kaiserin* were the first to open fire on *Barham* at a range of 21,000 yards even before she made her turn to the north, hitting her twice. When *König* reported Beatty's turn to the north, Scheer had ordered the fleet to make a two point turn to port by divisions, so that effectively at this point the battleships were steaming in six columns; it was only after this course alteration that Scheer could see the enemy ships for himself, ordering the flag signal 'Distribution of fire from the right, ship against ship'.

Goodenough's report of the sighting of Hipper's battlecruisers occasioned Jellicoe no anxiety. He immediately ordered Hood, with the 3rd Battle Cruiser Squadron (*Inflexible, Invincible* and *Indomitable*) to proceed at full speed towards Beatty to reinforce him, at the same time signalling the situation to his own fleet, and checking that Evan-Thomas was with Beatty:

> At this time I was confident that, under the determined leadership of Sir David Beatty, with a force of four of our best and fastest battleships and six battle cruisers, very serious injury would be inflicted on the five battle cruisers of the enemy if they could be kept within range.[38]

When the High Seas Fleet was reported, Jellicoe was in no doubt that the superior speed of the Battle Cruiser Feet and the 5th Battle Squadron would keep them out of danger from the enemy until the Grand Fleet came on the scene. He learned later, 'as an unpleasant surprise, that the 5th Battle Squadron, *when going at its utmost speed*, found considerable difficulty in getting away from Behncke's *König* class battleships.'[39]

Jellicoe's cruising formation deployed his battleships in six columns. The port column was headed by *King George V*, Jerram's flagship of the 2nd Battle Squadron, followed by the rest of the 1st Division, *Ajax, Centurion* and *Erin*. Next came the 2nd Division, led by *Orion* (Rear Admiral Arthur Leveson) with *Monarch, Conqueror* and *Thunderer*. Jellicoe led the third column in *Iron Duke*, followed by *Royal Oak, Superb* (Rear Admiral Duff) and *Canada*. This was the 3rd Division; the other half of the 4th Battle Squadron, the 4th Division, was led by Sturdee in *Benbow*, with *Bellerophon, Temeraire* and *Vanguard*. Next came the 5th Division, of the 1st Battle Squadron, headed by Rear Admiral Gaunt in *Colossus*, with *Collingwood, Neptune* and *St Vincent*; finally, on the starboard wing of the fleet, Burney led the 6th Division in *Marlborough* followed by *Revenge, Hercules* and *Agincourt*.

Aboard *Hercules*, the news that the German fleet was at sea lifted everyone's spirits. Commodore von Schoultz noted:

> As I passed along the various decks from the bridge to fetch my notebook I saw every face radiant with enthusiasm and delight. In my cabin my servant, Bathard, was packing the rest of my gear into a trunk and his face was flushed with eagerness.[40]

When he got back to the bridge, however, he found that Clinton Baker, the captain of *Hercules*, was gloomy; Beatty had all the luck, it was said, Baker adding: 'We shan't be in it. We're crawling like tortoises.'

The Grand Fleet had, since the first report from Alexander-Sinclair, been steaming at 18 knots. At 3.16, in anticipation of possible action, Jellicoe ordered his six divisions of battleships to steam 2000 yards apart; upon deployment this would make the gap between ships 500 yards. A minute later he ordered an increase of speed to 19 knots. As the minutes passed, the reports became more interesting, and at 3.22 Jellicoe ordered his destroyers to raise steam for full speed, but he remained doubtful of the strength of the enemy force with which Beatty's cruisers were in touch until at 3.35pm he received the latter's report of five battlecruisers. At 3.48 pm, when Beatty and Hipper both opened fire, he was 52½ miles from his battlecruisers.[41] So far, everything was falling into place for the Grand Fleet.

14

The Run to the North

The lateness of the 5th Battle Squadron's turn meant that it was dangerously close to the battleships of the High Seas Fleet, and was still of course within range of Hipper's squadron, with which it now engaged in a bitter gunnery duel. In spite of the ferocity of the earlier engagement with Beatty's fleet, Hipper's ships were still capable of giving a good account of themselves, even though Evan-Thomas had 15-inch guns with which to do business compared with the 11-inch and 12-inch guns of the enemy. During the first few minutes of this rearguard action, *Derfflinger* was firing at *Barham, Lützow* at *Lion*, *Seydlitz* at *Tiger* and *Moltke* at *New Zealand. Von der Tann,* reduced to one 11 inch gun, was firing at *Malaya.* Within ten minutes Beatty's ships were out of range, and the battle continued with the 5th Battle Squadron. *Derfflinger* hit *Barham* four times as the leading ships of the High Seas Fleet began to come within range.[1]

Correlli Barnett, commenting on Beatty's situation at this juncture, described him as 'heading for the Grand Fleet at his utmost speed, his guns silent from 5.10 pm to 5.40 pm, a third of his force sunk, a decisively beaten admiral.'[2] Professor Marder will not have this, saying 'that he was hardly fleeing from the enemy'; he points out that Beatty's role had now changed 'from that of a striking force to that of a reporting and reconnaissance force.' His mission was to lure an unsuspecting Scheer into the path of the Grand Fleet, reporting fully to Jellicoe as he did so.[3]

Nonetheless, it is not unreasonable to observe that, having seriously bungled his handling of the 5th Battle Squadron, Beatty's departure northwards at his maximum speed showed scant concern for the risk to which this might expose Evan-Thomas, whose ships sustained considerable punishment. The damage could, though, have been very much worse than it was. Even more seriously, however, Beatty's flight meant the abandonment of the opportunity, albeit brief, to inflict considerable further damage on Hipper's battlecruisers; he would have been fighting with eight ships against four, and he had the valuable advantage of the 15-inch guns of the 5th Battle Squadron.

Admiral Harper, perhaps understandably not the most dispassionate of commentators, following the difficulties which he had endured at Beatty's hands, after reviewing the strength of the forces engaged, put the matter bluntly:

> In spite of this overwhelming preponderance of power, we lost two battlecruisers, sunk by gunfire, while the enemy lost none. Considerably more damage was caused to our ships than they inflicted on the enemy. It *is* unpalatable – extremely unpalatable – but nevertheless an indisputable fact that, in this first phase of the battle, a British squadron, greatly

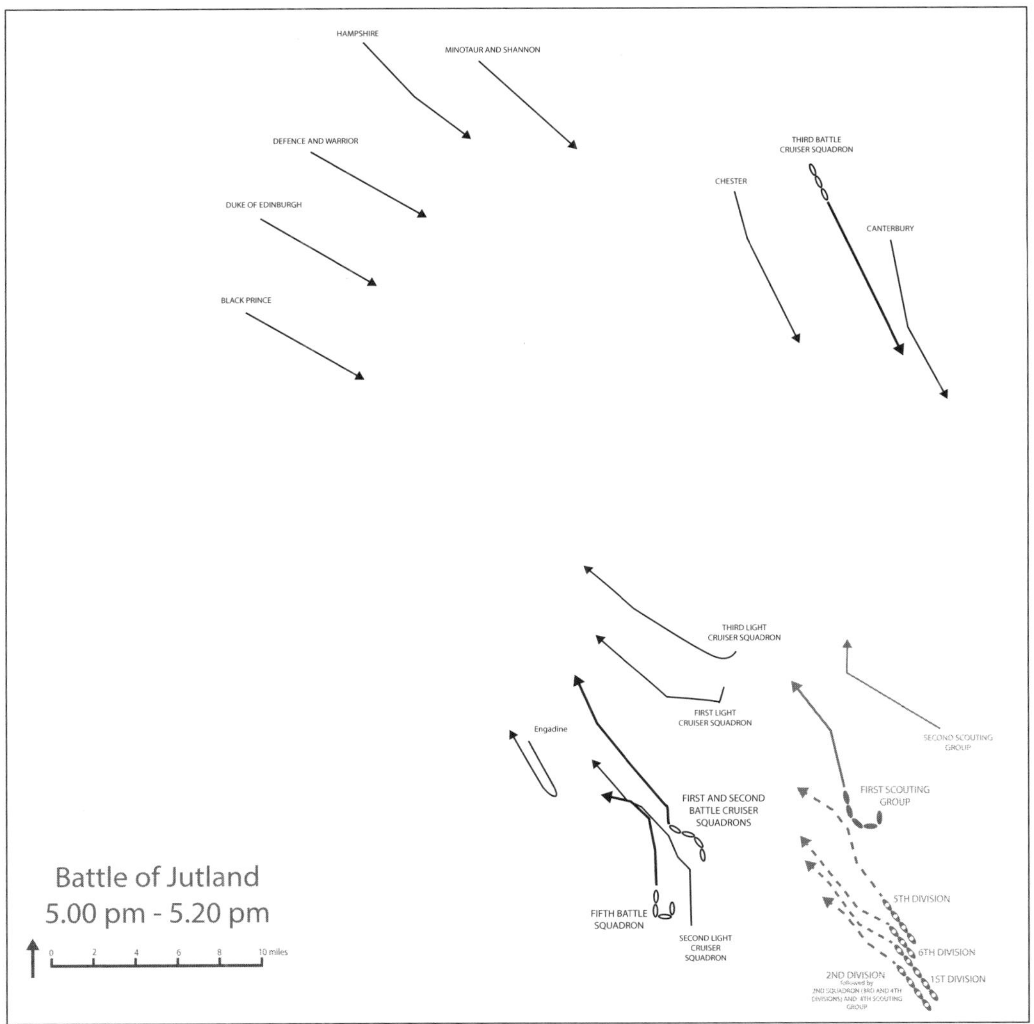

Map 9 Battle of Jutland: 5.00 pm to 5.20 pm.

> superior in numbers and gun-power, not only failed to defeat a weaker enemy who made no effort to avoid action, but, in the space of 50 minutes, suffered what can only be described as a partial defeat.[4]

John Brooks, noting that Beatty's despatch showed an awareness that he was liable to face reproach for his tactics, summarises the errors he made:

> He should be criticised for once again failing to use all the firepower at his disposal, for leading his battlecruisers out of action for the best part of half an hour, and for leaving the battleships under his command unsupported while they alone fought off the whole German battlefleet.[5]

As it was, for a short while after first Beatty and then Evan-Thomas turned to the north, it was the latter who was engaging Hipper's battlecruisers; Scheer's seven leading battleships were still too far off to be very effective, although by 5.15 all had opened fire. *Markgraf*, indeed, appears still to have been able to catch sight of *Tiger*, and for ten minutes fired on her from her forward turrets at extreme range:

> When Beatty disappeared in the mists, Scouting Group 1 ceased firing on his battle-cruisers. Hipper's vessels were pretty well exhausted after their long fight and the range to the 5th Battle Squadron was close to their maximum. There was no signal for them to shift target to the battleships. However, the *Lützow* at an unstated time commenced firing on the *Barham*. At 5.16 the *Derfflinger* commenced firing on the *Valiant* with high explosive shell. At 5.25 the *Seydlitz* fired on the *Warspite*. The *Moltke* did not fire on the *Malaya* until 5.27. The *Von der Tann* had been firing on the same target since 5.00 pm.[6]

During this period, however, the firing of Hipper's battlecruisers had become much less effective.

Hase noted that in fact, for the High Seas Fleet, the next phase of the battle was by no means as rewarding:

> The second phase was just as unsatisfactory as the first was successful and interesting from the point of view of gunnery. The enemy had learned the devil of a lesson and acquired a deep respect for the effectiveness of our gunfire. During the wild dash north they kept as much as possible out of our range, but kept us within reach of their own long range guns … I only fired to make quite sure that the enemy were still out of range, and then, to save ammunition, I contented myself with isolated shots from one turret. The guns were again trained on the upper edge of the funnels or the mastheads.[7]

At the extreme ranges at which they were firing, Hase observed that the British shooting was not good either; he speculated that the poor control was due to the limited visibility. Nonetheless, *Derfflinger* sustained three hits during this period, all from 15 inch shells; Hase recalled that 'when a heavy shell hit the armour of our ship, the terrific crash of the explosion was followed by a vibration of the whole ship, affecting even the conning tower.'[8]

Scheer's battleships maintained their fire as long as they could, but, as the German Official History explains, it became increasingly ineffectual:

> Only *Markgraf* had continued to fire at *Tiger* for some time, not however without interruption. But after the alteration of course by division, to NW, which brought the enemy still further ahead, only the foremost turrets would bear on the target, and finally at 5.25 she ceased fire when the range was 20,800 yards so as not to endanger the next ahead. The *Grosser Kurfürst*, on the other hand, transferred her fire from the *Princess Royal* to *Valiant* at 5.00 pm, the opening range being 19,000 yards and the *König*, from the *Tiger* to the *Barham* at 6.10 pm. But, after five minutes, only her two foremost turrets would bear; the *König*, therefore, also transferred her fire to *Valiant*. Then, at 6.16 pm the *Grosser Kurfürst* had to cease firing at this ship, the range having become too great.[9]

In spite of the fire from the leading German battleships, the 5th Battle Squadron, although suffering several hits, maintained an effective fire on both the German battlecruisers and the battle fleet. Meanwhile the destroyers *Onslow* and *Moresby*, seeking to rejoin Beatty's squadron after having screened *Engadine*, made a bold though unsuccessful attempt to mount a torpedo attack; *Onslow* was forced to turn away under fire from Boedicker's light cruisers, but *Moresby* was able to launch a torpedo at the third ship in Scheer's battle line before also turning away, and also escaped unscathed.[10]

As the battle moved steadily northwards, the effect of the worsening visibility tended more and more to the advantage of the British. As breaks began to appear in the clouds low on the western horizon, the sun, shining through, blinded the eyes of the German gunners. At 5.21 pm Evan-Thomas turned two points towards the enemy, later explaining that it was his intention to support the battlecruisers. This, as Frost points out, was quite unnecessary; for the moment Beatty's ships were safely out of range, and had the speed to avoid action if necessary.[11] At about this time Scheer ordered Hipper to pursue the enemy, a rash decision having regard to the existing tactical situation; Hipper had just then observed that Beatty had now begun to turn to the north east, which would have the effect of cruising ahead of the German battlecruisers, as well as postponing the moment when the Grand Fleet was spotted. However, at that moment the wireless aboard *Lützow* failed, and so Hipper had no alternative but to obey, turning to the NW and increasing speed; soon, though, he was obliged to turn back to the NE as Beatty continued his encircling movement. These movements had brought the two battlecruiser forces closer together, and at 5.40 pm Beatty opened fire.

Behind Hipper's squadron, Behncke had noted Beatty's move and himself turned to starboard to conform to it. At this point the German battlefleet was steaming in an extended line, seven miles astern of the I Scouting Group; scarcely visible on their port bow were Beatty's ships, firing so heavily on Hipper that at 5.47, unable effectively to reply due to the visibility he was obliged to turn away to the NNE.[12] By this time the German battleships were scarcely able to support Hipper, whose greater speed had resulted in the lengthening of the gap from the battlefleet. After four minutes steaming NNE, Hipper turned north, and ordered his destroyers to launch an attack. At 5.56 he turned east, to relieve the pressure from Beatty's battlecruisers, but soon after came under fire from a northeasterly direction. His immediate assumption was that this came from Jellicoe's battle fleet, and at 6.05 he altered course, steaming SW to fall back on the High Seas Fleet. As he ran back, his light cruisers suffered badly at the hands of Hood's squadron, *Wiesbaden* being heavily damaged and *Pillau* and *Frankfurt* both taking hits; Boedicker was able to relieve the pressure only by launching a torpedo attack which led to another fierce destroyer action.[13] Commander Loftus Jones, in *Shark*, had with him *Acasta, Ophelia* and *Christopher* and when he saw Boedicker's light cruisers steaming south east, he resolved to make the most of his chance both to attack them and frustrate the German destroyer attack on Hood's battlecruisers. During the ensuing engagement *Shark* was mortally injured; Jones refused a tow from *Acasta,* herself damaged, and continued himself to control the one gun he had left, even though his leg was shot away at the knee. When *Shark* finally went down, Jones was got into a life raft, but died a few hours later. There were only six survivors, rescued later by the Danish steamer *Vidar*. Commander Jones was later awarded a posthumous VC.[14] The other British destroyers also launched torpedo attacks, and were damaged in the process. *Acasta*, her steampipes cut, her steering gear wrecked and with her dynamo destroyed, could neither stop nor steer, and steamed slowly on through Jellicoe's

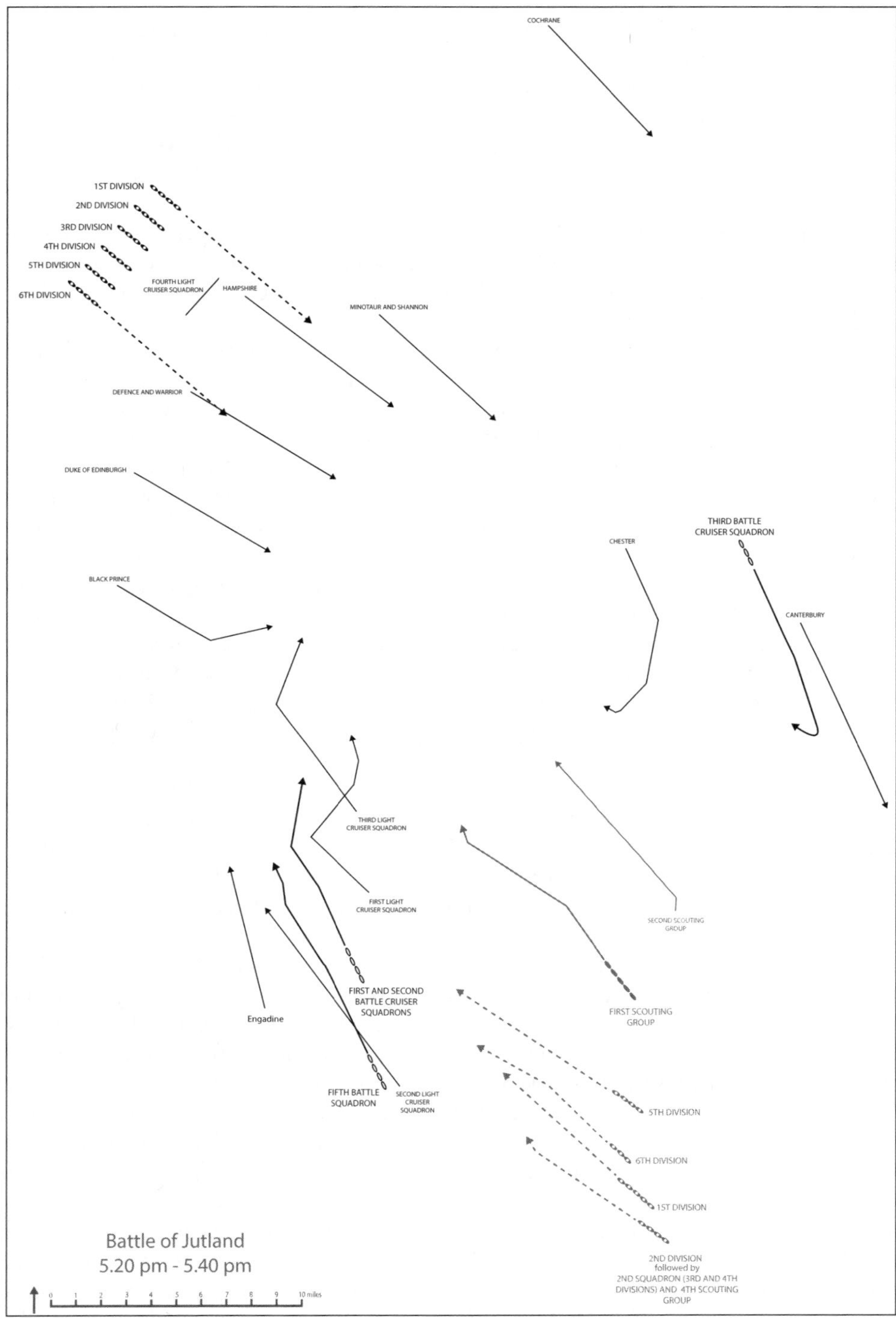

Map 10 Battle of Jutland: 5.20 pm to 5.40 pm.

battle fleet before coming to a halt. Lieutenant Commander Barron, her commanding officer, recalled her experiences:

> At about 6.30, having barged through our own destroyer flotillas ahead of the battle fleet – guided by Providence, for we we had no steering gear to guide the ship with – we at last got the ship stopped, and lying there only about 200 yards from the battleline, held a very fine review of the Grand Fleet coming in to action, as ship after ship they passed us. The men were very excited and cheered each ship as she passed, some to port and some to starboard, particularly the Commander in Chief in the *Iron Duke* ... Fortunately, they all dodged us.[15]

Prior to deployment, Jellicoe's battle fleet had continued to steam in six columns each of four battleships, led by the squadron and divisional commanders. The columns were some 2000 yards apart. The port column, consisting of the 1st Division of the 2nd Battle Squadron, was led by *King George V*, flying Jerram's flag as commander of the 2nd Battle Squadron; on his right came the 2nd Division, led by *Orion*, Leveson's flagship. Next came the column led by *Iron Duke*; on its right was the 4th Division, led by *Benbow*, bearing Sturdee's flag. The next column was led by *Colossus* (Rear Admiral Gaunt) and the starboard column was led by Burney's flagship *Marlborough*.

Hood's sudden arrival on the scene, and from an unexpected direction, resulted from Jellicoe's previous orders to steam on ahead of the battle fleet. He was, however, without any clear knowledge of where Beatty was; a wireless request from Hood to Beatty at 4.56 had asked for the latter's position, but produced no reply due to the damage to *Lion's* wireless. At 5.30 Hood had edged to his right, but he was still steering slightly to the east of Scheer's position as reported by Goodenough. His speed was 25 knots; he had with him four destroyers, and some five miles ahead of him, and to his right, respectively were the light cruisers *Canterbury* and *Chester*. At 5.36 *Chester* had caught sight of the four light cruisers of Boedicker's squadron, and came under heavy fire, suffering serious damage; she turned back to seek the support of Hood's battlecruisers, which finally opened fire on Boedicker at 5.55 as described above.

Although Beatty's turn to the NNE at about 5.35 had narrowed the range considerably, soon causing Hipper's alterations of course, the move represented a missed opportunity for the British. If instead Beatty had turned NNW, and been pursued by Scheer in that direction, it would either have led to the High Seas Fleet running straight into Jellicoe's battle fleet while strung out in a long column, or passing it in the deteriorating visibility, in which case Jellicoe would have been squarely between Scheer and his base. In such a situation, the German admiral would have found escape extremely difficult.[16]

As it was, Beatty was for the moment in a good tactical position to inflict damage on Hipper's hard pressed battlecruisers without their having much chance, with the sun in their eyes and deteriorating visibility, of making much response. He had not, however, been able to keep Jellicoe fully informed of the situation; the latter, as Beatty's battlecruisers came into view, sent a desperate message by searchlight at 6.01: 'Where is the enemy's battle fleet?' Five minutes later, Beatty signalled the unhelpful response: 'Enemy's battlecruisers bearing SE.' By this time Beatty's ships were passing across the track of the starboard column of the Grand Fleet, at a distance of only two miles from *Marlborough*.[17]

The arrival of Hood's battlecruisers and the contact with the light cruisers of II Scouting Group led to a serious misunderstanding by Boedicker of the force immediately opposed to him.

Hood's opening salvoes had at 5.47 inflicted fearful damage on *Wiesbaden* and left her effectively dead in the water. It was not until 5.58 that Boedicker could make out the capital ships from which came the heavy fire he was enduring and he at once reversed course in *Frankfurt*, followed shortly after by *Pillau* and *Elbing*. The first of these suffered heavy damage from a 12-inch shell, but was able to maintain her speed. Boedicker, having, as he thought, identified his opponents, sent a visual signal to Hipper: 'Am under fire of enemy battleships.'[18] After completing their turn, Boedicker's three cruisers immediately laid an extremely effective smoke screen which although preserving his ships from further damage, also prevented any further identification of the enemy.

During the confused destroyer actions which led to the sinking of *Shark*, the German captains had gone into action against what they supposed to be a squadron of Jellicoe's battleships, and had then become distracted by groups of British destroyers:

> It is interesting to note that at one of the critical moments of the action no less than three of the best German flotillas had allowed themselves to be drawn into engagements with small British detachments. The heavy blow in the air had first been caused by the erroneous belief that British battleships were present. The German commanders did not realise that they were firing at such a difficult target as three battlecruisers running at very high speeds. They thought that they recognised those ships as battleships and even believed they distinguished *Agincourt* among them. That indicated to them that the three ships in sight must be followed by at least five more (to complete one battle squadron) or probably the entire enemy battle line.[19]

Hood had steamed at his maximum speed to join Beatty's battlecruisers, but owing to the difference in the dead reckoning positions of *Iron Duke, Lion* and *Invincible* he arrived at the scene of the action some eighteen miles to the east of Beatty's force, and out of sight of them. It was, however, very much to the advantage of the British fleet that this error had occurred, as the German Official History noted:

> The position which the 3rd Battle Cruiser Squadron thus occupied, and which was neither contemplated nor due to skilled leadership, was, however, to influence later events favourably for the British fleet. While the head of the German line was hurrying on towards the advanced forces of the Grand Fleet, which were approaching from the north west, Hood's squadron suddenly appeared on the disengaged side of the High Seas Fleet.[20]

Hood's arrival not only enabled him to inflict severe damage on Boedicker's light cruisers, but also prompted the destroyer attacks, as well as causing Hipper to reverse his course in order to close up to Scheer's battle squadrons. As both Marder and the German Official History noted, however, Hood's appearance had an even more serious consequence:

> But for the intervention of this squadron the previously initiated attack of the German flotillas would have taken another direction, namely, at Beatty's force, and would probably have brought the latter's encircling movement across the head of the German line to a standstill, just as in the case of the British battle fleet later on. But in that case the German battlecruisers and ships of the 3rd Squadron would probably have surprised the enemy's

> fleet whilst still deploying, and would probably have succeeded in 'crossing the T,' instead of themselves being placed later on in a tactically untenable position by an outflanking movement of Beatty's.[21]

Marder quoted Levetzow, who wrote, many years later, of Scheer's disappointment at the missed chance:

> The German advance that had been launched could not be sustained, the powerful German spear … could no longer reach its target – and the English main force won time to deploy, luckily for England … Shortly before his death, Admiral Scheer told me in Weimar that the thought of how Providence had given them opportunities for a *complete* annihilation of the British fleet still robbed him of sleep.[22]

Jellicoe, by now aware that the High Seas Fleet was very near, but still in doubt as to where it actually was, was getting close to the point where he must make a decision as to the deployment of the battle fleet. Crucially, he lacked the kind of precise reporting that he might reasonably expect from the commander of his battlecruisers, as he pointed out:

> Had Sir David Beatty reported the position of the German Battle Cruisers at 5.40 pm when he once more came in sight of them and re-engaged, the difficulties of the Commander-in-Chief would have been greatly lessened, but he made no report of any kind between 4.45 pm and 6.06 pm, the latter report being in reply to urgent enquiries from the Commander-in-Chief … [Beatty] should have made it his principal duty to keep his Commander-in-Chief informed of the enemy's position. The Commander-in-Chief's battle orders laid the strongest emphasis on this duty.[23]

Frost reckoned that Jellicoe and Beatty should each bear part of the blame for the failure of the latter's light cruisers to provide information that would have been of immense value to Jellicoe, since their commanders had served for a long time in the Grand Fleet under war conditions, yet had evidently been inadequately trained in their duties. Only Goodenough, due principally to his initial reports of the High Seas Fleet, escaped serious criticism, but even he was guilty of supplying information that was incomplete or misleading.[24]

Jellicoe, at 6.08, ordered the disposition of his screening destroyer flotillas, two to the eastward and one to the westward of the battle fleet, an indication that he intended to deploy to the northeast:

> In other words, he had decided to make his first movement of the battle line away from, rather than towards, Heligoland. It was that decision that lost Jellicoe the last opportunity to surprise the High Seas Fleet. Beatty had first tried to beat them back or drive them to the eastward, rather than to lure them on to the north west into Jellicoe's hands. Jellicoe was now arranging to make the first general movement of the mass of his battleships away from the enemy rather than towards them. Thus, he could neither surprise them nor immediately cut their line of retreat.[25]

As the moments ticked away for Jellicoe to make his crucial decision as to the deployment of his battle squadrons, his light forces were getting into position and also, it appears, into rather a muddle. Alexander-Sinclair's 1st Light Cruiser Squadron had got mixed up with the battle line to such an extent that at 6.02 he signalled Napier, whose 3rd Light Cruiser Squadron was steaming ahead of the 2nd Battle Squadron: 'I was told to keep in touch with the battlecruisers. It seems to be getting a bit thick this end. What had we better do?'

Beatty signalled at 6.14 that the enemy's battle fleet bore SSW and this confirmed in Jellicoe's mind the decision that he should take. Even now, he had not yet himself sighted the enemy fleet. Captain Frederick Dreyer was standing amidships watching the steering of *Iron Duke*, which was the guide to the fleet, when he heard the distinctive step of Jellicoe approaching:

> He stepped quickly on to the platform round the compasses and looked in silence at the magnetic compass card for about twenty seconds. I watched his keen, brown, weather-beaten face with tremendous interest, wondering what he would do. With iron nerve he had pressed on through the mist with his twenty four huge ships, each weighing some 25,000 tons or more, until the last possible moment, so as to get into effective range and make the best tactical manoeuvre after obtaining news of the enemy Battle Fleet, which was his objective. I realised as I watched him that he was as cool and unmoved as ever. Then he looked up and broke the silence with the order in his crisp, clear-cut voice to Commander A R W Woods, the Fleet Signal officer, who was standing a little abaft of me: 'Hoist equal – speed pendant SE.'[26]

It was a decision of the utmost gravity, which Jellicoe had to take instantly, in the most unfavourable circumstance imaginable, as Corbett pointed out:

> There was not an instant to lose if deployment were to be made in time … Beyond a few miles everything was shrouded in mist; the little that could be seen was no more than a blurred picture, and with every tick of the clock the situation was developing with a rapidity of which his predecessors had never dreamt. At a speed higher than anything in their experience the two hostile fleets were rushing upon each other; battle cruisers, cruisers and destroyers were hurrying to their battle stations, and the vessels steaming across his front were shutting out all beyond in an impenetrable pall of funnel smoke. Above all was the roar of battle both ahead and to starboard, and in this blind distraction Admiral Jellicoe had to make the decision on which the fortunes of his country hung.[27]

Woods suggested it be made a point to port, so that it would be apparent that the deployment would be on the port wing column; Jellicoe agreed, ordering the equal-speed pendant SE by E, and Woods called to the signal boatswain. 'Hoist equal-speed Charlie London'. Moments later, Jellicoe ordered Dreyer to commence the deployment without waiting for all ships to acknowledge the signal. Dreyer blew two short blasts on the siren to indicate the turn to port, and put the helm over. The commanders of the columns on either side, watching for this, did the same, and the manoeuvre commenced.

For Dreyer, and for all Jellicoe's post-war supporters, it was 'the most brilliant sea-battle manoeuvre;' for Jellicoe's critics, it was a wasted opportunity. It was perhaps the most significant individual judgment that anyone was obliged to make throughout the battle, and as such has been debated at length. Most historians have expressed a view as to whether Jellicoe should have deployed on the port or starboard wing column, and have speculated as to what might have been the outcome if he had made the latter choice.

Jellicoe himself was in no doubt that he had made the correct decision:

> My first and natural impulse was to form on the starboard wing column in order to bring the Fleet into action at the earliest possible moment, but it became increasingly apparent, both from the sound of gunfire and the reports from the *Lion* and *Barham*, that the High Seas Fleet was in such close proximity and on such a bearing as to create obvious disadvantages in such a movement. I assumed that the German destroyers would be ahead of their Battle Fleet, and it was clear that, owing to the mist, the operations of destroyers attacking from a commanding position in the van would be much facilitated; it would be suicidal to place the Battle Fleet in a position where it might be open to attack by destoyers during such a deployment. The further points that occurred to me were, that if the German ships were as close as seemed probable, there was considerable danger of the 1st Battle Squadron, and especially the *Marlborough's* Division, being severely handled by the concentrated fire of the High Sea Fleet before the remaining divisions could be got into line to assist ... The final disadvantage would be that it appeared, from the supposed position of the High Sea Fleet, that the van of the enemy would have a very considerable 'overlap' if line were formed on the starboard wing division.[28]

In addition to these powerful considerations, a deployment on the port wing would enable Jellicoe to cross Scheer's 'T', while visibility was clearer to the southward.

The case against Jellicoe was led by Winston Churchill who, Marder thought, must have got hold of the Admiralty's *Naval Staff Appreciation* and used this in his description of the battle. Essentially, the complaint is that Jellicoe's decision delayed the coming into action of his battle fleet when only two or three hours of daylight remained; 'it increased the range of the enemy by at least 4,000 yards at a time when every 1,000 yards was of value, and every ten minutes of daylight was beginning to weigh in the scale of victory.'[29] And, it was suggested, the threat from the German destroyers was exaggerated. Among Jellicoe's admirals, Sturdee thought the deployment should have been to starboard, suggesting that Burney, on getting the order to deploy to port, should have disobeyed and gone the other way; if he had been in that position, Sturdee said, he would have been sorely tempted to do so.

Commander Frost is one of those who is critical of Jellicoe's decision, reckoning that the British paid dearly for not bringing their battle line, with its overwhelming strength, move quickly into action against the High Seas Fleet:

> This deployment had two important disadvantages. Although it was important to take the High Seas Fleet by surprise, the bulk of the Grand Fleet would for a considerable time be steaming away from, rather than towards, the enemy. Also, for a long time the 1st and 2nd Battle Cruiser Squadrons would be directly in the line of fire of the British battleships and their smoke would greatly interfere with the fire of the latter ships.[30]

Captain Bennett, on the other hand, rejects this argument, pointing out another advantage of the port wing deployment:

> Despite the difficult circumstances, Jellicoe's clear brain had made a decision which brought his fleet into line ahead by 6.20 pm, albeit with a bend of some 110 degrees in it,

> but *concave* to the enemy so that all ships could bring their guns to bear over a wide arc. He has, however, been criticised on the score that it led to an artillery duel at too great a range. In fact, it was soon inside 10,000 yards; moreover, the alternative of deployment on the starboard wing would have produced a bend *convex* to the enemy (unless Jellioe had sacrificed the advantage of the easterly position) masking the fire of many British ships for some 20 vital minutes.[31]

Among the most powerful supporters of Jellicoe's decision was the German Official History, which rejected the suggestion that a starboard wing deployment would have been advantageous:

> One must agree with the British leader that, had he acted in this way, he would in fact have led his ships into a position which would have been only too welcome to the German Fleet. The second possibility would have been for him to have led out into single line with his flagship from the centre columns, a manoeuvre which was certainly possible … but which was too complicated to be employed when already in contact with the enemy.[32]

The notion of a deployment on a centre column was particularly urged by Winston Churchill; but the German Official History, and Professor Marder, are undoubtedly right in concluding that it was out of the question at that time. It was a manoeuvre that had not been practised in the Grand Fleet, and must necessarily have led to great confusion.

Marder, after reviewing many of the arguments put forward for and against, came down firmly in agreement with Jellicoe and his supporters, concluding that 'it is difficult to conceive a method of deployment that offered greater strategical and tactical advantages than Jellicoe's.'[33] And Admiral Harper put it this way: 'What, however, is the use of conjecture as to the relative advantages of other means of deployment when we must admit that the manoeuvre, as ordered, was understood by the whole fleet; that it enabled our fleet to cross the enemy's "T", and placed our main force between the enemy and his base? A deployment which achieved these results is beyond adverse criticism.' Given what Jellicoe actually knew at the critical moment, and taking into account that he must at all times err on the side of caution, the decision he took was the correct one. But there was much fighting to be done, and it is surely overstating the case to suggest, as a recent historian of the battle has done, that 'it would be the decisive moment of the First World War.'[34]

15

The Fleets Engage

While Jellicoe was pondering his decision as to the deployment of his battle fleet, an unexpected drama was developing in advance of his battleships. The 1st Cruiser Squadron, led by Rear Admiral Sir Robert Arbuthnot, in *Defence*, had been in position ahead of the battle fleet when at 5.47 he caught sight of Boedicker's light cruisers. *Defence* and *Warrior* opened fire, but their shots fell short. Arbuthnot's blood was up; as Boedicker disappeared into the mist, he turned to starboard in pursuit, steaming recklessly across the bows of *Lion*; his immediate objective was the badly damaged *Wiesbaden*. Aboard the flagship, Chatfield was obliged to take avoiding action:

> It was clear that unless I altered course dramatically I should collide with one of his ships, so I jammed the *Lion's* helm hard over and swung her under the stern of their second cruiser, which only cleared us by a cable's length. By forcing the Battle Cruiser Squadron off its course in the low visibility, which was then only five miles, Arbuthnot caused us to lose sight of the enemy fleet and he himself took the place of the battlecruisers as their target.[1]

Marder suggested that Arbuthnot's move 'was inspired by a high and proper conception of his primary duty before battle was joined, namely, reconnaissance, and particularly in the existing circumstances, with Beatty engaged with the German advanced forces.'[2]

Watching Arbuthnot's manoeuvre, Chatfield recalled a conversation he had had with him earlier in the year. They had been discussing the way in which Arbuthnot should take up his station after the deployment of the battle fleet. Arbuthnot had already made up his mind about this:

> He could, he said, either do this by passing down the disengaged side of the Battle Fleet, which would, he felt, be a dull performance, or he could pass down on the engaged side between the two opposing Fleets. I said I thought he should go down the disengaged side. If he went between the Fleets he might find himself in a highly dangerous position, but what was even more, his smoke might well interfere with the fire of our Battle Fleet at a critical time. He was included to pooh-pooh both these objections, and I realised he was determined to go down between the two Fleets, which he said would only take a few minutes.[3]

Oddly, as Andrew Gordon points out, Arbuthnot's station was not on the far side of the Grand Fleet, but in the rear of the starboard wing, since the deployment had in fact been on the opposite wing, which makes his manoeuvre even more surprising.

Within minutes, Chatfield's warning of the danger into which Arbuthnot would be going was grimly justified. The 1st Cruiser Squadron was immediately exposed to heavy fire. Hase, in *Derfflinger*, recognised *Defence* as a British armoured cruiser, and authorised the secondary armament to open fire. Before the order could be given, he saw *Defence* struck by heavy shells, which came from Behncke's leading battleships:

> Something terrific happened: the English ship, which I had meanwhile identified as an old English armoured cruiser, broke in half with a tremendous explosion. Black smoke and debris shot into the air, a flame enveloped the whole ship, and then she sank before our eyes. There was nothing but a gigantic smoke cloud to mark the place where just before a proud ship had been fighting.[4]

The spectacle was observed from the British battleships. An officer in the foretop of *Neptune*, some way to the rear of the battle line, described what he saw:

> A few minutes after we opened fire, the *Defence* and *Warrior* appeared on our engaged side steering on an opposite course. The ships were practically continuously hidden by splashes, they were being repeatedly hit by heavy shell, and must have been going through hell on earth. The *Defence*, which was leading, was just about abeam of the *Neptune*, and barely a mile away, when she was hit heavily and blew up in one fearful cloud of smoke and debris. The foretop fell with a sickening splash into the water, and then the *Warrior*, herself damaged, listing to starboard and in places on fire, raced over the spot where the *Defence* had been, through the smoke cloud of her flagship's explosion.[5]

Credit for the destruction of *Defence* is usually assigned to *Lützow*; that was certainly Hase's opinion, although it was also variously claimed by *Markgraf*, *Kaiser* and *Kronprinz*, all of which were in action against Arbuthnot's squadron, as was *Grosser Kurfürst*, which observed two of her salvoes hitting *Defence*. At all events, *Defence* sank instantly, taking with her the entire crew of 903 men. *Warrior*, meanwhile, had been hit at least 15 times, and had suffered over 100 casualties; she was on fire and listing to starboard, and escaped destruction only because *Warspite* unexpectedly steamed between *Warrior* and Scheer's battleships.

This arose because Evan Thomas, leading the 5th Battle Squadron in *Barham*, had when first sighting *Marlborough* soon after 6.00 supposed her to be leading the battlefleet which had already deployed. His first instinct was to endeavour to take station ahead of her, and thus himself lead the battle line. Realising his mistake, however, he did not attempt to get across to the head of the battlefleet, and at 6.18 made a wide turn to port to enable him to follow *Marlborough's* division. To do so, he must then turn to starboard; as *Warspite* endeavoured to conform to this movement, and narrowly escaped colliding with both *Valiant* and *Malaya*, her steering jammed and she began turning in a circle around the crippled *Warrior*.

The point at which Evan Thomas turned to starboard to take up his position became known as 'Windy Corner', as scores of ships attempted to get into their proper battle stations under a heavy fire from the enemy. Captain Philpotts of *Warspite*, finding himself facing the enemy

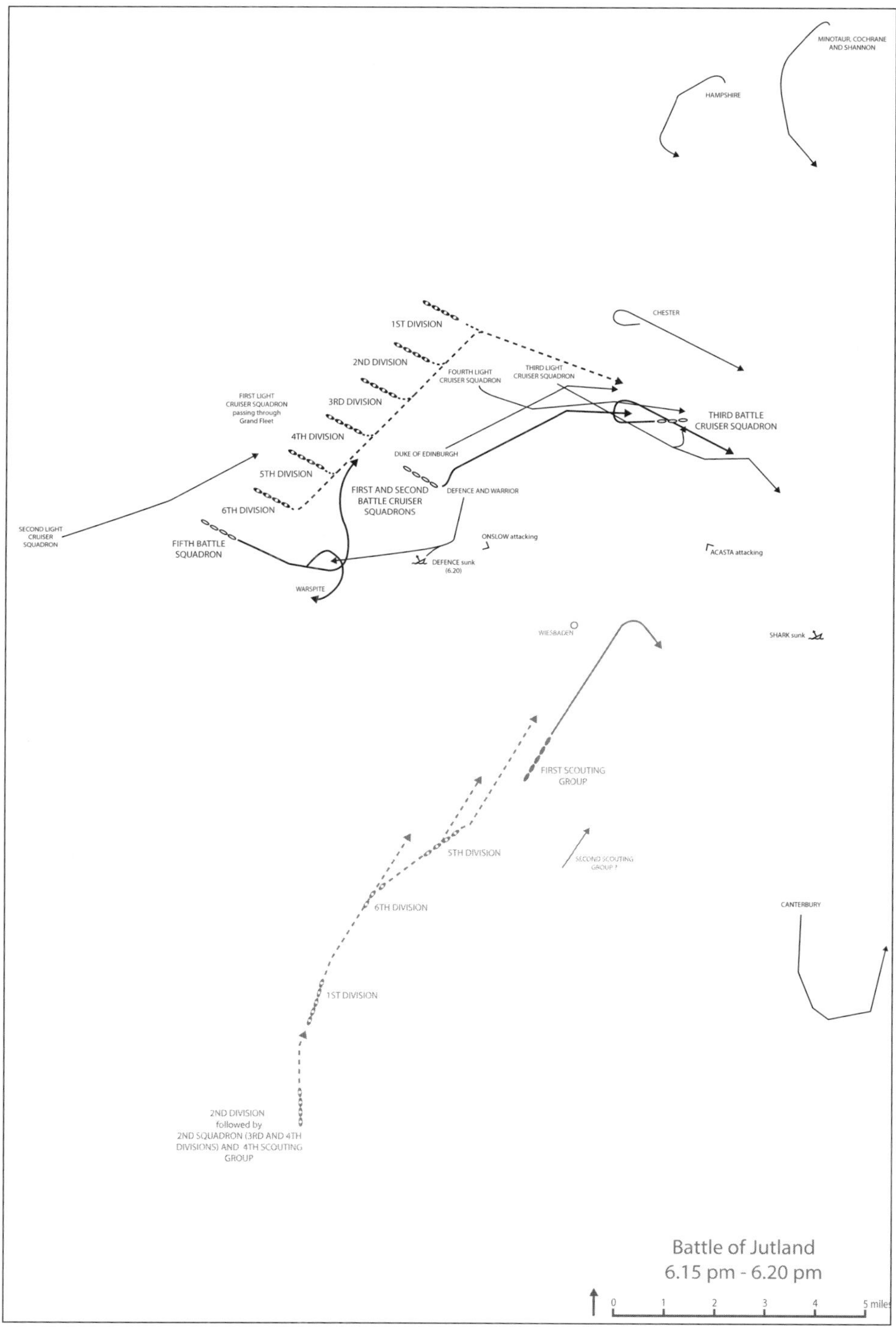

Map 11 Battle of Jutland: 6.15 pm to 6.20 pm.

fleet, decided it was safer to continue his turn; efforts to rectify the steering problem were for the moment unsuccessful, and *Warspite* set off again towards the High Seas Fleet, whose battleships hammered her mercilessly, hitting her a dozen times. Commodore Goodenough, following the 5th Battle Squadron with his light cruisers, found the *Warspite's* manoeuvres an inspiring sight:

> Heavily hit, her steering gear disabled, she turned a complete circle. 'There goes your old friend Captain Philpotts,' said my commander. But it was not so. The proper repairs were made, and, like a dog coming out of the water after a sudden immersion, she shook herself, her course straightened, her guns directed again towards the enemy, and she resumed her position in the line – her speed lessened, her action resolute.[6]

Although the unarmoured parts of the ship were wrecked, she had sustained only 33 casualties from the 13 hits she sustained during the action. So heavily had his battleships been concentrating on *Warspite* that Scheer, for one, was convinced that she had been sunk.

Meanwhile *Warrior*, seriously damaged and with her engine rooms flooded, endeavoured to make her way back to Cromarty. Barely able to keep under way, and having encountered the seaplane carrier *Engadine*, Captain Molteno ordered the latter to take the crippled cruiser in tow. For about 100 miles the two ships made their painful way across the North Sea, but by 7.00am next day, about 160 miles east of Aberdeen, it was clear that her bulkheads were giving way, and *Engadine* came alongside and took off her crew. When *Warrior's* commander reported that all the crew were on board *Engadine*, he and the captain jumped aboard. Molteno described the last he saw of his ship:

> *Engadine* went astern to clear the sinking ship. As we left the old *Warrior* we gave her three hearty cheers. Every big sea washed over her decks, and water poured down through the huge rents in the upper deck on to the main deck. As all the steam pumps and all but two of the hand pumps had been destroyed by enemy shells, we had no means of coping with the volume of water pouring into the ship, and the upper deck was now only about 2 to 4 feet above water. The whole main deck was flooded, and the ship was very much down by the stern.[7]

While Arbuthnot had been making his disastrous move, Hood's three battlecruisers had joined Beatty, after a series of fortunate escapes from the torpedo attacks that were made on the squadron. At about 6.17, sighting *Lion*, Hood countermarched his squadron and took up his station 3000 yards ahead on a south easterly course. The concentrated fire of the seven battlecruisers, supported by the fire of the battleships as they completed their deployment, brought not only Hipper's battered ships under intolerable pressure but also the leading ships of Behncke's squadron. The latter was injured when a heavy shell hit *König*'s conning tower, glanced off and exploded 50 yards beyond the ship:

> Suddenly, the German van was faced by the belching guns of an interminable line of heavy ships extending from north west to north east, while salvo followed salvo almost without intermission, an impression which gained in power from the almost complete inability of the German ships to reply to this fire, as not one of the British dreadnoughts could be made out through the smoke and fumes. The *Lützow* and the *König* came under particularly

heavy fire. Frequently it seemed as if several opponents had concentrated their guns on the two German ships. From 6.26 onwards the *Lützow* received hit after hit in the forepart of the ship, and from 6.32 onwards the *König* was also struck repeatedly.[8]

Michelsen, the commander of the German destroyer flotillas, ordered Hollmann, the commander of the III Flotilla, to launch an attack on the enemy lines, indicating that he was to proceed ahead on the port bow. Hollmann led his flotilla through the line of the battlecruisers, ordering his ships each to fire three torpedoes. As he emerged through the smoke, Hollmann sighted British battleships at a range of 7000 yards but then, incomprehensibly, Michelsen ordered him to break off the action. Three destroyers each got off a torpedo, none of which hit, although they nearly reached the leading battleships of the Grand Fleet.[9]

There now occurred another of the spectacular and tragic incidents of the battle. Since 6.23 Hood's squadron had been engaging Hipper's battlecruisers, and doing so to considerable effect, hitting *Lützow* and *Derfflinger* several times. Hood, on the forebridge of *Invincible*, called out to Commander Hubert Dannreuther, his Gunnery Officer in the fire control station, through a voice pipe: 'Your fire is very good. Keep at it as quickly as you can. Every shot is telling.'[10] They were the last words Hood is known to have spoken. His flagship was under heavy fire, at least from *Lützow* and *Derfflinger*, and from one of Behncke's battleships. Hase described the scene as *Invincible* came into his view:

At this moment the veil of mist in front of us split across like the curtain at a theatre. Clear and sharply silhouetted against the uncovered part of the horizon we saw a powerful battleship with two funnels between the masts and a third close against the tripod mast. She was steering an almost parallel course with ours at top speed. Her guns were trained on us and immediately another crashed out, straddling us completely. 'Range 9000!' roared leading Seaman Hänel. '9000 – Salvoes fire!' I ordered. 'Over. Two hits!' called out Lieutenant Commander von Stosch. I gave the order: '100 down. Good, Rapid!' and thirty seconds after the first salvo the second left the gun. I observed two short splashes and two hits. Lieutenant Commander von Stosch called: 'Hits!' Every twenty seconds came the roar of another salvo at this ship. At 6.31 the *Derfflinger* fired her last salvo at this ship and then for the third time we witnessed the dreadful spectacle that we had already seen in the case of the *Queen Mary* and the *Defence*. As with the other ships there occurred a rapid succession of heavy explosions, masts collapsed, debris was hurled into the air, a gigantic column of black smoke rose towards the sky, and from the parting sections of the ship, coal dust spurted in all directions. Flames enveloped the ship, fresh explosions followed, and behind this murky cloud our enemy vanished from our sight.[11]

Whether *Derfflinger* deserved the credit for the destruction of *Invincible* is a matter of some doubt; the German Official History credits *Lützow* with striking the decisive blow with her third salvo. The fatal shell hit *Invincible's* 'Q' turret, and she blew up at 6.32, taking with her 1,026 of her crew; there were only six survivors, one of them being Commander Dannreuther. Ordered by Beatty to pick up survivors, the destroyer *Badger* went to the scene of *Invincible's* sinking supposing the wreck to be a German vessel; her First Lieutenant posted an armed guard. In his surprise at finding British survivors he forgot to dismiss the guard, and was astonished at Dannreuther's calmness:

> The Commander was marvellously self possessed. I can hardly understand to this day how a man, after going through what he had, could come on board us from the raft as cheerily as if he was simply joining a new ship in the ordinary course of events. He laughed at the armed guard, and assured us he hadn't a scratch on his whole body, and that he had merely – as he put it – stepped into the water when the foretop came down.[12]

As other British ships came by the wreck of *Invincible*, with the bow and stern sections still sticking out of the sea, it was commonly thought at first to be the wreck of a German ship, and the crews cheered heartily until close enough to read her name.[13]

Throughout these events *Wiesbaden*, lying dead in the water between the two fleets, had continued to fire on the enemy with the few guns that she had until none remained, her flag still flying, and in her turn was attacked first by *Defence* and *Warrior*, then by *Falmouth*, then the British battle squadrons as they passed by. The Gunnery Officer of *Iron Duke* recalled the plight of the hapless *Wiesbaden*:

> Nobody dared to open fire before the *Iron Duke*. They all had a sort of sympathetic feeling that it was bad luck going on hammering a poor sinking ship. However, I asked Captain Dreyer if I might have permission to open fire. He said he would ask the Commander-in-Chief and after a bit of an argument the Commander-in-Chief gave permission. We then opened fire which I was very glad to do just to clear the bores, and the whole of the remainder of the Grand Fleet, as the *Wiesbaden* passed, opening fire too, and gave her an awful hammering. I think she fired a torpedo before she sank.[14]

By 6.30, however, the British battleships had more significant targets at which to aim, as Scheer's battle squadrons came into view.

The discovery that he was in the presence of the entire Grand Fleet no doubt came as a fearful shock to the German admiral, who until now had been the huntsman pursuing his prey. Andrew Gordon has written that if the story of Jutland had been a work of fiction, one of the improbable aspects of the plot would be the way in which Scheer had continued the pursuit of Beatty without divining that he was being lured into an extremely dangerous trap.[15] The principal reason for pursuing what might be a detached British force was the possibility that damaged ships under Beatty's command would fall behind to fall an easy prey to the pursuing Germans. This risk, that damaged ships were always vulnerable during any retreat, was ever present in the minds of the leaders on both sides. The Navigating Officer of *New Zealand*, describing the run to the north, expressed the fear that damage which was not in itself fatal could become so if the enemy caught up with a vessel that was obliged to fall behind:

> Could we keep them following us long enough, and could we avoid being hit? We had always to think that a ship damaged enough to lose only a few knots speed would be as good as lost, for she would drop behind into the open arms of the whole German Battle Fleet … the position of the *New Zealand*, now the rear of the four surviving battle cruisers, was not a very pleasant one. We felt any small hit in the engine-room would cause us at once to drop astern and we should lose the ship.[16]

Scheer, lacking the airship reconnaissance which would have told him of his danger, was left only with the consideration of how long to continue this pursuit. In his own memoirs he offered an account of his thinking at this time; it is difficult not to conclude that this was considerably informed by hindsight:

> While this encounter with the advance guard of the English Main Fleet was taking place, we, on our flagship were occupied debating how much longer to continue the pursuit in view of the advanced time. There was no longer any question of a cruiser campaign against merchantmen in the Skagerrak, as the meeting with the English fighting forces which was to result from such action had already taken place. But we were bound to take into consideration that the English Fleet, if at sea, which was obvious from the ships which we had encountered, would offer battle the next day. Some steps would also have to be taken to shake off the English light forces before darkness fell in order to avoid any loss to our Main Fleet from nocturnal torpedo-boat attacks.[17]

Scheer does not in this passage indicate at what point the actual presence of the Grand Fleet became obvious. Certainly a fight to a finish with the entire Grand Fleet was not, and never could have been, part of Scheer's plan; if he stood toe to toe with Jellicoe and slugged it out, there could only be one outcome.

Once, therefore, it was apparent that Jellicoe was among those present, Scheer's problem was to extricate his fleet with minimal losses. With the British battle line curving round the head of his own line, he had to act, and to act fast. The German Official History set out the situation in which Scheer found himself, and addressed to some extent the question posed by Andrew Gordon referred to above:

> The explosion which destroyed the *Invincible* brought to a close a phase of the daylight action during which the British, in spite of the intervention of the battle fleet, again suffered heavier losses than the Germans. But, favoured by the unexpected appearance of the *Invincible* on the disengaged German flanks and by a quite exceptional deterioration in visibility for the German ships, they had, by the end of this phase, reached an exceedingly advantageous tactical position. This was due in some measure to an endeavour of the German line to keep hold of the enemy at all costs, once contact had been established, a very natural and explicable tendency after so long a period of waiting. If the German leaders and subordinate commanders had not been so greatly swayed by a desire to press on, the presumption that there were strong enemy forces to the northward would probably have caused the Fleet Command to chase the British battle cruisers with less vigour.[18]

Scheer would also have concentrated his squadron to a greater extent, so that 'the van of the German line would then probably not have run into the bowshaped concentration of the British battlefleet.' Groos, in the Official History, went on to refer to the debate aboard *Friedrich der Grosse* as to how long to pursue the chase of Beatty's ships, describing it in much the same terms as did Scheer. When, the discussion not having reached a conclusion, the leading ships of the British battle fleet were encountered, Groos suggested that 'Admiral Scheer then determined to throw in all his forces and to fight out the impending action on the course he was then steering.'[19]

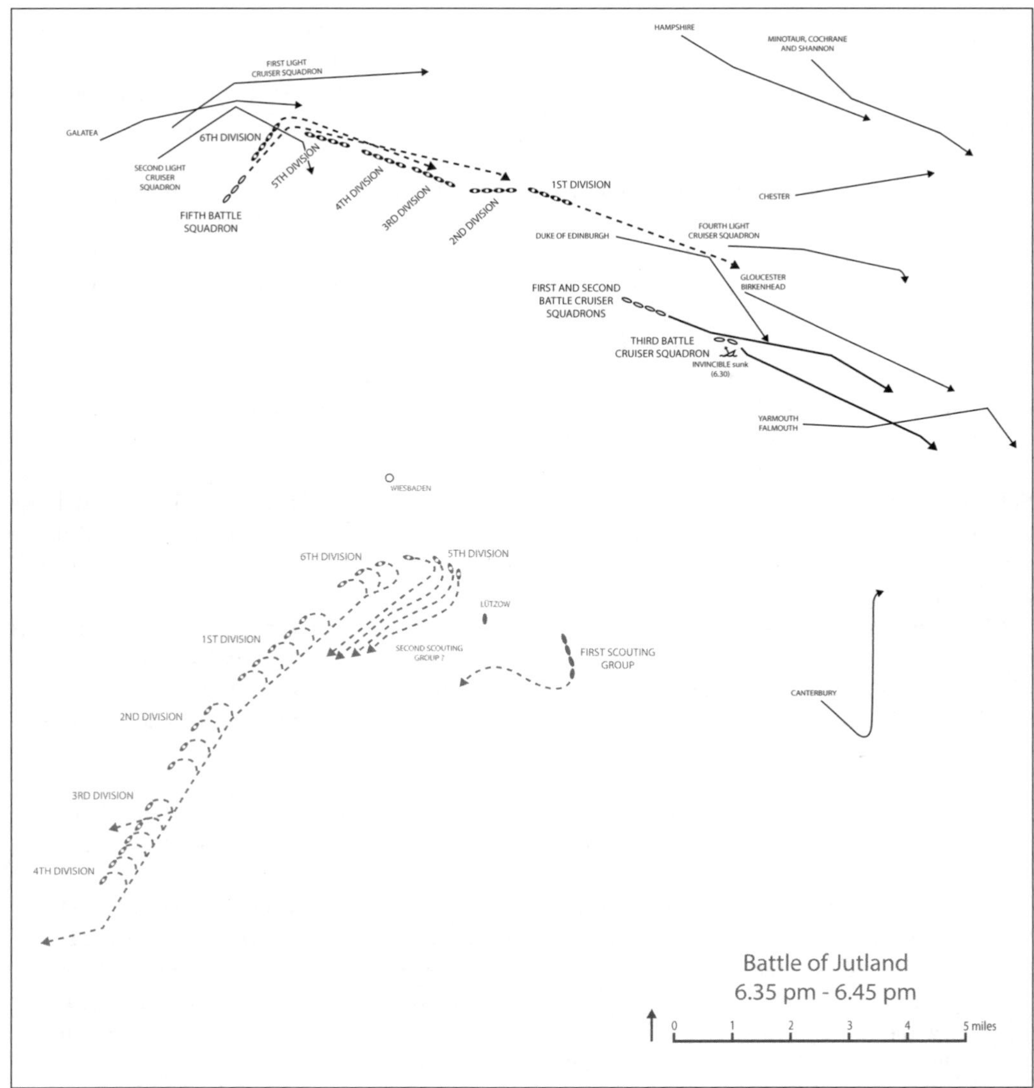

Map 12 Battle of Jutland: 6.35 pm to 6.45 pm.

If this had really been his intention, it did not long survive the first encounter with Jellicoe. It was at about this time that, unexpectedly, Scheer received news that confirmed the thought that the whole Grand Fleet might be in front of him. A radio message from V Flotilla stated that according to prisoners rescued from the destroyer *Nomad* 'there were 60 large enemy vessels in the vicinity, including 20 new battleships and six battlecruisers.' If Scheer kept on his easterly course, the situation would develop very unfavourably, to put it at its lowest, with Jellicoe's fleet curving around him, and with visibility deteriorating for the Germans, while against the setting sun the Germans stood out more clearly.

Scheer did not hesitate. At 6.33 *Friedrich der Grosse* made the following signal: 'Turn together 16 points to starboard and form single line ahead in the opposite direction.' This manoeuvre, known as the *Gefechts kehrtwendung* (battle about turn) had never been attempted under fire, but Scheer was sure that it could be done:

> The exceptional tactical training of the German fleet, the ground work of which had been laid by Admiral of the Fleet von Koester, made Admiral Scheer feel confident that, in spite of the bend in the line and the enemy's tremendous counter-activity, it would be possible to carry out the movements without serious difficulty, even under the heaviest of hostile fire, and his subordinate leaders and Captains fully justified the reliance he reported in them.[20]

In the German Official History Groos is at pains to explain that, contrary to the suggestion by Corbett and Jellicoe that this was 'a premeditated and frequently practised manoeuvre which the German fleet proposed to employ whenever the British battle fleet was encountered' in order to get away as quickly as possible from a superior force, it was only '*one* of the many tactical movements practised for the various eventualities of an action.' Scheer, says Groos, was not trying to break off the action as quickly as he could, but used the manoeuvre 'on sudden inspiration' intending to renew the action in more favourable circumstances.[21]

In a letter to Commander Frost, Scheer commented on the decision to carry out the battle turn away:

> While the battle is progressing, a leader cannot obtain a really clear picture especially at long ranges. He acts and feels according to his impressions. In looking at the diagrams that are made subsequently, it would seem as if we must have regarded our position as critical. In reality this was not the case. We were under the impression of the splendid effectiveness of our gunfire and of the fact that the entire battle line remained most conveniently arranged both while under fire and during the regrouping for the night march.[22]

Frost was persuaded by this, observing that except for the visibility the position of the High Seas Fleet was not particularly unfavourable, although Scheer's idea of the disposition of the Grand Fleet was incorrect, putting it to the east rather than the north, and necessitating a temporary disengagement.

Jellicoe made it clear in his own account that a retiring movement on the part of the High Seas Fleet had always been expected:

> The probable tactics of the German Fleet had been a matter of almost daily consideration, and all our experience and thought led to the same conclusion, namely that retiring tactics, combined with destroyer attacks, would be adopted by them... The difficulties resulting from the employment of these retiring tactics and the best method to adopt in the circumstances were, therefore the subject of constant thought, both by myself and by all the senior officers in the fleet, and the problem was very frequently discussed as well as being worked out on the tactical board. The difficulty is, to a certain extent, insuperable if retiring tactics are employed in conjunction with a free and skilful use of under-water weapons.[23]

The standing instructions for the *Gefechtskehrtwendung* provided for the turn to be begun by the rearmost squadron, in this case Mauve's II Battle Squadron, but since this had fallen behind and was still steering a northerly course Captain Redlich, in *Westfalen*, correctly assumed that Mauve's ships should be disregarded, and commenced the turn as the first ship; when at 6.39 Scheer signalled 'course west', *Westfalen* took over as leader of the line. Mauve now found himself on the disengaged site of Schmidt's I Battle Squadron; by altering course and speed he endeavoured to put his squadron ahead of Schmidt's squadron. The turn brought to an end the cannonade under which *Warspite* had been suffering so badly; as she faded into the mist, she seemed to be steering west, and Schmidt reached the incorrect conclusion that the whole of Jellicoe's line had turned about to follow the High Seas Fleet.[24]

By 6.45 this manoeuvre, described by Groos as 'difficult and dangerous' had been safely completed, a performance which reflected great credit on Scheer's battleship captains. Marder put it this way: 'Scheer's skill and resoluteness had extricated his fleet from a near catastrophe, though there was nothing skilful in getting into the mess in the first place.'[25] Dreyer, in *Iron Duke's* conning tower, had seen *König* turn away, but did not realise that Jellicoe, up on the manoeuvring platform, might not have done so.[26] In fact, the Commander-in-Chief had not, as he explained in his comments on the Admiralty Narrative:

> I imagined this disappearance of the enemy to be due merely to the thickening of the mist, but after a few minutes had elapsed it became clear that there must be some other reason and at 6.44 I hauled up one point to south-east and at 6.55 four more points to south, signalling at the same time to Sir Cecil Burney to ask if he could see any of the enemy's battleships, and received a reply in the negative.[27]

Jellicoe was now faced with a difficult problem, which was not that contemplated by his long held intention not to be drawn into a submarine trap or prepared minefield by a retiring enemy. In the way that the battle had developed, Scheer could not have been able to prepare such a trap for him, so he must necessarily get after the High Seas Fleet as quickly as he could. What he did not know was the course that the enemy had taken, which made it extremely difficult to decide what to do. Once again Jellicoe was let down by his cruisers. Napier, in *Falmouth*, was at 6.35 only about 11,000 yards north-east of the German battlecruisers, and he saw them turn to the west; he did not, however, make any report of this. Jellicoe had a number of possible options. A turn by divisions would expose the Grand Fleet to the risk of attack by long range torpedoes from the enemy battleships. A turn in succession would take the fleet directly into the waters now occupied by the enemy battleships, which Jellicoe, wrongly, thought carried mines which they could lay as they retired. Another alternative was to turn to the westward and then maintain the fleet's position to the north of the enemy, but this would not reduce the torpedo threat; and in the prevailing conditions to divide the fleet would be risky in the extreme:

> Nothing then remained for Admiral Jellicoe, since he could not tell in what direction the enemy had retired, but to place himself as soon as possible athwart their line of retreat to the Bight, for along that line, sooner or later, they were almost certain to be discovered. His ships were so disposed as to be able instantly to form line of battle on a course parallel to that line, and in order to maintain them in this disposition, Admiral Jellicoe now turned

> by divisions to south east (6.44) as the best means of attaining the required position, so far as he could divine the situation.[28]

It was a decision entirely consistent with the cautious approach which Jellicoe had followed throughout the battle, but it would be Scheer whose next decision answered the questions in Jellicoe's mind. Meanwhile, however, Hipper had been in considerable difficulty. When Scheer's battle squadrons made their 16 point turn, *Von der Tann* turned to port through east to north, in order to follow *König;* on the other hand, *Moltke, Seydlitz* and *Derfflinger* turned to the west with port helm with the same intention. *Lützow,* however, was by now in serious trouble; her speed heavily reduced, she steamed to the south west away from the enemy's fire which had been concentrated on her. *Derfflinger* had to stop engines for two minutes to secure torpedo netting which threatened to become entangled with the propellors, while *Seydlitz's* steering had been damaged. *Lützow's* plight meant that for the moment Hipper was obliged to order Captain Hartog in *Derfflinger* to take over leadership of the squadron, although he was hampered by the fact that his signal halliards had been shot away and his searchlights were for the moment unusable. Hartog wrote later:

> When the lead was transferred to SMS *Derfflinger* the ship had already suffered so heavily from the enemy's fire that only her wireless reception was clear. I had no means of signalling available to convey to the other armoured cruisers my order: 'Follow the leader; fire distribution from the right.' I therefore led the battlecruisers following me (without any signal to that effect) in starboard echelon on a northerly course at the head of our battle fleet towards the enemy.[29]

Michelsen, by now aware of the opportunity he had missed by recalling his destroyers, at 6.50 despatched the 1st Half Flotilla to *Lützow;* this arrived simultaneously with *G37* and *V45. G39* went alongside the stricken battle cruiser and took off Hipper and his staff, in order to take them to another battle cruiser. Raeder described the scene:

> The *G39,* under Lieutenant von Loefen, manoeuvred into position perfectly, despite the heavy enemy fire and the violent rolling. As fresh and cool as if he were merely leaving his breakfast table, Admiral Hipper climbed from the quarterdeck of the battle cruiser to the forecastle of the torpedo boat, and quietly gave the order to follow the Battle Cruiser Group, who were already speeding to the west to retain position with the main body ... Just as we were transferring to the *G39,* another shell hit on the *Lützow* blasted into a turret, and set off the powder in high leaping flames.[30]

Meanwhile there had been a story of magnificent heroism to match that of *Shark* and Commander Jones. As that destroyer, crippled by the damage she had sustained, had fought on with only one 4 inch gun remaining, she found a target among the German destroyers returning from their abortive attack on Hood's squadron. Jones, controlling the gun in person, was able to land a 4 inch shell in the engine room of *V48,* reducing her speed to a crawl. This was about 6.40; *Shark* had little time left to celebrate her success, being torpedoed by *S54* at a range of 4000 yards about five minutes later, sinking at about 7.00 pm. Soon after being hit, *V48* came under heavy fire from the British battle line:

> The *G42* turned back to her assistance, but had to retire again under the devastating barrage. Seeing that his battle line was suffering severely, the Captain of the destroyer, Lieutenant Commander von Arnim, laid a smoke screen that covered Battle Squadron III from the British fire. It was a splendid display of real initiative. It shows that even a little destroyer may play an important part in a fleet action.[31]

V48, although now lying crippled and barely able to move, also fought on in much the same spirit as *Shark,* firing two torpedoes at the British battle line, causing *Duke of Edinburgh* to manoeuvre to avoid one of them. Another may have hit *Marlborough* although, as we shall see, this may have been fired by *Wiesbaden*. At all events, *V48* had added to the lustre of the German navy; sadly, when she was sunk a little later, after firing her last torpedo which narrowly missed *Agincourt,* she went down with her captain, Lieutenant Commander Eckoldt and all his crew.

Wiesbaden's story was even more remarkable. As she lay, crippled, between the fleets, she sustained hit after hit from the British battleships; after Scheer's 16 point turn she was the only target visible to them, and they continued to pound her. It is noteworthy, however, that although *Wiesbaden* came under such heavy fire over such an extended period, it appears that she sustained a total of only about a dozen hits from Jellicoe's battleships between 6.20 and 6.45.[32] At 6.57 *Marlborough* reported that she had been badly damaged by a torpedo; it was unclear at first whether it was a mine or a torpedo, but almost at once it was confirmed as a torpedo hit. Whether it was *Wiesbaden* who fired it is unclear; at all events it brought upon the stricken cruiser the concentrated fire of practically the whole of Burney's 1st Battle Squadron. The third and fourth salvoes from *Marlborough* seemed to split her open, bringing down her funnels. Captain Reiss had fought her to the bitter end, and even now she did not sink at once; she was certainly still afloat at 2.00 am, when she was seen by *Acasta.* The few survivors finally took to rafts, but in the rough and icy waters they all died save one, Chief Stoker Zenne, who was rescued by the steamer *Willi* after having been in the water for 38 hours.

It was obvious to Scheer, when his 16 point turn set him on a westerly course, that he could not maintain this direction for long, and he now had another serious and difficult decision to make. This, too, has been the subject of considerable historical controversy in which hindsight and a certain amount of bias have played a considerable part. Perhaps the first evidence to be considered is that of Scheer himself in his memoirs:

> It was still too early for a nocturnal move. If the enemy followed us our action in retaining the direction taken after turning the line would partake of the nature of a retreat, and in the event of any damage to our ships in the rear the fleet would be compelled to sacrifice them or else to decide on a line of action enforced by enemy pressure, and not adopted voluntarily, and would therefore be detrimental to us from the very outset. Still less was it feasible to strive at detaching oneself from the enemy, leaving it to him to decide when he would elect to meet us the next morning. There was but one way of averting this – to force the enemy into a second battle by another determined advance and forcibly compel his torpedo boats to attack. The success of the turning of the line while fighting encouraged me to make the attempt, and decided me to make still further use of the facility of movement. The manoeuvre would be bound to surprise the enemy, to upset his plans for the rest of the day, and if the blow fell heavily it would facilitate the breaking loose at night. The fight of

> the *Wiesbaden* helped also strengthen my resolve to make an effort to render assistance to her and at least save the crew.[33]

Corbett was particularly scathing about Scheer's explanation of his intentions:

> It may well be that he justly gauged the appetite and ignorance of the German public in naval matters, but it cannot be reconciled with his high reputation as a tactician, or even with sanity. In the relative dispositions of the two fleets as he judged them to be, to thrust at the enemy's centre in line ahead was deliberately to expose himself to having his 'T' crossed by a superior fleet, and we may well believe, as is told, that subsequently his Chief of Staff remarked that had he attempted such a stroke in maneouvres he would have been promptly ordered to haul down his flag. Fortunately the ascertained facts of this phase of the action indicate clearly enough that his intentions were very different and much wiser.[34]

Marder takes the same view as Corbett of Scheer's motivation, noting Admiral Bacon's comment that if it was intended as a 'formidable thrust at the battleships of the Grand Fleet', it was incomprehensible that he should station his battlecruisers in the van. For Marder, 'it is extremely improbable that Scheer deliberately headed the High Seas Fleet towards the British battle line'. It was, he thought, more probable that his intention was to slip past the rear of the Grand Fleet and make for home.[35]

For Scheer's own unscripted comments on the issue, Weizsäcker's memoirs provide two comments. During the battle, it is recorded, Scheer said to a member of his staff: 'If I am chucked out of the Navy because of this, it's all one to me'. And later, one evening after the battle, there was a discussion with several admirals from Berlin, where the subject came up of what ideas might be attributed to the Commander-in-Chief in the years to come:

> Scheer, who was already in a mellow frame of mind, said: 'My idea? I had no idea. I wanted to help the poor *Wiesbaden*. And then I thought I had better throw in the cruisers in full strength. The thing just happened – as the virgin said when she got a baby'. To which Holtzendorff replied: 'But you must admit, Scheer, that one has to give the virgin some of the credit for what happened.'[36]

Gordon thought that Scheer's reasoning might 'never be convincingly explained', regarding the suggestion that he wanted to rescue the crew of *Wiesbaden* as ludicrous. He was inclined to adopt Marder's explanation; as an alternative, he cheerfully (and very improbably) suggested that Scheer's brain had entered into a state of denial of the way events had turned against him.[37]

An extended review of all the many opinions that have been expressed on the question would scarcely be productive, not least because 'in the avalanche of scholarship on Scheer's performance', practically all British historians have rejected Scheer's explanation, as Gary Weir has pointed out. Most scholars have, he observed, dismissed the acceptance of this by Otto Groos as 'far too simplistic'.[38]

Commander Frost, who reflected in some depth on Scheer's personality, looked at the spirit in which he conducted the battle:

> Scheer was an unusual man. He was as cool as ice, and just as unperturbed. His reactions were essentially direct and simple. Many writers in trying to attribute to him brilliant and far reaching plans have misjudged Scheer and have deceived themselves. He was the almost exact counterpart of our General Grant. In a letter to the author he makes the following interesting statement: 'While the battle is progressing a leader cannot obtain a really clear picture, especially at long ranges. He acts and feels according to his impressions.'[39]

Turning to the question of Scheer's decision to turn back again to the east, Frost wrote:

> In our opinion, Scheer did well to return to the attack. His reasons for doing so we thoroughly approve, but his manner of carrying his decision into effect could, we suggest, have been improved... It is difficult to say what he should have done, because we do not know exactly what information there was at his disposal. However, he did know that the enemy was generally to the eastward. Therefore, we suggest that he might to advantage have ordered a change of course in succession to about south (167°) or possibly SSE (145°). He could have commenced the movement at 7.00 and his 16 battleships would all have been on the new course by 7.16.[40]

This would have enabled his battleships to fight in line, and his light cruisers to get to the front of that line, while giving his destroyers their best opportunity to attack. The High Seas Fleet would thus be able to fight on a course towards its bases.

Groos, as indicated above, accepted Scheer's explanation. At 6.45 *Moltke* had reported that the van of the British line bore E by S:

> There was another hour before sunset and with the long twilight of these latitudes, it would be some time later before darkness put an end to engagements between squadrons. If under these circumstances he had adhered to the direction taken up after the 16 point turn, and if the enemy had then closed in again, the behaviour of the German fleet would very soon have been bound to assume the character of a retreat, with all the drawbacks associated therein. Quite apart from the fact that, under those circumstances, ships whose speed had been reduced would have fallen into the enemy's hands without more ado, the enemy would have been able, even before darkness set in, to compel the German fleet to accept action, to deprive it of all initiative, and finally to block its line of retreat to the German Bight.[41]

Groos, having thus adopted Scheer's thinking, went on to observe:

> The arguments in favour of this decision were almost the same as those employed by Nelson at Trafalgar. The latter wrote at the time: 'I think it will surprise and confound the enemy. They don't know what I am about'.

This similarity was, however, purely accidental.[42]

What Groos did *not* do was to suggest that Scheer intended to adopt Nelson's style of command. As the text makes clear, and Weir points out, Groos expressly rejected this. Marder, and other British historians, misguidedly reacted with hostility to the reference to Nelson; perhaps they resented the impertinence of a comparison with Britain's greatest admiral.

Iron Duke opening fire at Jutland.

High Seas Fleet.

High Seas Fleet in line ahead.

Westfalen.

High Seas Fleet at sea.

Gefechtskehrtwendung!

German battle cruisers in the North Sea.

Shells falling near *Lion*.

Damage to deck of *Lion*.

Damage to funnel of *Lion*.

Spitfire.

Invincible going into action.

Invincible blowing up.

Invincible blowing up.

Wreck of *Invincible*

Windy Corner at 6.15pm.

Lion hit on 'Q' turret.

Queen Mary blowing up.

Battle Cruiser Fleet sighting the enemy.

Chester after Jutland.

Seydlitz undergoing repairs at Wilhelmshaven.

Seydlitz down by the bow.

Seydlitz returning from Jutland.

König in dock.

Damage to *König's* main deck.

Sinking of *Indefatigable*.

Derfflinger in dock.

Derfflinger's quarterdeck after Jutland.

Seydlitz on fire.

Galatea class light cruisers.

Grand Fleet at sea.

In reviewing all this, it is possible to see that Scheer's principal concern was to regain the initiative. It must be acknowledged that his attempt to do so was bold in the extreme, even if the alternative possibility of getting around the rear of the Grand Fleet may also have occurred to him. At all events, by 6.55 the signal for another 16 point turn to starboard was again flying from *Friedrich der Grosse*; battle was about to be resumed.

16

The Second Engagement

The engagement brought on by Scheer's 6.55 signal for a second *Gefechtskehrtwendung*, this time towards the enemy, lasted only about twenty minutes. By 7.04 Goodenough was able to report: 'Urgent. Priority. Enemy battle fleet steering ESE. Enemy bears from me SSW. Number unknown. My position Lat. 57° 02'N,6° 07' E'.[1] A moment after Goodenough had despatched this message, his squadron was sighted by the High Seas Fleet. Although *Derfflinger* and five battleships at once opened fire on the four light cruisers at ranges between 9,800 and 18,000 yards, deluging them with falling shells, none hit as Goodenough twisted and turned away to the north.[2] At this point Jellicoe ordered his battle fleet to turn by divisions from south to south west by south; but reports from *King George V*, at the head of the line, and *Duke of Edinburgh*, about three and a half miles to port of *Iron Duke,* that U boats had been sighted, led Jellicoe at 7.09 to turn back by divisions to the south. He had also been influenced by the sighting of German destroyers approaching from the south west; these were however from III Flotilla, ordered by Scheer to attempt to rescue the crew of *Wiesbaden*.

These destroyers came under heavy fire from the British battle fleet in response to what was perceived as a torpedo attack, and it was soon clear that their mission was hopeless:

> Had they persevered in their undertaking, they would not only have interfered with the fire of the German line but would very soon have been exposed to the risk of complete destruction, without being able to reach the *Wiesbaden*. As they were still carrying a full complement of torpedoes, these boats were particularly valuable, and *Korvettenkapitän* Hollmann, leading the flotilla, did not feel justified in exposing them to further risks for such a hopeless undertaking. He therefore reluctantly decided to abandon the attempted rescue of the *Wiesbaden's* crew. But while they were turning back towards the German line the *V73* fired one torpedo and the *G88* three torpedoes at a range of 6,600 yards, at what they took to be enemy battle cruisers but which were in fact battleships of the *Colossus's* and *Marlborough's* divisions.[3]

None of these torpedoes found a target, but they caused first *Neptune,* and then the whole of *Benbow's* division to take avoiding action, and Jellicoe, fearing that his rear divisions were in grave danger, at 7.12 ordered them to take station astern of *Iron Duke's* division. The German Official History noted that the appearance of Hollmann's destroyers at the moment when 'the gunnery action recommenced under such splendid conditions for the British Fleet... sufficed

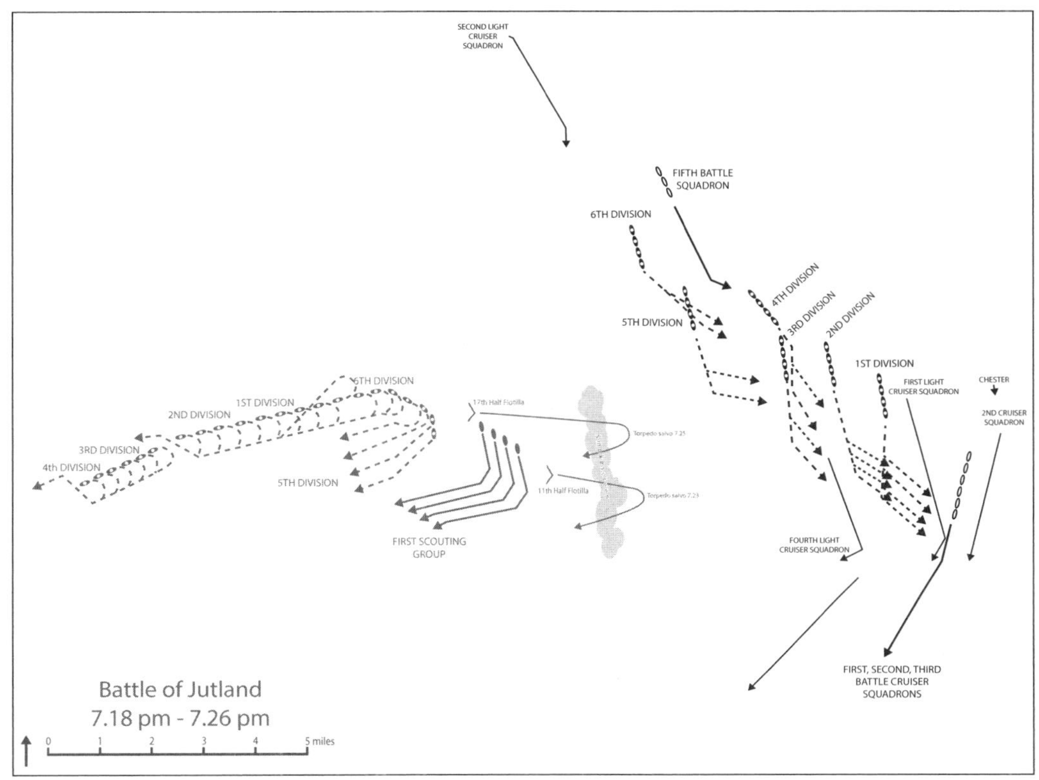

Map 13 Battle of Jutland: 7.18 pm to 7.26 pm.

to make Jellicoe draw back those of his divisions that were most advantageously placed for employing their guns.'[4]

While this was occurring there was a curious incident involving Beatty's battle cruisers, which reduced speed to 18 knots and began to circle to starboard. After the war Beatty was extremely irritated by the suggestion that he had made such a turn, and produced a chart showing a turn to starboard followed by a turn to port. Quite why he was so exercised about the matter baffled Admiral Harper, who considered it a natural manoeuvre to get within visual touch of the battle fleet without making a very large reduction in speed, undesirable if as reported submarines were about.[5] He showed beyond question that *Lion* did in fact make the 360° turn, as Corbett also concluded was the case; and Beatty's subsequent attempt to rewrite history is decidedly odd, although showing, not for the first time, that he was not always an entirely reliable witness as to events concerning him. His biographer suggests that the reason may have been that he 'wished to refute any suggestion that he had at this time turned his back on the enemy, or that he was not pursuing Scheer with the utmost vigour – as he wanted Jellicoe to do.'[6] Marder speculated that the reason for the fuss which Beatty made might have been because he thought a 360° turn would look silly on paper; while Admiral Chalmers, a great admirer of Beatty, wrote to Marder to say that 'none of us could understand why he preferred an "S" to a circle, unless it was sheer obstinacy, or possibly irritation with himself at not knowing that he had done it!'[7]

By 7.04 several British battleships had opened fire on the approaching High Seas Fleet, and more and more came into action in the following minutes. One of the first salvoes straddled *Derfflinger*, and *Lützow* was hit again. The range was rapidly shortening, but it was almost impossible for the Germans to make any effective reply:

> When the British shells commenced falling about the leaders of the German battle line, they could see nothing of their enemies but a continuous ring of flickering gun flashes. No range-finder readings could be taken of the British battleships. It was impossible to find any point of aim. Obviously, no effective reply could be made to the deadly fire of the British at very moderate ranges.[8]

The situation was, as the German Official History observes, 'the most unfavourable during the entire battle.' It looked, wrote Commander Frost, as if Scheer's miscalculation 'would prove to be one of the most colossal errors of all naval history, giving Jellicoe the opportunity for a 'victory of annihilation.' By 7.13 eight British battleships were firing on the German line; within seven minutes they had been joined by another twelve, and during this period 29 hits were claimed.[9]

To extricate his fleet Scheer had to act fast. At 7.13 he made a flag signal: 'Battle cruisers at the enemy! Give everything,' repeating this (in slightly different words) by wireless. Two minutes later he ordered his flotillas to attack and to make smoke to cover the retreat of his battle squadrons, and at 7.18 he ordered another sixteen point turn to starboard. The battle cruisers, in response to Scheer's order had at once, in spite of the battering they had already sustained, steamed at full speed towards the British line into an inferno of shell fire, to which they were able to make only a limited response. *Seydlitz*, however, scored two hits on *Colossus. Lützow* took five hits from *Monarch* and *Orion* at a range of 18,500 yards, while *Derfflinger* was hit no less than fourteen times, principally by shells from *Revenge* and *Colossus. Seydlitz* was hit four times and *Von der Tann* once. *Moltke*, astonishingly, was not hit at all. She had still not been able to take on board Hipper, who was in *G39* still amidst the German destroyers. Among the German battleships it was *Grosser Kurfürst* which suffered most, being struck seven times.[10]

The ordeal of the German battle cruisers was markedly eased when at 7.17 Scheer ordered them to engage the head of the enemy line, and Hartog turned onto a south easterly course in paralled with the British battle line.

Hase, describing the damage suffered by *Derfflinger*, was shaken by a shell which burst in front of the conning tower, causing 'poisonous greenish-yellow gases' to pour in; he ordered everyone to pull down their gas masks, and in spite of the difficulties of communication, continued the fight:

> The terrific blow had burst open the heavy armoured door of the tower, which now stood wide open. Two men strove in vain to force it back, but it was jammed too tight. Then came unexpected assistance. Once more we heard a colossal roar and crash and with a noise of a bursting thunderbolt a 38 cm shell exploded under the bridge… And one extraordinary thing happened: the terrific concussion of the bursting 38 cm shell shut the armoured door of the fore control. A polite race, the English! They had opened the door for us and it was they who shut it again. I wonder if they meant to? In any case, it amused us a good deal.[11]

Hase, unlike so many of the crews of each of the ships involved, could at least watch what was going on as the enemy fired continuously at both the battle cruisers and the battle squadrons. It was a daunting sight:

> I looked towards the enemy through my periscope. Their salvoes were still bursting round us, but we could scarcely see anything of the enemy, who were disposed in a great semi-circle round us. All we could see was the great reddish-gold flames spurting from the guns. The ships' hulls we saw but rarely. I had the range of the flames measured. That was the only possible means of establishing the enemy's range. Without much hope of hurting the enemy I ordered the two forward turrets to fire salvo after salvo. I could feel that our fire soothed the nerves of the ship's company.[12]

During this phase of the battle, the British battleships were not unscathed. An account, for instance, from *Colossus* described the situation from the other side:

> *Colossus* was being heavily shelled, apparently by the German battle fleet on the starboard bow, although they were invisible to us except for the flash of their guns, but, as far as I know, the return fire of the battle cruisers we were engaging, *Lützow* and her squadron, came nowhere near us. We were repeatedly straddled across the fo'csle, and a good many splinter holes were made forward from numerous 'shorts' which burst on hitting the water. One salvo hit us direct at 7.16 pm, two high explosive shells of approximately 12 inch calibre landing in the after end of the fore superstructure, and a third ricocheted on to the armoured pad abreast 'Q' turret, about three feet above the waterline after hitting the water a few feet short.[13]

Scheer's 7.18 *Gefechtskehrtwendung* was a good deal more difficult to execute than the two previous such manoeuvres. As they began the turn, Scheer's battleships were under heavy fire; predictably, *König* and *Grosser Kürfurst*, at the head of the line, suffered worst. Sensibly Schmidt, the commander of I Squadron, did not wait for his rear ships to turn but at once began the turn with his flagship *Ostfriesland,* while *Friedrich der Grosse* turned to port rather than starboard to give the ships of Behncke's III Squadron more room. As the ships bunched up, it required excellent seamanship to avoid collisions while avoiding the point on which the British fire was concentrating:

> As the *Markgraf's* port engine was out of action, Captain Seiferling, her commanding officer, considered it necessary to get away as soon as possible from the unfavourable line of bearing, *König-Kronprinz,* which was continuously under fire, and at the same time, in view of the reduced maximum speed of his ship, deemed it advisable to gain as much ground as possible at the start in the direction of the probable course of the Fleet, so as to be able to maintain his station in the line. But the *Grosser Kurfürst* was thereby forced to head south-west for a time, parallel to the *Markgraf,* until the latter was able to sheer into line astern of the *Kaiser* and *Grosser Kurfürst* and between the *König* and *Kronprinz.*[14]

Captain Bruninghaus of *König,* on his own initiative, hauled out of the line about 450 yards to windward and there laid a smokescreen to cover the German battle squadrons. As these drew away they were still pursued by heavy fire, principally from Beatty's battle cruisers, and *Markgraf* was hit at 7.35 by a heavy shell. Quite quickly, however, the danger began to pass by reason of the effect both of the charge by the battle cruisers and the destroyer attack.

The German flotilla attack was carried out by six flotillas having a total of 224 torpedoes available. First to move out towards the British battle line at 7.16 were the thirteen destroyers of VI and XI Flotillas, followed by the five destroyers of III Flotilla. Pressing forward to within 7,700 yards, the leader of VI Flotilla, *G41*, suffered a direct hit on the forecastle, while *G86* was also hit, as they came under fire from the secondary armament of Jellicoe's battleships. Commander Max Schultz, the leader of VI Flotilla, disposed a total of only four destroyers – *G41, V44, G86* and *G87*, and had almost immediately come under such heavy fire that he ordered them to fire their torpedoes and then withdraw under a dense smoke screen. A total of 11 torpedoes was launched.

Behind Schultz's destroyers came IX Flotilla, nine vessels under thte leadership of Commander Goehle in *V28* emerging through the screen some minutes after Schultz before turning south three minutes later. His flotilla launched eighteen torpedoes between 7.26 and 7.28, and two more a couple of minutes later, all the while under heavy fire. *S35*, with the survivors of *V29* aboard, was hit by a heavy shell, breaking in half and sinking almost at once. *V28's* speed had been reduced by a hit near her bow and Goehle passed the command to Commander Tillessen, who led the flotilla to safety behind a heavy smoke screen.[15]

These destroyer attacks were of course exactly what Jellicoe had been expecting. His first sight of the German destroyers was at 7.20 and his immediate reaction was to order the 4th Light Cruiser Squadron to attack them at once. Simultaneously, Commodore Hawksley led out the nearest half flotilla with the same object. At 7.22 Jellicoe took the decision, long planned, to turn away from the attack, by ordering two two point turns to port so that the battle fleet was on a south-easterly course. The effect of this was to delay the approach of the torpedoes launched by Schultz and Goehle to the point that when they arrived their speed had been so reduced as to make dodging them a relatively easy matter. In fact eleven torpedoes were observed as crossing the line of the 1st Battle Squadron, and all were avoided by skilful seamanship. At the moment he ordered the two turns to port Jellicoe was unaware of Scheer's 16 point turn, but taken together the two manoeuvres ensured that Scheer's hard pressed ships won the relief that was so necessary to them.

Jellicoe's decision was another of those at Jutland that has been minutely examined, both by his supporters and his detractors. The most comprehensive review of the issue was carried out by Professor Marder, who opened by making the point that although Jellicoe's decision appeared to have shocked a number of officers of the Grand Fleet, there was no reason why it should have. It was a policy decision made long before by Jellicoe, approved by the Admiralty and enshrined in the Grand Fleet Battle Orders. Marder suggests that the effect, in time and distance, has been overestimated. Between 7.22 and 7.35 the range was opened by the 2nd Battle Squadron by 1,200 yards; by the 4th Battle Squadron by 2,800 yards and by the 1st Battle Squadron by 3,800 yards. And Marder goes on to assert that much of the increase of the range of the two rearmost divisions would have happened anyway, because at 7.10 Burney's 1st Battle Squadron had been ordered to take station astern of the 4th Battle Squadron, and *Marlborough* and her division were already in the process of doing this at 7.22.[16]

The case against Jellicoe is, in summary, that at the particular moment of the turn away the German fleet was in flight; had he pursued actively he could have inflicted heavy loss. The torpedo threat was exaggerated, and in any event he could and should have turned towards the enemy rather than away.

On the other hand, his defenders argue that Jellicoe's ships were in close order, and well within torpedo range; he could not know the strength of the German destroyer attacks; these might attack in waves and hence launch torpedoes from different angles, which increased the danger of turning towards them; and it was settled policy to turn away. At the moment he did so, Jellicoe did not know of Scheer's 16 point turn. Marder develops Jellicoe's case by suggesting that even if he had known of Scheer's turn, he would not have turned towards the attacking destroyers in any case, and goes on to argue that, even if he had, he would not have inflicted a great deal of damage on the enemy. Finally, Marder relies on a witness from the Battle Cruiser Fleet, one who might have been expected to denounce Jellicoe's tactics; Chatfield, who was naturally disappointed to see the battle fleet turn away, wrote:

> The Battle Fleet could not envisage, and so had not been trained to meet, the peculiar conditions that it had suddenly to face in this fight. It had assumed, perhaps over confidently, that the action would take place in the circumstances in which it was accustomed to exercise – plenty of time to fight, to advance or retire as seemed opportune. A long range and good visibility were hoped for, which would give it that great gunnery duel in which the Battle Fleet was rightly confident its efficiency and its heavier guns would bring victory. None of these conditions existed that evening. Most experienced commanders would probably have acted as did Sir John Jellicoe. His was a weapon on which the world depended, and in the sudden and unexpected situation in which he found himself, of low visibility and a late hour, he was not prepared to take immeasurable risks with it.[17]

Among Jellicoe's sterner critics is Captain Roskill, who originally referred to 'the timidity of Jellicoe when the moment for arduous pursuit arrived' as one of the reasons why victory slipped through his fingers; when he came to write his biography of Beatty he felt that 'timidity' was too strong, and substituted for it 'centralisation and caution.' Broadly speaking, however, he stood by his criticism of Jellicoe.[18]

Commander Frost, on the other hand, as a more dispassionate commentator than most, concluded that Jellicoe could not be blamed too much for turning away from the German destroyers:

> He was a cautious commander, who had convinced himself that he could control the naval situation without running any risks. To turn away from the evident menace was surely the safest course of action. He had told the Admiralty he would play the game safe. It had agreed with his cautious attitude. It got from the Grand Fleet exactly the kind of a battle he had told the members they would get – to the last detail. If that was not what the situation demanded, the fault lies with the Admiralty, not with Jellicoe.[19]

The reason, thought Frost, was that the national policy of the British Empire was defensive rather than offensive. Since it now covered the globe, 'its task was not to get more, but to hold what it had,' which affected its naval strategy and turned the British navy to thoughts of defence. Frost did not concur in 'the new system of British strategy ushered in by the facile pen of Sir Julian Corbett'; he concluded that Jellicoe should have headed, in divisional column, directly towards the point from which the German destroyers had fired their torpedoes.[20] Gordon, looking back at the 1775 Fighting Instructions, concluded that Hawke or Duncan, and perhaps David Farragut, would have done just this, remarking that victories would not be won late in the day 'without radical action and a disregard of incidental risks.' The Grand Fleet Battle Orders appeared, thought Gordon, to be based upon the expectation that the High Seas Fleet would fight a fleet action as a set piece duel, by steering a course parallel to the Grand Fleet and waiting for the latter to open fire – in other words, that the chances of a decisive action depended on the High Seas Fleet adopting tactics contrary to its own best interests.[21]

The gallons of ink and acres of paper that have been devoted to this issue have not produced a decisive conclusion, and nor, given the context, could this be expected; and it is perhaps best left with Chatfield's grudging dismissal of the charges levelled against Jellicoe. His course of action was not bold; but in the situation as he understood it, it was entirely sensible.

However, coupled with Scheer's 16 point turn away, it meant that for the second time the High Seas Fleet had vanished. Scheer was quicker than his opponent to grasp the situation; by 7.30 he had realised that the British fleet had turned away from the torpedo attacks by his destroyers, and that as a result he had successfully extricated his own fleet from the dangerous situation to which he had exposed it. Now, however, he must decide what to do next, and he had little time in which to make up his mind. He could assume that Jellicoe would, in what daylight remained, endeavour to renew the action by following the High Seas Fleet on its westerly course and would certainly continue the fight at dawn:

> If Scheer could succeed in checking the enemy's encircling movement and reach the Horns Reef first, he would be able to retain the freedom of action which he had just won. The only way to achieve this was for the German battle fleet to shape course immediately for the Horns Reef in close order and by the shortest route, and to keep to this course in spite of attacks by the enemy. At the same time an attempt would have to be made to bring all the flotillas into action during the night, even at the risk of none of them being available for the fleet engagements which would probably take place at daybreak.[22]

Scheer's decision to head for the Horns Reef had been quickly made. The option of heading due east and passing round the Skaw and through the Kattegat was not viable. As the short summer night fell, the High Seas Fleet was some 340 miles from the Little Belt, and taking that route would give the faster Grand Fleet most of the following day to catch it and renew the battle. A more hopeful alternative was to take the southern route to the Ems estuary and then follow the Frisian coast line to the Jade. Against this was the fact that it was 70 miles longer than the route via the Horns Reef, and would also give Jellicoe a better chance of renewing the action at daybreak. The Horns Reef route meant passing astern of the Grand Fleet; Scheer's fleet did not overall have the speed to get far enough ahead of the enemy to pass ahead of it.

Jellicoe, however, had concluded that the Ems route was the more likely, and held on his course in order to be well placed to renew the battle if Scheer went that way, while at the same time covering the Horns Reef option. He wrote later:

> In view of the WSW course of the German fleet as received by me at 9.41 pm and remembering our submarine patrol so frequently maintained off the Horns Reef, it appeared to me that Admiral Scheer might consider that he had the best chance of evading the Grand

> Fleet if he made for the Ems route. To reach the Ems swept channel he would have had to steam a distance of about 180 miles, and half of this distance would be covered during the dark hours... My position at daylight would be between 80 and 90 miles from the Ems swept channel, about 40 miles from the gap between the British minefields to the WNW of Heligoland, and some 10 to 20 miles from a route which would pass through the British minefields lying NW of the Amrum Bank.[23]

With the dispositions he had made and the course he had set, Jellicoe was confident of bringing Scheer to battle next morning

Although the High Seas Fleet had entirely disappeared from Jellicoe's sight, he could hear that his rearmost divisions were still heavily engaged, and he took this to mean that they were firing at Scheer's battle line. In fact, they were firing at the German destroyers, and it was not immediately that Jellicoe realised that touch had been lost with the enemy, by his battle fleet at any rate. At 7.40 Beatty had reported that the enemy was still in sight, but this held good for only a few minutes. By 7.45, as Marder noted, *Lion* could not possibly have had the enemy in sight, being twelve miles from the German battle cruisers and thirteen and a half miles from the nearest battleship. It was at this point that Beatty sent a signal that quickly became famous, being seized upon by the British press as an example of Beatty's bold and determined tactics. Timed at 7.47, it read: 'Submit van of battleships follow battle cruisers. We can then cut off whole of enemy's battle fleet.'[24] Gordon commented on this to suggest that it was the most moderate of 'a range of insubordinate signals' contemplated by Beatty and his staff, and certainly it was a signal to which Jellicoe might well have taken offence. Years later, he did remark that he 'thought it was rather insubordinate.'[25] Marder had the benefit of a letter from Admiral Drax, who was serving on Beatty's staff, in which he explained that he had remarked to Beatty that Nelson would have signalled 'Follow me:' the admiral replied, correctly, that he could not do that, as he was not the commander in chief,' and as a result the longer signal was drafted and approved by Beatty.[26] A century on, there is just a touch of public posturing in the signal which makes it unsurprising that the Press seized on it.

Jellicoe read the signal at about 8.00, and was immediately aware that it could not have been sent at a time that the High Seas Fleet was in Beatty's sight. By that time, too, he had altered the course of the battle fleet to due west, which meant that he was more directly steering in the direction of the enemy than were the battle cruisers. Accordingly, he radioed Beatty to tell him he was steering west, assuming that the latter would alter to that course, and that he could then safely order Jerram to follow the battle cruisers, which he did at 8.07.

Admiral Harper was particularly unimpressed with Beatty's signal, noting that since the battle fleet was not in sight of the battle cruisers, it was not clear how he could have known its course; he could, but did not, find out by a visual signal to one of the vessels bridging the gap. Nor was it clear what cutting off meant; since presumably it referred to cutting off Scheer from his base, 'the position, course and speed of our battle fleet could not have been improved upon for this purpose'. At the time, it was practically following the battle cruisers, and was nearer to the enemy than *Lion:*

> An alteration in the course, to follow the battle cruisers, at the moment the signal was made would, therefore, have caused the van to converge less on the enemy's course than it was actually doing. The message sent was therefore, quite unnecessary, and likely to mislead the Commander in Chief.[27]

The controversy arising from this incident, on which neither Jellicoe nor Beatty commented publicly, damaged, as Marder said, morale and unity in the fleet. It was left to a former First Lord of the Admiralty, Reginald McKenna, to put the issue firmly to bed in a letter to Jellicoe in 1921:

> Perhaps the worst blow [to Beatty's supporters] was the final destruction of the 'Follow me' myth. The story current in London was that Beatty had signalled 'Follow me and we will sink the whole German fleet.' You refused and the result was the Germans escaped. The publication of the actual message and your reply has destroyed the fancy picture of a dare-devil hero held back from triumphant victory by a timid chief.[28]

By now the daylight was slipping away. Sunset was at 8.19, but there was sufficient light for firing for about another hour. It has been suggested that Jellicoe had had enough for the day, but in fact he manoeuvred his battle fleet to try and regain touch with an enemy at whose position he could only guess. By 8.00 he was squarely across Scheer's line of retreat, steering west in seven columns, while his opponent, some twelve miles away, was crossing the head of the British battle line. Beatty's battle cruisers, however, eight miles south west of Jellicoe, were converging on the head of the German line. *Falmouth,* the flagship of Napier's 3rd Light Cruiser Squadron, ordered to sweep west to detect Scheer's van, sighted Reuter's IV Scouting Group bearing N by W at 8.09, and at 8.15 Napier turned on to a parallel course and opened fire.[29] Hearing the gunfire, Beatty, who had just altered course to the west, turned to WSW to close the enemy; at 8.23 he opened fire on the German battle cruisers, hitting both *Derfflinger* and *Seydlitz.* It was at this time that Hipper, having ascertained which of his battle cruisers had suffered least damage, had gone alongside *Moltke* in *G39.* As Beatty's salvoes fell around *Moltke* had to pick up speed again before the transfer could be made, and it was not until the firing had ceased in the deepening twilight that Hipper and his staff succeeded in boarding her. Once aboard, they found that the battle cruiser's radio had been badly damaged, so Hipper kept *G39* close by in order to use her radio.[30]

The German battle cruisers responded as well as they could, hitting both *Lion* and *Princess Royal,* but by about 8.30 they were obliged to turn away to the west under cover of a smoke-screen. During this part of the engagement Beatty had closed to within 8,500 yards of the enemy, He was, however, prevented from following his old opponents by the intervention of Mauve's II Squadron, which, as I Scouting Group followed by I Squadron bore away to the west, held on its southward course. All six of Beatty's ships now turned their fire on Mauve's predreadnoughts, which altered course to SW to enable their guns to bear:

> The expectation that this would enable the enemy to be made out more clearly was not, however, realised. Owing to interference from smoke and the indifferent visibility, the *Pommern* and *Schleswig-Holstein* were unable to return the enemy's fire, and the *Deutschland* fired only one, the *Hessen* five, the *Hannover* eight and the *Schlesien* nine rounds from their eleven inch guns.[31]

At the short range of 8,000 yards the battle cruisers soon picked up their targets, and scored a number of hits before Mauve, judging that the risk to his poorly armoured ships was too great, at 8.35 turned away eight points to starboard. To their surprise, the British made no attempt to follow, and at 8.40 ceased fire. Hase wrote that the help that had come to save the German battle cruisers had come 'from the quarter from which it was least expected.' To him it seemed not long before the enemy had had enough:

> I wonder if they would have turned about had they known what kind of ships these were! They were the famous German 'five minute ships, to settle which the Englishmen could not spare more than five minutes, but bravely withdrew.[32]

Hase's comment was hardly fair; by 8.40 Beatty's ships had completely lost sight of the enemy in the failing light and mist.

As the daylight faded the fighting slackened. At 8.26 however, the light cruiser *Castor*, the leader of the 11th Flotilla, which with her destroyers and *Calliope, Constance* and *Comus* of the 4th Light Cruiser Squadron had been pursuing twelve German destroyers, suddenly found herself within 8,000 yards of the battleships of III Squadron. Three of them, *Prinzregent Luitpold*, *Kaiser* and *Markgraf*, opened fire; the British destroyers turned away, but the cruisers closed to 6500 yards, *Calliope* firing a torpedo before being hit by a shell which put two guns out of action. After this the cruisers also withdrew.[33]

This encounter, and Beatty's brief action against the German battle cruisers and predreadnoughts, gave Jellicoe some idea of the location of the High Seas Fleet. Additional information came from Goodenough, who was engaged with German destroyers seeking to attack the 5th Battle Squadron at the end of the British line. At this point also came the sound of firing from ahead, where the light cruisers *Caroline* and *Royalist* had sighted Mauve's predreadnoughts. In spite of a signal from Jerram not to attack, because he believed that the targets of the light cruisers were Beatty's battle cruisers, the two ships launched torpedoes at a range of 8,000 yards before making their escape under a storm of shell.[34] Aboard *Orion*, Rear Admiral Leveson's Flag Lieutenant was perfectly certain that the ships sighted were German, and he said: 'Sir, if you leave the line now and turn towards, your name will be as famous as Nelson's. Leveson hesitated a moment before his training kicked in and he replied: 'We must follow the next ahead.'[35]

As night fell, Jellicoe reviewed his options. He was quite clear in his mind that a night action between heavy ships was to be avoided, because it must expose his squadrons to attack from large numbers of destroyers, and his ships were not adequately equipped for such an encounter particularly as to searchlights and their control arrangements. He was sure that the enemy was well to the westward, having been turning on interior lines through the action. His concern was to keep his fleet between Scheer and his bases, so that he could renew the action at dawn. He must, therefore, at once decide on the formation to adopt during the night. He recorded his conclusions thus:

> The Grand Fleet was formed at that time in practically a single line, steering approximately WSW. I considered that a southerly course would meet the situation and would enable me to form the Fleet very quickly, and, if I put the destroyers astern, they would fulfil three conditions: first, they would be in an excellent position for attacking the enemy's fleet should it also turn to the southward with a view to regaining its bases during the night (which seemed a very probable movement on the part of the enemy); secondly, they would also be in position to attack enemy destroyers should the latter search for our fleet with a view to a night attack on our heavy ships; finally, they would be clear of our own ships and

> the danger of their attacking our battleships in error or of our battleships firing on them would be reduced to a minimum.[36]

His mind made up, at 9.00 Jellicoe ordered his battle fleet to alter course by divisions to the south, notifying his flag officers accordingly. The battleships were to steam in four squadron columns a mile apart.

Groos, in the German Official History, was critical of Jellicoe's decision:

> Jellicoe could have had little doubt as to the actual position of the German Fleet. At 9.00 he knew that the latter was on a converging course with the British line, and it would only have been necessary for him to have stood on with the course he was then following to have brought about a renewed action between the rival squadrons. He would at least have been justified in assuming that, in spite of all the incalculable factors of a twilight action, such a course would probably have enabled him to force the German Fleet still further to the west than the battle cruisers' surprise attack had already done, and would have allowed him to set in motion night attacks by his destroyer flotillas... But for this course of action Jellicoe no longer possessed the resolution.[37]

If this was a charge of timidity on Jellicoe's part, a similar charge could be laid against Beatty, who also did not consider it wise to close the enemy as night fell, because of his distance from the battle fleet; the damage his ships had suffered; the fact that the enemy was now concentrated; the number of enemy destroyers; and the fact that it seemed certain that the High Seas Fleet would be located at daylight. In all the circumstances Jellicoe and Beatty cannot fairly be criticised for the position they took. What now remained to be seen was whether Scheer would oblige them by being where he was expected to be when dawn broke.

17

Night

Jellicoe and Scheer now each had a simple, clear cut objective: for Scheer, it was to get home safely, and for Jellicoe to bring him to battle to prevent his doing so. As it turned out, neither of them had much influence over the events of the night, Jellicoe because his subordinate commanders failed to report to him what they had seen and done, and Scheer because his order to his subordinate commanders was simply to maintain their course at all costs. That this might mean the abandonment of the badly damaged *Lützow* was something he had to accept, as the German Official History relates:

> If he failed to get through, he would be in danger of being cut off from his base... It was, therefore, essential for him to be off Horns Reef by dawn. After that his decisions would have to depend on the outcome of the night actions and on the subsequent situation ... Even when, at 9.13, the *Lützow* was lost sight of from the last ship of the line, this did not alter Scheer's decision. Had the speed of the Fleet been determined by that of the damaged battle cruiser, or had the Fleet returned to her, it could not possibly have reached Horns Reef by dawn. As the weather had, however, become rather foggy, Scheer hoped that, even without help, the *Lützow* would be able to reach harbour unobserved by the enemy.[1]

Scheer's order for the night had been issued at 9.10. It was short and to the point: 'Battle fleet course SSE ¼ E (142°). *Durchhalten*. Speed 16 knots. II Squadron take station at the rear of the line. Battle cruisers are to prolong the line astern.'[2]

Durchhalten is described by Frost as 'picturesque but untranslatable,' but it is usually rendered as an instruction that 'this course is to be maintained,' and Scheer was merely emphasising his overriding tactical intention.[3] In fact, although the order was entirely straightforward in this respect, it was some time before the High Seas Fleet sorted itself out, and Frost finds that even the German Official History is sometimes confused as to how this was done, observing conflict between the text and the sketches, and sometimes between both of these and signal records. It is perhaps a statement of the obvious that making changes in the dispositions of a large fleet is never going to be easy after dark.

At 9.29 it was necessary for Scheer to repeat his instructions to Mauve and to the battle cruisers to take up their position astern of the main body, while Boedicker's II Scouting Group was to take station ahead and Reuter's IV Scouting Group to starboard. It was not until 9.58

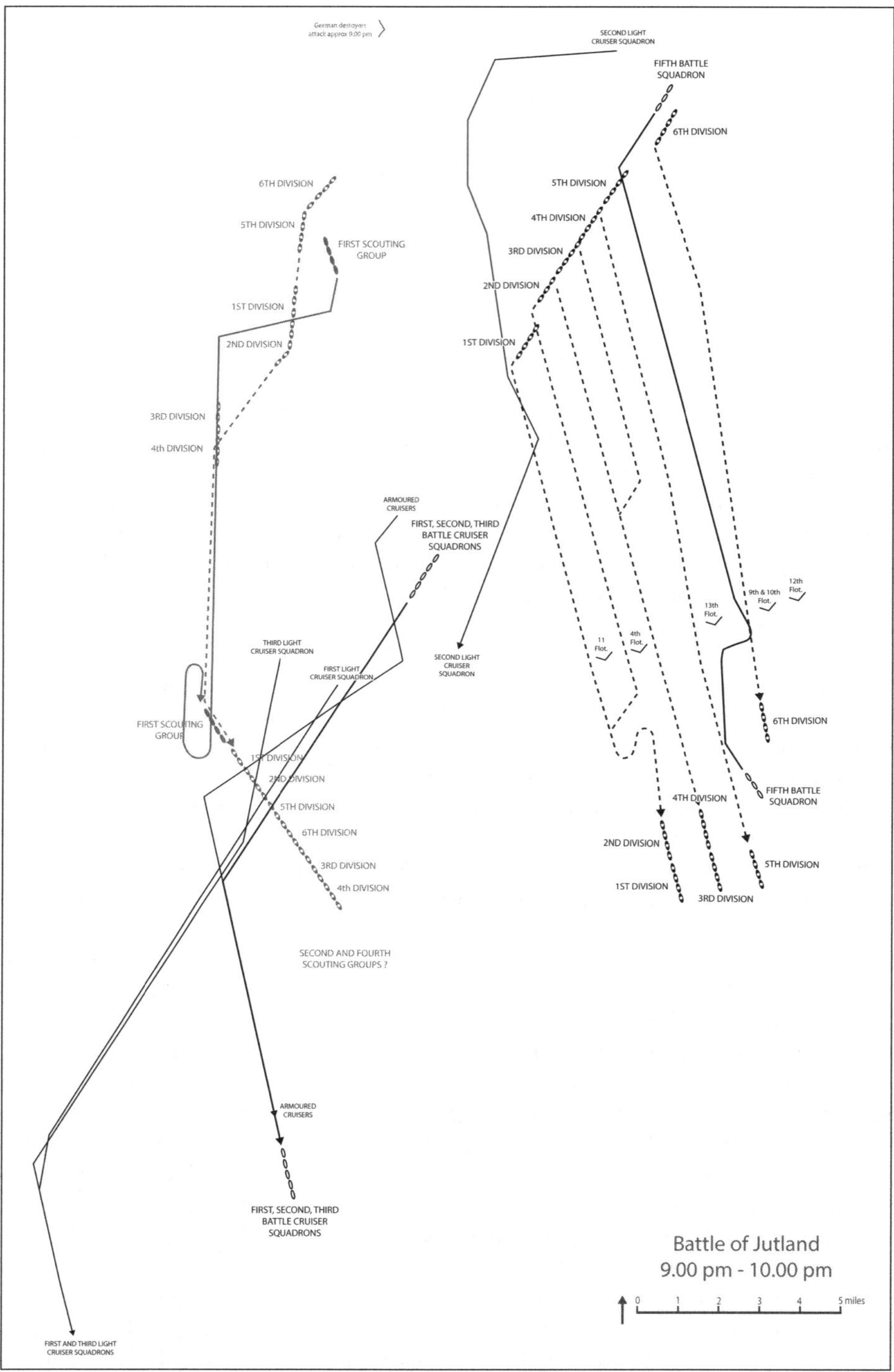

Map 14 Battle of Jutland: 9.00 pm to 10.00 pm.

that Mauve was able to complete his turn which involved a turn to port of 360° to the rear, in a manner that prompted Frost's admiration:

> That such a difficult manoeuvre was executed without lights on a very dark night speaks volumes for Mauve and his well trained captains. We know no one who would like to try that manoeuvre even under peace-time conditions.[4]

Reuter, however, was out of position as directed by Scheer; in response to an order from Rear Admiral Dalwigk in *Hannover*, who had sighted the armoured cruisers of Heath's 2nd Cruiser Squadron, he had turned to the southeast intending to take up a position ahead of the III Squadron. By 10.00 Reuter was on the course ordered for the fleet, although far to the south east of the battle line. Boedicker, meanwhile, had at 9.40 taken station well to the east of both the battle line and Reuter, instead of being ahead. Both Boedicker and Reuter may have been misled by the fact that Redlich, in *Westfalen*, had not immediately gone to course 142°.

The frequent course alterations of the battle line had made it impossible to get the flagships of each squadron to their proper place at the head of their units, and it was *Westfalen* that continued to lead the line during the night, at the head of I Squadron. Next came Scheer, in *Friedrich der Grosse*, followed by Behncke's III Squadron and Mauve's II Squadron. Astern of these came the battle cruisers. These changes of course had also hampered the development of the torpedo attacks by destroyer flotillas which had been ordered by Scheer. Heinrich, in *Regensburg*, had despatched the II Flotilla and XIII Half Flotilla to launch an attack at 8.10; this attack was driven off by Goodenough's 2nd Light Cruiser Squadron. In *Rostock*, Michelsen had earmarked the V and VII Flotillas to locate the enemy, calculating that Jellicoe would be steaming south torwards the coast of Jutland to intercept the High Seas Fleet at dawn. His hope was to inflict enough damage during the night to disrupt this. However, as Tarrant notes, when Michelsen finally launched his two flotillas at 9.00 they were further north than he reckoned and were to the west of the battle line, which meant that the destroyers must, dangerously, pass through the course of the battleships.[5]

These flotillas were composed of older, and slower vessels, which had been steaming at high speeds for many hours; their fires were dirty and their stokers exhausted, and their speed was now decidedly limited:

> For these reasons *Korvettenkäpitan* Koch, commanding VII Flotilla, had to refrain from spreading out his flotilla into groups as originally planned, although this would have extended its area of operations considerably, but had to proceed on close order on a SE course at 17 knots. In V Flotilla, commanded by *Korvettenkäpitan* Heinecke, which advanced on a S by ½ W course, smoke and the passage through the line of German battleships so greatly delayed the transmission of the signal to extend that this flotilla did not split up into groups until midnight. Unfortunately the torpedo boats were unable to establish touch with the enemy's battle fleet before dark, which was an essential prerequisite for a successful attack. Due to the large number of enemy light forces, there was also the danger that the flotillas, being dependent on their own resources, might be dispersed by them at dawn or least be driven off so far as to be unable to regain their station near the battle fleet in time for the expected resumption of action at daybreak. Scheer had already taken this point into account when he gave instructions for the flotillas to attack during the night,

> and Commodore Michelsen, at 11.30, therefore issued orders by wireless for all flotillas to be reassembled on the battle fleet off Horns Reef by 3.00 am. Only in the event of being driven off were they to take the route home round through the Skagerrak and round the Skaw, which they had already been ordered to do by Commodore Heinrich.[6]

It was not until about 9.55 that Hipper and his staff had finally been able to board *Moltke*, and when he did so he was evidently unaware of Scheer's order that the battle cruisers were to take up a position at the rear; his first act was to order them to go to the head of the line at 20 knots. This, however, was a speed that only *Moltke* and *Seydlitz* could do; *Derfflinger* and *Von der Tann* were limited to 18 knots, and Scheer repeated his order that they go to the rear. By 10.27 the whole of the fleet had taken up its night cruising formation and was proceeding on a course of SSE by ¼ E at 16 knots, with lights out and ready for immediate action.

By then, contact between the opposing light forces had already begun, as Scheer had no doubt anticipated. As Corbett writes:

> That he expected to find the way clear is hardly credible. Presumably he was feeling for his enemy, and as the courses of the two fleets were now fast converging his advanced guard cruisers came into action almost immediately. What they struck was the destroyer rear guard where the *Castor* with the 11th Flotilla had taken station on the wing nearest the enemy.[7]

At 10.15 Hawksley, aboard *Castor*, spotted ships on his starboard bow, but was uncertain about their identity, not least because the first two of the four signals made were correct for the British challenge of the day. Moments later, the leading ships switched on searchlights and opened fire at 2,000 yards, hitting *Castor* nine or ten times. *Castor* and the destroyers *Marne* and *Magic* each got off a torpedo before turning away, *Castor* with her motor boat burning fiercely and illuminating the whole ship: the enemy ships, which appear to have been *Elbing, Rostock* and *Hamburg,* did likewise.

The reference to recognition signals illustrated the importance that was attached to them, and it was particularly unfortunate therefore, that at 9.32 *Lion* had signalled *Princess Royal* by flashing lamp: 'Please give me challenge and reply now in force as they have been lost.' At the time, only two miles away, the light cruisers of II and IV Scouting Groups were able to read part of the reply from Princess Royal. As Marder observed, this was 'the final proof of the hopeless inefficiency of Beatty's signal department,' and was to have serious consequences later in the night. Jellicoe later described it as 'idiotic.'[8] It was an incident which Corbett tactfully forebears to mention.

Frost is severe on Hawksley's failure to follow up his brush with the German light cruisers by searching to the west to see what was behind them:

> He was distant only four miles from the German battle line and had available fifteen fine destroyers. It was another case of inert leadership for which Jellicoe must be charged with primary responsibility. To order destroyers to take station five miles in rear of the battleships without assigning any mission, without telling them the direction of the enemy, or without adding even a sentence to guide their conduct paralysed that powerful force to a great degree during all the night. His stated object of giving the destroyers opportunities to attack German battleships was not at all understood by the flotilla commanders.[9]

Hawksley continued south, reporting that his purpose was 'to be within reach of the fleet at daybreak.' This 'perfectly futile mission' was, Frost reckons, the natural result of Jellicoe's 'passive leadership.'

Meanwhile Goodenough had been exploring to the westward, and at about 10.30 came into contact with IV Scouting Group. The two squadrons were converging at a slight angle. The German cruisers had just been forced to alter course to avoid *Moltke* and *Seydlitz* as Hipper, steaming at 22 knots, endeavoured to get to the head of the German battle line. Reuter, who had seven light cruisers, having been joined by *Elbing* and *Rostock,* flew his flag in *Stettin,* which challenged the cruisers of Goodenough's squadron with coloured lights at 10.35. Almost at once both squadrons opened fire at the murderously short range of 800 yards; *Southampton* and *Dublin* switched on their searchlights, as did most of the German cruisers.

In the ensuing gun battle, the German came off rather the better. The upper decks of *Southampton* were wrecked and her gun crews almost wiped out. Powder charges caught fire and blazed as high as the masthead. In minutes some 90 of her crew were casualties, of which 35 had been killed; she took 18 hits in all.

Stephen King-Hall, aboard *Southampton,* wrote vividly in his diary of the experience of undergoing an ordeal such as she experienced:

> It is impossible to give a connected account of what happened. Many strange and unpleasant things happen when men find themselves in hell on earth. Men – strong men – go mad and jump overboard. Wounded men are driven to the oblivion of death in the sea by the agony of their injuries. It is not good to look too closely into these things which are the realities, the plain facts, of battle. The range was amazingly close – no two groups of such ships have ever fought so close in the history of this war. There could be no missing. A gun was fired and a hit obtained – the gun was loaded, it flamed, it roared, it leapt to the near, it slid to the front – there was another hit. But to load guns, there must be men, flesh and blood must lift the shells and cordite and open and close the hungry breeches. But flesh and blood cannot stand high explosives, and there was a great deal of H.E bursting all along HMS Southampton's upper deck from her after-screen to the fore bridge.[10]

Dublin was hit 13 times; her chart house was destroyed and her navigator and two men killed, and 24 were wounded. She lost touch with the squadron and did not regain it until 10.00 am next day. *Nottingham* and *Birmingham*, having turned on their searchlights, suffered little. On the German side, *Stettin* was hit twice, destroying a searchlight and puncturing a steam line. *München,* the only German cruiser to fire her torpedoes, was hit twice, and *Elbing* once, suffering 18 casualties. *Southampton*, before she turned away in flames, did fire a torpedo, as recounted by her torpedo lieutenant:

> On the bridge the full glare of the searchlights of the leading enemy ship was on us and we could see nothing, but I had already received enough impression of the general direction of advance of the enemy for the purpose of torpedo fire, so I passed down an order to the torpedo flat and waited impatiently for a reply. When it came through (the report 'ready') I fired at a group of hostile searchlights, which were the only things visible.[11]

Southampton's target was the unlucky *Frauenlob*; the torpedo hit her in the auxiliary ammunition space. Her lights went out and she listed steeply to port, while she was hit aft by shell fire:

> But nothing shook the heroic determination of her ship's company. Standing in water up to their waists, the crew of No 4 gun, under Petty Office Schmidt, continued to engage the enemy until fire and water put an end to the fighting. The *Frauenlob* capsized, and, with three cheers for the Kaiser and the German Empire, the Captain, eleven officers and 308 men attested with their deaths their loyalty to the Fatherland.[12]

Only five survivors were later rescued after many hours in the water.

Reuter's encounter with Goodenough resulted in his being left with only four cruisers. *Stuttgart* only avoided the stricken *Frauenlob* by a sharp turn to starboard, and lost touch with the squadron, joining I Battle Squadron. *Hamburg* likewise became separated when *Moltke* steered across her bow during the engagement and she made her way thereafter independently. During the confusion *Seydlitz,* which had been following *Moltke*, lost sight of her stern light. Unable to catch up with her – *Moltke* could still steam 22 knots – *Seydlitz* also made her own way home, leaving Hipper alone at the head of affairs but well to the starboard of the rest of the High Seas Fleet.

The two battle cruisers were, however, to have further adventures before the night was over. At about 10.40 *Moltke* sighted *Thunderer*, at the rear of the 2nd Battle Squadron in company with the light cruiser *Boadicea,* and challenged them with coloured lights. The Official Despatches set out *Thunderer's* report of the incident:

> An enemy cruiser challenged three times, switching on and off four red lights horizontal above four green horizontal. Fire was not opened as it was considered inadvisable to show up battle fleet unless obvious attack was intended. Our destroyers shortly after attacked this cruiser and a hot engagement followed. She was seen to be hit many times; she eventually turned to port.[13]

The 'hot engagement' appears to have been entirely fanciful if it really referred to *Moltke,* whose Captain von Karpf, having by now sighted the rest of the rear division of Jerram's 2nd Battle Squadron, had no intention of trying conclusions with four battleships. Accordingly, he gave the order to turn away, and *Moltke* disappeared into the night. Frost, considering the decision of Captain Ferguson of the *Thunderer* not to open fire, observes that for all he knew *Moltke* might have been the leader of a battle squadron that could have destroyed *Thunderer* at such close range. On the other hand, if he had in fact opened fire *Moltke* might have been seriously damaged, although this might have brought on an attack by German destroyers. 'The choice of decisions as to whether the *Thunderer* should or should not have opened fire is therefore quite evenly balanced.'[14] What can be criticised, however, is the failure to report the incident to Jellicoe.

As it was, Karpf twice more turned towards the east in trying to find a way through, and each time was headed off by the appearance of enemy battleships in her path. After his final attempt at 11.20, Karpf gave up and headed south at top speed until he was far enough ahead to cross ahead of the front of the Grand Fleet and head safely for home.

Captain von Egidy in *Seydlitz* also encountered possible trouble, sighting British battleships ahead of him. These were from the 6th Division of the 1st Battle Squadron, which due to the serious damage sustained by Burney's flagship *Marlborough* had begun to fall behind the main body of the Grand Fleet. At 11.45 *Seydlitz* was sighted by *Agincourt;* her captain reported this incident as follows:

> A ship or destroyer closed *Agincourt* at high speed during the night, her track very visible. I did not challenge her, so as not to give our Division's position away. She altered course and steamed away.[15]

In her present condition, *Seydlitz* was certainly not making a high speed. Once again no report was made to Jellicoe of the sighting. *Seydlitz* was also seen by *Revenge*, and by *Marlborough,* whose Gunnery Officer later mourned the missed opportunity:

> I missed the chance of a lifetime on this occasion. I saw the dim outline of this ship from the top and had the main armament trained on it and put a range of 4,000 yards on the sights and deflection of 24 right, then asked the Captain, who was in the conning tower, for permission to open fire. He replied 'No' as he thought it was one of our own ships. Of course what I ought to have done was to have opened fire and blown the ship out of the water and then said 'Sorry.'[16]

Seydlitz went on to pursue an even riskier route homewards than *Moltke*, passing through a gap between the 2nd and 5th Battle Squadron before pursuing her course eastwards to Horns Reef.

The damage sustained by *Marlborough* had in fact created a potentially dangerous situation for the 6th Division, which by 10.00 pm was already some four miles behind the 5th Division. This also created problems for Evan-Thomas's 5th Battle Squadron, and which had had to counter march first to starboard and then to port to keep that station. Finally, at 10.12, seeing that *Marlborough* was steaming quite slowly, Evan-Thomas overtook her in order to regain the battle line. Curiously, it was not until 2.00 am that *Marlborough,* unable any longer to steam safely at 17 knots, hauled out of line and allowed *Revenge, Agincourt* and *Hercules* to pursue the rest of the fleet, Burney transferring his flag to *Revenge.* Commodore Schoultz, on the bridge of *Hercules,* recorded the discussions of the situation:

> I remember being disappointed at the falling behind of our division, when we lost touch with the Battle Fleet and could not re-establish it for a considerable time. In the morning the last preparations for action were again made, for the general conviction on board was that the High Sea Fleet would not be able to overhaul our Battle Fleet, and would therefore fall in with us during the morning off Horns Reef, or a little to the northward of it. In the *Hercules* this question was discussed on the bridge and in the charthouse, and the general opinion was that gunfire would probably be heard again in a short time, after which we should come up with the Battle Fleet and so take part, if not in the beginning, at any rate in the later stages of the battle.[17]

It was not until 7.00 pm on the following day that *Revenge, Hercules* and *Agincourt* finally rejoined the rest of the Grand Fleet; *Marlborough,* her condition steadily worsening, had been ordered by Jellicoe to proceed to the Tyne or Rosyth.

At 10.41 pm the Admiralty sent a critically important message to Jellicoe which he read at about 11.30: 'German Battle Fleet ordered home at 9.14 pm. Battle cruisers in rear. Course SSE ¾ E, speed 16 knots.' Frost describes this information as 'one of the most remarkable feats of naval intelligence recorded by history.'[18] Unfortunately it had been preceded by a message that had further damaged Jellicoe's faith in the information provided by the Admiralty. This, sent at 9.58, (received at 10.23 and seen by Jellicoe at 10.45) was based on a signal from a German destroyer giving the position and course of the nearmost German battleship at 9.00; it put this at eight miles SW of the van of the Grand Fleet at a time when he knew that the High Seas Fleet must still be well to the NW of *Iron Duke*. Thus, when the 10.41 message arrived, he did not place much faith in the information it contained. In any case, since it did not give any news of the enemy's position, it left him in doubt of Scheer's probable route. However, Professor Marder has pointed out that if Jellicoe had taken the information at its face value, it told him what he needed to know:

> Although Scheer's objective was not mentioned in this message, the enemy's supposed course for home, if plotted from the accepted enemy position at 9.00 pm, pointed directly to Horns Reef and indicated that the High Seas Fleet would cross astern of the Grand Fleet. This intelligence was absolutely correct, and had Jellicoe acted on it and altered course and steered for Horns Reef any time as late as 12.30 am, he would have brought the High Seas Fleet to action at daylight.[19]

The Admiralty message was a summary of the information which the tireless cryptographers of Room 40 were passing to the Naval Staff as it came in. It did not include the conclusive information derived from Scheer's request, made at 9.06, for Zeppelin reconnaissance of Horns Reef early the following morning. This, as Patrick Beesly writes, 'should have settled all Jellicoe's doubts, but for some inexplicable reason this clinching intelligence was never passed out to him; Jellicoe did not even learn of its existence until some years after the war.'[20] Beesly rejects the suggestion that at the critical moment Oliver was taking a badly needed break and that Captain AF Everett, the Naval Assistant to the First Sea Lord was standing in for him. He points out that throughout the battle, 'Oliver drafted every single signal based on Room 40's decodes which was despatched to Jellicoe.'[21] Even more to the point is the fact that there were six other signals passed on by Room 40 which were not passed to Jellicoe; one of these, handed to the Operations staff at 11.15, was from Michelsen, the German destroyer commander, to the effect that all flotillas were to assemble at Horns Reef at 3.00 am. As Jellicoe was perfectly entitled later to write, these signals would have removed all doubt from his mind. It was, in Marder's words, a matter of 'criminal neglect to pass on these signals (all were in the Operations Division within three quarters of an hour of their being made) to the only quarter where they could be of use.'[22]

The problem for Jellicoe, and which caused the serious doubts he felt about the report from the Admiralty, was that at 11.30 Captain Duff, of *Birmingham,* reported that the enemy's battle cruisers were steering south, while at 11.38 a message from Goodenough, that had been greatly delayed, was received via *Nottingham* to the effect that IV Scouting Group was to the west of the course of the Grand Fleet. These certainly suggested that the High Seas Fleet was steering for the Ems route homewards. The ships reported by Duff were actually German battleships engaging the British destroyers of the 4th Flotilla. As Jellicoe wrote:

> Which should I trust? Reports from my own ships which had actually seen the enemy, or a report from the Admiralty which gave information as to their movements at a time over 2 hours earlier than the *Birmingham's* report?[23]

Perhaps, though, there should not have been doubt in Jellicoe's mind. The information received at 10.50 of Hawksley's clash with the German cruisers should have indicated that the High Seas Fleet was not making a westward detour to gain the Ems route. It would have been remarkable if the battle squadrons were to take that course while the cruisers made for Horns Reef.

The criticism of the Admiralty, entirely merited as it is, is rejected by Oliver's biographer, who quotes his subject's account of some of the pressures he was under that night:

> Balfour stayed in my office chatting all the afternoon and some of the evening and his Naval Assistant and his Private Secretary also, and if I went to look at a chart some of them were bound to be in the way and all the talk was distracting. When I could stand it no longer I went to Balfour and shook his hand and said, 'Good night, Sir,' and he said good night and took his supporters away with him. It was nice of him not to be offended.[24]

Out in the North Sea the two fleets were sailing on courses that were gradually bringing them together. In an often quoted passage Langhorne Gibson and Admiral Harper graphically described the situation:

> The fates were busy, weaving the threads of destiny. The blind fleets, unconscious of the workings of circumstance, steamed almost side by side, so close to each other in the darkness that they were like members of one great common formation. Their courses were slightly converging. They steamed down the sides of a very long, very slender V, and it was one of the most curious circumstances in history that they did not come together at the V's point. A matter of minutes – of a quarter of an hour – of the fact that Scheer had sent his leading ships back to the rear of his line, while Jellicoe had drawn the British rear up to form up on the Grand Fleet leaders; of the fact that Britain's speed was 17 knots, while the German speed was 16. Tiny factors, and no human plan, caused Jellicoe to arrive at the bottom of the V and pass through the junction point short minutes before the German ships arrived. The V became an X – the courses of the fleets crossed, neither side was conscious of what was happening – and from then onward, from the hour of midnight onward, they began to draw apart.[25]

Scheer's ignorance of the close proximity of the Grand Fleet was due to a complete lack of information as to the whereabouts of Jellicoe's battleships. He had received numerous reports of the British light forces which had made it clear that in holding his course for Horns Reef he would have to push his way through these. On the other hand, there was no way he could assess the likelihood of running into the enemy's battle fleet, apart from some important information deriving from a German radio intercept. The wireless station at Neumünster had picked up the general signal to the British flotillas to take station five miles astern of the battle fleet, and the reports from his light cruisers gave some information about the present position of some at any rate of the British flotillas.[26] One message from *Rostock* at 10.38 told him of having fired on enemy light cruisers and destroyers, a reference to the engagement with *Castor* and the 11th Flotilla. This put British light forces directly in the path of the High Seas Fleet:

> However, even that alarming information did not deter the calm and resolute commander-in-chief from holding his course towards Horns Reef. Here we see Scheer at his very best, prepared to cut his way through the enemy regardless of consequences.[27]

Confident in the high standard of training of his forces in night fighting, and especially of the gun crews of the battleships' secondary armament, Scheer was reasonably confident that he could beat off any destroyer attacks that materialised.

The British light forces had originally been organised in five groups behind the battle fleet. At 10.15 these consisted of *Castor*, with the 11th Flotilla, composed of 15 destroyers; the 4th Flotilla of 12 destroyers, led by Captain Charles Wintour in the flotilla leader *Tipperary; Champion*, with the 13th Flotilla of 9 destroyers; and finally the 12th Flotilla of 15 destroyers. Astern of this force of 2 light cruisers and 56 destroyers was *Black Prince*, which had survived the disastrous advance of Arbuthnot's squadron, but which had lost touch with *Duke of Edinburgh*, the only other survivor, and seemed to be trying to take up an appropriate station on the battle fleet.[28]

After the previous action in which *Castor* had been so badly damaged, Commodore Hawksley had taken her and his destroyers to the east in order to break off the action. Wintour, meanwhile, had had a brief encounter with German destroyers. A little later *Garland* reported to him a sighting of a German light cruiser heading south. Wintour continued on that course in accordance with his orders. He made no report of either of these contacts with the enemy, judging them of insufficient importance to risk disclosing the Grand Fleet's position to the enemy. Jellicoe, aware only that there had been action to the rear of the battle fleet, asked Hawksley just before 11.00: 'Are you engaging enemy destroyers?' What amounted to a reply to this had already been sent: 'Have been engaged with enemy cruisers.' Aboard *Iron Duke* this not very informative message was taken to mean that these were acting in support of destroyers.[29]

It was now that Jellicoe's failure to define any clear objective for his destroyers for the night was to have a pronounced effect. As Corbett puts it:

> At 11.30 the fight broke out again and the power of Jellicoe's massed flotillas to bar the escape of the High Seas Fleet was put to a fiery test. When the hour came – the hour that was to decide the question which had been the food of so much thought and experiment during the years of preparation – Captain Wintour was leading his flotilla south in line ahead. To the eastward, but nearly seven miles away, was Captain Farie in the light cruiser *Champion*.[30]

The wide gap was due to the fact that the eastern flotillas were keeping station on Burney's division which was dropping further and further astern.

Aboard the British destroyers there was no sense of the likely whereabouts of the enemy. At some time after 11.00, but before 11.30 – accounts vary as to the time – Wintour sighted a line of ships to starboard, apparently steering south east on a course converging with his own. It may be that he took them for Hawksley's ships, for he signalled to *Garland* that the 11th Flotilla was on their starboard beam. Still unclear as to the strangers' identity, he held on his course with all torpedo tubes trained to starboard, until the range was about 1,000 yards before making the recognition signal. He had encountered the head of the German battle line, led by *Westfalen*, which immediately opened fire with her secondary armament, followed by *Nassau* and *Rheinland:*

> Salvoes, accurate and rapid, at point blank followed instantaneously, and in a minute the *Tipperary* burst into flames, almost lost to sight in brilliantly illuminated splashes. Yet she fired both her torpedoes. The four boats of her division did the same, and so did the *Broke*. Some of the rear boats, still uncertain that a mistake was not being made, held their fire till accidentally one of the beams lit up the rear ship. Then it was plain to see what they had to deal with, and they also attacked.[31]

The first salvo hit *Tipperary's* bridge, killing everyone there. The second hit the main steam line, enveloping the after part of the ship in steam. The forward coal bunkers caught fire, and within minutes practically all the crew were down except those to aft, from which her 4 inch guns continued to fire at the enemy. The ship swung to starboard and by 1.35 had stopped in a sinking condition. Swerving to avoid her, *Spitfire,* the next in line, began a turn to starboard with the object of rescuing survivors from *Tipperary,* while firing at the German searchlights. After firing her torpedoes she turned away to reload, and at this moment was caught by a salvo which hit her amidships. Behind her, *Sparrowhawk, Garland* and *Contest* all fired torpedoes, as did *Broke*; but *Achates, Ambuscade, Ardent, Fortune, Porpoise* and *Unity* turned away without doing so. Frost observes:

> Those boats thus lost a marvellous opportunity for effective torpedo fire. The lack of an attack mission, which should have been assigned by the commander in chief, is very evident. The equal lack of initiative on the part of the captains shows a marked deficiency in their training and indoctrination.[32]

Captain Dorling, in his history of destroyer operations during the First World War, set out in detail the problems faced by the destroyer captains during the night:

> To the destroyers, ordered to take station five miles astern of the British battle squadrons, the position was just about as obscure as it could possibly be. All most of them had seen of the actions before dark was their own ships firing heavily into the banks of mist and smoke on the horizon wherever enemy hulls loomed up through the haze. They had no clear conception of what was happening around them, in which direction their enemy had last been seen, or from which direction they might be sighted. Such snatches of wireless conversations between the squadrons of heavier ships that may have been intercepted by their overworked telegraphists must have tended still further to confuse the situation, not to clarify it, Information of the enemy was what they needed, and information was what no senior officer seems to have been in a position to give them.[33]

Their duty was to make certain that they did not attack their own ships; they risked being fired on when approaching these at night, and were perfectly aware that giving the current challenge to an enemy by flashing signal at once revealed them as British, and would result in a hurricane

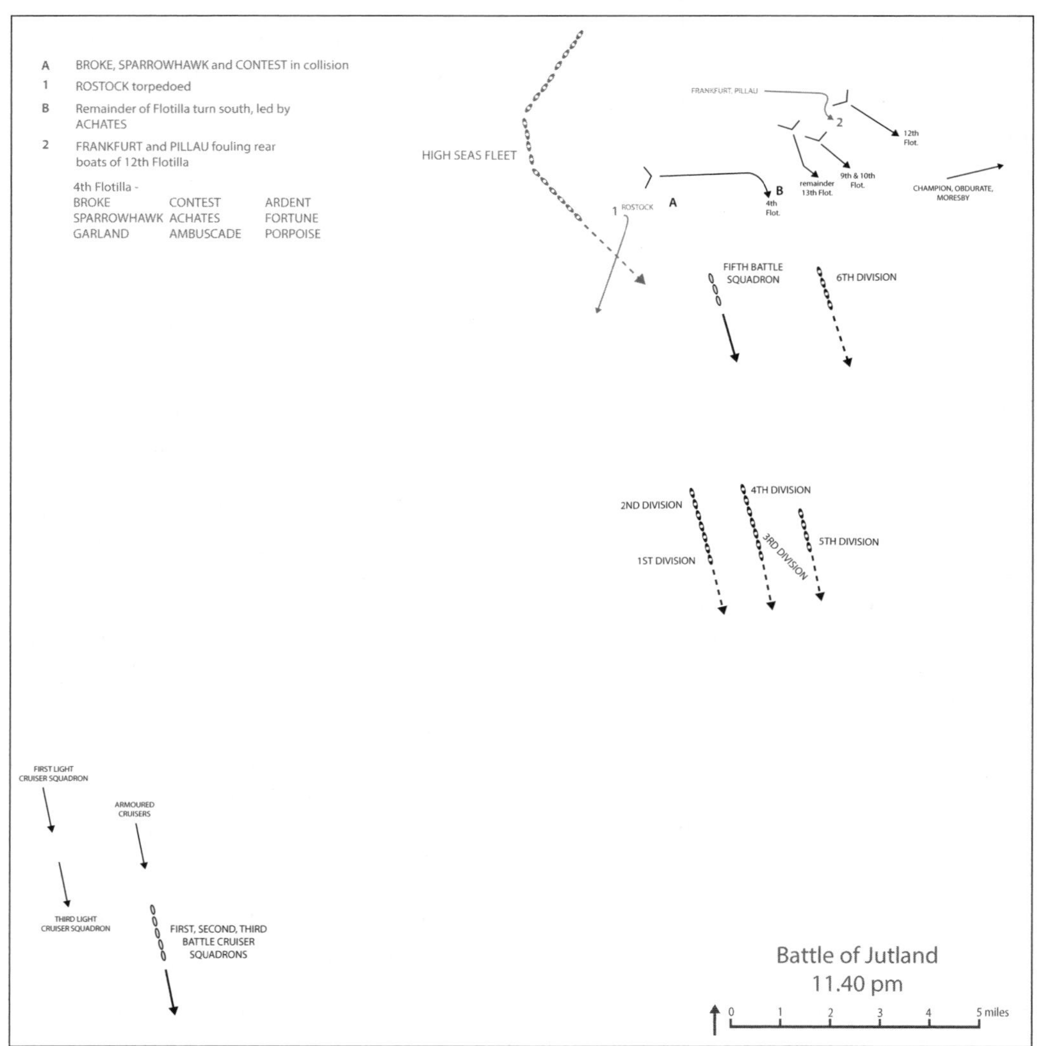

Map 15 Battle of Jutland: 11.40 pm.

of gunfire. 'In the strain and anxiety of the battle, nobody seems to have visualised the inherent difficulties of small craft at night, or to have realised the prime importance of telling them what to expect.'[34]

To the criticisms of Commander Frost and Captain Dorling, Admiral Bacon has an answer. The suggestion that Jellicoe should have explained the situation to his destroyers is, he says, splitting hairs:

> The destroyers knew perfectly well from their printed orders that their business was to attack any of the enemy battleships that were sighted by them. They also knew why they had been stationed well astern of the battle fleet.[35]

But this really will not do. What the destroyer leaders needed was explanatory information about the overall situation; merely knowing the course on which the Grand Fleet was steaming was not enough, not least because neither they nor the light cruisers supporting them were well enough informed to be able to evaluate the significance of the enemy's movements.

None of the German battleships had been hit by the torpedoes that had been launched. *Westfalen, Nassau* and *Rheinland* had turned sharply away to west by south while still firing heavily on the destroyers. *Westfalen,* for instance, in five minutes fired ninety two 5.9 inch shell and forty five 3.5 inch shrapnel. Following these three ships in his flagship *Ostfriesland,* Schmidt turned the rest of his squadron to the same course. Although the battleships had escaped torpedo hits, they did take a number of hits from the destroyers' gunfire, suffering a total of forty nine casualties in this action. The Germans did, however, suffer one serious blow during the engagement. The four light cruisers *Rostock, Elbing, Hamburg* and *Stuttgart* had been steaming on the port side of the column of battle ships, and as a result found themselves in a dangerous situation between them and the British destroyers. *Rostock* turned away at the same time as *Nassau* and *Rheinland* and thus followed them. Unluckily *Elbing,* which had been abeam of *Posen,* turned into the path of the oncoming battleship, which rammed her on her starboard quarter. Her engine rooms quickly flooded, and she listed 18°, drifting to the starboard of the German battle line.

As the Germans switched off their searchlights, the only illumination was the blazing wreck of *Tipperary*, and *Spitfire* turned back towards her with rescue in mind. Suddenly Lieutenant Commander Trelawny became aware of a large ship heading straight for him. Although he put his helm hard over to starboard it was too late to avoid a collision, and the two ships smashed into each other on their port bows. *Spitfire* was steaming at 27 knots; her adversary, the battleship *Nassau,* was doing some 16 knots:

> You can imagine how the one eighth inch plates of a destroyer would feel such a blow. I can recollect a fearful crash, then being hurled across the deck, and feeling the *Spitfire* rolling over to starboard as no sea ever made her roll. As we bumped, the enemy opened fire with their fo'csle guns, though luckily they could not depress them to hit us, but the blast of the guns literally cleared everything before it … The actual damage to the bows and ship's side was considerable. About 60 odd feet from our stern aft along the port side had been torn away, and in exchange the enemy had left 20 feet of her upper deck inside our mess deck.[36]

Garland also turned back to assist *Tipperary,* still burning fiercely. As she did so, *Hamburg* and S*tuttgart* came into sight and opened fire, forcing her away to the east, leaving *Tipperary's* survivors aboard a wreck which, despite her injuries, did not sink at once. Meanwhile the rest of the 4th Flotilla reformed behind the flotilla leader *Broke,* with the exception of *Unity* which had become detached and which joined the 9th Flotilla to the eastward. Commander Allen, in *Broke,* resolved to renew the attack, and led his eight ships on a southerly course, passing the wreck of *Tipperary* to starboard. *Rostock* fired on *Broke,* while *Westfalen* and *Rheinland* (now the second ship in the column after *Nassau's* collision with *Spitfire)* fired on *Sparrowhawk* before turning away. *Broke* took seven hits, causing heavy casualties, and her rudder jammed. Coming up behind, *Sparrowhawk* had been endeavouring to steam in parallel with her, but as *Broke* swung around was directly in her path; the flotilla leader drove into her just forward of the bridge, and the two crippled destroyers hung together, powerless to move. Next in line,

Contest, at full speed, rammed into *Sparrowhawk,* cutting her stern away for five fleet. Behind her, *Achates* narrowly avoided joining the pile up.[37] Commander Hutchinson, her captain, led the remnants of the 4th Flotilla away to the east, and then to the south, in order to rejoin the British battle fleet; unknowingly, however, his course took him back again towards the head of the German line.

At midnight, after exchanging recognition signals with *Pillau* and *Frankfurt, Westfalen* sighted an enemy destroyer to port, and switched on her searchlights and opened fire. She was *Fortune,* the third ship in Hutchinson's column, and she stood no chance as *Westfalen* deluged her with fire from her secondary armament. With her customary speed and accuracy, *Westfalen* fired seven 5.9 inch and eight 3.5 inch rounds in 28 seconds, reducing *Fortune* to a blazing wreck. The remaining five destroyers turned to port to escape the tornado of shells from the four leading German battleships, discharging torpedoes as they did so; in their turn, the dreadnoughts turned away, successfully avoiding them. *Porpoise* was hit by a heavy shell which severed her steam pipe and damaged her steering; the other four turned away in various directions. *Achates* and *Ambuscade* turned east, supposing that they were being pursued by a German cruiser approaching from the north.

It was however, *Black Prince,* still seeking to re-establish contact with the Grand Fleet, and which may have supposed it had done so when a line of heavy ships was sighted. If so, as Groos observed, 'never was an error to have such terrible consequences.'[38] She was first sighted at 12.00 by *Nassau,* which had fallen back to port of the German line, and by *Thüringen.* Challenged, *Black Prince* did not reply, but turned sharply away. In the beam of *Thüringen's* searchlights she was recognised as a British armoured cruiser, and the battleship opened fire with her 5.9 inch and 3.5 inch armament. A total of 51 shells were fired and practically all hit *Black Prince; Ostfriesland*, at 12.07, *Nassau* at 12.10, and *Friedrich der Grosse* at 12.15 joined in. The damage inflicted was fearful:

> She presented a terrible and awe inspiring spectacle as she drifted down the line blazing furiously until, after several minor detonations, she disappeared below the surface with the whole of her crew in one tremendous explosion.[39]

In her death agonies, *Black Prince* passed narrowly astern of the disabled *Spitfire:*

> To our intense relief she missed our stern by a few feet, but so close was she to us that it seemed that we were actually lying under her guns, which were trained out on her starboard beam. She tore past us with a roar, rather like a motor roaring up hill on low gear, and the very crackling and heat of the flames could be heard and felt. She was a mass of fire from foremast to mainmast, on deck and between decks. Flames were issuing out of her from every corner.[40]

Moments later *Westfalen* claimed another victim. *Ardent,* separated from the other surviving destroyers of the 4th Flotilla and seeking to rejoin them, sighted what was taken to be the *Ambuscade's* smoke. It was not; it was the four leading German battleships crossing in front of *Ardent.* The destroyer got off a torpedo before *Westfalen's* searchlights illuminated her, and her secondary armament blazed out. 22 rounds of 5.9 inch and 18 of 3.5 inch were fired at point blank range, reducing *Ardent* to a battered, smoking wreck, which at about 2.30 sank into the icy blackness of the North Sea. Only Commander Arthur Marsden, her captain, and one of her crew survived, the former after spending over five hours in the water before being rescued by the flotilla leader *Marksman*.[41]

Aboard the capital ships not actively engaged in the night action it was not at all clear what was happening. Hase, aboard *Derfflinger* at the rear of the German battle line, was able from time to time to glimpse something of what was going on:

> From our present position we were able to watch undisturbed the fighting which went on for the most part at a considerable distance from us. Searchlights flashed out and lit up the destroyers rushing to the attack. We saw the gun flashes of ships and destroyers, great splashes were lit by searchlights, thick clouds of smoke drove past the ships and destroyers. We were unable to distinguish details, but the result of the struggle was made clear to us when one blazing, red-hot vessel after another passed us ...We watched them with mixed feelings, for we were not quite sure whether any among them were German.[42]

From *Malaya* in the 5th Battle Squadron, the outcome of the engagements was no clearer, as a turret officer recorded:

> We heard and saw several destroyers' attack on the Germans. One especially we had an extremely close view of, some of the German shells fired at our destroyers actually falling around us. I have a very vivid impression of those destroyers dashing into the blinding searchlights and starshells, and into a perfectly furious fire. The leading boat was hit badly, and was soon ablaze from stern to stern. The others seemed to make good their escape after having fired their torpedoes. On this occasion, as during other attacks, we heard and felt heavy explosions as though a torpedo had hit, and one ship was actually seen to sink. One of the explosions lit up the whole sky. It seemed absolutely impossible to know what was going on all around us, and where was friend and where was foe.[43]

Notwithstanding observations of this kind, no reports of these engagements reached Jellicoe. It is, however, remarkable that Jellicoe and his supporting admirals did not react to the sounds of action from their rear, at least to the extent of directly enquiring what was going on. At some point during the night Jellicoe took a break, lying down for a while in his clothes on a settee in the so called 'admiral's shelter' on the bridge of *Iron Duke*.[44] He might reasonably do so, since he had received no information to suggest that the High Seas Fleet was not still to the westward of him. While the relatively low power of the destroyers' wireless made them susceptible to German jamming, so that such messages from them that were sent never reached him, there was at least one failure to report to him that was especially culpable. Admiral Bacon described it as 'an omission difficult to account for except that the human brain, unless thoroughly trained, is a poor reed to lean on in an emergency.'[45] The reference is to the sighting from *Valiant* and *Malaya* at about 11.30 of German battleships, lit up in the flashes of gunfire, in a position almost directly astern of the Grand Fleet. In his official report Captain Boyle of *Malaya* wrote:

> 11.40 Three points abaft starboard beam observed what appeared to be an attack by our destroyers on some enemy big ships steering the same way as ours, two of which used

> searchlights ...The leading ship of the enemy, which was seen by the flash of the explosion, had two masts, two funnels and a conspicuous crane (apparently *Westfalen* class).[46]

This, perhaps, was the most crucial failure of intelligence gathering, which occurred at a time when it would not have been too late to head off Scheer's progress towards Horns Reef.

The ferocious engagements involving the 4th Flotilla did not mark the end of the night's actions. When the first of these commenced at 11.30 the 11th Flotilla, led by Captain Farie in the light cruiser *Champion*, was immediately to the eastward; Farie had nine destroyers with him. A little further away came the 9th and 10th Flotillas, led together by Commander Goldsmith in *Lydiard*; he had a further four destroyers with him. Commander Frost is particularly critical of Farie's response to the situation; some of the German salvoes fell close to his ships, the third vessel *Nerissa* reporting salvoes falling between her and *Moresby*, while searchlights were seen to starboard. It was an opportunity to 'make torpedo attacks under the most favourable conditions against a single column of 24 capital ships, an opportunity of which a destroyer captain dreams.'[47] Farie could, Frost argues, easily have got into a position ahead of the German fleet and attacked on both bows. Instead of taking such aggressive action, Farie turned away, as he explained in his official report:

> About 11.30 pm heavy firing was opened on our starboard beam, apparently at some of our destroyers between the 13th Flotilla and the enemy. I hauled out to the eastward as I was unable to attack with any of our own flotilla, our own forces being between me and the enemy. I then resumed course south; firing was observed at intervals during the night on our starboard beam.[48]

Farie had, Frost points out, withdrawn from the scene of action before a single shell had hit one of his vessels. However, as he made his way eastward at top speed, only two of his destroyers actually accompanied *Champion*. In the darkness, and the confused situation, they would attach themselves to another flotilla. There would certainly be other opportunities for them before the night was over.

18

Dawn

Close beyond Farie's flotilla, and a little to the eastward, were the 9th and 10th flotillas, led by Commander Goldsmith in *Lydiard*, consisting of five destroyers. They were well placed to witness the action of the 4th Flotilla, but as Goldsmith later reported: 'Fire was opened on us by a line of large ships which we took to be our own.' *Landrail* also concluded that the shells falling near to Goldsmith's force were the result of friendly fire. *Liberty* clearly saw four heavy ships at a range of 4,000 yards. When Farie in *Champion* was seen to make off to the east, Goldsmith also turned away, taking a course south east. Unknown to him, his force had grown in strength, *Unity* from the 4th Flotilla having lost her companions and added herself to the tail of the 9th and 10th Flotillas, followed by *Nerissa*. By 12.15 *Lydiard* was five miles to the east of the German van, having witnessed the defeat of the 4th Flotilla and the destruction of *Black Prince*. Goldsmith should by now have been in no doubt that the battleships he had seen were German, but he made no move to attack them. Instead, altering course to cross their line of advance, his objective was merely to get to their other side.

However, to the east of the ineffectual Farie and Goldsmith there was a bolder flotilla commander. Captain Stirling, the leader of the 12th Flotilla, at 11.45 sighted *Champion* with her two companions steaming east at high speed. He was unaware that they had lost the rest of the 13th Flotilla and was obliged himself to turn eastwards to avoid colliding with what he supposed to be a column of ten vessels. Just then there was a brief encounter with *Frankfurt* and *Pillau*, which suddenly appeared, opened fire briefly and then vanished again; Stirling's destroyers were thrown into confusion by the sharp changes of course that became necessary, *Menace* narrowly avoiding being rammed and *Nonsuch* losing touch with the flotilla altogether. Stirling had had finally to turn north east to avoid *Champion* and her destroyers and it was 12.20 before he could turn south again.

Meanwhile the bulk of *Champion's* flotilla had joined Goldsmith's force, which he was steering to pass ahead of the German van. He was not aware of the additional destroyers accompanying him, but he would have been well placed to launch an attack. As it was, almost the entire force passed ahead of *Westfalen* and her consorts, only the last two, *Petard* and *Turbulent*, being in a position to attack. When *Wesfalen* switched on her coloured recognition lights she was no more than 500 yards away from the destroyers. Unluckily, *Petard* had fired all her torpedoes, so the blaze of searchlights which illuminated the four leading battleships displayed a target against which she was impotent. Under a hail of fire, *Petard* turned away, but not before she was hit six times out of nineteen shots. *Turbulent* was not so lucky, her path being barred by *Westfalen* and *Rheinland;* she

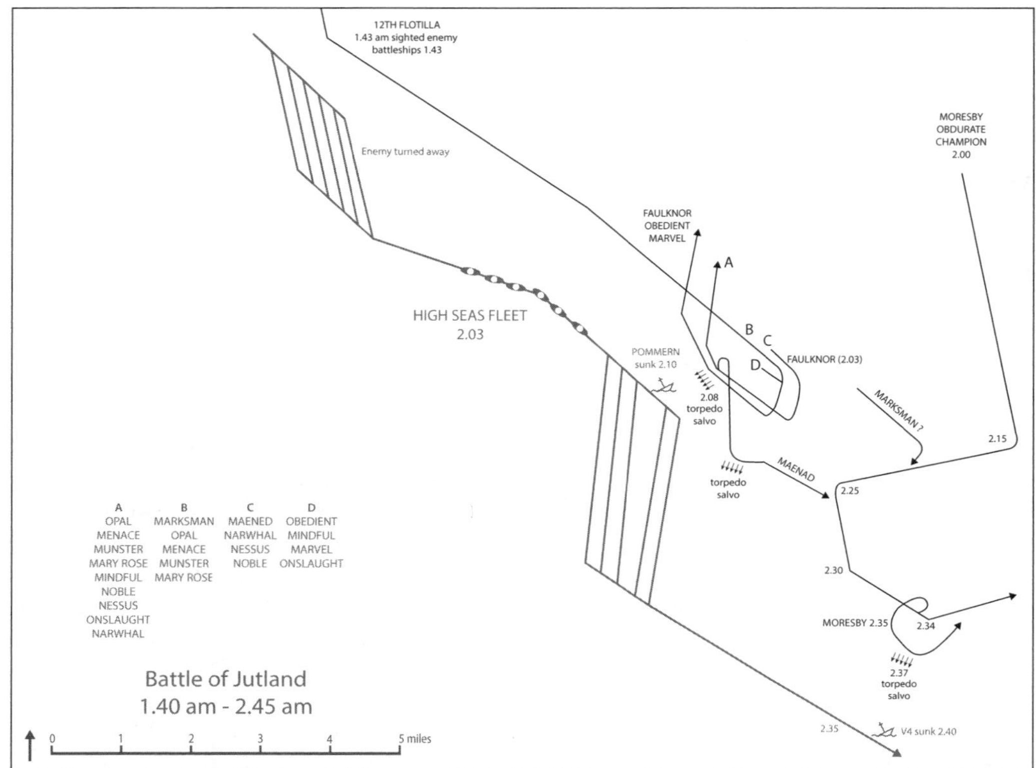

Map 16 Battle of Jutland: 1.40 am to 2.45 am.

put on full speed in an attempt to get ahead of them, but it was too late; spotted by *Westfalen,* that battleship's deadly 5.9 inch and 3.5 inch guns found another victim, smashing *Turbulent* with forty five shells at point blank range, and sinking her with all hands.[1] *Turbulent* went down at 12.32. The two destroyers ahead of *Petard, Pelican* and *Narborough,* were in an excellent position to fire torpedoes at the German battleships, but failed to do so, as did *Nicator,* the next ahead, which clearly observed the enemy. No reference to the incident was made by any other of the destroyers, while Goldsmith only learned of the increment to his force at 6.00 am. Frost comments, justly, that 'the whole episode is a glaring example of ineffective leadership and inertness.'[2] An account written from *Nicator* admitted that 'it somehow did not strike us that this was the German fleet breaking through the line unluckily at the weakest point,' which explains why no report was made.[3] There is no explanation for the failure of *Petard, Pelican* and *Narborough* to make a sighting report; but this is no more surprising than the curiously placid view taken aboard *Bellerophon*, stationed three ships from the rear of Sturdee's 4th Battle Squadron. In his report, Captain Bruen wrote:

> During the first watch there was quite a lot of firing going on to the NE and a cruiser seemed to be on fire pretty badly. At about 2340 there was further firing astern and for the first hour or so of the middle watch there was intermittent firing on the port quarter. Otherwise the night passed without incident.[4]

Following the destruction of *Turbulent* and the narrow escape of *Petard* there was a lull in the fighting, and the High Seas Fleet proceeded on its course. Only the 4th Flotilla had made any effective attempt to bar its way, and by 12.30 the only British units in a position to make a further attack on Scheer's battle line were Stirling's 12th Flotilla and Farie in *Champion*, with *Obdurate* and *Moresby*.

> It was doubtful whether those flotillas could make contact before daylight. At a cost of serious damage to two light cruisers, the German battleships had forced a passage through the very centre of the British destroyer mass, sinking 5 and seriously damaging 5 more. It was a brilliant feat of arms on the part of the Germans. High credit should go to the captains leading the battle line and particularly to Captain Redlich of the *Westfalen*, who had proved fully worthy of the high responsibility thrust upon him.[5]

Once Stirling had returned to his southern course he began to catch up with the German battle line and by 1.43 am the lead ship of his 1st Division, *Obedient* (Commander Campbell) reported enemy ships to the southwest; two minutes later, in the early dawn light they were recognisable from *Faulknor*, Stirling's ship, as *Kaiser* class battleships. He turned on a course parallel with the enemy and increased speed to 25 knots and ordered his 1st Division to attack. Before it could do so, the German ships disappeared again, as Campbell reported, and Stirling cancelled the attack. Campbell appears not to have made any very sustained attempt to follow the enemy. Stirling guessed that if the German battleships had turned away they would return to their south-easterly course, and he manoeuvred to get his flotilla into a good position to resume the attack. Unfortunately, he relied on the ships of his flotilla to follow *Fauknor* as she steamed at full speed to get ahead of the enemy, and the lack of a signal caused great confusion, not least because it resulted in the stringing out of his column.

What Stirling also did, however was to send a report at 1.56 by radio to Jellicoe: 'To C-in-C. Urgent. Priority. Enemy battleships in sight. My position is ten miles astern of 1st Battle Squadron.' In fact, his position was some 26 miles on the port quarter. Unhappily neither this message nor its repeating at 3.08, nor a third at 3.13, got through, due to the low power of the destroyers' wireless equipment which was unable to overcome the German jamming of British signals. If any of Stirling's messages were picked up by other British ships, they did not in any case reach Jellicoe.[6]

At 2.00 Stirling led his force around to starboard. He was followed by *Obedient, Marvel* and *Onslaught*. Almost at once he sighted the German battle line. Conditions for an attack were favourable; the increasing light reduced the effectiveness of the German searchlights, but it was still dark enough to allow the British destroyers to advance unseen. In addition to this, the move coincided with the arrival of German destroyers of V and IX Flotillas, with which the battleships were exchanging recognition signals. When *Faulknor* and her companions were spotted by *Markgraf* and *Kronprinz,* the battleships were at first in doubt as to whether they were German. Two minutes after *Faulknor's* turn, however, the battleships opened fire, while the destroyers all launched torpedoes. *Markgraf, Grosser Kurfürst* and *Kronprinz* all successfully took evading action, but the old predreadnought *Pommern* was not so lucky, hit by two torpedoes. An officer on the bridge of *Obedient* described her end:

> Right amidships on the waterline of the ship that we had fired at – the *Pommern,* now on our port quarter – appeared a dull red ball of fire. Quicker than one can imagine it spread

> fore and aft, until reaching the foremast and mainmast it flared upwards, up the masts in big red tongues of flame, uniting between the mastheads in a big black cloud of smoke and sparks. Then one saw the ends of the ship come up as though her back was broken, before the mist shut her out from view.[7]

844 officers and men went down with *Pommern*; there were no survivors. A section of her bow was still visible twenty minutes after the attack.

Following her, *Hannover* was obliged to turn to starboard to avoid the wreck, in the end as much as eight points, as did *Nassau*; torpedoes passed ahead and astern of her. *Schlesien,* opening fire on *Onslaught,* turned away to avoid two more torpedoes; *Schleswig-Holstein*, firing on *Onslaught*, remained on course, and her third salvo hit the destroyer's bridge, killing her captain. Meanwhile other destroyers of the flotilla had got into position to launch their torpedoes. None, however, found a target. Not all of Stirling's destroyers did, however, manage to launch a torpedo a failure which Frost calls 'an inexcusable lack of initiative.' As a result Stirling's bold attack failed to achieve the decisive success that might have been possible.[8]

While Stirling was attacking the rear of the German line, there was a mysterious incident at the head of the line, where *V2, V4* and *V6* of the V Flotilla had been steaming about 200 yards off the port beam of *Westfalen* and *Rheinland.* Suddenly a violent explosion blew off the bow of *V4*, killing 17 of her crew and wounding 2. No explanation was forthcoming; it was unlikely to have been one of Stirling's torpedoes, which could not have reached the German van. There had been no indication of any mines in the vicinity, nor were there any submarines, although her captain's first report was that it was caused by ramming a submarine.

It may be that one of her own torpedoes exploded accidentally. *V2* and *V6* rescued the surviving crew before sinking the stern section by gunfire and a torpedo from *V6*.[9]

Meanwhile Captain Farie, in *Champion,* still accompanied by *Obdurate* and *Moresby*, had been steaming SE until changing course to due south at 1.45. At 2.15, hearing the attack of the 12th Flotilla, he turned west, five minutes later encountering *Marksman,* one of the destroyers that had not participated in the flotilla's attack, and *Maenad,* which had done so. Farie signalled *Marksman*: 'Where are enemy's ships?' getting the reply that there were suspicious ships to the south. At 2.25 Farie accordingly altered course, asking *Marksman* where the British battle fleet was, to which the reply was 'Bearing south.' Five minutes later *Marksman* asked: 'What are ships bearing south,' to which *Champion's* reply was 'Germans, I think.' Although Farie now had four destroyers with him, he made no move to attack, turning to the SE. At 2.34 *Moresby* sighted four German predreadnoughts, and turned sharply to port, launching a torpedo which *Von der Tann* was obliged to turn to starboard to avoid. Farie, meanwhile, with the rest of his force, turned sharply to the east, directly away from the German battleships, although well aware of their identity. In his official report, Farie made no mention of this.[10]

As dawn began to lighten the sky Jellicoe, on the bridge of *Iron Duke,* anxiously sought signs or news of the High Seas Fleet. The weather was misty, and visibility not more than 7,000 yards. At 2.00 he learned from Burney that *Marlborough* could no longer maintain the Fleet speed of 17 knots, and must ease down to 12 knots. He ordered the battleship to return to the Tyne or Rosyth, and Burney transferred his flag to *Revenge*.[11] No enemy being visible, Jellicoe resolved to turn north if nothing materialised, and at 2.15 he ordered his battle squadrons to turn northward in single line ahead; he was prepared to take the risk of a submarine attack in order to be ready for the High Seas Fleet if sighted. His purpose in turning north was to collect his light forces, without which he felt decidedly exposed. He set out his reasoning and his firm conclusion:

> The difficulties experienced in collecting the Fleet (particularly the destroyers) ... rendered it undesirable for the Battle Fleet to close the Horns Reef at daylight, as had been my intention when deciding to steer to the southward during the night. It was obviously necessary to concentrate the Battle Fleet and the destroyers before renewing action. By the time this concentration was effected it had become apparent that the High Seas Fleet, steering for the Horns Reef, had passed behind the shelter of the German minefields in the early morning on the way to their ports.[12]

All through the night he had believed that Scheer was to the west of him; even now, as dawn broke, he had no idea that the High Seas Fleet had already forced its way through the Grand Fleet's destroyer screen. Beatty was even wider of the mark; as the eastern sky began to lighten he was still convinced that Scheer was not only well to the westward, but had been steaming southward in an attempt to get around the battle cruisers and the van of the Grand Fleet. He was on the point of seeking permission to reconnoitre to the southwest when at 2.22 he received Jellicoe's order to turn north to join the battle fleet:

> Neither of the British leaders' suppositions was correct. Neither of them had taken into account Scheer's bold determination to break through in the direction of Horns Reef regardless of any forces he might encounter on the way to his objective. While they still supposed that the German Fleet was to the north, west or south of the British Fleet, the High Seas Fleet was actually, at 2.30 am, only 16 miles to the west of the Horns Reef lightship and about 30 miles northeast of the *Iron Duke*.[13]

Groos goes on to observe that Jellicoe, who could at dawn have turned east towards Horns Reef, was evidently extremely conscious of the vulnerability of the Grand Fleet, notwithstanding its huge material superiority:

> Even if, during his march southward during the night, Jellicoe had decided to make for the Horns Reef at dawn should the German Fleet not have been sighted by then, he now considered himself no longer strong enough to do so, but decided to stand on to the northward, at least until his missing forces, particularly the destroyer flotillas, had rejoined. That this decision involved a complete renunciation of all hopes of bringing the German Fleet to action was indeed by no means clear to him; on the contrary, he still believed that he was between it and its base. He expected to encounter the enemy again at any moment ... But the enemy failed to appear, and neither Beatty's battle cruisers, the 6th Division, nor his cruisers and destroyer flotillas came into sight, for errors in the dead reckoning, which had steadily increased during the night, made it particularly difficult for the British forces to reassemble.[14]

The variation in the dead reckoning was very considerable; aboard *Hercules* it was ascertained from an observation of the sun that the difference between her dead reckoning and observed position was as much as 30 miles.

Scheer, on the bridge of *Friedrich der Grosse*, had during the night been able to see for himself the beating off of the British destroyer attacks, and had been receiving reports of these engagements, and particularly of the situation of the badly damaged ships. He was, however, no better informed of the position of enemy battleships than was Jellicoe. It was not until 1.27 that he received information of the contacts of *Moltke* with the enemy battle line. Sent via the destroyer *G39* because of the damage to *Moltke's* radio, Hipper's message reported the battle cruiser's position at 12.30, adding the vital news that he had been forced off his course by four hostile battleships but would attempt to rejoin the fleet at dawn:

> That was the first report of British battleships Scheer had received for many hours. Unfortunately, the report told principally of the *Moltke* and only incidentally of the British battleships. Had Scheer been given the time and place of the contact with them and their course, all of which were known to the *Moltke*, he could have estimated rather closely the position of the Grand Fleet. As it was, Scheer might have reasoned from the fact that the *Moltke* had been forced to the south to avoid the enemy, that the latter's course was either south or somewhat east of south, an indication that British battleships were in close proximity but probably were steering a somewhat divergent course. At any rate, regardless of what inference he may or may not have drawn from Hipper's unsatisfactory contact report, Scheer held to his course, determined to fight his way through at any price.[15]

Moltke had, by the time Scheer read Hipper's report, got far enough ahead of the Grand Fleet to turn east and pass closely ahead of it, and by 2.00 pm was 12 miles on *Iron Duke's* port beam and safe from danger.

Behind the High Seas Fleet the crews of three crippled German ships were struggling to keep their vessels afloat. Of these, much the most important was *Lützow*. As late as 12.00 there seemed some hope that she might make it back to port; but by 1.00 the huge volume of water that she had taken aboard in the forepart of the ship was overcoming even the stout bulkheads that were such a feature of her design. By 1.30 the waves began washing over her deck; an attempt to steam stern first to relieve the pressure failed when her propellers came out of the water. At 2.20 Captain Harder recognised that, to save her crew, the battle cruiser must be abandoned:

> The order to draw fires was passed to the engine room, the ship's company fell in on the quarterdeck and the torpedo boats *G37*, *G38*, *G40* and *V45*, which had been in company since the termination of the daylight action, came alongside. After three cheers for the Kaiser and for the *Lützow* had been given, the ship's company, the wounded first, left the sinking vessel quietly and in perfect order. By 2.45 am she was submerged as far as the bridge. Two torpedoes fired by the G38 gave the *Lützow* her *coup de grâce*, and two minutes later she disappeared below the waves. If there was anything that could console Captain Harder for the loss of his ship it was, as he states in his report, 'the military virtues displayed by his ship's company which had left in his heart an unquenchable pride that it should have been given to him to lead them.'[16]

At much the same time the remarkable *Wiesbaden* finally went down; of her brave crew only one survived long enough in the icy waters of the North Sea to be rescued. Two other German light cruisers went down, though only after prolonged efforts to keep them afloat. *Elbing*, some 30 miles south of *Lützow's* resting place, lay stopped, her engines flooded, and at about 2.00 am Captain Madlung recognised that he must discharge the bulk of his crew into the destroyer *S53* to save their lives; 477 men were transferred, but he remained aboard, with his executive officer, torpedo officer, and explosives party and the cutter's crew. He rigged a sail in the hope that with this he might drift towards the coast; but at 3.00, sighting enemy destroyers, he gave orders for her to be scuttled.[17]

Rostock, the flagship of Commodore Michelsen, crippled since being hit by a torpedo at 11.50, was making directly for the German Bight in a southerly direction, at a reduced speed of 10 knots, with the assistance of *S54*. At 2.25 she was also joined by *V71* and *V73*. At 3.55 she was sighted by *Dublin*, but, by using the British recognition signal persuaded the light cruiser that she was British. A report from the Zeppelin L11 that a squadron of British battleships was approaching, however, convinced Michelsen that *Rostock* must be abandoned; her crew was transferred to the escorting destroyers and she was sunk by torpedo.[18]

The four destroyers carrying the crew of *Lützow* had got to within thirty five miles of the Horns Reef lightship when they encountered *Garland* and *Contest*. Captain Beitzen, the senior officer, decided to attack; there was a brisk exchange of fire as the destroyers approached and then passed each other, after which the British destroyers turned away. The Captain of *Contest* described the affair somewhat differently in his report:

> 2.23 sighted four German TBDs heading SSE at full speed. Altered course to cross their bows and opened fire at about 5000 yards. Germans at first began to turn on a parallel course and returned our fire. At least one shot was seen to take effect on the stern of one German TBD.[19]

Beitzen was not yet out of the wood. At 3.20 he sighted *Champion* with the destroyers *Obdurate*, *Maenad*, *Marksman* and *Moresby* in position to cut off his route to Horns Reef. Again he resolved to attack, a decision which, since his opponents were led by Captain Farie, was probably the wisest course. Groos described the encounter:

> The torpedo boats turned towards the enemy, opened rapid fire and at about 3.30 am the *G40* fired one and the *V45* two torpedoes at ranges between 2400 and 2700 yards. A fire was observed almost at once in the cruiser and a big explosion in one of the destroyers. The hostile vessels turned away and did not take up the chase. The *G40* suffered a hit on her after turbine but was able to maintain 26 knots for another ten minutes in spite of considerable danger to the engine room personnel from escaping steam. She was then, however, forced to stop and was taken in tow by one of the other boats.[20]

In fact, none of the British ships were hit; claims of imaginary hits were frequently made on both sides in good faith throughout the battle, illustrating just how easily such mistakes could be made. Farie's account of the engagement was contained in his official report:

> At 3.25 am four destroyers, steering southward, were sighted; owing to the mist I was uncertain at first who they were; but at 3.30 am I made them out to be the enemy, and opened fire, range about 3000 yards. Two torpedoes were fired at *Champion*, the first one

> passing under our bows, the second just missing close astern. Enemy passed on opposite course, and when ship had been steadied after avoiding torpedoes, the enemy had disappeared in the mist, and I resumed my same course.[21]

Given the superiority of his force, it seems surprising that he made no attempt to re-establish contact.

Aboard Jellicoe's battleships as the sun rose there was a strong feeling of expectation, as a midshipman in *Neptune's* foretop recorded:

> Shortly before three we heard heavy firing to the eastward. The visibility was quite good, and gave promise of a better day; we had plenty of ammunition left, and felt that, given the chance, we could make short work of what remained of the enemy. Was this the chance? All quarters were warned. The guns had been left loaded all night, and were as ready as we were to start again. The silhouette of our battle cruisers became faintly visible, but there was no sign of the enemy. We searched the horizon all round with glasses, hoping to find some target, but there was nothing.[22]

Jellicoe's decision to turn northwards to collect his light forces, rather than east to Horns Reef, did not indicate that he had entirely rejected the idea that this would be Scheer's target. It was always a live possibility in his mind, as he had demonstrated as night fell, ordering the minelayer *Abdiel* to proceed to a point fifteen miles west of the Vyl lightship, there to lay a minefield which might catch returning vessels of the High Seas Fleet. She successfully carried out the task, although in the event with no result. In fact, however, when close to home, *Ostfriesland* struck a mine laid previously, although not seriously damaged.

The operation that Scheer had previously planned had had to be given up, and the advance towards the Norwegian coast substituted for it, because the weather deprived him of airship reconnaissance. Now, on the morning of June 1, the Zeppelins had a chance to prove their effectiveness. Ironically, Scheer's message calling for airship reconnaissance off Horns Reef, which had provided the Admiralty with such valuable intelligence, never reached its destination. However, *Korvettenkapitän* Strasser, the commander of the Airship Division, acted on his own initiative, ordering five Zeppelins to reconnoitre the North Sea at dawn as far as the Skagerrak. Soon after 11.00 pm *L11, L13, L17, L22* and *L24* took off on this mission, but with the coming of daylight visibility was extremely poor, and the information which they furnished was correspondingly inaccurate.

At 3.40 one of the Zeppelins briefly revived the hopes of the Grand Fleet that the battle might be resumed, when it flew over Beatty's battle cruisers. It was driven off by gunfire from *Indomitable* and ships of the 3rd Light Cruiser Squadron. The sound of the gunfire led Jellicoe at once to alter course by divisions in the direction whence it came. But disappointment quickly followed when the cause became apparent, and by 3.52 he had turned the battle fleet back on its original course. Shortly after this the Zeppelin came in sight of the battleships, most of which fired at her before she disappeared into the clouds.[23]

At 3.55 there was received in *Iron Duke* a message from the Admiralty, sent at 3.29, which finally put paid to Jellicoe's last hopes of finding the enemy again. It was to the effect that at 2.30 am the German battle fleet was 17 miles from Horns Reef, steering SE by S at 16 knots. Beatty, unaware of this crushing news, was still convinced that Scheer was to the west or southwest, and that the turn north was a mistake. At 4.05 he sent a message repeating his desire to scout to the southwest; repeatedly jammed by German interference, it was delayed in transmission until after Jellicoe had received the Admiralty message and he naturally refused permission. Notwithstanding this, Beatty was still certain that he was right and he pushed his light cruisers further to the west to look out in this direction. Even as late as 4.30 he felt able to make a characteristic sub-Nelsonian signal to his battle cruisers:

> Damage yesterday was heavy on both sides, we hope today to cut off and annihilate the whole German Fleet. Every man must do his utmost. *Lützow* is sinking and another German Battle Cruiser expected to have sunk.[24]

Mindful perhaps of his own losses, he found it necessary to allude to those of the enemy in a message which, it is not altogether fanciful to conclude, like his suggestion the previous evening was written with an eye to posterity.

At 2.55 Scheer received from Hipper, through *G39,* a report as to the condition of his battle cruisers which made clear that they could not be counted on to contribute a great deal should there be a resumption of the fighting. *Derfflinger* and *Von der Tann* both had only two guns of their main armament in working order, *Moltke* had taken on 1000 tons of water and *Seydlitz* had suffered heavy damage.[25] Scheer ordered Hipper to return to port, while he waited off Horns Reef with the battle fleet to await developments.

Meanwhile *L24*, after having been fired on several times by vessels she could not identify, flew on towards the Skagerrak. At 3.00 she made what seemed an important discovery, reporting the sighting of 12 large units and many cruisers in Jammer Bay, on the northwest coast of Denmark. It was certainly a sighting error; there were no British warships there and Corbett suggests it was possibly a convoy.[26] When it was reported to Scheer, however, it seemed a possible explanation of what had happened to the British battle fleet after night had fallen.

A more accurate sighting report came from *L11,* who reported at 4.00 sighting what she supposed to be the Grand Fleet as it headed northward; in fact it was Beatty's fleet, the Zeppelin having counted cruisers as dreadnoughts in its assessment. It was *L11* who had attracted the gunfire first from Beatty's ships and then from the Grand Fleet. At about 3.50 *L11* reported sighting what she reported as three battle cruisers and escorting destroyers; in fact she had seen Burney's three remaining battleships with three destroyers which had not yet rejoined the Grand Fleet.[27] Reviewing these reports, Scheer erroneously concluded that the ships in Jammer Bay were the Grand Fleet, and accordingly discounted the more accurate reports from *L11*; he supposed that the ships reported were a new force, possibly from Harwich.

It was worth considering the possibility of bringing this force to action but, Groos observes, it must have seemed hopeless:

> The encounter and its consequences would have remained entirely a matter of chance, and that was a risk that Admiral Scheer did not feel justified in incurring until his ships had replenished with fuel and ammunition and had had their more serious defects remedied. The leading ships of III Battle Squadron, if not the others, had suffered a serious diminution of fighting power, and after the experiences of the night (*Pommern)* it was clear that the older ships of II Battle Squadron must not be exposed again to the effects of modern weapons. In addition, almost all the torpedo boats had expended the greater part of their

> complement of torpedoes and no longer possessed the necessary radius of action for an immediate repetition of the undertaking. The Commander-in-Chief therefore very rightly gave up all idea of further operations, and at 3.45 pm directed II Battle Squadron to return to harbour.[28]

Forming his battle fleet into a single line, he remained off Horns Reef in the hope that *Lützow* might be escorted back; but after hearing from Beitzen that she had been sunk he ordered his fleet back to port. Apart from *Seydlitz,* the injuries to which made the task of bringing her in extremely difficult, the fleet was back in the Jade by the afternoon of June 1. *Seydlitz* grounded briefly at 2.40 east of Horns Reef North Buoy and then again abreast of Hörnum Island:

> Consequently, the *Seydlitz*, assisted by two salvage steamers, did not arrive at the Jade until dawn on June2, and even then much strenuous work was necessary before the battle cruiser reached the dockyard lock. Only the conspicuous seamanship displayed by Captain von Egidy, Commander von Alvensleben (the executive officer) and her war-tried crew enabled the ship to be saved.[29]

While the High Seas Fleet made its way back into harbour, Jellicoe was steaming north in cruising order in search of damaged enemy ships. He was aware that *Lützow* at least had been far behind Scheer's battle fleet. A report from *Dublin,* which had become detached from Goodenough's Squadron, that she had sighted an enemy cruiser with two destroyers, did not affect his movements. Beatty, thinking that *Dublin* had sighted *Lützow,* turned at 5.40 to the south east, but saw nothing. In fact *Dublin* had sighted *Regensburg,* which had gone towards Beitzen's destroyers to offer assistance. At 7.00 Beatty radioed Jellicoe to say that if he sighted nothing by 7.30 he would make a sweep NE; Jellicoe replied that he would sweep northward and that Beatty should keep to the eastward of him. At 8.00 Beatty turned up north in the wake of *Iron Duke*, some thirty miles astern.[30]

For the next two hours Jellicoe cruised among the wreckage which was scattered over a wide area, steaming back to the SSW before turning back to the north. After two hours nothing had been seen of the enemy, nor any crippled ships found:

> Admiral Jellicoe now therefore made up his mind that further search was useless, and at 10.44 he so informed the Admiralty. 'The Harwich Force,' he signalled, 'not required except for destroyers to screen *Marlborough.* Am ascertaining no disabled ships are left and am returning to base. Whole area swept for disabled enemy cruisers without result.' That was the end, and just after 11.00 he turned NW direct for Scapa, while Admiral Beatty, still apparently unwilling to admit the disheartening truth, diverged NNE.[31]

The world's greatest sea battle had ended.

19

Aftermath

The weather in the North Sea, which had been bright and clear on the previous day, began to deteriorate during the morning of June 1. Soon after 11.00 am, after the hours spent searching for an enemy fleet which long since had turned for home, Jellicoe had reluctantly given the order for the Grand Fleet to return to base. During the search many relics of the fight were to be seen:

> Patches of oil, with in the centre some wreckage or even the bows of a ship still sticking up, and floating bodies around. It was even possible in a very few cases to rescue a man here or there from the wreckage still alive, but very few were these, for the cold of the North Sea is soon numbing in its effect, and humans floating in it mercifully soon lose their senses, become drowsy, and then drown.[1]

Throughout the rest of that day and the following night the battle-scarred ships of the Grand Fleet wearily made the long journey home. Some, seriously damaged in the previous day's fighting, steamed back individually under escort, facing not only the bad weather which sprang up during June 1, but also the risk of enemy action from the U boats posted across their course:

> Struggling back across the North Sea on June 1, June 2, and even on June 3, there were half a dozen or more crippled British ships, some in the tow of another ship or some in tow of another cripple – *Onslow* and *Defender*, for example, almost all with their wireless shot away, their navigational appliances gone, and for many their seaworthiness dangerously impaired by the damage received in action. *Marlborough*, *Warspite*, *Southampton*, *Broke*, *Spitfire*, *Onslaught*, these and a number of other damaged ships were struggling back, some at no more than 4 or 5 knots speed, or some even, as was the *Broke* on account of her bows being smashed up, forced to turn stern to sea and making back on June 2 towards the coast of Germany, before the dying down of the gale allowed her to make good some ground on a westerly course.[2]

Not all of them made it home; the armoured cruiser *Warrior*, towed by the seaplane carrier *Engadine* since 8.00 pm on the day of the battle, finally had to be abandoned at 7.00 am on the following day, when all her surviving crew were rescued. During June 1 the Grand Fleet was devoted to the mournful task of committing to the deep the bodies of those killed in the battle, wrapped as tradition demanded in their hammocks. The crews of all the ships were utterly exhausted and not a little confused about what had transpired, and a sense of anti climax pervaded the fleet. For some, the battle had been especially traumatic; for those in the battle cruisers, the sight of the sudden destruction of three of their number had affected them deeply, as it had many of their leaders. After the funeral service for the ninety nine men killed aboard *Lion*, Beatty, deeply moved, came into his flagship's chart room. Rear Admiral Chalmers, his subsequent biographer, at that time a young officer serving on his staff, later recorded his demeanour:

> Tired and depressed, he sat down on the settee, and settling himself in a corner he closed his eyes. Unable to hide his disappointment at the result of the battle, he repeated in a weary voice, 'There is something wrong with our ships,' he added, 'And something wrong with our system.' Having thus unburdened himself he fell asleep.[3]

The battle cruisers reached Rosyth on the morning of June 2; the main body of the Grand Fleet entered Scapa Flow that afternoon. There were cheers at Rosyth from the civilian population that witnessed the arrival of the battle cruisers, but this was by no means a unanimous reaction. Bill Fell, a midshipman on the battered *Warspite*, recorded the vessel's reception when she limped home:

> I don't think we gave any thought to how we would be received at home. But as we passed up the Firth of Forth and under the bridge, all the railway people were lined along it. To our dismay they shouted 'Cowards! Cowards, you ran away!' 'and chucked lumps of coal at us. We were received at Rosyth with very, very great disapproval by the local people. They were all in mourning black hats and black arm-bands. They all felt the Grand Fleet had suffered complete defeat and that some ships, like the *Warspite*, had run away. That was the news that had reached Scotland and it was twenty four hours before things got better, when the other ships returned and more facts were known.'[4]

There were other such scenes, prompted by the rumours that the Grand Fleet had suffered a heavy defeat. These, rapidly disseminated, were partly triggered by the Admiralty having issued precautionary orders to dockyards all along the East Coast to be prepared to receive badly damaged warships. Such a public response came as a horrifying surprise to those that encountered it. Ralph Seymour, Beatty's Flag-Lieutenant, wrote to his mother on June 4:

> It was probably one of the most fiercely contested and bloodiest naval battles in history, and the most powerful fleet but one was put to flight in exactly ten minutes, and escaped annihilation by the skin of their teeth. We have returned and are told there has been a disaster! Our losses are grievous! and our Admirals fools![5]

Officers were in a better position to know something of what had occurred during the battle; for most of the seamen it was a matter of optimistic guesswork:

> We on the lower deck had no means of telling the outcome of the Jutland Battle, and we were quite confident that the German Fleet had been sent to the bottom. In the early morning light, on June 1, we saw much floating debris as we swept over the scene of the

> fray, but, save for a solitary airship, there was no sign of the enemy. The previous night we had clashed with what we had imagined to be a ghostly remnant of Scheer's Fleet, and were sure that our victory was complete. But now, back at Scapa, amidst the bustle of refuelling, reports were fluttering through that the honours were with the Germans and that we had suffered a moral defeat. It was beyond belief, and we concluded that the news was German-inspired; but it did have a chilling effect upon our self-confidence.[6]

The public mood was not improved by the release of an official communiqué from the Admiralty, at 7.00 pm on June 2, following receipt of Jellicoe's first report and prompted by the announcements from the other side of the North Sea. The communiqué, drafted in a flat, official tone, conveyed a sense that the Grand Fleet had, indeed, suffered a defeat. Authorship of this document was ascribed to Arthur Balfour, although Admiral Sir Frederick Hamilton, the Second Sea Lord, noted in his diary that it had been written by Balfour's private secretary.[7] The Chief Naval Censor Douglas Brownrigg, on the other hand, was quite clear that it was composed by Balfour, Jackson and Oliver, the Chief of Naval Staff.[8] At all events Balfour, not perhaps the politician most sensitive to popular reaction, was content that the announcement should stick to the truth as it was known, and not put any spin on the facts.

Not surprisingly, the Grand Fleet's leaders were furious at the slightest suggestion that they had been defeated. Hamilton, visiting Rosyth, found Beatty well and cheerful, 'but very angry with the Admiralty for their very stupid communiqué.' He also noted the first hints that there might be issues as to who was to blame, Beatty showing traces of indignation that he had not been supported earlier by Jellicoe. Beatty expressed his anger in a letter to HA Gwynne, the editor of the 'Morning Post' on June 18, complaining that although the Admiralty communiqué had been 'downright bloody foolishness,' it was not to be expected that the Press should put on it the interpretation that they did; it did not say much for their faith in the Navy. Naturally, he wrote, his men were furious; they had done gloriously, and none could have done more.[9]

Jellicoe was equally upset. Following his first reports to the Admiralty he sent a priority telegram at 2.40 pm on June 3:

> Submit communication to Press re enemy casualties and our own and general history of action may be amended to agree with my reports in my 994 and 995. Last night's communiqué magnifies ours and minimises enemy casualties and gives somewhat false impression of action generally.[10]

Jellicoe followed this up next day by suggesting to the Admiralty that there should be immediate publication of the fact that 'the British Fleet remained on and to the southward of the scene of action during the greater part of June 1, looking for the enemy.'[11]

Lord Fisher, always ready to jump to conclusions, was entirely bowled over by the German claims of victory, even though he really should have known better to await a fuller statement of the facts. On June 2, the physicist Sir Joseph Thomson visited him in his office at the Board of Invention and Research. He found him 'more dejected than any man I have ever seen.' Fisher was taking the apparent setback extremely personally, repeating: 'They've failed me, they've failed me! I have spent thirty years of my life preparing for this day, and they've failed me.'[12] To be fair to Fisher, he wrote a handsome letter on June 18 to Jellicoe when he knew more of the facts:

I hear from an onlooker that your deployment into battle was Nelsonic and inspired, as you could see nothing, and that in consequence you saved Beatty from destruction, and in one hour (given vision) you would have ensured Trafalgar. I got this from a most disinterested observer, *so I bless you with all my heart*.'[13]

Perhaps feeling some sensitivity at the way in which the Admiralty's first announcement had been so badly handled, Balfour wrote a soothing private letter to Jellicoe on June 6:

If the Grand Fleet had some reason to feel disappointed over the public attitude on Friday night and Saturday morning, they certainly have no reason to be dissatisfied now. Opinion has undergone a revolution, both rapid and complete. You were robbed by physical conditions of a victory which, with a little good fortune, would have been complete and crushing; and I feel deeply for your disappointment. But your reasons for satisfaction are many and great. You have dealt a heavy blow at an enemy who, for nearly two years, has contrived to evade you; you have had the opportunity of testing for the first time the efficacy of your fleet under modern conditions of warfare; and you have gained a victory which is of the utmost value to the allied cause. You may well be content![14]

The subsequent communiqués from the Admiralty, issued in obedience to Jellicoe's requests, had indeed had to a large extent the effect which Belfour claimed. At 1.15 am on June 3 the Admiralty announced that the disparity in losses was not as great as had first appeared. And on the late evening of the following day the Admiralty went a good deal further in claiming victory. It gave a much higher estimate of German losses, and noted that Jellicoe had driven the High Sea Fleet into port, before returning to the scene of action in search of disabled vessels. In this communiqué, to which Winston Churchill made a substantial contribution, the Admiralty followed the example of its German counterpart, and boldly departed from the truth, boasting that two German battleships and two battle cruisers had been sunk.[15] This was loosely based on Jellicoe's telegram to the Admiralty of 10.48 pm, and was much more to the taste of the Commander-in-Chief, who had been putting together a much rosier picture of the battle's outcome. Since he had been told by Jackson in a letter dated June 1, based on wireless intercepts, that apart from the loss of *Lützow, Derfflinger, Seydlitz* and *Moltke* were going into dock, and in a letter dated June 3 that *Von der Tann* was the only battle cruiser fit for service, the question arises whether by June 4 he had received these letters. If he had, it is difficult to see how he could claim that 3 battle ships and battle cruisers had certainly been sunk and probably two more. Beatty supported these claims in his report of June 12.[16]

Jellicoe was certainly very unhappy about the outcome; but he would have been comforted by the letter he received from Captain WW Fisher, the Captain of *St Vincent*, dated June 2:

May I go outside strict service custom and say that every officer and man in *St Vincent* believes in you before anyone? And this feeling is broadcast throughout your fleet and I believe a Commander-in-Chief should know it, and therefore I write whatever other motive may be imputed to me.[17]

King George V was quick to express his gratitude, sending a message to Jellicoe, which he followed up with a visit to the Grand Fleet:

> I mourn the loss of brave men, many of them personal friends of my own, who have fallen in their country's cause. Yet even more do I regret that the German High Seas Fleet, in spite of its heavy losses, was enabled by the misty weather to evade the full consequences of an encounter they have always professed to desire, but for which when the opportunity arrived they showed no inclination. Though the retirement of the enemy immediately after the opening of the general engagement robbed us of the opportunity of gaining a decisive victory, the events of last Wednesday amply justify my confidence in the valour and efficiency of the fleets under your command.[18]

A monarch could do no less, particularly as the King was so bound up with his navy; and, of course, his son, the future George VI, served on *Collingwood* during the battle.

Beatty later claimed that Jellicoe's immediate reaction was to acknowledge that he was to blame for the outcome. Many years later Beatty's son told Professor Marder on his father's authority that when visiting Beatty on June 24, Jellicoe 'was obviously very depressed as, seated with head in hands, he made the doleful confession, "I missed one of the greatest opportunities a man ever had."' A similar account of Beatty's recollection was given by Leo Amery who wrote that Beatty

> once gave me a vivid description of Jellicoe, two days after Jutland, breaking down completely in his cabin at the thought of his failure, and only gradually coming round later to convince himself that he had done the best possible in the uncertainties of the situation.[19]

This self serving account by Beatty is to be taken with a considerable pinch of salt. It took him only a day or two to evolve his own account of the battle and the responsibility for its outcome. In spite of a careful letter on June 9 to Jellicoe full of supportive phrases, he was behaving in a thoroughly two faced manner, as Commander (later Rear Admiral) Dannreuther makes clear in his account of his meeting with Beatty after their arrival at Rosyth:

> I spent an hour or more alone with him in his cabin on board the *Lion* while he walked up and down talking about the action in a very excited manner and criticising in strong terms the action of the Commander-in-Chief in not supporting him. I was a young Commander at the time and still regard that hour as the most painful in my life.[20]

Regrettably Beatty's much later behaviour in seeking to falsify the Harper record lends Dannreuther's evidence the ring of truth. While it does not add to the consideration of the long running debate as to who won at Jutland, it does not reflect much credit on Beatty, who thereafter energetically held firmly to his belief that the victory which he could have achieved was undermined by Jellicoe's caution.

This conviction, widely known and energetically supported by his adherents, led inevitably to bitter recriminations as Jellicoe's supporters hit back. The effectiveness of the Royal Navy cannot have been improved by the culture of blame which resulted.

While Lady Beatty certainly could never be regarded as in any way a reliable source of information, a letter she wrote on July 10 to Commander Dennis Larking, a family friend, gives some idea of the views that Beatty was expressing in the privacy of his home:

> Now that it is all over there seems to be very little to say except to curse Jellicoe for not going at them as the BCs did and never stopped until we had annihilated them. I hear he was frightened to death in case he might lose a B ship. I think the real truth he was (sic) in a *deadly* funk and of course it makes one perfectly sick with the Admiralty trying to make out he is a great man and did all he could and that he is a great leader. He failed hopelessly and not only that but he does not tell the truth in his dispatch. He says he was in action for over two hours and all the others say it was quite [-] and that none of the BS's were in action more than 15 minutes. The map he has made is also untrue and the Admiralty know it. It makes one boil, as now one feels the BC's will have to fight again and one has less confidence than ever in the Commander in Chief, and they will not make any change and seem quite pleased with lies and mistakes.[21]

At this stage Jellicoe was not pointing the finger of blame at Beatty. To Balfour, he expressed the hope that if his actions were not considered correct, they would be enquired into; and to Jackson he wrote: 'I often feel that the job is more than people over 55 can tackle for very long. However, I will do my best, and I have a splendid staff.'[22] Jackson sent a reassuring reply to the effect that 'no criticism has emanated from those qualified to judge.' When Jellicoe's despatch was officially published on July 6 it contained no criticism of Beatty, and was couched in terms which appeared to confirm the British victory. The British Press were entirely satisfied that this was the case and printed triumphalist leading articles accordingly.

Richmond's first reaction to the news of Jutland was characteristically outspoken. He wrote in his diary on June 2:

> It is a nasty knock and there is no denying it. We have engaged an inferior force and got the worst of it. We cannot afford to do this at any time. The effect of this engagement, palliate it how we may by saying that the enemy retreated, will be very bad in Europe. We deliberately engage them at a disadvantage, and Jellicoe's doctrine that the gun decides the battle receives a shock which I hope we shall be quick to recognise.[23]

Two days later he noted that the Admiralty news was worse, and was especially censorious about the gap between Beatty's force and the rest of the Grand Fleet, which he considered had violated one of Nelson's most quoted dicta. He cheered up on June 7 when he heard the Grand Fleet's claims about German losses; sadly, of course, these turned out to be wildly exaggerated, and Richmond had a good deal more to say about the battle once the war ended. He was a regular correspondent of the violently anti-Jellicoe writer, Commander Bellairs. In a letter to him on June 26 1919 he mocked the claims of one of Jellicoe's supporters, the naval journalist John Leyland, who had claimed that Jutland would probably be regarded as one of the decisive battles of the world, because thereafter the German fleet had not thereafter put to sea until it crossed the North Sea to surrender:

> Is he sure it never came to sea again? What force came to sea in April 1918 when the *Moltke* was torpedoed well outside the German minefields. Was she alone? … Because Mr Leyland has not heard of a sally of the German Fleet, it does not follow that they never put out. He says that the battle was decisive because the enemy Fleet never came to sea again.

> If this is so, we can add Matthews's battle off Toulon to the decisive battles of the world, as the Spanish Fleet never put to sea again. But Matthews was cashiered all the same.[24]

Whether Beatty's rashness had cost Jellicoe the chance of a great victory, or Jellicoe's caution had thrown away the opportunity presented by Beatty's boldness was an argument that continued to rage. Indeed, it has never stopped. Lord Fisher, not someone whose expressions of opinion enjoyed much by way of consistency, was quickly assuring Beatty that 'rashness in war is prudence, as prudence in war is criminal.' It was nearly eleven years after the battle before the most graphically expressed explanation for what might have been Jellicoe's excessive caution was published, when Winston Churchill's account of the battle in his *The World Crisis* appeared.[25] Although it made for a fine journalistic flourish for him to suggest that Jellicoe was the only man on either side who 'could lose the war in an afternoon,' it was of course not to be taken literally. It would have required several decidedly unfortunate afternoons for the Grand Fleet to be so reduced by casualties to the point where this would ultimately have any practical effect on the outcome of the war. On the other hand it was certainly true that Jellicoe bore an enormous responsibility, quite sufficient to justify a cautious approach to risk in any engagement with the High Seas Fleet. Politically, a defeat would be of the greatest significance.

On the other side of the North Sea there were no such internal recriminations. The main body of the High Seas Fleet had steamed into the Jade between 1.00 and 2.45 on June 1. Some of the ships required immediate docking, and presented an even more battered appearance than their adversaries. It was only now that Scheer became aware of the extent of the losses which he had inflicted on the Grand Fleet, as it became evident that no less than three British battle cruisers had been destroyed. For the first time he felt that he had something to celebrate; as dawn had broken he had felt sufficiently pessimistic about the outcome of the battle to tell Ernst von Weizsäcker that he had better cancel a dinner invitation to General von Heeringen. Weizsäcker's reaction, seeing the damaged ships steaming home, had also been downbeat at first:

> But the enemy, who had had a two to one superiority, had also suffered heavy damage, and when at last better reports began to come in, Scheer came up to me and said 'I really don't see why General von Heeringen shouldn't have dinner with us after all. We'll let the invitation stand.' And a few hours later, as we put into Jade Bay, glasses of champagne were handed round on the conning-bridge on Scheer's orders. Scheer was the first of us to form an accurate assessment of the situation. The English had in fact lost twice as much as we had in men and tonnage.[26]

Weizsäcker recorded that for the next week he was fully occupied in drafting letters of thanks for congratulations sent to Scheer.

Scheer himself quickly prepared a preliminary report, containing all the information thus far available to him, and expressly referring to the loss of *Lützow*. Unwisely, the German official communiqué announcing the battle, which was based on his report, was couched in boastful and inaccurate terms; it was issued on June 2 before the whole of Jellicoe's fleet had returned to base. In particular, the communiqué failed to mention the loss of *Lützow*, an omission on which Scheer commented:

> The announcement of this loss was suppressed by the Naval Staff, though not at my request. The enemy could not have seen the ship go down. In the interests of naval warfare it was right to suppress the news. Unfortunately the secrecy observed produced the impression that it was necessary to enlarge our success to that extent.[27]

Groos, in the Official History, justified this in more detail, pointing, out that it was 'one of the principles of the conduct of war … to avoid disclosing in official statements losses that the enemy cannot himself ascertain,' in order to keep the enemy in ignorance as long as possible. He compared it to the British suppression of the loss of *Audacious* early in the way; he noted that *Lützow, Rostock* and *Elbing* had been sunk on their way home rather than in battle. The regrettable result, 'due to large masses of the people lacking comprehension of the military requirements of this sort,' was that it was wrongly interpreted, and the later reluctant admission of the losses of these vessels was detrimental to the public perception of the final outcome. The Official History added, however, that 'even after the publication of all the German losses the result of the battle, judged solely on this basis, still remains a German victory.'[28]

William II was in no doubt that this was just what it was. On June 5 he made his way to Wilhelmshaven to visit his fleet. Euphoric in his celebration of the victory, he kissed Scheer on both cheeks, conferring on both him and on Hipper, the Order *Pour le Mérite*, and promoting both men. Before touring the other ships of the fleet, he delivered to the crew of the flagship an emotional address:

> The journey I have made today means very much to me. I would like to thank you all. Whilst our Army has been fighting our enemies, bringing home many victories, our Fleet had to wait until they eventually came. A brave leader led our Fleet and commanded the courageous sailors. The superior English armada eventually appeared and our fleet was ready for battle. What happened? The English were beaten. The spell of Trafalgar has been broken. You have started a new chapter in world history. I stand before you as your Highest Commander to thank you with all my heart.[29]

Beatty's opposite number, Hipper, could perhaps claim to have come out best among the leading admirals, decisively defeating the Battle Cruiser Fleet during the run to the south, and sensibly ignoring Scheer's order to pursue the enemy closely when the respective battle cruiser forced reversed direction. Thereafter, he had fought his damaged ships with consistent skill, while unaware of the true extent of the battering they had taken. In this state of mind he was still full of fight on the morning of June 1, writing before he got the damage reports: 'My only thoughts were that we should have the whole English fleet before us at Horns Reef the next morning and there decide the issue.'[30]

Trotha, Scheer's Chief of Staff, was decidedly less bullish about the prospects for the High Sea Fleet if the fighting had been resumed. He wrote to Tirpitz on July 18 that although it was a pity not to be able to strike a blow at the southerly group of the Grand Fleet on the morning of June 21, 'perhaps it was just as well that we didn't.'[31]

Stephen King-Hall, ashore after *Southampton* entered the dockyard, had an experience which stayed in his mind:

> It was on June 3, and the embargo on people leaving the dockyard had been removed. I decided to go to Dunfermline and walking past the shell-scarred battle cruisers I went through the gates and boarded a train. It was packed, and the air of excitement and babel of noise were intense. Doubtless the action, I thought, and listened to hear what they were saying.
>
> Not so.
>
> The cause of the excitement was a football match in which Dunfermline and Cowdenbeath strove together in a League semi-final.[32]

Churchill, in an article in the *London Magazine* in October 1916, argued that although a great victory had not been won at Jutland, Britain still possessed the 'full and unquestioned command of the sea:

> We are entitled to be quite satisfied with [the current] situation. The war function of the British Navy is being discharged with absolute thoroughness and success. Without a battle we have all that the most victorious of battles could give us... No obligation of war requires us to go further. The next move is with the Germans. It is a perfectly simple and obvious move. If they do not take it, it is because they are not strong enough to take it, and do not dare to take it.[33]

It was an attitude which was roundly criticised in letters to *The Times* from Lord Sydenham and Admiral Sir Reginald Custance, who complained that Churchill's views were gravely mistaken, in failing to emphasise the importance of engaging and destroying the High Seas Fleet. Although in part probably written to bolster public confidence in the navy, Churchill was sensibly enough adopting Jellicoe's strategic view. For the Grand Fleet to take chances in seeking out the High Seas Fleet was just what Scheer would have wished. However, it was not a position which Churchill continued to hold for long, to the fury of many in the navy.

The experience of fighting the battle of Jutland left many of the participants overcome with emotion. Trotha, for instance, wrote to his wife two days after returning to port:

> It was a great day in world history and Our Lord God held his hand, wonderfully gracious, above us. I have received impressions that will never leave me. During the night, after a salvo from *Friedrich der Grosse,* the *Black Prince* 800 metres distant blew up in one single enormous explosion, the wall of flame was probably 100 meters high. You will sense how deeply grateful I am. I cannot put it into words.[34]

Nicholas Wolz has written of Scheer's report to the Kaiser, which altogether amounted to sixty two typed pages, that in it he 'admitted that the capital ships built with such great hopes were more or less useless for military purposes.'[35] In fact, he did nothing of the kind. He correctly pointed out that a successful battle would not of itself compel Britain to sue for peace; but he did not say, and did not believe, that the High Seas Fleet was useless, as his employment of it subsequent to Jutland amply demonstrated.

Fate was to write a grim postscript to the battle of Jutland. Field Marshal Lord Kitchener arrived at Scapa on June 5, en route to Russia for talks with the Russian government. Although not personally optimistic about what he could achieve, he was looking forward to a break after two stressful years, as he told Jellicoe at lunch that day. Nonetheless, he did not want to prolong the trip unnecessarily, intending to return within three weeks, and he asked Jellicoe what was the shortest time in which the passage to Archangel could be made. During the day the weather had been steadily deteriorating, and by afternoon was blowing a north easterly gale, causing a heavy sea on the eastern side of the Orkneys, the route which would normally be taken, which the escorting destroyers could not face at high speed. Jellicoe discussed the matter with his staff and it was decided that *Hampshire,* the armoured cruiser in which Kitchener was to sail, should go up the western side of the islands, keeping close inshore. It would, it was reasoned, have been impossible for any surface minelayer to have mined these waters.[36]

However, one of the submarines Scheer had sent out was the large submarine minelayer *U75*, one of three directed to lay mines off the Forth, Moray Firth, and to the west of the Orkneys. On the night of May 28/29 the commander of *U75* in fact laid his mines in the wrong place off Marwick Head, a prominent headland on the northwest coast of the main Orkney Island, having mistaken it for Hoy Island.[37]

Kitchener and his staff boarded *Hampshire* at about 4.00 pm, and she sailed at 4.45 with orders to proceed at a speed of at least 19 knots. At about 7.00 pm Captain Savill sent back the two escorting destroyers, since they could not cope with the heavy seas at that speed. At about 7.40 *Hampshire* struck a mine 'which seemed to tear the centre of the ship right out' and she sank within 15 minutes. Survivors reported that after the explosion Kitchener came on deck, but he was not seen again after the ship went down. As soon as news of the disaster was received, nine of the Grand Fleet's destroyers were sent out, but by the time they reached the scene there was hardly a trace of wreckage. Fourteen men reached the shore on a Carley raft, but two died before rescuers could reach them. It was a grim place for a shipwreck:

> The *Hampshire* went down about a mile and a half from the shore, between the Brough of Birsay and Marwick Head. It is one of the wildest parts of the coast, where a dark rampart of cliffs rises sheer out of the foam and spray which storm against the wind-beaten shore line.[38]

Jellicoe was dismayed, writing to Jackson next day to say that the 'national disaster of the first magnitude' had naturally caused him the deepest distress; since he had ordered the cruiser's movements he felt partly responsible. His luck, he thought, was 'dead out for the present.'[39]

The loss of *Hampshire* was a further demonstration of the extreme vulnerability of older warships to modern weapons; on both sides, predreadnought battleships and the armoured cruisers that had preceded the battle cruisers had suffered a fearful toll from mines, torpedoes and large calibre guns.

20

Who Won at Jutland?

The fact that the question of who won at Jutland has been posed so often and continues to be debated so hotly suggests that the simple and obvious answer is that nobody did. Certainly that is the view of a number of the distinguished historians who have reviewed the battle. Commander Frost deals with the matter in this way:

> It would be futile for us to attempt to discuss that oft-debated question: who won the battle. In land warfare it usually is possible to say that one army or the other won a tactical victory because it held the battlefield. Even then a tactical victory often has been without any strategical significance. In other words, it has had no effect upon the campaign in progress or upon the war as a whole. In naval war it means nothing to hold the battlefield. What we really want to know are the effects of the battle upon the naval campaign in its entirety and upon the ultimate consummation of the pending hostilities.

The issues, he suggests, are the losses, the effect on the opposing plans and the effect on the morale of the respective belligerents.[1]

Reviewing first the direct losses, he assesses the ships sunk, those damaged and the human casualties. A ship that is sunk is gone for good. Its replacement takes a long time, and consumes a lot of money, materials and labour; a ship that is damaged, however, can be repaired in a fraction of the time and at far less cost in resources than the replacement of a ship that is sunk.

The ships lost at Jutland, and their tonnage, were as follows:

British		German	
Queen Mary	26,350	*Lützow*	26,700
Indefatigable	18,800	*Pommern*	13,200
Invincible	17,250	*Wiesbaden*	5,600
Defence	14,600	*Rostock*	4,900
Warrior	13,550	*Elbing*	4,400
Black Prince	13,350	*Frauenlob*	2,700
Tipperary	*1,430*	*V48*	1,170
Turbulent	1,100	*V27*	960
Fortune	965	*V29*	960
Ardent	935	*S35*	956

Shark	935	*V4*	687
Sparrowhawk	935		
Nestor	890		
Nomad	890		
Total	111,980	Total	62,233[2]

Of these, the three British armoured cruisers and the German destroyer *V4* are classed by Frost as second line ships, and *Pommern* and *Frauenlob* as third line ships; the loss of these was of much less significance than the first line ships. Overall, the losses were roughly in the same proportion as the total of the ships engaged, although the British loss of three battle cruisers, taken with the imminent arrival of the new German *Hindenburg*, reduced the Grand Fleet's margin in these vessels to 7:5.

Examining the statistics of ships damaged during the battle, Frost concludes that the German capital ships received slightly heavier damage than the British, receiving 83 hits against 73. The British light cruisers received 66 hits against 15 sustained by the Germans; while as to destroyers, the British had seven out of action against the German one. The British superiority in dockyard facilities meant that in any case they could repair damaged ships more quickly; it was mid August before the High Seas Fleet could resume operations, and at that date they were still without *Derfflinger* and *Seydlitz*.

In terms of human loss the British suffered much more severely; their total casualties amounted to 6,945 against 2,921 for the Germans. This was due to the greater loss in ships, and to the fact that the Germans were able to rescue almost the entire crews of *Lützow*, *Rostock* and *Elbing*.[3]

Overall, therefore, the outcome of the battle was that in absolute terms the weaker fleet had inflicted greater losses on the stronger. As Andrew Gordon puts it, 'the Germans could claim victory in *Ausfallsflotte* terms – that is, in terms of an erosion of British numerical superiority. The fright of their lives, but an *Ausfallsflotte* victory nonetheless.'[4] He goes on to say, however, that victory must be defined in terms of the subsequent battle; and this was never to take place.

Dealing with the second of Frost's key issues, the effect on the subsequent plans of the opposing forces, we come to a question of interpretation that has caused great controversy. Some historians, not being naval historians but who should nevertheless have known better, have written that after Jutland the High Seas Fleet did not again emerge from its harbours. This is, of course, wholly wrong. Scheer, in his report, wrote of the success that had been obtained, while observing that even the most complete victory in a sea battle would not compel Britain to make peace. He intended, as soon as the repairs to most of his damaged ships had been completed, to resume operations, and this is what he did; Jellicoe, on the other hand, made it clear that 'he intended to operate in the future with even more caution than he had exercised prior to and during the battle.'[5] Following the battle, he ceased to plan any offensive operations intended to lure the High Seas Fleet out from its harbour; and, when he succeeded to the command, Beatty was, if anything, even more cautious. The interpretations of these facts by a number of other historians, taking a different view to that of Commander Frost, are referred to below. There was, however, no reason for Jellicoe to adopt a riskier strategy; his overall superiority remained intact, and he still enjoyed an enormous advantage by reason of this geographical situation.

Frost's third issue is that of morale. He notes the overall position of the conflict which, in mid 1916 was not favourable to Germany and Austria. Against that background, reports of the battle in the North Sea were of considerable significance:

> Is it any wonder that the news of Jutland was heartening to the Germans. Previously, the Fleet had remained safely in port while the Army was being decimated time after tine. The Navy had proved now that it too could do something when the opportunity was presented. It had shown that it could fight. It could relate tales of heroism of its own officers and men. At least the Fleet had met the overwhelmingly stronger enemy face to face and had come home after inflicting heavier losses than it had sustained ... The authoritative accounts are unanimous in declaring that the effect of the battle upon the morale of the High Seas Fleet itself was excellent. The report of the Austrian naval attaché, not meant for publication, is particularly convincing in that respect.[6]

Certainly the account of Richard Stumpf, whose accurate and comprehensive diary covered the whole of the war, does not suggest that naval morale was other than high after the battle. The causes of the later mutinies in the High Seas Fleeet are to be found elsewhere.

As for the Grand Fleet, notwithstanding the distressing spectacle of the disastrous blowing up of a number of major vessels, Frost observes:

> However the deep-seated British courage and determination were not affected, and there is every indication that another fight would have been as fiercely, if not as gaily, fought by them as was Jutland. In one respect Jutland benefited the British Navy. The over-confidence of certain elements was rudely shattered. That caused many improvements to be made in both material and training.[7]

The opinion of participants as to the outcome of the battle may perhaps be heavily discounted, for obvious reasons. Likewise, it is not to be expected that official historians should be entirely free from what is, after all, a natural bias. Both Corbett and Groos are from time to time occasionally guilty of this, although not to the same extent as Newbolt. Corbett completed the manuscript of Volume III of the Official History in September 1922, just a few hours before he died, and it was left to Newbolt, at the start of Volume IV, to express a view about the outcome. Corbett was, though, a fair-minded historian, who wrote of Scheer:

> Who shall blame his judgement, though it involved declining an action with a fleet obviously bent on fighting and leaving an undefeated enemy in possession of the field? That after being surprised by the Grand Fleet he had so cleverly drawn his head out of the noose, and with so much success to his credit, was enough to enrol his name high upon the list of fleet leaders.[8]

Newbolt summed up the result of the battle 'from the purely strategical point of view':

> Admiral Scheer had failed in his object of cutting off and overwhelming part of our advanced forces, and had found himself unexpectedly entrapped into meeting the Grand Fleet. From this encounter he had succeeded in extricating himself at considerable expense, but, on the other hand, both before and after the main action he had inflicted upon us more serious losses than he could ever have contemplated. Admiral Jellicoe had outmanoeuvred and surprised the High Seas Fleet, and for him the net result of the action had been to increase the Grand Fleet's large margin of superiority as a combative force, a defence

> against invasion, and an instrument of blockade. The control of the North Sea remained in our hands, and any expectation that this control might be weakened or taken from us had been finally dissipated.[9]

Newbolt, therefore, pinned his claim of British victory upon the doubtful proposition that a battle that had changed nothing was capable of being, in strategical terms, so described. As for morale, he wrote:

> Private letters from officers and men present in the action, which were being published in many papers, proved that the navy's one desire was to meet the enemy again as soon as possible with a few more hours of daylight in hand for a fight to a finish. In short, the position was intact, and the question of victory had been shown to be a merely verbal one.[10]

Professor Marder, of all the historians of the battle entitled to be heard with the greatest respect, accords greater importance to the damage inflicted on ships which did not sink:

> The Germans based their claim to victory chiefly upon the infliction of greater losses, in ships particularly, despite heavy odds. They could fairly congratulate themselves on this achievement, as well as for escaping annihilation. But the raw figures tell the lesser half of the story; much more significant than ships sunk are the ships ready to continue fighting.[11]

Judged by this, of course, the Grand Fleet suffered proportionately less than its opponent, and the advantage in dockyard facilities meant that it was fully ready for battle well before the High Seas Fleet. His conclusion is that from the tactical point of view the battle 'belongs to the series of inconclusive battles or partial victories which are the rule in naval warfare'; but that from the strategical point of view 'the Grand Fleet was, beyond a shadow of a doubt, the winner.'[12] This he bases on the fact that the British control of the sea communications was unimpaired.' It follows from this that even a more resounding defeat for Jellicoe would have been a British victory strategically, since it is unimaginable that another action could inflict so much damage to the Grand Fleet that its numerical superiority, allied to its favourable geographical situation, would be lost. Marder's view is largely adopted by Tarrant, who finds that, from a strategic point of view, 'the German cry of victory had a hollow ring.'[13] Professor Halpern emphatically agrees: 'One can state unequivocally that Jutland was a strategic defeat for the Germans. It changed nothing.'[14]

Gordon makes a pertinent point when he observes that if there had been another battle, it is unlikely that anyone would care much about the answer to the question of who won at Jutland. 'The imperative to attach to it the label of 'victory' – and even to describe it as a great battle – derives at least in part from its being the only meeting of the two fleets in the entire war.'[15] To satisfy that imperative some rather artificial elements have been created in order to assess the outcome as a victory. One of the most striking of these inventive historians was Admiral Bacon, who in his biography of Jellicoe claimed that 'Jutland was a substantial victory,' on the basis that 'there was little to choose between the losses in the main battle;' this conclusion was possible by entirely discarding what he dismissed as 'the preliminary cruiser action.'[16]

A number of recent historians of the battle have concluded that the battle ended in a British victory. Daniel Allen Butler, in *Distant Victory,* is in no doubt of this, arguing that the results 'went far beyond mere arithmetic.' He contends that what made Jutland decisive was the way in which it altered German strategic thinking, leading to decisions which ultimately brought down disaster. This, as do others, he bases on the fact that nothing had changed.[17]

Robert Massie notes that the Germans, in claiming victory, could compare the number of ships sunk and of seamen killed and wounded, and that here they had the advantage. However, he goes on to add 'significant footnotes' to these figures, pointing out that British losses in personnel were due to the fact that five large British vessels had blown up each destroying nearly 1,000 men, and that in terms of proportionality, when ships available were added up, Britain's superiority was as overwhelming as ever. Although 'blurred,' it was, he concludes, a British victory.[18]

Jon Sutherland and Diane Canwell observe that 'although this was not a clear cut victory, Jellicoe had succeeded inasmuch he had control of the battle field with his enemy in retreat.' However, they think that the best that can be said is that the battle was indecisive.[19] George Bonney, writing in 2001, does not attach the label of victory to either side. He notes the grief and gloom of the British public at the failure to win another Trafalgar. Scheer, he writes, had skilfully extracted the High Seas Fleet from two difficult sitiuations, had damaged an important part of the Grand Fleet, had crashed through the British screen and had returned to port with the loss of one capital ship. He makes the interesting comment that Scheer may have underestimated the technical superiority of the German fleet and the tactical skill of its commanders.[20] John Costello and Terry Hughes raise the question of whether any Admiral could have won a decisive victory at Jutland, given the circumstances of uncertain visibility and weather, the limitations of materiel and communications and the overriding strategical situation. Their conclusion, which might well be correct, is that dreadnought technology and tactics may well have outstripped the human capacity to control it.[21] Of these elements it was perhaps the poverty of the communication systems that was the most significant.

In a more recent book, also entitled *Jutland 1916*, Nigel Steel and Peter Hart assert that the great question of the naval war had been answered. The High Seas Fleet would never again seriously threaten the British command of the seas; whatever specious claims could be constructed from an analysis of losses or casualties, the fact was that the Grand Fleet won the battle. They rely on Hase's comment on the situation after the battle:

> The English fleet, by remaining a 'fleet in being,' by its mere continued existence, had so far fully fulfilled its allotted task. The Battle of Skagerrak did not relax the pressure exerted by the English fleet as a 'fleet in being' for one minute.[22]

Steel and Hart warn that one of the problems arising from an analysis of the battle 'is that experts will not consider what actually happened, but constantly imagine what might, or should, have been.'[23] It is a historical failing not confined to the battle of Jutland.

Another historian rejecting the validity of numerical comparisons is Keith Yates, whose *Flawed Victory* was published in 2000. For him, Jellicoe had won a partial victory, 'the typical outcome of most sea battles.' Smashing victories such as Trafalgar and Tsushima, he argues, are the exception rather than the rule. 'Jutland was a flawed victory, but a victory nonetheless.'[24]

Admiral Harper, both in *The Truth About Jutland*, and later in *The Riddle of Jutland*, written with Langhorne Gibson, was in no doubt that Jutland ended in a British victory. In his earlier book, he writes:

> Scheer's tactics were chiefly devoted to extricating his command from situations in which he was threatened with annihilation. This, to give him his due, he achieved with considerable ability; but he was like a boxer, knowing himself to be outmatched and outfought, who concentrates his wits on avoiding punishment, while he waits anxiously for the call of 'time'... To Jellicoe, therefore, must go the verdict of that impartial referee – accurate history.[25]

Writing with Langhorne Gibson, Harper expresses the matter in more highly coloured terms:

> Jutland determined Germany's future. Its effect was decisive and fateful and influenced profoundly all the military and political events which came after it. History, in the most emphatic of terms, gave the palm of victory to Jellicoe and Britain.[26]

It is possible to feel that there was a considerable over-statement in this proposition.

One of the earliest books on the battle was that written by Commander Carlyon Bellairs MP soon after the end of the war. A passionate admirer of Beatty, he devoted his book to a sustained attack upon Jellicoe, whom he blames for just about everything that went wrong for the Grand Fleet. As a historian, he deserves no respect; his opinions are violently expressed but display only the extent of his partiality. Jutland, he writes, impressed on the Germans 'the cautious tactics which it was to our interest they should not practise':

> It left them in numbers, both of personnel and material, stronger than they were before, but the *moral* was broken in the sense that they realised that a real battle meant their annihilation. So they inflicted on us a sustained agony which is prolonging its effects into the years of peace. The High Seas Fleet remained the great controlling factor behind a two years' submarine campaign which nearly lost us the war. Its existence completely deterred us from action in the Baltic, and was therefore a great factor in the downfall of Russia. For two and a half years after Jutland it forced us to maintain the Grand Fleet under continuous steam with all the immediate diversion of personnel and material urgently needed for the anti submarine campaign.[27]

Extravagant nonsense though a lot of this book is, written to support his absurd demand for a public enquiry, it provides an indication of the intensity of the partisan campaign fought to apportion the blame for Jutland.

A much more measured judgment, written not long after the end of the war, appears in Commodore von Schoultz's account of the time he spent with the Grand Fleet. He regarded the question of who won at Jutland as superfluous, since the two fleets did not meet again, and summed up the battle in a paragraph which has been adopted by a number of historians as a neat expression of the outcome:

> From the tactical point of view the Battle of Jutland belongs without doubt to the series of indecisive battles which constitute the greater part of the history of naval warfare. The fall of darkness, combined with the bad visibility, led to the breaking off of a battle which neither side wished to continue.[28]

Schoultz, for all his admiration and sympathy for the Royal Navy, was a thoughtful and dispassionate commentator on a battle which he witnessed and the effect of which he was required to analyse. He addressed the question of its strategic consequences:

> Was the battle of Jutland a strategic victory for the British, as some naval writers maintain? I must admit that personally I cannot associate myself with this view. Naval history knows no such thing as strategic victory. True, successful operations have occurred which, regarded in the light of their political consequences, are equivalent to victory; but a victory, as such, can only be won tactically, and its result must be that the enemy is either destroyed or at least so seriously weakened as to be forced to abandon the objective for which he is striving. The Battle of Jutland had no real effect on the strategy of either of the two sides. England continued the blockade of Germany, extended it to include neutral countries bordering on Germany, and tightened the iron ring round the Central Powers.[29]

Two other more recent historians of the battle have contributed some telling conclusions about technical aspects of the fighting which deserve immense respect. In a detailed and scholarly appraisal of gunnery during the battle, John Brooks has drawn attention to a number of the key conclusions that can be drawn from the evidence. Beatty's gunnery defeat in the Run to the South was, he concludes, 'due primarily to the consequences of his tactics, compounded by the inefficiency of his battle cruisers' gunnery.' He observed that Beatty's own account of the Run to the South is 'directly at variance with other sources.' It leads back, he finds to a number of assertions made by Beatty designed apparently to answer criticisms of his conduct of the fighting:

> What began as an investigation of fire control at Jutland has led to a critical reappraisal of Beatty's tactics and leadership in action. As the First World War ground on, the British people badly needed a naval hero, and Beatty, square-jawed, handsome and with cap rakishly atilt, certainly looked the part. But, among fighting admirals, he cannot be ranked highly ... the reality of his leadership fell far short of his carefully cultivated image.[30]

John Campbell, in his thorough analysis of the fighting at Jutland, did not attempt to answer directly the question of who won the battle. His extraordinarily detailed examination of the actual damage sustained by the ships that took part in the battle is of outstanding value to historians, and his technical conclusions can hardly be challenged. He makes the point, however, that 'it had never been any part of Scheer's plan to engage the whole of the Grand Fleet, and though he had doubtless hoped for a still more favourable loss ratio, he could at least claim partial success.'[31]

One of the most striking conclusions reached was that of Corelli Barnett, who found an even more profound significance in the outcome of the battle. He noted that, for the British, it had proved 'that the relative qualities of the two fleets were such as to make great caution necessary'; while for the Germans it had demonstrated that the chance of falling upon a detached British force and thereby reducing the British superiority was remote. However, he went on to argue that Jutland represented 'a defeat for British technology.' The outcome of the battle had exposed Britain's social system as 'decadent and uncreative.' It proved, he writes, that already by 1914, when Britain seemed at the height of its power, wealth and technological ability, 'dry rot was crumbling the inner structure of the vast mansion.' It showed, he contends, that the collapse of British power and industrial vigour in 1945 was merely 'the final acute phase of industrial decline.'[32]

As the centenary of the battle approached there have been, naturally, a considerable number of new books on the battle published, offering a wide range of interpretations. Jellicoe's grandson, Nicholas Jellicoe, has written a detailed and even handed account of Jutland before turning, understandably, to the controversy that followed, carefully reviewing many of the studies made of the battle. He makes the point that, in the official British accounts, the Admiralty could not have it both ways; a neutral report of the chronology and actual events of the battle could not strike a 'tone of victory,' such as the navy might have wished.[33]

Among German writers on the battle, Jörg Hillmann has produced a comprehensive review of the way in which it has been remembered in Germany. In the course of this he quoted the opinion of another German historian, Jürgen Rhades, who wrote in 1967 that the battle had, psychologically, 'for the Germans, for the navy, for the hard fighting land army, indeed for the entire German people at that time, it demonstrated at least a moral victory.'[34] The writer of another article in the same volume, Werner Rahm, notes that the fact that there was greater personnel and material loss for the Grand Fleet 'brought a predominating sense of victory for the German side.' Scheer wanted, he finds, to continue to deploy the fleet in the North Sea, seeking a further success, while the High Seas Fleet remained as it had been throughout the war, 'a fleet in being' which tied up the Grand Fleet and a large number of lighter warships that were needed elsewhere for escort purposes. In his view, however, the strategic analysis in *Der Krieg zur See* fell short in its claims of victory.[35]

Angus Konstam, in *Jutland 1916: Twelve Hours to Win the War*, is firmly on the side of those who see the battle as a British victory. Rejecting any suggestion that it was indecisive, he concludes that it led to the abandonment of surface operations in favour of U-boat warfare and, in the longer term, ensured that the blockade ' would completely undermine German morale,' and hence did more to bring about an Allied victory than 'any amount of fighting in Flanders, the Somme or Verdun.' The end of the war came, he argues, because one side maintained its control of the sea.[36] This school of thought argues that a battle that changed nothing can nonetheless be described as a victory; in fact, it was geography, and an almost overwhelming naval superiority that gave Britain control of the North Sea from the outset.

A book describing the battle as seen through German eyes is Gary Staff's *Skagerrak*. Himself an Australian, he is rather more forthright than most modern German historians in rejecting claims of a British victory, pointing out that far from it being the case that the High Seas Fleet remained bottled up in harbour while the Grand Fleet continued to sweep the North Sea, the reverse was true. It was the Grand Fleet that stayed clear of the actual site of the battle, and never again sailed with the intention of luring its enemy into a pitched battle. On the other hand, on August 19 Scheer undertook a major operation which would have led to a fleet action had not the British reversed their course in the face of threats from U-boats; while in 1917 and 1918 German heavy units frequently entered the battle zone in support of minesweeping operations. The continuing significance of the High Seas Fleet was noted by Beatty, writing on October 23 1918: 'The power behind the submarine warfare of the enemy is the High Seas Fleet. Remove that power and the submarine menace would completely collapse.'[37]

Perhaps the most authoritative of recent studies of the battle is that by John Brooks, following up his previous work on dreadnought gunnery at Jutland. He concludes his latest, definitive account with a more detailed assessment of the major decisions of the principal commanders.

His view of Hipper is particularly favourable, whom he praises for his leadership of the German scouting groups. Although noting that Scheer enjoyed some good fortune, and made several mistakes, one of which was serious, he finds that 'when the dangers were greatest, he acted coolly and promptly.' For Jellicoe, he has words of sympathy; having been resolute during the gun actions, it was fair to conclude that if during the night he did not live up to the Nelsonic ideal, it was due to fatigue and 'a profound anxiety about underwater threats.' When turning to Beatty, Brooks is again sharply critical of his disregard of his own precepts about keeping in touch with the enemy; in addition, he steered the wrong course as night fell, and failed to press his gunnery advantage. He is also severe on Beatty's post war attempts to obscure his mistakes. Brooks ends by saying that a British strategic victory had been bought at 'a disconcertingly high cost.'[38]

This survey of the opinions of many of the historians of the battle may be concluded by considering the opinion of two distinguished naval officers writing on the battle. Captain Geoffrey Bennett published his account in 1964. He analysed the outcome of the battle by dividing it into five rounds. The first went to the Germans because Hipper succeeded in enticing Beatty within range of the High Seas Fleet. The second round was Jellicoe's, because Beatty lured Scheer into a confrontation with the whole of the British battle fleet. In the third round points were equal; although Jellicoe succeeded in engaging the High Seas Fleet on a course which cut it off from its base, he failed on two occasions to follow it after its turns away. The fourth round belonged to Scheer, because he escaped from Jellicoe's trap and reached safety. There was, however, a fifth round, albeit bloodless, when Jellicoe found himself in undisputed possession of the North Sea. This, of course, sets up again the disputed proposition that possession of the battlefield is a relevant consideration after a naval battle.[39]

Captain Donald McIntyre firmly concludes that the battle ended in a draw;

> The battle was never fought out, and neither side can justly claim a victory. Both countries can be proud of the way their navies, the oldest and youngest in the world, upheld their national traditions and honour. Heroes emerged on both sides ... Jutland was nobody's victory. Perhaps the forces involved were too large, with the technique of those days, with no radar and primitive communications, to be brought effectively into action in the concentration necessary for a decision. Yet, Jutland will always merit its place in history as the greatest of sea fights from the very magnitude of its scope, the majestic but awful spectacle of the tremendous fleets arrayed against each other.[40]

The comments reviewed above represent only a fraction of the extensive literature on the battle of Jutland. In 1992 Professor Eugene L Rasor published a bibliography in which he identified no less than 528 works dealing with the battle; since then there have been many others published and it is a safe bet that there will be many more. It is an even safer bet that no consensus will be arrived at either as to the battle's outcome or the assessment of the performance of the leaders.

From the strategic point of view Jellicoe, with the stronger fleet, had failed to inflict a defeat on the weaker High Seas Fleet; but his command of the sea, and his numerical superiority, remained undisturbed. Scheer had failed to break Jellicoe's control of the North Sea, but had emerged with his fleet more or less intact. Strategically, therefore, neither fleet was in a worse nor a better position than it was before the battle was fought. That looks a lot like the definition of a drawn battle. Tactically speaking, and to a very limited extent, it can be argued that Scheer had emerged the victor; perhaps a very narrow win on points. However, taking everything together, Jutland is perhaps best described as a moral victory for the High Seas Fleet, although moral victories do not win a war.

This explains, and perhaps at the time justified, the euphoria with which the news of the battle was greeted in Germany. Historians have perhaps been a little unfair in scoffing at the Kaiser's extravagant reaction when he visited the fleet in the days after the battle, but given all the circumstances it was not surprising. He was entitled to feel a considerable relief that his heavily outnumbered fleet had come out so well from the encounter. In any case, his response was not so greatly different in intent from that of King George V when he visited his fleet. Both monarchs had an obvious duty publicly to recognise on behalf of their people the courage and sacrifice of their sailors.

The alternative history industry, which frequently confuses the writing of fiction with a sober assessment of how events might have developed if certain essential conditions had been different, will always be able to have a field day over Jutland and its outcome. However, the suggestion by Beatty's supporters, including Churchill and Dewar, that 'there would have been a different story to tell' if Beatty had commanded the Grand Fleet, has been comprehensively demolished by Professor Marder. Reflecting on the abilities and personalities of Jellicoe and Beatty, he does not believe 'that Beatty would have tried anything sensational. If he had, he might well have lost the war there and then.'[41]

A powerful argument for the proposition that Jutland represented a moral victory for the High Seas Fleet is to be found in Beatty's own appraisal of the situation before Jutland was fought. In a thoughtful and prescient letter to Admiral Sir Henry Jackson, the First Sea Lord, ten days before the battle, he observed:

> I quite agree, that if after an action with the High Seas Fleet our losses equalled but did not exceed those of the Enemy, the proportion of forces would be in our Favour. But I think morally victory would rest with the Enemy, who would still have a Fleet in Being. And I think it would be difficult to convince the Navy, the British Public and the world generally, otherwise. They would only recognise that the Superior Sea Power had inflicted the same loss on the Inferior Sea Power as they had suffered themselves. And that the Superior Sea Power had missed an opportunity of annihilating the Enemy and settling the Command of the Sea forever.[42]

A more accurate comment when applied to the outcome of the battle of Jutland it would be hard to imagine.

21

Lessons

The outcome of the battle of Jutland sent a wave of dismay throughout the British navy. The extent of the shock felt by the naval establishment can be gauged by the number of specialist committees set up to enquire into a very wide range of matters that might bear upon the performance of the Grand Fleet. Committees were established to investigate questions of gunnery (one each for battleships and battle cruisers), protection (one each for battleships and cruisers), torpedoes, wireless, anti-flame and gas, signals, searchlights, engineering and shell. Dreyer chaired the committees on battleship gunnery and shell; Chatfield that on battle cruiser gunnery.[1] It reflected the greatest credit on Jellicoe that he saw clearly that there were many lessons to be learned from the battle, and wasted no time in examining them in the greatest detail. It was one of his greatest strengths that he was prepared to think through a problem to its logical conclusion; an innate pessimism, however, meant that caution usually characterised his decisions.

The questions relating to gunnery were, with those relating to protection, the most urgent. The committees chaired by Dreyer and Chatfield submitted their conclusions to a further committee, also chaired by Dreyer. He described in his memoirs some of the key conclusions:

> The question of fire control was closely examined. We were well satisfied with our Dreyer fire control tables, but longer base range-finders were a requirement. There was also a call on the Admiralty to experiment further with stereoscopic range-finders.... *We retained the bracket system for use* once we had crossed the target but lessened the time taken to cross it '*by laddering up or down*,' when our shots were in line with the target for direction. We introduced the firing of rapid double salvoes in the ladders. These were incorporated in new standardised spotting rules.[2]

Jellicoe was pleased with the new rules:

> These had already produced a most convincing and most satisfactory advance in accuracy and rapidity of fire before I gave up command of the Grand Fleet. It is no exaggeration to say that the average time taken to find the gun range of the enemy with these new methods was about one half of that previously required.[3]

Dreyer also chaired the Anti Flash Committee, the work of which was seen as particularly crucial in the light of the fate of the three battle cruisers destroyed at Jutland. It was a matter which, naturally, occupied Chatfield's attention especially, as Beatty's Flag Captain. What concerned everyone was the fact that the British battle cruisers, when hit near a turret, blew up, while those of the enemy, more heavily hit, did not. The explanation was not far to seek. *Lion* had only narrowly escaped the fate of *Queen Mary*, when the shell which struck 'Q' Turret penetrated the front armour plate at its joint with the roof plate, blowing off half the roof which ignited the cordite in the loading cages about to be entered into the guns:

> The explosion and the fire caused, had killed every man in the gun house and working chamber. The igniting of the charges in the gunhouse did not at once ignite other charges, which were in the loading cages a little further down in the turret; but there must have been a good deal of smouldering material, which needed only a draught of air to burst into flame. This air current was provided when the battle cruisers altered course 180 degrees to the northward, bringing what wind there was ahead. It was at that moment that the other charges, eight in number, in the supply hoist, caught fire and a considerable explosion took place... The turret's magazine and shell room crews, however – some seventy men – were all instantly killed.[4]

Dreyer's committee quickly introduced anti-flash arrangements which corresponded closely with those introduced in the High Seas Fleet after the experience of *Seydlitz* during the battle of the Dogger Bank. The British turret gun charges were much more susceptible to flash, in single thickness silk cloth bags with a black powder igniter sewn on to each quarter charge, than the German system, with the main portion of each charge in a brass cartridge.[5] The new measures did not completely solve the problem; it was widely felt that the magazines themselves were inadequately protected. The question of armour protection in the capital ships had been identified by Jellicoe in his official despatch as one needing urgent attention, particularly in the earlier dreadnoughts, because their side armour was not carried to the upper deck level. Because of the long range of gunnery action, the trajectory of the shells made these ships very vulnerable.[6]

When the subject was brought up at a crucial Admiralty conference on June 25, it was agreed that the decks required additional protection. This provoked a huge row with the Director of Naval Construction, Eustace Tennyson-d'Eyncourt, who produced a strongly argued analysis of the evidence to show that 'there was nothing wrong with the design and construction of the battle cruisers;' and that the problem was with the cordite charges, which the new arrangements had dealt with.[7] His fear was that demands for additional protection would make future capital ships far heavier, and that a greater proportion of the total displacement would be accounted for by armour protection. He was supported by Rear Admiral Tudor, the Third Sea Lord; but the pressure from the Grand Fleet was overwhelming, and additional thicknesses of armour plating above the magazines and in the embrasures of the secondary batteries were provided for the majority of capital ships before the end of the year. On the day of Jutland a new battle cruiser, *Hood,* had been laid down. The experience of the battle led at once to increases in the vessel's protection, particularly in the thickness of her vertical armour.

There was also a marked suspicion in the fleet that there was a problem with the British armour piercing shell. Chatfield discussed the matter with Dreyer; both were equally perturbed. However, as Chatfield wrote: 'The Admiralty were informed as to our grave doubts of our shell, but reassuring replies were received. There was no reason to doubt that our shell were the best in the world, they said.'[8] Their suspicions were confirmed in August, when a Swedish naval officer, visiting *Lion* for a luncheon party in August, told Chatfield that it was the view of German officers that the British shell broke up on their armour. He wrote to Dreyer to report the conversation and asking him again to take the matter up with the Admiralty:

> A few weeks later a long reply came from the Admiralty. This letter, full of technical detail and reports of previous experimental firings carried out, denied that there could be anything wrong with our shell. A copy of this letter came to Beatty, and I suggested that we should decline to accept it; that we should again write to the Commander in Chief and request that the further trials asked for should be carried out at once. Eventually the Admiralty consented. These trials exposed a situation so disturbing, as seriously to affect the fighting power of the Fleet.[9]

It was not until Dreyer was transferred to the Admiralty and subsequently became Director of Naval Ordnance in March 1917 that significant progress was made to rectify the situation. Chatfield described his success in the post: 'Outstandingly able, and of great energy and pertinacity, he set to work to rearm the Grand Fleet with a new shell with the greatest skill.'[10] He ordered batches each of a dozen of a new design of armour piercing shell of 12-inch, 13.5-inch and 15-inch from each of four manufacturers, each of which was to use its own steel and hardening. By the summer of 1918 the Grand Fleet had been rearmed with 12,000 of the new type of shell.[11] The new shells were known as 'green boys,' because they were painted with that colour; in Jellicoe's opinion they doubled the offensive power of the heavy guns.

Another important reform was in the adoption of German methods of night fighting. This included the introduction of the use of star shell which, bursting by a time fuse, released a parachute which carried the illuminant and lit up a large area. In 1917 a star shell was perfected which did not reveal the firing ship and her course.

Having regard to the failings displayed by the Admiralty in the use of intelligence gathered by Room 40, the most important administrative reform to flow from the Jutland experience was for Room 40 to be treated as an intelligence centre rather than merely a cryptographic bureau. Hall, as Director of Naval Intelligence, pressed Oliver strongly to implement this suggestion. This, for a long time, fell on deaf ears:

> The Operations Division could not be expected to agree readily to accepting Intelligence reports instead of the signals from men whom they did not credit with sufficient knowledge of naval affairs to understand all that the signals might imply, and to transform several signals or parts of signals into Intelligence reports.[12]

Hall, however, stuck to his guns, and in July 1917 was able to persuade Oliver that it would be a better system, and Room 40 became part of the Intelligence Division.

Jellicoe introduced a submarine patrol off Horns Reef in order to get information about the movement of enemy surface vessels, but its effectiveness was badly hampered by the poor wireless equipment carried by British submarines, with a range limited to about 50 miles. Jellicoe insisted that it be improved:

> As soon as submarines were attached to the Grand Fleet, I represented strongly the absolute necessity of effecting an improvement in this particular, stating that I was quite prepared

> to sacrifice some of the torpedo armament should this be necessary, but that it was a vital matter to install efficient wireless apparatus in the only class of vessel that could carry out a watching patrol in the vicinity of German bases. Eventually arrangements were made to provide them with a wireless installation which gave a range of 300 to 400 miles.[13]

Newbolt, who to a much greater extent than Corbett was inclined to follow the Admiralty line, wrote that there was little doubt that the recommendations of the Grand Fleet Committees were sufficient to avoid further disasters, 'and that the Board of Admiralty were right in deciding that the basic principles of British warship design needed no revision.'[14] More significantly, in a section devoted to the effects of Jutland on fleet tactics, he concluded that 'no drastic change in our tactical methods was called for as a result of the action,' after examining the basic tactical rules in Jellicoe's original battle orders and the revision issued by Jellicoe on September 11, and his memorandum of October 17 entitled 'Notes on the defence of the battle fleet against torpedo attack':

> The first of these rules was that the command was to be entirely centralised in the Commander-in-Chief, the Dreadnought fleet was to keep together, and squadron Commanders were not to make independent tactical movements unless ordered to do so. The second rule, equally important in the Commander-in-Chief's plan of battle, was that the destroyer flotillas were to be used defensively until the enemy was beaten by gunfire. It is very significant that each of these governing rules was reprinted, without alteration, in the new Fleet Orders issued by the Commander-in-Chief on September 11.[15]

Marder, however, notes the important movement towards decentralisation and flexibility contained in Jellicoe's reissue of the Fleet Orders, which was due to 'the difficulty, always clearly recognised, and confirmed at Jutland, which the Commander-in-Chief would experience in controlling the movements of the whole fleet in the heat of action.'[16] This amendment provided that the signal 'MP' might be made to remind squadron commanders that they should manoeuvre their squadrons independently in circumstances in which the Commander-in-Chief was experiencing difficulty in controlling the whole battle fleet. Another significant change was to give the flag officer leading the van of the fleet discretionary power to press on if the enemy, in conjunction with a battle turn away, launched a destroyer flotilla attack. The new rules went on to define the steps that each section of the battle line should take in the face of a torpedo attack. This was clearly a response to criticism of the policy of turning away in the face of such attacks; and the change was followed up in the memorandum of October 17, which emphasised that the first defence against an enemy torpedo attack was a rigorous counter attack by light cruisers and destroyers, while the second defence was a turn away.[17]

Other changes included a more advanced position for the 5th Battle Squadron to enable it to reach either flank more easily; and a provision that one or more light cruiser squadrons should have the responsibility of maintaining touch with the enemy during the night. All in all, Marder is clearly right to say that 'post-Jutland tactics did mark a very real advance on the GFBO's in effect at Jutland.' And Newbolt is wrong in suggesting that no drastic change was called for.[18]

The important conference of June 25 also addressed the concerns that Jellicoe had expressed to Jackson on June 14, when he wrote:

a) Our lightly armoured BCs are not a match, ship for ship, for the Germans. The result is they must not be too far from the Battle Fleet.
b) Our 5th BS is not fast enough to get away from the German 3rd BS and cannot therefore be used as a backing up force for the BCF, far from the main Fleet.[19]

It would have been surprising had such a conference, attended by both Jellicoe and Beatty, not in the end adopted policies agreeable to the Commander-in-Chief, and this is what it did. It reiterated the importance of concentrating the battle fleet, except for the 4th Battle Squadron, at Rosyth as soon as the necessary facilities were completed, so that it would operate from the same base as the battle cruisers. It was agreed that, where the Grand Fleet had the initiative, the battle cruisers would not in future operate so far ahead; and that where the battle cruisers were ordered south to deal with a German raid, they were not to become 'seriously engaged with superior forces until the Battle Fleet is within supporting distance,' unless the Admiralty ordered otherwise.[20]

The reference to 'superior forces' did not please Beatty at all. He was mindful of the instructions to Troubridge at the time of the escape of *Goeben* and *Breslau,* which led to a court martial. He wanted to know whether he was to be allowed freely to exercise his judgment and discretion, arguing that there might arise circumstances in which it would be important for an inferior force to engage a superior force even if unsupported. Jellicoe forwarded the letter from Beatty on the subject, dated July 27, to the Admiralty, recording his view that the expression 'superior forces' referred to the 1st Scouting Group supported by a battle squadron. He added the significant comment:

> Any misconception existing in the mind of the Vice Admiral may, to some extent, be due to the use of the term 'Battle Cruiser Fleet,' to describe the force under his command. This nomenclature may be taken to imply that it is a force distinct from, and not an adjunct to, the battle fleet and that, owing to its advanced position, it is expected to fulfil the role of a first battle squadron.[21]

Jellicoe had put his finger on one of the aspects of Beatty's leadership of the battle cruisers that explained some of the difficulties that arose in action.

By the time of the conference at the Admiralty Beatty's discontents were assuming a public form. Evidently mistrustful of any record that might be kept by the Admiralty (or by Jellicoe) he recorded his notes of the meeting of June 25 at the Admiralty (he dated them June 26). Also present were Jackson, the First Sea Lord, Commodore Everett, the First Lord's Naval Secretary, and Jellicoe. Beatty said that if it had been settled to send the 5th Battle Squadron to Scapa Flow, he 'wished to enter a protest in the strongest and most emphatic manner possible.' He argued that until the Grand Fleet could come to Rosyth in October, the 5th Battle Squadron should support the Battle Cruiser Fleet. Jellicoe remarked that the squadron's speed was insufficient for this; Beatty denied that there was any evidence for this. Jackson remarked, to Beatty's annoyance, that he hoped that the next time he had the 5th Battle Squadron, he would keep them in line with him.

Beatty went on to blame the lack of opportunity for the squadron to work with him:

> That if I had had them with me constantly as I had asked and so enable them to be trained with me so that the RA and myself should have thoroughly understood each other they

would have been at 2 miles. But as this was the first time we had ever been to sea together, it was considered advisable to give them more sea room. Squadrons of the heaviest ships moving at 25 knots require room unless they have been previously manoeuvred together.

After a lengthy explanation by Beatty of the movements before and during the run to the south, Jackson further annoyed Beatty by observing that it was a pity that on sighting the enemy battle cruisers he did not turn away to join the 5th Battle Squadron, and that he would probably have done better to have done so, as the enemy battle cruisers might have followed him.[22]

Taking together the technical, tactical and strategic reforms directly flowing from the Jutland experience, it is reasonable to go further than Marder in rejecting the complacent views expressed by Newbolt. These reforms represented an enormous shake up of the way in which the Grand Fleet was to do its business in the North Sea for the remainder of the war. Rather than reflecting discredit on the Navy because they were found to be necessary, as Newbolt appears to suppose in dismissing their significance, they demonstrated the Navy's professionalism and dedication.

There was no similar comprehensive overhaul of materiel or tactics as far as the High Seas Fleet was concerned. The ships had stood up to considerable punishment, and there was, therefore, no anxiety about their design; and in most respects their equipment had performed entirely satisfactorily. The obvious lesson to be learned, and it was no more than a confirmation of what was well understood, was that the great numerical advantage of the Grand Fleet made it extremely hazardous to do battle with the whole of it. The policy of seeking to engage only part of it was obviously correct. Strategically, however, Scheer's report of July 4 provided him with an opportunity to assert the reality of the situation in the North Sea:

> With a favourable succession of operations the enemy may be made to suffer severely, although there can be no doubt that even the most successful result from a high sea battle will not compel England to make peace … A victorious end to the war at not too distant a date can only be looked for by the crushing of English economic life through U-boat action against English commerce.[23]

The suggestion that a further battle or series of battles would not win the war, and that a submarine campaign was the only way to achieve this, has been taken by historians to indicate that the outcome of the battle of Jutland was a revelation to Scheer, causing him to argue for a change of strategy. From this has been developed the argument that Jutland therefore represented a strategic victory for the Grand Fleet. This may, however, somewhat misrepresent Scheer's position. He had always been a proponent of an all out submarine campaign, and Jutland did not change his view. His report of July 4, however, gave him an opportunity of emphasising his opinion, and if anything was intended to operate as a corrective to any suggestion that the relatively favourable outcome of the battle might support the arguments of those opposing a submarine campaign.

This was bound to provoke a violent debate among Germany's military and political leaders. Events on the Western Front, and Romania's entry into the war on the Allied side, sharpened the calls for an unrestricted U-boat campaign, and Trotha wrote to Levetzow to say that they must use every opportunity to develop the understanding of the navy by Hindenburg and Ludendorff.[24]

Reviews of tactical aspects of the battle did, however, reveal dissatisfaction with the performance by the light cruisers of their reconnaissance duties. Raeder, for instance, noted that Boedicker's cruisers had reported the appearance of Hood's battle cruisers, but had identified them as battleships. As to the battle cruisers, once they had joined the battle fleet, they had lost much of their value for scouting:

> In the engagement with the enemy's 5th Battle Squadron and his battle cruisers, their assigned position at the head of the fleet was not well adapted to reconnaissance … As a result, in order to improve our reconnaissance in the future, at the suggestion of Admiral Hipper the Commander in Chief directed that action reconnaissance be made the duty of the 2nd Torpedo Boat Flotilla, which, on account of the size and speed of its units, was well suited to the task.[25]

Part III

After Jutland

22

The August Sortie

Scheer's plans for the operation on May 31 had been marred by the disappointing performance of his U-boats, and by the lack of airship reconnaissance. He was, however, undaunted by the outcome of the battle, and was resolved to continue his policy of seeking to erode the Grand Fleet's numerical superiority. He was satisfied with the effectiveness of the High Sea Fleet as a weapon, and had no intention of letting it sleep in his hand. It is hardly just for Professor Marder to comment that 'there was even less desire than there was before 31 May to stand up to the Grand Fleet in a fair fight.'[1] Scheer had never intended to meet the whole of the Grand Fleet in a 'fair fight.' It would have been the height of folly for him to do so given the disparity of force that he would meet.

It was, however, still his intention to catch part of the Grand Fleet at a disadvantage, and he planned to do so as soon as the bulk of the repairs required by the ships of the High Seas Fleet had been completed. By mid-August he was ready to move; he was, though, still without *Seydlitz* and *Derfflinger*, so he attached the newly completed *Bayern,* with *Grösser Kurfürst* and *Markgraf* to I Scouting Group. The other key change in his deployment was his decision not to sail with II Battle Squadron; the low speed and high vulnerability of the pre dreadnoughts made this decision inevitable, and they were assigned to cover the German Bight. In planning his next operation, Scheer revived his original intention for May 31. I Scouting Group was to bombard Sunderland, supported by the rest of the High Seas Fleet. He described his plan:

> The Fleet was to put out by night, to advance through the North Sea towards the English coast, so that the line of U-boats might come into action if required. If no collision with the enemy occurred, and there were no indications that the English Fleet would cut off our retreat from the sea, the ships were to push on to the English coast and bombard Sunderland at sunset. After the bombardment, while the Fleet returned in the darkness to the German Bight, the U-boats were to take up their second position in the direction of the probable approach of the enemy, if, as was expected, he should come up as a result of the bombardment.[2]

The plan was based on a different scheme of operation for the U-boats; that on May 31 'had resulted in no success worth speaking of,' partly because the Grand Fleet had already put to sea before the U-boats were in position, and partly because the deployment was so arranged that they got in each other's way. The new scheme involved them taking up positions on moveable base lines in the direction of the probable approach of British forces. U-Line 1 covered the northern flank of the advance towards Sunderland, running ENE from a point opposite Blyth, and U-Line III covered the left flank, running due east from Flamborough Head:

> A third group, formed from the Zeebrugge flotillas, was to take position on two separate lines in the approaches to the Flanders Bight, to the north westward of the Texel. Yet another line of five U-boats was stationed across the north western approaches to the Bight, at about one hundred and twenty miles from Heligoland. Lines I and III were to serve as a kind of long-distance cover to the main fleet, when it was under the British coast; and the lines off the Texel were intended as a trap for the Harwich forces.[3]

All told, twenty four U-boats were deployed in the five groups. In order to coordinate their movements with those of the High Seas Fleet, the overall commander of the U-boats, Captain Hermann Bauer, sailed aboard *Prinzregent Luitpold*.[4]

The risk of encountering opposition early in the operation, foreshadowed in Scheer's exposition of his plan, meant that effective reconnaissance was of crucial importance. Scheer arranged for eight Zeppelins to ensure that he got early warning of British movements. Four of these would patrol a line between Peterhead and Norway. Another would watch the Firth of Forth, and another would cruise off Sunderland. One more would cruise off the Outer Silver Pit between the Humber and the Wash, and the last would patrol the Flanders Bight. As the High Seas Fleet advanced therefore, it would be encircled by airships able to keep a constant watch for the enemy.

Commodore von Schoultz, the Russian attaché, had collected a great deal of material on the battle of Jutland, and spent most of June writing up his notes. At the end of the month he was ordered to London to serve on a commission examining Russia's needs of war material, and it was not until August 4 that he rejoined the Grand Fleet. He was assigned to *Benbow*, lying at Cromarty, the commander of which was Captain Clinton Baker, with whom Schoultz had served in *Hercules* during the battle of Jutland. He was impressed to see the work that was being done to address some of the problems that the battle had exposed, not only in *Benbow* but in all the battleships of the 1st Battle Squadron:

> The work was carried out by dockyard experts, who were fetched from the shore every morning. It was proceeding rapidly, for the armour had already been ordered some time before to templates and the main task was the pneumatic drilling of holes for the rivets and the bringing of plates into position. The number of dockyard experts was comparatively small, but part of the ship's company, about sixty men, were also engaged on the work. When I came on board armour plates were lying in different parts of the upper deck and casemates, and it was most astonishing how the work progressed. The routine of the ship went forward as usual, and in the evenings, when the shore workers had left, the ship's artificers got everything so far ship-shape that, if necessary, we could have put to sea during the night.[5]

With *Benbow* at Cromarty Firth were the battleship *Monarch* and the armoured cruiser *Minotaur*.

Meanwhile Roger Keyes had been brought home from the Mediterranean. His promotion to Rear Admiral being imminent, he was advised to take command of a battleship at once, rather than wait for a battle cruiser for which he had been hoping; although he could remain in command of a ship once promoted, he could not be appointed to command a ship after he had become a Rear Admiral. Accordingly, at the end of June he went north to take command of *Centurion*. In August, he took his new command to Invergordon for a refit, and, as a result, was to miss Scheer's planned operation. Meanwhile his wife had brought his family north to join him, taking a house on the Cromarty side of the anchorage:

> She had given up our Fareham house, sold the cows and pigs, and transferred herself, three children, seven servants, two dozen chickens, two prams and about two tons of luggage there, a day or two before the *Centurion* arrived. No mean feat in wartime.[6]

In those days a senior naval officer's family evidently did not travel light.

As the summer wore on, Jellicoe had been feeling the strain, and responded at once to Jackson's suggestion that he ought to have a break, writing to the First Sea Lord on July 31:

> It is very kind of you to suggest some leave for me. I dislike going intensely, but I do feel quite played out and with your permission I will try and get away in about ten or twelve days' time when Burney returns … It is very annoying but I feel so constantly tired that I am afraid of not doing justice to the Fleet should we succeed in meeting the enemy and I can only hope that a rest will put me right. I suppose it is the incessant strain.[7]

He went to stay at Kilpurnie Castle, a house belonging to his father in law. It was arranged that the light cruiser *Royalist* should be posted at Dundee; Jellicoe could be on board her within an hour and a half of getting news that required him to rejoin the fleet.

By August 15 he was feeling better for the rest, although as he told Jackson, the first few days had had the opposite effect. He thought that it was time the Grand Fleet did more exercises: 'I hope the Battle Cruiser Fleet have been able to do some full calibre firing … They want it badly.'[8] He was, however, sceptical about the prospects for enticing out the High Seas Fleet: 'They will only come out when they want to do so, and nothing that we can do will bring them.'

As usual Room 40 was well informed that something was in the wind, noting on August 15 some preliminary movements which were significant of impending activity: 'Two and half flotillas of destroyers were detailed as outposts at Schillig Roads and none for Heligoland. This procedure being unusual presaged something.'[9] Room 40 continued closely to monitor German wireless traffic; by now it was able to assess with a good deal of accuracy the meaning of the movement which it was recording:

> It was also learned that the 1st and 3rd Battle Squadrons, at full strength, and the 2nd and 4th Scouting Groups plus two of the battle cruisers and the usual destroyer flotillas, were assembled in the Jade. All the usual portents followed – mine sweeping, instructions to light vessels and, on the morning of August 18 the information that the 3rd Battle Squadron would pass the outer Jade at 10.30 pm that evening. Airships were given orders to take up prearranged positions.[10]

With such comprehensive intelligence available, the Admiralty had no hesitation in sending the Grand Fleet to sea, at 10.56 am ordering Burney to concentrate in the Long Forties east of Aberdeen. By 4.00 pm the Grand Fleet had cleared Scapa; the Battle Cruiser Fleet sailed from the Forth at 6.20 pm. Thus the British were at sea the best part of three hours before the Germans left the Jade. Altogether they had a total of twenty nine dreadnoughts (the 1st, 2nd, 4th and 5th Battle Squadrons) and six battle cruisers (the 1st and 2nd Battle Cruiser Squadrons). Against them Scheer had eighteen dreadnoughts, three of which had been attached to Hipper's I Scouting Group, which had only two battle cruisers available. The High Seas Fleet sailed as planned at 9.00 pm on August 18. Interestingly, in the light of the issues raised about the appropriate distance between the battle cruisers and the battle fleet, Scheer had decided that Hipper should be stationed at a distance of twenty miles.[11]

Meanwhile the Admiralty had been busy making other preparations to meet the threatened German advance. At 11.37 am Tyrwhitt was ordered to sea, with instructions to be at Brown Ridge, about 50 miles east of Yarmouth, by dawn on August 19. The 3rd Battle Squadron was to assemble in the Swin by 8.00 pm with steam at one hour's notice. Orders went out for the disposition of the submarines; three off Terschelling, two to the north of Heligoland, two each off Yarmouth, Lowestoft and Harwich; and the remainder in two groups to await further orders. Later, the minelayers at the Nore were ordered to the Swin, and Vice Admiral Bacon was ordered to concentrate the Dover Patrol, while all aeroplanes on the coast were to go up at dawn.[12] *Benbow, Monarch* and *Minotaur,* from Cromarty, were to rendezvous with the Grand Fleet.

Jellicoe, as soon as he heard the news, set off at once for Dundee, where he boarded *Royalist,* which was waiting for him with steam up. By 2.00 pm she had cast off, and was heading north at maximum speed. Burney, meanwhile, ordered a rendezvous of the Grand Fleet 100 miles east of the River Tay, while the Battle Cruiser Fleet was to take station 30 miles to the south. *Iron Duke,* in response to a request from Jellicoe, was sent on ahead of the rest of the fleet, steaming southward for a rendezvous with *Royalist,* escorted by the destroyers *Marvel* and *Onslaught.* Just as *Iron Duke* met *Royalist,* and the challenge was being made by searchlight, the track of a torpedo was seen heading for *Onslaught.* Dreyer was on the bridge of *Iron Duke* at the time, and was taking in a message from Jellicoe about his transfer from *Royalist* when he spotted the torpedo:

> I was leaning over the fore bridge rail, and as the last word of the signal was called I suddenly saw a circular 'slick' form close on our starboard bow, out of which ran the track of a torpedo towards the destroyer *Onslaught.* I flashed to her 'Torpedo coming.' It missed just astern. I ordered the *Iron Duke's* tiller to be put hard to starboard in the hope that as our stern swung to starboard it would bump the submarine, which was inside our turning circle, but no such effect occurred.[13]

The Naval Staff Monograph records the subsequent action taken:

> It missed, but the long line of bubbles revealed the immediate danger. It was clearly no place to transfer the Commander in Chief, and the *Iron Duke* held on at 21 knots, with the *Royalist* following in her wake … Admiral Burney was some 12 miles astern of the *Iron Duke* at the time, and on receiving the report altered course four points to port, and turning east a little later, made a wide detour which carried his squadron well to eastward of the spot.

It was 9.00 before Jellicoe was able to board *Iron Duke*, although he did not yet resume command. At 10.00 pm the Grand Fleet altered course to the south.[14]

Aboard *Benbow*, Schoultz had been asleep in an armchair when he was woken with the news that the Grand Fleet was in sight:

> It was 4.00 am and the day was beginning to break. The sun was still below the horizon when I saw the black silhouettes of the approaching ships against the bright sky. The picture was as unusual as it was impressive. An hour later we had taken our station in the squadron, astern of the *Emperor of India* ... We were following a southerly course, with slight zig-zags as protection against submarine attack. From the foremast of my old ship, the *Hercules*, was flying the flag of Admiral Sturdee, commanding the 4th Battle Squadron. Above the ship a captive balloon hung at a height of over 300 feet. The balloon was sausage-shaped, but instead of the usual tail had three small balloons attached. Under way she remained perfectly steady, and the observers were connected by telephone with the ship.[15]

What struck Schoultz particularly was the cruising formation of the Grand Fleet. He had not previously had time to investigate whether there had been significant changes in tactics since Jutland:

> At this moment, when I saw the disposition of the Grand Fleet,, I realised for the first time that the tactics had remained unchanged; to approach the enemy as closely as possible in parallel lines ahead and develop at the last minute a battle line whose unwieldy length and awkwardness made envelopment or pursuit of the enemy difficult. In order to have my observations confirmed I questioned Clinton Baker, and he told me that no alterations in the tactics of the Fleet had resulted from the Battle of Jutland. My Captain hit off these tactics pointedly by expressing his personal opinion with a dry humour which went very well with his Mephistophelean beard: 'We're still geese after all, and can only move like geese.'[16]

Tyrwhitt, meanwhile, had sailed from Harwich in accordance with his orders, reaching the Brown Ridge at about 3.00 am. He had with him five light cruisers, the flotilla leader *Lightfoot* and 19 destroyers. He flew his flag in *Carysfort*. At this point he had not even been told that the Grand Fleet was at sea, let alone its position, course or intentions. He assumed, of course, that it must have sailed, but for the moment he could do no more than patrol the Brown Ridge, hoping in due course to sight the enemy.[17]

By 5.00 am the Grand Fleet had reached a point a few miles to the northward of the rendezvous. *Iron Duke* was in sight ahead and at 5.25 the flagship had taken up its position ahead of the division led by *Colossus*. The armoured cruisers *Shannon, Duke of Edinburgh* and *Minotaur* were ordered to take station twelve miles ahead of the battle fleet. The Battle Cruiser Fleet had been approximately 35 miles ahead of the battle fleet; it turned northwards for ten minutes to close the gap, before again turning to the south. By 5.40 the entire fleet was steaming southwards at eighteen knots.[18]

Jellicoe was still concerned about the distance between the Grand Fleet and the battle cruisers, however, and at 6.04 am he ordered Beatty to close within visual distance. Beatty complied with this order at 6.17 am, but as he did so he received a signal that *Nottingham*, one of his light cruisers, had struck a mine or torpedo. This signal emanated from Goodenough, to whose squadron *Nottingham* belonged, and was passed on by Beatty to Jellicoe, although the latter did not receive it until 6.50 am. The uncertainly as to the cause of the explosion had a serious consequence. Taken with an Admiralty signal of 6.15 am, received in the flagship at 7.00 pm, which put the German fleet at 5.25 am 200 miles to the south eastward of him, Jellicoe decided to turn 16 points to the northward until the cause of the damage to *Nottingham* had been clarified. The battle fleet turned at 7.03 and the battle cruisers at 7.30.[19]

In fact *Nottingham* had been struck at 5.57 am by two torpedoes fired by *U52*, at the eastern end of U-Line I; a third torpedo hit was scored half an hour later, and she began to settle by the head:

> By about 6.45 the forecastle was under water; all the boats manned, except the second cutter, which had been blown from its davits; the five Carley rafts had been launched, and mess stools and extempore floats followed them over the side. The cyphers and codes coming up in sacks from the wireless office were deluged with a 'huge quantity of paraffin' and burnt merrily in an extempore fireplace between two doors until they were consumed … At 7.00 am all officers and men had left the ship, and Captain Miller left her as the water rose around him. She heeled heavily to port and sank by the head about 7.10 am.[20]

Away to the east, the British submarine *E23* had also struck a shrewd blow, torpedoing *Westfalen*, the last ship in the German line, at about 6.05 am, hitting her on the starboard side. Although the battleship was not seriously damaged, Scheer was afraid that she might be attacked again and possibly, in her vulnerable state, sunk. Accordingly, at 6.30 am he ordered her home, escorted by two destroyers. As he feared, *E23* did launch another attack, but the torpedo missed, and *Westfalen* returned to the Jade under her own steam.[21]

Her wireless signal reporting the hit and the damage, in violation of Scheer's express orders as to wireless silence, had been picked up, and decoded by Room 40, and the vital information as to the whereabouts of the High Seas Fleet sent by the Admiralty to Jellicoe; it was received by him at about 8.00 am.[22]

The fact that this told him Scheer's position did not change Jellicoe's mind about the risk of steaming into a trap, and it was not until 9.00 am that the Grand Fleet turned back to the south, followed by the battle cruisers at 9.30. Jellicoe's decision was criticised by Churchill, who wrote in *The World Crisis* that 'a comparatively slight alteration of course would have carried the Grand Fleet many miles clear of the suspected mine fields.'[23] Jellicoe explained his position in terms which suggested that there was no sensible alternative:

> Until it was clear that a minefield did not exist, it was prudent for the fleet to avoid this locality, and course was accordingly reversed until it was ascertained that damage was due to torpedoes; when this became clear, the southward course of the Fleet was shaped to pass to the east of the submarine.[24]

Dreyer thought simply that 'it would have been lunacy to steer the Grand Fleet into a minefield.'[25] It meant, however, the loss of four hours, which had a significant effect on subsequent events.

Professor Marder argues that the consequence of the Grand Fleet's turn back to the northward should not be overstated, relying on the points made by Sir Henry Newbolt, who pointed out that although if the turn had not been made, contact might have been made with Hipper's squadron between noon and 1.00 pm:

> But only on the supposition that the British advance was not held up by the submarines of U-boat Line I, and that Admiral Scheer held on for Sunderland, in ignorance of the tremendous force which was steadily approaching his communications with Germany. But it is in the last degree improbable that the German Commander-in-Chief would have known nothing of our Grand Fleet until it was close upon him; and, once he knew that it was approaching, he would no doubt have endeavoured to gain time. It is certain that never, if he could possible have avoided it, would he have joined battle with the Grand Fleet to the eastward of him, and with the prospect of an eight hours' daylight battle before night could bring him a chance of breaking away.[26]

Tyrwhitt's patrols around the Brown Ridge had been observed by the Zeppelin *L13*, which at 6.30 am correctly reported to Scheer that his force consisted of a cruiser squadron and two destroyers flotillas.[27] *L13* was driven off by gunfire from the cruisers, but reappeared at 8.20 and sent a further report, before again retiring. She sighted the Harwich force again at 11.30; her report of what she thought she had seen was to be of crucial importance. Tyrwhitt maintained his patrol until picking up the signal from *E23* at 9.16 which reported the attack on *Westfalen* and the course of the High Seas Fleet. It had been sent to all ships, and on the basis of this information Tyrwhitt hurried north.

The report from *E23*, however, was not received in either *Iron Duke* or *Lion*. It was, however, picked up by one of Tyrwhitt's light cruisers; subsequent events illustrated the communications problem that bedevilled both sides during the war:

> The *Canterbury* took it in at 9.19 am, but unfortunately the last and most important words of the signal, namely '4.00 am' were jambed (sic) The *Canterbury* passed it at 9.45 am by semaphore to [Tyrwhitt] who sent it on in cipher at 10.10 am and it was received by the battle fleet about 10.18 am. It read as if the enemy had been sighted at 9.19 am which would place the German Fleet some four hours to the eastward of its actual position, but fortunately the Admiralty directionals, received earlier by the Commander in Chief and evidently referring to the same incident, supplied a valuable check.[28]

Scheer, who had been informed by Neumünster that intercepted messages showed that the Grand Fleet was at sea, had been getting a good deal more in intelligence reports from his U-boats and Zeppelins than had been the case at Jutland. After *L13's* report of the sighting of the Harwich Force, *U53* reported three enemy battleships with four cruisers steering north at 8.10 am. Just before 10.00 am *L21* reported enemy ships heading north east; and at 11.40 *U52* reported Goodenough's cruisers and the news that she had sunk one of them. It was not clear what all these reports added up to:

> From all the information received no coherent idea of the counter measures of the enemy could be formed. We could safely assume that he was aware of the fact that we had put to

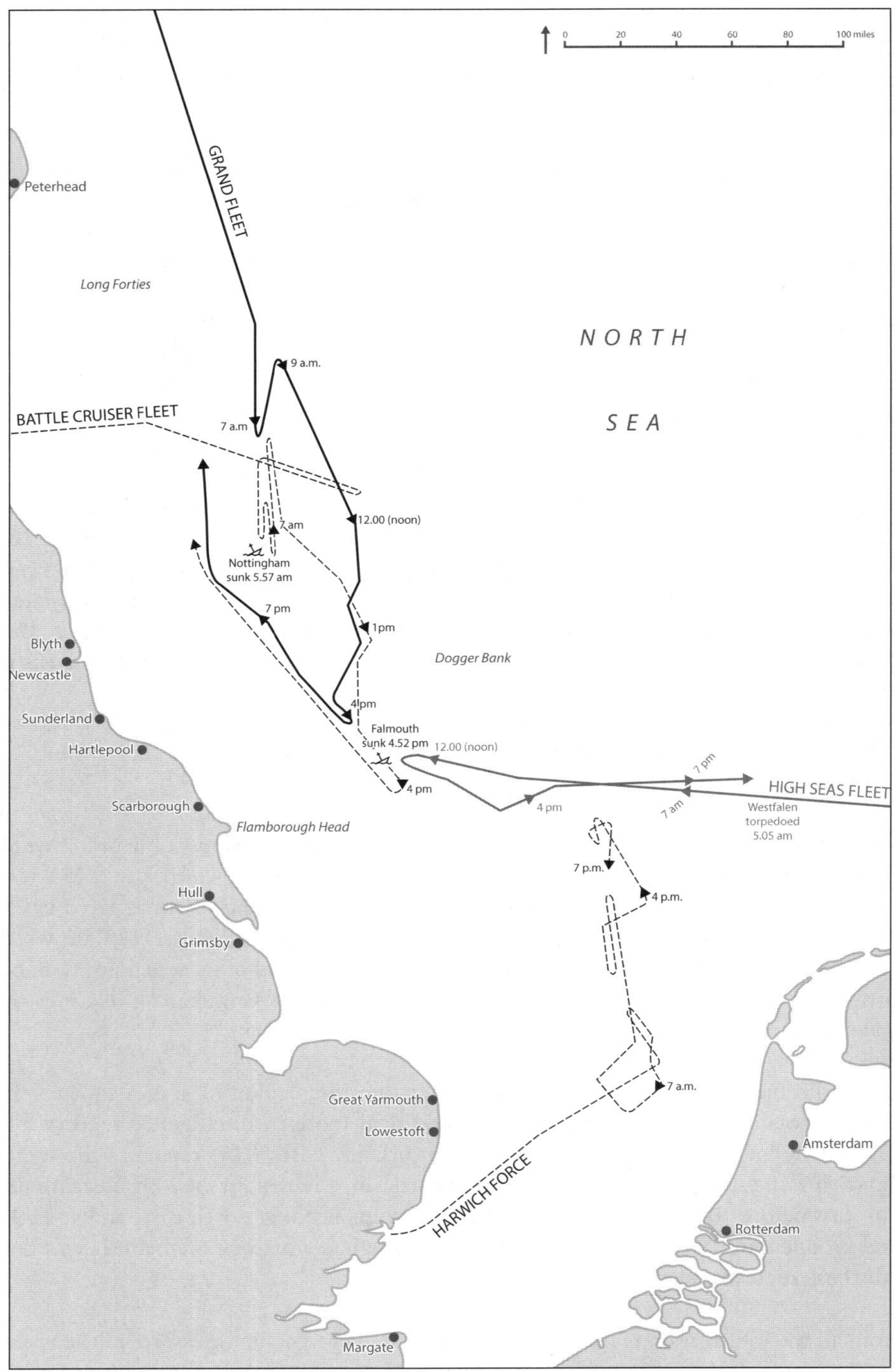

Map 17 The August Sortie: August 19 1917.

> sea, for the submarine that had hit the *Westfalen* had had ample time since 6.00 am to send messages to England. Up to this time the remaining airships had reported no movements of larger forces, and the visibility in the locality of the Fleet justified the assumption that our airships commanded a clear view over the whole sea area.[29]

At 12.03, however, the situation changed dramatically. *L13* reported that at 11.30 am it had sighted strong enemy units, comprising 30 units, on a northerly course, some 60 miles east of Cromer, which would put it about 60 miles to the south of Scheer's position at 11.30. At 12.23 L13 followed this up with the information that the enemy force consisted of 'about 16 destroyers, small and large cruisers, and battleships.' This, it seemed to Scheer, was exactly the opportunity for which he had been looking; with the forces at his disposal he could be confident of inflicting a decisive defeat on an isolated British squadron. On receipt of *L13's* first report he had marked time to enable Hipper to rejoin him; the second report at 12.23 confirmed him in his intention to abandon the attack on Sunderland, and go after the prey apparently spotted by *L13*, only 65 miles to the south and steering north east.[30]

It was, of course, not a detached battle squadron, but the Harwich force which had been seen, but there was no chance of a correction, because a thunderstorm at 1.20 caused *L13* to lose touch with Tyrwhitt's ships. Scheer had, at 1.00, turned his whole fleet to the south east in pursuit of what he believed was his best chance of denting the Grand Fleet's overall superiority. Ironically, Tyrwhitt, totally unaware of the situation, had himself turned south at 12.45 and was hence steaming away from the High Seas Fleet, which Scheer had calculated would be able to fall on its prey by about 2.30. As he continued southward, however, without making any contact, he received fresh intelligence which further changed the situation. At 2.13 he read a report from *U53* to the effect that the Grand Fleet was coming south and at 1.15 had reached a point 65 miles north of the High Seas Fleet.[31]

This news obviously put a different complexion on the situation, as did the failure to make the expected contact with the enemy, and Scheer clearly had an urgent decision to make. With Jellicoe heading towards him, it would be extremely risky to pursue the will of the wisp too far, particularly without effective airship reconnaissance:

> I hoped, however, soon to get news of the enemy from our ships, since, according to our reckoning, it was now the hour when the encounter should take place; but I received no information from them. Either the enemy had changed his course, because he was disquieted by the presence of the airship which he assumed was scouting for the Fleet, or the airship, owing to its unreliable navigation, had incorrectly reported his position.[32]

Scheer pressed on for some twenty minutes after he had heard of the Grand Fleet's advance; but at 2.35, approaching the area of known minefields, he gave up the pursuit and turned his fleet to the course ESE, to return home. It was obviously too late to retrace his steps to bombard Sunderland, not least because that would almost certainly have brought him face to face with Jellicoe. Levetzow, his Chief of Operations, rather improbably claimed after the war in a letter to Hermann Goering that but for *L13's* intervention, if the High Seas Fleet had maintained its course for Sunderland, it would have achieved 'a substantial success. The fate of the war turned on this battle, which was the last chance to end the war by a naval success.'[33]

Jellicoe, as he steamed south, was extremely hopeful of an encounter with the High Seas Fleet. He had chosen not to come south down a swept channel which would take him further east:

> It is fairly clear that he thought the best means of getting hold of the enemy was not to go too far from their probable objective, the British coast; for at 12.32 he altered course to the westward, so as to pass between the Humber minefield and the land. No news was coming in from his advanced force or from the Admiralty; but, from time to time, his wireless room picked up signals from a fleet sweeper reporting a Zeppelin in the Sunderland area: and the ships round him, and on the screen, were reporting that the enemy's *Telefunken* signals were increasing in strength.[34]

Instead, therefore, of coming down the 'L' Channel further to the east, he opted for the 'M' Channel. It was the more cautious option; had he chosen the 'L' Channel he might have stood a better chance of getting between Scheer and his base, but he would not have been able to prevent a bombardment of Sunderland or anywhere else on the east coast, had Scheer got that far. To have allowed such a bombardment to take place, and then not catch the High Seas Fleet would have been disastrous in terms of public relations. At 2.00 pm he received an important message from the Admiralty, informing him that intercepts put Scheer only 60 miles south of Beatty's battle cruisers at 12.33. By the time he read this message an hour and a half had passed, which should mean that Beatty was less than 40 miles away from the High Seas Fleet and at 2.15 preparations were made for an imminent encounter. Jellicoe signalled his fleet: 'The High Seas Fleet may be met at any moment. I look with entire confidence to the result.'[35] A message from the Admiralty at 2.30 that suggested that Scheer was at 12.30 pm coming north seemed to confirm that action might be about to commence.

Jellicoe's confidence that a battle was imminent was absolute, as he wrote in his memoir:

> The meeting appeared to be so certain that I arranged the distribution of gunfire of the Battle Fleet. On the assumption that the enemy would turn to the eastward on meeting us, I directed a concentration of fire of ships that would be ahead of the *Iron Duke* on deployment, of two ships on one, leaving the *Iron Duke* to deal with one ship singly, as a compliment to her accurate firing at Jutland. The conditions were eminently favourable to us. The weather was clear. There seemed to be a very good prospect that we might, on gaining touch with the enemy, find that the Grand Fleet was in a position to cut off the High Seas Fleet from its base, as it was probable that we should be to the eastward, although farther north.[36]

This was an understandable hope, but it would have only been realised if Scheer, once contact had been established, had shown an uncharacteristic passivity in allowing the Grand Fleet to get around his eastern flank.

The tension soon relaxed, however. By 3.00 pm, no contact with the High Seas Fleet having been made, Jellicoe had to accept that the chances of encountering Scheer had faded. He ordered Beatty, if no sighting was made by 4.00 pm, to turn north to return to base. At 3.46 news came from the Admiralty that Scheer had turned for home, and at 3.57 pm the Grand Fleet turned north, its immediate rear covered by the 2nd Cruiser Squadron, six miles astern, and the 5th Squadron two miles astern.

Just as Beatty received Jellicoe's signal that he was to turn at 4.00 pm, two of his light cruisers, *Phaeton* and *Chatham*, reported submarines ahead. The cruiser screen was now running into the edge of U-Line III off Flamborough Head. *Phaeton,* on the east wing of the cruiser screen, spotted a submarine on the surface seven and a half miles ahead; *Chatham*, in the centre, sighted a conning tower six miles ahead. *Lion* increased speed to 22 knots, and began zigzagging with her destroyers, when at 3.35 *Birkenhead* and *Falmouth* reported smoke to the south. At 3.40 *Dublin* reported another submarine six miles off, running on the surface north eastwards, which then dived. The smoke was a false alarm, turning out to be a trawler, and Beatty duly turned north at 4.03pm, to follow the battle fleet.

To the discomfort of the battle cruisers, they were being shadowed by Zeppelins most of the time, and the light cruisers were ordered to try to drive them off. It was while engaged in this task that *Falmouth* suddenly spotted two torpedo tracks;

> The *Falmouth's* helm was put hard to port. The first torpedo just missed ahead and the second hit the ship close to the stern. A huge column of water rose 100 feet high and fell on the deck, sweeping everything out of its way. The petty officer at the port foremost gun was blown out of his seat and picked himself up by the gallery 50 feet away. Another explosion aft told that a third torpedo had hit the ship astern ... The stern on the ship had been 'concertinaed' and, standing on the quarter deck, one could look right down into the wreckage of the tiller compartment. The main deck was split open up to the centreline, and the upper deck bulged 1 ½ feet to 2 feet.[37]

However, the engines were still intact, and Captain Edwards resolved to make for the Humber, 65 miles away. *Chester* kept her company, steaming around her to discourage further submarine attack. The U-boat that torpedoed Falmouth was *U-66;* when three destroyers came up to relieve *Chester,* one of them, *Pelican*, dropped a depth charge, which shook the submarine badly. She had unsuccessfully fired two more torpedoes before making off. *Falmouth* continued to crawl homewards, by now escorted by seven destroyers. By 9.00 am on August 20 two tugs had arrived to take the light cruiser in tow, with two more destroyers. In spite, however, of this impressive screen, another U-boat, *U63*, pounced and hit her twice, and reluctantly Captain Edwards accepted that his ship must be abandoned. She was still under tow, although proceeding very slowly; and it was not until 8.00 am on August 21 that *Falmouth* finally sank.

When turning for home with the Grand Fleet, Jellicoe was perfectly aware that the danger to his ships was not past:

> It seemed fairly certain to me that the enemy would leave a trap behind him in the shape of mines or submarines, or both; and, indeed, the numerous submarines already sighted made it probable that the trap was extensive; it was therefore unwise to pass over the waters which he had occupied unless there was a prospect of bringing the High Seas Fleet to action.[38]

Although in fact there were no new minefields to threaten him, he was repeatedly made aware of the threat from submarines, as reports reached him from various of his ships. Newbolt described the uncomfortable journey home:

> The fleet's movement up 'M' Channel between 4.00 pm and dark is a fair test of risk incurred by a large force when it moves over an infested area. Their north westerly course carried the battle squadrons straight towards the line which the U-boats off Blyth had been ordered to occupy, and everything favoured the enemy submarines. In order to keep inside the channel our screens were closed up; the spaces between the squadrons were considerably less than those prescribed for the formation in which they were then cruising; and as the channel was narrow, the ships could not zigzag freely. The whole target was at once massed and hampered. Without counting the submarines which torpedoed the *Falmouth,* eleven reports of U-boats in dangerous positions came in to the flagship between 4.00 and 9.00 pm … the experience seems to have made a strong impression on the Commander-in-Chief.[39]

For Scheer on his way home, there remained only one other possible threat, and this was provided by Tyrwhitt and the Harwich Force. He had been the recipient of a series of confusing messages from Jellicoe, which caused him to make a number of changes of course. At 3.00 pm he received Jellicoe's order to be ready to attack the High Seas Fleet as it returned to base; after an hour on the course indicated, he heard that the order was cancelled, and so returned to his original northerly course. Next, Jellicoe warned him that Scheer might be retiring by way of Terschelling; and finally he received the Admiralty message locating the High Seas Fleet at 2.45 in a position 75 miles NW of the current position of the Harwich Force. Pondering the conflicting information, Tyrwhitt decided he had better act on that received from the Admiralty, and he continued on his existing course. At 5.20 a Zeppelin was seen, and shortly after *Lightfoot* reported seeing a considerable number of large vessels steering east. For a brief while Tyrwhitt turned south to avoid being cut off and then, when he had enough room, he turned back to follow what he realised was the High Seas Fleet.[40]

On seeing that Tyrwhitt was following him, Scheer disposed his fleet to prepare for a night attack. On the basis of what he described as his 'lucky experience on the night of June 1,' he decided against using his destroyers and light cruisers to drive off the Harwich Force, reckoning that the enemy had the advantage in speed. Instead, he put a strong force of destroyers in his van, to guard against a surprise, and a further large group at the end of his line. To his surprise, Tyrwhitt did not take the opportunity of making a night attack, and by 8.10 pm he had learned from *L11* that the enemy was moving away south eastwards.[41]

Tyrwhitt had reported the contact with the High Seas Fleet to Jellicoe at 6.00 pm; in reply, he was told that the Grand Fleet was too far away to give him any support. It was clear to Tyrwhitt that he was on his own, and that if he attacked, he could not hold up the High Seas Fleet long enough to bring about a fleet action. Although he attempted by increasing to full speed to get ahead of the High Seas Fleet it was soon apparent that he could not get into an attacking position before the moon rose; and he turned away, reporting to Jellicoe at 7.32 that night attack conditions were unfavourable.[42] On August 21 he wrote to Jellicoe in what his biographer thought were unnecessarily apologetic terms:

> I am afraid we failed you on Saturday and I am kicking myself for not standing on for another hour instead of turning at 12.45 pm. I imagine I should have sighted the enemy if I had. It will probably seem inexplicable to you, but I had not the slightest idea where you were … I hope I was right in not making a night attack. I could have made one, but I don't think I should have succeeded in doing any harm and should most certainly have

> been badly cut up as the night was not very dark. There was not time to make a detour to get ahead of them, especially with their Zeppelins in close attendance so I turned away and came home. I also gathered you did not want me to go in when you said you were too far off to support me. This all seems very feeble and I am afraid you will think so too, but I was groping in the dark all day.[43]

Commander Frost's criticism of Tyrwhitt's failure to attack is extremely severe:

> To be in plain sight of 20 capital ships at dark is a wonderful opportunity for any destroyer commander. Any situation, except possibly a full moon, would be favourable for a night attack. On the other hand, destroyers making a night attack do not need or desire any support from their capital ships, as that would expose those ships to the attacks of the enemy's destroyers. That the British deliberately refused the opportunity for a night attack and Scheer was perfectly willing to risk it disproved the claim that the British had gained a moral ascendancy over the Germans as a result of Jutland. The British forces on August 19 were certainly handled with more caution than on May 31.[44]

Predictably, the German Official History takes the same view of Tyrwhitt's decision:

> The reasons which caused him and Admiral Jellicoe not to attack the heavy German forces … and to leave them entirely unmolested stand in basic opposition to the German conception of the use and independent attack of torpedo boat forces.[45]

Professor Marder, on the other hand, exempts Tyrwhitt from criticism, arguing that he had a reason with more validity that Frost admits, in his belief that an attack would be useless and too hazardous. This, rather than the impossibility of delaying the High Seas Fleet long enough for the Grand Fleet to arrive, was the reason for not closing the enemy.[46] However, the moon did not rise until midnight, and Tyrwhitt had made contact at 6.00 pm; it does seem that he had an opportunity to attack before moonrise, even if he could not get into the preferred position of attacking from ahead.

23

Strategic Changes

Apart from some ineffective shots at the Zeppelins that frequently appeared, the Grand Fleet had not been in action on August 19, but the events of the day had, as Newbolt observed, made a great impression on Jellicoe. He was particularly exercised by what he saw as the inadequacy of the force of destroyers necessary to screen the battle fleet. He set out the risks to which he was exposed:

> The experience of August 19 showed that light cruisers, proceeding at even the highest speed unscreened by destroyers, ran considerable danger from enemy submarines. The enemy's submarine commanders were no doubt increasing in efficiency, and risks which we could afford to run earlier in the war were now unjustifiable. Representations were made to the Admiralty to the effect that it was considered that in future light cruisers should be screened by at least one destroyer per ship; the number of destroyers available for the Grand Fleet did not at the time admit of this, but as the total complement of 100 (the number intended to be appropriated to the Fleet) was reached, destroyers could be allotted to most of the light cruisers in the advanced line, provided there were not many absent from the Fleet carrying out extraneous services.[1]

He also drew the firm conclusion from the events of the day that it was extremely risky to take the Grand Fleet into the southern waters of the North Sea unless there was a really pressing need to do so, and that there had to be an adequate destroyer force to act as a submarine screen for all ships. He sensed that the partial success of Scheer's submarine traps on August 19 would encourage him to repeat operations of this kind.

Over the next few weeks Jellicoe hammered home his need for destroyers, to the point where Oliver, the Chief of Naval Staff, found him becoming a distinct nuisance; he endorsed Jellicoe's letter of September 13 with the words 'keeping up an argument will not provide any more destroyers.'[2] Jellicoe wrote also to Balfour explaining that the issue was of the utmost gravity, calling for urgent pressure to be applied to the shipbuilders producing destroyers. Until he got more, he wrote, he could not guarantee that there would not be further heavy losses in cruisers, if not in battleships.[3] To Jackson he wrote on August 23 to regret his losses on August 19:

> The only way of avoiding them in future when submarines are so numerous will I fear be to screen all cruisers and light cruisers, and I am afraid the number of TBD's won't run

> to it until I get the 15th Flotilla. I don't understand why Beatty did not screen his light cruisers as he had 24 TBD's out and only six battle cruisers. I am enquiring. His screen was three or four times as thick as that of the Battle Fleet. Of course his numbers that day were abnormal and are gradually being reduced. It is bad that our submarines miss so much but the Germans miss too. There were many misses on the 19th besides the hits. I am always ready to give the submarines some practice here against fast ships. I do it for the Blyth submarines.[4]

The events of August 19 had caused Balfour a good deal of anxiety about how they should be reported publicly, as Jackson told Jellicoe on August 20:

> The First Lord is very worried about what to say to the Press. As they would not stop to face you, I don't think he need worry even if we have lost two cruisers … I think no one can take exception this time, and when our submarine returns we can add the torpedoing of the German battle ship. I still think they were going for a raid as their principal object, laying a trap for you at the same time.[5]

Beatty's first reaction to the outcome of the day was to bring up again his request that the 5th Battle Squadron be attached to his command, since 'three or four of the fastest and newest German battleships are believed to be attached to the First Scouting Group.' This meant that Hipper would now have 'a position of definite superiority.' Jellicoe was unimpressed; forwarding Beatty's suggestion to the Admiralty, he pointed out that at Jutland the 5th Battle Squadron had only been with Beatty because Hood's battle cruisers were with the Grand Fleet. Had Hood been with Beatty, there would have been nine battle cruisers to Hipper's five, and unlike the 5th Battle Squadron they would have been able to get out of range of the High Seas Fleet.[6]

In his reply of September 6, Beatty accepted Jellicoe's view with a good grace; he went on to show that he was entirely in sympathy with the strategic changes that Jellicoe was proposing for the Grand Fleet:

> I am very firmly of the opinion that the war has reached a stage when it behoves us in the Navy to move very circumspectly. The old proverb that 'when you are winning risk nothing' might well be applied now, and I think the North Sea south of latitude 55° 30 N is a very unhealthy place for capital ships and should be left entirely to submarines who should be able to deny the use of it to the enemy except at very grave risk. If they are willing to take that risk it would surely be for an objective of great importance … in which case we ought to be able to guess and counter it. The enemy's fleet is no use to them unless they can perform some such duty as breaking up the blockade which is really now having a strangling effect and in that case they have to fight us, and in waters of our selection and not of theirs.[7]

The important strategic decisions that must be made as a result of August 19 were to be discussed at what Marder describes as 'one of the most important naval conferences in the war.' Oliver journeyed north to meet, on September 13 aboard *Iron Duke*, Jellicoe and Madden, his Chief of Staff. Before the conference took place, however, Jellicoe had entered into a remarkably irate correspondence with Jackson, in the course of which both men departed from their usually urbane mode of expression. It arose from a visit to the fleet of the Fourth Sea Lord, Captain Cecil Lambert, on which he reported, on his return to the Admiralty, to the other three Sea Lords. The correspondence began with a letter from Jackson of September 11 and continued with some vigorous exchanges until September 17. The full correspondence is contained in Volume II of the *Jellicoe Papers*, and very clearly illustrates the strains of high command.[8] It may be that Lambert was predisposed to paint Jellicoe in a poor light; after Jutland, he was reputed to have said that Jellicoe 'ran away.'

The lack of sympathy between Jellicoe and Lambert was mutual; Jellicoe told Hamilton that the feeling against Lambert in the Fleet 'was very strong and we should all welcome a change there.'[9] Hamilton thought Lambert fraternised too much with politicians and had got some of 'their silly impracticable habits of thought.'

Even before this furious correspondence, Jackson was privately very dissatisfied with Jellicoe's defensive strategy. On August 29 he had written a minute on a letter from Jellicoe of August 4 which was extremely critical. Its contents were not however, embodied in any letter to Jellicoe, and merely remained on file:

> It cannot be overlooked that the Commander-in-Chief lays great stress on the injury the enemy can inflict on our forces in the North Sea, but offers no suggestion as to the employment of his forces to inflict similar losses on the enemy. It is also to be noted that practically all large movements of the Fleet have to be initiated by the Admiralty. I suggest the Commander-in-Chief might again be informed that we should welcome any suggestions from him as to the employment of any of the vessels under his command with the object of inflicting similar injury to the enemy.[10]

It was against this background of mutual dissatisfaction that Oliver held his meeting on September 13 with Jellicoe and Madden. A note of the matters discussed was set out in a memorandum which Jellicoe sent to the Admiralty on the following day. Essentially, they revolved around the extent to which risks could be taken with the Grand Fleet in the face of German minefields and submarines, and the willingness of the Government to accept the consequences of following an even more cautious strategy. This would mean, for instance, the inability of the fleet to prevent the bombardment of East Coast towns or interfere with any German attempts at a landing. More generally, it was necessary to consider just how bold the Grand Fleet should be in going into areas that might be mined or infested with submarines. Jellicoe was emphatic in his view that such risks were unacceptable:

> The Commander-in-Chief stated that his view was that the main fleet should not go south of Lat. 55.30N in longitudes east of Long.4.OE, unless under exceptional conditions, the reason being that waters so far to the eastward cannot be watched by our cruisers or our submarines, and they therefore offer to the enemy facilities for preparing a trap of mines or submarines on a large scale.[11]

Jellicoe went on to restate the consequences of his lack of sufficient destroyers, observing that having regard to the threat from submarines 'it should be perfectly understood that the fleet should not go to the southward of the Dogger Bank unless the number of destroyers is sufficient to furnish thoroughly efficient screens for all ships.' He was also uneasy about the risk that the

Germans might have grasped that their secret wireless traffic was being monitored; in order that it should not appear that the presence of the Grand Fleet in the North Sea always coincided with the departure of the High Seas Fleet from its bases, he wanted there to be a more constant patrol of the North Sea by cruisers. An additional reason was to put the Germans on notice that there was a great risk of their being sighted if they put to sea. This would, he thought, be a deterrent against raids. It would also, although he did not say so, render a fleet action less likely – a very clear indication of his reluctance to provoke such a thing.

Jellicoe was also worried about the possibility of the Germans putting two and two together in another respect. Although there is no evidence that this was so, he feared that the enemy had discovered the position of the 'L' and 'M' swept channels, and demanded that a new channel should be swept without delay.[12] If it had been the case that the Germans knew this particular secret, it would have been extremely serious, since, as the operations on August 19 had demonstrated, the battle fleet would be extremely vulnerable in the confined area to U-boat activity; the swept channels could become a death trap for the Grand Fleet's battle squadrons.

Following the conference on September 13, Oliver next day paid a visit to Beatty, whom he found to be entirely in agreement with Jellicoe's cautious strategy, as he minuted on the latter's report of the conference:

> Both the C-in-C and the VA, BCF hold very definite views as to the Fleet not coming south on every occasion of the German Fleet approaching the East Coast of England, but only when there is a really good chance of engaging it in daylight .... The VA was if anything more emphatic on this point than the C-in-C.[13]

Given the evident unanimity on the part of the leadership of the Grand Fleet, it would have been extremely difficult for the Admiralty not to endorse the strategy prescribed by Jellicoe. On September 25 a letter went to the Commander-in-Chief approving generally the conclusions reached on September 13, and enclosing revised fleet orders embodying these; they were to come into force during the winter months and would be reviewed in the following spring as the days lengthened.[14]

Nonetheless, the Admiralty recognised that periodical fleet exercises would be necessary to maintain the efficiency of the fleet, which would inevitably involve some risk; but it would not be sound strategy to take large risks with capital ships if there was only a slender chance of bringing the High Seas Fleet to action in daylight. This was a further restatement of Jellicoe's refusal to become involved in a night action.

Although Jackson might complain that Jellicoe did not bring forward proposals for damaging the enemy, the Admiralty retained a tight control over the movements of the Grand Fleet. When ordering the Grand Fleet to raise steam it would themselves determine the level of urgency; thereafter, when the fleet was ordered to put to sea, it would concentrate east of the Long Forties, and Jellicoe would arrange the rendezvous. In rough weather, which would hamper destroyer operations, it would not be ordered further south.

Richmond, serving in the 3rd Battle Squadron as captain of *Commonwealth,* was prompted on August 22 by two officers of *Lion* (Lieutenant Chalmers and Captain Plunkett-Ernle-Drax) to set out in characteristically pungent terms the strategy which he believed should henceforth be followed:

1. Take no risks with the GF. The whole operations all over the world depend on it.
2. The GF is doing its job and will complete it even if it never fights the HSF. It is better to stifle our disappointment than to weaken, without adequate compensation, this supremely important force.
3. Endeavour to confuse the enemy by a variety of measures.
4. Relegate the defence of coast towns to a few long range guns. (Objection – expense and time. But the Germans could do it. So could we).
5. Let's free ships for active operations, offensive, in the regions where they can do service and assist the common cause.
6. Keep the GF at maximum strength and aim only at a decisive blow.
7. A decisive blow can only be obtained in a spot remote from enemy's harbours ...[15]

By now, Professor Marder reckons, stalemate had set in in the North Sea. The Naval Staff Monograph saw August 19 as having been 'one of the great beacons of the war at sea:'

> It was the last time that the German Fleet pushed right out against the English coast. It was the first and last day on which German submarines worked in close conjunction with the Fleet controlled by their leader's signal from the bridge of a battleship. On the British side, too, it was a red letter day of reconnaissance, for it was *E23* which sighted the German Fleet as it left the Bight, and announced its position to the Commander in Chief, hastening down from the north. Strategically its outcome was of the first importance, for it was decided that it should be the last time that the Fleet should push so far down the North Sea, and on the German side it was practically the last effort of its kind.[16]

After reviewing in considerable detail the events of August 19, the Naval Staff Monograph developed its thesis of the far reaching results of the day:

> It is typical of the vagaries of naval war that while the Battle of Jutland, whose name is a household word, had no immediate effect on fleet strategy, August 19, a day when not a shot was fired on either side marks a definite turning point in the war at sea. On the German side, Scheer thought he saw a door of high promise opening before him. But for the elaborate machinery of reconnaissance, essential to his plan, every available submarine and airship had to accompany the battle fleet whenever it put to sea. All these auxiliaries had to be at the admiral's disposal, and it followed that if the submarines were required for the war against commerce, the operations of the High Seas Fleet must cease ... thus a deadlock arose in the North Sea. It may be said that Admiral Scheer could not sally out without submarines and Admiral Jellicoe could not drive him back without destroyers. On the one side the apparatus of reconnaissance, on the other side the apparatus of screening broke down. August 19 was thus at once both a finale and a prologue. The curtain rang down on the excursions of the German Fleet just as they began to offer a promise of success. It was to rise again, not on serried fleets seeking one another in the North Sea, but on submarines toiling night and day in tireless search for prey, while behind them a host of relentless pursuers followed hard. It is in the light of these far reaching decisions that August 19 ranks with Heligoland Bight, Dogger Bank and Jutland as one of the red letter days in the calendar of the North Sea.[17]

This emphatic conclusion perhaps slightly overstates the case, particularly if is read as suggesting that Scheer, after August 19, had had enough. This was far from the case. He was sufficiently encouraged by the outcome of the day to plan another sortie for the beginning of September. It was to be similar to the August sortie, with the submarines deployed to protect the flanks of the High Seas Fleet, but their disposition was to be modified. With the single base lines there was no certainty that the U-boats could be certain of a chance to launch a torpedo if the enemy ran into the line; the destroyer screen might be able to prevent the first U-boat to sight the enemy from attacking, while the others were too far away to assist. This time, only the enemy's probable direction of approach was taken into account; 'the U-boats covered a larger area, altogether 100 nautical miles, and were placed in three rows, opposite the gaps between the leading craft.'[18]

Unluckily, Scheer was unable to put this plan into effect because unfavourable weather prevented effective airship reconnaissance, and the operation had to be cancelled. Undaunted, Scheer planned another operation for early October, intending it to be on the same lines. Now, however, he ran into another difficulty, since the U-boat campaign against commerce had been resumed, albeit under prize court rules, and he had to think again. His solution was, instead of advancing on the English coast, to operate with a wide screen of destroyers into the middle of the North Sea, to take stock of the commercial traffic encountered there, and to take prizes. The High Seas Fleet was to serve as a support to the light craft. Scheer was obliged to choose the battle ground with care. Based on his experience at Jutland, 'the position with regard to wind and sun must play an important part in the outcome of the artillery battle.' In addition, the timing of any engagement was crucial; he did not want to be exposed to too lengthy a daylight action in which the British advantage in numbers could overwhelm him.[19] The German Official History noted that if Scheer 'hoped to clash with enemy surface forces, the chances were slight due to the limited extent of the advance.' It added that Scheer intended, if he could, to launch a night torpedo attack.[20] Certainly, in view of the new Grand Fleet strategy, a fleet action was unlikely; it was even less likely that Jellicoe would allow himself to be attacked at night.

At 5.30 pm on October 18 Scheer radioed his orders for his forces to put to sea. As usual, the signal was picked up, and at 7.46 pm the Admiralty ordered Jellicoe to be at short notice for steam. Other intercepted signals confirmed that a German sortie was under way, and precautionary orders went out to Immingham, Harwich and the 3rd Battle Squadron. Following the new strategy agreed upon in September, Jellicoe did not put to sea, since the enemy intentions were unclear. Jellicoe appears to have considered that the Germans intended to draw the Grand Fleet south and west, so that surface raiders might slip past and on October 19, and the two days following, he sent two cruisers, *Achilles* and *Minotaur,* two light cruisers, *Weymouth* and *Melbourne,* and eight destroyers to patrol the northern end of the North Sea.[21] Tyrwhitt was ordered to put to sea, and to assemble to the west of the North Hinder, while the 3rd Battle Squadron was sent into the Swin.

Not for the first time, the weather took a hand. Scheer put to sea at midnight on October 18/19, steering west for a point east of the Dogger Bank. As he advanced into the centre of the North Sea, his flanks were covered by a widely extended destroyer screen. For reconnaissance he relied on ten Zeppelins, spread in a wide semicircle across the Bight, two of which suffered breakdowns and returned to base. However, the destroyer screen was handicapped by rapidly deteriorating weather, and was unable to go as far afield as Scheer had intended. As he proceeded northwest, the British submarine *E38* was able to get inside the screen, firing two torpedoes at the light cruiser *München*; although damaged, she was able to return to base under tow from the light cruiser *Berlin*. A report of *E38's* attack had reached the Admiralty; no more was heard of the movements of the High Seas Fleet until 5.00 pm, by which time Scheer was about ninety five miles north west of Heligoland, steering for the Horns Reef, evidently on his way home. The various British forces that had been alerted were accordingly stood down.[22] Scheer had continued his advance until 2.00 pm, at which time he ordered his Zeppelins back to base, and turned back himself, having, according to the German Official History, concluded that night time conditions would be too bright for an effective torpedo attack. He was, in any case, aware since 11.35 am that his movements were known; with the heavy sea hampering his destroyers, a decision to abort the operation was inevitable.[23] Deprived of his submarines, Scheer was reluctant to take any chances with the High Seas Fleet.

This caution was greatly increased when he got into trouble with the Kaiser for sending Hipper to sea on November 4 with the battle cruiser *Moltke* and the battleships *Grosser Kurfürst, König, Markgraf* and *Kronprinz,* with a half flotilla of destroyers, to attempt to rescue two U-boats which had been stranded on the coast of North Jutland in a fog. One of the U-boats could not be shifted, and was abandoned and blown up. At about 1.05 pm, as the squadron was returning home, both *Grösser Kurfürst* and *Kronprinz* were hit by torpedoes from the British submarine *J1,* in heavy seas. Neither was seriously damaged, and they returned home safely, but William was not at all pleased, as Scheer recorded:

> Upon receipt of the news of this incident, His Majesty the Emperor expressed the opinion that to risk a squadron for the sake of one U-boat, and in so doing almost lose two battleships, showed a lack of sense of proportion and must not occur again. Now this dictum might easily have imposed too great a restraint upon the Fleet merely for fear of submarines. We should have lost the confidence in our power to defend the Bight which we had gained as a result of the sea fight, and which became manifest when we sent these scouts 120 nautical miles from Heligoland, a distance which had hitherto been regarded as the ultimate limit to which our Fleet could advance.[24]

For the moment, therefore, as far as the battle fleets were concerned, deadlock had now been reached in the North Sea.

24

The Submarine Threat

Tirpitz had not been an early exponent of the submarine as a naval weapon. In a speech in the Reichstag in 1901 he said that, thanks to the configuration of her coasts and the location of her ports, Germany had no need of submarines, which he regarded as a purely defensive weapon. In his memoirs he explained his attitude to their development:

> I refused to throw away money on submarines so long as they could only cruise in home waters, and therefore be of no use to us; as soon as sea-going boats were built, however, I was the first to encourage them on a large scale, and, in spite of the financial restrictions imposed upon me, I went as far as the limits of our technical production would permit. The question as to how the submarines were to be used could not be answered practically until the instrument itself was there. The immediate question, therefore, was to construct boats which could operate overseas, and, as soon as this was possible, build as many of them as we could. This was done, and consequently nothing was neglected.[1]

By the outbreak of war the German Navy had begun to catch up, and it had been able to develop the most advanced submarines of the time. Numerically speaking, however the British still had a considerable advantage. The U-boat campaign of 1915 had, before they were withdrawn from the waters around the British Isles, achieved considerable success. By the end of the year the total number of U-boats in service had risen to fifty eight; this included the new *UB* class of coastal submarines and the *UC* class of small minelayers; both of these types were, due to their size and relatively simple design, suitable for rapid production. Later developments of these, however, saw them grow considerably in size.

Although Fisher had foretold that Germany would employ submarines in a war against British trade, a concept rejected by Churchill and Battenberg as uncivilised, there was no plan to do so before the war broke out. Hermann Bauer, the commander of the U-boat forces, who began the war as a commander but ended as an admiral, wrote in his memoirs that 'cutting England off from its sea supply by U-boats had in no way been considered, since such a submarine war against English sea trade would not have conformed with the London Declaration.'[2] This was also the view of Rear Admiral Spindler, the Director of Submarine Construction, and of Scheer, who wrote in his memoirs that 'simple and straightforward reflection' on how to avoid defeat in the war at sea pointed to a U-boat campaign against commerce:

> Of course it was our duty thoroughly to weigh its political consequences, its practicability from the military point of view, and its chances of success on a careful estimate of English economic conditions. But the study of these points ought to have preceded the war. It was neglected then because no one foresaw that a fight with England would mean a fight against her sea traffic with all the consequences it would entail. For who anticipated that we could possibly be in a position to inflict as severe an injury on English trade as that which we must expect to receive from the effects of the English blockade? It is no reproach to anybody not to have foreseen this.[3]

In fact, one theoretical study of the possibility had been made before the outbreak of war. Lieutenant Commander Ulrich-Eberhard Blum, of the U-boat Inspectorate, wrote a staff study in May 1914. In this, he calculated that the number of submarines necessary to conduct such a campaign against British trade was 222. Dan van der Vat speculates that Blum's paper would have landed on Tirpitz's desk, and notes that there is no evidence that he was impressed.[4] The question of an attack on British shipping was apparently considered in September 1914; it was not pursued, because the number of U-boats available was quite insufficient for such a campaign. Frequent changes of policy with regard to this were determined in part because of international pressure, but also because of the resources actually available.[5] It was what was seen as the British disregard of international law which first prompted the German navy to argue for the U-boat war against commerce.

Following the withdrawal by Scheer and Schröder of their U-boats from the war against commerce, in April 1916, the debate in the highest echelons of German naval command about the resumption of unrestricted submarine warfare continued. And although the abandonment of the campaign brought, for the moment, a considerable relief to Great Britain, her naval leaders remained profoundly anxious about the U-boat threat, and anxiously sought ways to meet it. The Admiralty had established the Board of Invention and Research, chaired by Fisher after he resigned as First Sea Lord. It explored many research possibilities, some of which were bizarre in the extreme, and in particular looked at ways of listening for submarines underwater. These mirrored developments in Germany of similar hydrophones, capable ultimately of detecting ships at a range of twenty five miles. The depth charge, invented in 1915, was not brought into use until the spring of the following year, but soon was widely employed by surface vessels hunting U-boats.

Müller faced mounting pressure from the Navy on the issue of resuming the unrestricted U-boat campaign. Trotha, for instance, wrote to him in May a passionate letter complaining of what he called 'the failure of a grand-style leadership, at the gradual decline in the morale of the nation and the catastrophic submission to America.' He found incomprehensible the behaviour of Holtzendorff, who had sided with the diplomats. If the U-boats were not to be used, he said, 'the Navy would be blamed for losing the war and would have no future.' Müller replied on May 23 to put Trotha right about Holtzendorff's position:

> He was all in favour of unrestricted U-boat warfare … In his report to the Kaiser and certainly at conferences with the Chancellor the Chief of Naval Staff stressed emphatically what a great sacrifice the 'kowtowing' to America signified. When His Majesty and all the political leaders of the Empire found it necessary to give way on the U-boat question, the Chief of Naval Staff was forced to comply.

As to the suggestion that Holtzendorff should have resigned, Müller was firm that an officer's duty was to comply with a decision and carry out his orders. He went on to appeal to Trotha and his colleagues to keep things in perspective:

> In my opinion the Navy's expectations regarding the effect of the U-boat blockade are just as exaggerated as their under-estimation of the effect that a break with America would have had. That is humanly understandable, but it is unfortunate when reigning moods descend to a personal plane and people in leading posts, who have to view things from all angles, give up the ghost because their views on a very two-edged weapon do not coincide with those of their representatives. Let us pray that we shall soon have political freedom of action which will allow us to beat even American hostility. Then we shall introduce unrestricted U-boat warfare against our enemy England.[6]

Scheer had withdrawn his U-boats from the war against commerce because he regarded the insistence that they should act in accordance with prize law as futile. It was his understanding that the Kaiser approved his decision, which had at least made available his U-boats for his operations against the Grand Fleet. However, he was under some pressure to withdraw his objections to the limited campaign. On June 20 he was invited to set out his position. His reply was blunt:

> I replied that in view of the situation I was in favour of the unrestricted U-boat campaign against commerce, in the form of a blockade of the British coast, that I objected to any milder form, and I suggested that, if owing to the political situation we could not make use of this, there was nothing for it but to use the U-boats for military purposes.[7]

This refusal on Scheer's part to compromise prompted Müller to attempt to mediate. With the attitude displayed by Scheer, there was little chance of avoiding a lengthy and bruising contest at Imperial Headquarters. On June 23 he wrote to Scheer, saying that he understood Scheer's position to be 'either everything or nothing,' and that although he sympathised with this point of view, the matter was not so simple. It was the task of the Chief of Naval Staff to find a way to carry out attacks in British waters:

> I am of the opinion that the C-in-C High Seas Fleet should help him by discovering a compromise between the boorish tribal views of the U-boat arm and those of the Chief of Naval Staff, bearing in mind general military and political requirements. It is obviously vital that the C-in-C recognise the decisions of the All-Highest, which are the result of serious deliberations of a military, political and economic nature – something one can hardly expect of a soldier – and that he agrees to use the U-boats to their best advantage in the aforementioned manner to destroy or threaten goods reaching Britain. I do not presume to make suggestions as to the methods to be employed because I realise that these measures are far more difficult against the English coast than in the Mediterranean.[8]

Müller went on to add that he himself believed in the possibility of unrestricted U-boat warfare. In spite of Müller's patient attempt to get a positive response, Scheer was having none of it, replying merely that he had done his duty and written of his conviction to the Chief of Naval Staff.

Holtzendorff maintained the pressure, submitting a further report, with Falkenhayn's support, on June 30, calling for 'the most ruthless form of submarine warfare,' but without success. It was agreed to postpone the issue further in the light of the political situation in the United States, and the Mexican crisis, which had led to American troops being sent to the border. Müller continued to defend Bethmann-Hollweg from those critics in the navy and the army who raged against his opposition to all out U-boat warfare, and who absurdly suggested that it was based on a pro-British policy.[9]

The dispute rumbled on throughout the summer. Scheer was contemptuous of the various shifts of policy on the part of the government with regard to the U-boat campaign, and the inconsistency between its domestic pronouncements and actual policy:

> Our attitude gave our people the false impression that, despite America's objections, we were still going to use our U-boat weapon with all our might. The people did not know that we, pledged to the nation by our big talking, were only pretending to carry on the U-boat campaign, and America laughed because she knew that it lay with her to determine how far we might go. She would not let us win the war by it. So we did not wield our U-boat weapon as a sword which was certain to bring us victory, but, as my Chief of Staff, Rear Admiral von Trotha put it, we used it as a soporific for the feelings of the nation, and presented the blunt edge to the enemy.[10]

While the U-boat dispute continued to occupy the attention of the admirals, another crisis had been brewing for some time at Imperial Headquarters. Falkenhayn had, since the failure of his additional strategy at Verdun had become apparent, been the subject of mounting criticism. On August 29 Falkenhayn was dismissed, leaving Pless at once for Berlin. He was succeeded by Hindenburg, who was appointed Chief of the General Staff with Ludendorff as First Quartermaster-General. Holtzendorff had come to Pless at this critical moment, and seized the opportunity again to press for the introduction of unrestricted U-boat warfare. By now, Müller was prepared to support him, arguing that a bumper harvest made Germany less dependent on imports, that there were more U-boats available, and that the neutrals were resentful of Britain, and more disposed to the wholesale blockading of her coasts.[11]

On August 31 there was a large scale high level conference on the war situation. Holtzendorff read a carefully prepared paper calling for the immediate resumption of unrestricted U-boat warfare. He argued that even if the United States declared war, there was nothing she could do about it; Denmark and Holland would remain neutral in any case, and the South American nations would be helpless. Germany's allies were failing fast; neglect to employ the weapon would mean *Finis Germaniae.*[12] Although Holtzendorff was supported by the War Minister, General Wild von Hohenborn, the civilian minsters were still against it, and Hindenburg wanted to see the outcome of the campaign against Romania before a decision was taken. When Scheer heard of this, he sent Trotha to see Ludendorff; the Chief of Staff came back with encouraging reassurances that it was agreed that to win the war a ruthless U-boat campaign was essential, with no half measures. It should be begun as soon as possible. Scheer was able to confirm this for himself when he met with Hindenburg and Ludendorff on November 22.[13]

In the meantime on October 6 an express order had been issued resuming U-boat warfare against commerce in Northern waters, albeit under prize rules. Contrary to Scheer's belief, the campaign quickly enjoyed considerable success, as RH Gibson and Maurice Prendergast noted:

> The new orders brought about an immediate rise in the shipping casualties, and from 131,000 tons the monthly average of sinkings rose to 276,000 tons. The anti-submarine measures were becoming patently inadequate to hold heir own against the growing danger; and when the British losses in October were found to have almost doubled the September toll of 84,600 tons, the severity of the menace could not be minimised.[14]

Captain Gayer, the German naval historian of the submarine arm, estimates that the pause in the U-boat war on commerce between May and September 1916 had conserved some 1,200,000 tons of merchant shipping that might have been destroyed during that period, excluding the 400,000 tons which Schröder's U-boats based in Flanders might have sunk in addition. He noted also that the rate of commissioning new U boats during the same period was at its highest, averaging ten per month between April 1916 and January 1917. Nonetheless, he is critical of the failure of the Pless conference to approve any substantial increase of orders for new boats in preparation for an all out offensive. Up to this time no large orders for new submarines had been placed with the shipyards, due in Gayer's opinion to the constant changes in the tactical employment of U-boats, and the desire to see that new designs were successful in operational conditions. The conference should, he argued, have approved a large programme, utilising the shipyards which normally produced merchant vessels much earlier than was generally the case. The narrow mindedness of some naval leaders was illustrated by the opposition faced by Rear Admiral Spindler, the Director of Submarine Construction, before he could place new orders:

> Admiral von Capelle, State Secretary for the Navy, was averse to embarking on an ambitious programme, considering that a surplus of submarines would be decidedly disadvantageous for the administration and further expansion of the navy as a world power after the war![15]

Both at Scapa Flow and in Whitehall there was deepening anxiety about the threat from submarines. Jellicoe addressed a series of letters on the subject to Jackson. On October 17, for instance, he wrote to the First Sea Lord:

> I am sending in some remarks about the activities of enemy submarines off New York which I hope will not be considered out of place. It is of course outside my province entirely, but one can't help thinking about these things and I am afraid there will be much trouble in the spring from these overseas submarines.[16]

It was, however, a paper which he wrote for Balfour on October 29 on the subject of the submarine menace that was of decisive importance:

> The very serious and ever increasing menace of the enemy's submarine attack on trade is by far the most pressing question at the present time. There appears to be a serious danger that our losses in merchant ships, combined with the losses in neutral merchant ships, may by the early summer of 1917 have such a serious effect upon the import of food and other necessaries into the allied countries as to force us into accepting peace terms, which the military position on the continent would not justify and which would fall far short of our desires. The methods which have been used in the past for attacking submarines are not

> now meeting with the success which has hitherto attended them … It is therefore essential for the successful conclusion of the war that new methods of attack should be devised, and be put into execution at the earliest possible moment.[17]

Jellicoe went on to give examples of the research that was being conducted into various methods of dealing with U-boats. He was not, he said, putting forward concrete proposals. He added:

> My objective in writing this memorandum is to press for the formation of a committee, whose one and only aim should be the production in the shortest possible time, and not later than the spring of 1917, of methods for overcoming the most serious menace with which the Empire has ever been faced. If this committee included officers possessing the necessary qualifications, I should have great hopes that it would be the means of producing quickly some methods by which we should be able with some measure of success to cope with this ever-growing menace.[18]

He sent a copy to Jackson as well, suggesting that he could come south to talk things over. Balfour, who induced Asquith to read Jellicoe's paper to the War Committee on October 31, took him up on the offer, and arranged for him to attend the next meeting of the War Committee on November 2.

Dissatisfaction among senior politicians with the performance of the Admiralty under Balfour and Jackson was growing. In the Press, too, there was a mounting concern that the conduct of the naval war was insufficiently aggressive. The morose and pessimistic Jackson had begun to exert a fatal influence over Balfour's attitude. His 'Report on Recent Naval Affairs,' which he presented to the Cabinet on October 14 1916, offered a shockingly negative view of the situation of the U-boat campaign against commerce:

> Of all the problems which the Admiralty have to consider, no doubt the most formidable and most embarrassing is that raised by submarine attack on merchant vessels. No conclusive answer has been discovered to this mode of warfare; perhaps no conclusive answer ever will be found. We must for the future be content with palliation.[19]

The Press was never likely to find this kind of helpless thinking acceptable, and there was a continuing agitation for effective action. Lord Charles Beresford and most naval journalists, together with leading newspapers, stridently demanded that all merchantmen should be armed without delay. This would, as Marder points out, be a huge exercise, there being thousands of merchant vessels, while the army, the anti aircraft services and the Navy itself had an insatiable appetite for guns.[20] But other voices were beginning to call for new blood at the Admiralty; the *Daily Mail* on November 13 was among those insisting that the country must see results:

> If the present Board of Admiralty cannot declare that the new submarine menace is 'well in hand,' we must have such changes as will ensure the country's safety.[21]

One of the issues considered by the War Committee at its meeting of November 2 was the convoy question. It had been suggested in various quarters that this might at least increase the possibility of defeating U-boat attacks. With Jackson, Jellicoe and Oliver all in attendance, the War Committee did not lack for professional advice. Unfortunately none of them was enthusiastic about the adoption of a convoy system; Jackson's attitude, for instance, reflected his concern that it would make an already chaotic situation in Britain's ports even worse.[22] Not surprisingly, therefore, the introduction of a convoy system 'was not generally accepted' by the War Committee. Jellicoe's key proposal, the formation of an expert committee to explore methods of anti-submarine warfare, was not discussed.

Next day, however, there was an extremely heavy-weight conference at the Admiralty to look at measures which might be introduced. It was attended by the Sea Lords, Jellicoe, Oliver, Wilson and a number of key members of the Naval Staff. Among the questions discussed was that of the ineffectiveness of destroyers in sinking U-boats; the possibility of employing submarines to tackle U-boats; a new mine laying programme; and the further development of a new depth charge mortar, which was showing promise. The principal recommendation derived from Jellicoe's paper of October 29:

> Some Flag Officer of authority and energy should be employed at the Admiralty for the exclusive purpose of developing anti-submarine measures, to follow through suggestions with all speed, and press their execution. His duties however, should not extend to the movements of ships.[23]

The decision was not, however, immediately acted upon, and in the meantime the extent of the general defeatism of the Admiralty was chillingly revealed by a paper which Jackson and Oliver circulated on November 20:

> It may definitely be stated that naval resources are practically exhausted as far as small craft for hunting submarines are concerned .... It is therefore suggested ... that the question be considered whether it is not worth while shaping military strategy as far as can now be done to assist in the reduction of the submarine menace through the destruction of as many of their home bases as is practicable.[24]

The direct reference here was to the proposal that an attempt be made to capture the Flanders bases from which Schröder's U-boats were operating with such success; more would be heard from the Admiralty in the future with regard to this.

As to the proposal that a 'Flag Officer of authority and energy' be appointed to head the anti submarine campaign, Jellicoe at first contemplated that he might take the post. On reflection, however, as he explained to Balfour in letters of November 3 and 6, he thought this not such a good idea. He felt that he should either be an embarrassment to the First Sea Lord or alternatively denied the power to be of much use. Better, he considered, for such a post holder to be not so senior; he suggested Sturdee's second in command, Rear Admiral Duff.[25]

Jackson had an alternative suggestion to make to Balfour on November 6; Jellicoe could come to the Admiralty as his understudy, on the understanding that he would in due course succeed him:

> The only point for consideration would be the date for relief. If it is in the interests of the Country and will help to bring the war to a more satisfactory ending, I am willing to vacate my post at any time and turn over my duties to him or any other more energetic officer who

> has had more experience of modern war at sea than I possess, and I should have the satisfaction of feeling I was doing my duty by retiring from this onerous post before it becomes too heavy a burden for me. I am not, however, ready to do this voluntarily, now, as a sacrifice to the discontented and ill informed (or misdirected) party in the House of Commons and the Press, who, I understand, are attacking the Government through any channel that gives them a chance of defeating or discrediting it.[26]

Balfour told Hankey on November 8 that Jellicoe's offer had been declined; Hankey urged that Vice Admiral Bacon, the commander of the Dover Patrol, be appointed, having on October 31 suggested to Balfour that he should 'pick Admiral Bacon's brains on the subject of measures against submarines.' He had an extremely high opinion of Bacon's 'extraordinary ingenuity, technical ability and driving power.' Hankey's biographer, Captain Stephen Roskill, considered this to be 'a considerable overestimate of Bacon's abilities,' however.[27]

25

The Dover Straits

As it happened, Bacon was in the autumn of 1916 under something of a cloud. Until then, there had not been a great deal of activity on the part of the German surface fleet off the coast of Flanders, from which Schröder's submarines had operated with considerable success. Now, however, it was resolved to try something new, as Scheer explained:

> The resumption of the U-boat campaign against commerce, which was to begin early in October, had to be supported as far as possible, even though it was little to the taste of the Naval Corps in Flanders. After our sortie on October 19, two torpedo boat flotillas were sent to Flanders, and from that base they were to attack the guard boats at the entrance to the Channel, so as to make it easier for our U-boats to get through.[1]

Commodore Michelsen, the commander of the High Seas Fleet's destroyers, accompanied the two flotillas as they made the journey from Heligoland to Zeebrugge, a journey which at one time would have been regarded as extremely hazardous, but which was now accomplished without incident.

Preparations were at once made to launch an attack on the ships of the Dover Patrol guarding the entrance to the Channel, and any transports found to the west. The British Admiralty had however learned that some movement was afoot, and put the Grand Fleet on standby, and at 6.45 am on October 24 ordered Tyrwhitt to sea. He was at the North Hinder by 1.00 pm, but Michelsen had taken his destroyers close along the Dutch coast, and there was no contact. Their arrival brought Schröder's strength in destroyers up to a total of twenty three, and he and Michelsen planned a quick raid before the reinforcement was discovered.[2] It was evident, though, that some new operation was planned, and Bacon was warned accordingly. Tyrwhitt was now ordered to reinforce the Dover Patrol with the light cruiser *Carysfort*, and the destroyers *Laforey*, *Liberty*, *Lucifer* and *Laurel*, and these vessels arrived at Dover on October 25. Bacon now had to decide which of his various responsibilities should have priority in preparing for the expected attack.

He had a lot of potential objectives to cover:

> Besides the seaward flank of the Allied armies, which seemed immediately threatened, he had to make a provision for defending the route between Beachy Head and the Downs, the mass of shipping which collected every night in the Downs anchorage, the barrage and

> the drifters watching it, and the transport route behind the barrage, between Folkestone and Boulogne. Of these targets the Downs appeared to him the most important, for it was there that the food supplies of the capital were assembled. The political effect of a serious and sustained raid against this central point of our vast network of communications would hardly have been less than that caused by the Dutch expedition to the Medway in 1667.[3]

Although defending the submarine barrage was less important, 'it had been established at a very great expenditure of material and labour,' and it was believed to have been an effective obstruction to the passage of U-boats. It consisted of a net running from the South Calliper, on the southern end of the Goodwins, to the south western end of the Outer Ruytingen shoal. The barrage was protected by a considerable number of drifters, unarmed save with rifles, and lacking wireless; they were organised in groups of six to eight.

Newbolt observes that Bacon's position was very difficult; his forces were inadequate, and in recent days there had been a lot of U-boat activity, requiring him to double the number of vessels engaged in escort and patrol duties:

> He could not attempt to direct operations by going to sea himself; his problem was one of defence, and could only be solved by his remaining ashore at the telephone centre and signal station. There he must wait in the black darkness of a raid-night, with lights out and windows open, to hear the sound of gunfire or to receive reports of it from the many stations strung on the long line between Beachy Head and the North Foreland or Dunkirk. His decisions must be doubly embarrassed, both by his knowledge of the many vulnerable points which he had to defend, and his complete ignorance of the force and direction of the enemy's attack.[4]

Bacon had two light cruisers (although *Attentive* had her boilers open for cleaning); one flotilla leader; 32 destroyers and 12 monitors (three of which were under repair). He also had a very large collection of other vessels of various types, including 78 trawlers and 130 drifters. The Harwich division was to sail to Dunkirk to reinforce the 5 destroyers there; the division led by *Lawford* went to the Downs and anchored there: *Flirt* was to support the drifters; six 'Tribal' class destroyers were held as a striking force at Dover, and four 30 knotters formed a general reserve.

At dusk on October 26 Michelsen sailed from Zeebrugge. The III Flotilla was to attack the drifters and the barrage, while the IX Flotilla was to raid the transport line. Michelsen himself led the 5th Half Flotilla (seven destroyers) north of the Colbart and Sandettie shoals, while the 6th Half Flotilla (six) took the southern area. The 17th Half Flotilla (six) was to operate north and west of the Varne, while the 18th Half Flotilla (five) searched the Pas de Calais.[5] It was a clear starlit night, with a new moon.

At 9.20 the lookouts of the 18th Half Flotilla reported four British destroyers to port, steaming on the opposite course; the Germans held off attacking, and were not spotted by *Laforey* and her consorts en route for Dunkirk. At 9.35 *Flirt* sighted the five German destroyers, which after being challenged repeated the signal; her captain assumed that these were *Laforey's* division and that they were returning to Dover. Again the Germans held their fire. Meanwhile the III Flotilla was approaching the barrage and the drifters guarding it. Michelsen's 5th Half Flotilla was the first in action, encountering five boats led by *Paradox*. Three were immediately sunk and a fourth, *Waveney II* was damaged and set on fire, while *Paradox* escaped north westward. Hearing the gunfire, *Flirt* turned back and ran into the 6th Half Flotilla, sighting also the damaged *Waveney II.* The destroyers were taken to be French; Flint stopped and lowered a boat to pick up men seen in the water; as the boat drew away the Germans opened fire, sinking *Flirt* in a few minutes; only her boat's crew survived.

At Dover, Bacon at 10.50 ordered his 'Tribal' destroyers to sea, led by *Viking,* while *Laforey's* division was en route to Dunkirk. The light cruiser *Carysfort* began to raise steam, but it would be some time before she could sail. The two half flotillas of the IX Flotilla had crossed the barrage at about 10 pm and pressed on through the Straits, finding no targets before turning back. First to turn was the 17th Half Flotilla, which between 11.00 and 11.30 encountered the transport *Queen*; an officer from *V80* boarded her, and allowed her captain and crew to take to the boats, before she was sunk by gunfire.

To the eastward Michelsen's destroyers had encountered two more groups of drifters, sinking four and damaging another. Bacon's orders to *Lawford's* division were mangled in transmission; when Lieutenant Commander Scott, the latter's captain, encountered *P34,* which had picked up survivors from *Queen,* he reckoned that he should leave the Downs to search for the enemy. This was not at all what Bacon intended, and he ordered Scott to return to the Downs; unfortunately the message was sent in error to *Laforey.* The shipping in the Downs was therefore temporarily uncovered, but Michelsen was unaware of this, and did not turn into the Downs.[6]

On leaving Dover, the 'Tribals' had become scattered. By 12.30 *Viking, Mohawk* and *Tartar* were crossing the barrage SSE; *Nubian* and *Amazon* separately were steering south, while *Cossack* was further off. *Nubian* ran into the 17th Half Flotilla, and was heavily damaged by gunfire before being hit by a torpedo which blew away her bow section. Her petrol tanks caught fire, and clouds of flame and smoke lit up the central part of the Straits, attracting both *Lawford's* division and *Laforey's* division toward the scene. Next, *Amazon* met the 17th Half Flotilla, which put two shells into her as it steamed past, putting her after gun and two boilers out of action.

The 18th Half Flotilla had met with *Viking, Mohawk* and *Tartar,* damaging *Mohawk* as it steamed past the British destroyers. *Laforey's* division was not far away, and *Lucifer* and *Laurel* were sent to assist; but by the time they arrived all the German destroyers, none of which were damaged apart from one which had had a chance collision with a drifter burning out of control, had returned home.

Nubian, completely disabled, was taken in tow by *Lark* at about 1.00 am. She could only be towed stern first. As dawn broke the wind got up and at 5.45 am the tow parted, and she drifted on shore between the South Foreland and St Margaret's Bay, but not before the tug *William Gray* had gone alongside to take off the wounded. *Nubian* was eventually salvaged, and her missing bow section was later replaced by that of *Zulu,* which had lost her stern when striking a mine. With a nice sense of humour, the new vessel thus created was commissioned as *Zubian.*[7]

Understandably, when reporting to the Admiralty, Bacon was somewhat defensive, pointing out that the raid had been the kind of operation that succeeded 'mainly by knowing at what point, and when, the blow will fall, and exactly what it is intended to carry out.' The enemy had had, he said, the advantage of knowing whether a boat was friend or foe, had a definite objective and a pre arranged plan:

> It is as easy to stop a raid of express engines with all lights out, at Clapham Junction, as to stop a raid of 33-knot destroyers on a night as black as Erebus, in waters as wide as the

> Channel … My defence against night raids has been to have the Downs protected, and the transport of troops stopped, since the obvious response to a raid that cannot be prevented is to have nothing the enemy can raid.[8]

Bacon developed the point in the history of the Dover Patrol which he published after the war, pointing out that no attempt at defending the Straits against a raid could be effectively made with the number of vessels he had at his disposal:

> To defend the Straits against a raid a considerably greater number of destroyers than that which a raiding force could bring to bear would have been required in order to cover successfully the twenty-mile line of approach and yet to be in reasonable force at any point where the enemy might turn up. Of course these numbers were not available.[9]

The outcome of the raid had prompted more public criticism of the Admiralty, which did not improve matters by claiming in its first communiqué of October 28 that two enemy destroyers had been sunk, and omitting to mention the loss of the drifters. The problem was compounded three days later when Balfour retreated somewhat as to the claim of having sunk the two destroyers, and admitted the loss of the drifters. The *Daily Mail* wrote of the feebleness which characterised the voice of the navy on this occasion as after Jutland, while the *Nation* wrote on November 4 that the enemy

> made a surprise attack on the Narrows, which all of us thought either securely blocked or watched with a jealous care, and succeeded in getting through, inflicting a not inappreciable amount of damage, and returning without harm to Zeebrugge. There is little comfort to be gained from a contemplation of that sequence of events.[10]

Jackson, worn down by overwork, was becoming very tired of what he regarded as the hostile and ill informed criticism to which the Board of Admiralty was daily subjected. He suggested that it might do some good if Balfour candidly admitted that there were limits to the power of the Navy to prevent tip and run raids. Balfour duly did so in his speech to the Lord Mayor's Banquet on November 9, referring to the fact that 'on a night of pitch darkness, no moon, clouds and storm, a few fast torpedo boats had entered the Channel and went as far west as Folkestone.' They had done not the smallest military damage to the lines of communication. He went on:

> I do not think it will be repeated, because I doubt it being worth the enemy's while. But it can be repeated. I have confidence that if it is we shall be able to show that if destroyers can enter the Channel on a night which they choose they will not be able to get out of the Channel without heavy disaster.[11]

Unfortunately for Balfour, the Germans did try another raid. Although it was not pressed very far, and the results were limited to the damage to one drifter and a few shells fired into Margate, the Press was outraged. *The Daily Mail* on November 27 put it thus: 'The Germans, to put it plainly, have pulled Mr Balfour's nose.' It went on grimly to observe that it was not the rank and file of the Navy that was at fault; they were beyond praise. The explanation must be sought elsewhere: 'The enemy is not to be beaten by the smart phrases and threats which chloroform

Parliament or an after dinner audience. Will and energy and insight and the resolutely offensive spirit are required.'[12]

By then, however, the position at the Admiralty had changed. The need to replace Jackson as First Sea Lord had now become obvious to many of those in government, and when Asquith took a hand by writing to Balfour on the subject on November 20, Jackson's removal became inevitable. Asquith generously conceded the First Sea Lord's 'very special attainments' and 'great tenacity and staying power,' but considered that 'in view of the increasing seriousness of the submarine situation' and other questions hardly less grave, Jackson should be replaced by 'the best naval expert' available. This was, of course, Jellicoe. Asquith ended his letter with sentiments which, in view of subsequent events, were ironic in his misapprehension of the real situation:

> I need scarcely add the assurance of my perfect confidence, which is shared by all our colleagues, in your supreme control in all that concerns the Navy. I regard it as one of our principal assets in the conduct of the war.[13]

Jellicoe will have seen what was coming, although not when it would arrive. In the meantime he had a bone to pick with the Admiralty, as he told Jackson on November 19:

> Mr Balfour has written that he proposes to relieve Burney at the end of his two years and to make Beatty second in command. I am intensely sorry to lose Burney. He is a splendid seaman and handles ships second to no one, and if his health were above suspicion he should certainly remain, but I do honestly think that he might not bear a great strain for long. I assume the decision re Beatty is irrevocable, so whilst giving my opinion (which you know) I have only said that I hope he will remain in the Battle Cruiser Force as long as he is second, and not come to the First Battle Squadron. I don't see any use in his doing so and I see very many objections. He will require a very able chief of staff, of that I am convinced, and I can think of no one better than Duff, if Duff would take the job.[14]

As far as Beatty was concerned, Jellicoe was swimming against the tide, as he well knew.

Having waited a while in the hope that the Press uproar would cool down, on November 22 Balfour telegraphed Jellicoe to offer him the post of First Sea Lord. Jellicoe accepted at once. Following a meeting with Balfour and Beatty in Edinburgh, he asked Duff to accompany him to the Admiralty as the flag officer charged with dealing with the submarine menace; he also proposed to take Dreyer with him. The formal order to transfer command of the Grand Fleet to Beatty arrived by telegram at 1.22 am on November 28. At the same time a message went to Beatty appointing him Commander-in-Chief with the acting rank of Admiral. Madden was to be second in command as Admiral Commanding the 1st Battle Squadron. Burney and Jerram were relieved. Pakenham was to command the Battle Cruiser Force, the title of Battle Cruiser Fleet being discontinued. Brock was to be Beatty's Chief of Staff.

The choice of Beatty to lead the Grand Fleet had probably become inevitable, for it was the choice which the politicians expected would be made. Nonetheless, from the point of view of the British Navy, it raised a number of problems. Admiral Burney, and Vice Admirals Jerram and Sturdee were all senior to him. Burney, as has been seen, was not thought to be physically up to the job. Jerram had done his reputation no favours by his performance at Jutland. Sturdee was not seen as appointable; as Professor Marder puts it: 'His ideas were considered too dangerous, his personality rubbed many people the wrong way, and his powers of commanding a big fleet, if he ever possessed them, had waned by this time.'[15] That, among the senior admirals, left only Madden and Beatty, and to the end Jellicoe pressed Madden's case. Even Asquith had some doubts about Beatty's lack of experience in fleet administration on a large scale. When it came to it, however, Beatty was seen as the only possible successor to Jellicoe.

Sturdee was greatly put out by these decisions; but following a telegram from Balfour which hinted that he might ask to be relieved as well, he replied that, the nation being at war, he felt it was his duty to place his services 'entirely at the disposal of Their Lordships.' Jellicoe wrote to Sturdee on November 28:

> I fear it is useless for me to tell you how much I feel for you in your present position, but I can at any rate say how very much I admire the spirit of self-sacrifice and patriotism which prompted your reply to Mr Balfour's telegram which I have seen. From the point of view of the welfare of the Fleet it is of course an immense gain that you decided as you did, and I can well understand how difficult was the course you took.[16]

In reply, Sturdee thanked Jellicoe for his 'very kind letter,' and asked that in due course Jellicoe should tell him whether he was to remain in command of the 4th Battle Squadron; not knowing was unsettling to both the squadron and himself.

Jellicoe received a shoal of letters on his giving up the command, but the most outspoken of these, as was to be expected, came from Fisher on November 28:

> Never in my life have I written a letter with deeper reluctance than this. I have been hoping against hope you would have listened to my entreaty not to give up command of the Grand Fleet ... You have the absolute unbounded confidence of the whole Grand Fleet and the whole Nation! Your leaving the command of the Grand Fleet at this juncture is absolutely parallel to Nelson coming home to sit on an office stool the week before Trafalgar! <u>There is no one comparable to you to command the Fleet!</u> It is absolutely certain also that you never could have chosen Beatty as your successor and what reply can you have if as First Sea Lord you allowed a man to succeed you that you did not choose? <u>You know a better!</u>

Fisher went on to condemn the move as a 'political appointment to prop up an administration of naval affairs that has proved itself absolutely incapable of recognising the first principles of naval strategy.' He concluded by saying that this was the saddest letter of his life.[17]

Jellicoe endorsed the letter with a note on the reference to Beatty: 'I recommended Madden as my successor. Beatty had not experience enough, and had made many mistakes. J.RS.' To Fisher he wrote that he was grieved to have disregarded his advice but did so because he agreed with Fisher that the great danger was the submarine menace. As to Beatty, he mildly commented that he did not know Fisher's opinion as to the succession to the command, reminding him of a letter he had written saying 'We want more Beattys.' Fisher replied at once, to the effect that it was 'one thing to praise a man for a subordinate command, but quite another for the chief command.' Jellicoe was the 'sole man for it' and failing him it had to be Madden. Fisher hoped that somehow, sooner or later, Jellicoe might go back, and added that his opinion of Beatty had 'greatly altered because of Jutland Battle episodes, whatever high opinion I might have previously had.'[18]

Beatty marked his elevation with a letter to his old friend Walter Cowan with an unmistakeable if oblique criticism of his predecessor:

> We have been through some odd times together and have had some successes, and there is no reason why we should not have more and greater ones. As you well know my heart will always be with the Battle Cruisers who can get some speed, but I'll take good care that when they are next in it up to the neck, this old Battle Fleet shall be in it too.[19]

Beatty arrived aboard *Iron Duke* on December 3, and next day wrote to his wife with his first impressions:

> Poor Sturdee was very piano but is eating out of the hand and ready to help all he can. Madden, Evan-Thomas are the other two squadron commanders here and they are alright. Generally speaking I have not much time to think but am wrestling with the multitude of things to be done and think with a little reorganisation I can put things on a better footing. There seems at present to be such an enormous amount of time wasted on details which can be much better performed by others than by me, and so free me for the more important things. I fancy the late C-in-C loved detail and messing about finicky things, and consequently the big questions got slurred over and overlooked altogether.[20]

Jellicoe was under no illusions about the immensity of the problems which he inherited as First Sea Lord. While relieved to leave behind him the stresses of commanding the Grand Fleet, he well knew that he was jumping from the frying pan into the fire, as he wrote after the war:

> The attacks already made upon the Admiralty in connection with the shipping losses due to submarine warfare, and on the subject of night raids upon our coast, which it was impossible to prevent with the means existing, fully prepared one for what was to come … in bidding farewell to the officers and men of the *Iron Duke* (a very difficult task in view of the intense regret that I felt at leaving them), I said that they must expect to see me the object of the same attacks as those to which my distinguished predecessor, Sir Henry Jackson, had been exposed. I was not wrong in this surmise.[21]

Jellicoe was not destined to serve as Balfour's First Sea Lord for long. Within a week of his arrival in Whitehall the government was plunged into a major crisis. A general sense of dissatisfaction with the government's conduct of the war in all its aspects had meant that there was a lot of inflammable material lying about, and it was extremely likely that a crisis, when it came, could mean the downfall of the First Coalition government. When it erupted, the trigger was David Lloyd George's insistence on the formation of a War Committee of three members with sweeping powers; the Prime Minister would not be a member. Asquith resisted, insisting that the Prime Minister must be a member. Lloyd George, who had the support of Bonar Law, Carson and Beaverbrook, pressed his point; after twisting and turning Asquith resigned. At first the King invited Bonar Law to form a government; when he declined to do so, the King sent for Lloyd George. This certainly meant the end of Balfour's tenure of office at the Admiralty; Lloyd George had for some time regarded him as unfitted for the post:

> The First Lord during a Great War ought to be a man of exhaustless industry and therefore of great physical energy and reserve. It was an office that called for unceasing attention to detail. It meant long hours, early and late. Mr Balfour was obviously unsuitable for such a post.[22]

Balfour, who perhaps accepted office as Foreign Secretary with a feeling of relief, was succeeded by Sir Edward Carson. Lloyd George thought that, lacking administrative experience, Carson would have been better employed in a consultative role as a member of a remodelled War Cabinet with Lord Milner as First Lord, but this (according to Lloyd George) was unacceptable to some of the Conservative leaders. Accordingly, Lloyd George switched the two posts and Carson went to the Admiralty. He was greatly distrusted by Hankey, who became Secretary of the War Cabinet; but he was soon to develop a good working relationship with Jellicoe.

The latter had been able to insist on the composition of the new Board of Admiralty; Burney was to be Second Sea Lord, Rear Admiral Tudor Third Sea Lord, and the former Captain of the Fleet, Commodore Lionel Halsey, was to be Fourth Sea Lord. A new post was created of Fifth Sea Lord, responsible for Air Services. The new team would be sorely tested.

26

Blockade: the Northern Patrol

Blockade, in the sense of action to prevent an enemy's warships from entering or leaving port, raises no particular question of international law; but when used in an economic sense to interdict an enemy's commerce, it gives rise to a number of extremely complex issues. As a matter of law, the Entente Powers were never during the Great War able to declare a blockade of the coasts of Germany and Austria Hungary, entitling them to prevent neutral ships proceeding to hostile ports. This was because although the Allies enjoyed command of the sea in many areas, they did not do so in the Baltic. For a blockade to comply with international law it must not only be fully effective, but must bear with equal severity on all neutrals. It was not possible to prevent Sweden and Denmark from communicating freely with German ports.[1]

By the Declaration of Paris of 1856, the foundation on which the modern international law stood, Great Britain surrendered her traditional right to seize enemy property found abroad neutral ships, a concession made in order to obtain the abolition of privateering. The Declaration provided:

> A neutral flag covers enemy goods with the exception of contraband of war; and neutral goods, with the exception of contraband of war, are not liable to capture under an enemy flag.[2]

The exception of contraband of war, however, was not defined in the Declaration, and this, in the years before 1914, was the subject of intensive international debate and negotiation. The Russo-Japanese War of 1904-1905 had caused serious damage to the commercial interests of Great Britain as a neutral during the war, due to the Russian decrees as to contraband. In 1907 an international conference at The Hague reached agreement on eight conventions intended to regulate maritime warfare, the most important of which was to establish an international prize court to protect the interests of neutral states. The Hague Convention, in the absence of further international definition or of generally recognised principles of international law, provided that the court should proceed according to general principles of law and equity.

However, although the proposal had been put forward by the British government, it was not well received by British public opinion, and it was evident that it would not be ratified by Parliament unless there was a clearer definition of the powers of the international prize court. This led to a further conference in London, which met from December 1908 to February 1909. There, the British delegation proposed to suppress the principle of contraband altogether; but although twenty five of the nations represented accepted this, ten did not; it was opposed by Germany, Russia, France and the United States, the French arguing that since a neutral could under its own laws carry on a trade in arms, the right to prevent this was a legitimate interest on the part of belligerents.

The London Conference considered the definition of contraband, concluding that there was a distinction between absolute contraband, which applied to goods 'susceptible exclusively of military use,' and conditional contraband which might be used for either military or civil purposes. Initially eleven items were defined as absolute contraband, including arms, ammunition and equipment. A belligerent could add other exclusively military goods on notifying neutral states of this. Conditional contraband included food, fodder, clothing for military use, fuel and lubricants; again, a belligerent could add to the list. A third list defined seventeen items which could not be treated as contraband at all, including cotton, rubber, fertilisers and paper.[3] Article 30 of the Declaration provided that absolute contraband was liable to capture if destined to an enemy, even if it was en route discharged at a neutral port. Conditional contraband was liable to capture if destined for the armed forces or government of an enemy state; it was not liable to capture if it was to be discharged at an intervening neutral port.

Even as it stood, the Declaration of London provided considerable scope for argument. In Great Britain, however, a violent campaign against the Declaration arose, based on the presumed risk to neutral vessels bringing food to the country. As a result, the House of Lords in 1911 rejected the essential terms of the Declaration, which accordingly the government was unable to ratify. Louis Guichard has noted, however, that the principles enshrined in the Declaration were carried into practical effect:

> It is fair to add that the instructions given by the principal Powers to their navies were nevertheless closely adapted to the terms of the Declaration. The French instructions drawn up in 1912 contained the principal articles of the Declaration *verbatim*, as did also the German instructions of 1909 which were in force when war broke out.[4]

As soon as war broke out, the US government asked all the belligerent nations how they proposed to conduct their operations in the light of international maritime law, suggesting that they should all adopt the Declaration of London as it stood. Almost at once, however, the Allied governments were dismayed to learn that cargoes of corn were coming into Rotterdam and then being shipped to Germany along the Rhine. The Dutch government refused to ban this transit trade, being bound by neutrality and by the Convention of Mannheim of 1868 which regulated the Rhine traffic. This trade would deprive the Allies of the benefit of their command of the sea, and accordingly in reply to the United States they announced that although they would apply the Declaration of London, they would depart from it in respect of conditional contraband. If such goods were destined for Germany, they would be liable to capture no matter to which port they were bound. This was a complete perversion of the Declaration of London, designed to allow the Allies grounds for stopping conditional contraband; for their part the Germans predictably told the United States that they would fully comply with the Declaration.

In seeking to placate the United States, the Allies slightly moderated their position, removing the right of capture where goods were addressed to a consignee not resident in an enemy country; but the burden of proof as to that was shifted to the consignee. As a result of all these issues there was a more or less continuous stream of complaints from the United States, but to these the Allies could afford no more concessions. Indeed, they strengthened their position by extending their right of search to the sending in of suspect vessels to be searched at a convenient port, using the existence of German minefields to justify the measure. This, too, prompted further American protests, rejecting the British argument that search at sea was often impracticable due to adverse weather. The Allies, however, paid no attention other than to pray in aid the opinions of Jellicoe and the French Admiralty that the measure was necessary.

Controlling the passage of ships through the English Channel was of course a relatively easy matter. On November 2 1914 the British Admiralty declared the North Sea to be a military area, and all neutral vessels entering it would be subject to Admiralty direction. Scandinavian ships were ordered to pass through the Straits of Dover, which was very inconvenient to them; they were usually granted permission to go north about provided that they put into Kirkwall for inspection. Intercepting vessels before they entered the northern part of the North Sea meant that effectively the area to be patrolled was now in the North Atlantic.

This meant that while the Grand Fleet, whether based at Scapa Flow or on the mainland, was poised to intervene in the event of any substantial advance by the High Seas Fleet, it could not effectively close the door to any German vessels entering or leaving the North Sea. The conduct of a blockade of the waters north of the British Isles thus became the responsibility of the 10th Cruiser Squadron, under Rear Admiral Dudley de Chair. This squadron comprised eight old protected cruisers, two of the *Crescent* class (*Crescent* and *Royal Arthur*) and six of the *Edgar* class (*Edgar, Endymion, Gibraltar, Grafton, Hawke* and *Theseus*). All were completed between 1893 and 1894. They were of 7,700 tons; the first two had one 9.2 inch gun and twelve 6 inch guns; the others had two 9.2 inch and ten 6 inch guns. Their speed was said to be 19.5 knots, but it was almost certainly much less. Immediately on the outbreak of war, de Chair took his squadron northwards, and by August 7 was patrolling the area between Orkney and the Norwegian coast.[5]

Designated the Northern Patrol Force, the task assigned to de Chair's squadron was to watch the northern exit of the North Sea. Its function was defined as being to intercept German warships and merchant vessels, and sink or capture them; to stop all neutral vessels proceeding to German ports; and to deny the anchorage of any harbour in the Shetlands or Orkneys to the enemy. The passage between the Shetlands and the Orkneys is about forty miles wide, while from the Shetlands to the Norwegian coast the distance is about 100 miles. The key patrol area was around latitude 62° N; the coast of Norway, fringed with islands, provides a route through territorial waters to this point, but here any traffic must emerge into the open sea.[6] The squadron was based initially at Scapa Flow, but was soon transferred to Lerwick in the Shetlands.

De Chair, aged 50, was an outspoken individual, who had become famous during the Egyptian War of 1882, and had served as Naval Attaché in Washington between 1902 and 1905. After two seagoing commands he went to the Admiralty in 1910, first as Assistant to Jellicoe who was Controller of the Navy, and then as Naval Secretary to Winston Churchill. He was disappointed to be told in May 1914 that he was to be in charge of training for the whole Navy, but jumped at the chance to command the 10th Cruiser Squadron.

The Northern Patrol was almost at once strengthened by the assignment of armed merchant cruisers to join the squadron; in the first instance there were four of these. On October 14, while de Chair in *Crescent* had gone into Cromarty for urgent repairs, the squadron suffered its first casualty when Weddigen, in *U9*, sank *Hawke,* demonstrating again the vulnerability of these elderly vessels to torpedo attack. The scale of de Chair's task was, it was soon realised, much too large for the ships which he had, and these were supplemented by more armed merchant cruisers.

They had not really been designed to cope with the sustained battering to which they were subjected in northern waters. De Chair's Report of Proceedings of December 3 described the damage to his flagship *Crescent* during a gale on November 11:

> During forenoon heavy seas came over forecastle of *Crescent,* wrecking fore bridge, sweeping overboard Admiral's Sea Cabin, carrying away ventilator cowl of foremost stokehold (a considerable amount of water getting down and putting fires out), breaking hammock nettings and damaging beyond repair Port Cutter which was turned in, removing bodily a whaler at davits abaft cutter; various hawser reels and other fittings fastened to the deck were torn away from their securings owing to woodwork being rotten.[7]

Endymion had to make for Scapa for immediate urgent repairs, while *Theseus*, *Edgar* and *Gibraltar* had to take shelter in Busta Voe. *Edgar* had lost two men overboard during the gale. Jellicoe was clear that the ships could not cope with this kind of weather; sending for de Chair, he ordered that all the ships be refitted, the first three to go to the Clyde at once.

By November 15, when *Crescent, Royal Arthur* and *Grafton* had been sent in and inspected in the dockyard, it was clear that these old ships were no longer capable of keeping the sea. The Northern Patrol was reorganised to consist of 24 armed merchant cruisers, manned by the crews of the old ships now paid off. The AMCs were of 4000-6000 tons, with speeds between 14 and 17 knots. Security was a constant problem, as de Chair recalled; a number of unexplained explosions caused great anxiety:

> Enemy agency was, however, suspected, and when taking in coal or stores a good lookout was kept to see that no bomb was hidden in them. We had to be specially careful in the 10th Cruiser Squadron, as our complement of 9800 men was a mixture of Royal Navy, Mercantile Marine, and longshoremen, including Newfoundland fishermen, who turned out to be some of our best boatmen in boarding prizes in heavy seas.[8]

De Chair hauled down his flag in *Crescent* on December 3; his new flagship was *Alsatian.* Originally armed with 4.7 inch guns, she was reequipped with 6 inch guns. The total of 24 ships now at his disposal enabled de Chair to organise his force in four divisions, distributed in such a way as to make it difficult for a ship to get through undetected. Area A was north of the Faeroes; Area B north of the Shetlands; Area C to the west of a line between the Faeroes and Sule Skerry; and Area D was west of the Hebrides. By the beginning of January, when the Northern Patrol was at full strength, twenty ships were intercepted and sent into Lerwick for inspection.[9] The squadron was in future to use Liverpool as its base for coaling and repair. It was not ideal, being 600 miles from the Shetlands, and the squadron frequently coaled at Busta Voe and Olna Firth in Swarbacks Minn on the west side of the Shetlands, as well as at Loch Ewe.[10]

In order to avoid the long voyage to Liverpool, the Admiralty suggested as an alternative base West Loch Roag, in the Island of Lewis in the Hebrides. De Chair visited on April 15, and was not impressed. He preferred Busta Voe and Olna Firth, as better suited for coaling and nearer to his patrol ground. In addition, there was a good deal of U-boat activity around the Hebrides, as more of the submarines were going north about in order to avoid obstructions in the English Channel. De Chair reported that at Swarbacks Minn seven of his ships could lie at single anchor, shielded from the continuous winter gales. Jellicoe agreed, and so this became the base for the 10th Cruiser Squadron.[11] The old cruiser *Gibraltar*, formerly part of the squadron, was moored there as a depot and repair ship, together with a coal hulk and four colliers. The squadron consumed coal voraciously, burning some 1,600 tons a day. An anti submarine boom was sited at the entrance to the anchorage; minesweeping trawlers patrolled regularly.

Life on the Northern Patrol was extremely hard. There was a constant risk of encountering the enemy, and the weather was almost perpetually hostile. Nor was the task of boarding the ships intercepted by the Patrol at all easy, as Commander Barry Bingham described:

> Some of these boarding trips were anything but pleasant. To be lowered in a cutter from a height of fifty feet, with the ship rolling heavily, and the boat itself swinging wildly from the davit heads, is bad enough, even when the cruiser is not moving above six knots. And then there is the final drop of some feet that gives you a hearty shake-up as the boat falls on the water. You feel it still more if, by a piece of faulty judgment on the part of the officer lowering her, the boat happens to strike a hollow between two seas.[12]

De Chair described the experience of his ships, always cleared for action:

> Men on the lookout, guns' crews at their stations, miserably wet and cold, captains and officers on the bridge, peering into the darkness. Dawn breaks over a grey and stormy sea, ships rolling and pitching heavily. As the horizon lightens it is scanned by the lookouts in the crows' nests far and wide, for any sign of blockade runners or enemy craft. A special lookout is kept for submarines, many of which we know to be lurking round about. These first hours of daylight are always the most trying and anxious, as a battle cruiser might easily have approached the patrols during the night, without being discovered.[13]

The risk of encountering a major warship was something that de Chair had discussed with his captains. There was no doubt that an AMC would be quickly sunk. Calling for help from the nearest ship of the squadron would achieve little; the patrols were thirty miles apart, and another ship would not only arrive too late, but would inevitably also be sunk. De Chair and his captains reckoned that the only thing to do 'would be to steam straight for the enemy at full speed, hoping to get him within range of our guns before we were knocked out.'[14] Fortunately the occasion did not arise to test this plan.

Throughout the early months of the war, the British government had kept its policy as to trade conditions under constant review, in the light of practical experience. On March 11 1915 it published an Order in Council that was to be the effective policy for the remainder of the war. It set out what had been more or less the actual position for several months, prohibiting any vessel from entering a German port and authorising the seizure of any goods leaving a German port or ultimately destined for Germany. Any vessel attempting to conceal a cargo destined for Germany was liable to be condemned. Neutral ships were now examined more thoroughly, and most were sent into Kirkwall, Lerwick or Stornoway for inspection. Their fate was determined by committees in London, which decided either on release or reference to the Prize Court.[15]

John D Grainger, in his introduction to *The Maritime Blockade of Germany in the Great War: The Northern Patrol 1914-1918*, observed that the principal response on behalf of the neutral states was a determination to remain neutral, and to make as much profit as possible at the expense of both sides. They used the opportunities to replace the German mercantile marine in the carrying of goods to Germany to a considerable extent. More surprising was the way in which British merchants and shippers took advantage of the same opportunity. Exports and re-exports from Britain to Norway, the Netherlands, Denmark and Sweden rose from £11.5 m in the first quarter of 1913 to £16.5 in the first quarter of 1915. The move meant some commodities increased particularly; exports of cocoa increased threefold, those of grain and flour quadrupled and lubricating oil and meat doubled. It took a protest from France to check this energetic trading with the enemy.[16]

The scale of the operations of the 10th Cruiser Squadron was considerable, covering an area of 200.000 square miles. At the end of 1915 de Chair reported that during the year his ships had intercepted 3,098 merchant vessels; of these, 743 found to be carrying contraband or other suspicious cargoes had been sent into port for further inspection. He estimated that of almost 4,000 ships traversing the patrol area only eight whose interception was considered significant had managed to evade his patrols. Typical of the work of his ships, de Chair's flagship *Alsatian* had spent 262 days at sea, steaming 71,000 miles. In that time she had burnt almost 41,000 tons of coal, which illustrates the extent of the supply problems that had had to be overcome. Two of his ships had been sunk by U-boats; another had foundered in heavy weather; another had gone down with all hands from an unknown cause, while another had been damaged by a mine. 86 officers and men had died.[17]

In order to impress the United States authorities that the blockading activities of the Northern Patrol which they found so objectionable were the work of the Allies as a whole, it was decided in November 1915 to transfer two of de Chair's ships to the French navy. *Digby* became *Artois* and *Oropesa* became *Champagne*. The performance of his allies did not impress the admiral:

> I went into Busta Voe to meet them, and give them their instructions as to blockade work. From the first I had trouble with *Artois*. When ordered to sea her captain said, 'But really, Admiral, it is so much safer in harbour!' However, I eventually got *Artois* to sea, and in order to help I sent the gunnery lieutenant to show them what to do and how to do it. At first I placed *Artois* on a patrol line that would be easier for her, and where there was not much doing. Meeting her on patrol afterwards, I sent for the gunnery lieutenant and asked him how things were working. He told me it was really very funny. If by day they sighted a ship all the officers would rush up on deck and excitedly gesticulate towards the horizon, but if it were by night they would pretend not to see any light, as they said it was much too dangerous to board a ship in the dark.[18]

Champagne was eventually sunk by a U-boat in October 1917, while at that time it was concluded that *Artois* was not fast enough for patrol work, having a maximum speed of only 13 knots; she often had difficulty in overhauling vessels while on patrol, while her slow speed made her vulnerable to torpedo attacks.[19]

Lieutenant Kenyon, *Alsatian's* Gunnery Lieutenant, wrote a formal report to de Chair on the French Captain:

> The Captain of *Artois* … has little or no experience as a captain of a ship, and, although I gather that he has considerable capacity for directing and staff work, he does not figure

> equally well in the capacity of captain. There is evidence of a very marked lack of self confidence, which results in a desire to avoid to the greatest possible extent any unusual work, or any unusual work which might lead to any unusual situation.[20]

The British do not seem to have treated their allies very fairly, as Grainger points out. *Digby* was the oldest and slowest ship in the squadron, and had frequent mechanical problems, while the self confidence of the unfortunate captain of *Artois* was not improved by having Lieutenant Kenyon breathing down his neck.

Among the commodities which the Germans particularly needed, and of which the supply was considerably restricted by the blockade was rubber. The Washington correspondent of the *Morning Post* reported on December 22 1916 on one failed attempt to beat the blockade:

> Fancy a woman imagining in these times that she could leave New York on an ocean trip with nearly two tons of personal baggage and escape observation; yet that is what a female agent of the German Government attempted, and, naturally, she has landed in the police net. So desperately hard up are the Germans for rubber, especially for motor car tyres for military use, and so effective is the British Naval blockade, despite German statements that a blockade does not exist, that in their extremity they have tried to smuggle in rubber from the United States as the personal baggage of women travellers.[21]

Anna Dekkers, who had 3500 lbs of rubber in trunks and packing cases, which she declared simply as her personal belongings, was arrested as she was about to board a ship for Rotterdam.

The Order in Council of March 11 1915 had left a large number of commodities outside the list of absolute contraband, but the list was steadily increased, so that by October 1915, it contained 42 articles of absolute contraband, in addition to 14 of conditional contraband. The process continued throughout the war so that by the end 'practically every single article of commerce' had become contraband.[22] In addition, as a response to the huge increase of imports into neutral countries, with a corresponding increase in their exports to Germany, the Allies began to develop a quota system. This took as its basis a decision of the British prize court in a case where a cargo was confiscated 'on account of the extreme probability of its being destined for the enemy.'[23]

This was, of course, an extremely flexible concept, and it did not go down well in the United States, from whence emanated vigorous protests. Nonetheless, governments and commercial undertakings had to walk a fine line, as Guichard pointed out:

> It must be remembered in all these discussions that the United States could not push matters to a rupture with the Entente without seriously compromising its own industry and trade; the Allied orders for arms and ammunition were increasing month by month, and if the United States felt some bitterness at its exclusion from the German market it was much too sensible to lose all its foreign markets except South America and China.[24]

For both neutrals and belligerents, self interest was more powerful than narrow concepts of international law and morality.

The 10th Cruiser Squadron had another task, which was to prevent German warships slipping out of the North Sea. It was not something with which they had had to deal to any great extent; the German AMCs which had been employed as raiders in the early months of the war had set out on their careers from ports overseas. In February 1916 however, Jellicoe was notified by the Admiralty that a German AMC, escorted by submarine, had been sighted off the Skaw, steering westward. The 10th Cruiser Squadron was alerted, and Jellicoe sent out a number of light cruisers and destroyers to search for the intruder. De Chair deployed those of his ships in the area of the probable line of approach to patrol to the north; both *Andes* and *Alcantara* were also ordered to remain in the area. They had been due to rendezvous NE of the Shetlands late on February 29; that morning both were warned that a disguised AMC might be coming up from the south to cross the patrol line. Captain Wardle, of *Alcantara*, sighted smoke to port, and received at the same time a message from *Andes* to his north; 'Enemy in sight steering north east 15 knots.' Two further messages followed, the first of which informed him that the enemy ship had two funnels and the second that she was painted black, with one funnel.

Wardle turned northwest, between the position of *Andes* and the stranger, which he soon sighted; it was a single funnelled ship named *Rena* flying the Norwegian flag, with the same colours painted on her sides. Wardle, who had now seen *Andes* heading away to the NE, lowered a boat to investigate *Rena*, which had stopped; he signalled *Andes*: 'Is the enemy still in sight? This ship is the *Rena*, armed guard being put on board.' The response was immediate: 'This is the suspect ship.' Before Wardle could do anything about it, *Rena* dropped the flaps concealing her guns and opened fire. She was in fact *Greif*, formerly the *Guben*, of 4962 tons, a newly built 13 knot ship that had been armed with four 5.9 inch guns and two torpedo tubes. Her first salvoes caused serious damage to *Alcantara* which, however, replied to such effect that Captain Tietze of *Greif* gave orders to abandon ship. However, *Alcantara* had also been heavily damaged in the fierce exchange of fire and she too began to sink, and was abandoned, sinking at 11.10 am. *Andes* had by now come up, and had joined in the action, although scoring no hits on *Greif*. She rescued one officer and 110 men. *Greif* sank at 1.00 pm, after having taken several hits from the light cruiser *Comus* which had now arrived on the scene. 209 out of *Greif's* complement of 306 were rescued by *Comus* and *Andes*.[25]

This was the 10th Cruiser Squadron's last action under de Chair, who was relieved on March 6 by Vice Admiral Reginald Tupper, hitherto employed as the senior naval officer for the West of Scotland and the Hebrides. Based at Stornoway, he commanded a force of small patrol craft, trawlers and yachts in the narrow waters of the West Coast of Scotland. Grainger remarks that Tupper's appointment was 'rather odd.' He comments that appointing a Vice-Admiral to a post previously held by a Rear-Admiral was 'an example of that tendency of war to enlarge the rank of post holders.' Whatever the reason for the appointment, he considers that Tupper 'brought a more vigorous style of command than de Chair.'[26]

The latter was disappointed to give up his command. He was not mollified by Balfour's explanation of the importance of his new post, which was to be professional adviser to the newly appointed Minister of Blockade, Lord Robert Cecil:

> I went out of the Admiralty that day with my mind in a whirl. To say I was disappointed would be to put it mildly. I was almost heart-broken, in spite of all the nice things the First Lord had said to me. But there it was. It was wartime, and one's own feelings had to be put aside at such a time.[27]

Wiesbaden sinking between the battle lines. (Bergen)

Shark at Jutland. (Pears)

A sweep in the North Sea. (Wyllie)

Saving the crew of *Audacious*. (Wyllie)

German minelaying U-boat. (Wyllie)

Bringing in the wounded *Lion*. (Wyllie)

Revenge and *Lion*. (Wyllie)

Dropping depth charges. (Wyllie)

A swept channel in the North Sea. (Wyllie)

Benbow with others deploying into line. (Wyllie)

Repulse. (Wyllie)

Glorious and *Furious* in a gale. (Wyllie)

Armed merchantman boarding neutrals. (Wyllie)

Valiant and *Malaya*. (Wyllie)

Queen Mary, *Princess Royal* and *Lion* at Jutland. (Wyllie)

Champion and the 13th Flotilla. (Wyllie)

Defence and *Warrior* in action. (Wyllie)

Chester in action. (Wyllie)

Tiger with *Princess Royal*, *Lion*, *Warrior* and *Defence*. (Wyllie)

Second Division at Jutland. (Wyllie)

Royal Oak, *Acasta*, *Benbow*, *Superb* and *Canada* in action. (Wyllie)

Crew of *Acasta* cheering the C-in-C. (Wyllie)

Warspite and *Warrior*. (Wylie)

Hipper in the control station.

In response to an increasing number of rumours that the German Admiralty was planning to send out a number of AMCs as commerce raiders, Jellicoe had devised plans to intercept these vessels, employing the 2nd Cruiser Squadron from the Grand Fleet to reinforce the 10th Cruiser Squadron. This consisted of five armoured cruisers which were also based on Swarbacks Minn. They were not, however, able to prevent the escape of the German raider *Möwe,* which slipped through the patrol line on November 23 1916. It was her second cruise; under the command of Count zu Dohna-Schlodien, she had operated between December 1915 and March 1916 sinking or capturing fifteen vessels of a total of 57,520 tons. During her second cruise she sank a further 25 ships, totalling 123,265 tons. She returned safely, again passing undetected through the waters of the Northern Patrol.[28] Dohna was especially cautious as he prepared to run the blockade for the fourth time, reckoning that he was by now so well known that the British would be looking our for him. Fortunately the weather was foul, and although he caught sight of smoke on the horizon, he encountered no other vessels as he ran far to the north before entering Norwegian territorial waters. On March 19 he entered the three mile limit, and made his way down the Norwegian coast to the Skagerrak, from where he sailed through the Sound to Kiel. He arrived there at 2.00 am on March 22, and in spite of the lateness of the hour was greeted in the harbour by many boats anxious to welcome *Möwe* home. Among them was Prince Henry of Prussia, who came aboard to honour Dohna and his ship.[29]

One of her captures, *Yarrowdale* (which in due course became the raider *Leopard)* had embarrassed Tupper by returning to Germany through the patrol area with some 400 British prisoners aboard. Tupper was obliged to explain himself, which he did in a letter to the Admiralty of February 22. The principal cause of *Yarrowdale* being able to get through was, he said, because there were only five ships actually on patrol at that time. The rest were on special service, or in the dockyards or, in the case of six of them which should have been on patrol, had been delayed at Liverpool.[30]

Möwe was followed by *Wolf* (Captain Nerger) who also passed through the British patrol lines at the end of November, en route for a cruise which lasted fifteen months, in the course of which she sank twelve and captured and made use of two more of a total tonnage of 38,391. Nerger, like Dohna, was fêted as a great naval hero on his safe return. So was Count von Luckner, the captain of the fully rigged *Seeadler,* a former American sailing ship fitted out as a commerce raider. He too slipped through the patrol lines, having sailed on December 21 1916. After a cruise in which Luckner sank sixteen ships, of a total of 30,099 tons, *Seeadler* was driven ashore and wrecked on a deserted island in the Central Pacific.

These successes prompted the German Admiralty to fit out another raider early in 1917. This was the *Yarrowdale,* captured by Dohna on his first voyage. Commanded by Hans von Laffert she was not as fortunate as her predecessors, sinking with all hands after a furious action with the armoured cruiser *Achilles* and the armed boarding steamer *Dundee,* armed with two 4-inch guns.[31]

Tupper, on taking command, had no need for any reorganisation of his force; for him, it was, it would appear, a matter of continuing the work of his predecessor. He was, though, rather more conscious than de Chair of the contribution of all the men serving under him, naming both officers and men who lost their lives on duty. In this, he displayed a more creditable attitude than Commodore Robert Benson, his second in command and the captain of *Teutonic.* The latter faced what he termed 'open mutiny' on the part of eight stokers, who complained that unless they could be messed on the same scale as they had enjoyed under the White Star Line, they refused to continue duty in the ship. This had come about due to the introduction of general messing, which provided them with food that was not what they had been accustomed to. They also complained of being paid at less than the port rate prevailing.

Benson was furious; reporting to the Senior Naval Officer, Liverpool, on March 28 1916 he wrote of the eight men in terms which, a century later, still have the power to shock:

> They are almost without exception of the lowest scale of humanity found in Great Britain. They have been accustomed to engage for a cruise of three weeks under mercantile regulations, to have plenty of food served in any unsystematic way they liked, and untrammelled by discipline or restrictions, except to keep their watches, to be treated not as men in a fighting ship, but as animals necessary to the steaming of an Atlantic liner. They have no patriotic, social, or moral conceptions, and their ideas, ingrained from their earliest training, go no further than lots of food in as savage and uncivilised a way as possible, and the greatest amount of pay that their earning capacity can obtain, to enable them to spend as long as possible away from work when they return to port.[32]

They were tried by court martial for 'mutiny not accompanied by violence,' a charge to which they were 'advised' by their defender, an officer, to plead guilty. They were all sentenced to two years hard labour and were dismissed from the service. As Grainger remarks, 'their experience in the prison cannot have been any worse than two years stoking a steamer in the North Atlantic, and they were in much less danger of death.'[33] It is not a matter for regret to learn that Benson was relieved from command a few weeks later, Tupper diplomatically recording that he had done 'excellent work.'

It is worth recording what the fuss was about. Where the food was provided by the owners of the AMCs, the rates provided were from six shillings to seven and sixpence per day for officers and for the men one and ninepence to two and sixpence. There were special rates for Petty Officers. The Director of Victualling, JH Brooks, explained the new arrangements to the First Sea Lord on May 9 1916:

> Under the Admiralty system the officers are credited with an allowance of 3s 6p a day, and arrange their own messing as in all other HM Ships. The men are messed under the General Mess System, as in force in Naval Barracks and other Shore Establishments, at a rate not exceeding 1s 3d a head.[34]

He was confident, he said, that this amount was ample. One wonders what the household of Mr Brooks spent daily on food.

There was a considerable disagreement between Beatty, as Commander-in-Chief, and Jellicoe as First Sea Lord as to the importance of the blockade to the outcome of the war. It was Beatty's opinion that, at the beginning of 1917, the blockade was 'the only offensive policy apparently carried on,' as he told Carson on January 13.[35] A fortnight later he expressed himself even more strongly in a letter to Jellicoe:

> The 10th Cruiser Squadron is the one unit that could win us the war, if up to the fullest strength. You are up against the biggest proposition any man has had to tackle. You have the support of the First Lord and the whole Fleet, and you may have to thump the table and

> dictate what is going to be done. There are two things which are going to win or lose this war and nothing else will affect it a damn. Our armies might advance a mile a day and slay the Hun in thousands, but the real crux lies in whether we blockade the enemy to his knees, or whether he does the same to us. Our blockade rests on the 10th Cruiser Squadron.[36]

Jellicoe's response to this flamboyant letter was, characteristically, in much more measured terms:

> I think you are wrong in assuming that the blockade will ever cause the enemy to give in. That certainly is the opinion of those who are in a position to know. We may cause them a great deal of suffering and discomfort by the blockade, but we shall not win the war by it. The war will not be won until the enemy's armed forces are defeated – certainly on land and probably on sea, and therefore it is essential to get our troops to France and keep our communications open.[37]

The effectiveness of the Northern Patrol was, by mid 1917, steadily increasing. The number of vessels sent in for inspection was, however, falling. This was due to the introduction of a system of Letters of Assurance or 'Navicerts.' These documents were issued to vessels travelling through the patrol area after they had been carefully investigated at the point of loading, and showed that the goods were as stated, consigned to permissible recipients and were within the quota for the relevant country. In this way neutral merchant vessels were interfered with to a much reduced extent. If a ship had a Navicert for each item of its cargo there was no need for its interception. By May 1917 it was becoming apparent that the Northern Patrol had, with the entry into the war of the United States, become redundant, and at the end of June ships were being transferred to convoy duties. In November 1917 Beatty agreed that the 10th Cruiser Squadron should be abolished. In its place a small squadron of three AMCs, two armoured cruisers and two armed boarding steamers was established, based at Scapa, and known as the 2nd Cruiser Squadron.[38]

The effectiveness of the blockade, claimed as crucial in the defeat of Germany, has more recently been called into question. Guichard, in his history of the naval blockade, concluded:

> It seems impossible to deny that the enfeeblement of Germany by reason of her economic encirclement was one of the main factors of victory. Economic encirclement after all was only an achievement incidental to the successful accomplishment by the Allied navies of their main task of acquiring and maintaining the mastery of the sea without which victory would have been impossible.[39]

Another French historian, Jacques Dumas, concluded that on the whole the naval economic was not a profitable operation for the Allies:

> By the exercise of the right to capture the Allies succeeded in partially drying up the sources of Germany's supplies, but were unable to obtain a decisive result. On the other hand they supplied Germany with a pretext for waging war by means of her submarines upon commerce, a war which proved ineffective, as the Allied ports were never so busy as in the years 1917-1918.[40]

Grainger's view is that the blockade had only a limited effectiveness, although its effects increased with time to be fully effective after the United States' declaration of war and the introduction of the Navicert. On the other hand, he finds, the effects on Germany were perhaps marginal, and these were greater than they need have been due to the systems of allocation utilised by the German government. By blaming the blockade for the shortages, it was able to transfer the responsibility for shortages to the enemy rather than acknowledging its own failings. His conclusion is that 'The effectiveness of the blockade was thus neither so great as the British navalists claimed nor so minimal as the latest revisionists suggest.'[41]

27

Tyrwhitt and the Harwich Force

The operations of the Harwich Force under Tyrwhitt really deserve a detailed history of their own. From the outbreak of war until its end the force was more or less continuously engaged, and its activities were characterised throughout by an energy and boldness which soon caught the public imagination. The Harwich Force took part in all the fleet actions (except for Jutland, in which it was expressly forbidden to participate by the direct order of the Admiralty) but its reputation really rested on its ceaseless activity in the North Sea. Professor Marder wrote of it:

> The heaviest and most dangerous services were demanded of the Harwich Force; no other unit experienced so many sea days and suffered such great losses. And yet for no other force was there so much enthusiasm.[1]

As has been seen, Marder had a justly high opinion of Tyrwhitt, whom he regarded as 'completely successful' in his command of the Harwich Force. He was ably supported by his Flag Captain, Barry Domvile, who had begun the war as captain of the destroyer *Miranda*, which joined the Harwich Force on August 29 1914.

Tyrwhitt himself had been, since December 13 1914, Commodore (Second Class) in command of all the destroyer flotillas of the Home Fleet; on the outbreak of war he was ordered to take command of the 1st and 3rd Destroyer Flotillas, to be based at Harwich. Tyrwhitt flew his flag in the light cruiser *Amethyst*; the 1st Flotilla of twenty destroyers was led by Captain W Blunt in the light cruiser *Fearless*, and the 3rd Flotilla of nineteen destroyers by Captain CH Fox in the light cruiser *Amphion*. The latter became the first British ship to be sunk when she struck a mine on August 5. Tyrwhitt had complained bitterly that *Amethyst* was 'damned slow;' but was soon delighted to be given the brand new light cruiser *Arethusa*, writing to his brother on August 26:

> From the oldest and slowest to the newest and fastest light cruiser ... She's a regular flyer and a ripper but I have no time to get her into fighting trim ... I am of course delighted at getting such a splendid new ship, but it is rather a trial having a new ship's company and new guns. Everything new – officers, guns, ship and men. I expect we shall soon get into order, but I would like to have had a week to do it in.[2]

Arethusa was not to remain Tyrwhitt's flagship for long, having been badly damaged during the battle of Heligoland Bight; while she was being repaired, Tyrwhitt was given one of

Goodenough's light cruisers, *Lowestoft;* he found her too large for the job, as well as being slower. He was glad, at the end of October, to get *Arethusa* back, and she was to serve as his flagship until February 11 1916, when she struck a mine returning to Harwich. Efforts to get her under tow failed, and she drifted on to the South Cutler Shoal and broke in two. Tyrwhitt was the last man to leave her. By then *Arethusa* had become identified in the public mind with Tyrwhitt and the Harwich Force, and her exploits had contributed to the making in the press of Tyrwhitt as a genuine naval hero, alongside the dashing Beatty. Tyrwhitt's biographer described the effect of their creation as celebrities:

> The fact that both Beatty and Tyrwhitt were striking-looking men (perhaps especially Tyrwhitt, who looked so completely the keen-eyed and hawk-faced seaman the public expected) encouraged the press to continue publicising them until some of the more sensible and responsible papers began to hint that there were other naval leaders about whom people might like to hear something. Both of the victims of what Tyrwhitt called 'this paper humbug' felt this strongly; and he even feared, not entirely without justice, that this excessive adulation might prejudice other members of the service against him.[3]

From the outset of their cooperation at Harwich Tyrwhitt and Keyes had an excellent working relationship, as well as being good friends. The stresses that they were under meant, however, that misunderstandings could easily arise. Although of the same rank, Keyes had been senior to Tyrwhitt; but on December 5 1914 his friend was promoted Commodore, First Class, over his head. Keyes took this as a sign that Fisher, as First Sea Lord, was pursuing a campaign against him, and allowed himself in his chagrin to make some bitter remarks which greatly offended Tyrwhitt. The row lasted only a few days before Keyes apologised, and all was peace between them. However, at the end of January 1915 another quarrel arose. This concerned the suggestion that Keyes had made that he might be allocated a light cruiser of the *Arethusa* class as his flagship to lead his submarines; hitherto, when accompanying them to sea, he had done so in one of the destroyers *Lurcher* or *Firedrake* under his command.

This proposal was disagreeable to Tyrwhitt, who seems to have thought that if Keyes was able to go to sea in a cruiser it might upset the delicate balance of seniority at Harwich, of which Keyes might then be given overall control. For his part Keyes suspected that Tyrwhitt, who was much more highly regarded at the Admiralty, might be using his influence to scupper his request. The row again related to Fisher's unfavourable impression of Keyes; the First Sea Lord was reported to have said of him: 'Why can't that fellow go to sea and fight like Tyrwhitt?' It was a remark that was wholly unjust, but fairness never was a characteristic of the old admiral.[4]

The Admiralty had reserved to itself the control of those forces not directly based with Jellicoe and the Grand Fleet, including both Beatty's battle cruisers and the Harwich Force, although it was understood that they would come under Jellicoe's operational control once he put to sea. A number of the operations carried out by the Harwich Force were therefore undertaken independently of the Grand Fleet. On the other hand, on occasion a sortie by the Harwich force would be supported either by Beatty alone or by the whole Grand Fleet.

One example of this was an air raid planned on the Cuxhaven Zeppelin sheds. This was to take place on Christmas Day 1914. Nine seaplanes, aboard the seaplane carriers *Engadine, Riviera* and *Empress* were to bomb the sheds. The Harwich destroyers and submarines, led by the light cruisers *Arethusa, Fearless* and *Undaunted,* would support the operation, which it was hoped might provoke the High Seas Fleet into putting to sea. With this in mind, the whole of the Grand Fleet was concentrated in the middle of the North Sea.[5]

The raid proved abortive. Seven of the seaplanes took off, but when they passed the German coast they ran into thick fog and were unable to find their target. On the way back, only two got back to the carriers. Keyes, in *Lurcher*, rescued another; and the submarine *E11* rescued the crew of three others in spite of the efforts of a Zeppelin to sink her while doing so. When Tyrwhitt went to the Admiralty to report on the events of Christmas Day, he found that it had not been realised there that the raid had failed. He wrote to his wife:

> They are awfully pleased with the Raid and most complimentary. Couldn't be nicer! I was really surprised at everybody's pleasure and delight. They want more and I expect they will get it before long.[6]

There were further air raid attempts in the early months of 1915, as well as frequent sorties into the Bight. Inevitably, there were casualties, from mines and from collisions, as ships of the Harwich Force responded to the many calls on them. Commander Domvile, still commanding *Miranda,* described the kind of duties required:

> I was here, there and everywhere. In the early spring, working with minelayers from Sheerness ... Later escorting six-knot monitors down the Channel to Ushant with my 35-knot destroyer – a particularly brilliant brainwave of someone's at the Admiralty ... Then getting a dicky propeller-shaft put to rights in the Clyde ... then fetching the *Tipperary* [a new flotilla leader, of which he took command] from White's yard at Cowes [and] shortly afterwards having a hole driven through her starboard side into my cabin by one of our own submarines just outside Harwich in a fog – a hole you could have driven a coach and four through: we nearly went down, but the bulkhead held.[7]

The Harwich Force was sometimes required to operate far afield, but as Domvile wrote, they were never happy far from home, as there was a fear of missing something in the North Sea.

In some respects Tyrwhitt had been sorry to see Churchill and Fisher leave the Admiralty, correctly believing that they held a good opinion of him. He found that the new regime did not adopt as bold a policy with regard to offensive operations, although he soon developed a good personal relationship with both Balfour and Jackson. He was allowed, however, to undertake a number of sorties in the hope of tempting out part of the High Seas Fleet. One such was on December 20 1915, when he went into the Bight to the Danish coast; the Battle Cruiser Fleet was put under short notice for steam. Tyrwhitt was very disappointed, as the weather turned foul, and he was obliged to turn back. He wrote to his wife:

> I hope we shall be able to try again before long. It really will knock August 28 into a cocked hat if it comes off. I have not been so excited for a long time. We left in a gale and returned in the same gale ... Snow, hail, sleet and rain and constant gale ... I gave up all idea of carrying the job out at 11.30 am yesterday and I had just turned round for home when I received a wireless message from the Admiralty telling me to do the same![8]

One of the most onerous duties imposed on the Harwich Force was the so called 'Beef Trip.' In June 1916 the British Government had concluded an agreement with the Dutch Government for the allocation to Britain of a large amount of food which had previously gone to Germany. The goods delivered consisted of butter, cheese, eggs and other foodstuffs (although not actually including beef). The route was from the Shipwash Light Vessel, off Orfordness, to the Maas Lightship, off the River Maas which leads to Rotterdam. The total distance was about 120 miles. It was a route particularly vulnerable to attack, especially from destroyers, and for the protection of the convoys the Admiralty ordered Tyrwhitt to provide two light cruisers and up to ten destroyers as escorts. The problems which this task presented were described by Captain Dorling:

> It would have been easier if the ships of the convoy had all steamed the same speed. But they did not. There were ships of all ages, speeds and sizes, some of which could steam 10, 12 or even 14 knots, and others no more than 7. They all put their best foot foremost, so that the head of the convoy lengthened out from the tail at the rate of seven miles an hour. When the leader arrived at the Maas the convoy was spread over fifty miles of sea, with sometimes no more than four destroyers to guard it.[9]

One such operation was on July 22/23. 1916 Tyrwhitt, his flag in *Carysfort,* took *Canterbury* and eight *M* class destroyers to sea to cover the crossing. *Canterbury* (Captain Percy Royds), with four destroyers, watched the route near the North Hinder, while *Carysfort,* with the other four destroyers, patrolled the Maas section. Tyrwhitt had sailed at 9.00 pm on July 22; unknown to him, a German flotilla sortied from Zeebrugge at the same time. At 1.15 am *Carysfort* sighted three enemy destroyers steering north; they turned east at high speed, and the flagship followed, opening fire for a few minutes before a rain squall blotted out the target. The German destroyers laid a heavy smoke screen and turned sharply to starboard; when visibility improved, they were out of sight. Tyrwhitt now headed for the Maas, hoping to cut them off, and ordered Royds to try to catch them near the Schouwen Bank. Royds had already turned east on seeing the gun flashes from *Carysfort;* on getting the order he altered course SE at 28 knots, and at 1.45 was rewarded with the sight of six enemy destroyers heading for Zeebrugge. At 2.10 he opened fire; the enemy replied. *Matchless* could not keep up and *Milne* stood by her; Royds thus had only two destroyers in company. The German destroyers were by 2.25 approaching the minefield off the Schouwen Bank, though, and Royds called off the chase.[10]

While this brief encounter satisfied the Admiralty that the escort arrangements were working well, it was resolved to impose a more effective organisation on the convoys, which were to run every two or three days under the direct escort of a light cruiser and four destroyers, eastbound and west bound convoys being synchronised. A second force, similarly composed, patrolled the Schouwen Bank. However, the tendency for the merchant vessels to straggle obliged Tyrwhitt to change the system. In October 1916 he replaced the direct escort by a system of destroyer patrols along the route, which would be confined to daylight hours. Later, he reverted to the convoy system, after eliminating the use of slower ships.[11]

The scale of the task may be shown by the fact that during 1917 the Harwich Force was responsible for the passage of 520 eastbound and 511 westbound merchant vessels travelling by this route. During the same period, Tyrwhitt lost four destroyers by mines and one by collision. Three more destroyers were damaged by mine or torpedo, and a light cruiser and five destroyers were damaged by collision.[12]

The most dramatic illustration of the dangers faced in providing escorts for the Dutch convoys came on December 23 1917. The destroyers *Surprise, Torrent*, *Tornado* and *Radiant* were accompanying a convoy off the Dutch coast, when they ran into a new German minefield:

> One of these vessels struck a mine, and a second went to help her, only to be blown up herself. A similar fate met the third ship while she was trying to rescue the crews of the other two. The *Surprise, Torrent* and *Tornado* had gone. Only the *Radiant* was left. Her captain, Commander Geoffrey FS Nash, knew what had happened; but, undeterred by the horrible danger, steamed his ship to the spot where the survivors were struggling in the icy water, lowered his boats and was the means of saving many lives. Seven of the *Radiant's* officers and men jumped overboard to save drowning men. Barely a quarter of the crews of the three ships survived. But not one of them would have been saved if it had not been for the coolness and gallantry of the *Radiant's* captain.[13]

In addition to providing escorts for the Dutch convoys, Tyrwhitt had a series of other responsibilities which meant that his force was almost constantly in action or on standby. These other tasks were summarised by Jellicoe. First, it was intended that the Harwich Force would come out in support of the Grand Fleet if the High Seas Fleet put to sea. Next, he was responsible for the reconnaissance of the southern part of the North Sea and the Bight. He was also required to provide cover for seaplane carriers involved in air raids on the German mainland, to cut off any German light forces in the southern area, and to attack any Zeppelins returning from raids on England. Finally, Tyrwhitt was constantly called on to provide reinforcements when required by the Dover Patrol.[14]

As with other units watching for the emergence of German naval forces, Tyrwhitt benefited from the intelligence provided by the cryptographers of Room 40. On January 22 1917 the Admiralty learned that a German destroyer flotilla was about to sail to reinforce the light forces based at Zeebrugge, and Tyrwhitt was ordered to intercept it with his destroyers, holding his light cruisers in support. Bacon was ordered to send six destroyers to Harwich to supplement Tyrwhitt's force, which sailed at 5.30pm with six light cruisers, two leaders and sixteen destroyers. Tyrwhitt had to cover two routes; the enemy might come either down the Dutch coast by the Maas and Schouwen Bank light vessels, or down the central part of the Flanders Bight past the North Hinder. Led by *Grenville,* a fore of seven destroyers covered the Maas route and eleven, led by *Nimrod*, were stationed off the Schouwen Bank. Tyrwhitt, in *Centaur*, led *Aurora* and *Conquest* to a patrol line 25 miles NE of the north Hinder; *Penelope*, (Captain H Lynes), *Cleopatra* and *Undaunted* were ten miles to the west.[15]

The German flotilla was the VI Flotilla, led by Commander Max Schultz. It consisted of a flotilla leader and ten destroyers. It was midway between the North Hinder and the Maas when at 2.45 it encountered Tyrwhitt's division of light cruisers, crossing astern of *Conquest* at the end of the line. Tyrwhitt, swerving to avoid a torpedo, tried to head the German flotilla north eastwards, but Schultz, laying down a heavy smoke screen, regained his course for Zeebrugge. However, his flotilla leader *V69* was struck by a shell and his helm jammed, and he turned in a circle, before being rammed by *G41.* Both damaged, the two destroyers limped away. Meanwhile, another destroyer, which had been following *V69*, turned away and lost touch with the rest of the flotilla. Tyrwhitt sent two signals, one to say the enemy was steering NE and one to say that they had scattered. This caused confusion; while Commander Dundas, in *Grenville,* thought that he should remain on his patrol line, two of his destroyers, *Meteor* and *Rigorous,* assumed that they should steer NE. The captain of *Nimrod* took the same view, and also set off in that direction. In *Penelope*, Lynes steamed towards the sound of the guns. When he realised the confusion, Tyrwhitt signalled all ships to return to their stations; Dundas, who did not receive the signal, steamed north in order to avoid confusion with *Nimrod's* group. Meanwhile *Penelope* had encountered the damaged *V69,* and in a brief engagement it was thought had sunk her; in fact, however, she escaped to Ymuiden, where the Dutch refused to intern her. *G41* reached the Dutch coast and headed into Zeebrugge.[16]

The rest of the flotilla, there being no British forces south of the Schouwen Bank, safely reached Zeebrugge. This left *S50,* following behind at some distance. Soon after 4.00 am she encountered *Nimrod* and her detachment, which steered to close her; and then by a line led by *Simoom*, followed by *Starfish, Surprise* and *Milne,* all of which opened fire. *S50,* however, was nearly at the head of the British line, and concentrated her fire on *Simoom.* Within a few minutes she also launched a torpedo at her, causing *Simoom's* magazine to blow up. Tyrwhitt's Flag Captain, Domvile, in *Centaur,* to the north, saw the detonation: 'A most terrific explosion reddened the lovely starlit sky far away to the southward.'[17] And Captain Howard, aboard *Mansfield,* in *Nimrod's* detachment wrote:

> We were still proceeding in the direction of the gunfire when the whole sky was lit up by a heavy explosion. It seemed as if a giant had taken a running kick at a huge bonfire. Sparks flew up several hundred feet and came down in a beautiful golden rain.[18]

The commander of *S50,* realising *Nimrod* and her destroyers were working round him, abandoned the attempt to reach Zeebrugge and returned home through the Bight. Morris picked up the survivors from *Simoom*; still afloat at 7.15, *Nimrod* was then ordered to sink her. Thus ended an unsatisfactory night for Tyrwhitt and the Harwich Force:

> The results of the night's work were extremely disappointing. In spite of our knowledge of the enemy's movements, and our great superiority in strength, the bulk of the enemy flotilla got past our intercepting forces, and inflicted in passing more injury than they received.[19]

Tyrwhitt learned later, when he visited Jellicoe at the Admiralty on January 26, that the unsuccessful outcome of the action had been the subject of sharp criticism by Lord Curzon during a meeting of the War Cabinet, but that Balfour had stoutly defended him, as had Jellicoe himself.[20]

By the end of 1917, Tyrwhitt commanded nine light cruisers, four flotilla leaders and twenty four destroyers, an increase in the size of the Harwich Force which reflected the continued increase in its duties. During the year his achievements were recognised by the award of a knighthood; his substantive rank was still only that of a post captain, and it was said to be only the second time it had been given to a post captain. In the House of Commons Commander Bellairs demanded that Tyrwhitt should be given flag rank and 'should not wait until over fifty captains senior to him have been promoted to Rear-Admiral.' This was extremely embarrassing to Tyrwhitt, who wrote a sharp note to Bellairs:

> I should be grateful if in future you will refrain from taking a personal interest in my professional career. I am perfectly content to leave my advancement, etc, in the hands of my superior officers, who have risen by merit to the positions they hold in the Admiralty.[21]

Tyrwhitt was, however, promoted to Acting Rear Admiral on January 14 1918, over the heads of forty eight captains.

He got a new flagship, the light cruiser *Curaçoa*, on February 20 1918, which he considered 'a great improvement even on *Centaur*.' The latter was mined on June 13, and had to steam stern first 250 miles across the North Sea to the safety of the Humber; and the incident followed the mining the day before of *Conquest* just off the Sunk, outside Harwich; she was taken in tow by *Curaçoa* to Sheerness. The Harwich Force had been used as bait on May 31 1918, being sent in through the minefields of the Bight, while the Grand Fleet cruised outside; but the High Seas Fleet did not appear. Domvile complained of 'mad expeditions' into the Heligoland Bight, and 'cursed the genius at the Admiralty who first mined the Bight and then sent us into our own minefields.'[22]

For the rest of the war, it was business as usual for the Harwich Force, which continued to meet the demands made upon it until the armistice. On November 11 Tyrwhitt was able to send a signal to all his ships, thanking them for 'the unbounded gallantry, zeal and endurance they have invariably displayed during the war.[23] 'It was no more than they deserved.

Tyrwhitt was a man of strong opinions, which he expressed trenchantly but by no means always consistently in his correspondence. His attitude to Winston Churchill was an example of this. In the early days of the war he enjoyed a good relationship with the First Lord. In January 1915 he told his wife that he and Roger Keyes knew Churchill 'better than anyone else in the Navy does,' and that he liked him 'in spite of his bad points. He is extremely brave and I am sure longs to up and do things himself.'[24] When the crisis came which led to Churchill's fall from office, he wrote to her on May 18:

> I am v. sorry about the Fisher-Winston wrangle. Such bad form in these days of war. I hope they will both get the sack! They are both dangerous people, who working together rather cancel one another's dangerous qualities but working alone I should be very much afraid of either.[25]

Within a month, however, Tyrwhitt had changed his tune completely, writing to Keyes:

> I am very sorry Winston has gone. I am sure you are of the same opinion. He was always charming to me and I believe in him. He was absolutely fearless and if he had any faults they were his unfortunate journalistic characteristics which kept popping out. Of course he's made mistakes but tell me who hasn't during the war. I saw a good deal of him and I have no hesitation in saying I hope I shall see him again in office and it is quite possible.[26]

This roseate view of the former First Lord did not, however, survive the latter's speech in the House of Commons on March 7 1916, when he attacked the Admiralty for 'an attitude of pure passivity,' and called for the return of Fisher. Tyrwhitt was outraged, writing to his wife on March 9:

> I hated Winston's reappearance and have wiped him off my list. He has done a bad piece of work and has made himself ridiculous to the world. As for old Fisher, if he gets back he will create Hell at the Admiralty and will do any amount of harm.[27]

Tyrwhitt expressed himself forcefully with regard to a number of prominent naval personalities. He shared with Keyes a profound distaste for Bacon, whom they derisively referred to in correspondence as 'the streaky one' or 'the porker.' He was not at all impressed with Oliver, and most of the time was disrespectful of the Admiralty as a whole. On the other hand, he had a great and enduring admiration for Beatty. After a visit to the Grand Fleet in mid February 1917, he told Keyes:

> DB was splendid ... he impresses me more every time I meet him. He has a wonderful grasp of the situation and absolutely fills me with confidence and hope of the future.[28]

In June, after another visit to the Grand Fleet, he wrote:

> It fills me with admiration the way he has captivated everybody and the absolute faith that everybody has in him. There's no doubt that he is the right man in the right place.[29]

His admiration for the new Commander in Chief continued to deepen; he remarked to Keyes at the end of the war: 'He is a great man and becomes greater in my estimation every time I see him.[30]

28

New Ships, New Men, New Strategy

Bringing back Fisher to the Admiralty had been, as Churchill wrote, for him personally the most disastrous step he had ever had to take. Even so, he did not repent of the decision:

> Fisher brought to the Admiralty an immense wave of enthusiasm for the construction of warships. His genius was mainly that of a constructor, organiser and energiser ... To build warships of every kind, as many as possible and as fast as possible, was the message, and in my judgment the sole message, which he carried to the Admiralty in the shades of that grim critical winter of 1914.[1]

Unlike many at the Admiralty and in government, Fisher believed that it might be a long war. Churchill described how, 'in four or five glorious days, every minute of which was pure delight to him,' Fisher presented a huge array of construction schemes. On November 3 he held a meeting at the Admiralty to arrange the programme of ship building on which he had set his heart, and with the energy that always characterised his implementation of his ideas made plain his insistence that it be achieved in the shortest time possible. It has been calculated that some 600 ships were planned that day, producing what Churchill called a 'tremendous new Navy.'[2]

At the top end of Fisher's programme came new capital ships. The *Royal Sovereign* class had been intended to consist of seven ships. Two of these, *Renown* and *Repulse,* ordered before the war, had been suspended on August 26 because it was considered that they would not be completed before the war ended. One of Fisher's first schemes on his return to the Admiralty was for a 32 knot battle cruiser carrying four 15 inch guns, which he christened 'Rhadamanthus.' He at once proposed to Churchill that the contracts for *Renown* and *Repulse* should be converted to provide battle cruisers. It has been pointed out that it was in reality not at all a matter of conversion, since building work had not commenced.[3] However, it probably made the suggestion more palatable. Churchill, not sharing Fisher's view of a long war, was at first opposed to the scheme, but Fisher did not give up his campaign. Asking Jellicoe to write him an unofficial letter which he could show to the Cabinet complaining that the apparent British superiority in fast battleships was fallacious, he added:

> None of our existing ships have the necessary FUTURE speed! The new German *Lützow* battle cruiser, with possibly 14-inch guns, or even 16-inch, will have certainly over 28 knots

> speed! We must have 32-knots speed to give us a margin for being long out of dock, and to give the necessary speed to CATCH a 28-knot ship! …SPEED IS EVERYTHING.[4]

Armed with the letters he besought from Jellicoe and Beatty, Fisher continued to hammer Churchill with his arguments for his 'Rhadamanthus.' On Christmas Day 1914 he despatched another thunderbolt to the First Lord:

> Our fastest ship is the *Tiger*. She cannot exceed 29 knots. The German battle cruiser *Lützow*, now completing, aims at that speed also. But we don't want equality of speed; we MUST have excess of speed, a large excess of speed to catch the enemy. The greyhound is much faster than the hare! Ever so much faster! We have nothing to 'catch' the German *Lützow*. We must have something.[5]

By now Fisher had already given instructions to the Director of Naval Construction, Sir Eustace Tennyson d'Eyncourt, to prepare a design for his new battle cruisers. Churchill finally succumbed to Fisher's pressure, and procured Cabinet approval on December 28 for two new battle cruisers, to take the names of the battle ships they replaced. They were now to have six 15-inch guns, and twenty five 4-inch, with a radius of action of 12,000 miles. The DNC's department moved swiftly, completing the whole of the design by April 12 1915, both ships having been laid down on January 25. It was a feature of the design that, in accordance with Fisher's constant desire to sacrifice protection for speed, their armour was extremely light. As John Roberts has pointed out, their scheme of defence 'varied little from that originally provided in the *Invincible* class,' He concluded that Fisher must have expressly stipulated that this should be so.[6] In the course of the Jutland post-mortem it was 'decided that the protective decks in the *Repulse* and *Glorious* classes should be thickened in the manner which has been approved for ships already completed.'[7] However these were apparently piecemeal additions, and little more than temporary expedients. Following her completion, *Repulse* ran her trials in August 1916, achieving 31.7 knots; in the following month, *Renown* made 32.6 knots. They were large ships, with a displacement of some 32,700 tons, and were 794 feet long with a beam of 90 feet. They had a draught of some 26.5 feet. As completed, they had a secondary armament of 17 4-inch and 2 3-inch AA guns. In terms of speed as against armour, therefore, Fisher had got what he wanted.

With the lessons of Jutland firmly in his mind, however, Jellicoe was clear that they were 'really not a match for vessels of such protection as that given to the German battle cruisers.' This was in a report to the First Lord of July 21 1917; when comparing *Repulse* and *Renown* to *Hindenburg* and her sister ship, he commented: 'The British vessels are absolutely outclassed and are not fit even to engage the German ships. They are really freaks.'[8]

In the autumn of 1914 Fisher had been greatly interested in the possibilities of action in the Baltic, sharing with Churchill the view that by entering the Baltic they could turn the German flank. The difference between them was that Fisher believed, characteristically, that such an operation could be launched without preparing the way by seizing Borkum and blockading the Bight. Churchill believed that Fisher completely failed to address the question of how the Elbe was first to be blocked. No detailed plans for such an operation into the Baltic as Fisher proposed were ever worked out, but it was this scheme that played a large part in another construction project. This was the building of three of what he called 'Big Light Cruisers,' a term which appeared likely to be more politically acceptable to the Cabinet. These, he told both Churchill and Jellicoe in January 1915, would act as support vessels for the Baltic operation, being designed with a very shallow draught. They were a development of the *Renown* class, with one of the forward turrets omitted and the hull armour reduced to that of a traditional light cruiser. Fisher, as usual, was extravagantly enthusiastic, telling D'Eyncourt that his design of the class had impressed him by 'its exceeding excellence and simplicity – all the three vital requisites of gunpowder, speed and draught of water so well balanced.'[9] The first two, *Courageous* and *Glorious* were laid down on March 28 and April 20 respectively. As completed, in November and December 1916, they were 786 feet long, with a beam of 81 feet and a displacement of 22,700 tons with a designed speed of 32 knots. They were armed with four 15-inch and eighteen 4 inch guns, and two 3 inch AA guns. The third ship of the class, *Furious*, was slightly larger, and was armed with two 18 inch, ten 5.5 inch and four 3 inch AA guns She was completed in July 1917. Only the after 18 inch gun was mounted, since the vessel was completed with her forward section as a flight deck; her monstrous gun was found to be a shattering weapon on such a lightly built vessel, and in 1918 she was transformed completely into an aircraft carrier.[10]

But it was not in capital ships, but in the hundreds of smaller craft that were built as a result of Fisher's determination to fit the navy for a long war, that is to be found his real achievement. In the forefront of his mind was the pressing need for more submarines, and it was with these that he began the meeting of November 3 1914. Keyes, who had been invited to attend, recalled Fisher's conduct of the proceedings:

> He opened the meeting by telling us his intentions as to future submarine construction, and turning to the Superintendent of Contracts, he said he would make his wife a widow and his house a dunghill, if he brought paper work or red tape into the business; he wanted submarines, not contracts. He meant to have them built in eight months; if he did not get them in eight months he would commit hara-kiri. Addison, in an aside which I think that Fisher must have heard, remarked, 'Now we know exactly how long he has to live.' I laughed, and I suppose looked incredulous. It seemed absurd; we had not been able to wring submarines out of Vickers and Chatham Dockyard under two and a half years. He fixed me with a ferocious glare, and said, 'If anyone thwarts me, he had better commit hara-kiri too.'[11]

Fisher wrote later that day to Jellicoe:

> We have made a wonderful coup (after you left) with someone abroad for very rapid delivery of submarines and small craft and guns and ammunition. I must not put more on paper, but it's a gigantic deal done in five minutes! That's what I call war![12]

The 'someone abroad' was Charles M Schwab, the chairman of the Bethlehem Steel Corporation, with the shipbuilding yard of which was placed an order for 20 submarines. Twelve of these, the '*H*' class, were promptly delivered in 1915, after which when the US Government clamped down on delivery of the rest as being an activity inconsistent with neutrality. In the United Kingdom the building continued of additional units of the '*E*' class, which formed the backbone of the British submarine fleet. These were of 660/800 tons, were 181 feet long and capable of up to 16 knots on the surface and 10 knots when submerged. The first of these had been completed in 1913. In all, 57 of the class were built. They were followed by the '*G*' class, the first British ocean going submarines, which were slightly bigger, most of these being completed during 1916. These were followed by the much larger '*J*' class, capable of speeds of 19.5 knots, and which at that time were the fastest submarines in the world. They were built in response to rumours, later found to be untrue, that the Germans were building large submarines capable of 22 knots. In 1917 the Navy took delivery of the even larger 'K' class, of 1883/2565 tons, 338 feet long, and capable of 25 knots on the surface. These were designed to operate with the Grand Fleet. Steam driven, they were designated 'Fleet submarines.'[13]

What the Grand Fleet really needed above all else were destroyers, as Jellicoe repeatedly insisted. The '*M*' class, which represented no great departure from the immediately preceding designs, were steadily coming into service. There were some variations from the basic design, according to the shipbuilder. They were, however, of between 994 and 1042 tons, being between 271 and 276 feet in length and 26 ¾ feet in breadth. Their design speed was 34 knots. The armament consisted of three 4-inch guns and a 2 pounder. They mounted two pairs of torpedo tubes. Although personally doubtful about the future of the destroyer, as soon as he came into office, Fisher placed large emergency orders for additional destroyers of the '*M*' class. Nine of these vessels had come into service during 1914, followed by a further thirty one in the following year. 1916, however, saw no less than sixty eight of these vessels delivered to the navy; the ever increasing need for more destroyers was not, of course, solely for the Grand Fleet; the Harwich Force and the Dover Patrol required more and more of them, not least to replace losses, which were high.

The next class to come into service was the '*R*' class of 55 ships, most of which were completed during 1917. These again followed the general design of the '*M*' class, being of a similar length and breadth but of a slightly higher displacement. They were, however, faster, attaining 36 knots; five of this class, with engines capable of 29,000 horsepower compared to the 27,000 horse power of the rest, were capable of speeds of between 37 and 40 knots.[14]

Early in the war it had become apparent that ships of the former coast defence type or monitors could be used effectively for the bombardment of enemy shore positions. Fisher included a number of these in his Emergency War Programme. He and Churchill were agreed on the potential of such vessels, Churchill because he saw them as valuable for an attack on the German coast, and Fisher because they would support his Baltic project.[15] Three river monitors being built for Brazil were taken over, and two of them, *Mersey* and *Severn*, were successfully employed in the destruction of the German light cruiser *Königsberg*, which had been blockaded in the Rufiji Estuary in East Africa. These were joined by the four monitors of the *Abercrombie* class, mounting two 14 inch guns, followed by the eight ships of the *Lord Clive* class, mounting two 12 inch guns. Both classes had secondary armament of from one to four 6-inch guns, and two 3-inch AA guns. They were all about 6000 tons in displacement, but speed being inessential were designed to attain only 6-8 knots. All came into service during 1915.

Among the smaller vessels ordered, a large number of small patrol vessels were built, called P Boats or PC Boats. These began coming into service in 1915. Of between 578 and 613 tons, they carried a four inch gun. They were principally designed to hunt U boats, and were fitted with a hardened steel ram in the bows. They had a design speed of 20-23 knots. The so called PC Boats, which were slightly larger, were completed as Q ships, disguised as coastal freighters, and came into service in 1917 and 1918.

The needs of the German navy were much more limited in scope, since its responsibilities were much narrower than its opponent. In fact, following the outbreak of war, only the first two battleships of the *Bayern* class joined the dreadnoughts of the High Seas Fleet, and *Bayern* and *Baden* were not destined to see action. Their sisters *Sachsen* and *Württemberg*, as previously noted, although launched in 1914 and 1915 respectively, were never completed. Of the battle cruisers, only the three ships of the *Derfflinger* class joined the fleet during the war; rumours of new construction, however, kept the British Admiralty and the leaders of the Grand Fleet in a constant state of apprehension. Fisher, in particular during his brief second term of office, exploited these fears to press for more construction to meet them.

The delay in construction of new capital ships, and their eventual abandonment, ensured that the superiority of the Grand Fleet over the High Seas Fleet steadily increased throughout the rest of the war. Both fleets having recognised that stalemate had been reached in the North Sea, however, this increasing imbalance had relatively little strategic consequence. Beatty, from the moment he assumed command, pursued a policy which was even more cautious than that of his predecessor, while the attention of the German navy was focused on the rapidly increasing U-boat fleet. This, if it was to be able to mount an effective campaign against Allied commerce, had to be of enormous size, and required the commitment of a great deal of German shipbuilding activity. HM Le Fleming summarised the needs of the U-boat fleet:

> The largest number of U-boats known to have been at sea at one time was 61, in June 1917. To maintain operations on this scale would require nearly 200 vessels (as estimated before the war). Apart from the replacement of losses, much time had to be spent in docking, training, replenishment and in moving to and from war stations. Before the days of nuclear generators and peroxide turbines, the great weakness of the submarine was its dependence on heavy batteries for submerged running. Any increase in battery power had to be balanced by reduced fuel capacity and armament, thereby seriously decreasing the vessels' effectiveness. Broadly speaking, the larger submarines could travel submerged for 100 miles at 3 knots (30 hours), or for about 20 miles at 8 knots (2½ hours).[16]

Marder, relying on the statistics provided by Gibson and Prendergast, puts the largest number of U-boats at sea at any one time at 70. In the event, this proved insufficient, although only narrowly.

What is remarkable, therefore, is the failure of the German leaders to launch a major programme of U-boat construction in 1916. The explanation appears to be partly that it was supposed that an unrestricted U-boat campaign would achieve its objective within six months, and partly that it was thought that German industry would be unable to cope with a huge additional burden. Both suppositions were to be proved wrong; the U-boat campaign, though it was to come close to success, was much more prolonged, and in the event, when massively increased orders were placed for additional submarine construction, Germany's shipbuilders rose to the task. This, at any rate, was Gayer's opinion, as Marder observes.[17] As it turned out, these orders came much too late; new U-boats were being delivered at the rate of about eight per month in 1917, and the same rate prevailed during the first ten months of 1918. Had the war continued, of course, the rate would have increased considerably. The British, however, persistently overestimated the rate of U-boat construction, calculating that 316 U-boats would be available by January 1918, compared with an actual total of 165. They also estimated that another 130 would be added during the year, against the 80 actually completed.

Following the changes in leadership, the Grand Fleet settled down under the new men in charge. Understandably Beatty had been particularly sensitive to the question of who should lead the battle cruisers, and it had been at his insistence that Pakenham be appointed. William Pakenham was in many ways an eccentric; Marder has written of him that he played tennis at Rosyth in a boiled shirt, and that he always went to bed fully dressed in order to be ready for any emergency. Born in 1861, he had entered the navy at the age of thirteen. He had been present as an observer at the battle of Tsushima in 1904, where he displayed notable sang-froid. Thereafter he was seen as a coming man; he became Fourth Sea Lord in 1911; then, as Rear Admiral, he commanded first the 3rd Cruiser Squadron and then in 1915 the 2nd Battle Cruiser Squadron. It had been intended than he should hoist his flag as commander of the Battle Cruiser Force in *Australia*; Beatty was emphatic, however, that he should do so in *Lion*.

At first entirely confident in his subordinate's competence, Beatty began to have reservations about Pakenham's abilities, particularly his administrative skills. As early as February 1917 he was expressing his concerns in a letter to his wife:

> The battle cruisers arrived safely and I had a long talk with Packs, and I think he is alright. He has the right ideas in his head and I feel would do the right thing in the presence of the enemy, which, after all, is something. It is his administration work which is badly done and things are forgotten, which means bad staff work, and he hasn't the knowledge or imagination to keep them right, but that will come and he will learn, especially as I am continually pointing out his mistakes and never lose an opportunity, but it is tiresome. Still, he is such a gentleman that he (like many others would) never takes offence or tries to shirk the question.[18]

By May things were rather worse. Beatty wrote to Ethel to say that he was 'rather disappointed with old Packs, (but don't think of saying a word to a soul), he does not seem to possess quite the right flair.' Beatty's complaint was that Pakenham was not quick enough at grasping a situation which, at high speeds, was a major worry. He was clearly fond of him, however, expressing his pleasure that 'dear old Packs' was to be made a vice admiral in June.

Regrettably, matters did not improve. In a letter to his wife on October 3, Beatty wrote:

> I am sorry to hear your opinion of old Packs. I hope he is not going to crack up. I really do not think he bears any malice against me because I took his light cruisers away. I haven't taken them away in the things that really matter, i.e. operations etc, and only in matters of administration, which had become too big for him to deal with, and required decentralising. He has only himself to blame.[19]

Beatty recalled that he had 'a devil of a fight to get him the appointment at all;' but concluded that he did not anticipate Pakenham causing trouble, as he was, after all, a gentleman. By February 1918, Beatty had found, as he thought, the cause of the problem:

> I am afraid old Packs is soft or weak or something, which prevents him from making firm decisions. For instance, he wrote to me that the disaster to the Ks had had a very shaking effect on the officers and men in the other submarines, and suggested that they should all be given leave!![20]

Beatty was having none of that: the submariners needed, he thought, to be not softened but hardened, and his prescription was to send them all to sea.

With Madden, the commander of the 1st Battle Squadron, and second in command of the fleet, Beatty seems to have got on reasonably well. He always valued Madden's good opinion of him, not least because he was a reserved individual, and perhaps too because as Jellicoe's brother in law he might be supposed to be making comparisons. Nonetheless, Beatty's judgment of him was not entirely favourable; he was able to write in May to his mistress Eugénie Godfrey-Faussett, when contemplating the possibility that he might himself have to become First Sea Lord: 'For the life of me, I do not know who to put into the Grand Fleet.'[21]

For his part, Madden noted in 1918 of Beatty: 'He is very shrewd and takes no risks. Responsibility is a great steadier.'[22]

Sturdee's disappointment at being passed over has already been described. Beatty was pleased that their relationship survived this, and in May 1917 wrote to his wife:

> He is a great supporter of mine now, Sturdee. I have humoured the old beggar, and he is loyal and helpful, and we get on very well. In fact all my admirals are splendid and help me enormously to keep things going, and all our relations are harmonious.[23]

He was equally pleased with de Robeck (commander of the 2nd Battle Squadron) of whom he had always a good opinion. In the same letter he described him as being like a two year old, 'and you wouldn't believe he is the same man as joined up six months ago. He is 15 years younger and as cheerful and happy as a sandboy.'

Beatty had, of course, had occasion to work closely with Evan-Thomas when the latter's 5th Battle Squadron was attached to the Battle Cruiser Fleet, and may well have had reservations about him. Immediately after Jutland he had been able to write to Evan-Thomas to thank him 'for your gallant and effective support on Wednesday. It was fine to see your squadron sail down as it did.' It was not until after the war that the handling by Evan-Thomas of his squadron became a source of such controversy between the two men, and during Beatty's appointment as Commander-in-Chief they worked well together. Certainly Beatty accorded Evan-Thomas a striking compliment when, as the latter knelt to receive the accolade of knighthood from King George V on *Queen Elizabeth* in June 1917, he drew his own sword and presented it, hilt-first, to the King. Andrew Gordon, while observing that paying such a compliment to the man who had supported him at Jutland may have been Beatty's sole motive, suggests that it is permissible on the other hand 'to allow a smidgen of cynicism to intrude.'[24] Beatty liked gestures like that.

Jellicoe, when taking up his duties as First Sea Lord, could at least feel that he had around him the men that he wanted. Whether they were the best men for the positions which they held is another matter. As Second Sea Lord he had obtained Burney, for whom he had always had a great respect, but of whom many in the service had a low opinion. The Permanent Secretary, Sir William Graham Greene, wrote of him:

> He was not a man of strong and decided character and had not the gift of independent judgment, but his knowledge of the details of the Naval Service was deep and his advice on all that concerned the routine and inner life of officers and men afloat was very valuable … As Second Sea Lord during the war his administrative functions did not call for much display of special abilities.[25]

In his position he was principally concerned with matters of personnel, the manning and training of the fleet and the appointment of officers. His health was poor. Beatty for one did not see him as an adequate deputy for Jellicoe, writing in 1917 to his wife, when Jellicoe had had to go away for a rest: 'What a situation with an old mummy like Burney to do his work.'

The Third Sea Lord was the able Rear Admiral Sir Frederick Tudor, who remained from the previous administration. His post was responsible for all matters of materiel. The Fourth Sea Lord was Lionel Halsey, who had been Jellicoe's Captain of the Fleet; he was concerned with all questions of logistics. Richmond thought him 'a very good chap, but as mutton headed as he can be.' A Fifth Sea Lord, Commodore Godfrey Paine, was appointed in January 1917 to be responsible for all matters concerned with aviation. Oliver, the Chief of the Admiralty War Staff, retained his position, and so did Hall, the Director of Naval Intelligence.

The key appointment was, however, that of the Director of the newly constituted Anti-Submarine Division, Rear Admiral Alexander Duff, whom Jellicoe greatly admired and brought down with him from the Grand Fleet, together with the staff appointed to the Division. This consisted of two captains, four commanders, three lieutenant commanders and two engineers. They joined the four captains already engaged on anti-submarine experimental work. Dreyer, of whom of course Jellicoe had the very highest opinion, was appointed as Assistant Director; as his Flag Captain aboard *Iron Duke*, he was probably closest of all to Jellicoe. Duff, second in command of the 4th Battle Squadron at Jutland, was a torpedo officer who had been Director of Mobilisation at the outbreak of war; in 1916 Jellicoe had selected him to be his Chief of Staff if anything happened to Madden.

Much the most significant new appointment was naturally that of First Lord. Sir Edward Carson, passionate supporter of the Protestant resistance in Ulster to Home Rule, had served for five months as Attorney General in Asquith's first Coalition Government. He had been a Conservative Member of Parliament since 1892, and was the most renowned lawyer of his day. Lloyd George described him thus:

> He had the supreme gift of getting to the point that mattered in the formation of opinion and of presenting and pressing it with words, voice and emphasis that moved those who heard him in the direction he wished their sentiments to travel … As soon as he joined the Asquith Coalition in 1915 he penetrated all the greatest weaknesses of the War Administration and was aware of the fatal defects of the two personalities upon whom the potency of direction must depend – the Prime Minister and Lord Kitchener.[26]

Lloyd George, however, later considered that bringing Carson into the Cabinet had been a mistake, remarking that 'he had no aptitude for administrative office.'

Carson at once gave his most loyal support to Jellicoe and his team. He was, though, in Marder's view, too loyal, allowing his legal training and sense of propriety to prevent him ever seeking guidance outside the Admiralty. This self imposed restraint and lack of assertiveness, apart from his lack of administrative talent, 'largely nullified his powerful assets of energy, courage, independence, and intolerance of complacency.'[27] He was, however, popular with the Navy, and Beatty's first thoughts on his appointment were probably fairly typical:

> Well, now that Carson is at the Admiralty we shall see what manner of man he is. But I fancy you will find Jellicoe will stop there longer than you think. I certainly hope he will,

> as he knows the Grand Fleet conditions, and, if Carson supports him strongly, he will do. The trouble with him, ie J, is that if Carson doesn't support him, he, Jellicoe, is not strong enough in character to make him.[28]

In this letter to his wife, written on December 15 1916, Beatty made clear that, although thinking Lloyd George was 'a dirty dog,' he was probably right to displace Asquith from power.

Richmond confided to his diary on January 3 1917 his hopes that the new Anti-Submarine Division might indicate fresh thinking:

> The establishment of the new section at the Admiralty under Duff for taking charge of the submarine side of the business is a sign of a change of heart. It is rather comical, but rather sad, that it should have taken so long to recognise the necessity for something of the sort.[29]

His optimism was short lived. A colleague, Lieutenant Commander Isaacson, had visited the Admiralty and had returned with a depressing report:

> Apparently things are quite chaotic as far as this new submarine department is concerned. Nothing organised, no principles, everyone scratching his head and wondering what to do … Whether Duff will succeed remains to be seen. But what is clear is that his department is starting *ab ovo*; they are all amateurs in strategy and have first to learn the rudiments of their business. We are a wonderful people, truly.[30]

There had been no comparable changes in the leadership of the German navy. Much the most important development had been the fall of Tirpitz in March 1916. Fisher amused himself by writing an open letter to Tirpitz on March 29, which he prevailed on one newspaper to publish. Addressing the Grand Admiral as 'Dear old Tirps,' he wrote:

> We are both in the same boat! What a time we've been colleagues, old boy! However, we did you in the eye over the battle cruisers and I know you've said you'll never forgive me for it when bang went the *Blücher* and Von Spee and all his host! Cheer up, old chap! Say 'Resurgam'! You're the one German sailor who understands war! Kill your enemy without being killed yourself. I don't blame you for the submarine business. I'd have done the same myself, only our idiots in England wouldn't believe it when I told them. Well! So Long! Yours till hell freezes, Fisher.[31]

Capelle, Tirpitz's successor, had very much less political clout. He was competent, but lacked the force of personality to be able to assert his will in the complex structure of German naval governance. Marder notes that he was averse to embarking on any crash programme of U-boat construction.[32]

In October 1917 Capelle was asking Holtzendorff to rescind 'unlimited submarine construction orders,' because it would provoke union demands for higher wages, and because the emphasis on submarine warfare would reduce the number of posts for admirals.[33] Throughout his term of office he was frequently the target of criticism, both from politicians and from the fleet. Scheer recorded the failure of Capelle as State Secretary to respond to the fleet's request for a better organisation of the U-boat war:

> It had taken six months of urging, from July 1917, to December of the same year, before a central organisation for U-boats – the U-boat Office, demanded by the Fleet Command – had been instituted. Such was the delay in carrying out demands or suggestions as the case might be – whether they referred to personnel, armament, or technical matters pertaining to shipbuilding and so on; the working of the different departments was inadequate for the needs of the times.[34]

Capelle had served as Under Secretary to Tirpitz; it is surprising, therefore, to read that Bachmann, who was one of Tirpitz's most loyal supporters, wrote to Tirpitz after they had both left office to include Capelle among their opponents. He described Capelle as being 'a successor who has fled from the banner and passed over to the opposing party.'[35] Capelle, after his appointment, was received very coldly by the Crown Prince, a warm adherent of Tirpitz.[36] Throughout his period of office. Capelle was obliged to resist attempts by the Admiralty Staff to encroach on his authority, no doubt because he was seen as a weaker man than his predecessor.

His position was not helped, of course, by the fact that Tirpitz remained in constant touch with very many senior officers, and continued therefore to exercise a not inconsiderable indirect influence while being seen as one who might at any time make a comeback. The exchanges were valuable both to Tirpitz and his correspondents:

> The battle of Jutland in May 1916 – although the outcome was undecided – meant a considerable gain in prestige for Scheer and Trotha, who were regarded as 'coming men' in the navy. Through the continued contact, Tirpitz was able to keep *au fait* with the developments in the navy and to exert a continued influence; for Scheer and Trotha it provided the opportunity to utilize and refer to Tirpitz for support in the furtherance of their own careers.[37]

Nonetheless, even in the Byzantine complexity of the management of the German navy, Capelle's office gave him a considerable power in decision making. In August 1916, for instance, he firmly decided on retaining both battleships and battle cruisers, but wisely insisted that no ships older than the *Nassau* class should remain with the High Seas Fleet. What put him at odds with Scheer, however, was his refusal to countenance larger guns than the 15 inch of *Baden* and *Bayern*. He prepared a building programme based on two capital ships a year, starting with eight battle cruisers, thereby ditching Tirpitz's plan for sixty capital ships. Scheer demanded greater speed, and larger guns, and urgent priority for the building of battle cruisers. Capelle also later insisted that no ships larger than 41,000 tons be built, to avoid the need to enlarge harbours, locks and canals.[38]

Throughout 1916 it had been Holtzendorff who had been making most of the running in the campaign to introduce unrestricted submarine warfare. In February 1916 a paper was produced by Dr Richard Fuss, the director of a banking institute, which calculated that if U-boats were able to sink enemy merchant shipping at the rate of 630,000 tons per month, Britain would be brought to her knees within five or six months. There would then no longer be enough merchant tonnage to bring in sufficient food imports and sustain the war economy. Holtzendorff, making the maximum use of this plausible analysis, was emphatic that here was the means to win the war. The failed grain harvest of 1916 in the UK lent weight to his argument, which he set out in a paper of August 27 1916. He presented this just two days before Hindenburg and Ludendorff succeeded Falkenhayn; their views on the issue would in the end be decisive. Müller, at the meeting which confirmed Falkenhayn's supersession, recorded Holtzendorff's presentation:

> Holtzendorff proposed both verbally and in a memorandum, unrestricted U-boat warfare. I supported him on three grounds: 1. Thanks to a bumper harvest, we shall be less dependent on imports than in the spring. 2. We have more U-boats available than last spring. 3. The neutrals are resentful of England and are more disposed to our wholesale blockading of Britain.[39]

Bethmann-Hollweg, with whom Müller had a long discussion after the meeting, was not persuaded; the diplomatic consequences of an unrestricted submarine campaign remained in his mind as an absolute bar to taking such a step. The decision was postponed, in part to await the outcome of the campaign being waged in Romania, but the issue remained the subject of constant discussion. Scheer embarked on some lobbying on his own account, when in September he sent Trotha to visit Ludendorff. A firm agreement was reached between them:

1. There is no possibility of bringing the war to a satisfactory ending without ruthless U-boat warfare
2. On no account must a half and half campaign be started, which could not achieve anything of importance, but involved the same military dangers, and would probably result in a new limitation for the nation.
3. The U-boat campaign should be begun as soon as possible. The Navy is ready.
4. The separate treaties with the Northern States, who had received considerable concessions in the matter of exports to England, must be cancelled with all speed, so that we can act without interference
5. In no circumstances must there be any yielding.[40]

Scheer was able to confirm the understanding between Army and Navy when he visited Hindenburg and Ludendorff himself on November 22. The position of the High Command on the issue was not, however, disclosed to Bethmann-Hollweg at this time. He was steering a difficult and dangerous course, both asserting that a decision about submarine warfare was one for him to make, while at the same time acknowledging that he must take the views of the High Command into account.

Holtzendorff had adopted an extremely cautious policy, as he explained in a letter to Müller:

> For a year I have followed the principle which Hindenburg has recently adopted for his slogan: 'First weigh the cost and then dare,' and I have weighed up things for so long that there are no longer any grounds for wavering or for half measures. Let us attack England now and destroy her shipping with all the means in our power or else we shall bleed to death and we shall have deserved our collapse, towards which we have steered without resolution, guidance or sense .... Our whole position when weighed up carefully demands that we force a decision. England has good reason to tremble on this score and to fling all her might on to the Somme front before we cut her lifeline on the seas. Conditions have changed. We now enjoy considerable military supremacy. England as far as we can see is faced with famine and inflation.[41]

Holtzendorff, visiting Müller on September 19 soon after writing this, had come to Imperial Headquarters to lobby for the removal of Jagow, the State Secretary at the Foreign Office, whom he saw as the principal opponent of unrestricted submarine warfare.

Holtzendorff was now cranking up the pressure. Between August 31, when the meeting at Imperial Headquarters resolved to defer the issue, and December 22, Müller's diary records no less than ten discussion with the Chief of the Admiralty Staff on the subject of unrestricted submarine warfare. On the latter date Holtzendorff produced a further memorandum on the subject which was to prove decisive. It produced an immediate response from Hindenburg, who next day telegraphed the Chancellor to express his opinion that the unrestricted campaign should begin at the end of January. This in turn exerted further pressure on the Kaiser, who was also in receipt of persuasive arguments from both his wife and the Crown Prince in favour of the campaign. By now Jagow had gone, and had been replaced by Zimmerman, who supported Bethmann-Hollweg in his continued opposition; but the Chancellor's position was steadily weakening.

In his memorandum Holtzendorff repeated the arguments that he had been putting forward throughout the year. A decisive outcome to the war was required by the autumn of 1917 to avoid it ending in 'the mutual exhaustion of all parties and thus in a disaster for us.' He went on:

> Of our enemies, Italy and France are economically so hard hit that they are only upheld through England's energy and activity. If we can break England's back, the war will at once be decided in our favour. Now England's mainstay is shipping which brings to the British Isles the necessary supplies of food and materials for war industries, and ensures their solvency abroad.[42]

He went on to restate the conclusion of the Fuss memorandum that the volume of seaborne trade with Britain could be reduced by 39% within five months. His case was that Britain would be smashed before the United States could intervene militarily. He acknowledged that 'war with the United States is such a serious matter that everything was to be undertaken to avoid it,' but argued that fear of the diplomatic consequences 'should not lead us to recoil from the use of a weapon that promises victory for us.'

On the day before the formal discussion of Holtzendorff's paper, to take place on January 9, he had a private meeting with Hindenburg and Ludendorff in which they reviewed what Bethmann-Hollweg would say at the coming meeting. Notes of the conversation record their anguished discussion. Holtzendorff asked what they should do if the Chancellor did not join them. Hindenburg replied that he was racking his brains about it. Holtzendorff said that he must become Chancellor. No, said Hindenburg, he could not and would not do it; he could not deal with the Reichstag. There is a note of despair in Hindenburg's final resolve:

> Well, we shall hold together, anyway. It simply must be. We are counting on the possibility of war with the United States, and have made all preparations to meet it. Things cannot be worse than they are now. The war must be brought to an end by the use of all means as soon as possible.[43]

Holtzendorff's paper was considered at the meeting at Imperial Headquarters next day attended by the Kaiser, the Chancellor, Hindenburg, Ludendorff, Holtzendorff and the three

Cabinet Chiefs. Bethman-Hollweg, warned by Müller before the meeting of the overwhelming strength of military opinion against him, finally withdrew his opposition to the proposed U-boat campaign. The Kaiser, therefore, signed the order for the campaign to begin in February 1, and instructed Holtzendorff to telegraph Scheer accordingly. Bethmann-Hollweg remained profoundly pessimistic, and refused to allow Müller to cheer him up after the meeting, remarking:

> Yes, I had to give way to the military arguments but, as I see the future, we shall make the enemy tire of the war in the end, but not until they have achieved notable successes by pushing us back in France and Belgium to the Maas, with the capture of many guns and the taking of a host of prisoners. Then we shall be forced to sign an exceedingly modest peace.[44]

Thus Holtzendorff and the admirals got their way. Both Müller and the Chancellor were realistic; this was, the former thought, the last shot in Germany's locker.

Scheer, aware that a decision was approaching, had sent Levetzow to meet Holtzendorff on January 4, and was disconcerted to learn from this that for the moment permission might be given only to sink armed liners, which led him to fear that the situation of a year previously was about to be repeated. Levetzow went on to see the Chancellor, to stress again that a middle course would be the worst of both worlds, giving offence and being ineffectual if the United States objected. When Scheer got the order on January 9 for unrestricted submarine warfare he was relieved, but puzzled that it was immediately preceded by the order which Holtzendorff had foreshadowed. Maybe, he thought, the middle course against which he argued so passionately, had already been enshrined in some communication to the United States which it was too late to withhold. At all events, the task now was to launch the campaign. He was under no illusions as to the immensity of the task:

> With the unrestricted U-boat campaign we had probably embarked on the most tremendous undertaking that the world war brought in its long train. Our aim was to break the power of mighty England vested in her sea trade in spite of the protection which her powerful fleet could afford her. Two and a half years of the world war had passed before we addressed ourselves to this task, and they had taxed the strength of the Central Powers to the uttermost. But if we did not succeed in overcoming England's will to destroy us then the war of exhaustion must end in Germany's certain defeat ... <u>In such a situation it was not permissible to sit with folded hands and leave the fate of the German Empire to be decided by chance circumstances.</u>[45]

For Holtzendorff, however, the explosive and emotional situation that continued among Germany's leaders had thrown up a new anxiety. By January 30 he was writing to Müller about it:

> To my great personal disappointment I am coming more and more to the conclusion that the highly-talented and worthy Ludendorff, like Tirpitz, is over reaching himself and succumbing to ambition. At this juncture, when the final decision may be reached at sea, he tries, in an excess of zeal, to take a hand in the waging of naval warfare and to subordinate the plans of the Admiralty Staff to his own plan of operations. I shall resist him until His Majesty intervenes. But any slip here can prove fatal.[46]

Müller, expressing his complete agreement, replied that it would be preferable 'to have an Admiral take over the Army Command;' unity of policy and leadership was, he thought, the first condition for success in a world war. He also floated the uncomfortable possibility that, in certain circumstance, both Hindenburg and the Kaiser might consider making Tirpitz Chancellor.

It was in this fevered atmosphere that preparations for the campaign went forward. On January 31 the German government formally notified the United States of its intention to commence an unrestricted submarine campaign on the following day in which all Allied or neutral shipping entering British and French coastal waters might be sunk on sight. The area covered included the Channel, the western half of the North Sea, and the western coasts of the British Isles and France. It extended some 400 miles into the Atlantic.[47] The challenge was thus thrown down; it remained to be seen how the British government, the Admiralty and the British people would respond to it.

29

The Convoy Debate

John Winton, in his comprehensive analysis of the use of convoy to defend seaborne trade, summarised its historical importance:

> In all the naval wars under sail (there were ten major wars between 1659 and 1815, with innumerable other alarms, emergencies and skirmishes) convoy was the one crucial doctrine of naval warfare on which all else turned. Generations of British naval officers were brought up in the convoy tradition. To them, convoy was as natural and as obvious a tactic as, say, gaining and keeping the weather gauge. Convoy was the one sure and proved defence against an organised attack on commerce, the *guerre de course* as it was called, employed by enemies, and especially by the French and the Dutch, over and over again through the centuries. Nelson himself believed that all ships, fast or slow, big or small, should always sail in convoy.[1]

'Convoy,' a term which relates to ships being escorted, is defined by Marder as consisting in the despatch of merchant ships in organised groups accompanied by one or more warships.[2] The magisterial conclusion of Alfred T Mahan in his history of the Napoleonic wars put the value of a system of convoy beyond doubt; taking as an example the use of convoy in the Far East, he wrote:

> In fact, as the small proportionate loss inflicted by scattered cruisers appears to indicate the inconclusiveness of that mode of warfare, so the result of the convoy system, in this and other instances, warrants the inference that, when properly systematised and applied, it will have more success as a defensive measure than hunting for individual marauders, – a process which, even when most thoroughly planned, still resembles looking for a needle in a haystack.[3]

Huge convoys were assembled during the Napoleonic Wars, with escorts the size of which were determined by the extent of the perceived threat, sailing together down Channel past the many ports in which lurked French privateers constantly on the lookout for valuable mercantile prizes. Only a tiny percentage of merchant vessels sailing in convoy were lost; the percentage of those lost sailing independently was ten times as great. Convoy, as Winton points out, also made a direct contribution to the destruction of enemy ships while helping to preserve one's own. It combined the best defence with the most effective attack; 'yet, astoundingly, incredibly, by the end of the nineteenth century this priceless piece of naval knowledge had been lost by the Royal Navy.'[4] Marder observes that the lessons of old wars had been forgotten, because the study of history was regarded as a waste of time.

By the time Lloyd George came to power in December 1916, the losses in merchant shipping had risen to the point where Sir Walter Runciman, the President of the Board of Trade, could report to the War Committee (in November 1916) that 'a complete breakdown in shipping would come before June 1917.'[5] The new Prime Minister made 'the institution of a regular system of convoys for all the merchant shipping from the moment it reached the danger zone' one of his first priorities. He encountered, as he wrote, 'amazing and incomprehensible difficulties' in inducing the Admiralty even to try the convoy system. It was the plan, he considered, which produced the 'most implacable and prolonged resistance.' As has been noted, an attempt to overcome the 'blind obstinacy' of the admirals had been made at the War Committee meeting of November 2 1916, but foundered on the objections not only of Jellicoe, Jackson and Oliver, but also of Runciman. The minute of the decision reached recorded the latter's view:

> The President of the Board of Trade pointed out that from an economical point of view the system of convoys was extremely unsatisfactory since it involved the whole convoy proceeding at the speed of the slowest ship and the simultaneous arrival of all the ships at the port of destination, which would then become congested.[6]

The astonishing change of policy towards convoy on the part of the Admiralty went back some way. In December 1874 the First Sea Lord, Admiral Sir Alexander Milne, published a War Plan that reflected the contemporary focus on sea routes and their protection. The prevailing philosophy was that the navy should at all times act offensively rather than defensively, and that the provision of escorts to merchant shipping was essentially defensive. On the other hand, to employ warships to patrol the crucial trade routes was to act offensively, and this became the core of naval thinking. John Winton has pointed out that this policy had a major effect on the design, range and armament of the warships ordered for the navy which would be required to execute this policy.

In 1885, following the Penjdeh Incident which had given rise to expectations of war with Russia, the issue of trade protection was again revisited by a committee, entitled the Foreign Intelligence Committee. This, however, merely endorsed current thinking that called for the patrolling of key trade routes and the blockading of enemy bases; raiders were to be hunted down. The committee dismissed convoy as a policy, taking the view that to provide protection in this way for fast steamers, such as 'those on the Transatlantic routes or on the principal ocean mail routes, by men of war, is out of the question, for the simple reason that the British Navy contains no vessel at the present time capable of keeping pace with them.'[7]

A different view was taken in 1887 by Captain Philip Colomb in a paper presented to the Royal United Service Institution. Having addressed the practical and legal implications of imposing a convoy system, Colomb concluded that the introduction of steam might be expected to lead to a revival of convoy in the next naval war. This, however, he did not expect. Convoy on the old system was 'dead beyond recall' because of changes in the course of trade and in the course of opinion.' The changes in the trade system arose from the introduction of faster merchant vessels which would be able to outrun a pursuer. The drawback of a convoy system, he argued, was that this meant the concentration of a large number of merchant vessels protected by a force inadequate to meet an enemy determined to attack such a tempting target. As a result, he considered that it 'would be opinion rather than impracticability which would forbid the revival of convoy in modern naval war.'[8]

There was a vigorous debate on Colomb's paper. Among his hearers, one Lloyds underwriter observed that 'as far as I can see the opinion (of underwriters) is greatly in favour of convoys for slow steamers – steamers carrying coal and grain and suchlike. As for the fast steamers which carry the mails and perishables, they can look after themselves.' A naval opinion was put forward by Captain WH Henderson:

> As things are, at present, in any maritime war our naval strength will be frittered away in trying to protect our commerce instead of striking effective blows against the enemy.[9]

The RUSI chairman, Sir Donald Currie, described the British navy of the time as inadequate for its purposes. Convoy, as a policy, depended on whether the nation was prepared to pay for it. He concluded:

> So I venture to say in regard to this convoy question, if the mercantile marine is to be of some use it is the duty of all who are interested in the protection of trade and commerce to impress upon those in authority to be in time with their preparations and to have those preparations adequate.[10]

The problem was that, for naval officers, the destruction of enemy fleets was a far more exciting objective that shepherding unwieldy convoys of merchant ships across the ocean, as Captain Henderson's contribution demonstrated.

In 1888 Admiral of the Fleet Sir Geoffrey Phipps Hornby, speaking to the Chamber of Commerce, had expressed some anxiety about current thinking. He argued for light convoys in the Mediterranean and on the principal ocean routes, and called for more small escort craft. Even he, however, saw the principal defence of trade routes to be provided by cruising squadrons. The navy required, he said, 186 cruisers to protect Britain's huge merchant fleet of 36,700 vessels. Sir John Laughton, writing in 1894, supported the case for more small escort vessels: 'Numbers, not strength, are what is wanted.' In 1904 the distinguished military historian Colonel Sir Henry Hozier, who was Secretary of Lloyds, suggested that it was 'doubtful whether the system of convoy will ever again be practised on a large scale.' He was conscious that while it had been effective on occasion, it had also enabled the enemy to make large hauls. His concern was that the navy was unable to conduct a system of convoy effectively. He argued, nonetheless, that it was absolutely necessary for all merchant vessels incapable of doing more than 14 knots. This prompted a stern rejection from Commander Bellairs, who wrote in the 1904 Brassey's Annual:

> The convoy system is at best a distasteful system of dragooning commerce and under the above proposal could apply to 80 per cent of British shipping. I do not think Sir HM Hozier took sufficiently into account the waste of naval force defending the convoys, and the operations of torpedo craft against them … The safety of commerce is in the superiority of our fighting force in the face of the enemy's force.[11]

Another distinguished writer, James Thursfield of *The Times*, addressed the subject in the 1906 Naval Annual, in an article which did not mention the word convoys. His thesis was that the defence of commerce was only a secondary object; the command of the sea, he wrote, was always the primary object. A dispersion of force either for the attack or defence of trade was 'the strategy of the weak, and cannot materially influence the ultimate result of the war.'[12]

This central precept, that the command of the sea was the primary aim, and once achieved, that trade was thus capable of being protected, created the climate of opinion that formed the Admiralty's policy on trade protection. In the early stages of the debate, there was of course no conception of any threat from submarines; but even after they began to come into service on a large scale in the twentieth century, no account was taken of them in considering the utility of a convoy system. Practically no one, apart from Fisher, had perceived how submarines would be employed in a war on trade.

Reviewing the convoy system in operation during the Napoleonic Wars, Sir Julian Corbett found that there were times when it 'seriously disturbed our dispositions.' He cited the effect of the escape of the Toulon squadron, which forced a close concentration on the British Western Squadron; it was felt impossible to retain the mass for more than two days because the great East Indies and West Indies convoys were approaching, and would be exposed to attack by Villeneuve from Ferrol. It was the liability to deflection of this kind that Corbett considered was 'the most serious strategical objection to the convoy system.'[13]

Corbett, who was writing in 1911, concluded that the equipment of most large merchant men with wireless had greatly improved their security; an enemy raider could not attack a single one 'without fear of calling down upon her an adversary.' The much more limited range of steam powered warships further reduced the capacity for mischief of such enemy raiders, so that distant operations would be much more difficult than in the days of sail:

> Upon the great routes the power of attack has been reduced and the means of evasion has increased to such an extent as to demand entire reconsideration of the defence of trade between terminal areas. The whole basis of the old system would seem to be involved. That basis was the convoy system, and it now becomes doubtful whether the additional security which convoys afforded is sufficient to outweigh their economical drawback and their liability to cause strategical disturbance.[14]

Thus the intellectual case for the abandonment of convoy as the key means by which trade could be protected had been made out so successfully that, with the outbreak of war in 1914 the official Admiralty policy had been firmly adopted. The key feature of this was the reliance upon the distant blockade of the High Seas Fleet, together with a system of patrols and the arming of merchantmen. Merchant vessels were advised as to the routes to be taken to minimise the risk of attack. Other than those sailing in coastal waters, merchantmen operated singly, depending on such defensive armament as they possessed, and on zigzagging and smoke screens.[15]

Winton summarises the Admiralty policy as it stood at the outbreak of war in these terms:

> Had the Germans carried on the war against commerce entirely with surface warships then, just conceivably, the confident pre war forecasts and opinions about the impracticability and undesirability of convoy might have seemed nearer the truth. It might, just, have been possible to 'guard the sea lanes' against surface raiders (although later experience with

> *Wolf* and *Möwe* demonstrated how much damage these single raiders could do, and how very difficult it was, and how expensive in time and ships to catch them). But the submarine gave commerce raiding, literally, another dimension.[16]

A system of convoy had been introduced, as has been seen, to protect the trade between Britain and the Netherlands. The 'beef trip' had been extremely successful, in spite of the not inconsiderable cost in destroyers escorting these convoys, five being lost. Its success, however, went unremarked at the Admiralty, doing nothing to affect the official view. Lloyd George's outrage is easy to understand:

> Looking back, it seems amazing that the system of escorting our ships in convoys was not adopted earlier. Yet in the teeth of the fact that other methods were proving futile and disastrous, and our sinkings were increasing at an alarming rate, the Admiralty stubbornly refused to consider adopting the convoy system and thus extending to the mercantile marine the same guardianship as that upon which they relied for their own safety in the Grand Fleet.[17]

In January 1917, the Admiralty's official policy on the convoy issue was expressed in a pamphlet which Winton, quite reasonably, describes as 'stupid' and 'one which pigheadedly ignored all the lessons of past naval history:'

> Whenever possible, vessels should sail singly, escorted as considered necessary. The system of several ships sailing together in a convoy is not recommended in any area where submarine attack is a possibility. It is evident that the larger the number of ships forming the convoy, the greater is the chance of a submarine being enabled to attack successfully, the greater the difficulty of the escort in preventing such an attack. In the case of defensively armed merchant vessels, it is preferable that they should sail singly rather than that they should be formed into a convoy with several other vessels. A submarine could remain at a distance and fire her torpedo into the middle of a convoy with every chance of success. A defensively armed merchant vessel of good speed should rarely, if ever, be captured. If the submarine comes to the surface to overtake and attack with her gun the merchant vessel's gun will nearly always make the submarine dive, in which case the preponderance of speed will allow of the merchant ship escaping.[18]

Winton remarks that this document was 'all the more dangerous because it was not obviously the work of a lunatic.' It sounded reasonable. 'It was not the product of a single deranged mind;' it represented the collective opinion of the Admiralty at the time.

The struggle with the Admiralty over the convoy issue profoundly damaged Lloyd George's respect for the admirals; once in power he went out of his way to assert his control over them. It took, however, some time. He found that Carson, his new First Lord, while personally sympathetic to the idea of trying the convoy system, had met a brick wall at the Admiralty. This resistance to the idea of convoy remained as resolute under Jellicoe as it had done previously. Reluctant to insist on a direct order being given to Jellicoe and Oliver, whom he accepted had 'an unparalleled knowledge of the technique of their profession,' which might precipitate the resignation of the whole Board, Lloyd George arranged a breakfast meeting on February 13

1917 to discuss the issue. It was attended by Carson, Jellicoe, Duff and Hankey, and had before it a memorandum prepared by the latter. This contained a detailed exposition of the objections raised to the convoy system, and set against these the failure of the existing system of trade protection. This memorandum originated on February 11, as Hankey wrote in his diary:

> Had a brain wave on the subject of anti-submarine warfare, so ran down to Walton Heath in the afternoon to formulate my ideas to LL. George, who was very interested. I sat up late completing a long Memo on the subject. My Memo was an argument for convoys, but contained a great number of suggestions.[19]

Hankey's biographer, Captain Roskill, considers that it is entirely possible that his brain wave originated with a suggestion from Commander Reginald Henderson, serving on the War Staff of the Admiralty; he was one of a number of junior officers who did not accept the official line on the subject of convoy. He had discovered that the information given by the Admiralty as to 'safe arrivals' and 'losses' gave a false picture, because the figure of arrivals included every arrival including those of coasters which called at a great many ports. He had also been engaged since February 7 in the organisation of an elementary convoy system to protect the coal trade between Britain and France.[20] In support of his theory, Roskill cites a letter from Churchill to Hankey written in 1937, recalling 'how when young officers came to you and told you the truth, against service rules, you saw that the seed did not fall on stony ground.'[21]

Hankey, in his paper, which he emphasised was not written in a critical or aggressive spirit, nonetheless contained hard hitting recommendations:

> The general scheme submitted below entails ultimately an entire reorganisation of the Admiralty's present scheme of anti-submarine warfare, although it might, in the first instance, be adopted experimentally on a smaller scale. It involves the substitution of a system of scientifically organised convoys, and the concentration of this service of the whole of the anti-submarine craft allotted to the protection of our trade routes, excepting only those vessels devoted to the anti-submarine service of our main fleets. It further involves the concentration on to the convoy system of every means of anti-submarine warfare – the gun, the submarine, the net, the depth charge, the mortar, the hydrophone, and wireless telegraphy. It aims at the utilisation of the slower, as well as of the faster anti-submarine craft for the convoy system, and it contemplates ultimately the provision of special salvage and life-saving craft and plant to accompany the convoys. The Memorandum also contains suggestions for investigations of technical character for combating the submarine, which may or may not be entirely new.[22]

Hankey ended his paper with the point of which Lloyd George invariably made much: 'Perhaps the best commentary on the convoy system is that it is invariably adopted for our main fleet, and for our transports.' During the meeting, as Hankey recorded, Jellicoe and Duff 'resisted a good deal,' but he thought that the discussion had done some good. Newbolt, however, notes that the paper did not bring Lloyd George and the Admiralty any closer together. 'To the Admirals the paper read merely like an abstract statement of strategical principle;' they were considering not the principle itself but its effect on the disposition of the navy's forces. The subject was not immediately pressed further by the Prime Minister; for the moment the War Cabinet's attention was focused on the planned Nivelle offensive in France.[23]

Nothing more for the moment was done. Shipping losses continued to mount. Not even the announcement by the Germans of their introduction of unrestricted submarine warfare had prompted any rethinking in the Admiralty. In the last month before this came into effect, the U-boats had sunk 368,521 tons of shipping, and could soon be expected to double this figure. 46 U-boats were at sea on February 1; in the first week 35 ships were sunk in the Western Approaches and the English Channel alone. For the month of February, total losses reached 500,500 tons; in March the figure was 556,000 tons and in April it was 870,000 tons. By then there were over 70 U-boats at sea.

There was, of course, public disquiet about the submarine menace; but the official posture of the Government was reassuring. Jellicoe had made a speech at the Fishmonger's Company on January that the menace must and would be dealt with; of that he was confident. Beresford, speaking in a debate in the House of Lords on February 13, was similarly bullish, declaring that he had 'absolute and complete faith in the ability of the present Board of Admiralty successfully to combat the German submarines.' On February 21, watched by Jellicoe and by Fisher, Carson made his maiden speech as First Lord. He, too, was upbeat about the situation, expressing his confidence that 'in the development of measures which have been and are being devised its seriousness will by degrees be greatly mitigated.[24] All this sort of thing greatly cheered the Press; the *Morning Post* next day observed that 'the country imposes an absolute confidence in the Board of Admiralty and in the Admirals at sea. The country is right, for never has it been better served.' For the *Spectator*, Carson's statement had been 'thoroughly informing, bracing, and reassuring.' Just how misplaced all this nonsense was must surely have been apparent to Jellicoe and his colleagues, but for the moment they were not under pressure, either from Lloyd George and the War Cabinet or from public sentiment.

The grim reality of the situation, as the shipping losses remorselessly increased, meant that this honeymoon for the new Board of Admiralty could not last long. In April there began to be heard mutters of anxiety in the Press, and it was not long before this gave rise once again to a rising demand for the recall of Fisher, who was seen by many in the Press and elsewhere as the one man who had the necessary genius to defeat the German submarine fleet. On January 31 he had offered to serve under Jellicoe as Third Sea Lord and Controller, with a brief to do just that. Jellicoe, after thinking it over, turned the proposal down, writing to Fisher on February 13:

> I have thought a great deal over the suggestion which you made to me during your visit, but I have been forced to the conclusion that it would not be practicable for such a scheme to be adopted. There are only two posts which, in my opinion, you could hold here – those of First Lord or First Sea Lord. In any other position, I cannot help feeling that difficulties are bound to arise.[25]

Fisher, hugely disappointed, was also extremely angry, not just with Jellicoe, but with the entire Board of Admiralty and the War Staff. Hall, the Director of the Intelligence Department, was 'a peculiarly incompetent crank – nearly a lunatic.' Tudor, the Third Sea Lord 'ought to go,' and the sooner the better.' Oliver's faulty strategy had failed, and he had also failed to force the other two 'to do their business, so he too ought to go.' All this was set out in a letter to an unknown addressee in February, and he continued to rage against the Admiralty in the following weeks.[26]

Jellicoe, while allowing Carson and others to offer their generally encouraging views to the public, was privately even more pessimistic than ever. On February 21 he submitted a paper to the War Cabinet to the effect that so far 'no complete and practicable cure for the submarine menace has been, or is likely to be, discovered short of the destruction of the bases, which is obviously a military measure of great magnitude.'[27] In his memoirs, somewhat ingenuously, Jellicoe wrote of the early part of 1917 that it was impossible to effect any fresh means of dealing with submarine warfare for many months, because of the time required for production; 'all that could be done was to try new methods of approach to the coast' and, as he went on, to extend the convoy system already in force for the French coal trade and the Scandinavian trade.

However, Henderson's experimental convoys, running between Mount's Bay and Brest, Weymouth and Cherbourg, and Weymouth and Le Havre were beginning to show impressive results. Crossings took place daily; they sailed either in groups proceeding by special route instructions or under the escort of armed trawlers. Eleven of these protected the Mount's Bay convoys; fifteen covered the two Weymouth routes. In the three months ending on May 31 4016 ships were convoyed and only nine lost.[28]

In addition to this, there had also been a very considerable success in limiting the losses to shipping operating between Scandinavia and the North Sea ports. On December 15 1916, in an effort to placate Norwegian and Swedish ship owners, the Admiralty had instituted a system of 'protected' or 'controlled' sailings between Norway and the Shetlands, which came into effect at the end of January. The Naval Staff Monograph *Home Waters: December 1916 to April 1917* recorded February 24 1917 as 'a date of no small importance in the history of the war. On it sailed the first convoy from Lerwick to Bergen.'[29] However, the system of controlled sailings did not at first work well. A conference met at Longhope, in the Orkneys, on April 4, and it unanimously recommended that a full convoy system should be introduced. Convoys would consist of a maximum of nine vessels, with an escort of two destroyers, a submarine if available, and four to six armed trawlers. When Beatty received the report of the conference, he forwarded it to the Admiralty with a strong endorsement.[30]

Lloyd George was relieved to learn that the Admiralty had on April 11 agreed to allow Scandinavian convoys to run on an experimental basis. This, together with the success of Henderson's coal trade convoys, would, he hoped, lead to a more proactive stance on the part of the Admiralty. In this, however, he was disappointed. Jellicoe reported regularly to the War Cabinet, but his reports almost entirely consisted of accounts of single ship actions with U-boats. His gloom was increasing. In response to a War Cabinet enquiry in March about the possible introduction of convoy, he replied only that the matter was still being considered.

In March, however Henderson's discovery of the misleading nature of the Admiralty's statistics began to erode the blind obstinacy of those at the top. Lloyd George noted that, far from a weekly figure of 2,500 arrivals, the actual number was about 140; this could easily be handled in the arrival ports under convoy arrangements. It also meant that the number of escorts required would be far less than had previously been supposed. Even this, however, did not alter the Admiralty's official position; on April 22 Jellicoe wearily put before the War Cabinet a paper saying that 'the only immediate remedy that was possible was the provision of as many destroyers and other patrol vessels as could be provided by the United States.' He did not mention convoys.[31] Inside the Admiralty, the introduction of convoy was not proceeded with, according to Duff, 'owing to strongly adverse criticism from both Naval and Mercantile Officers. The more experienced the officer the more damning was the opinion expressed against mercantile convoy.'[32] Ship owners, too, were opposed to convoy; the Admiralty continued to be impressed by their arguments as to delays that that would be caused by its introduction. Another argument, which in April became largely irrelevant with the entry of the United States into the war, was that the assembly of a convoy in a neutral port could legally be objected to by a national government on the ground that this might 'attract foreign combatants to their national waters.' They could create such administrative difficulties as to make the work of assembling a convoy almost impossible.[33]

Jellicoe's pessimism about the overall situation had been dramatically expressed in his meeting with the American Rear Admiral William S Sims, who had come to London to discuss how best the United States could cooperate with Britain's naval war effort. On April 10 Jellicoe gave him a note of the actual and anticipated losses of merchant shipping tonnage in February-April. Sims was astounded. He had never imagined anything so terrible. It looked, he said to Jellicoe, as if the Germans were winning the war:

> 'They will win, unless we can stop these losses – and stop them soon,' the Admiral replied. Is there no solution for the problem?' I asked. 'Absolutely none that we can see now.' Jellicoe announced. He described the work of the destroyers and other anti-submarine craft, but he showed no confidence that they would be able to control the depredations of the U-boats.[34]

The War Cabinet discussed the situation on April 23 and again on April 25. Jellicoe's paper of April 22 made a marked impression. Lloyd George referred to Beatty's endorsement of the adoption of a convoy system. Jellicoe repeated that the matter was under consideration, again referring to the lack of sufficient destroyers. Lloyd George had had enough. After discussing it privately with Carson, he announced to the War Cabinet that he proposed to visit the Admiralty on April 30 'and there take peremptory action on the question of convoys.' He stipulated that he would require the attendance of any officers, whatever their rank, from whom he desired information.[35]

When he got there, however, he found that he was pushing at an open door. The ice at last had begun to break up. On the evening of April 25, after the War Cabinet meeting, Duff came to Jellicoe's room at the Admiralty. Reflecting on the apparently unstoppable rise in the rate of merchant shipping losses, he had come to the conclusion that a general system of convoy must be tried. Jellicoe asked him to draw up a minute embodying this recommendation which Duff submitted to him on the following day:

> It seems to me evident that the time has arrived when we must be ready to introduce a comprehensive scheme of convoy at any moment. The sudden and large increases of our daily losses in merchant ships, together with the experience we have gained of the unexpected immunity from successful submarine attack in the case of the French coal trade, afford sufficient reason for believing that we can accept the many disadvantages of large convoys with the certainty of a great reduction in our present losses. Further, the United States having come into the war eliminates some of the apparently insuperable difficulties to a comprehensive scheme of convoy. The number of vessels roughly estimated in the attached paper as the minimum necessary for escort work is large, but the necessity of further safeguarding our food supply is becoming vital. The attached paper is merely an outline proposal giving certain figures to enable a decision to be given as to whether the scheme is to be proceeded with and worked out in detail. The work will be heavy, and if approved, I suggest the appointment of a Captain for a special purpose, in the first place to work out the scheme and afterwards to superintend its practical application.[36]

The paper made little attempt to save the face of those who had argued so long and so stubbornly against the introduction of a convoy system. Jellicoe resisted not at all, approving the minute on the following day.

Thus when Lloyd George visited the Admiralty on April 30 he discovered that the battle he had come to fight was already won. He found the Board in a chastened mood:

> Apparently the prospect of being overruled in their own sanctuary galvanised the Admiralty into a fresh inquisition, and by way of anticipating the inevitable they further examined the plans and figures which Commander Henderson had prepared in consultation with Mr Norman Leslie of the Ministry of Shipping.[37]

The Prime Minister was thus enabled to report back to the War Cabinet that he had been gratified to find that Duff 'had completely altered his view in regard to the adoption of a system of convoy' and that Jellicoe shared his view, at least to the extent of experiment. Lloyd George did not, however, think that Jellicoe and Duff really believed in the principle of a convoy system, and he realised that ceaseless pressure on the Admiralty would continue to be necessary. The suggestion that it was his impending visit which had led to the Admiralty's change of position, which Lloyd George made in his *Memoirs,* naturally caused extreme offence. Carson told the *Morning Post* in 1934 that this was 'the biggest lie ever was told;' and Duff wrote of 'the monstrous charge we are asked to believe is that on a threat of "act or go" the naval chiefs turned a complete somersault in order to retain their position.'[38] It was, he said, the rising loss of ships, and America's entry into the war, that prompted his minute to Jellicoe, and was unconnected with Lloyd George's visit. Marder sees no reason to doubt Duff's view; Roskill on the other hand, suggests that the Admiralty must have been perfectly aware that convoy would be on the agenda on April 30. He does, however, point out that Lloyd George had had Hankey's memorandum for six weeks before forcing the issue, and that it is unfair that he should have all the credit for saving the country from the Admiralty's ineptitude.[39]

At all events, the visit to the Admiralty appears to have passed off entirely agreeably, as Hankey recorded:

> This morning LL.G. and I went to the Admiralty and spent the whole day there very pleasantly lunching with Adl. Jellicoe and his wife and four little girls – LL.G. having a great flirtation with a little girl of three. I spent the whole evening up to 8.30 dictating a long and epoch-making report, embodying a large reconstruction of the Admiralty and more especially of the Adty. War Staff.[40]

Hankey's paper would, in due course lead to a major reorganisation at the Admiralty. For the moment, the convoy issue had been decided; but it had not at all resolved the Prime Minister's serious reservations about the Admiralty, and he was determined to do something about it.

In the meantime Jellicoe had decided to make a major effort to impress on his political masters just how serious the naval position was, and to attempt to make them consider it from a naval perspective. It was, Winton considers, 'the last message from the old pre-convoy world, the last despondent account before the end of an era.' Addressed to Carson on April 27, Jellicoe's memorandum expressed the fear that the War Cabinet was not as yet fully impressed with the gravity of the situation. He put the matter bluntly; Newbolt describes the paper as a document of great historical importance, 'because it is the only statement we possess, written with complete knowledge and the highest responsibility of the one mortal danger which has ever threatened this country in war.'[41] This perhaps is putting it a little high; but it was certainly Jellicoe's intention to make his point as emphatically as he could. Observing that it was for the Government to decide the policy of the war, it was his duty, he said, to advise whether the Navy was in a position to give effect to that policy. He wrote his memorandum in the hope that, through the First Lord, its contents might have some influence on the War Cabinet. The government should, he wrote, shape its policy in the light of the true situation:

> The real fact of the matter is this. We are carrying on the war at the present time as if we had the absolute command of the sea, whereas we have not such command or anything approaching it. It is quite true that we are masters of the situation so far as surface ships are concerned, but it must be realised – and realised at once – that this will be quite useless if the enemy's submarines paralyse, as they do now, our lines of communication. History has shown from time to time the fatal results of basing naval and military strategy on an insecure line of communications. Disaster is certain to follow, and our present policy is heading straight for disaster. It is useless and dangerous in the highest degree to ignore that fact.[42]

By the time the War Cabinet had read this, Duff's memorandum of April 27 had been approved. In it he proposed convoy for all vessels, (except for those capable of above fifteen knots), including British, Allied and neutral, from North and South Atlantic ports to the United Kingdom. They would assemble at 'Convoy Depots' at Gibraltar, Dakar, Louisbourg and Newport News, and appropriate escorts would be provided for the various stages of their journey.

The first convoy was intended to sail from Gibraltar about ten days after the new policy was approved; it would contain no more than twenty ships, and would include only the slower steamers. It was assembled by May 7, and what was to become a standard conference of the ships' masters was held on the same day, so that they should be aware of what was required of them in the matters of signalling, station keeping and limiting funnel smoke. The convoy sailed on May 10, in three columns. No submarines were encountered before the ships finally arrived in the Downs on May 22, after a passage of two days less than would have been the case if they sailed singly. They were escorted at various times by two Q-ships, three armed yachts, a flying boat and four destroyers.[43] The exercise was regarded by the Admiralty as having been a success. In principle it had been agreed to set up a scheme for transatlantic convoys; but here the Admiralty encountered a problem. In Washington, the Navy Department had serious misgivings. Evidently cooperation with the new ally was not going to be entirely straightforward. Commodore Gaunt, the British Naval Attaché, reported that the Navy Department considered that the hazards of attempting convoy such as fog, gales, inexperience and general tension were very great; nonetheless the Department was 'most courteous and evidently very anxious to fall in with the Admiralty's views.'[44] In the end the first convoy, of twelve ships, sailed from Hampton Roads on May 24.

30

America Enters the War

The participants in the momentous Crown Council meeting at Pless were in no doubt that the decision to introduce unrestricted submarine warfare meant, as Gerhard Ritter has put it, 'that the great power beyond the seas would now be inevitably swept into the war, torn from its traditional isolationism.'[1] It also meant, as Ritter observes, that 'for Germany it was a turn that not only tragically prolonged its grim struggle, but made that struggle truly hopeless in a military sense.' Bethmann-Hollweg, seeing all too clearly what was to come, contemplated resignation; but seeing this as a kind of desertion, which would have the effect of passing all power over both domestic and foreign policy to the military, felt his duty was to stay on.

In Washington the German Ambassador, Count von Bernstorff, was dismayed when confidentially told the news of the U-boat decision. He was told that he could not pass the information to the US Government until January 31; his plea for a month's postponement to allow a period of grace for American vessels already at sea, and to allow President Wilson's mediation efforts to continue, fell on deaf ears. Bernstorff knew what the consequence would be. Indeed, the US Secretary of State, Robert Lansing, was hoping for just such a development, as he wrote in his diary:

> War is certain to come, but we must wait patiently for the Germans to do something that will cause general indignation and clearly show all Americans the dangers of a German victory. When that time comes, it will be on account of some German stupidity … I hope these German fools will soon blunder into it, for without a doubt the Allies in the west are having a hard time of it, while Russia is making no progress, despite its masses.[2]

Lansing was an important influence on United States policy towards Britain, described by one observer as 'an able lawyer, wise, far sighted, level headed and a steady friend of the Allies.'[3]

Although diplomatic relations between the United States and Germany were at once broken off, and the ambassadors withdrawn, it was another two months before Wilson finally reached the decision to declare war. He still hoped that somehow war might be averted; that Germany might realise what it had done, and draw back from the brink. It was not to be. On February 26 Wilson asked Congress for authority to arm American merchantmen. As late as March 27, in conversation with his particular adviser and confidant Colonel House about a declaration of war, he is said to have cried out: 'What else can I do? Is there anything else I can do?' There was not, and on April 2 Wilson went before a special session of Congress to advise that it declare that the German actions constituted war against the United States. In his speech he declared: 'The world must be made safe for democracy. Its peace must be planted upon the tested foundations of political liberty.'[4]

Thus a war proceeded which Germany and her allies might well have won but which she must now almost inevitably lose. Only if the unrestricted U-boat campaign was even more successful than its authors hoped was there now any prospect that Britain and her Allies would contemplate throwing in the towel, and that success would have to be achieved within a very few months indeed.

Well before the American declaration of war, Rear Admiral Sims had departed for London. He was to become a profoundly influential figure in the conduct of the naval war. Born in 1858 in Ontario, Canada, he graduated from the US Naval Academy in 1880. After a period of sea service, in which he became a gunnery specialist, he served three overseas assignments as a Naval Attaché, and then became a Naval Aide to President Theodore Roosevelt. The latter was extremely impressed with Sims, and appointed him Inspector of Target Practice. Well known as an extreme Anglophile, Sims had some years before the war got into trouble for the outspokenness of his remarks about the relationship between Britain and the United States. In February he had become President of the Naval War College, having previously been in command of the battleship *Nevada*; at the end of March, with the outbreak of war apparently inevitable, he was summoned to Washington. He described what followed:

> The Department … wished me to leave immediately for England, to get in touch with the British Admiralty, to study the naval situation and learn how we could best and most quickly cooperate in the naval war. At this moment we were still technically at peace with Germany.. Mr Daniels, the Secretary of the Navy, therefore thought it wise that there should be no publicity about my movements.[5]

He was to remain ostensibly as head of the War College, where his family would continue to occupy the official residence, and to sail on a merchant vessel, in civilian clothes under a false name.

Sims arrived in London on April 10, after a scare in which the vessel in which he was travelling hit a mine as it approached Liverpool. He brought with him a belief that in the circumstances it was impossible for Germany to win the war; the Allies had practically an unchallenged command of the sea, 'and that in itself, according to the unvarying lessons of history, was an absolute assurance of ultimate victory.' Sims then had his first and thoroughly unsettling meeting with Jellicoe on April 10; he came to it quite certain that the British fleet had the situation well in hand:

> Yet a few days spent in London clearly showed that all this confidence in the defeat of the Germans rested upon a misapprehension. The Germans, it now appeared, were not losing the war – they were winning it. The British Admiralty now placed before the American representative facts and figures which it had not given to the British press. These documents disclosed the astounding fact that, unless the appalling destruction of merchant tonnage which was then taking place could be materially checked, the unconditional surrender of the British Empire would inevitably take place within a few months.[6]

Sims knew Jellicoe well; they had first met in China in 1901 and, both being gunnery specialists, soon became fast friends. The admiration he felt for Jellicoe's character and intelligence was, he wrote, something which he never lost:

> He was then, as he has been ever since, an indefatigable worker, and more than a worker, for he was a profound student of everything which pertained to ships and gunnery, and a man who joined to a splendid intellect the real ability of command. I had known him in his own home with his wife and babies, as well as on shipboard among his men, and had observed at close hand the gracious personality which had the power to draw everyone to him and make him the idol both of his own children and the officers and jackies of the British fleet.[7]

Jellicoe reciprocated this friendship and admiration, observing not only that his new colleague held the soundest views, but that he was 'able, by dint of the tact and persuasive eloquence that had carried him successfully through his gunnery difficulties, to impress his views on others.'[8] The arrival of such a man afforded the hope of a particularly fruitful and effective cooperation. Sims, however, had to guard against the impression back home that his Anglophilia led him too readily to acquiesce in the demands of his British friends. Admiral Benson, the Chief of Naval Operations, had found it necessary to use strong words to Sims before his departure to London: 'Don't let the British pull the wool over your eyes. It is none of our business pulling their chestnuts out of the fire. We would as soon fight the British as the Germans.'[9]

While Sims was thus meeting with Jellicoe, the British and French commanders in the West Indies, Admirals Browning and Grasset, had gone to Washington for a meeting with Benson and two other American admirals. This produced a number of important agreements. The US would maintain flying squadrons in both the North and South Atlantic, and would patrol their own coastal waters. Their forces in the Far East would remain on station. Some small patrol boats would go to the French coast and, perhaps most importantly, six destroyers would be sent to European waters.[10] Meanwhile the Germans, in a futile attempt to avoid inflaming American opinion, had withheld any operations on the American coast or any attacks upon American shipping in the blockade zone around the British Isles. This restraint continued until May 22, when Holtzendorff lifted the embargo on such attacks.

The six destroyers of the 8th Destroyer Division, led by Commander Taussig, sailed from Boston on April 24, arriving at Queenstown on May 4, where they were placed under the command of Admiral Sir Lewis Bayly, who was Commander-in-Chief of the west coast of Ireland. In due course Sims was to forge a close friendship with Bayly, and this was by no means the least of his wartime achievements, since Bayly was renowned for being an extremely difficult man to deal with.[11] Sims was invariably sensitive to the importance of cultivating good relations, as he wrote to his friend Captain William Pratt in the Navy Department on June 7:

> I believe there is no case on record where Allies have cooperated together for any considerable length of time without more or less serious friction. I am out to make an exception … There has been to date material for any amount of friction, due to peculiar personalities, but I believe that they [disputes] have been successfully overcome. That other causes [of tension] will arise is perfectly certain … if we can get by these for a certain length of time, so as to really get into the game with these people, all danger of friction will disappear.[12]

Page, the American Ambassador in London, was delighted with the excellent impression which Sims had made on his arrival. It was, however, not long before Benson's suspicions that Sims was under the thumb of his British hosts were aroused; he commented that Sims and others were obsessed with all things British.

Meanwhile an important ministerial mission, headed by Balfour and including representatives of key departments, had arrived in Washington. The Admiralty member of the mission was de Chair, who had been so dismayed to be taken from the Northern Patrol. Before he left, de Chair had spoken to Sims, who warned him that he would find it very difficult to convince the Navy Department at Washington how necessary it was that they should lend all their destroyers to us.'[13] The warning proved well founded, and it was only after repeated discussions of the issue that Franklin D Roosevelt, the Assistant Secretary of the Navy, was able to overcome his colleagues' reluctance and obtained agreement for 36 destroyers to be sent. Balfour's mission had, overall, proved a great success; de Chair was rewarded, in September, with the command of the Third Battle Squadron at the Nore where he hoisted his flag in *Dreadnought*.

Sims soon became intimately familiar with leading politicians and others, in addition to his professional colleagues at the Admiralty. He got on particularly well with the King, and was impressed by 'his familiarity with all naval questions and the intimate touch which he was evidently maintaining with the British fleet.'[14] Generally, Sims found that most of the influential men in British public life were extremely pessimistic. The exception was Lloyd George:

> I met the Prime Minister frequently at dinners, at his own country place and elsewhere, and the most lasting impression which I retain of this wonderful man was his irrepressible gaiety of spirits. I think of the Prime Minister of Great Britain as a great, big, exuberant boy, always laughing and joking, constantly indulging in repartee and by-play, and even in this crisis, perhaps the darkest one of British history, showing no signs of depression.[15]

Lloyd George's readiness to remain cheerful, and to entertain his colleagues with humorous anecdotes, reminded Sims of Lincoln at the darkest moments of the American Civil War. His picture of the Prime Minister, however, was not one which would have been recognisable to his colleagues at the British Admiralty.

Almost at once Sims had grasped the importance of introducing a convoy system, and got to work on the Admiralty. His influence there on the issue was probably considerable. It was apparent that, once the decision had been taken, a good deal more assistance would be required from the United States, and Sims was obliged constantly to press Secretary of the Navy Daniels for more escorts. By June 21 he was writing in extreme terms:

> I consider it my duty to report that if we cannot offer more immediate actual assistance, even to the extent of sending the majority of the vessels patrolling our own coastlines which cannot materially affect the general situation, we will fail to render the service to the Allied cause which future history will show to have been necessary.[16]

In response, Daniels assured Sims of his readiness to cooperate and to send every destroyer that could be spared. When Sims suggested that battleship and cruiser escorts would be required for protection against German raiders, however, the Navy Secretary was not so keen, quoting

Mahan's doctrine that the future of the United States must never be jeopardised by any disintegration of its main battle fleet.

The success of the earliest transatlantic convoys confirmed the advice which Sims had been consistently giving both to his own Navy Department and to the British Admiralty. By July 21 he was able to write to Daniels: 'The success of the convoys so far brought in shows that the system will defeat the submarine campaign if applied generally and in time.'[17] He was, however, mindful that it was the Grand Fleet that made the victory of the destroyer over the U-boat a possibility. Without its power to hold the High Seas Fleet in check, allied commerce would have been destroyed. The result would have been the surrender of the Allies, leaving the United States to face Germany alone, and to do so before it could assemble its resources and equip its armies:

> The world was preserved from all these calamities because the destroyer and the convoy solved the problem of the submarine and because back of these agencies of victory lay Admiral Beatty's squadrons, holding at arm's length the German surface ships while these comparatively fragile craft were saving the liberties of the world.[18]

Sims had soon been able to speak with much more authority than that of a liaison officer, however senior. In May, he was designated as the commander of the US destroyers based in Britain, with the rank of Vice Admiral, and in the following month he was appointed commander of all US Naval Forces in European Waters. His diplomatic position was confirmed when he was also, in December 1917, appointed as Naval Attaché at the London Embassy.

President Wilson had been a strong proponent of the idea of close blockade of the German submarine bases, something that Sims regarded as completely impracticable, and which he had hoped he had successfully squashed. Wilson, however, having remained silent on naval policy for the first three months of the war, had been harbouring a mounting discontent with the effectiveness of the British Admiralty. On July 3 he sent to Daniels a draft cable to Sims, following a letter of the previous day in which he wrote:

> As you and I agreed the other day, the British Admiralty had done nothing constructive in the use of their navy and I think it is time we were making and insisting on some plans of our own, even if we render some of the more conservative of our own naval advisors uncomfortable.[19]

Daniels noted in his diary that the President 'wanted offensive in submarine warfare and merchant ships to be convoyed. I wrote that England had decided to convoy.'[20] As David Trask observes, if the President was still unaware of the adoption of a convoy system, albeit experimentally, at this date, it was a sad commentary on the communication between the President's office and the Navy Department. At all events, the cable to Sims was sent on July 4. At the back of Wilson's mind there was an awareness of the Anglophilia of Admiral Sims, which he deemed it necessary to correct:

> From the beginning of the war I have been surprised by nothing so much as the failure of the British Admiralty to use Great Britain's great naval superiority in any effective way. In the presence of the present submarine emergency they are helpless to the point of panic.

> Every plan we suggest they reject for some reason of prudence. In my view this is not a time for prudence but for boldness even at the risk of great losses ... I would be very much obliged to you if you would report to me, confidentially of course, exactly what the Admiralty have been doing and what they have accomplished and add to this report your own independent judgments already arrived at on that side of the water ... I beg that you will keep these instructions absolutely to yourself and that you will give me such advice as you would give if you were handling an independent navy of your own.[21]

It was not a memorandum with which Lloyd George would have found much reason to disagree. Page, reporting the receipt by Sims of the cable, was reassuring, telling the President that Sims did not always or wholly agree with the Admiralty, which had made 'considerable reorganisations' on his advice, adding that 'They defer to him greatly.' Lloyd George, meanwhile, had employed Lord Northcliffe to ascertain American opinion on naval matters; he reported on the belief in the US that the British navy was inactive against submarines, and that a much more offensive policy should be adopted, including attacks on German bases, closure of the North Sea with nets and mines, and convoy through the submarine danger zone. Benson, he told the Prime Minister, was reluctant to see shipbuilding concentrated on anti-submarine vessels because he did not want delays in the battleship programme.

Sims replied promptly to Wilson's cable, sending a detailed response on July 11. He was sensitive to the implication that he had become the mouthpiece of the Admiralty:

> I wish to make it perfectly clear that my reports and dispatches have been in all cases an independent opinion based upon specific facts and data which I have collected in the various Admiralty and other Government Departments. They constitute my own conviction and hence comply with your request for an independent opinion.[22]

He went on to reiterate his view that close-in blockade and mining operations were impracticable. The war would, he said be decided by the success or failure of the submarine campaign; and he put forward seven suggestions as the basis of American naval policy. First, as much of the US fleet as possible should be sent to European waters. Secondly, the advance force should be committed to anti-submarine and convoy operations. Thirdly, supply and fuel ships should be prepared at once to support the land campaigns in Europe. Fourthly, naval construction should be concentrated on destroyers and light craft. Fifthly, all other construction should be concentrated on merchant shipping. Sixthly, the emphasis should above all be on convoy operations. Finally, an organisation should be established in London to oversee the actual fighting. In his paper he repeated his often expressed view that 'regardless of any future developments we can always count upon the support of the British Navy.' This last was not a view which Benson and Daniels shared, of course, and merely reinforced their suspicion that Sims remained dangerously Anglophile in his perceptions.

The idea of dispatching the main fleet to Europe was thoroughly objectionable to both men, and Daniels opposed it in reporting to the President; all the other points made by Sims were, he said, being acted upon. This was not entirely true; there were considerable reservations in Washington about the building up of an effective naval headquarters in London which, it was feared, would always be subject to undue British influence. Ultimately, however, Sims was able to create the kind of organisation which he had in mind.[23]

Sims did not give up on the question of the best utilisation of the main US battle fleet, although he recognised that this was a very sensitive issue. This was especially so after he learned from Pratt that the Navy Department had with a heavy heart resolved to postpone the battleship construction programme until the end of the war. Pratt, writing on July 2, warned Sims that it was seen as leaving the United States with its guard down in case of complications, and that that was where Sims came in; they trusted to his good offices, in his diplomatic way 'to make the solution safe for the future.'[24] Sims responded to Daniels' policy statement to the President tactfully. He argued that the US battle fleet must be seen as a reserve to the Grand Fleet. He accepted that shifting part of it to Europe transgressed the almost sacred principles of Mahan, and that caution was therefore understandable. But, he said, the war would be won or lost in European waters. The whole of the battle fleet could not go there, as there were insufficient destroyers to screen it; but a battle squadron could join the Grand Fleet as an advance force, and it could always recross the Atlantic if necessary.[25]

On July 19 Sims went with Jellicoe to pay a visit to the Grand Fleet, following which the First Sea Lord applied to the Navy Department for the dispatch of four coal burning battleships, with a screen of six destroyers, to join the Grand Fleet. This would allow a reshuffle of predreadnoughts after which the older vessels could be paid off, and their crews employed in anti submarine operations. Daniels and Benson would have none of it. With the support of Admiral Mayo, the commander of the US Atlantic Fleet, Benson decreed that, applying Mahan's doctrine, the American battleships should remain concentrated, certainly until the British Admiralty developed a more aggressive policy.

However, when Mayo came to Europe himself, ostensibly to improve relations with the Allied navies but also at Wilson's request to keep an eye on Sims, Jellicoe had an opportunity to renew his request for battleship support. This came after the Inter Allied Naval Conference of September 4/5, when the British put forward a scheme to block the channels used by U-boats when leaving port. A request was made for the ten oldest US predreadnoughts and eight old cruisers, to be sunk in the fairways.

Jellicoe went out of his way to empasise the scale of the operation that would be required:

> The scheme was one of vast magnitude and the blocking operation would necessitate the employment of all the old British battleships prior to *King Edward VII* class, all the French Battleships of older classes, all the Italian Battleships, and about 10 American battleships. Altogether there would have to be employed about 40 battleships, 43 old cruisers, and for the shallow part, to prevent exit of submarines, about 55 class *A*, 45 class *B* and 177 class *C* vessels. In addition it would necessitate the capture of Heligoland and Wangeroog.[26]

It is difficult to believe that he supposed that such a proposal was likely to go down well with his audience. Mayo, agreeing to put this before Benson, warned that it was unlikely to be agreed, and this proved to be the case. The Navy Department immediately lost interest in the close blockade idea, and the Admiralty were entirely content to abandon the proposal.[27]

Mayo's mission, following which he reported favourably on the work of Sims in London, greatly improved transatlantic relationships. Sims, for his part, wrote to Benson to explain that he recognised the difficulties, but that his complaints arose from his impatience, not ill feeling. Benson responded well, expressing his hope for better cooperation between them for the future and this, for the moment, proved to be the case. It enabled Sims to continue to press the case for US dreadnoughts to be sent to join the Grand Fleet. He pointed out to Pratt that German battle cruisers under construction were nearing completion, which was another good reason to make the reinforcement. In October the General Board of the Navy Department held hearings to consider the request, in the course of which it appeared that there was considerable uneasiness about the Japanese and what they might intend.[28]

Benson himself came to London in November; three days of talks with Jellicoe and Sims brought him round to their point of view, and on November 10 he cabled Daniels to suggest that the four dreadnoughts be despatched. It was, as he saw it, now a matter of prestige, and he was prepared to modify his interpretation of Mahan's doctrine. The principle thus bent, the British now sought to increase the size of the reinforcement, aiming at a total of ten battleships which, allowing for two in dock at any time, would constitute a complete squadron. For the moment, though, Jellicoe had to be satisfied with four, and on December 7 1917 Battleship Division Nine, commanded by Rear Admiral Hugh Rodman, steamed into Scapa Flow, after a testing passage across the Atlantic. It consisted of the flagship *Wyoming*, with *Florida, Delaware* and *New York*.[29]

Delaware was the oldest of these. Completed in 1910, she displaced 20,000 tons, and mounted ten 12 inch, fourteen 5 inch and four 3-pdr guns. She was capable of 21 knots. *Florida* was completed in the following year; she displaced 21,815 tons, and had a similar armament; her speed was 20.75 knots. *Wyoming* was completed in 1912, and was significantly larger at 26,000 tons displacement. She carried twelve 12 inch, and twenty one 5 inch guns. Her speed was 20.5 knots. All three of these ships had an 11 inch armoured belt, and 12 inch turret armour. *New York*, completed in 1913, was slightly larger again, at 27,000 tons. She carried ten 14 inch guns and twenty one 5 inch. She could do 21 knots. Her armoured belt was 12 inches, and her turret armour 14 inches. The first three were equipped with two torpedo tubes; *New York* had four.[30] All were coal burners, as requested; this was due to the oil shortage in the United Kingdom. These battleships, designated as the Grand Fleet's 6th Battle Squadron, represented a considerable reinforcement as well as a powerful symbol of Anglo-American cooperation. The Kentuckian Hugh Rodman had been well chosen to effect the integration of these ships into the Grand Fleet. He had a considerable reputation for seamanship, but he was also noted for his social skills, as one junior officer, later to command *Iowa* in the Second World War, described him:

> An excellent ship handler, quick witted, excellent at cribbage, played a good game of bridge ... He considered himself an authority on the qualities of Kentucky bourbon whiskey, and yielded to no one when it came to making a mint julep.[31]

Beatty got on extremely well with Rodman, and was soon able to give an encouraging report of the American battleships in a letter he wrote to the King on January 28 1918. He reported that they were gradually getting into the Grand Fleet's way of doing things, and were 'desperately keen.' Their signalling and wireless, however, was of 'a very primitive kind,' and there had been a wide ability range in their performance at target practice. Beatty hoped that the King would visit Rodman's squadron before long, which he was sure would be 'enormously appreciated not only by them but by the whole American Nation.'[32]

The development of a trustful relationship between the British and American navies went only so far. Benson and Daniels always retained a suspicion of British intentions, particularly looking ahead to the post war period; and for their part the British were prepared to disclose only a limited amount of information as to their intelligence sources, and particularly with regard to their ability to decrypt German signals. When Benson, on his trip to the United Kingdom, went north to visit Beatty and the Grand Fleet, Jellicoe was careful to instruct the latter as to how far he could go:

> You will find Benson very willing to help, but very ignorant of sea warfare. He has never had his flag up afloat and has odd ideas, but as I say he is very willing and friendly. He has agreed to send the 4 battleships but proposes changing them periodically. He does not know anything about our secret information and he will not be told, so please don't mention it. All he knows is that our secret service is very good. Will you warn Brock, etc, about this.[33]

Part IV

The Crisis of the Naval War

31

Admiral Bacon and the Dover Patrol

While the main battle fleets lay at anchor at their respective bases, scowling at each other from opposite corners of the North Sea, there was continuous activity around its periphery. In the north, the Northern Patrol continued its blockade operations, although in 1917 these were gradually winding down, and patrolled on constant watch for German raiders both outbound and inbound. The developing Scandinavian convoy system ran its regular transits across the North Sea, escorted by destroyers and armed trawlers. The Harwich Force engaged in frequent operations into the Bight – 'prowling around,' as Tyrwhitt put it – and continued its supervision and escort of the Dutch convoys.

And, in the south eastern corner of the North Sea, there was constant activity in and around the Dover Straits. This zone was of crucial importance; across it passed the troopships and supply ships vital to the operations of the Allied armies in France, which required protection at all times. The area for which the Dover Patrol was responsible lay on the left flank of the Allied armies, and was vulnerable to the German destroyers and submarines based at Zeebrugge and Ostend; it was a key point in the German war on commerce. Accordingly, the Dover Patrol provided plenty of copy for the national Press, which naturally focused much attention on its commander.

Rear Admiral Reginald Bacon had left the navy in 1910 to become Managing Director of the Coventry Ordnance Works, his last posting having been Director of Naval Ordnance at the Admiralty, and it was in this commercial position that he was still serving on the outbreak of War. Early in 1915, having volunteered for active service, he was supervising the 15-inch howitzers in France, which had been constructed at his factory; in April he was asked by Churchill and Fisher to take one of these out to the Dardanelles. Before, however, he could set off, he was recalled to London:

> I saw Mr Churchill, who asked me to take command of the Dover Patrol. I was not at all anxious to do so, as I was looking forward to going to the East; I knew nothing of Dover and the work being done there. Nevertheless, I left the next morning for Dover, and found that Rear Admiral Hood was no more anxious to go in charge of a division of light cruisers off the Irish coast than I was to relinquish my guns. However, the change was made, and the next morning I took over the command, not without considerable misgivings, as I understood from Lord Fisher that the tenure of the Dover Command varied directly with the number of submarines sunk! Apparently this was to be quite independent of the

> difficulty of the problem of tackling them, which was one to which, at that time, not much attention had been given.[1]

Bacon was highly regarded by Churchill and Fisher; he had served as the latter's Naval Assistant in 1904-1905, and the First Sea Lord had described him as 'the cleverest officer in the navy.' It was not long before, in Fisher's eyes, he was living up to expectations; he wrote to Jellicoe, who was also one of Bacon's admirers, in 1915: 'Bacon is so splendidly energetic in the Dover Straits that no more submarines come that way.'[2]

Bacon's appointment was not universally looked on with favour. His popularity in the service had been damaged with the publication of letters he had written from the Mediterranean to Fisher during the latter's first stint as First Sea Lord, while he was serving under Beresford. The issue arose because Fisher, in 1906, had sought the opinion of junior officers in the Mediterranean Fleet as to the mood of seamen and officers and their reaction to his reforms. Two of them, Troubridge and Bacon, obliged by writing letters; a third, Sturdee, claimed that he had indignantly refused to do so. Bacon wrote six or seven letters; in none of these did he made specific criticisms of senior officers. He did, however, pass on to Fisher the comments made to him by the Prince of Wales, adding a comment of his own suggesting that Beresford and Lambton had been complaining about the reforms.[3] In another letter he told Fisher that the King and Prince of Wales still supported him, 'although they were very much disturbed at the Service agitation headed by Lord Charles Beresford and Admiral Lambton.'

The existence of these letters only became known because of the publication of one of them by Sir George Armstrong, an opponent of Fisher who in 1909 was campaigning for election to Parliament. It created an instant furore, with a lengthy series of questions raised in the House of Commons prompted by Beresford's supporters. Fisher, accused of having instituted a system of spying on fleet commanders, was ably defended by the First Lord, Reginald Mckenna. Bacon insisted that his authorship of the letters, which Armstrong had not revealed, should be mentioned in the Commons; McKenna did so, saying:

> The letter in question was written by Captain RH Bacon … I have read the letter; it is a perfectly proper letter to have been written by Captain Bacon and I cannot find in it the smallest ground for any of the calumnious charges which have been based upon it. It contains no opinion of Captain Bacon of any officers of the Fleet.'[4]

Both the original incident, and the extent to which it affected the perception of Bacon on the part of many naval officers, illustrate the polarising effect of the bitter fend between Fisher and Beresford and their respective supporters. It is impossible, of course, to assess the extent of the damage which this did to the service.

Tyrwhitt's reaction, in a letter to Keyes of April 25 1915, was not untypical: 'Hood has as I suspect you know been replaced by Bacon. It is a d – d shame but I believe Hood rather asked for trouble by his 'back chat' to their Lordships'.[5] Bacon's return to the navy, with his seniority intact, after having left it for a commercial appointment, did not go down well. De Robeck wrote to Keyes on the subject on August 14 1916:

> I am much annoyed to find that Bacon, a retired officer, is my senior in accordance with an Order in Council, if one is to be allowed to leave the Service *entirely* for one's own

> convenience and benefit and come back and take command over those who have worked on through the dull days; it seems as if there is not much object in serving except when convenient to one's self.[6]

Apart from twelve 'Tribal' class destroyers which arrived at Dover on the outbreak of war, the Dover Command was in its early days very poorly equipped. It collected together a remarkable array of different types of ship with which to discharge a complex range of responsibilities. These included monitors, destroyers, armed trawlers and drifters, paddle mine sweepers, armed yachts, motor launches, coastal motor boats and submarines. It also employed land based aircraft, seaplanes and airships. The duties of the Dover Patrol, which soon established a high profile in the Press, included anti submarine patrols; the escorting of merchantmen, hospital ships and troopships; the laying of mines and the construction of mine barrages; sweeping minefields laid by the enemy; and the bombardment of German positions on the Belgian coast. It was, however, the war against the U-boat that was the Dover Patrol's most important function, as Bacon had been told at the outset of his appointment.

Hood had made efforts during October 1914 to bombard German positions, employing a motley collection of vessels, including the aged battleship *Revenge*; she mounted four 13.5-inch guns which, relined, were reduced to 12-inch. A slightly younger predreadnought, *Venerable,* joined the bombardment force briefly, but it proved a generally ineffective operation. In the summer of 1915, when the Dover Patrol had been reinforced by some specially designed monitors, bombardment was resumed. Six were ultimately delivered. The eight *Lord Clive* class monitors were 351¼ feet long, with a beam of 87¼ feet, and displaced 5,900 tons. They were equipped with two 12-inch guns, taken from the old battleships of the *Majestic* class. In addition, they carried up to four 6-inch and two 3-inch AA guns. They could crawl along at a maximum speed of eight knots. The four *Abercrombie* class monitors, slightly larger, carried two 14-inch guns, but were otherwise similar. Later there came the two ships of the *Marshal Ney* class and the two ships of the *Erebus* class; these later vessels carried two 15-inch guns as their main armament, and were somewhat larger. None of them had much in the way of protection, the deck armour being about 1½ inches, although slightly greater in the last two classes; they were all fitted with bulges.[7]

Bacon designed observation platforms to be fixed to the sea bed off the Belgium coast to spot the fall of shot from his monitors. On the night of August 15 1915, flying his flag in *Sir John Moore*, with *Lord Clive* and *Prince Rupert*, Bacon made his way to the position selected for the bombardment, escorted by destroyers, drifters, yachts and minesweepers. By daybreak the observation platforms were in position, and the bombardment commenced. The operation was repeated a number of times, although in September morning mists severely reduced visibility.[8] *Revenge,* which had in the meantime been renamed *Redoubtable* as her original name was required for a new battleship, joined the force on September 7. Two weeks later the unwieldy *Marshal Ney* arrived to take part, but her unreliable diesel engines failed, and she had to be towed back to Dunkirk.

Bacon became sceptical about the effectiveness of these operations, but the Admiralty insisted that they continue; difficulties of spotting remained, however, and in January 1916 he ordered the bombardments to cease until *Erebus* and *Terror* arrived with their 15-inch guns. In June, bombardments began again, in support of the Somme offensive; rumours that a landing on the Belgian coast was imminent were spread widely and, it appears, these did cause the German

High Command some apprehension. In 1917 a fresh series of bombardments was carefully planned, and began in April. The weather was, however, extremely adverse for much of April and May; during the rest of the year a number of bombardments were undertaken, with some success in destroying buildings in harbour installations; in October a U-boat torpedoed *Terror*, and in the same month *Erebus* was damaged by an electrically controlled motor boat.[9]

The raids by the German destroyer flotillas led by Michelsen and Goehle in October and November 1916, which so seriously damaged Bacon's credibility, have already been described. One significant advantage possessed by the Germans was their ability to deploy more modern destroyers, whereas those available to the Dover Patrol were to a considerable extent elderly and outdated. Destroyer flotillas could temporarily be released from the High Seas Fleet, to make their way along the coast to the Belgian bases, before commencing an operation, and could then return. It had proved disadvantageous permanently to station a large number of destroyers at Zeebrugge due to the danger of air attacks; it was necessary to send them up the canal to Bruges, a process which took an unacceptable time.[10]

Michelsen's raid in October 1916 had, however, led to a prolonged investigation by the British Admiralty into the way in which the attack by the German destroyers had been met. In general, it had approved Bacon's dispositions and strategy. However, Courts of Inquiry into the losses suffered were critical of the tactics adopted by the *Tribal* destroyers:

> The *Tribal* destroyers proceeded to sea without any previous formation or orders; some left by the eastern and some by the western entrance; and as soon as they got outside they proceeded to lose touch with one another.[11]

Forwarding the minutes of these Inquiries to the Admiralty, Bacon expressed his approval of the tactics employed, remarking that it was far more important to get boats early to the point at which the drifters were being attacked than for them to hold back and wait for others. The Admiralty did not agree:

> All experience of night fighting in this war has shown that it is absolutely essential to keep the forces concentrated at night in order to avoid the great danger of our vessels mistaking one another for enemy ships. They consider that in all circumstances destroyers proceeding at night to gain touch with an enemy should be kept in company, and that it is further essential that, if two separate forces are working from different bases, each should, on dark nights, be confined to certain areas so as to avoid the possibility of meeting one another.[12]

The principal objective of the German destroyer raids was the so called 'Dover Barrages.' In April 1916 Bacon, in an effort to protect his monitors from U-boat attacks, had conceived the idea of running a net barrage ten miles offshore for the whole length of the Belgian coast. He was convinced that with the aid of the deep sea fishermen who manned the drifters which would patrol the nets, it would be feasible. He described his thinking thus:

> The danger to the monitors lay chiefly in attack by submarines; the net barrage would be an efficient protection provided such an attack were made from the shore flank of the patrol, and the 12-pounder destroyers having one flank only to guard, should be able to ward off submarines on the other flank, the one that was open to the North Sea. It was, however,

> also necessary to guard against a sudden daylight attack by cruisers. Speaking generally, the shoals to seaward provided a good measure of defence, but there was still a considerable area of open water by which large ships could approach the patrol line.[13]

The barrage itself consisted of nets carrying mines; Bacon's solution to the problem of its protection was to lay two rows of mines, at different depths, close inshore of the net line. He considered that 'the whole scheme was a rather pretty self compensating arrangement.'

In September the Admiralty took up the concept as a way of controlling U-boat access to the Channel and began to lay a similar barrage of mine nets across the Channel from the southern end of the Goodwin Sands to the south western end of the Outer Ruytingen Shoals. The barrage thus lay just to the east of the line Dover-Calais. It was protected by a line of deep mines laid half a mile to the west of the barrage, These mines, however, dragged into the nets and were accordingly a danger to the drifters on patrol. This barrage was not completed until December 1916, but in the event did not prove an effective barrier to submarines.[14]

Jellicoe, pondering the difficulties faced by the Dover Patrol in meeting German destroyer attacks, saw the latter as possessing a considerable superiority:

> The enemy, who possessed the incalculable advantage of the initiative, had at his disposal, whenever he took heart to plan an attack, a force of at least twenty-two very good destroyers, all unfortunately of higher speed than anything one could bring against them, and more heavily armed than many of our destroyers. This force was based within seventy miles of Dover, and as the Germans had no traffic of any sort to defend, was always available for offensive operations against our up and down or cross Channel traffic. Our Dover force was inferior even at full strength, but owing to the inevitable absence of vessels under repair or refitting and the manifold duties imposed upon it, was bound to be in a position of marked inferiority in any night attack undertaken by the Germans against any objective in the Straits.[15]

Towards the end of February 1917 the Germans planned another attack. By now, mindful of the inferiority described by Jellicoe, Bacon's force had been considerably strengthened. On February 25 it consisted of two light cruisers, two flotilla leaders (*Broke* and *Faulkner*), twelve *L*, four *H* and one *I* class destroyers, which with *Viking* and two monitors were stationed on the Dover side of the Straits. In addition there were the older destroyers and patrol boats employed on escort duties and traffic control.[16] For their latest venture the Germans adopted a different plan of attack, widely dispersing their force in order to attack a number of targets. These were the traffic route between England and the Hook, the Downs anchorage, and the outpost forces on the Channel barrage. Against the Dutch traffic route there was sent the second Zeebrugge Half Flotilla; the first Half Flotilla under Commander Konrad Albrecht was aimed at the Downs, while the VI Flotilla under Commander Tillessen was to attack the barrage. These forces sailed between 6.00 and 7.00 pm on February 25.

On this occasion Room 40 failed for once to detect the German movement. The weather was fine but overcast, and the four day old moon was hidden by clouds. The raid, however, proved ineffective. Tillessen's flotilla was encountered by the destroyer *Laverock* which, by remarkable good fortune, survived the meeting with little damage; Tillessen formed the view that he was in touch with a detachment of destroyers and, on intercepting *Laverock's* report of the contact, concluded that his intended surprise attack on Dover must be abandoned, and he returned to base. Albrecht, having unwisely detached two destroyers towards the Gull, achieved little, briefly bombarding Margate and Westgate. His two destroyers, whose presence was not detected, escaped the advancing destroyers from Dover which Bacon had sent to sea. The remaining half flotilla also returned to base without having achieved anything significant.

Three weeks later Tillessen tried again. On the night of 17/18 March he launched the VI Flotilla and the First Zeebrugge Half Flotilla (Commander Albrecht), totalling twelve destroyers, in a raid on the barrage, while the second Zeebrugge Half Flotilla, (Lieutenant Commander Zander) of four destroyers attacked shipping in the Downs. Adopting the same prescription as the British Admiralty, he gave each unit a separate line of operation. On this occasion Room 40 was able to give a warning that an operation was intended. The German destroyers sailed between 6.00 and 8.00 pm. Tillessen, steaming across the barrage to the east of the line he had himself prescribed, happened upon the destroyer *Paragon*; opening fire at once, Tillessen's destroyers launched torpedoes, one of which struck *Paragon's* engine room causing her depth charges to explode; she sank in minutes, leaving only two survivors.[17]

The destroyer *Llewellyn,* sighting the explosion, reported 'hearing firing from the direction of Calais;' *Laforey* thought a destroyer had been mined, and signalled *Llewellyn* for assistance. At this point Tillessen, who had turned back past the wreck of *Paragon*, came up with *Llewellyn; G87* and *S49* each fired a torpedo, one of which struck the British destroyer's fore part, bringing her to. Tillessen's guns had remained silent, leaving *Laforey's* captain now to conclude that both destroyers had been attacked by a submarine. Meanwhile Zander had found the merchant vessel *Greypoint* anchored a mile east of Broadstairs Knoll, sinking her with a torpedo. By the time any vessels of the Dover Patrol could get to the scene of either action, the German destroyers had slipped away.[18] Bacon reported gloomily to the Admiralty:

> The enemy need only keep a rigid lookout, when close to the Straits, for one hour, and fire a torpedo at everything he sees and run away … The enemy can vary the time of attack at will and choose their night. They can predetermine whether to 'shoot and scoot' or to carry out a more or less prolonged attack. The best disposition of my destroyers differs in each of these two forms of attack.[19]

The Germans now made a change not only in the units assigned to operate in the Channel, but also in the way in which operations were to be conducted. The III Flotilla(Commander Kahle) now took the place of the VI Flotilla, which returned to support the High Seas Fleet. Albrecht's destroyers were raised to full flotilla status and Assmann's torpedo boats, which had been largely successful in clearing the old Belgian coast barrage, were similarly reinforced.[20] Kahle was ordered to take command of all these forces, and to do so from the headquarters of the Naval Corps at Bruges. This was, as Newbolt observed, a new way of exercising command:

> We had certainly never centralised the control of offensive operations in the Flanders Bight, in anything like the same degree. During raids Admiral Bacon did, it is true, control the movements of our destroyers from ashore; but this was very different from what the Germans were doing. Admiral Bacon commanded from ashore when he was taking counter measures against a surprise attack; Commander Kahle was ordered to control a deliberately planned operation from an office, many miles away.[21]

The British Admiralty would, on occasion, abort or postpone an operation but once the ships were at sea the senior officer was in absolute control.

Kahle's first operation was not, however, destined to mark a success for the new system. Twelve modern destroyers, capable of 34 knots and armed with 4.1 inch or 3.4 inch guns, were launched on April 20 in two groups, one on each side of the Channel. There was no advance warning from Room 40 of an impending attack. On the French side, four British destroyers led by Commander Cardale patrolled to the east of the barrage, while at 7.45 pm the destroyer leaders *Broke* (Commander Evans) and *Swift* (Commander Peck) left Dover Harbour on a regular patrol to the South Goodwins. The German forces under Albrecht bombarded Calais at about 11.10 pm, and then drew off. At about 11.30 the northern group under Commander Gautier appeared off Dover, and began an ineffectual bombardment before turning eastwards.

On reflection, he seems to have thought he should achieve rather more than this, and for a while reversed his course; this took him straight towards the British forces, By 12.30 he was steaming towards the centre of the barrage when he met *Swift* and *Broke.* A fierce action broke out, in the course of which *Swift* torpedoed *G85*, while *Broke* rammed *G42*. Behind the latter came two more destroyers, which poured a heavy fire into *Broke* before making off. As *Broke* headed towards the blazing *G85,* the crippled destroyer opened fire; Commander Evans silenced her, but as he did so his engines failed, and his ship drifted closer to the wreck, which he feared might blow up and destroy them both.[22]

Soon, however, a further subdivision of destroyers came up from Dover, and took *Broke* in tow. It had been the first setback for the Germans for some time, having lost two destroyers in the action. Both *Broke* and *Swift* had also suffered seriously however, and were in dock for several weeks, having sustained a total of 45 killed and wounded. The press seized on the night's work, and thereafter *Broke's* captain was always known as 'Evans of the *Broke*.'[23]

Kahle, three days later, launched an attack against Dunkirk. A group of destroyers came down the coast and shelled the town for several minutes; turning for home, they encountered the French destroyer *Etendard,* and sank her after a brisk action, and severely damaged a patrolling trawler. The British monitors anchored off Dunkirk, and the destroyer *Greyhound,* opened fire on the enemy, but to no effect.[24]

Jellicoe had been monitoring Bacon's programme of bombardments of the Belgian coast, and was extremely impressed:

> The carefully organised arrangements made by Admiral Bacon for these coastal bombardments excited my warm admiration. He left nothing to chance, and everything that ingenuity could devise and patient preparation could assist was done to assure success.[25]

A rather more jaundiced view of Bacon's methods was taken by Admiral de Robeck, who had written to Keyes in the previous year to describe one of Bacon's operations; 'I went over with Bacon and saw all his show in France, quite interesting, but such a lot of 'swank' – a huge force under him carrying out a minor operation.'[26]

Jellicoe, however, during the visit of the commander of the US Atlantic Fleet, took Admiral Mayo and his staff to witness one of the bombardments of Ostend in September 1917. Bacon described the visit:

> It was a quaint experience for them. Half an hour after leaving Dunkirk in the *Broke* we lost sight of the shore. After an hour's steaming we sighted the *Terror* and destroyers in the open sea, and the motor launches just starting their smokescreen. Nothing else was in sight except a small monitor five miles away right out at sea, burning her searchlight as an aiming mark. Really our visitors must have thought we were humbugging when the *Terror* opened fire and fired single rounds at fixed intervals. While steaming about in the *Broke*, a few minutes after we had altered course three points, a splash came from a Tirpitz shell about 300 yards off; it fell very near the spot where we would have been if we had kept our original course.

The Tirpitz battery, established on the coast by the Germans, had been giving a lot of trouble to the bombarding units. Bacon jokingly apologised for not having maintained his course and thus given his visitors a near miss to report. Mayo cheerfully replied: 'Don't mention it, Admiral; by the time we get to New York that shell will have been close alongside right enough.'[27]

Bacon's efforts in the Channel continued to attract snide comments from those with a low opinion of him. Tyrwhitt wrote to Keyes at the end of 1918 to complain of his influence at the Admiralty:

> 'The Streaky One' has obsessed everyone at the Admiralty and does exactly what he pleases with them. I am not going to bore you with what he does and does not do, but you will understand when I tell you he is not a white man … I was also very sad when the streaky one got round JJ. The bug here said that you were going to Dover. I don't know what you would have said but I can imagine it would have suited you down to the ground.[28]

Richmond, likewise, was contemptuous of Bacon, and hoped that Keyes would succeed him. He wrote to Keyes on May 17 1917:

> If there's any chance of your going to Dunkirk in place of Porky, make a note that I should be more than delighted to serve under you in any capacity you would like. Porky *may* have saved his bacon by bombarding Zeebrugge after months of inactivity; but if this is only going to be a spasmodic effort it will be useless waste of energy. There will then be a great outcry as to why it has not been continued and he will have to shift.[29]

32

Shake up at the Admiralty

The visit of Lloyd George to the Admiralty on April 30 had consequences which went far beyond the policy to be adopted with regard to convoy. The attitudes which he there encountered confirmed his darkest fears as to the lack of an offensive spirit. Although he had reported that the views of the Admiralty were 'now in complete accord with the views of the War Cabinet' on the question, he was not in the least surprised to find that this was a considerable overstatement:

> Neither Admiral Jellicoe nor Admiral Duff really believed in the principle of convoys, though they were willing to assent to a cautious trial of this experiment. They had been convinced against their will and at heart remained of the same opinion still ... They acted as men whose doubts are by no means removed, and who therefore proceed with excessive caution and with an ill-concealed expectation that their forebodings will be justified by the experience. When anything went wrong with convoyed ships, it was reported with an 'I told you so' air to the War Cabinet.[1]

This experience left Lloyd George with the firm conviction that Jellicoe should be replaced. For the moment, however, that was not possible; Carson stood loyally behind the First Sea Lord and would entertain no question of his removal.

What was possible, though, was a major reorganisation of the administrative structure of the Admiralty, and Lloyd George at once pressed forward with this. The size of the Admiralty had enormously increased as the war went on; by the end of hostilities the total work force was 10,637, five times what it had been at the war's outbreak, and managing this put an enormous strain on the men at the top.[2] The problem was exacerbated by the fact that Jellicoe and Oliver in particular found it extremely difficult to delegate, due both to the traditions of the service and their own personalities.

There had, for some time, been a considerable press campaign calling for Admiralty reform, so Lloyd George had a considerable wind in his sails when he became involved in the process. With Hankey's active support, a scheme of reorganisation was presented to the War Cabinet on May 2. It was intended to relieve Jellicoe of responsibility for the materiel of the navy. This was to be achieved by the appointment of a Controller who would supervise the entire shipbuilding responses of Great Britain. At Hankey's suggestion, this took in the mercantile shipping programme hitherto the responsibility of the Ministry of Shipping. He would also set up an organisation which matched that of the Ministry of Munitions in its relationship to the Army.[3]

Lloyd George knew the man he wanted for this crucially important new post. Sir Eric Geddes had been a considerable success, first as Deputy Director-General of Munitions Supply in 1915-1916 and then as Director-General of Military Railways in France, with the honorary rank of Major General. His previous career, in business, had been in the railways, becoming Deputy General Manager of the LNER in 1911. In his new role he was to be supported by Rear Admiral Halsey, who replaced Tudor as Third Sea Lord. The new Fourth Sea Lord was to be Rear Admiral Tothill. Geddes was reluctant to take on the job, having no knowledge of the navy and its supply system, but Lloyd George overcame his diffidence, confident that he had the personality to get thing done. Sims shared this view, quickly coming to admire Geddes, observing that he 'acquired, in an astonishingly short time, a mastery of the details of naval administration;' he was, thought Sims, the 'type of man that we like to think of as American … a man after Roosevelt's heart – big, athletic, energetic, with a genius for reaching the kernel of a question and of getting things done.'[4] Within a month Jellicoe was noting that this last was certainly true.

Jellicoe had warmly welcomed the arrival of Geddes at the Admiralty, writing to Beatty on May 10:

> Eric Geddes comes here as Controller and takes over Third Sea Lord's and Assistant Civil Lord's duties subject of course to naval requirements being met. As to this Halsey will look out as Third Sea Lord. Leveson would never have accepted the job or suited it. I expect great increase in rapidity of production from the change. Geddes is a superman, an excellent fellow and has the complete whip hand of LG so we shall get all the steel we want. He will take over mercantile building too and thus bring it under Admiralty. This is an immense advantage. I am very sanguine of the result of the change. I spent a long time with Geddes in France talking and consulted Haig and those who have dealt with him.[5]

In reply, Beatty said that he was sorry that a civilian had had to be introduced, but that he was glad it was such a good one as Geddes. He assumed that it was important to go outside the Navy for political reasons, and hoped, a little doubtfully, that it would turn out all right.

The admirals, however, were by no means pleased by the award to Geddes of the temporary rank of Honorary Vice Admiral; Tyrwhitt thought it odd that a person could become 'a real live admiral by the stroke of a pen,' and there was some dismay when Geddes insisted on wearing his new uniform. The arrival with him of other civilians, especially from the railways, did not go down well either.

The reorganisation also extended to the Staff. Jellicoe now became Chief of the Naval Staff in addition to his post of First Sea Lord. He claimed later that the reorganisation came from within the Admiralty:

> In the early spring of 1917 the illogical nature of the War Staff organisation became apparent, in that it had no executive functions, and as the result of discussions between Sir Edward Carson and myself the decision was taken that the duties of the Naval Staff (the term decided upon in place of that of War Staff) should be made executive, and that the First Sea Lord should assume his correct title as Chief of the Naval Staff, as he had, in fact, already assumed the position.[6]

Oliver and Duff became respectively Deputy Chief and Assistant Chief of the Naval Staff. They would continue to work with Jellicoe in the same relationship as before. Regrettably, the new arrangement, under which Oliver and Duff formally joined the Board of Admiralty, did not result in the speeding up of business that had been hoped. Oliver was responsible for dealing with the German surface fleet, and Duff continued to cover commerce protection and anti-submarine warfare.[7]

These changes meant that the admirals concentrated on operations, while the incoming civilians provided the business management. As Marder notes, the new department under Geddes performed the same kind of functions as the Navy Board, abolished in 1832. The reforms meant other changes of personnel. Jackson, the Director of Operations, departed; Richmond, who wrote that he was 'universally execrated as the source of all this inertia and opposition,' was profoundly relieved by his replacement by Rear Admiral Hope. Duff's role as the Director of the Anti-Submarine Division was taken over by Captain WW Fisher, the highly regarded commander of *St Vincent* in the Grand Fleet.

Richmond observed of Halsey's promotion that he was 'a very good chap, but as mutton headed as he can be. They would not have Leveson, the man best fitted for it, as he has too strong a personality. Nonentities they want and they can get them very easily.'[8] One possible candidate for a post in the new structure would of course have been Richmond himself, but there was no way in which Jellicoe would have him there, as Richmond well knew. He thought that the changes were 'eyewash,' and was particularly acid about the freeing of, for example, the Second Sea Lord (Burney) and Fourth Sea Lord (Halsey) from departmental responsibilities, asking in his diary if either were men who had given their life to the study of war:

> Burney's methods and views when in command of the Channel Squadron shew him to be a most ignorant man. Halsey, a good administrator, has never studied war at all. They will 'practically' devote their whole time etc. What does 'practically' usually mean?[9]

Nor was Beatty much impressed with the reforms, writing to Tyrwhitt, who shared his views:

> The same as before, but with new labels and Tothill instead of Tudor, but it seems to please the Critics, which is apparently all that is desired. It is not the system which is wrong, but those that run it.[10]

He wrote an extended note, evidently for a conference with Jellicoe in July, offering his own views on what should be done, and strongly criticising the way in which the Admiralty received new ideas, which he thought amounted to a positive dislike which discouraged thought:

> Every proposal for offensive action has been systematically shelved, or so picked to pieces and sent back for correction, that time – the most decisive factor – has been lost. Every objection has been found to new proposals; they were never encouraged.[11]

Somewhat contradicting his own letter to Tyrwhitt, Beatty in this paper found that 'the remedy lies in a thorough reorganisation of the staff system at the Admiralty,' while adding that there should be personnel capable of running the system.

Public criticism of the Admiralty at this time was not solely focused on its administrative structure but was also concerned, as Beatty's note reflected, with a perceived lack of offensive will. A violent controversy blew up when Admiral Sir Reginald Custance wrote to *The Times* on May 7. In this he complained that the current naval strategy was based on a belief that success could be achieved without battle, and that the destruction of the enemy's fleet came second to the control of his sea communications. The U-boat threat could be met by smashing the High Seas Fleet:

> If the massed fleet is destroyed the action of the submarine is weakened, since its exit is impeded by the small surface craft and submarines of the victor, which are then free to pass into gun range in the enemy's waters with mines, nets and every new device.[12]

Beatty, who told his wife, as he had Tyrwhitt, that 'it is not the organisation that is wrong but those who form the organisation who are not equal to the job,' observed that he had pointed this out until he was tired. He could, he said, do no more unless he left the Grand Fleet and went there himself, which he would not do. This came in a letter of May 10 in which he reacted violently to Custance's letter. Calling him a 'nebulous old fool,' he described the letter as 'destructive, cheap and nasty.' Picking up a reference Custance had made to 'directing naval minds,' he asserted rather pompously that he and not the Admiralty was the controlling mind of the Grand Fleet, and he was not aware that his actions during the war had been such as to permit 'such an appalling statement: '

> In any case, it does not make it any easier for me, and he should make his statements clearer as to what he does mean, instead of damning wholesale the senior officers of the service which has suffered him for so long. Anyway he has roused a considerable feeling of resentment in the fleet.[13]

Beatty was, however, even more upset when Churchill joined in to support Custance. In an article in the *Sunday Pictorial* on June 24 he emphatically called for an aggressive naval policy. In a further but not uncharacteristic U-turn, he complained that the fleet had been reduced merely to 'keeping the ring.' A way must be found to 'get at them.' For at least two years the Admiralty had adopted the opposite principle, 'wait about till they come out:'

> The problem of 'how to get at them,' which is essentially a problem of mechanical preparation for a supreme act of naval aggression, has been entirely laid aside … is all this accumulation of deadly war energy to wait idly on the off chance of the German fleet emerging from its harbour to fight a battle until peace, perhaps an unsatisfactory peace, is declared.?[14]

He did not go into details, but clearly he wanted to use the predreadnought battleships to smash their way into the German harbours, a project that was entirely fanciful.

Beatty, having discovered the article, wrote furiously to his wife about it:

> In it, apparently having forgotten the article he wrote some months ago in which he pronounced the absolutely opposite opinion, he stated that the Navy was doing nothing and must become more aggressive … It is disgusting that a man who has been a Cabinet

> Minister and First Lord of the Admiralty should be allowed to write articles in a rag of a paper, belittling the officers and the great Service of which he was once the head.[15]

Beatty added that he would not fuss himself, however; there would always be dirty dogs in the world who endeavoured to make capital of others, and he was in no doubt that Churchill's article was part of an intrigue to regain office.

Richmond, who had been extremely bored while commanding *Commonwealth* in the 3rd Battle Squadron, and was relieved in April 1917 to be appointed to the Grand Fleet as captain of *Conqueror* in the 2nd Battle Squadron, wasted little time in putting himself about to promote his ideas. His particular scheme was the delivery of diversionary attacks on the Syrian coast-line, in order to tie down large numbers of Turkish troops, and he advocated it incessantly. He also, however, spent a lot of time with senior commanders. On April 30, he saw de Robeck, Beatty, Brock (Beatty's Chief of Staff) and Brand (the Captain of the Fleet), and was 'very much encouraged,' as he wrote in his diary:

> Here are men who see what is wanted, who are ready to take risks with the Fleet, who have no prepossessions for this deadening strategy of defence, but, on the contrary, a longing for offence and active measures. De Robeck was as keen as myself could be on the importance and value of diversionary operations in Syria.[16]

Quite what risks Beatty was prepared to take with the Grand Fleet were not explained; Richmond, not for the first or last time, was decidedly overstating the case.

He found, he wrote later, that the Grand Fleet captains were 'unanimous' that Jutland was a 'failure,' and that they could 'hardly bear to speak of it. 'To me, the more I hear of it, it appears the most disgracefully mismanaged thing in our naval history.' He continued his regular visits to the upper echelon, seeing Brock and Beatty again on May15. The latter told him that Jellicoe's ignorance of war was astonishing:

> He had never read a book in his life before the war. He had found at last in reading Mahan's *Influence of Sea Power* – Good Lord! for the first time – some quotation about Nelson, and had joyfully showed it to Beatty as a wholly new discovery, to which Beatty told him if he would read further – Nelson's life by Mahan, or his despatches – he would find the same idea constantly repeated throughout them. How childish this pleasure at discovering something. Fancy beginning to read about war when you become Commander-in-Chief in War!!![17]

It is hard to say upon which of them these distasteful exchanges of contempt for the First Sea Lord reflect more badly – the junior officer or the C-in-C.

On June 5 Richmond went to see Lloyd George at the latter's invitation, which gave him an opportunity, of which he made the most, to put his ideas forward at the highest level. He had a lot to say, on the subject of Admiralty organisation, on Jellicoe, and on the strategy that should be employed. He offered his views on a number of others, such as Oliver, Wemyss and Browning. He suggested Walter Roch, MP or General Smuts, as First Lord. And, of course, he had something to say about the Syrian coast. With that, and his own proposals no doubt in mind, he wrote in the paper which he prepared for the meeting:

> Matters have thus come to such a pitch that young officers with ideas are in despair, and yet, still hoping to get their schemes considered, they send them to the Commander-in-Chief of the Grand Fleet, where they receive sympathy from that broad-minded officer. But this is most improper. He has other work to do commanding the Fleet, and it is the duty of the Admiralty Staff to deal with these things.[18]

As to Jellicoe, Richmond was scathing. His comments were music to Lloyd George's ears:

> As to personality, the First Sea Lord is by temperament defensive. His tactics at sea were defensive. He did not intend to fight a decisive action if the enemy adopted tactics of an awkward character. He would not risk the loss of ships. His employment of destroyers was defensive. They were to defend the Battle Fleet, not to attack the enemy. He has revised those ideas since Jutland. But no man who possesses the true spirit of attack would ever have held such views. Sir David Beatty's use of destroyers was from the beginning of an offensive character ... The First Sea Lord failed at Jutland. This has surely impressed itself upon him by now. It has not made him bolder. And, while he was a defensive tactician, he is now a still more defensive strategist.[19]

Richmond spent over half an hour with the Prime Minister at the end of which, he recorded, he told him that things were being concealed from him 'because they would give too much ammunition to the politicians.' Lloyd George thanked him, saying that he had learned a great deal, and sent him off to see Carson, which Richmond did on the following day. In this meeting he 'went much further, going into details of changes.' Carson gave him the opportunity of making suggestions for a reconstituted Board of Admiralty:

> I said Wemyss for First Sea Lord, Duff for Second, Hope for Third and HF Sinclair for Fourth. So far as I was concerned, I should prefer to command a fighting force somewhere, above all off the Syrian coast, but if he wished me anywhere in this place, I thought I could be of most use as Deputy C.O.S.

According to Richmond's account of the interview, Carson told him that the Cabinet had ceased to take Jellicoe seriously, saying 'if we were to believe and act upon all that he says, we might as well give up the war at once.' Richmond said Burney must go – Carson agreed that 'we have enough old women as it is' – and that Keyes should replace Bacon. After an hour and ten minutes the meeting ended, and Richmond visited the Naval Secretary, Rear Admiral Everett, where they exchanged further disparaging comments about Bacon.[20] Richmond returned to *Conqueror* on June 15, somewhat pessimistic as to the outcome of his visit; Corbett had told him that in conversation with Hankey, who asked the Prime Minister whether he had been impressed by what Richmond had said, Lloyd George's reply was 'partly yes and partly no.'

Long after the war Carson gave an interview to the *Morning Post* which conveyed a very different account of Richmond's meeting with him:

> Once at his request I saw a junior officer who Mr Lloyd George thought was going to save the situation. Well, I said I would gladly see the young gentleman and he came to my room. I told him that as there was no one present but myself he could speak with complete

> freedom. He said, 'Thank you Sir, since you ask me to speak freely let me say that I have no confidence in Admiral Jellicoe'... So we went over the First Sea Lord's record together and he could find no fault with it; and, beyond that, he had no practical suggestion to offer at all. The tittle-tattle grew to be such a plague that I had to issue an order that, if officers were found to be gossiping about the affairs of the Admiralty at people's luncheon tables, I would take a serious view of it. But I suppose Mr Lloyd George must have listened to it.[21]

Jellicoe was aware of Richmond's visit to Lloyd George although he may not have realised the energetic manner in which Richmond was intriguing against him. If he did, it would certainly explain his lack of enthusiasm for having Richmond at the Admiralty. Nonetheless, as explained below, he was prepared to tell Carson that 'if Captain Richmond is likely to be suitable in other respects, I think he would probably be useful at the Admiralty, and I therefore suggest his appointment as a preliminary step.'[22] Perhaps he preferred the idea of Richmond being inside the tent.

A fortnight later Richmond again visited Beatty to report on his meetings in London. The C-in-C told him that he had heard from Carson and was aware of Richmond's visit, and that he had complained to the First Lord of the 'preposterous' way in which the war was being run, and that he should be consulted and have a voice. Carson had made encouraging noises in response. Richmond 'came away with the feeling that he does not intend to allow things to rest where they are, which is a great comfort'.[23]

In the following months Richmond continued to see Beatty on a regular basis to express his views on a wide range of strategic and tactical issues. Enchanted to have such an appreciative audience for his opinions, Richmond recorded in his diary a meeting on September 22:

> A most interesting conversation, which confirmed my opinion that in Beatty we have a man with the makings of a real statesman. The question of whether he should not be at Whitehall intrudes itself more than ever upon me. The second rate man we have there now will never see further than his own interests, nor than the purely naval defensive operations. He cannot see things on a big scale. It is natural that he should be unable to do so. His training has not fitted him for it, nor is his intelligence of a high enough order to overcome the defects of his training.[24]

Carson had been pressed by Lloyd George, much influenced by what he was hearing from Hankey, Richmond and others, to create a section of the Naval Staff devoted to the planning process; this, he hoped, would provide the offensive approach which he felt was lacking. Carson proposed to Jellicoe that such a section be formed under the Director of Operations. It would be concerned solely with planning offensive naval operations, and would be entirely free from all administrative duties. Carson set out in some detail his proposals for staffing the section, which should consist, inter alia, of two or three Captains. Jellicoe was not keen, but dutifully responded:

> In order to carry out your wish I would suggest that as a preliminary step a Captain should be appointed additional to the Operations Division of the War Staff, and that he should then select the officers to work in cooperation with him.[25]

He presumed that Richmond's visit to the Prime Minister was connected with the proposal, and was at Hankey's instigation. He forbore to comment on 'this interference with Admiralty administration by Colonel Hankey,' but reminded Carson that it was for the senior officers of the War Staff to in initiate offensive operations. He added:

> At the same time I would remark that I have been considering possible offensives ever since the commencement of the war and I am fairly certain that there is no possible operation … which has not been considered a great many times. However I quite realise that there is plenty of criticism of Admiralty methods due to the want of knowledge of the circumstances … The sooner Captain Richmond is appointed, the better.[26]

In the event, however, Richmond's appointment to the Admiralty did not occur during Jellicoe's time; he went there as Director of Training in April 1918.

For his part Beatty was, outwardly at any rate, entirely supportive of Jellicoe, offering on June 27 to come down to London so that between them he and the First Sea Lord could 'knock out any hare brained schemes.' He felt that when the two of them met and talked things over, they always agreed, and should present a broad front. In response, Jellicoe stressed his desire to keep in the closest touch. He told Beatty:

> I fancy there is a scheme on foot to get rid of me. The way they are doing it is to say that I am too pessimistic. This is because I point out the necessity for concentration of forces on the submarine menace and the great danger of not being able to feed the country… Of course putting aside one's duty to the country I should be delighted to go, and have done with all politicians, but if I am of use here in the opinion of the Navy I certainly should not volunteer to go. I am not conceited, nor ambitious in the least, but I believe I am of use here because I have both sea and office experience.[27]

Beatty replied with advice which, in the light of his own private correspondence and his discussions with such as Richmond, does not make comfortable reading:

> I do not think you should permit yourself to be worried by what the intriguers set themselves to do. And you must stick at all costs to your intention of not volunteering to go; that would be fatal. Do not be goaded into any step of that kind no matter what the Press or anybody else says… If we keep together and have plenty of opportunities to discuss the many questions I have no fear we could improve matters and defeat the manoeuvres of the intriguers.[28]

In May, Beatty had written to Eugénie that Jellicoe 'was always a half hearted man,' adding that he would do very well as First Sea Lord if he had the right sort of men behind him, but that he was 'totally incapable of selecting good men to serve under him' and that he disliked men of independence and character, and loved 'sycophants and toadies.'[29] And he told his wife that he had half a mind to invite Fisher to visit the Grand Fleet, observing: 'He is a man, unscrupulous, but still a man. Which is more than anybody at the Admiralty is.'[30]

Since Carson was resolutely opposed to Jellicoe's dismissal, it was necessary for Lloyd George to remove the First Lord. This was an operation that would require the greatest care, if he was to retain the support of the Conservative Party. He had originally, he wrote, wished to appoint Carson to the War Cabinet and Lord Milner to the Admiralty, but at the time Conservative leaders, most of whom 'admired but disapproved of him,' were opposed to this, 'so Carson had been kept out of a place for which he was qualified and given a post for which he was unsuited.'[31] In mid 1917 the Prime Minister decided that what was needed at the Admiralty was someone 'with a greater reserve of vitality, with more resource and mastery of detail.' As ever, ready to seek other opinions, Lloyd George consulted Haig:

> He was apprehensive that the War might be lost at sea before he had an opportunity of winning it on land. He had great admiration for Jellicoe's knowledge as a technical sailor, but he thought him much too rigid, narrow and conservative in his ideas. As to Sir Edward Carson, I am afraid Sir Douglas Haig had no opinion of his qualities as an administrator. He thought he was distinctly out of place at the Admiralty. He strongly urged upon me the appointment of Sir Eric Geddes to the post. The power, and especially the punch, which Sir Eric had displayed in the reorganisation of transport to and in France had made a considerable impression on the Commander in Chief's mind.[32]

Haig's immediate concern was his planned offensive in Flanders, intended to clear the Belgian coast and drive back the right flank of the Germans on the Western Front. When Lloyd George's new War Policy Committee had considered the plan, Jellicoe had been asked whether the navy could destroy the U boat and destroyer bases without the need for a military advance. No, said Jellicoe; a bombardment by monitors at a range of 12 to 14 miles could not destroy these harbours, while the suggested use of battleships was an operation which 'no responsible naval officer would recommend.' On June 18 Jellicoe presented a paper to the War Cabinet insisting that the capture of Zeebrugge and Ostend was essential. Two days later he astounded the War Cabinet by asserting that it would be impossible to continue the war in 1918 as a result of the loss of shipping. No one else present shared this view, and this further instance of Jellicoe's pessimism caused, according to Hankey, 'great irritation.'[33]

Haig's plan was for the navy to land an infantry division near Westende once the army's advance reached Roulers, estimated at between August 4 and 8. It was an operation which Beatty, Madden and de Robeck thought was unlikely to succeed. Jellicoe, while supporting the plan, was doubtful if it would bring out the High Seas Fleet; more probably the Germans would intervene with light cruisers and destroyers, so it might be necessary to reinforce the Harwich Force. Haig, during his visit to England, had a breakfast meeting with Lloyd George, Milner and Geddes on June 26, at which the Prime Minister discussed his intention to do something about the Admiralty, although as Haig noted in his diary he was 'uncertain as to what was the best decision to take at present.[34] That day Milner made a suggestion, which in the light of the history of Lloyd George's relationship with the Admiralty, seems unsurprising; promote Carson to the War Cabinet and make Geddes First Lord. Lloyd George seems for a while to have contemplated appointing Hankey, who had asked the Prime Minister if he had considered this; but on mature reflection Hankey backed out of the suggestion, saying that he would only accept the appointment 'under pressure of a very high sense of national duty, and under persuasion from the whole Cabinet.'[35] By July 5 Lloyd George's mind was made up, and he went to tell the King of his intention to put Carson into the War Cabinet and to appoint Geddes as First Lord. Next day he wrote to Carson with the proposal; the latter was unenthusiastic, and Lloyd George drew back for a few days until Milner, on July 16, put some backbone in him, protesting at further delay which would inspire public criticism. Next day the changes were announced, and Geddes took up his duties on July 20.

Within the navy, Carson's departure was regretted. Jellicoe wrote that when he left the Admiralty it was 'to the intense regret of those who had been privileged to work with him.'[36] Tyrwhitt wrote to Keyes: 'I weep to think that Carson has gone … I think he was the best 1st Lord we've had for years and knew a great deal more than people thought.'[37] Richmond made no comment in his diary at the time, but a few weeks later he saw his father in law, who told him something of Geddes' views of the Admiralty, including his 'astonishment at the lack of any method of conducting board meetings – the vagueness, the lack of preparation, and the absence of minutes, the amateurishness of the whole concern.' Richmond added, with considerable satisfaction, that it was exactly what he would have expected.[38] Evan-Thomas wrote to his sister in law on July 26 expressing what was perhaps a view common to many officers:

> We have made the great Enrico Geddes now First Lord of the Admiralty – the other day assistant manager of a railway – a bullet-headed sort of cove who anyway looks you straight in the face which is more than those confounded Politicians will do. So perhaps he will suit us quite well.[39]

The appointment of Geddes led at once to a number of changes of personnel, and these brought an immediate crisis for Jellicoe. As Controller, Sir Alan Anderson, a director of the Orient Line, took over from Geddes. Graham Greene, the Permanent Secretary, was at Hankey's suggestion removed and replaced by Sir Oswyn Murray, the Assistant Secretary. However, it was the demand by Lloyd George that both Burney, as Second Sea Lord, and Oliver, as Deputy Chief of the Naval Staff, must be replaced which brought matters to a head for Jellicoe. He was prepared, reluctantly, to lose Burney. At his meeting with the Prime Minister on July 17 he put his foot down, saying that if Oliver left, he must consider his own position:

> The Prime Minister thereupon remarked that I was bound by the same rules as any midshipman, and must do as I was told. But I informed him that there was no Board in existence owing to the change of 1st Lord and that I should certainly consider myself free to decline an invitation to join the New Board were Sir H Oliver omitted. A prolonged discussion took place but I refused to alter my decision. Sir Eric Geddes argued with me at some length after the meeting broke up, but failed to shake me.[40]

Jellicoe was going next day to the Grand Fleet and said he would consult Beatty and Madden, which he did. Both counselled him against resignation.

While there, he discussed with Beatty the apparent superiority of the High Seas Fleet in battle cruisers, based on the latest intelligence available. It is hardly too strong a word to use panic to describe the way in which Jellicoe and Beatty analysed the situation. Jellicoe reported to Geddes on July 21, in a paper to which he attached the latest information about the German battle cruisers:

> By the end of the present year the situation in regard to the comparative strength of the British and German Battle Cruiser Forces will be serious. Owing to the inadequacy of the armour protection of the majority of our battle cruisers as compared with those of Germany, our advantage in point of numbers will be more than balanced and the superiority will be on the German side.[41]

The only solution that Jellicoe could see was to use Japanese battle cruisers, the only other nation possessing such vessels. There was little likelihood of the Japanese agreeing to their joining the Grand Fleet, and in any case if they did it was 'doubtful whether they would be a match for German battle cruisers when manned by Japanese.' He proposed, therefore, to ask the Foreign office to sound the Japanese about their willingness to sell two of their battle cruisers. Not altogether surprisingly, this remarkable suggestion was politely but firmly rejected, as was a further proposal that Japan should send the ships with Japanese crews to serve with the Grand Fleet.

When Jellicoe returned from his visit to the fleet, he made an attempt, unsuccessfully, to save Burney; and as to Oliver, insisted that he 'should view with the very greatest apprehension his removal from his present position.' Lloyd George, presented with the chance to rid himself of Jellicoe, blinked first, and a compromise was reached, permitting Oliver's retention but providing for Burney's supersession by Vice Admiral Sir Rosslyn Wemyss.

Geddes had, in any case, made his acceptance of the post of First Lord conditional upon Jellicoe remaining for the time being. Lloyd George wrote that Geddes was aware that Jellicoe 'had the confidence of the senior officers of the navy, and that it would therefore be a distinct advantage to secure his cooperation if that were at all possible.' Geddes promised to report if he found that he could not work with Jellicoe. Lloyd George was soon hearing from Geddes what he expected to hear:

> It was not long before he discovered that the proper coordination and full efficiency of the Admiralty were being seriously handicapped by personal factors, among which was the lack of sympathetic confidence between Admiral Beatty, commanding the Grand Fleet, and Admiral Jellicoe, the First Sea Lord. This disagreement had existed since differences had arisen between them about the battle of Jutland.[42]

The solution, Geddes decided, was to make Wemyss Deputy First Sea Lord; he intended initially that he should combine the duties of this post with those of Second Sea Lord, responsible for naval personnel. It was soon evident to Wemyss that this would not work, and he persuaded Geddes to appoint a separate Second Sea Lord, leaving him free to concentrate on staff duties as Jellicoe's deputy; Vice Admiral Heath took over the role of Second Sea Lord on September 27.

Wemyss had not at all wanted to come to the Admiralty, having been offered and accepted the new appointment of Commander-in-Chief of the British Fleet in the Mediterranean; the French had put up a struggle for one of their admirals to have overall command, but finally assented. Wemyss had, all his career, had the ambition to become C-in-C Mediterranean, and was proud to have attained it. He wrote in his diary for June 12, at Ismailia, where he had been conducting naval affairs in the Eastern Mediterranean and the Middle East:

> I shall be very sorry from a professional point of view to leave here, where the work has been so interesting, and of course it is a much more difficult business I am going to, but it's a great compliment to me for it is an enormous affair I am going to take up and will require an enormous amount of organisation.[43]

Wemyss had demonstrated his loyal and public spirited character when, at the outset of the Dardanelles operation, Carden, the C-in-C had fallen ill; Wemyss, at that time engaged in setting up the naval base at Mudros, was senior to de Robeck, Carden's second in command, but waived his right to take command, suggesting that de Robeck should succeed Carden with the acting rank of Vice Admiral. Lloyd George was pleased with his appointment, both because he was 'neither a Jellicoeite nor a Beattyite,' being quite friendly with both, and because he was willing to listen to young officers with ideas. 'He never stared them out of the room. His eyeglass greeted them with a friendly gleam.'[44] Wemyss, in accepting his new appointment, albeit with reluctance, had to overcome his wife's furious objections:

> Above all she dreaded the Admiralty, which during the war had proved the grave of so many reputations, and the spirit of intrigue which ever since Fisher's reign had clung to its walls and with which she full well knew he was so unfitted to deal. She therefore besought him to refuse – but in vain! He was adamant.[45]

Another product of the new regime was the establishment of the Plans Division, based on an enlargement of the responsibilities of the Plans Section which Jellicoe had set up. Jellicoe objected strongly, on the basis that plans could not be made independently of the Operations Division. Geddes was determined, however, and Jellicoe mournfully concluded that it would be useless to press his objections to the point of resignation, and that he must give in, although he intended that the new Director of Plans should work in the closest cooperation with the Director of Operations. So far so good; but the First Lord selected Keyes for the new post, without Jellicoe's approval. Jellicoe took exception to this, as he wrote in his autobiographical notes:

> I considered him quite unfitted by temperament and brain power for the post, although I knew of course of his other sterling qualities, but the appointment had been made and I agreed to let it stand. The organisation never worked well and I found that my work was increased by the necessity for constantly dealing with two people.[46]

Keyes was dismayed at his appointment, having very happily settled into his post in the Grand Fleet. He was painfully clear as to what lay ahead:

> But how I hated the whole business, and the thought of all the unpleasantness in front of me. I had spent so many years striving for things other people did not want to do, and I was under no illusions as to the hostility I would encounter if I did all that I knew I should feel impelled to do. It seemed indeed hard to have to leave all my good friends and my happy life in the Grand Fleet for such a prospect, while there was the chance of a battle in the North Sea.[47]

His friend Tyrwhitt tried to cheer him up, writing to say that it was very hard luck to lose his command, and that he had all his sympathy; but it was 'a very high compliment;' he was, he said, 'inwardly delighted, as he knew that their efforts to do things would at least get a hearing, 'instead of being put in old Oliver's wastepaper basket.'[48]

The practice of intriguing against brother officers was of course by no means confined to the Royal Navy. The German navy contained just as many opinionated individuals readily inclined to put pen to paper, as has already been seen. Perhaps it was the immense but shadowy presence of Fisher and Tirpitz in the background which contributed to the atmosphere in which this sort of thing was apt to occur. Certainly, each of the former leaders had extremely strong views which they energetically promoted through their acolytes. Among prominent German naval personalities, it has been seen that Trotha, Levetzow and Eckermann were particularly busy correspondents. Much of the gossip passed over the desk of Müller, who as Chief of the Naval Cabinet had an enormous circle of contacts with whom he exchanged correspondence. Tirpitz, correctly, saw him as one of his principal opponents within Imperial Headquarters; when Bethmann-Hollweg finally left office in the summer of 1917, he denounced both the outgoing Chancellor and Müller to Trotha. He accused them of collusion with high finance and indirectly with Wall Street and its interests.[49] For his part, Müller had always loyally supported Bethmann-Hollweg against his many enemies. Among them, he believed, Hindenburg and Ludendorff were conspiring to remove the Chancellor and replace him with Tirpitz. Müller was especially suspicious of Ludendorff, observing to Holtzendorff in a letter of January 31 1917 that he had 'grave doubts about Ludendorff's hunger for power, he being, moreover, very easy to approach for intrigues by the enemies of the Chancellor.'[50]

Trotha, ever a supporter of Tirpitz, did all he could to promote a relationship between the former State Secretary and Hindenburg and Ludendorff, of which he had high hopes. He wrote to Tirpitz on January 15; 'Everything now really depends on Ludendorff ... Our hope lies in cooperation between the High Seas Fleet and Ludendorff-Hindenburg seems to be more easily persuaded by the other side.' As Scheer's Chief of Staff, Trotha occupied a position of great influence on German naval strategy, and he made the best use of it that he could.

Scheer does not appear directly to have engaged in the kind of *ad hominem* criticisms referred to above. He had, of course, sought Hipper's replacement before Jutland; and although reconciled to his retention in command of the battle cruisers, he was still inclined to be critical of his subordinate, as for instance in the final fitness report on Hipper which he wrote at the end of 1917:

> Very active as a man and a personality; perhaps he even stands out too much (which may be) the beginning of his downfall. His performance as a leader – for it is as such he has been in the forefront of all operations and he served with special distinction in the battle of the Skagerrak – is that of performing well at the right tactical moment. At the same time, when he is in charge of subordinate forces, he does not supervise the tactical commanders closely enough and turns too much of the tactical work over to his staff. As a combat commander his temperament and competence cannot be faulted. He remains always a good leader. I don't know about peace, though, if one would want him as a fleet commander.[51]

From the headquarters of the High Seas Fleet there was expressed much the same discontent with those in Berlin as was felt in the Grand Fleet with those in Whitehall. Not surprisingly, it was Trotha who most persistently articulated this, observing in August 1917:

> The Imperial Navy Office can properly only be called a ruin and the Admiralty Staff grows or rather swells over everything in an unhealthy ambition to possess everything without being able to master it.[52]

33

The Problem of the Neutrals

The principle that necessity knows no law had been ruthlessly applied by Germany to justify the violation of Belgium. Thereafter, both sides were prepared to contemplate further violations of neutrality if it was considered that there would thereby be gained a net benefit; and neither side displayed much concern with the morality of such a step.

Different considerations arose at various stages of the war, but on each side there was a pronounced concern with what the other might do. It was, or might be, crucial to anticipate this, so the question of whether to infringe the neutrality of Denmark, Norway and Holland, and even Sweden, was perpetually on the table.

Starting with the conclusion of the Franco-Russian alliance in the 1890's, the German Admiralty Staff had to reckon with the need to block the passage of a Russian fleet into the North Sea, which meant controlling the Sound and the Danish Belts. Once it became necessary to plan for a naval war against Great Britain, the memory of the actions taken against Denmark during the Napoleonic Wars demonstrated the importance of pre-empting such a move. The Admiralty Staff therefore strongly favoured the occupation of Danish territory. The General Staff, however, was opposed; every soldier committed to such an operation meant one less for the crucial offensive against France. Danish neutrality, if benevolently applied in relation to Germany, might answer best.

In Britain, in the years before the war, the Ballard Committee had produced naval war plans which included, as a tempting objective, a German army which, having occupied Zealand and Funen, would be dependent on seaborne supplies; such an occupation was 'considered probable by those who have had opportunities of studying the German military organisation for war, though it is difficult to understand what Germany would hope to gain from such a move.'[1] In 1911, at the famous meeting of the Committee at Imperial Defence on August 23, Sir Arthur Wilson, outlining the navy's Baltic strategy, thought that the Germans would not outrage the Danes by mining their territorial waters; thus the fleet would be able to enter the Baltic. There, so far as Denmark was concerned, British strategic thinking for the moment remained.

Once war had broken out, however, Churchill and the British Admiralty looked again at the strategic options as they affected Denmark; one, of these, to support the navy's bid for control of the North Sea, involved the seizure of the Danish port of Esbjerg; the Foreign Office was appalled. There was no prospect of Denmark voluntarily entering the war on the side of the Entente; determined to preserve her neutrality, Denmark had reached agreement with Germany to close its territorial waters to belligerents by mining the Belts and the Sound.[2] When

Fisher returned to the Admiralty, his Baltic plans would, he hoped, provoke the Germans into violating Danish neutrality and hence opening the opportunity for British operations there. At this stage Asquith and the Cabinet would not entertain the prospect of Britain herself violating Danish neutrality.

Although Ingenohl, and later Pohl, his successor, called for the abrogation of the agreement with Denmark so that the High Seas Fleet could make use of the Belts and the Sound in order to sally out into the Skagerrak from a protected position, the advantages of Danish neutrality were well understood by most of the German naval leaders. Lans, for instance, argued that holding back the High Seas Fleet in the North Sea was important to ensuring Danish neutrality; it was a view which Tirpitz roundly denounced in a letter to Trotha in March 1915.[3]

The possibility that Denmark might be drawn into the war on the side of the Entente remained a grave concern to the German naval leadership. In August 1916 both Prince Henry, commanding in the Baltic, and Scheer asked the Admiralty Staff what it intended to do about this. As in the past, the General Staff position was that there were no troops to spare for such an operation, so it would be up to the navy to deal with the issue. Holtzendorff informed Prince Henry and Scheer of this on September 2, but discussions with the military continued. Ludendorff was adamant that the most the army could do was to hold a defence line across Schleswig-Holstein. Holtzendorff pleaded that, at least, Fredericia should be captured. Since this would require a major offensive, his pleas fell on deaf ears. By the spring of 1917, however, the inter-service negotiations had reached the conclusion that the occupation of the whole of Jutland would be feasible.

Meanwhile the British Admiralty had been considering the case of Denmark. There was no immediate intention to violate her neutrality, even though she represented an enormous hole in the British blockade of Germany. This fact generated bitter complaints in the Press; the *Daily Mail* in March 1917 thought that the fault lay in interference by the Foreign Office, as a result of which 'food in enormous quantities is reaching the enemy … Food is no longer imported into Germany, it is true. But we permit neutral ships to carry fertilisers and fattening stuffs, which are the raw materials of food, to neutral countries, such as Holland and Denmark, where they are properly worked up into food and sent to the Germans.'[4] It was certainly true that a great deal of food crossed the Danish border into Germany, which meant that a German invasion of the country would be very much a last resort. If, however, that happened, the question was whether Britain could give effective help to the Danes. An Admiralty appreciation in October 1916 concluded that it was not possible; and although it was looked at again in the following year, the answer was still the same. It was left to the more extravagant strategists to argue for such an operation. Fisher, for instance, repeating his usual mantra that 'rashness in war is prudence. Prudence in war is criminal,' wrote to Jellicoe in May 1916: 'You know as well as I do the beautiful landing sites for our British Army in Danish territory on both sides of the Promontory of Schleswig-Holstein.'[5] He was still advocating this eighteen months later, but by then even his most devoted adherents had abandoned any hope of his return to power or influence.

The case of Norway was somewhat different. The supply of Norwegian and Swedish iron and steel, nitrates, zinc and aluminium was crucial to the success of British arms production, and Norwegian merchant shipping was carrying a great deal of Allied trade. For these reasons it would be essential to protect Norway from invasion, if the Germans took that step. On the other hand Beatty, as C-in-C, demanded the right to enter Norwegian territorial waters to hunt raiders and check the supply of contraband goods to Germany. However, the violation of Norway's territorial rights in this way was regarded as politically unacceptable, due to the effect on other neutrals. Beatty did not give up on the idea. In July 1917 he asked Richmond to produce a paper on the effect on naval operations if Norway came into the war. Richmond started his paper in the belief that this might be beneficial, but in the end concluded:

> Unless therefore Norway could give us an assurance, and reasons for that assurance that carry conviction, that she can guard her own bases, towns and shipping against minor raids, military, naval or aerial, without help from us, or with as much help as we can spare without influencing our operations detrimentally elsewhere, it is not to our advantage that she should come into the war.[6]

However, as the German submarine campaign continued, it began to appear to the Admiralty that getting a naval base in Norway might help in dealing with the U-boats. In the autumn of 1917 plans to establish an advanced base at Kristiansand were worked out; but this would only be pursued if the Germans moved first, and in the event they did not do so. The German Admiralty Staff continued to study the possibility, but the lack of available troops meant that a military operation was scarcely feasible. In any event, if it was decided to act against Norway, it would be necessary to occupy Jutland, even if Denmark sought to remain neutral. However, in 1917 the General Staff was more cooperative, and promised troops for a move into Jutland. On the other hand, it was not contemplated at that stage that Norway be invaded, although Scheer saw the scope of operations being widened: 'Case N [the plans against Norway] requires in the first phase the control of the Kattegat and Jutland and as the final goal control of the Skagerrak and the Scandinavian countries grouped around it.'[7]

Scheer's attitude to the control of the Skagerrak and the Kattegat was close to the arguments in the strategic papers of Wolfgang Wegener which had caused such a stir in 1915. Leaving aside the important advantages that flowed from Danish neutrality, he had been emphatic that the possession of a flanking position in the Skagerrak was of 'a totally offensive nature: so offensive, indeed, that Heligoland Bight, by comparison, will become a flanking position.' In the Skagerrak, the German fleet would exercise some measure of sea control:

> We stand in the way of the English; therefore, <u>they</u> must attack. If they want to deprive us of this measure of sea control, they must come to us; and the battle will take place in our waters, under strategically and, as proven in manoeuvres, tactically advantageous conditions for us. These are advantages that we attempt in vain to attain from the Heligoland Bight.[8]

To achieve this advantage, however, Danish neutrality must be violated. As things stood, Wegener saw Danish neutrality as benefiting only the enemy, which contradicted the spirit of neutrality:

> In the struggle for survival among large nations, a small state simply cannot be accorded the right to neutralise the power of a fleet, schooled over years of hard work, in favour of the [other] side, or to force that fleet to undertake detrimental operations – like an offensive with insufficient means, emanating from the Helgoland Bight.[9]

Although generally it was the case that German plans for attacks on the Scandinavian neutrals would come into effect only if one of them joined the enemy, of if the latter forced its way into national territorial waters, there were some who argued for such action even without the need for preventive measures. Holtzendorff argued against this; it would serve no purpose to force neutral states into the enemy camp, a view that was strongly supported by Count Rantzau, the Ambassador in Copenhagen, and by the Foreign Office. The Danish Prime Minister, Scavenius, was seen as strongly pro German.[10]

In general, neither side was keen to see Holland involved in the war. For Britain, it was a source of a lot of food, as well as of information about Germany, while the Dutch often turned a blind eye to brief infringements of their territorial waters. It would be a different matter if the Germans violated Dutch neutrality, particularly if their objective was to seize the mouths of the Scheldt. From time to time there seemed indications that Germany might be planning to do so, and Beatty in particular was hawkish on the action that should be taken. He argued that plans should be prepared, and the necessary forces be made ready if it seemed that the Dutch were about to join the enemy or if the Germans were about to move. Beatty was indignant about the insistence by the Foreign Office that no action be taken unless the Germans actually crossed the frontier; the delay would, he thought, be fatal. 'This provides an instance of the Foreign Office dictating Military Policy which is obviously wrong. I gather further that any Force we should employ would be a small Force. Again, this is wrong.'[11] It was his hope that the employment of a large force might bring all or part of the High Seas Fleet out. However, as the year drew to a close, it seemed that Holland would defend her neutrality against all comers. Meanwhile, although plans were continuously worked on for action by German forces against Holland, these were all based on the possibility of a British violation of Dutch neutrality or of Holland voluntarily joining the Allies. So long as the Belgian coast was in German hands, there was no interest in the Scheldt. For Germany, as for Britain, the balance of advantage lay with the maintenance of Dutch neutrality.

34

Brummer and *Bremse*

On Monday, July 9 1917, aboard *Benbow*, Commodore von Schoultz had retired for the night at about 10.30:

> I was still not completely undressed when I suddenly heard a dull roar and felt the ship shudder as from the firing of a heavy gun. The door banged to, and the open scuttles of my cabin clattered against the bulkhead. My first thought was, an explosion on board.[1]

As he pulled on his boots, Captain Clinton Baker came to him, saying something had happened. When they went on deck, they could see beyond their division 'a great column of smoke which seemed to be illuminated from within.' It was *Vanguard,* which had suddenly blown up. Only two of those on board survived; 'of the ship herself not the least trace was to be seen; nothing but a thick streak of oil on the surface showed the spot where she had gone down.'

The cause was not immediately known; but it followed similar devastating explosions which had destroyed the battleship *Bulwark* and the armoured cruiser *Natal* in 1914 and 1915, and was probably due to deteriorating cordite which reached a state of spontaneous combustion.[2] Whatever it was, it was almost certainly not the result of action by enemy agents, as was rumoured at the time. Beatty, writing to his two daughters of the 'terrible calamity,' still found it hard to grasp the loss of nearly 1,000 lives, in twenty five seconds.[3]

During the first three quarters of 1917 the High Seas Fleet had been quiescent. It was a period when it had to give up some of its most experienced officers and men required to commission the new U-boats coming into service, as Scheer observed:

> The commanders had to be officers who had sufficient experience to navigate and handle the boats without assistance in the most difficult circumstances. That meant a big demand for officers of the watch, because they, by age and seniority, were best fitted for such service. The fleet had to train men to take their places, so younger officers were promoted to be officers of the watch, and the training of midshipmen was accelerated. The substitutes for the latter were taken direct on board and received their training as naval cadets with the fleet. This entailed a very extensive shifting of all ranks which was bound to have a deleterious effect upon the efficiency of the ships.[4]

Nevertheless, the fleet continued its regular exercises in preparation for its next operations.

In March 1917 Scheer had planned a raid with the High Seas Fleet into the Hoofden, to attack the Dutch convoys. This never took place, however, because until March 11 the weather had been continuously dreadful, and by then the clear nights were over, which he regarded as 'a necessary preliminary condition for the enterprise.' The weather again deteriorated, preventing air reconnaissance, and the gale force winds prevented a night time cruiser raid. In the following months the fleet's activities were in the main limited to the support of the U-boat campaign, and to extensive and continuous minesweeping operations. These required a very large number of vessels; Scheer noted that whereas at the beginning of the war there were only thirty three small old torpedo boats available, the minesweeping forces in the North Sea by the end of the war comprised seventeen torpedo boats, twenty seven U-boats, seventy one M-boats (new purpose built minesweepers) four FM-boats (shallow draught minesweepers), twenty three trawlers, fifty eight motor boats, twenty two UZ boats, four parent ships and a repair ship.[5] Manning these absorbed a huge number of trained officers and men. In addition, convoying U-boats both outwards and inwards required about a hundred torpedo boats and smaller steamers; their extremely dangerous role was an essential support for the U-boat campaign.

Between July 6 and August 16 there was unrest in several vessels of the High Seas Fleet involving insubordination including refusals to obey orders, hunger strikes and acts of sabotage, apparently linked to the extremist Independent Social Democratic Party. Richard Stumpf recorded in his diary the state of feelings among enlisted men which had led to the outbreak:

> High state of excitement caused by a total lack of confidence in the officers. Persistence of the fixed notion that the war is conducted and prolonged solely in the interests of the officers. Manifestations of bitter anger due to fact that the enlisted men are starving and suffering while the officers carouse and roll in money.[6]

Prompt action was taken; on September 3 five of the ringleaders were sentenced to death, and two of these sentences were carried out, while sixteen others were sentenced to long terms of imprisonment. On August 18 the Kaiser visited the Fleet, putting briefly to sea on board *Baden,* to visit Heligoland. Scheer reported on the mutiny, and the actions taken. Müller recorded that 'sharp measures were demanded against the Socialist deputies involved. Capelle poured oil on the troubled waters by quoting the immunity of Reichstag members.'[7] Scheer felt that prompt action had nipped in the bud what might have become a much more serious outbreak of mutiny, adding:

> Most of those implicated had not realised the consequences of joining the organisation; to many it had not even been explained. Compared with the total numbers of the crews, those who had joined the movement were very few … Conditions on the big ships in particular unfortunately provided fruitful soil for such activities, as the crews were all the time in close communication with their homes and could, therefore, not be kept immune from the prevailing depression. These men performed the same service on the big ships all the year round, and they lacked the refreshing stimulus of meeting the enemy in battle.[8]

That autumn a large part of the High Seas Fleet, under the command of Vice Admiral Erhard Schmidt, took part in the successful operations to capture the Baltic Islands. Schmidt had no less than ten battleships with which to conduct Operation Albion, as it was known, and which proved a text book example of inter-service cooperation in the amphibious landings undertaken. Scheer, reflecting that a North Sea operation with surface vessels would not be expected while so much of the fleet was engaged in the Baltic, resolved to take advantage of this by launching an attack on the Scandinavian conveys. To carry out this operation he selected the fast 5.9 inch light cruisers *Brummer* and *Bremse*; although fitted as minelayers, the mine laying apparatus had been removed. In conducting this raid, Scheer had in mind not only the destruction of the convoy actually encountered, but also that the British would have to strengthen the escorts for future convoys at the expense of the forces engaged in antisubmarine warfare.

As it happened, this plan coincided with an operation which Jellicoe had proposed should be undertaken while Schmidt and his battleships were engaged in the Baltic. It was intended to carry out extensive mine laying operations close to the principal German bases, and Beatty had assigned a force of four light cruisers, twelve destroyers and a leader to attack the German minesweepers working in the Bight as a preliminary. However, as he was preparing to launch this venture Room 40 reported that a German operation, with an unknown objective, was in the wind, and Beatty was ordered to raise steam in all his light cruisers and in twelve destroyers: 'As the enemy's intentions were quite unknown Admiral Beatty was virtually ordered to place the whole North Sea under observation.'[9] Beatty accordingly set in motion his light cruiser squadrons to establish a series of patrol lines on October 16. The 6th Light Cruiser Squadron was sent to the NW coast of Jutland; it arrived minus one of its light cruisers, *Caradoc* and four of the six destroyers that were to accompany it. The 4th Light Cruiser Squadron was to patrol the Skagerrak between Norway and Denmark. The 3rd (from Scapa) and 1st and 2nd Light Cruiser Squadrons (from Rosyth) were to be on patrol lines in the centre of the North Sea, while to the south of them *Furious,* with four destroyers, was to patrol along the 56th parallel. The 1st Light Cruiser Squadron took up its position without destroyer escort, due to the change of orders. During the day Beatty added *Courageous* and *Glorious* to the patrol line of the 2nd Light Cruiser Squadron, with four destroyers, while in the evening the Admiralty ordered Tyrwhitt to sea with seven light cruisers, three leaders and twelve destroyers. These were to establish patrol lines in the southern part of the North Sea.[10]

There were, therefore, a large number of British warships searching the haystack for an unknown number of needles. The historian of Room 40, however, has pointed out that rather more information was available than Newbolt suggests. At 4.23 pm on October 15 a message from *Brummer* was intercepted, postponing an operation until the following day, and requesting minesweeping. An hour later Oliver notified Beatty: 'Minelayer *Brummer* leaves via Norman Deep tomorrow 16 to northward probably for mine laying. She should be intercepted.'[11] He told Beatty that if further information was received it would be signalled direct to ships at sea. However, although further decodes became available, they were not passed on, even though obvious deductions could have been drawn from them that a raid by more than one light cruiser was in the offing, including references by *UB 64* to heavy convoy traffic off Lerwick, and orders to all U-boats not to attack light cruisers unless positively identified as British. *Brummer* and *Bremse* were thus able to make their way northward without any of Beatty's ships being given any clue as to what was about to happen. A possible explanation for the Admiralty's failure to grasp the threat is that put forward by Newbolt as the reason why the current Scandinavian convoy was allowed to sail: 'It seemed to them improbable that the enemy would carry out his operation very far to the north, and so the Scandinavian convoy was not held in harbour.'[12]

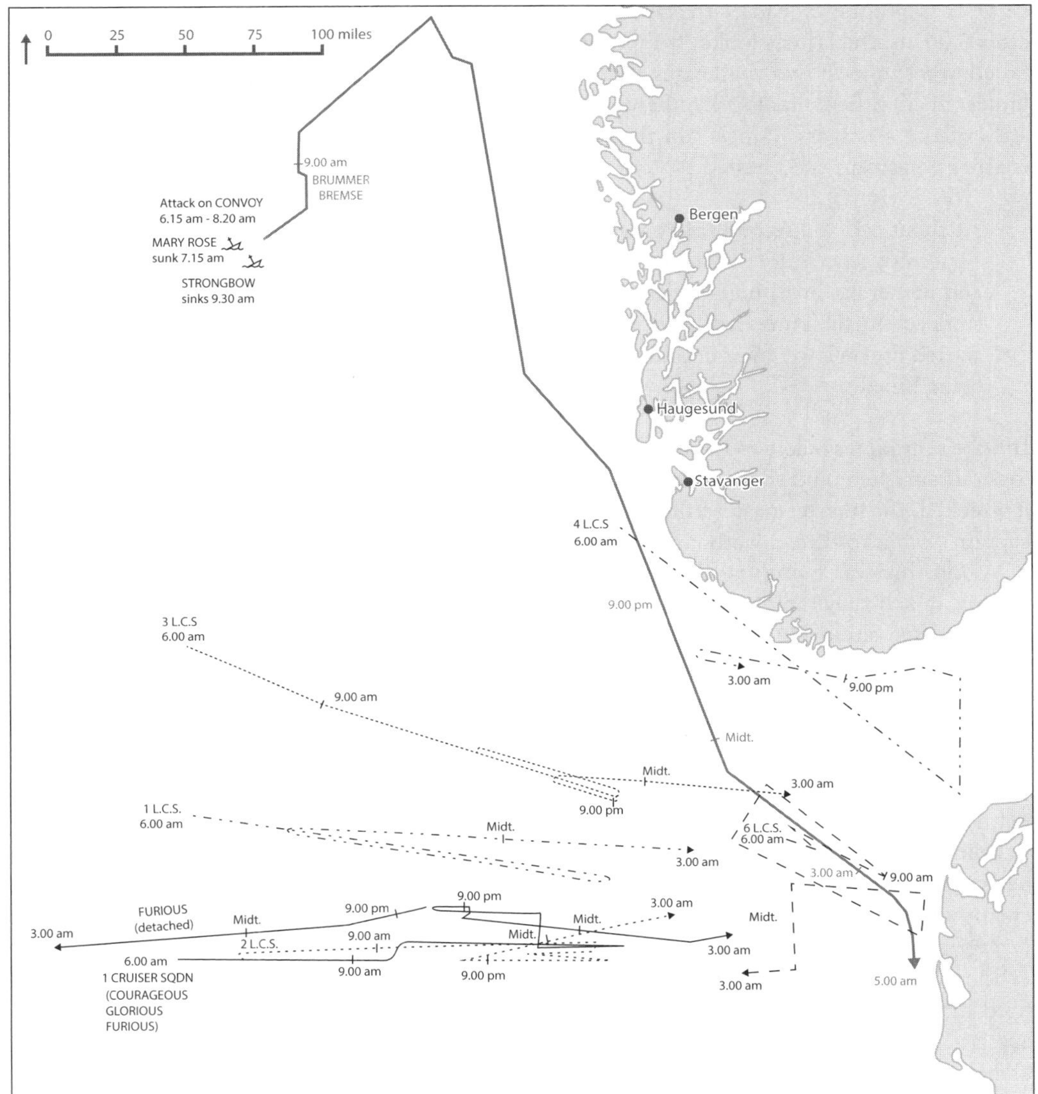

Map 18 First Scandinavian Convoy Attck: October 17 1917.

Escorted by the destroyers *Mary Rose* (Lieutenant Commander Fox) and *Strongbow*, and the armed trawlers *Elise* and *P Fannon*, the eastbound convoy had left Lerwick on October 15. At noon next day *Mary Rose* went ahead to collect the next westbound convoy in the Bergen leads, while *Strongbow* dispersed the ships of the eastbound convoy to their destinations. During the afternoon Fox sailed with twelve ships in convoy, and *Strongbow* rejoined after dark. Lieutenant Commander Brooke, her commanding officer, was unable to make contact with Fox, and so took up a position on the port quarter of the convoy. Soon after dawn next day *Mary Rose* was some eight or nine miles ahead of the convoy, with *Strongbow* still on the port side. A few minutes after 6.00 am the latter's lookouts reported two unknown vessels on a converging course; these failed to respond to two challenges and Brooke went to action stations, after asking Lieutenant James, his first lieutenant, if he knew of any German, or any Norwegian vessels of the appearance of the strangers. James said that he did not. He described to the subsequent Court of Inquiry what happened nest:

> At about 6.15 am second ship opened fire, foremost ship being more end on than second. First salvo entered fore of engine room, bursting main steam pipe and making a large hole and numerous small holes in ship's side above waterline. Ship was covered in steam and stopped. At the same time foremost ship opened fire, second salvo hitting forecastle and started fire on lower mess deck. Foremost gun was put out of action, most of the gun's crew being killed.[13]

Brooke sent James below to throw overboard the confidential books in the wireless room; James found it smashed, and the wireless operator killed. When he went back to the bridge he found it wrecked, the quartermaster killed and Brooke badly wounded; he was sent below again to the captain's cabin to throw overboard the steel chests there.

While this was going on *Brummer* and *Bremse* had turned away towards the ships of the convoy, which they rapidly began to sink. James saw nothing of *Mary Rose*, and presumed that she had been sunk. He and the gunner got the captain onto a raft before one of the cruisers returned to finish off *Strongbow*.

In fact, Fox in *Mary Rose*, having heard the firing astern of her, had turned back, thinking at first that the convoy had been attacked by a submarine. Soon, though, he sighted the cruisers and at once rapidly closed them, opening fire at about 6.20 at a range of between 6,000 and 7,000 yards. He stood no chance; by the time the range was down to 2,000 yards he put his helm hard over, and German gunners got the range as he turned. By 7.00 am, with *Mary Rose* in a sinking condition, he gave the order to abandon ship. Meanwhile the trawler *Elise,* which had contrived to avoid being sunk – James told the inquiry that there was nothing to prevent the enemy sinking her as well – went to look for survivors of *Mary Rose* before returning to pick up *Strongbow's* survivors who were still in the water.

The Court of Inquiry looked particularly into the allegation that the German cruisers had fired on survivors in the water, and concluded that they had. Newbolt wrote that, 'to their everlasting discredit fire was opened and maintained upon the *Strongbow's* survivors.' It was an allegation vehemently denied by the German Official History:

> Some of *Strongbow's* crew, who had taken to the lifeboat, and others who had leapt into the water, became additional victims of the gunfire, possible from shots falling short; it stands to reason that there was no intention whatsoever of firing on them. The statement of the British Official History, that defenceless survivors from the *Strongbow* were deliberately fired on, cannot be refuted strongly enough.[14]

The master of the Swedish ship *Visbur*, which was sunk in the attack, was quoted in the Swedish press as saying that reports that the German ships had fired on lifeboats with crews from sunken steamers were untrue. On the other hand he was critical of *Elise*, saying that she had 'rescued and carried off Englishmen from wreck of British destroyer *Strongbow* which was still afloat without caring for lifeboats of neutral steamers or investigating whether anybody on board three wrecks still afloat.[15]

Neither destroyer had got off any wireless messages about the attack, and the Admiralty remained in ignorance of what had occurred. It was not until the morning of October 17 that the later decodes were reported to Beatty; then at 2.20pm Oliver sent a personal update to the C-in-C:

> It is just possible *Brummer* may be accompanied by one or perhaps two light cruisers but if this is the case she has not yet left. Enemy has warned all submarines not to attack light cruisers unless certain they are hostile. This may indicate intention to operate on East Coast or to attack Lerwick or other convoys. In order to be prepared it seems desirable to withdraw *Courageous* and *Glorious* to Scapa to refuel and also 1st Light Cruiser Squadron.[16]

About an hour later Oliver had second thoughts, telling Beatty that it was now practically certain that *Brummer* was not accompanied by light cruisers. Beesly is justly extremely critical of the Admiralty's performance: 'It really is difficult to find any excuse for this incredible delay in passing out intelligence at this late stage in the war.' It was, he suggests, one more of Oliver's 'inexplicable failures to make proper use of the priceless intelligence at his disposal.' Newbolt glosses over this failure by saying only that 'during the forenoon of the 17th the Admiralty could get no further indications of the movements which they had detected two days before,' which of course missed the point entirely. Richmond, writing in his diary in December after the report of the Court of Inquiry, had discussed the matter with Commander Roger Bellairs of Beatty's staff, who had recently been to the Admiralty:

> They let the C-in-C down entirely over the convoy business when *Mary Rose* and *Strongbow* were lost. The Cruiser Squadrons were sent out by C-in-C on information from Adty, but important particulars were not sent, which, if sent, would greatly have modified his dispositions. This is the old stupidity the Admiralty have been guilty of so often – not acquainting commanders with the whole situation.[17]

By now Richmond's diary entries on the subject of the Admiralty were becoming more and more extreme; on the previous day he had written that 'Jellicoe himself is as ignorant as a pig, a weak-minded man with all the obstinacy of small natures.'

The later recollection of Admiral Sir William James, in letters to Marder of 1966 and 1968, who at the time was responsible for Room 40, was that they knew the call signs of both the German cruisers, and that their movements meant that 'they were obviously about to carry out some operation:'

> I remember Keyes, the Director of Plans, coming into our chart room and speculating on what these two ships were going to do. We did not of course have on our charts the position of any British ships: they were all shown on charts in Operations Division. If the convoys had been shown on our charts, it is probable that Keyes or someone else would have seen the possibility that the *Brummer* and *Bremse* objective was a convoy.[18]

During the rest of October 17, when *Brummer* and *Bremse* were making their way back to base, there were a great number of British ships at sea, but it was not until between 4.00 and 5.00 pm that Beatty was told that the convoy had been destroyed. He did his best to position his squadrons to cut off the German retreat, but his chance of doing so had been greatly reduced. It was calculated that if the two cruisers had steamed directly back for home at twenty knots they would be off the entrance to the Horns Reef channel by about 2.00 am on the following day, and at 6.15 pm new orders were issued to all the squadrons to take up positions to intercept. Before they could do so, however, the German cruisers had passed the cordon; at 5.00 am on October 18 they were reported to have reached Lyngvig, and all the squadrons returned to base.[19]

Commenting on the findings of the Court of Inquiry, Beatty wrote:

> As regards *Mary Rose*, the most remarkable point elicited by the Court of Inquiry is that although *Mary Rose* recognised the hostile character of the light cruisers she apparently made no attempt to communicate with her consort or to report the presence of enemy vessels to Lerwick by W/T… While admiring the spirit which actuated the captain of the *Mary Rose,* it is considered that in this case, where a single destroyer was engaging an overwhelming force of light cruisers in the daytime, more discretion would have been shown by keeping at long range. It is neither politic nor possible to keep destroyers informed of the movements of British forces when the latter are at sea, owing to the danger of revealing our dispositions.[20]

While it is obviously right that the enemy should be reported, the suggestion that *Mary Rose* could have kept out of range was scarcely reasonable; the speed of the German cruisers was such that she would almost certainly in any case have been caught. However, it was a view shared by the German Official History:

> The heroic fight put up by the two British destroyers *Strongbow* and *Mary Rose* had been in the highest British tradition, but it had achieved nothing. On the contrary; in consequence of their determination to give battle, they had not been able to carry out their essential task, which was to report the attack and thereby facilitate effective and adequate counter measures. If they had done this and later joined in the rescue operations after the withdrawal of the German Cruisers, they would have done better service.[21]

In fact Fox in *Mary Rose* did endeavour to report the presence of the German cruisers:

> Just as the *Mary Rose* was closing to attack the *Brummer*, a weak signal was heard. It was repeated on request from another station, but was jammed by the *Brummer.* If British observation stations had been alert then, it should perhaps have been possible to ascertain or at least suspect the position and time of the action. But this was not so, for throughout the forenoon British W/T traffic continued normally.[22]

In practice, however, getting a signal off would have been extremely difficult; the Germans were well aware of the importance of keeping news of their operation from other British forces, and the two light cruisers successfully jammed every attempt to transmit.

Beatty immediately promulgated fresh instructions to destroyer officers, emphasising the importance of treating every strange vessel as hostile 'until her friendly character is unmistakeable.' Since there were no current instructions as to what should be done in the event of an attack by surface vessels, he set these out plainly:

> In the event of a convoy being attacked by enemy surface craft, the signal to scatter is to be made by escorting Destroyers... The Destroyers themselves, while using their utmost endeavours to damage the enemy, are not to engage superior forces. They are to use their speed to maintain a safe distance from the enemy; they cannot protect the convoy after it has scattered and Destroyers are not to be risked uselessly. Their most important duty is to report enemy vessels and position immediately.[23]

Inevitably, when details of the action became known the Admiralty faced severe criticism in the press. The *Daily Mail* was particularly outspoken, complaining of a lack of intelligent initiative to deal with the submarine menace, or with German naval strategy or to use the naval forces to prevent such incidents as that of the attack on the convoy. The 'High Command ashore' stood indicted by the unanimous opinion of the country. All of this was somewhat unfair, as Geddes pointed out to the House of Commons on November 1. It was the first occasion on which a vessel in one of the Scandinavian convoys had been lost to an attack by enemy surface ships; some 4500 vessels had been safely convoyed since the system was introduced in April 1917. The Admiralty's case, not unreasonably, was that it would always be effectively impossible to prevent the occasional determined and well managed raid by fast, well armed surface ships breaking through a convoy's defences. On October 22 he attended a conference at the Admiralty to consider what might be learned from the affair, and a fortnight later detailed proposals were put forward for an extensive revision of the whole Scandinavian convoy system.[24]

Meanwhile, so seriously had the Government taken the savage criticism contained in the *Daily Mail* articles that FE Smith, the Attorney General, was asked to write an opinion as to whether the newspaper could or should be prosecuted under the Defence of the Realm Regulations. This he did on October 31. He explained to Geddes that criticism of the War Office or Admiralty was permitted under the existing law, unless the statements made were likely to 'interfere with the success of His Majesty's Forces' or 'likely to prejudice the discipline or administration of His Majesty's Forces.' Reviewing the language used by the *Daily Mail*, which said that the affair of the Scandinavian convoy was a grievous humiliation, and that those responsible should be punished, that the Admiralty was to blame and made no attempt to cut off the raiders, that Whitehall had got to 'answer this – if it can,' and that a naval enquiry would come to comfortable conclusions on the matter, he concluded that it *was* likely to prejudice the administration of the navy. The question of prosecution however, was one of expediency; not only whether it would succeed but whether the Admiralty High Command should be made the subject of issues in a civilian court. That said, he thought that a magistrate ought to convict, and probably would:

> But it is not certain. The case would be tried at the Mansion House – an incalculable and not specially competent tribunal. Such a prosecution raises questions of grave policy which the War Cabinet ought to consider. I should not refuse to direct a prosecution if in the opinion of the War Cabinet the objections of policy are superable.[25]

Not altogether surprisingly, in the light of this advice, it was decided to take no action, not least perhaps because the Prime Minister's views were not far different from those of the newspaper.

35

The Second Battle of Heligoland Bight

In November it was the turn of the Grand Fleet to launch a major operation. This was to be a large scale attack on the German minesweeping operations in the North Sea. For some time these had been escorted by light cruisers and destroyers; more recently it had been observed that they were increasingly being supported by an entire battle squadron from the High Seas Fleet. The possibility of being able to engage this meant that a very substantial force must be committed to the operation. Madden, as commander of the 1st Battle Squadron, was to take overall charge of the attack, designated as 'Operation FR.'

The vessels to be employed would be divided into three groups. Force A, under Vice Admiral Sir Trevelyan Napier, comprised his 1st Cruiser Squadron *(Courageous,* his flagship, with *Glorious* and four screening destroyers); 1st Light Cruiser Squadron (Cowan) (four light cruisers and two destroyers); and 6th Light Cruiser Squadron (Alexander-Sinclair) (four light cruisers and four destroyers). Force B, commanded by Pakenham, consisted of his 1st Battle Cruiser Squadron of four battle cruisers, reinforced by *New Zealand*, and the light cruiser *Champion* with nine destroyers. Force C was Madden's 1st Battle Squadron, with eleven destroyers, which was to play a supporting role. Forces A and B, together under Pakenham's command, were to sail from Rosyth and arrive at a point 'about half way across the outer edge of the quadrant of mines in the Helgoland Bight. They were to approach this point from the western and southern sides of the large German minefield in the central part of the North Sea.'[1] Thereafter, they were to sweep NNW at high speed. They were to be in position by 8.00 am on November 17. Force C was to take up its supporting position at the same time. Madden's written orders, issued on November 16, had originally prescribed 10.00 am for the cruisers' rendezvous, but this was brought forward. Two submarines were patrolling to give intelligence of enemy movements.

The plan was, however, marred by a remarkably bad piece of staff work, the significance of which was explained in detail by Newbolt:

> As the squadron commanders were instructed to strike at a force of enemy ships on or near the outer edge of the mine barrier, it followed that if it found them, the British squadrons might be obliged to press on into the mined area in pursuit. If they were so compelled their movements would obviously be restricted by those minefields which they believed to lie within the zone of their operations.[2]

The Admiralty, in the person of the Hydrographer of the Navy, issued a monthly chart showing the British and German minefields in the Heligoland Bight. A copy went to the Commander-in-Chief, but it was not circulated to the fleet. Pakenham had either been given a copy or at any rate had seen one; but it was not shown to the admirals commanding cruiser squadrons. They, and their captains kept their own charts, updated by the 'mine memoranda' issued from time to time by the C-in-C. Unlike the monthly chart which he had, these memoranda did not locate the lines of mines laid, but merely indicated dangerous areas. The chart which Pakenham possessed or had seen showed a zone of clear water to the southeast of the general rendezvous. Pakenham therefore knew that his squadrons could safely go into the mined areas for some thirty miles, but Napier was quite unaware of this. What he did know was that Beatty had banned operations beyond a line just south of the rendezvous unless the ships involved had full information as to the minefields.[3]

Napier's chart differed from those in the possession of Alexander-Sinclair and Cowan, in that it marked as a danger area a 1915 minefield in the centre of the Heligoland Bight, which had been strengthened in July 1916. This large danger area was, Napier considered, an absolute barrier to further advance; on the other hand, the light cruiser squadron commanders knew nothing of it.

In addition there existed a chart showing the approximate positions of the German swept channels. Beatty had a copy, but he showed it to none of the admirals taking part in Operation FR. Madden's orders of November 16 stated, under the heading of 'enemy intelligence,' that 'enemy submarines on passage are following the route from Muckle Flugga to the Doggerbank Nord light vessel.'[4] He gave no information as to the likely enemy movements or lines of retirement. Taken overall, these lapses in efficient preparation for a major operation were inexcusable.

There was no doubt a good deal of discussion between the commanders while the operation was at the planning stage, at which the objective would have been thoroughly explored. All the same, Madden's order of November 16 was laconic in the extreme, and cannot have helped Napier much with the decisions which he would have to make once the operation was under way.

At all events the British forces intended to take part in the operation duly assembled at Rosyth, and all of them left harbour at 4.30 pm on November 16. By 7.00 next day the cruiser groups were approaching the barrier. Napier, with the 1st Cruiser Squadron, was leading the way, with Alexander-Sinclair's 6th Light Cruiser Squadron on his port beam and Cowan's 1st Light Cruiser Squadron some three miles astern. Pakenham, with the battle cruisers, was steaming ten and a half miles on the port quarter of *Courageous*. Apart from some indications of wireless traffic which had been picked up during the morning watch, there was nothing to indicate that German forces were at sea in the vicinity. Visibility was about seven and a half miles; the sea was smooth and light, and the westerly wind was force two.

As it happened, the Germans had planned a large minesweeping operation for October 17 in the very sector to which Pakenham's forces had been directed. This involved three minesweeping half-flotillas, and two destroyer half flotillas, reinforced by two additional destroyers, making eight in all, and a barrier breaking group, consisting of mine explosion resistant trawlers. The covering force was the Second Scouting Group under von Reuter, consisting of the light cruisers *Königsberg, Nürnberg, Pillau* and *Frankfurt*. There were two battleships, *Kaiserin* and *Kaiser*, in support near Heligoland.[5]

The objective of the German operation was to obtain accurate information as to the whereabouts of British minefields, and to devise ways of circumventing them. Once the location of all of these had been identified, it would next be necessary to determine which should be cleared away. The operation on November 17 was aimed at searching from about the centre of the line Horns Reef – Terschelling in the direction N by W. Reuter ordered his group to assemble at 7.00 am; Captain Grasshoff, of *Kaiserin,* reported that at that time the two battleships would be in position west of Heligoland. Airship reconnaissance was impossible due to the thick weather, which also prevented Reuter shipping any seaplanes on his light cruisers; sea planes were, however able to fly from Borkum.[6]

Aboard his flagship *Königsberg,* Reuter saw that two of the minesweeping half flotillas had not by 7.30 am, yet reached the rendezvous, and since they could not be far behind, he turned away from the rest of his squadron to bring them up. As he did so he suddenly came under fire from the NW; Napier's flagship *Courageous* and her consort *Glorious* had sighted *Königsberg* on their starboard bow, and at 7.37 opened fire with their 15-inch guns. They were aided by the fact that whereas the western horizon was misty, obscuring the German's ability to discern them, the eastern horizon was bright; the German vessels showed up distinctly. The surprise was complete; but the German destroyers and minesweepers at once made smoke screens, and by 7.51 the German ships were lost to sight. Reuter ordered the German cruisers, which had advanced to cover the retreat of the minesweepers, at 7.53 to turn southeast through the British minefields, falling back towards the support of the two battleships. One armed trawler, *Kehdingen*, had been serving as a mark boat for the sweeping forces; anchored in her position, she was hit almost at once by a shell, and thereafter lay immobile.

Although Napier had achieved a surprise of the enemy, he was far from clear about what he had encountered. Soon after opening fire he reported to Madden that he had an unknown number of light cruisers in sight, bearing east. Pakenham picked up the signal, and almost at once heard the sounds of gunfire, but was uncertain as to the enemy's strength. A report from Cowan at 7.45 that the enemy bore ESE was accompanied by a warning that he could not tell how many enemy ships were present, so Pakenham was still none the wiser.

Nor was Napier, whose first report to Pakenham after the action was extremely inaccurate:

> Soon after 0730 the enemy were sighted ahead consisting of five to eight submarines escorted by two or more destroyers, some minesweepers to port of them, and four light cruisers gradually coming into view to starboard of them. Four of the submarines appeared to be of unusually large size, either with funnels or with two conning towers and no masts. The light cruisers were probably *Stralsund, Pillau*, *Regensburg* and one other.[7]

He went on to describe how these entirely fictitious submarines began to submerge and, more accurately, how the minesweepers disappeared NE while the destroyers made smoke:

> The smoke screen was skilfully managed by the enemy, and soon reduced the shooting greatly to a matter of chance, crippling the range finding and spotting, and the point of aim was often only flashes.[8]

When, at 8.00 am, Napier reached the smoke screen he turned sharply to the south. Once clear of the smoke, at 8.07 he sighted Reuter's cruisers to the southeast of him, apparently heading

ENE. Four minutes later he could see that they had turned southeast, and he reported these sightings to Madden. Pakenham, picking up these messages, ordered Rear Admiral Phillimore, in *Repulse,* to steer to the support of Cowan's light cruisers, and turned his remaining battle cruisers to port to follow Napier.[9] In his report to Beatty, Napier described how the action had now 'settled down into a chase at ranges of 15,000 to 10,000 yards, the enemy still making heavy smoke, and steering down what was probably a swept channel as a pillar buoy was passed presumably marking an outer end.'[10]

Although Reuter, having turned to the southeast, had completed his concentration, and his auxiliary forces were safely retreating to the north east undisturbed, his position was still hazardous. He had drawn all Napier's forces after him, and could now only head for the support of *Kaiserin* and *Kaiser* as fast as he could. Newbolt points out the danger that he faced from the heavy guns of the light battle cruisers:

> He was being followed by a force of overwhelming strength; and although he had gained a forward position against which the British broadsides could not be brought to bear, the forces against him were so numerous and powerful that a single mischance might bring disaster on his squadron. One 15 inch from the *Courageous* or *Glorious,* falling in the after part of any of his ships, might at any instant reduce her speed by a few knots: if it did he would have to abandon her as Hipper had abandoned the *Blücher* nearly three years before.[11]

By 8.20 Reuter was under very heavy fire from all three British squadrons. Early in the engagement *Ursa,* one of Napier's destroyers, had launched one torpedo unsuccessfully; now *Vanquisher* and *Valentine,* two of Alexander-Sinclair's destroyers, attempted a torpedo attack but were driven off under heavy fire. Reuter now put up another smoke screen, and the two forces steamed on, with the British steadily reducing the range. Fifteen minutes later, as the smoke had cleared, Reuter again put up a particularly dense smoke screen, behind which his forces entirely disappeared. This gave Napier a problem. All the time he could directly follow Reuter he could safely assume that he would pass through waters that had been cleared of mines; now, this huge smoke screen might be intended to conceal a crucial change of course. Napier was approaching a line marked on his own chart, labelled 'Line B,' which he had drawn to show the point twelve miles beyond the rendezvous which, as he later wrote to Beatty, was 'the limit I had in mind of, at any rate, British minefields, and to which I could go if necessity arose.'[12]

To continue on his present course was obviously dangerous, and at 8.40 Napier turned his squadron eight points to port, to a north easterly course; Cowan and Alexander-Sinclair followed suit. At this point *Courageous* was about two and a quarter miles north of the two light cruiser squadron; Cowan was just then crossing the stern of Alexander-Sinclair at a very short distance while *Repulse,* which had not yet come into action, was six miles on the port quarter of *Courageous.* Napier reported to Madden that he had lost sight of the enemy, but that the light cruisers were in pursuit.

Twelve minutes later the smoke screen began to clear, and Napier could see that Reuter had, in fact, continued on his course; he altered course eight points to starboard and resumed the chase, having lost five precious miles by his original turn. By now the 6th Light Cruiser Squadron was in the lead, having had to make the smallest turn, and it was upon the ships of Alexander-Sinclair that Reuter's vessels concentrated their fire. *Cardiff* sustained three hits, one on her forecastle, which started two fires, one on her superstructure above the after control position, and one in her torpedo department.

At 9.00 Phillimore, in *Repulse,* had finally caught up. He had been warned by Pakenham not to take her into the minefields, which the British were fast approaching and which obviously presented serious hazards. Pakenham had taken in Napier's report that he had lost sight of the enemy, and was extremely anxious about the risks that were being run:

> Although he possessed better and more detailed information with regard to the minefields than any of the other Admirals in the operating squadrons, Admiral Pakenham was very doubtful whether any good purpose would be served by pursuing the enemy through the intricate and twisting passages through the fields … now, on receiving Admiral Napier's signal, he decided that our pursuit of the enemy ought to cease. The signal read as though contact with the enemy had been completely lost, and gave him no inkling that the enemy had temporarily disappeared behind a smoke screen; he therefore ordered all squadrons to join him at the general rendezvous.[13]

Napier got this recall at about 9.00 am, by which time all the British ships, now including *Repulse*, were again in action. He was reluctant to comply, having just decided to advance further into the minefields. He thought, incorrectly, that Reuter had been reinforced, and that Alexander-Sinclair and Cowan would continue to need the support of his 15 inch guns; accordingly, in two messages to Pakenham he said that he had sighted the smoke of six ships 'in addition to those reported at 7.30,' and that he was still engaging the enemy. Accordingly, he did not act upon Pakenham's signal of recall, and pressed on. This was in spite of the fact that following the turn to port *Courageous* and *Glorious* had fallen back so far that at 8.07 they were obliged to cease fire. In addition, the 4 inch guns of the *Galatea* class cruisers (*Galatea, Royalist* and *Inconstant)* were also out of range, only their two 6 inch guns being effective.

Just now, Reuter decided to launch a torpedo attack to slow down the British pursuit, under cover of a fresh smoke screen at about 9.15. For the next ten minutes torpedo tracks were repeatedly sighted by all three squadrons. Scheer records that six torpedoes were fired by the German destroyers, and that *Königsberg* and *Frankfurt* also fired torpedoes; but none hit.[14]

It was not at all clear what hits had been scored on the enemy, although British fire control officers believed that one light cruiser had been damaged. At 9.30 Reuter again made smoke, preparatory to launching a fresh torpedo attack; again, no hits were recorded. By now, however, Napier had reached a point which he had marked on his map as 'Line C,' representing a 'dangerous area;' it was in fact a British minefield laid in 1915, and it was, for Napier, the absolute limit of his advance. At 9.32 he ordered his own squadron to turn sharply to starboard. Eight minutes later he signalled Pakenham and his own light cruiser squadrons: 'Battle cruisers and cruisers should not go further through the minefield. Light Cruisers use discretion and report movements.'[15] At 9.49, he signalled *Repulse*: 'Heavy draft ships should not go further into minefields.' Since neither Alexander-Sinclair nor Cowan had the danger zone marked on their maps, they carried on the chase, trusting to their quarry to lead them through safe waters. *Repulse* appears to have continued to follow them, and all concerned had high hopes of achieving a decisive victory.

Reuter, too, now felt able to hope of achieving a success, as he wrote in his battle despatch:

> Up to this point the action had been fought with a calm that may well be called exemplary. Everyone manned his post, carrying out the duties assigned to him as in manoeuvres. In spite of the tremendous impression caused by the mixed salvoes and the ensuing effects of the enemy's fire... we were animated only by the fervent desire, filled only with the one thought: to destroy the enemy. This moment had arrived; calm yielded to a certain feverish expectation. It could only be a matter of minutes until the fate of the enemy was sealed.[16]

His optimism was justified; with the British light cruisers in hot pursuit of him, there was every chance that he would be able to deliver them to *Kaiserin* and *Kaiser.* If they tried to escape by turning north or northwest, they would be heading straight into the minefields, where they might suffer heavy losses.

In the ongoing exchanges of gunfire between the respective light cruisers, *Calypso* suffered serious damage when a shell hit the conning tower, destroying the bridge, and killing all those on the lower bridge and wounding her navigating officer and mortally wounding her captain. The other light cruisers pressed on until at about 9.50 am they found themselves under fire from *Kaiserin* and *Kaiser.* Alexander-Sinclair at once ordered his own ships, and Cowan's squadron to turn sixteen points and make their way at high speed out of the trap into which they had nearly stumbled. *Kaiserin* got a shot home on *Caledon,* which caused no damage; as *Königsberg* turned to pursue the retreating British, she was hit by a shell from *Repulse,* which caused a fire in a coal bunker. No further pursuit was undertaken.

While this had been going on, Napier had been hovering outside the danger zone awaiting reports. At 10.00 *Galatea* signalled: 'Enemy battleships, battle cruisers and light cruisers bearing southeast, steering east.' Napier's subsequent report to Pakenham spoke of the arrival of four enemy battleships.[17] Any momentary alarm which this may have caused, however, was dispelled by later messages that the light cruisers had successfully extricated themselves, and were no longer being pursued. By 1.00 pm these had rejoined Napier, and all the British forces at sea made their way back across the North Sea without further incident. Meanwhile *Hindenburg* and *Moltke,* which had set off towards the scene of action when the first contact with the enemy was reported, had now joined *Kaiserin* and *Kaiser,* too late, however, to take any part.[18]

Both sides claimed considerably more hits than was in fact the case. The Germans scored seven hits on the British light cruisers, while being hit themselves five times. They had been surprised by the appearance in battle for the first time of *Courageous* and *Glorious,* noting correctly that so far as they could see they had only two turrets; they were also struck by their high speed. The fact that *Königsberg* had suffered so little from a direct hit by a 15 inch shell was considered remarkable:

> It passed through all three funnels of the ship, went through the upper deck into a coal bunker – the inner wall of which it burst; there it exploded and caused a fire. The fragments of this shell were picked up and its calibre determined. This proved to us that the English had built a new class of cruiser armed with a 38 cm gun.[19]

In fact, of course, it was not one of the light battle cruisers that had fired the shell, but *Repulse,* which was also making its maiden appearance in a North Sea engagement. Considering the high speed of the British ships, Scheer correctly concluded that they must be lightly armoured.

The lesson which he learned from the engagement was in future to bring the support groups further forward, so far as the minefields allowed:

> The demands thus made upon the battleships of our outpost section increased considerably. The field of operation of the minesweepers extended 180 sea miles to the north and 140 miles to the west of the Jade. Work at such distant points was impossible without strong fighting support.[20]

Half of the supporting vessels were located immediately behind the minesweepers, with the rest about 50 miles further back. In 1918 an anchorage in the Amrum Bank area was made secure from submarine attack, surrounded by nets, where the support ships could anchor in safety, thus avoiding the need to make the long journey back to the Jade.

The British performance in the engagement had not been very distinguished; Marder calls it a 'fiasco,' and this is not an overstatement. Beatty was extremely disappointed. He was displeased not only with Napier, but also with Pakenham. In his formal report to Beatty of November 26 Pakenham had done his best to talk up the operation as being in some way a success. He found it creditable that in spite of the difficulties created by the German smoke screens 'all singled out the most important military force present as the object for collective attack.' He noted the caution with which the Germans treated the minefield, concluding that 'in dashing into it our forces performed a feat of a high order.' Finally, he noted the value and loyalty of Phillimore's support, but observed that *Repulse* was too valuable to be hazarded in minefield other than in extreme circumstances: 'Success entitles the venture to rank as an achievement.'[21]

This did not go down well with Beatty. In his first report to the Admiralty of December 1, which stimulated a considerable exchange of correspondence and the expression of a large number of opinions, he said that he did not agree with Pakenham as to the risks run by Phillimore:

> The information given to the latter officer as to the position of minefields was incomplete and showed clear water after passing mined area W6. I consider that under the circumstances Rear Admiral Phillimore… was justified in the steps he took to carry out the orders given to him to support the light cruisers. Having regard also to the fact that he had the enemy light cruisers as a guide down a channel which had obviously been swept and marked with buoys, I consider his determined support was most effective and valuable in assisting the light cruisers to retire before the enemy battleship supports. His action undoubtedly served as a deterrent to those supports, which otherwise might have inflicted considerable damage on our light cruisers.[22]

Phillimore was always something of a favourite of Beatty.

It was for Napier that Beatty reserved most of his wrath. He was displeased that no arrangements had been made to deal with the German minesweepers when sighted, ' the destruction of which was one of the objects of the operation.' He observed that Napier did not place his squadron between the enemy and his base: 'a determined effort to do this at the beginning of the engagement might have met with success and cut the enemy's line of retreat.' He found it regrettable that when the action had developed into a chase, 'the high speed of the squadron was not utilised to close the range.' His most serious discontent was with Napier's most crucial decision:

> It is unfortunate also that the 1st Cruiser Squadron turned eight points away and gave up the chase at 0840, subsequently turning again at 0852 and following at a distance which had now been increased by five miles.[23]

He also, not unreasonably, picked up Napier's first report of large submarines in the German force, which had subsequently been reported by *Glorious* to be minesweepers and other small craft. He wanted this information checked, 'which is important in view of the tendency to too readily assume that every low lying craft sighted is a submarine.' Prisoners from the outpost boat *Kehdingen* confirmed that no submarines were present on November 17.

Beatty's report duly made the rounds of the senior officers at the Admiralty, working its way up from an initial critique of December 7 by Hope, as Director of Operations. He noted the lack of any operational signals by Napier, and that his movements indicated 'an absence of decision as to tactics to be employed.' He was also struck by the fact that 'no attempt was made by anyone to follow up the minesweepers, all attention being devoted to the light cruisers.' For the future, he considered that the Admiralty should issue definite instructions on the use of heavy ships in the minefields:

> The question as to whether the heavy ships should have entered the area of minefields is a difficult one. The orders issued for the operation contained no instructions on this point So long as our ships could remain on the track taken by the Germans they were comparatively safe, but if they were manoeuvred off this line they might easily have got into an unswept area. If a ship was mined and her speed reduced, she must have been lost, owing to the presence of strong German supports, as it would have been impossible for our supports to extricate her.[24]

Hope was perfectly right to point out the unfairness of leaving it to an admiral to take such a decision in the heat of battle. Nonetheless, it does seem surprising that neither Pakenham nor Napier raised the issue beforehand. Oliver concurred with Hope's comments, adding his regret that Napier did not close the enemy at full speed as soon as they were sighted. He also observed that the Commander-in-Chief had known that there would be enemy battleships in support, but that there was nothing to show that the squadrons engaged knew this.

Wemyss, too, felt that Napier should have at once altered course and increased to full speed when he sighted Reuter's ships. He did not think much of Pakenham's recall signal, which he regarded as ambiguous. When the papers reached Jellicoe, he had a number of serious criticisms to make. Napier's failure to close the enemy he found inexplicable; he should be asked for an explanation. He proposed to ask Beatty whose fault it was that no provision was made to deal with the minesweepers. He could see no reason why *Repulse* should not have followed the light cruisers, and wanted to know what was known about the minefields, and by whom. As for the enemy battleships, he wanted to know whether Beatty warned Madden or Pakenham of the possibility that these might be met. Finally, when all this got to the desk of the First Lord, Geddes minuted that a telegram should be sent to Beatty expressing the view that Napier's failure to close was inexplicable.[25] The telegram when sent caused understandable confusion, since Jellicoe inadvertently referred to VABCF (Pakenham) when he meant VALCF.

On December 16 Napier produced his explanation, enclosing a tracing showing what he knew about the minefields and the conclusions he drew from that information, particularly as to his first turn away, and his subsequent decision to go on further, to the limit of the 'dangerous area.' As to Beatty's complaint that he had not put himself between Reuter and the latter's base, he pointed out that he did not have information about the swept channels, 'so could not act in the way in which in open water would no doubt have been sound.' What he did not do was to offer any reasons for not increasing his speed from 25 knots, other than a plaintive reminder that what looked so clear afterwards when all information was known was 'anything but clear at the time when surrounded by smoke in all directions; and also that the loss of heavy or comparatively heavy ships by mines would have converted an action with somewhat negative results into a disaster.' As the editor of Jellicoe's papers points out, the resemblance of this paragraph to the case for Jellicoe at Jutland against his critics is noteworthy.[26]

At all events, it did not impress Oliver, who wanted to know more about the minefield charts, or Jellicoe, who still wanted to hear why speed was not increased. Napier was required to submit a further lengthy explanation, which on December 22 he did. Having increased to 25 knots it appeared that the enemy was then on a course opposite to his own, so a further increase would not have enabled him to close. His chief consideration, he wrote, had been to get through the smoke screen and determine what the situation really was. This was hardly a complete explanation, and it did not satisfy Oliver, who minuted that it did not appear to explain why no increase of speed was made between 0859, when fire was reopened, until course was altered on Line C and the action abandoned.'[27] *Courageous* and *Glorious* were certainly capable of something of the order of 32 knots, and working up to this speed might well have made a difference, even if it meant going on ahead of the light cruisers. The German Official History offers Napier no comfort:

> Minesweeping forces, closely supported only by light cruisers, encountered heavy enemy forces and found themselves in a situation which should have ended in the destruction of both minesweeper and light cruisers; if the enemy had acted with vigour, the *Kaiserin* and *Kaiser*, well to the rear, would have arrived too late to prevent it... Correct tactical behaviour on the part of the German units, together with the weak and hesitant attack by far superior British forces, provided the essentials for this unexpected outcome ... Only the conduct of the 1st and 6th Light Cruiser Squadrons left nothing to be desired; they were least concerned with worries about mines, since their mine charts were the most incomplete and, unlike the charts of Admirals Pakenham and Napier, theirs did not show the extensive mined area to the west of List. But the decision of the day lay less with the leaders of the light cruisers than with those of the capital ships.[28]

Napier wrote privately to Tyrwhitt on December 8 to express his chagrin at the way things had turned out for him:

> Have you ever experienced the chill down your back when – after an exciting and tiring day's shooting, you return well pleased with yourself – and the house party immediately asks what is in the bag. With a sudden revulsion you are obliged to admit it is only several pheasants and hares wounded and dying in their holes! This is somewhat our feelings on returning to harbour on 19th Nov. – and incidentally is much what we felt after that rotten entertainment called the Battle of Jutland. It seems that we are expected to sink them all, but we found that they were difficult to sink, especially when enveloped in smoke, with nothing showing except gun flashes.[29]

Geddes, who had been dismayed by the fiasco, had picked up on a visit to the Grand Fleet the extent of Beatty's disapproval of Napier's actions, and wished to make the latter a scapegoat for the failure. He was impatient at the delay in receiving Beatty's report, announcing that in his opinion the Commander-in-Chief was trying to shield Napier, as Jellicoe recorded:

> This was having the effect on him (Geddes) to make him all the more determined to make a scapegoat of Napier. I said this was unjust and wrong and that he must await the receipt of the report. This happened more than once and as I thought showed a want of justice on the part of Geddes.[30]

Candour of this kind on Jellicoe's part was unlikely to have gone down well with the First Lord.

Cowan wrote to Keyes on November 23 with a brief account of the action from a somewhat different perspective:

> So far as A-S's and my outfits were concerned it was a good hard straight for'd chase and shoot, bothered to death by smoke screens, far too busy and interested to think of torpedoes and mines of which there were plenty and at the latter end rather anxious about ammunition, my bow gun shot away all its outfit (200) and 20 as well, we'd 50 rounds a gun left. We really had great hopes towards the end as the 2nd ship was nicely on fire and the rear one slowly coming back to us, but then up hove those battleships and it was no good going on was it to let them score off us.[31]

As the extent of the criticisms being heaped on him became apparent, Napier's reaction was to suggest to Beatty that he should be relieved. Beatty, however, had had enough of the inquest, and told Napier that he still had confidence in him, and wanted him to stay. This may have been, as Marder suggests, due to his 'characteristic magnanimity;' or it may have been because the inefficiency at various levels reflected on him as well. In order to bring the matter to a close, he wrote to the Admiralty on December 24 to express his view that Napier had made an error of judgment and that he had pointed this out and explained the consequences. He thought that the experience would be of the greatest value in the future to Napier, who had 'hitherto shown skill and judgment in command of light cruiser work and notwithstanding the disappointing results which attended the recent operation in the Heligoland Bight,' he would be very loath to part with his services. He suggested that the matter would be sufficiently met by an expression of their Lordships 'displeasure'.[32]

This, on January 31, was the course taken by the Board of Admiralty, which formally concurred with Beatty in the conclusion which he had reached, and so informed Napier. Their Lordships went on to receive a report that arrangements had been made for full information as to the location of British minefields to be given to the flag officers of all the Grand Fleet squadrons to prevent the problem recurring. It was agreed to leave the item on the agenda in the future so that the question of whether there had been bad staff work on Pakenham's part might be considered. This does not, however, appear to have been pursued further.[33] Beatty certainly considered Pakenham to blame for an omission that went a considerable way to excusing Napier for his failure; and it had been immediately apparent to Madden that it was essential that the light cruisers should have comprehensive charts of the minefields if they were to be expected to pursue the enemy in mined areas, as he told Beatty. The affair, which had demonstrated failings that might not have been expected after all the Grand Fleet's experiences, had ended in humiliation, as the prolonged investigations into the reasons for its outcome starkly demonstrated.

36

The Second Convoy Attack

There was much concern at the Admiralty about the best way to improve the security of the Scandinavian convoys. A proposal to lengthen the intervals between sailings, not yet implemented, risked disturbing the normal flow of trade, particularly in respect of the transport of coal to Norway. The solution proposed was to shorten the route, and on December 10 1917 Captain Henderson visited Longhope for a meeting with the officers responsible for the convoys. The suggestion was that the convoys should sail from Methil instead of Lerwick, which was in any case a more logical point of departure for Sweden and Denmark, and this was generally agreed. Beatty, however, while accepting this, pointed out that the new route was much closer to the German bases, thus increasing the risk of attacks from surface ships.[1]

It so happened that at this moment Scheer was perfecting his arrangements for another attack on the Scandinavian convoys. For this he selected the II Flotilla, commanded by Commander Heinecke, which consisted of eight of the latest destroyers. Larger and faster than their predecessors, they carried three 4.1 inch guns, and were capable of 36 knots. The plan was to launch two attacks simultaneously. The 3rd Half Flotilla, under Lieutenant Commander Holbe, was to go north and attack the convoy traffic on the Bergen-Lerwick route, while the 4th Half Flotilla, under Heinecke, was aimed at the convoy traffic close to the English coast near Newcastle. The flotilla sailed on the morning of December 11 and was escorted as far as the north eastern end of the Dogger Bank by the light cruiser *Emden*, where the two half flotillas went their separate ways.[2]

Following the October attack by *Brummer* and *Bremse,* the Grand Fleet had been sending out cruiser squadrons to make regular sweeps to cover the Bergen-Lerwick route; these were also intended to give early warning of any German units coming out of the Bight. Naturally it was hoped that Room 40 would be able to discern if any German operation was imminent, but on this occasion there was no indication that anything was in the wind. During the afternoon and evening of December 11 two cruiser squadrons sailed. The 3rd Light Cruiser Squadron, consisting of *Chatham, Yarmouth* and *Birkenhead*, commanded by Captain Woollcomb, left Rosyth with four destroyers at 5.15 pm. Their route was to take them to thirty miles WSW of Jaederen by 8.30 am next day, after which they were to sweep across the entrance to the Skagerrak towards Bovbierg, returning the same night. Meanwhile at 10.00 pm the 2nd Cruiser Squadron sailed from Scapa; it consisted of the armoured cruisers *Shannon* and *Minotaur*, with four destroyers. Captain Molteno commanded this force, with orders to cover the Bergen-Lerwick route. He was to meet the westbound convoy on the morning of December 12. Thereafter he was to return along the convoy route to cover the eastbound convoy which would be crossing on that day.[3]

As Heinecke approached the English coast he intercepted a number of British wireless messages which seemed to indicate that a southbound convoy escorted by destroyers would leave the Firth of Forth between 8.00 and 11.00 pm. Accordingly he steamed northwards up the 'war channel' towards Berwick, expecting to meet the convoy between 3.00 and 6.00 am on December 12. Other wireless intercepts suggested that there were eight British cruisers in the Firth of Forth with a number of destroyers in the Tyne and the Humber; taken together these forces rendered his advance towards the convoy very hazardous, or should have done if the reports of their location were accurate. In fact they were not; the only convoy in the area was that coming south from Lerwick, escorted by the destroyers *Ouse* and *Garry*, which had sailed on the afternoon of December 10. At just before 11.00 pm on the following night, the convoy reached the Longstone Light, unaware that Heinecke, coming north, was to the east. As the weather deteriorated, two vessels lost touch with the convoy, the Danish *Peter Willemoes* and the Swedish *Nike*; the escorting destroyers assumed that they had deliberately parted company to head for Blyth.

At 12.30 Heinecke encountered *Peter Willemoes*, and sank her with torpedoes; he then went on towards the coast where he found to his surprise that the Longstone Light had been extinguished. He was unaware that Trinity House only lit the light when it was required by the prearranged passage of ships. As a result Heinecke had to steam around the Farne Islands, giving them a wide berth. At 4.00 am he encountered *Nike,* off Blyth, and torpedoed her; he made no attempt to collect intelligence by taking prisoners, as a result of which he remained unaware that the rest of the convoy with *Ouse* and *Garry* was only twenty miles to the south. As Heinecke turned away, he sighted four small steamers, which he erroneously took to be part of the convoy. Opening fire, he sank one of them; in the poor weather conditions the other three escaped, and Heinecke turned for home. By dawn he was well out of sight of land.[4] The convoy, its escorting destroyers unaware of what had occurred, continued on its way, not knowing of how narrowly it had escaped destruction.

Meanwhile Holbe, with the 4th Flotilla, was running into increasingly bad weather as he headed north. By 4.00 am on December 12 he had to reduce speed, first to 15 and then to 12 knots. In the heavy seas it was soon clear that it would be impossible to fire either a gun or torpedo, and Holbe headed for Utsire on the Norwegian coast, which he sighted at 7.00 am. There was some moderation in the weather at about this time, and he hopefully turned north again. After four hours of battling against the mountainous seas, he was reduced to a speed of 9 knots, and accordingly turned south again in the hope of picking up some merchantmen there. During the morning *G104* developed condenser trouble; Holbe had to choose between sending her home alone, or keeping her with him, reducing the speed of his force to 25 knots. He took this course, since the journey home would have been long and hazardous.[5]

As Holbe steamed south he sighted the east bound convoy from Lerwick. Escorted by the destroyers *Pellew* (Lieutenant Commander Cavendish) and *Partridge* (Lieutenant Commander Ransome), with the armed trawlers *Livingstone, Tokio*, *Commander Fullerton* and *Lord Alverstone*, it consisted of six ships, and had left Lerwick on the previous day. The convoy, too, was battered by the waves in the stiff north west breeze, and had also been obliged to reduce speed. *Pellew* was leading with *Partridge* astern of her, the convoy and the armed trawlers following. By now the convoy was approaching the position of its second rendezvous position, twenty five miles south west of the entrance to Bjorne Fjord. The destroyers had not been told of the intended movements of the 2nd Cruiser Squadron.

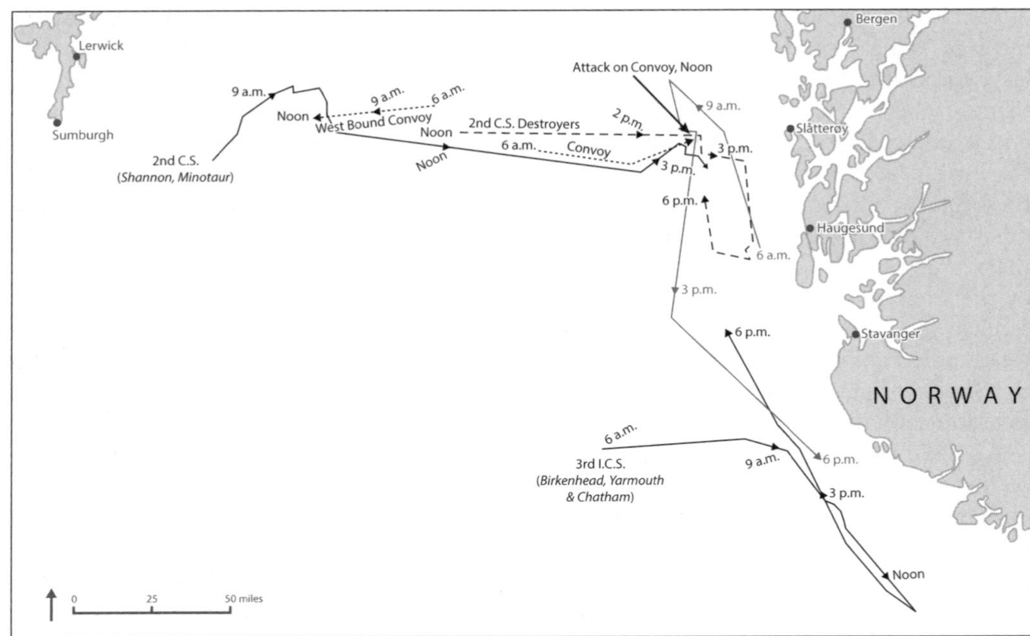

Map 19 Second Scandinavian Convoy Attack: December 12 1917.

They sighted Holbe's force almost simultaneously; *Partridge* endeavoured to challenge the strange vessels, but was handicapped by her searchlight being out of order; it was ten minutes before she could make the challenge, which was wrongly answered. By now Holbe's destroyers, approaching from the north, were only five miles away. *Partridge* sent an urgent signal, addressed to the Commander-in-Chief of the Grand Fleet, reporting that she was going into action, but giving no more information. *Pellew* also attempted to send a signal at 12.10 but her wireless was out of action. *Pellew*, ordering the convoy to scatter, steamed across its bows to get on its exposed flank; *Partridge* followed suit. Cavendish, in *Pellew*, the senior officer, aimed to gain enough time for the convoy to get away by a vigorous attack on the enemy.

Holbe, however, was quite able to deal with this, sending *G104* to destroy the convoy while he engaged the British destroyers, opening fire at 11.55 am. The waves were so high that at times nothing could be seen of the German destroyers but the tops of their funnels and their masts. Newbolt describes what followed:

> The Germans made admirable use of their advantage; and, as usual, their fire was extremely accurate and rapid. Although the terrible precision of the enemy's shooting meant death to most of those who saw it, the officers and men in the British destroyers watched the fall of the German salvoes with a sort of bitter admiration. From the very beginning matters went badly with the British destroyers, and both began to suffer.[6]

Within a few moments *Partridge* was hit, a shell exploding in her engine room which severed the main steam pipe, filling the space with scalding steam which killed everyone there. Minutes later another shell struck the after gun, and then a torpedo hit the ship forward. Ransome ordered the ship to be abandoned; but as the crew took to the rafts and boats, one of the German destroyers came within the arc of fire of *Partridge's* torpedo tubes; two officers launched a torpedo, which struck the target without exploding. Another German torpedo struck the doomed destroyer, and finally a third and she sank quickly in the heavy seas.

Pellew, too was hit in the engine room, and lost speed; fortunately, however, a sudden blinding rain squall covered her, and the three destroyers with Holbe turned towards what remained of the convoy. *G104*, a fox in the henhouse, had already sunk several of the ships, and it took little time for the remainder to be finished off, all six ships and four armed trawlers being sunk by 12.40 pm. The German destroyers rescued four officers and forty eight men from *Partridge* and the trawlers and twenty three from the convoy; a further 115 survivors from the convoy managed to reach the Norwegian coast. Later, 88 more were rescued by the British destroyers which first arrived on the scene. Meanwhile *Pellew*, badly holed and partially disabled, limped towards the Norwegian coast, where she entered Brandersund Inlet and anchored about a mile from Slottero.

Molteno, in *Shannon*, had picked up *Partridge's* first signal to Beatty, and at 12.15 picked up a further signal, which had been badly mutilated by German jamming. This, however, confirmed the approximate position of the attack, and Molteno sent on his destroyers while following at 20 knots with *Shannon* and *Minotaur*. The destroyers arrived at about 2.00 pm and were able over the next half hour to pick up survivors; by then, of course, there was no sign of the enemy. *Partridge's* first signal, prevented by jamming from reaching Scapa Flow, was forwarded by Molteno to Beatty, reaching the latter at 12.25. He at once ordered the 5th Battle Squadron, the 2nd and 4th Light Cruiser Squadrons, and the entire Battle Cruiser Force to raise steam; it seemed to him entirely possible that the High Seas Fleet might be at sea.[7] When he received the second signal from *Partridge*, also forwarded by *Shannon* at 1.03 pm, he ordered Woollcombe to head for the area in which the enemy force had been reported. At this time the 3rd Light Cruiser Squadron was some 150 miles SE of the convoy's eastern rendezvous. Woollcombe had, however, also picked up *Partridge's* first signal, and was already steaming north to the scene of the action.

Picking up all this news at the same time as receiving information about Heinecke's activities on the East Coast, the Admiralty ordered the rest of the Grand Fleet, and the Harwich Force, to raise steam, and to be at one and a half hour's notice.

If Holbe had returned to the Bight by the way he had left it, he might very well have been intercepted by Woollcombe's cruisers; but he did not. The foul weather which he had encountered while he was engaged in the destruction of the convoy persuaded him that it would be more sensible to return home via the Skagerrak where he would find more sheltered water, and by about 5.00 he passed unseen astern of the 3rd Light Cruiser Squadron.

Cavendish, with the damaged *Pellew*, reported by wireless to Molteno that he had reached Slottero, and was unable to steam. One of Molteno's destroyers, *Sabrina*, after having engaged in the rescue operations, arrived on December 13 to find *Pellew* with the Norwegian torpedo boat *Brand* alongside. After some delicate diplomatic negotiations involving the British Vice Consul, the British Ambassador and the Norwegian Government, in the course of which the latter took a decidedly generous view of its obligations as a neutral, *Pellew* was sufficiently repaired to enable her to leave Norwegian territorial waters and make her way across the North Sea to Scapa Flow; her journey was covered by the units of the Grand Fleet which Beatty had sent to sea.[8]

Beatty was, not surprisingly, dismayed at this disaster, writing to Jellicoe on December 14:

> We do have the most cursed luck. The *Shannon* and *Minotaur* should have been alongside the convoy exactly at 12 o'clock after sighting the westbound convoy. Why they were not I do not know yet. I never anticipated that the Huns would send TBDs so far afield and the 3rd LCS could only have missed [them] going north by very little.'[9]

Beatty was under no illusion about what would be the press reaction to the affair when news of it was published, as it soon was to the House of Commons on December 17. Next day the *Daily Mail* described it as 'a humiliating reverse,' and the *Daily News* wrote that the disaster should cause public indignation and deep concern; while the *Pall Mall Gazette*, mindful of it following so closely on the previous incident, spoke of the public's 'considerable need of reassurance as to the state of our commerce defences.'[10]

Geddes seems usually to have burned on a short fuse when getting bad news, and was extremely upset to hear of the destruction of the convoy. Jellicoe described his angry reaction:

> The loss of the second Norwegian convoy caused a good deal of comment, and it was not clear why the protecting cruisers *Minotaur* and *Shannon* were not present at the time of the attack. Sir D Beatty, in a reply to an enquiry of mine, told me the orders under which they acted and this showed that they should have been there at the time of the attack unless something prevented them carrying out the orders. I had a bad cold during the weekend after the attack and was in bed on the Saturday when Sir H Oliver was sent over by Sir E Geddes to see me. He said that the First Lord desired an immediate enquiry ordered, and that it was to be composed of very senior Flag Officers whose names were to be reported for approval, and that all the facts were to be brought out. He added that if I refused to order this sort of enquiry he intended to send up Lord Fisher to enquire into it. Sir R Wemyss also saw me and said he had told the First Lord that Naval Courts of Enquiry were quite common, and that there was no need to make a fuss about them as the procedure was well understood, and Sir D Beatty in ordering the enquiry could be directed to include enquiry as to the dispositions for the protection of the convoy, and the subsequent escape of the raiding destroyers.[11]

The threat to send Fisher to look into the matter was of course calculated by Geddes to ensure that he got a prompt reaction and this he duly received in a letter from Jellicoe which enclosed a draft of his proposed telegram to Beatty. He told the First Lord that it would be very foolish to send Fisher on such a mission, 'and would cause great ill feeling in the Fleet, and would moreover produce no good result.' Geddes next made matters worse by substantially amending Jellicoe's draft without telling him he had done so, making it offensive to Beatty. He then compounded this by a letter to Beatty saying that 'nothing but a full and searching enquiry would satisfy the public.'

Geddes was evidently embarked on a collision course with his admirals, as Jellicoe next recorded:

Other aspects

Lion with repair ship *Assistance*.

Sinking of *Blücher*.

Destroyers raising steam after submarine alarm.

First obstruction at Scapa Flow.

Smokescreen by destroyers.

Dummy battleship, March 2015.

U-boat of UC type.

U-boat of cruiser class.

A convoy zigzagging.

A convoy with an airship.

AMC *Alsatian*.

Alsatian's 6-inch guns.

Miranda at sea off East Coast.

Smokescreens and monitor.

German torpedo boat.

Destroyers at sea.

Battle cruisers in the Forth.

Battle Cruiser Fleet carrying out a sweep.

Second Battle Cruiser Squadron.

New Zealand in the Firth of Forth.

British armoured cruisers.

Tiger at sea.

German and British fleets saluting the Kaiser at Kiel.

Second Battle Cruiser Squadron.

German battery at Zeebrugge Mole.

Zeebrugge canal entrance.

Blockships fitting out.

Vindictive before fitting out.

Bayern sinking at Scapa Flow.

Colossus at Scapa Flow.

Friedrich der Grosse at Scapa Flow.

Hindenburg en route to Scapa Flow.

König at Scapa Flow.

> On Sunday he sent over to me the draft of an announcement he proposed to make in Parliament. It was worded so as to throw blame on Sir D Beatty, and in such a way as to give the idea that the loss of the convoy was a disaster of the greatest magnitude as well as preventable. I objected to this wording, altered it a great deal and sent it back. Most of my alterations were adopted, but not all, and the announcement was not a very happy one.[12]

On December 22 Jellicoe paid a visit to the Grand Fleet at Rosyth, and found Beatty in a furious rage at the way he was being treated by Geddes. Always extremely sensitive to personal criticism, he had reacted badly, not only to Jellicoe's telegram as distorted by Geddes (which the First Sea Lord now saw for the first time) but especially to the personal telegram from the First Lord, which he had found particularly insulting. Jellicoe agreed, and promised that when he got back to London he would take the matter up with Geddes. This he did, noting that the First Lord did not like his frankness. As was shortly to become apparent, Jellicoe was skating on increasingly thin ice.

Although outraged at the suggestion that in choosing who should sit on the Court of Inquiry he might effectively pack the Court, Beatty proceeded to establish it without delay; he selected Sturdee, de Robeck and Goodenough. They, plainly, were sufficiently senior for their findings to be accepted. When in the New Year Geddes visited the Grand Fleet Beatty told him that he and his flag officers had been deeply offended by the terms of the Admiralty's order convening the inquiry; evidently by now anxious to draw a veil over the incident, Geddes asked what action Beatty wanted him to take. Beatty asked for a letter of apology; he cannot have been pleased that he was obliged to send a reminder before the apology eventually arrived. When it did, it assured him that the Admiralty order had not been intended to convey 'any lack of confidence in yourself, or any desire to subject your own dispositions to a Court of Inquiry.' It was a more or less complete climbdown, and Beatty took satisfaction in calling together his flag officers in his cabin aboard *Queen Elizabeth*, and reading it out to them.[13]

In its formal findings the Court of Inquiry exonerated everyone concerned. Neither Beatty, nor Molteno, nor the commanders of *Partridge* and *Pellew* were in any way to blame; all possible steps to prevent the enemy's escape were taken; and the forces assigned to the protection of the convoy were sufficient. Owing however to the arrangements for the disposition of cruisers, 'and the methods employed for the sailing of the convoys, one convoy was left unprotected from surface attack.'[14] It was in other words, the system that was at fault, and the three admirals on the court had, in an annex to their findings, some suggestions to make to address the lack of coordination and the division of responsibility. In future, the escorting forces required strengthening:

> The attacks on the convoy have shown the necessity for a force of sufficient strength being in company with the convoy to meet the probable enemy's attack. The attacks the convoy may expect are:
>
> a) Submarine attack
>
> b) Surface attack by
>
> i) Destroyers
>
> ii) Light Cruisers
>
> iii) Battle cruisers or Battleships. It should be noted that the Germans have no ships between the light cruiser and the battle cruiser which may reasonably be expected to be employed in these raids.[15]

They proposed that in future armoured cruisers of the *Shannon* class and her predecessors should be employed for the protection of the convoys in the North Sea. If this policy was adopted, in conjunction with the use of older light cruisers, destroyers and submarines, it would, they felt, greatly improve the security of the convoys, releasing the newer classes of light cruisers and destroyers for service with the Grand Fleet.

They also suggested that in future 'the control and immediate responsibility for these convoys should be undertaken by a Flag officer afloat (under the Commander-in-Chief, Grand Fleet,' since the admiral commanding in the Orkneys and Shetlands was unable to have adequate supervision of the work. With this, Beatty did not agree, minuting: 'The control is largely based on communications which are obviously more efficient when the controlling authority is situated on shore with shore telegraph and telephone systems at his disposal.'[16]

The future arrangements for the convoys were discussed at conferences held at the Admiralty in December and at Rosyth in January, following which a new system was introduced with effect from January 19. Thereafter the Admiralty was to be responsible for the organisation and routing of the convoys, which would sail to and from Methil on the Firth of Forth instead of Lerwick; they would sail at intervals of three days instead of daily, which reduced the strain on the escorting forces considerably; and significantly stronger covering forces would be at sea in the vicinity of the convoys. This last caused Beatty real anxiety, amounting as it did to a dispersion of force which carried with it the risk that a more powerful raiding force might fall upon the British covering force and destroy it. The same thought occurred to Scheer, who wrote that there was thus 'little further prospect of our light forces being able to destroy any more convoys. Stronger forces would have to be employed for this purpose.'[17] This, in due course, was to lead to a further sortie of the entire High Seas Fleet.

Richmond, in a note to Roger Bellairs on December 15, put his finger on the problem of providing a sufficient escort for the convoys:

> It will develop into a struggle as to which of us anticipates the other by bringing up a superior force. If we increase our escorts by driblets, he will always be able to put up something a little bit stronger. The advantage is all on his side, he being the attacker who chooses his time.[18]

He followed this up two days later, commenting on the impossible situation of the Commander-in-Chief of the Grand Fleet, who was tied by requirements always to have the fleet as well as light and other cruisers at the call of the Admiralty:

> Hence, his attention is divided, and also his power of command. He has to defend convoys, intercept raiders, and be ready to conduct some minor offensive initiated at a moment's notice on the grounds of information that must be acted on at once. If this is to continue, it appears to me that it will become impossible to continue the N Sea convoy. It is only a matter of time before the enemy sends out a larger force to attack the escorts. We send 2 TBDs – he sends 4. We lose the two and add two cruisers. He soon learns this and sends 2 battle cruisers. We lose 2 cruisers and send 4 battle cruisers. He sends 5 and some battleships. We send a battle squadron. He sends a large number of submarines. So the game goes on. But we lose something at each step unless we can surprise or outbid him – make

> an increase before his, and eventually make it necessary for him to risk so large a force that the game is not worth his while.[19]

Richmond sailed as part of the 3rd Division on December 28 as a covering force, and crossed to the Norwegian coast, coming upon the convoy on the following morning. He could not see that there was anything to have prevented the enemy falling on the convoy between daylight and the time the covering force arrived; 'we were miles away and could have given no protection at all against an attack by battle cruisers ... To my mind, the whole thing was futile and dangerous.'[20]

37

The Submarine Campaign in 1917

Jellicoe's profound pessimism about the outcome of the war was already well established before the German campaign of unrestricted submarine warfare took effect. The restricted campaign which Holtzendorff had begun in October 1916 in the teeth of Scheer's opposition, and which was conducted according to prize rules, had achieved considerable success. In September, sinkings by U-boats had already risen to 172 ships amounting to 231,573 tons. Professor Halpern has pointed out that this increase was principally due to the entry into service of the larger UB II boats of the Flanders Flotilla, which were capable of operating well into the Western Approaches or south towards the Gironde.[1] Merchant shipping losses continued to rise; in October 185 ships totalling 341,363 tons went down; in November the figures were 180 ships of 326,689 tons; and in December 197 ships of 309,847 tons. The antisubmarine activities of the British navy achieved only limited success during this period. The U-boats were especially successful in the Mediterranean, where individual commanders achieved huge success.

It was apparent to Jellicoe even before the advent of unrestricted U-boats operations that it would take time to develop a successful defence against them; as has been seen, he was not at all convinced that the introduction of convoys was the answer. In 1917 the U-boats continued to enjoy considerable success; in January, they sank 195 ships of 328,391 tons. When the unrestricted campaign began there was a total of 105 U-boats available. They were scattered across a number of bases; the High Seas Fleet had 46 boats; 23 were based in Flanders, 23 in the Mediterranean, 10 in the Baltic and 3 in Constantinople.[2]

The blockade zone established by the Germans, known as the *Sperrgebiet,* ran from 20 miles from the Dutch coast to the Terschelling light vessel, and thence across the North Sea to Utsire off the Norwegian coast. From there it ran northwest to 62° W, and then down to a point three miles south of the Faroes. Running west as far as 20° W, it then ran down to 20 miles off Cape Finisterre, and southwards to the Spanish coast. There was also a *Sperrgebiet* in the Arctic Ocean covering the approaches to Archangel and the Kola Peninsula. Within these prohibited zones neutral traffic would sail at its own risk, and might be sunk without warning. The Mediterranean was also declared a prohibited zone, although certain limited areas were excluded from the prohibition to allow for the needs of the neutral states of Spain and Greece.

Colonel Repington, the influential journalist who was Military Correspondent of *The Times,* and who kept an outspoken diary, thought in January 1917 that 'it was at present a question whether our armies could win the war before our navies lost it,' and noted the remark of an officer in Naval Intelligence that 'frankly he knew no way of combating the submarine menace.'[3] In the following month he spoke with another naval officer at the Admiralty:

> He is not at all sanguine about overcoming the menace, and thought we should tunnel the Channel and improve our air transport service. What a prospect for the Navy! He thought it had become a disadvantage to be an island.[4]

These views of course, reflected the opinion of Jellicoe and others at the Admiralty, and the first results of the unrestricted submarine campaign went a long way to confirming their worst fears. In February the total of losses shot up to 540,006 tons, a figure surpassed in March, where the tonnage sunk amounted to 593,841. Worse was to come; in April the staggering total of 395 ships was sunk, a total tonnage of 881,027 tons. Of these losses, 4% were due to mines; the rest were sunk by U-boats.[5] About one third of the total was lost in the Mediterranean, which throughout the war proved a happy hunting ground for the U-boats.

The bare figures were bad enough, but as Gibson and Prendergast point out, the whole picture was even worse:

> Appalling as these figures of British losses were, they presented neither the full sum of devastation nor the extreme gravity of the situation. Besides ships destroyed, there were many damaged and temporarily out of useful employment. In April about 80,000 tons were crippled by torpedo attack, and mines wounded another 47,587 tons. An average of 150 ships repaired each month was maintained for a considerable period. In one particular week there were actually under repair the colossal figure of 2,120,301 tons – more than one ninth of British mercantile tonnage in 1914. To give a more graphic idea, those two million odd tons represented on an average 600 ships, of 3500 tons each, out of cargo carrying service.[6]

It was the urgent need to maximise the building of new tonnage that had led to the appointment of Geddes as Controller in May 1917, responsible for the construction of both naval and mercantile tonnage. At the rate of the April losses, however, it would be impossible for them to be made good. New construction in the whole of 1915 had been 688,000 tons; in the following year it was 538,000 tons. In the first half of 1917 484,000 tons were built, and the target figure for the second half was a million tons; in the event only a total of 620,000 tons was produced. Sir Joseph Maclay, who followed Geddes when the latter became First Lord, grimly warned the Americans that they must turn out six million tons of new shipping.[7]

During the dreadful month of April there were 21 U-boats at sea from North Sea bases, while 8 from Flanders were in the Channel or in the waters south of Ireland; 13 more were operating in the Mediterranean. It was a force well below the maximum possible, and well below the figures attained later; but although neither the British nor the Germans could know this, it represented the high point of U boat success. In his paper of April 23, Jellicoe reported to the War Cabinet:

> It was quite obvious that such a rate of loss, if continued, would bring about a crisis. The First Sea Lord's remedy was that more destroyers should be built, that the United States should be asked to send more ships; and that more merchant shipping should be laid down, either in the form of small ships or of very large unsinkable ships for which he could provide escort.[8]

Jellicoe also had hopes that the policy of extensive mining in the Heligoland Bight would take a higher toll of U-boats setting out and returning. He feared that the existing pattern of mines was not satisfactory against submarines, but hoped that the new pattern of mine coming into production would do better. It would not, however, be available before July.

At this point in the U-boat campaign Jellicoe's gloom was naturally matched by optimism on the part of the German naval leaders. Their success was even greater than they had hoped; Holtzendorff's assessment that a six month campaign would bring Germany within sight of victory at sea appeared entirely reasonable.

The situation was dramatically highlighted by Gibson and Prendergast:

> Everywhere the submarines were succeeding in the predicted decimation of England's vital trade; everywhere the defence seemed to make little or no headway against the vindictive and determined onslaught. Upon the graphic chart the line denoting losses had leapt upwards at an appalling slant. Let that gradient be prolonged onwards a few months into the future; it would inevitably intersect the ordinate that meant Starvation! – Defeat! – Surrender! The crisis of the whole naval war – of her very existence – was upon Great Britain.[9]

One particular reason for German optimism was the failure of British light craft to inflict heavier losses on the U-boat force. Since the outbreak of war until the end of Mach 1917 it was calculated that there had been 142 actions in which British destroyers had engaged U-boats, and only on six occasions had the U-boat been sunk. As Newbolt points out, a U-boat commander must necessarily fancy his chances of emerging unscathed from a confrontation with a British destroyer.[10]

And it was not only submarines that escaped destruction at the hands of British light forces. On April 7 information was received indicating that a force of German auxiliaries (later, and predictably enough, found to be minesweepers) would be operating near the Horns Reef light vessel. Beatty despatched the 2nd Light Cruiser Squadron together with a force of twelve destroyers led by the light cruiser *Champion* to attack them. The attack was a complete failure, perhaps because of the difficulty of coordinating the forces engaged, and perhaps because an unexpectedly strong current carried them away from the line on which the minesweepers were operating. All through the night of April 8/9 the British forces were inside the operational area of the German units, but the minesweepers were able to complete their mission and return home unscathed. Maintaining the effectiveness of the British minefields intended to inhibit the U-boat campaign was clearly no easy matter.

These minefields were a vital part of the British anti submarine activities. A close study had been made of the routes used by U-boats when leaving and entering the Heligoland Bight, and a good deal of information had been assembled.. Based on this, a constant programme of minelaying was undertaken in the Heligoland Bight; in the first quarter of 1917 nearly 5000 mines were laid at the ends of the U boat routes. It was not until April 6 that these claimed a victim, when U-22 struck a mine north west of Horns Reef, and had to be towed home for repairs.[11]

The process of mining selected areas of the Bight, and the German response in locating these new minefields as well as laying further minefields themselves, continued throughout 1917. Newbolt's conclusion is that the attempts to close the Bight with a quadrant of mines proved fruitless:

> During the spring of the year the Bight was practically encircled by mines, but the German naval command successfully combated the danger. Instead of searching for British mines whenever and wherever they were to be found, they marked and buoyed a certain number of entrance channels and swept them continually. By thus restricting the zones which had to be kept clear they completely thwarted our original plan. Very few U-boats were lost upon the minefields.[12]

Grant, however, takes issue with this, arguing that mining operations in the Bight in the autumn of 1917, which were generally carried out by submarines rather than surface vessels, actually achieved rather good results, considering the small number of mines laid. During the year as a whole, the Germans lost one U-boat in the spring and another on their own defensive mines; and six more in the last four months of the year. These later successes were due not only to improved mines but also to the high quality of British information.[13]

In May 1917 there was a sharp reduction in the tonnage lost, to 616,316 tons gross. This was not due to the introduction of convoy, which had not yet had much effect, but to the inability of the U-boats to maintain the efforts made during April, when U boats had been at sea for the total equivalent of 660 days. In May the number of active submarines dropped, for the equivalent of 535 days at sea. Walter H Page, the American Ambassador in London, pithily summarised the situation:

> At the present rate of destruction more than four million tons will be sunk before the summer is gone. Such is this dire submarine danger. The English thought that they controlled the sea; the Germans, that they were invincible on land. Each side is losing where it thought itself strongest.[14]

However, the peak of the U-boats success had, in fact been reached. Losses rose again in June, to a total tonnage of 696,715, but never again reached the total achieved in April. What has been described as 'the primal wane of the German drive had begun.' For this there were many reasons, not the least of them being the almost immediate success of the convoy system, which came as a marked surprise to those that had so reluctantly accepted that it had to be adopted. Churchill vividly set out the reason for this:

> The size of the sea is so vast that the difference between the size of a convoy and the size of a single ship shrinks in comparison almost to insignificance. There was in fact very nearly as good a chance of a convoy of forty ships in close order slipping unperceived between the patrolling U-boats as there was for a single ship; and each time this happened, forty ships escaped instead of one. Here then was the key to the success of the convoy system against U-boats. The concentration of ships greatly reduced the number of targets in a given area and thus made it more difficult for the submarines to locate their prey. Moreover, the convoys were easily controlled and could be quickly deflected by wireless from areas known to be dangerous at any given moment. Finally the destroyers, instead of being dissipated on patrol over wide areas, were concentrated at the point of the hostile attack, and opportunities of offensive action frequently arose.[15]

In this passage Churchill somewhat overstated the ease with which convoys could be rerouted; local commands did not always have the latest intelligence, while the suspension of traffic did or course have the effect of enforcing the German blockade.

The commencement of the unrestricted submarine campaign had an immediate effect on neutral shipping; ship-owners ordered their vessels to remain in port. This had been anticipated and the British response was immediate:

> As a first step the Government gave instructions on February 1 that all neutral vessels, to the number of some 600, in the ports of the United Kingdom, should be provisionally detained, pending some assurance against the general laying up or withdrawal of neutral shipping trading with or for the Allies. Harsh as this measure may appear, it must be remembered that, for a long time, neutral countries had been receiving supplies and bunker facilities under agreements which involved the employment of their shipping in British and Allied trade, and it was of vital importance to secure that such agreements, whether express or implied, should continue to be carried out despite the new German threat.[16]

It came at a bad moment for Britain's relations with the European neutrals; only with Norway were these on a friendly footing. Against Sweden, Denmark and Holland a strict 'ship for ship' policy was applied, whereby clearance was only granted for their ships bound to their own country, whether in port on February 1 or arriving subsequently, on the arrival at a British port of a similar vessel under the same flag.

The unrestricted submarine campaign hit many neutrals hard; in the first six months of its operation, in addition to about 2,350,000 tons of British shipping, about 1,500.000 tons of shipping under Allied or neutral flag was lost. The heaviest sufferer was Norway, with 440,000 tons; France and Italy each lost over 200,000 tons, and Greece and the United States over 100,000 tons.[17]

Among the measures adopted to beat the submarine was a system of hunting patrols in areas where U-boats were expected to be active. One weapon which patrolling or escorting warships could use with good effect was introduced in 1916, when depth charges were used for the first time. A number of U-boats were successfully destroyed by this means, and it was some time before the Germans realised that this potent new weapon was being employed, because there were no survivors from these boats. The first report came in May 1917:

> The Commander of *U49,* returning to Emden from a special duty cruise – observation of the East Coast Traffic conditions – reported that he had passed through a new ordeal. He had been attacked by 'marine bombs.' The findings created a sensation at the Ems base of the U-boats; it was patent that a new peril had to be faced. No longer was the sea a protective cloak; no longer was safety to be found in diving.[18]

The fitting of hydrophone listening devices to destroyers, trawlers, P-boats and motor launches was another addition to the armoury of anti-submarine measures available. It was early days for a system that developed much more effectively in the Second World War; it was too rudimentary to be a serious threat, sometimes necessitating the stopping of engines to enable the sounds of a submarine to be detected. As Halpern observes, this was not an attractive option for vessels operating in areas where submarines were known to be about.[19]

The use of Q-ships, decoy vessels that appeared to be innocent merchantmen but which were in reality heavily armed, enjoyed some success in destroying U-boats that came to the surface to sink a merchantman by gunfire. As time went by, however, U-boat commanders became smarter at identifying such vessels, and in any case, once the unrestricted campaign had begun, they sank their victims by torpedo without surfacing.

Anti submarine operations consumed enormous resources, as Beatty explained in a letter to his wife on June 19:

> I am in the middle of a big operation against enemy submarines which I pray may be successful. I have denuded myself of all destroyers, SMs, patrol vessels, seaplanes, airships etc. in the effort so that the fleet is immobilised for the time being. It's no use pecking at it and have taken the largest steps I can. No result to date, but I live in hope. It is time our luck turned, it has been dead out for a long time. Mercifully the weather helps us and it is not hard on our small craft which is something to be thankful for.[20]

The operation to which Beatty referred was known as Operation BB, covering a large area around the north of Scotland; five destroyer zones and four submarine zones were located along known routes used by U-boats, a number of which were expected to be at sea in the area. The plan was to force them to dive to avoid the destroyers so that they would then have to surface in the areas patrolled by submarines. 4 flotilla leaders, 49 destroyers and 17 submarines were committed to the operation which, however, failed to destroy a single U boat. During the operation *K7,* one of the large steam powered 'K' boats, lying in wait in the Fair Isle Channel, was chased by the destroyers *Observer* and *Rocket,* which, convinced that it was a U-boat, attacked with depth charges until it was able to surface and signal its identity. Nonetheless Beatty was convinced that the operation put pressure on the enemy, and persuaded Jellicoe that it should be repeated when forces were available. This came in October, when Operation HS was mounted, which involved a flotilla leader, 21 destroyers, 4 submarines, 24 armed trawlers and 42 net drifters. The plan was for four areas to be heavily patrolled along the routes expected to be used by homeward bound U-boats; three or four were expected to be traversing these during the first week of October. A mine net barrage was laid in one of the areas, between the latitudes of the Firth of Forth and Flamborough Head. The Admiralty convinced itself that the operation had been successful in destroying three U-boats; these, however, had fallen victims to other minefields farther to the south.

Nonetheless, the total monthly tonnage of sinkings worldwide continued to decline. In July, the figure was 555,514 tons; in August it was 472,372 tons; in September it was 353,602 tons. There was a rise in October, to 446,542 tons; in November the figure was down to 302,599 tons, rising to 411,766 tons in December. For the German naval command these figures represented an unmistakable defeat; colossal though the total figure of sinkings was, it was apparent that the six months which had been described as sufficient to bring Britain to her knees had passed without this result:

> Bitterly have the naval leaders since regretted that this stipulated period, put forward with the greatest secrecy, should ever have come to the public knowledge. Too many had come to know of the undertaking to force a decision before the harvest reaping. The German nation expected the U-boats would be triumphant by the autumn. They knew the campaign

> still raged furiously. It was possible for the naval leaders to conceal from public sight the ominous fact that the sinkings achieved in August were but a third of the fearful April total. The question confronting the German naval authorities was simply this: How long could the deception last?[22]

Not only had the rate of sinkings declined, but also the losses of U-boats gradually reduced the number available of experienced commanders and their irreplaceable crews. As a result the periods of refit and overhaul were progressively shortened, with consequent effects on morale. By these means, and with the completion of new submarines, the number of boats in commission rose to a peak of 140 at the end of October 1917.

Nevertheless, as 1917 drew on, with no sign of the ultimate British defeat at which their campaign had been aimed, even the most optimistic U-boat commanders began to have doubts. Typical of these was Lieutenant Commander Werner Fürbringer, who wrote in his memoirs:

> It was of course our duty to maintain the level of buoyant optimism which had been characteristic of unrestricted submarine warfare at its outset. In this we were assisted by the continuing descriptions made by our foreign agents as to the degree to which our sinkings were having their effect on the comforts of English life. But we saw what we saw, and in discussions between intimates the first doubts had begun to emerge about the possibility of victory. I must emphasise that only in the most intimate circles did these conversations take place, but they cast a long shadow.[23]

Captain Bauer, the *Führer der U-boote*, suggested that in order to overcome the problems which the convoys were causing individual U-boats, a group of them should operate jointly. His plan was to put a flotilla commander on one of the large submarine cruisers of the *U151* class, converted to a command U-boat, and for him to coordinate by radio an attack by the group of U-boats on a convoy. It was a forerunner of the 'wolf pack' organisation of the Second World War. Bauer however, was relieved of his command in June 1917, being promoted to the command of a squadron, and replaced by the successful destroyer commander Commodore Andreas Michelsen, now serving in Flanders, who was given the title of *Befehlshaber der U-boote*.[24] Scheer explained the reason for the new appointment:

> When … owing to the increasing activity in construction, the number of U-boats grew to such an extent that their organisation far surpassed that required for a squadron and demanded a significant increase in authority, Commodore Michelsen, who had hitherto commanded the torpedo boats, was placed at the head. His great knowledge and experience of the department of torpedoes designated him as particularly suitable for this post, and he completely fulfilled all expectations in this respect.[25]

In September Michelsen took a significant decision, expressly ordering the large North Sea boats to recommence using the passage of the Dover Straits. It was a decision which, perhaps, in due course contributed to yet another crisis at the British Admiralty; it was prompted by the success of the convoy system, as Newbolt explains:

It was in September that the U-boat commanders changed their tactics for the first time since the campaign began. The change was not a startling one; it was only that they abandoned areas which they had found fruitful for months, and shifted their principal operations eastward into the Channel and southwards into the Bay of Biscay. But this change of plan is the first visible, salient result of our counter-measures. For the first time since submarine warfare began the U-boat commanders were confronted with a form of opposition which threw their plan of attack completely out of gear.[26]

38

Keyes

Michelsen's directive that North Sea based U-boats should use the Dover Straits in order to reach their cruising grounds may not have meant any substantial increase in traffic, but it was not long before Keyes, after taking up his post as Director of the Plans Division, became closely involved with the issue. In October he learned from Hall in his capacity of Director of Naval Intelligence that 'enemy submarines use the Straits practically unmolested, suffering little or no inconvenience from the mobile patrols or the explosive barrage.'[1] This intelligence derived from a report on the passage of the mine net barrage in the Dover Straits which was among the papers recovered from *UC 44*, sunk in a German minefield off Waterford on August 4, and subsequently raised. This disclosed that between December 23 1916 and June 6 1917, 190 submarines had made the passage through the Straits, an average of more than 30 per month. During the same period there were only eight reports of U-boats touching the nets and only eight occasions on which it had been necessary to dive to avoid patrols. It was apparent from the interrogation of prisoners, and other information, that most of these passages were made at night, and on the surface.[2] The papers also included a copy of the instructions given to U-boat commanders for passing through the Straits and avoiding the net defences:

> It is best to pass this on the surface; if forced to dive, go down to 40 metres .... As far as possible, pass through the area between Hoofden and Cherbourg without being observed and without stopping; on the other hand, the boats which in exceptional cases pass round Scotland are to let themselves be seen as freely as possible, in order to mislead the English.[3]

The statistics of sinkings by U-boats in the Channel, which amounted on average to about twenty per month, made it essential that something be done to increase the effectiveness of the barrier intended to close the Straits. Keyes had been asked by Beatty to find out what had happened to a scheme put forward in April 1917 by Captain Donald Munro, who had been particularly successful in improving the security of both Scapa Flow and Rosyth. When submitted to Bacon, the latter had dismissed it out of hand, writing that 'a glance at the scheme was sufficient to condemn it. Captain Munro's scheme would not last a single tide in the Channel.' The Captain of the Drifter Patrol, Captain Frederick Bird, was similarly dismissive, calling it 'entirely impracticable.' Keyes reopened the question in a minute dated October 19:

> Information recently circulated by the ID clearly establishes the fact that enemy submarines use the Straits practically unmolested, suffering little or no inconvenience from the mobile patrols or the explosive barrage. Under the circumstances I submit that too much weight should not be attached to the opinions of the Officers who have been responsible for this area for over two years. I do not say most definitely that Captain Munro's net barrage is the solution of the difficult problem before us, but I do say most definitely that the passage of the Straits of Dover can and ought to be made a most hazardous proceeding, and that we are not likely to arrive at the solution if suggestions are subjected to criticisms such as that contained in the letters of the Vice Admiral, Dover, dated May 4, and the Captain of the Dover Drifter Patrol dated May 3.[4]

This was trenchant stuff, and on November 13 Geddes, after a meeting at the Admiralty involving among others Jellicoe, Wemyss and Keyes, appointed a Channel Barrage Committee. Headed by Keyes, the other members were Colonel Alexander Gibb, who had been responsible for building the Rosyth Dockyard, Mr W McLellan, a civil engineer, Captain Learmonth, the Assistant Hydrographer, Captain Litchfield Speer, the Director of Mines and Torpedoes, and Captain Cyril Fuller, one of Keyes's Assistant Directors. The Committee had wide terms of reference; it was to consider how and why the existing net barrage had not succeeded, and to consider from all points of view the practicability and probable efficiency of any schemes which could be put forward.[5]

On November 20 Keyes and his colleagues visited Dover to see for themselves, and to meet with Bacon and his senior officers. At this time Bacon was about to lay a deep minefield, approved by the Admiralty, between the Varne and Cap Gris Nez. Keyes told him that this would be useless, unless it was closely patrolled night and day. Bacon said that he had one P-boat on patrol there, and would add three more when the minefield was completed: he did not propose to do more. Keyes argued for the use of light vessels carrying searchlights, and suggested that in the meantime, pending their arrival, the minefield could be lit by flares and by the searchlights of the patrols. Bacon was completely opposed to this; he had no intention, he said, 'of burning searchlights and flares from vessels that could be stalked and torpedoed by enemy submarines.' On November 23 he put forward a scheme based on the use of powerful shore based searchlights on both sides of the Channel (three each at Cap Gris Nez and Folkestone) and three or four shallow draught bulged vessels, with searchlights and guns moored across the Straits. For Keyes, the objection to this scheme was one of time:

> Only we simply could not afford to wait while special ships and devices were being constructed. During the month of October, 289,000 tons of shipping had been sunk in the Atlantic, and 62,500 tons in the Channel by enemy submarines, most of which had passed through the Straits of Dover; and although the losses in the Atlantic were at a somewhat lower rate at the moment, those in the Channel showed no sign of declining.[6]

Not surprisingly, the Channel Barrage Committee entirely adopted the position taken by Keyes, and rejected Bacon's proposal, in an interim report dated November 29 which was, as Keyes wrote, 'a scathing indictment' of the existing anti-submarine measures. Since it was so very critical, Keyes sent a copy direct to Bacon. The Committee found that the 'complete ineffectiveness' of the existing barrier was proved by the Intelligence Department's information, and that even apart from this an examination of the present arrangements led to the same conclusion. The Germans evidently wanted the British to think these arrangements effective. Minefields, patrols, illumination and an explosive surface obstruction should all be applied as soon as possible, and other new devices should be experimented with and pushed forward. Bacon's suggestion of a parallel line of buoys to carry a horizontal floating net was rejected. Finally, the 'construction maintenance, defence and patrol' of any barrage scheme across the Channel should be under the control of one officer responsible directly to the Admiralty. Any other course would lead to failure.[7]

Bacon was outraged by the report, later describing it as merely 'a fifth wheel to what was an intricate and very technical coach:'

> The Committee of amateurs, so far as conditions of war in the Channel were concerned, was to be given sole charge of the central slice of the Dover Command, and was to use the vessels of the Dover Command as it wished without any reference to the Admiral who was responsible for the protection of traffic, raids, cooperation with the Army etc. Was there ever a more impossible suggestion made by any committee.[8]

Enlarging on this, he quoted the saying that 'a committee has neither a body to be kicked nor a soul to be damned.' It could force action on others, but escape all blame in case of failure.

By now Keyes was hell bent on getting Bacon removed from his post. He wrote to Beatty on December 5, saying that it was almost time he went up to get a breath of fresh air:

> I do think Bacon has been delivered into the hands of the Board. They have ample grounds for kicking him out – on his own showing … Our interim report is a very strong indictment of Bacon and all his works. We will make Dover Straits unhealthy for submarines, but Bacon's presence adds to our difficulties – and I am afraid the Board won't kick him out. He was all over us when we went to Dover and apparently all out to help – but not really. However he is badly rattled and making an ass of himself.[9]

And, indeed, Bacon's reaction justified the way in which Keyes described it. In the words of Professor Marder, it was 'a classic example of how personality can be a determining factor in history,' as demonstrated in a number of extracts from Bacon's letters to Geddes. As he well knew, it was ultimately the latter who would determine his fate; he could depend on Jellicoe to support him as far as he was able. He later wrote:

> No suggestions of any proved value emanated from the Committee which had not already been put forward by Admiral Bacon and approved to be carried out as material and vessels were available.[10]

The tone of Bacon's letters to Geddes, hectoring, arrogant and pompous, was hardly likely to strengthen his position with the First Lord:

> The reason for my writing is to say that if the Admiralty are wholehearted in the matter and will provide me with the material and follow my plan we can practically close the Straits but if the proposals are emasculated by makeshift light vessels or fears – groundless – of

> loss of shipping it will be a failure. I think I know … more about conditions obtaining in the Straits than any other officer … if the Admiralty place their confidence in me I have no doubt of the final result.[11]

A few days later he was writing that there was no reason 'if a little energy is used at the Admiralty' why the scheme should not be completed and the Channel practically blocked. To Wemyss, writing to Jellicoe on December 5 after reading effusions of this kind, it was necessary for the Board to give the whole matter the most careful consideration; Bacon's letters showed 'an impossible attitude of mind' on his part. He had had a free hand for two and a half years of unavailing attempts to stop the passage of submarines, and that being so it was 'inadmissible to write such letters.'

Bacon's most revealing letter to Geddes was sent on December 12. He was, regrettably, continuing to make an ass of himself; his letter demonstrated graphically his total lack of understanding of the effect it would have on its reader:

> I own I like my own way. I own in some matters I have firm convictions. But then I know the place and am generally right!!! I own I do not suffer fools gladly … I have no use for the imperfectly informed. I hope perhaps that it is to some of the latter, of whom I have met a good many in the last few years, that I owe my evil reputation and this made the Committee wary.[12]

It is not difficult to see why Fisher liked him so much.

Under pressure from Keyes and the Plans Division a telegram went to Bacon on December 7 to ask what steps he was taking to illuminate and patrol the deep minefield which had now been laid between the Varne and Cap Gris Nez. He replied that search lights were necessary both at Folkestone and Cap Gris Nez and that by December 12 the minefield would be sufficiently extended to warrant the use of searchlights from patrol boats. He was still anxious to limit the use of searchlights because these rendered the patrol boats and, particularly, destroyers vulnerable to the risk of being torpedoed. Keyes regarded the response as extremely unsatisfactory and minuted Jellicoe to say so. He pointed out once more the ease with which U-boats were passing the Straits, and the ineffectiveness of the barrage, and that Bacon's anti-submarine activities were thus confined to patrol craft, and were ineffective. He set out a detailed response which he suggested should be made to Bacon. When this reached Oliver for comment he minuted on December 12 that it was 'undesirable to give senior officers detailed orders as to the disposition and working of vessels under their command.' It was not easy to slap Keyes down, and he responded next day that in the present case 'some departure from established custom is necessary.' By now he had the latest report from Hall, to the effect that at least 35 U-boats had definitely passed the Straits between November 1 and December 9, and probably 15 others. Moreover 21 had gone through since the start of laying the deep minefield on November 21. This intelligence, coupled with the sinking of 11 vessels in the Channel during the first week of December, greatly strengthened the case for the instructions that Keyes proposed should go to Bacon.[13]

Thus, when these minutes reached Jellicoe, he was now somewhat more sympathetic to the need for urgent action. True, he did in his minute seek to defend Bacon:

> I am not able to accept the sweeping indictment of the work of the VA Dover, as stated by the Director of Plans. The VA's dispositions are based on experience, not only of submarine

> action but of destroyer attacks, and he is naturally reluctant to ignore the latter in the attempt to deal with the former… However, it is indisputable that the barrage is not effective against submarines and some risk in regard to destroyers etc. must be run in order to cope with the submarine menace.[14]

Accordingly, an order went to Bacon calling for a strong patrol over the deep minefield as soon as possible, even at the expense of reducing forces elsewhere, and for destroyers and P-boats to use their searchlights intermittently. Drifters were to use flares. Bacon's response to this on December 15 was as characteristic as it was unwise. He was increasing the number of patrolling drifters, but insisted that changes in the arrangements must be gradual. He devoted a lot of space to the question of the destroyers at Dover, and the problems of keeping them under way; a force at anchor at Dunkirk not only rested the boats but was a bigger deterrent to German raids than a similar force at Dover. He ended his letter:

> I have gone into this explanation of a single detail to point out that I have reasons for all my dispositions which may not on the face of them be apparent. I know the wishes of their Lordships, and it is needless to say I will carry out these wishes whole heartedly and at the same time provide as best I can for the safety of the Straits; but I must have latitude in my dispositions, and I must vary them as necessary; and I submit that, having expressed their wishes, their Lordships should leave the executive dispositions of forces to me and to vary them as I consider necessary.[15]

In his history of the Dover Patrol, he later wrote: 'Just fancy an Admiral in command in war time having to write in this strain to the Admiralty to answer the meddlings of an irresponsible committee!' Oddly the same day he wrote to Keyes acknowledging receipt of the interim report in unexpectedly moderate terms, saying that the only paragraph with which he was in total disagreement was that concerning the old Folkestone-Cap Gris Nez barrage which 'never stood winter weather.' It was hopeless to get it effectively completed.

The Admiralty response to Bacon's letter was to send for him to explain himself, and at a conference in Jellicoe's room on December 18 he was expressly ordered to institute a twenty four hour patrol of the deep minefield, illuminated as ordered. He grudgingly agreed to do so next day. Before, however, he left the Admiralty, the meeting went on to consider the plans for an assault on Zeebrugge and Ostend. Bacon had given an outline of his proposal to Captain Fuller in December; Keyes described it as 'a combination and an ingenious development' of the successive schemes which Tyrwhitt had put forward, all of which Bacon had rejected. The development, which he thought brilliant, was to assault the mole at Zeebrugge from its seaward site. He could see serious flaws in the detail, but, he says, he accepted that the Admiral commanding must have a free hand. Jellicoe agreed, subject to two points; he agreed with Keyes that the men to be employed as a storming party should be blue jackets and marines, and not an army battalion, and he asked Keyes to prepare a list of old cruisers to be used as block ships, those of the *Blanche* class asked for by Bacon being unable to be spared.

Bacon was as good as his word, and implemented next day Jellicoe's order as to the patrols and the illuminations. As a result *U 59*, which had embarked on a passage through the Straits, was forced to dive by the searchlights and flares and ran into the minefield and was blown up. When the news of this reached the Admiralty on December 20, Keyes was exultant:

> This was a stroke of good fortune for Plans Division. The odds were all in favour of the submarine getting through, as the patrol vessels were a considerable distance apart; and the minefield … had been rapidly deteriorating, a number of mines having broken adrift in the winter gales. However, *U 59* provided an overwhelming argument in support of the policy Plans Division had so insistently urged, and Sir Reginald Bacon had so strenuously resisted. *U 59* actually sealed Admiral Bacon's fate, for the First Lord – Sir Eric Geddes – had been watching the battle about the Dover Straits with the keenest interest.[16]

Geddes may well have decided that Bacon must go, but he faced a serious obstacle. Jellicoe was still not prepared to agree to Bacon's dismissal and this sooner rather than later, could mean only one thing. Matters were coming to a head; it was the intervention of Wemyss, however, that was critical. In his unpublished memoirs he wrote of the proof that the enemy was passing the Straits successfully:

> Sir R Bacon on the other hand maintained that they did not, that his system of nets was satisfactory and that the proof of this lay in the fact that no ship had ever been torpedoed in his area. He brushed aside as puerile my contention that naturally the enemy left alone an area that he wished to pass unmolested and took other areas for his nefarious activities. Towards the end of December I brought the subject very insistently before both the First Lord and the First Sea Lord, and my contention was that Bacon was not being successful in his anti-submarine measures, that we should leave no stone unturned to try and stop the passage of these craft and that we had better try somebody else and go on changing until we found somebody who could. Jellicoe maintained that Bacon was the best man we had for the job and should remain. I on the other hand maintained that he was not. The interview at which all this happened took place in the First Lord's room, and I came away feeling that matters could not go on in this manner.[17]

With Geddes, from above, and his Deputy from below, so sharply opposed to him on a significant issue, Jellicoe's position was becoming impossible. Meanwhile the final report of the Channel Barrage Committee was completed on December 21; it contained a large number of technical recommendations, and it repeated the serious criticisms that had been made of the existing arrangements. It reiterated that 'the whole of the arrangements in the Dover Straits should be in the hands of one Officer, with an adequate staff.' Oliver, predictably, minuted that such an officer 'should be under the orders of the SNO or confusion will result.' As matters turned out, this issue was not to be tested.[18]

39

Jellicoe's Dismissal

Even in a democracy the power of a Prime Minister in wartime is enormous. It does have its limits, however, as Lloyd George's handling of Haig and Jellicoe demonstrated. In both cases he would like to have seen them removed, but it was not an easy task, bearing in mind the resistance which he knew this must encounter both from politicians and from the professionals involved. In the case of Haig, of course, Lloyd George was unsuccessful; in the case of Jellicoe, the process took a considerable time. Lloyd George had taken office as Prime Minister immediately after Jellicoe had been summoned to the Admiralty over the issue of the introduction of convoy. Writing in his memoirs of the situation in February 1917, he observed what a serious thing it was for amateurs to interfere and 'recklessly exercise their authority by overriding the opinion of the most famous specialists that are available in the Kingdom.' There was no one whose reputation in naval circles stood as high as Jellicoe. Accordingly, 'Jellicoe had to be given a fair trial.'[1]

Lloyd George's famous breakfast with Jellicoe, Duff and Hankey on February 13 1917 immediately followed the production by Hankey of his 'brain wave' about convoys of two days earlier. The latter noted in his diary that Jellicoe and Duff 'resisted a good deal,' and Lloyd George, in his account of the meeting, wrote that it 'evoked a restatement of the Jellicoe objections against convoys with which we were already familiar.'[2] If for a while after this Jellicoe was still undergoing a fair trial, the coming to a head of the convoy dispute at the end of April brought the fair trial closer to a conclusion in Lloyd George's mind, as the tone of his language about the First Sea Lord makes plain. By June Lloyd George plainly had reached a conclusion:

> I made up my mind to effect a change at the top in the Admiralty. Obviously unless I were present at the Admiralty every day to supervise every detail of administration, it would be impossible for me promptly to remove all hindrances and speed up action. I therefore contemplated a change in the First Lord, Lord Carson, and the First Sea Lord, Admiral Jellicoe. They were both men of great influence and authority, and both possessed a formidable following, one political, the other naval.[3]

The extent of their influence and authority made it impossible for them to be removed simultaneously; replacing Carson by Geddes had necessarily been the first step. But only the first step:

> Sir Eric Geddes, in his acceptance of the position of First Lord, stipulated that Jellicoe should not be immediately removed. Geddes knew that Jellicoe had the confidence of the senior officers in the Navy, and it would therefore be a distinct advantage to secure his cooperation if that were at all possible. He promised to tell me without delay if he found that he could not work with or through him.[4]

Although Lloyd George in this passage appears to suggest that he still had an open mind about Jellicoe's possible retention, his determination to remove him was in fact as strong as ever. Hankey, in his diary on July 3 1917 recorded that the Prime Minister 'was hot for getting rid of Jellicoe.'[5] Captain Roskill is of the opinion that the change at the Admiralty was largely due to a strong campaign by Haig to get rid of Jellicoe as well as Carson; Haig's motives were, he considers, 'obscure,' but 'genuine dissatisfaction with the pessimism of the Admiral was probably among them.'[6] Haig had been highly critical of Jellicoe for some time, being gravely alarmed by the Admiral's defeatism.[7] He continued his campaign, and had had a lot to say about the Admiralty when he breakfasted with Lloyd George and Geddes on June 26. For the moment, Jellicoe's removal was postponed, since Carson had made plain that, as a term of his agreement to leave the Admiralty himself, Jellicoe must remain.

It was not for long. On October 26 Hankey recorded in his diary:

> Earlier in the day Balfour had told me that he and Carson (as ex-First Lords) had been summoned to meet the PM and Geddes to discuss the question of superseding Admiral Jellicoe. It appears that from the Adty. Inquiry it has transpired that the latter had been fully warned by highly secret, but absolutely reliable information, of the probability of the recent attack on the Norwegian convoy, and had neglected to act. Geddes regards this as an example of Jellicoe's lack of energy, if not timidity, and wants to replace him by Adl. Wemyss.[8]

This was only the first of a series of sticks with which to beat Jellicoe which events that autumn were to provide.

By now the *Daily Mail* had embarked on the vicious campaign of denigration of Jellicoe previously referred to. The reason for the hostility of Lord Northcliffe, its proprietor, towards Jellicoe might, Marder suggests, derive from an incident in 1915 when he refused to allow a *Daily Mail* reporter to visit a squadron of the Grand Fleet at Invergordon. 'Given Northcliffe's inflated notions about himself and his newspapers, it would have been natural that he should thereafter harbour a grudge against the Admiral.' Marder also recounts an incident in 1917 when Northcliffe visited the Admiralty to complain about air raids at Ramsgate and met with Jellicoe and Commodore Paine; the latter, replying to Northcliffe's unjustified criticism of the RNAS, did so in a manner which Jellicoe later recalled. 'Godfrey Paine, head of the RNAS at the time … did not mince matters in replying to Northcliffe and (in his usual somewhat heated manner !!) gave Northcliffe "What for," pointing out that the RNAS did not pretend to stop air raids.' Northcliffe later complained to Carson about the matter in terms which suggested that it was Jellicoe rather than Paine who had spoken so aggressively.[9] Another, and perhaps even more convincing explanation for Northcliffe's hostility is that he was very probably encouraged by Lloyd George to attack Jellicoe and blame him for all the bad news; it deflected criticism from others and steadily weakened Jellicoe's position. Regrettably such a course was entirely consistent with the Prime Minister's record for deviousness, and there is some evidence to suggest that this is what in fact happened.

On October 19 the *Daily Mail* asked 'whether the recent changes in Whitehall had gone far enough.' On October 30 a leading article asked 'What is wrong at the Admiralty?' It concluded that it was because Jellicoe was not a strategist and was hence 'not the right man in the right place.' On November it complained that the strategical direction, 'for which the First Sea Lord is primarily responsible, has shown signs of weakness in three various theatres of war during the last few weeks.' Jellicoe was himself in no doubt as to what was going on:

> Northcliffe was pressing the PM to get rid of me, the PM was pressing Geddes, the latter wanted to avoid trouble and so tried to get away from the Admiralty but failing this carried out the desire of Northcliffe.[10]

The King, writing to Beatty in the following year, observed that Lloyd George 'had his knife into him [Jellicoe] for some time and wished for a change.' Beatty, like most of the military and naval leaders, profoundly despised the popular press, and could see what was going on: he wrote indignantly on November 30:

> I see or rather read that the *Daily Mail* is conducting a most outrageous campaign vilifying the Admiralty in general and the unfortunate Jellicoe in particular. This is against all fair play. He cannot reply, and as long as he occupies the important and responsible position he does, he is entitled to some measure of protection against the Press... it looks to me as if somebody in the Government was at the bottom of it. LG probably, or it would not be permitted. Fair criticism is one thing, but this is another. And if it continues, nobody is safe and nobody will be trusted.[11]

There was perhaps a degree of hypocrisy in this; Beatty was perfectly prepared to encourage such as Richmond to develop the most severe criticism of Jellicoe.

Robertson, the Chief of the Imperial General Staff, reckoned that Lloyd George took exception to the fact that 'Jellicoe was always pouring cold water on LG's fervent imagination and bringing him down to earth, and LG did not like it.' Newbolt, anxious as ever to paint those in authority in roseate colours, writes of the burden that Jellicoe had for nearly three and a half years had to bear, first as Commander-in-Chief and then as First Sea Lord:

> It was a burden in itself great beyond all experience, and since the contest and the hazard were on a Titanic scale, the anxieties of these high offices were even more exhausting than the incessant labour. Great as were Sir John Jellicoe's powers, and admirable as were his devotion and endurance, there was among those who met him frequently at the council table no doubt that the strain was bearing hard upon him, and could not be further prolonged with justice to him or advantage to the Service.[12]

Marder's conclusion is that while 'there is a considerable body of evidence that Jellicoe was physically fit and under no great mental strain during 1917,' he was in fact, mentally and physically, a very tired man. This accords with Balfour's belief that, as he wrote to Carson on January 3 1918, 'it may be that Jellicoe is now an overtired man. He certainly has every right to be.'

Marder thus more or less adopts the position put forward by Newbolt, which was really Lloyd George's justification for his determination to get rid of Jellicoe:

> In short, Jellicoe's ability to grapple with his problems as First Sea Lord was sapped by the cumulative mental and physical pressures of three years and a by product of these – the intensification of his latent pessimistic streaks to the point where he saw all problems through the darkest of glasses.[13]

Jellicoe wrote in his autobiographical notes of what he considered was the underlying reason for Lloyd George's sustained hostility towards him:

> My consistent support of the policy of concentrating our military efforts on the Western front, and my criticism of the secondary Eastern campaigns as placing a strain on our naval and shipping resources which resulted in heavy losses elsewhere, undoubtedly tended to inspire Mr Lloyd George (a convinced Easterner) with hostility towards my views, and was no doubt one of the factors leading up to my dismissal from the Admiralty at the end of 1917. A second factor was my opposition towards futile bombardment operations (including the bombardment of Heligoland) during 1917.[14]

These various explanations for the progress of the campaign that was to lead to Jellicoe's dismissal are no doubt all background contributions to what can be seen as the inevitable denouement. If it was Lloyd George who was hell bent on getting rid of him it was Geddes who would have to do the deed, and in the last months of 1917 there were a lot of issues to impel him to do so. One of these was the complaint which Jellicoe made more than once of the slowness of ship construction; his comments did not, he wrote, cause a serious disagreement, although it is easy to see that they may not have pleased Geddes:

> I had said that I feared that the organisation set up by him as Controller had failed to produce better results – if as good results – as the old organisation in the hands of naval officers and Admiralty officials. I mentioned that information reached me from various sources that the shipbuilders disliked the organisation and could not work with the new officials as well as with the old ones, and that their methods caused great and avoidable delays.[15]

In October had come the raid of *Brummer* and *Bremse*; in November there was the fiasco of the operation for which Geddes wanted to scapegoat Napier; and then in December came the second attack on the Norwegian convoys, and the perversion by Geddes of Jellicoe's draft telegram to Beatty. These, taken together, amounted to a less than satisfactory performance, as the *Daily Mail* had been so quick to point out. And for this, someone must take the blame. There was, however, an even more pressing reason for Jellicoe to be sacked, and that was his continued resistance to Bacon's removal. The conflict with Jellicoe over this led Wemyss to consider resignation; as he dined alone on the evening of December 22 he was considering how best to proceed when he received a message from Geddes asking him to come to see him after dinner.

When Wemyss arrived, the First Lord told him that he had made up his mind to get rid of Jellicoe, and asked if Wemyss was prepared to take his place:

> I certainly did not wish to, and I had some doubts as to whether I should be able successfully to grapple with the enormous problems that confronted the First Sea Lord, but the last three years had taught me a good deal of self confidence, and I also felt that I at any rate would bring to the office a wider outlook than it had before had. As on a former occasion I therefore dealt as freely and openly as possible with the First Lord – told him what points I considered were in favour of accepting and what I considered were my disabilities. He replied that he had been studying me for the last three months and that in his opinion I was the best man. On this I accepted, believing that under the circumstances it was my duty, but by no manner of means pleased at my sudden elevation.[16]

Geddes asked him to say nothing at present, because he had first of all to consult the King and Prime Minister, and because he wished to choose the right moment to tell Jellicoe. The consultation process was a formality and would not take long; Geddes would not have gone as far as he had without the warm encouragement of Lloyd George, and the King, however distasteful he might think the process, would not stand in the way.

Discreditably, Geddes chose not to face Jellicoe personally to tell him of his dismissal; instead, he wrote him a letter which the admiral received at 6.00 pm on December 24. It cannot have been an easy letter to write, as its weasel words make clear:

> After very careful consideration I have come to the conclusion that a change is desirable in the post of First Sea Lord. I have not, I can assure you, arrived at this view hastily or without great personal regret and reluctance. I have consulted the Prime Minister and with his concurrence I am asking to see the King to make this recommendation to him. The Prime Minister asks me to tell you that in recognition of your past very distinguished services he proposes to recommend to His Majesty that a peerage should be bestowed upon you. I have thought that you would prefer me to convey this decision to you in writing but, should you wish to see me, I shall of course be at your disposal at any time. My regret at having to convey this decision to you is the greater in view of the very cordial personal relations which have existed between us throughout.[17]

The letter was marked 'Personal and Strictly Private,' which Jellicoe felt inhibited him in consulting anyone as to how he should respond; but feeling that he must speak to someone, he saw Halsey, the Third Sea Lord, to tell him what had happened. He felt he could hardly carry on under the circumstances, so proposed to go on leave, telling Wemyss to carry on. Halsey agreed with this course, and Jellicoe wrote that evening a dignified letter to Geddes assuming that the reason for his dismissal was due to 'a want of confidence in me,' and going on to tell Geddes what he proposed. The same night Geddes, profoundly relieved that Jellicoe was evidently going to go quietly, acknowledged the letter and agreed. Next day, after seeing the King, Geddes wrote again, to ask if Jellicoe would accept the offer of a peerage.[18]

Jellicoe's first reaction was to decline the offer; but after talking it over with his wife he changed his mind. He decided to accept, first, 'for the sake of the service, which got so few honours;' secondly, because it would give him a platform from which to speak out if he thought it necessary, and finally for the sake of his children, 'as History might never know the truth and might say I was kicked out, evidently justly as no honour was conferred.'[19] Several of those to whom he spoke advised him for these reasons to accept the offered peerage, including Beresford;

others, including Beatty and Madden took a different view, the latter writing to Jellicoe on December 27:

> Just received your letter and I am more than ever astounded at not only your dismissal but the manner of it, and I hope you will refuse the Peerage. It is bound to come in time and please don't receive it at Geddes' hand – bad for the Service to feel its most trusted men can be turned out at a moment's notice and squared by a peerage... I really cannot believe Geddes who has benefited so much by your help could behave as he has done.[20]

Madden was, as he said, 'full of fear for the future;' he told Jellicoe that his own feelings were 'mutinous and explosive and very bitter.'

These feelings were shared by the remaining Sea Lords, who went as a body to see Wemyss on the late afternoon of Christmas Day. There they learned that Wemyss was to be the new First Sea Lord; after this conversation they wrote to Geddes seeking an interview. Geddes consented to see them two at a time. In the course of these meetings he disputed their right to ask for an explanation of his action, but said: 'As man to man I am prepared to tell you what I will not tell you as First Lord.'[21] The first reaction of the Sea Lords, who felt that Jellicoe had been 'kicked out without warning like a housemaid' was collectively to resign in sympathy, but they recoiled from this on reflection that it might 'do great harm to the country.'[22]

This was not, however, the end of the matter. In the course of his meetings with them, Geddes told the Sea Lords of the meeting which he and Lloyd George had held with Balfour and Carson, and suggested that Balfour and Carson had agreed that a change of First Sea Lord was desirable. When this came to the ears of Carson, he expressly denied that he had said any such thing, both in a letter to Jellicoe and personally at a meeting with Halsey on January 2. Seething with fury at what appeared to be Geddes'deceitfulness, the Sea Lords wrote a detailed, and angry, letter to Geddes to the effect that they could not continue as his colleagues until the 'misunderstanding' was cleared up.[23]

This was getting very close to mutiny, and Geddes responded strongly. The letter from the Sea Lords had, unwisely, appeared to suggest that they had some right to interfere in the appointment or dismissal of the First Sea Lord, which was simply wrong, and Geddes was quick to seize on this, writing on January 4 that the concluding paragraphs of their letter filled him with amazement:

> They imply that you and your co-signatories propose to tender your resignation unless the First Lord affords an explanation which you consider satisfactory upon a private and personal conversation which he had with you and Admirals Halsey and Tothill upon a matter in no way coming within the scope of your duties.[24]

Faced with this response, and having been advised by Jellicoe that their resignation would do no good, and would be harmful, the Sea Lords backed down. Duff, later reflecting on an affair which he thought had been mismanaged, considered that the line which should have been taken was simply that they would resign because they thought that Jellicoe's dismissal was disastrous. The decision by the Sea Lords to remain, he wrote, 'was very much against their inclination, and was come to on purely patriotic grounds.'[25] Duff, who did not enjoy a comfortable relationship with Geddes, had orally resigned as Assistant Chief of Naval Staff on December 28, and Geddes had accepted this. Subsequently he was persuaded to stay on.[26]

Wemyss was formally appointed on December 27. With Jellicoe, his protector, gone, Bacon had little chance of survival, as he recognised in a letter he wrote to Jellicoe that day:

> I was very sorry to see this morning's papers. Sorry from every point of view, that of the country, the Navy yourself, and lastly myself. It is bad news … Personally I care not much what happens regarding myself. I have for three years nearly carried a weight of responsibility few realise.[27]

Wemyss, with Geddes, had made a hurried visit to Scotland on December 26 for a meeting with Beatty, meeting him next day. In a letter to Jellicoe written in haste before the meeting Beatty expressed amazement at Jellicoe's departure and the manner of his dismissal. He said that he did not know what experience Wemyss had to run the 'complex and great machine,' but promised to write again. In fact he did not do so until January 26, when he told Jellicoe that he got 'nothing of a definite character out of Geddes, as to the reason of your departure.'[28] Wemyss and Geddes returned at once, and on December 28 Bacon was sent for and summarily dismissed, as he had expected; he took the news with great dignity, and his departure was greatly mourned by his men of the Dover Patrol.

His successor was Keyes, who was at once sent for by Wemyss, who said: 'Well Roger, you have talked a hell of a lot about what ought to be done in the Dover Area, and now you must go and do it.' This, Keyes writes somewhat unconvincingly, came to him as rather a shock; it seemed to him hardly decent that he should fill the vacancy after all he had done 'to put an end to the passive resistance at Dover.' He told Oliver, who was himself leaving the Admiralty to command a battle cruiser squadron in the Grand Fleet, in a prearranged move, how badly he felt about superseding Bacon. Oliver replied, dryly: 'Well – now it is up to you to deliver the goods.'[29]

Wemyss now settled down to his new post; he made no secret of the reluctance with which he had taken it on, writing to Calthorpe, his successor in the Mediterranean, on December 31:

> People write and congratulate me, but you – more than most people – will easily understand that it is hardly a question of congratulations, but rather one of condolences. However, in these damnable times of war one can only do what one is told and not what one likes. If the service is content with my appointment, then I am content to do my best in it. The results we can only wait for.[30]

In the new composition of the Board of Admiralty, the post of Deputy Chief of Naval Staff went to Rear Admiral Sir Sydney Fremantle; Heath, Halsey, Tothill and Paine continued as Second, Third, Fourth and Fifth Sea Lords. Fremantle had previously been in command of the British Aegean Squadron. He came to the Admiralty with a great respect for his new chief, and his wide experience, writing later:

> Wemyss, whose merits have, in my opinion, never received the appreciation which is their due, was a man of optimistic and sanguine temperament. While not to be compared with Jellicoe as a great professional sailor, he was a widely read and well informed man, whose war experience had brought him into contact with military affairs and with the functions of the Royal Navy abroad, as contrasted with those in Home Waters of the Grand Fleet,

> the supreme importance of whose efficiency and constant readiness for action, as well as their continued exile at the base in the Orkneys, tended to produce in its officers a limited outlook.[31]

The shock waves following Jellicoe's dismissal reverberated throughout the navy, and he received a flood of letters of sympathy from senior officers across the service. There was widespread outrage at the manner of his departure; Marder calls it 'squalid,' and much stronger terms than this have been used to describe a process that reflected no credit on the Prime Minister or the First Lord. It is not altogether easy to see how much real difference his sacking made to the course of the naval war, apart of course from the inevitable dismissal of Bacon. A widely held view was that of Sir Arthur Wilson, who wrote:

> The dismissal of Sir John Jellicoe is a disgraceful concession to an unscrupulous press agitation, and they have also dismissed Bacon from Dover, who was far the best man in the Navy for that particular work. I think Oliver will also go, so we shall have lost the three ablest men in the Navy.[32]

De Chair, by now serving in command of the 3rd Battle Squadron, received the news that Jellicoe had resigned, and at once wrote to him. In reply, Jellicoe said that he did not resign, but had been 'dismissed very curtly by the First Lord without any reason at all being given.' A few days later de Chair was asked to go to the Admiralty to see Wemyss:

> I was still boiling over with indignation about Jellicoe's dismissal, and the way Wemyss had betrayed him. When Wemyss began talking of filling vacancies at the Admiralty, and asked me to take one of the posts on the Board of Admiralty vacated by one of the admirals who had resigned in consequence of Jellicoe's dismissal, I told him that I would not and could not take any post at the Admiralty, as I felt so keenly the disgraceful manner in which Jellicoe had been treated ... In fact I expressed myself forcibly, and let myself go, and left him after a scene which did me no good and had disastrous results, in so far that, shortly afterwards I was relieved of my command and put on half pay.[33]

There were of course contrary views. Typical of these was the opinion of Richmond, who wrote in his diary:

> Jellicoe has fallen. One obstacle to a successful war is now out of the way. Of course he gets a peerage. What for, goodness knows! I expect the last convoy miscarriage was the cause of the dismissal. The Court of Enquiry held by Sturdee, de Robeck and Goodenough put some pretty frank criticism of the Admiralty on their report – so I gather from Goodenough. It is possible, from what Bellairs said, that Beatty had something to say of the neglect of all that he has proposed and the failure to take any serious steps in the sea war.[34]

Jellicoe himself believed at first that his dismissal was due to the fact that he had stood up to Geddes, objecting to the latter's treatment of senior officers. Writing to Beatty immediately after his dismissal, he predicted the reason that would be advanced:

> I have no doubt the country will be told I am war weary, lacking in the offensive spirit etc. I incline to the opinion that the true reason is that I will not agree to the Navy being run by an autocrat like a Railway!![35]

There was, naturally, widespread comment in the Press on Jellicoe's departure; Northcliffe's newspapers, the *Daily Mail* and *The Times*, welcomed the news enthusiastically, as did many other newspapers. The *Morning Post,* with several papers not expressing a view on the wisdom of the decision, did some months later note that Jellicoe had been 'most discourteously treated, and the whole business wears an ugly complexion.'[36]

40

Zeebrugge

The appointment of Keyes to the Dover Command was not unanimously welcomed within the navy, as Richmond recorded in his diary on January 4:

> Leveson came over to see me. Does not agree with R Keyes's appointment. Says K has not 'made good' and does not deserve it. Question is, I think, who is a good fighting man for Dover Command? Keyes has courage and independence at all events, though very little brains – rather like Vernon's 'fighting blockhead.'[1]

Richmond also had a lot to say about the new Board. He complacently observed that the arrangement of the staff was on the lines which he had recommended to Lloyd George and to Carson, although he objected to submarine operations being treated separately from general operations, and to the failure to make the Plans Division directly responsible to the First Sea Lord. He thought that Hope, the Director of Operations, was 'useless – sees nothing but difficulties, loss of matériel and life if such and such a thing is done. Any risk is vetted, as if you could make war without risk!' And this, he noted, was at a time when weak divisions of battleships were being sent out at risk of being 'mopped up by any German superior force that comes out.' Winding himself up to fresh heights of invective, he accused the Admiralty of being 'as timid as kittens when they smell danger,' but doing dangerous things, in defiance of all established principles of war, due to their stupidity and ignorance.[2]

Whatever Richmond thought about Keyes, the latter at least paid him the compliment of writing to him in late January to ask if he had any suggestions about his new job. Richmond had nothing to put forward, but congratulated Keyes on his appointment, and told him that he looked to him to do great things. He wished that Keyes had taken him with him to Dover; ironically, he was to learn two weeks later that Keyes had in effect described him as a 'visionary and unpractical.'[3]

Tyrwhitt, naturally, was particularly pleased to hear the news, writing to Keyes on January 3:

> I only heard the news yesterday. I am truly delighted and I now look forward to a very different state of relations between Dover and Harwich. I wonder how the 'streaky one' took his dismissal. Anyhow it is a great triumph and I am glad you have left the Admiralty! It is no place for a white man. I was there yesterday and I did not like the atmosphere a little bit.[4]

In fact, as Keyes found a little to his embarrassment, Bacon was both kind and helpful to his successor. Keyes observed to de Robeck that if he himself was removed, he hoped that he would take it as well as Bacon: 'I must say I take my hat off to him for the way he has behaved since he heard of his supersession.'[5]

When Keyes arrived at Dover he called together the senior officers of the Dover Patrol on January 2. They exhibited a good deal of reserve, as he recorded in his memoirs:

> At once I sensed an atmosphere of hostility and resentment, which was perhaps not surprising, after the summary supersession of their chief. I told them how desperately serious the situation was, and said, as they no doubt knew, submarines were streaming through the Straits, unhampered by the Dover Patrol anti submarine measures, and they were inflicting terrible losses on shipping in the Channel and its western approaches. It was absolutely necessary to take drastic steps to deny the Straits to them.[6]

They were at first extremely sceptical, taking what had been Bacon's position; but in the end Keyes was able to convince them of the need for an entirely fresh approach.

He selected for his Chief of Staff Captain the Hon. Algernon Boyle, at that time commanding *Malaya* in the Grand Fleet; he was promoted to the rank of commodore. Command of the Dover Patrol destroyers went to Captain Wilfred Tomkinson. The Intelligence officer was Captain Herbert Grant, who had known Keyes when they were both at Britannia Royal Naval College, and where he 'formed a contempt for him that time has by no means eradicated.'[7] Keyes, who told Beatty that he was 'very conscious of being thick headed,' claimed with some justice that he had 'the knack of getting the right people about me.'

He abandoned Bacon's mine-net barrage, satisfied that it had proved ineffective in preventing the passage of U-boats, and instead introduced massed patrols together with the brilliant illumination of the deep minefield between Folkestone and Cap Gris Nez. These patrols, carried out by trawlers and drifters, were covered to the north by two groups of destroyers. The constant illumination, and the density of the patrols, compelled U-boats to dive; it was no longer possible to pass the Straits on the surface at night. These measures soon brought success; between December 19 and February 8 five U-boats were destroyed, four of them by mines and one by depth charges.[8] Michelsen, who in November had ordered that the High Seas Fleet U-boats operating from Germany should generally use the Channel to get to their cruising grounds, in February, revoked the instructions, allowing their commanders to make their own choice of route.

Keyes expected that the difficulties now being experienced by the U-boats would provoke enemy offensive action, and on January 14 received information from Room 40 that a strong force of enemy destroyers was apparently at sea. All the available forces were alerted, as was Tyrwhitt at Harwich, who put to sea soon after midnight with *Conquest* and four destroyers. Keyes had sailed in the light cruiser *Attentive* at 8.00 pm and taken charge of all the covering forces, which included one light cruiser, four flotilla leaders, and six large destroyers in two divisions, one either side of the probable line of approach of the enemy. The weather, however, steadily deteriorated, and no contact was made; the German destroyers had gone north, and shelled Yarmouth and Southwold before returning to their base at Zeebrugge.[9]

Keyes was disappointed, but comforted himself with the thought that the Germans would soon launch another raid. In this, he was perfectly correct. Admiral Ludwig von Schröder, the commander of the *Flandern Marine Korps*, appealed to the High Seas Fleet for help to destroy the light barrier that was causing such problems for the Zeebrugge based U-boats. Scheer assigned the task to Heinecke's II flotilla which would sail direct from Germany and thus ensure surprise. The operation was planned originally for February 7, but continued bad weather caused its postponement. Heinecke proposed to sail with his whole flotilla to the Sandettie Bank, where the two half flotillas would then separate. He would attack the barrier west of the Varne Bank, while Kolbe would attack to the east.[10]

In misty weather on February 13, Heinecke's flotilla sailed from the German Bight, anchoring for the night off Norderney; next day, the weather having cleared, he first steamed westward, but once out of sight of land turned south, and slipped along the Dutch coast. At the Hook of Holland he had to send one of his destroyers home with condenser trouble, but carried on to the Sandettie Bank, where at 11.30 pm the two half flotillas separated. On this occasion Keyes was given no advance warning of the raid by Room 40; all that Hall was able to tell him was that it was expected that a large U-boat, homeward bound, would attempt to break through the Straits, and all vessels were told to look out for this.[11] Such information as he was to get would have to come from the British vessels upon which the attack fell.

On the night of February 14/15 there were nine divisions of drifters on patrol, amounting to a total of 58 vessels. *Attentive*, and the destroyers *Murray, Nugent* and *Crusader* were anchored in the Downs; *Swift* and *Marksman* were on the West Barrage Patrol, and *Termagant, Melpomene, Zubian* and *Amazon* constituted the East Barrage Patrol. Groups of trawlers were stationed to the north east and southwest of the drifter line, with another group off Cap Gris Nez. Two paddle minesweepers, *Lingfield* and *Newbury,* were patrolling between the south eastern gate and the Varne lightship. In addition the monitor *M 26* (Commander Mellin) was stationed near the north east Varne buoy, with the destroyer *Racehorse* between the Varne lightship and the Colbart. There were also a number of P-boats and two French torpedo boats on patrol. These dispositions were entirely directed at intercepting U-boats that might attempt the passage; Keyes realised that the two barrage patrols might be unable to stop a destroyer raid, and ordered that green Verey lights were to be fired if enemy surface vessels were spotted.[12]

At 11.30pm the drifter *Shipmates* sighted a submarine heading eastward, and sent up red and white Verey lights, the signal for a submarine; but in the hazy conditions soon lost sight of her. At about 12.30 as *Newbury* turned towards the Varne buoy:

> No signal or warning for special vigilance had been received, and the commanding officer was in his cabin. A few minutes after the ship had been turned, two destroyers steamed up out of the darkness, on a course parallel to hers, and riddled her with shells. Every part of the ship suffered equally; the steam pipes were severed and sent out sheets of steam, the woodwork caught fire and blazed furiously; the men on deck were shot down. The destroyers passed on rapidly.[13]

Although the sound of the firing was heard by many of the British vessels in the Straits, both the direction from which it came, and what it portended, were widely misunderstood. There followed a series of destructive attacks by both of the German half flotillas, which wreaked havoc upon the drifter patrols. Even now, the cause of the firing was not generally understood, being supposed by some to indicate that a submarine was being attacked and by others that

Dover was experiencing an air raid. The commander of one motor launch, heavily shelled by two destroyers from which he only narrowly escaped, believed he had been attacked by British destroyers.

Keyes, at Dover, though aware of the firing, had received no reports of green lights; it seemed to him that the drifters must be engaging a submarine. By 1.15 am he was beginning to feel extremely anxious, as the firing had gone on so long; he signalled to *M 26* to ask what the firing was. He got no reply until 1.53, when he got a signal (timed at 1.37) that the firing was south of the Varne and that the monitor was proceeding to investigate.[14] At 2.30 *M 26* reported that a trawler had fired a green light, but that all was now quiet. In fact *M 26* had seen a green light at 1.00 am. A few minutes later Keyes received a message which suggested that it was all a storm in a teacup, when the trawler *Goeland* II reported to the captain of the patrol that it was a fine clear night with a light east wind:

> It could hardly have been guessed from this that the stout-hearted but not very active-minded man, who sent in this report, had been seeing and hearing gunfire for the last hour and a half, had spoken the motor launch which had been under fire, and was quite convinced that German destroyers were about.[15]

Meanwhile the German destroyers, who turned for home at about 2.30 am, had a stroke of luck. Kolbe's half flotilla crossed the track of the East Barrage Patrol, and was spotted by the last vessel in the British line, the destroyer *Amazon*, commanded by Lieutenant Adam Ferguson. Three challenges were made without reply; but Ferguson was certain that the three destroyers he had seen were British, and reported this up the line to Commander Bernard, the senior officer of the patrol, in *Termagant*. The latter asked why he thought they were British, but by then in any case they had disappeared.

When dawn came up, the full extent of the disaster became apparent. Seven drifters and one trawler had been sunk, while five other drifters, one trawler and the paddle minesweeper *Newbury* had been severely damaged. British casualties amounted to 76 killed and 13 wounded. Heinecke's flotilla suffered no casualties. Newbolt, observing that this was the last of the German raids on the Dover Straits, summed up their achievement:

> Their destroyer attacks upon the Straits are indeed a brilliant episode in German naval operations. Seven times in all the German destroyers burst into the Straits and inflicted loss and damage on our watching forces; on one occasion only had they themselves suffered. But although the enemy's raiding was well conducted it was never more serious than mere raiding. The shortest interval between any two successive attacks was about a month; the longest nearly nine. The German commander in Flanders was never able to shake our hold on the Straits by continuous attacks, with the consequence that the damage done by any one raid had been made good by the time the next raid was started. The last raid, the most destructive, perhaps also the best executed of them all, laid singular emphasis upon the difficulties of interception.[16]

Scheer, who considered that the results of the raid were 'brilliant,' noted that the conditions made life difficult for the attackers as well as the defenders:

> The demands made on the skill of the officers commanding these boats were very great, as it was difficult to distinguish things clearly because of the gunfire, and particularly because of the smoke on the water from the magnesium lights.[17]

For his part, Keyes was livid; his anger was particularly directed against Ferguson, whom he had court martialled. He was sentenced to be severely reprimanded, and was relieved of his command, as was Commander Bernard. Of Mellin, the commander of *M 26*, he wrote that he did not believe that he lacked personal courage; his failure, he thought, was due to 'thick headed stupidity,' as he told Beatty. Mellin, too, was relieved of his command.[18] Jellicoe, writing after the war, concluded that 'the heavy losses sustained were due to the system of patrols adopted by Keyes against the advice of Bacon.'[19] The War Cabinet was sufficiently disturbed by the disaster to comment in its minutes on 'the bad results which had attended so many naval actions during the last year or so.'

Keyes was by now heavily involved in the planning of a major operation against the German bases at Zeebrugge and Ostend. Throughout the war it had been recognised that to deal with the U-boat threat from these bases it would be necessary to block them, and a number of proposals had been put forward by, among others, Bayly, Tyrwhitt and Bacon. In September 1917 the Plans Division was instructed to prepare plans for such an operation, about which Keyes was predictably very enthusiastic. When the scheme was reviewed by Bacon he dismissed it as 'unworkable,' preferring his own proposal for a landing from monitors on the outside of the mole at Zeebrugge while the lock gates were bombarded by other monitors; this, he argued, would block the canal efficiently against small craft for some weeks, which blocking ships did not do. In his *Concise Story of the Dover Patrol*, published in 1932, Bacon explained his scheme in great detail, still arguing its superiority over that put forward by Keyes.[20] Jellicoe, approving Bacon's scheme, wanted it combined with a blocking operation. Before this could be worked out both Jellicoe and Bacon had been sacked, and Keyes was free to proceed with the planning for his blocking operation, designed to close the Bruges ship canal, to block the entrance to Ostend harbour, and generally to smash up the two ports as much as possible.

Beatty agreed to help the enterprise by releasing officers and men from the Grand Fleet to take part, for which Keyes was profoundly grateful:

> A thousand thanks for your promise of help – without it I don't think we could take it on with any great confidence. Now I am absolutely full of it! – And am delighted to know that the Grand Fleet is going to share in an enterprise, which if it fails even, and it is not going to, can only bring credit to the Service.[21]

Keyes kept Beatty constantly informed as preparations continued, and sent him the final outline of the plan on February 22. It was reviewed by the Sea Lords at a meeting two days later, and over the next few days it was circulated to them for comment. There was general approval of the plan, and praise for the care taken in its preparation; the propaganda value of a successful operation was noted by Hope, the Deputy First Sea Lord, who observed: 'If successful, the operation may have far-reaching political and moral effect.'[22] This was obviously true; it indicated the readiness of the Admiralty to make the most of such a daring and high profile operation.

The scheme involved the use of the elderly cruiser *Vindictive*, of 5,750 tons, built in 1899, which was to lay alongside the stone mole, 1,850 yards long and 80 yards wide, that covered the entrance to the Bruges ship canal and which, curving out north and east, formed the harbour. *Vindictive* was armed with two 7.5 inch guns, to which had been added an 11 inch howitzer. Two shallow draught ferries, *Iris* and *Daffodil*, would accompany her, and shove her against the mole, and hold her in position, while a storming party of 200 blue jackets and 700 marines landed. These were all drawn as volunteers from the Grand Fleet. The sailors were to storm the guns at the northern end of the mole, and the marines the fortified zone from inside, in order to enable three concrete laden block ships to enter the harbour. These were three even older protected cruisers of the *Apollo* class, of about 3500 tons, built in 1892 – 1894, *Thetis*, *Intrepid* and *Iphigenia*. The first was intended to sink herself in the lock, and the other two across the mouth of the canal. Two more of the same class, *Brilliant* and *Sirius*, were to proceed to Ostend and block the harbour there. Finally, two old submarines, *C1* and *C3*, each loaded with five tons of explosives, would be driven under the 580 yard long railway viaduct which linked the mole to the shore, and there blown up. The practicability of the scheme depended on the weather. It was intended to launch the operation on the night of April 11-12; high water and a moonless night were prerequisites, as was a calm sea. Ninety minutes before the expedition was due to arrive, the wind changed, blowing off shore; with a heavy heart Keyes aborted the operation. On April 13 Keyes tried again; but high winds developed before his ships could sail, and it was again postponed. Next day, Wemyss came to Dover to tell Keyes that by now surprise would have been lost and the operation should be cancelled. Keyes pleaded for another chance, opting to launch the operation between April 22 and 26; there would be high water, but there would be a full moon, which increased the risks.

Wemyss consented, and on April 22, the weather being favourable, the expedition sailed; always having a good eye for a flamboyant gesture, Keyes made before night fell a general signal by semaphore; 'St George for England,' having been reminded by his wife that next day was St George's Day. Keyes flew his flag in the destroyer *Warwick*. A total of 76 vessels took part in the expedition, which included the monitors *Erebus* and *Terror*, which were to bombard German positions. Unknown to Keyes, the Germans had obtained a copy of the orders for the operation when a coastal motor boat (CMB) had run aground off Zeebrugge during the abortive operation of April 11-12. It does not appear, however, that they did much about it, apart from putting some sections of the coast defences on a higher alert.[23]

About ten minutes before *Vindictive* could reach the mole, a change in the wind blew away the smoke screen that was supposed to mask her approach, and the Germans opened a heavy fire under star shells and search lights, wrecking her upper works and causing heavy casualties. Acting Captain Alfred Carpenter, commanding *Vindictive*, increased speed, but this had the effect of her reaching the mole more than 340 yards beyond the intended position; this meant that the guns at the end of the mole were out of reach of the storming party, and her guns could not bear on the defenders. *Daffodil* held *Vindictive* in place while the landing parties clambered up the special brows on to the mole, and for the next fifty five minutes, while they fought with great gallantry to establish a position. Under heavy fire they made little progress. One of *Vindictive's* 7.5 inch guns was knocked out, and the other never opened fire, two successive crews being wiped out by shell fire. Carpenter, seeing the block ships entering the harbour, sounded the recall soon after 12.50 am; as many as possible of the storming parties regained *Vindictive* and *Iris*, and with *Daffodil* they retired under heavy smoke screens. That *Vindictive* and the others did not suffer fatal damage was due to the height of the mole, which to some extent shielded them from the enemy fire.

Meanwhile the block ships, taking advantage of the diversion caused by *Vindictive,* had reached the end of the mole before they were detected. At once, they were subjected to a heavy fire at point blank range. *Thetis* suffered particularly severely, and finally grounded in a sinking condition before she reached the canal entrance. *Intrepid* and *Iphigenia* did reach the entrance, and there scuttled themselves in a position which appeared to have blocked the canal entrance.

Meantime *C1* had parted her tow and failed to arrive at the viaduct before the recall, but *C3* got there, and was rammed into position between two piers. Her crew escaped in a skiff after setting the fuses; the resulting explosion was successful in cutting the viaduct. Meanwhile *Warwick* and her supporting destroyers, *Phoebe* and *North Star,* which had been covering the approach of the block ships, were also subjected to a heavy fire. Before long, Keyes lost touch with them in the smoke, having frequently to alter course to avoid the motor launches which were working close inshore:

> On two or three occasions, finding them exposed and under fire, the *Warwick* laid smoke between them and the mole extension battery, which opened fire promptly upon anything that appeared out of the smoke. On about four occasions we all felt very naked when we emerged from the smoke and salvoes splashed round us, but the *Warwick* was only hit in the rigging.[24]

North Star lost her bearings in the smoke, and found herself close to *Intrepid* and *Iphigenia;* picked up by a searchlight, she came under heavy fire as she stood out to sea, firing her torpedoes (to no effect) at the destroyers alongside the mole as she passed. However, after passing the lighthouse she was hit at point blank range in the engine and boiler rooms, and lay stopped about 400 yards north east of the Mole at 1.25. *Phoebe* attempted to take her in tow, but by now *North Star* was in a sinking condition and was abandoned.

By then the Zeebrugge force was on its way home, *Vindictive* under tow by *Daffodil.* A destroyer and two motor launches had been lost, in addition of course to the block ships and *C3.* Total casualties were 170 killed, 400 wounded and 45 missing.

Meanwhile the attack on Ostend had been a complete shambles. The wind changed at a critical moment, depriving *Brilliant* and *Sirius* and their attendant destroyers of the cover of the smoke screens, and exposed the calcium light buoys that had been laid by the British to mark the harbour entrance; these were soon destroyed by gunfire from the shore. Unknown to the British, the Germans had moved the light buoy which normally marked the entrance about a mile to the east. Deceived by this, *Brilliant* and *Sirius* missed the entrance and ran aground where they supposed the entrance to be. The ships were blown up, and their crews rescued by three motor launches.[25]

When he got back to Dover, Keyes at once reported to the Admiralty that the operation had been carried out according to plan, apart from the supporting aerial attack which was prevented by the weather. The news of the apparent success was electrifying. Within an hour or two, Keyes received a telegram to say that the King had appointed him a Knight Commander of the Bath; Carpenter's acting rank as Captain was confirmed. The public relations machine of the Admiralty at once swung into action; a sensational communiqué declared that the harbour and canal had been blocked. The Press lapped it up; it had clearly been a magnificent enterprise and a huge success. The *Daily Mail* cried that it was 'an immortal deed,' exulting that 'our High Command today believes in using our sea power to strike, and not merely to fend off blows.' Congratulatory messages poured in to Keyes, especially from naval colleagues. Beatty sent a 'short line to convey my most sincere and warmest congratulations on your well earned honour. A KCB won under such circumstances is something worth having.'[26] Captain WW Fisher told him that he had 'earned the gratitude of the whole Navy. We feel vindicated. We can put our heads up again.' Wemyss wrote to Lady Keyes:

> You will know how delighted I am at Roger's great and deserved success, and at his reward. It was splendid. The loss alas was heavy and I have lost one or two real friends, but one has the happy feeling that these gallant fellows haven't given their lives in vain.[27]

Keyes was determined to make another attempt on Ostend. The block ships this time were *Sappho,* another of the *Apollo* class, and the poor old battered *Vindictive.* Filled with concrete, they sailed for Ostend on the night of May 10-11. *Sappho* never made it, being forced to return after a boiler accident, which reduced her speed to six knots. *Vindictive,* unable clearly to see the harbour entrance in the fog and smoke, came under heavy fire and ran aground. Commander Godsal, her captain, was killed; Lieutenant Crutchley, who took command, tried to swing the ship across the channel, but, finding she had stopped swinging, gave the order for her to be abandoned. *Vindictive's* final resting place blocked about a third of the fairway. Keyes, in *Warwick* out at sea, was meanwhile 'having a hateful time, the roar of guns was intense, rockets, star shells and "flaming onions" lit up the sky. *Warwick* was able to rescue many of *Vindictive's* crew, but on the way back she was mined, and was lucky to make it to Dover under tow from another destroyer.[28]

Keyes had still not given up on Ostend, and planned another attempt for June, using *Sappho* and the old battleship *Swiftsure* as block ships; but in the event the Admiralty cancelled the operation. Intelligence reports suggested that Ostend could only be used by small submarines and torpedo boats; since these could get past the block ships at Zeebrugge there was no point in incurring heavy losses to block Ostend.

Following the second attempt on Ostend the Admiralty, still on the crest of a wave of favourable publicity, sought to improve the shining hour with a further laudatory press release:

> The operation designed to close the ports of Ostend and Zeebrugge was successfully completed last night, when the obsolete cruiser HMS *Vindictive* was sunk between the piers and across the entrance of Ostend Harbour. Since the attack on Zeebrugge on April 23, *Vindictive* had been filled with concrete and fitted as a block ship for this purpose … Our casualties were light.[29]

Keyes was 'very annoyed' about this, since his chief of staff's report of the operation gave no grounds for claiming that the operation had been 'successfully completed.'

In his report of the Zeebrugge operation, Keyes claimed that the operations had been 'completely successful in attaining their first and most important object. The entrance to the Bruges Ship Canal was blocked.' He went on to say:

> The main results achieved have, however, proved greater than I expected when the fleet returned to port on the morning of April 23. Aerial observation and photographs up to

the present day (May 9) show clearly that even the lighter craft in the Bruges ship canal and docks have so far been unable to find an exit through the smaller waterways to Ostend harbour.[30]

It was a judgement that the Admiralty was entirely ready to accept. Keyes went on to claim that 23 destroyers and torpedo boats and not less than 12 submarines had remained 'sealed up,' at Bruges since the attack. All his life Keyes seems to have believed that this was true, almost certainly in good faith; he was about as cockeyed an optimist as it was possible to be, and he was very ready to believe what he wanted to believe. He was not alone. As late as 1958, Barrie Pitt in his account of the attack wrote that 'there is no valid reason for decrying the success of the Zeebrugge Raid.' He was particularly angry at what he saw as the preference for the German records:

> Why our own material should be brushed aside so contemptuously and the German picture avidly accepted, is difficult to appreciate upon any reasonable grounds; if our own evidence is considered to have been manufactured for devious purposes, surely the same scepticism at least should be extended to that of an enemy whose political history reveals little in the way of naïve simplicity.[31]

The Admiralty's claims, however, were false. Room 40 knew at once that the raids on Zeebrugge and Ostend had failed. At Zeebrugge, the gap had not been completely closed. Small destroyers were able to leave the port within twenty four hours and U-boats within forty eight hours. Only the larger U-boats were obliged for a short time to use Ostend. Keyes, predictably, refused to accept that this was the case; Admiral Hall drily observed:

> At the Admiralty we knew five hours after the attempt from an intercepted signal that the canal had not been blocked, but no good purpose would be served by publishing this.[32]

As far as the Admiralty was concerned, the British public wanted and badly needed a victory, and this was what the British public was going to get.

The German Official History reflected soberly on the chances that had led to the unfavourable outcome:

> Daring and bravery, great as it was, could not compensate for such things as the partial failure of the smoke screen in the latter stages of the approach until *Vindictive* was alongside, going alongside at the wrong spot, the destruction of *Vindictive's* landing gear, and the loss of leading men. These and other divergences from the minutely worked out and exercised plan, were bound to have such a strong influence on the total success that all the great daring displayed was in vain, and the aim not achieved.[33]

Bacon, in his history of the Dover Patrol, was highly critical of the tactics employed. A monitor would have offered greater protection against shell fire than *Vindictive*; a division of destroyers should have engaged the mole batteries; the movable gangways fitted to *Vindictive* were more or less useless; *Vindictive* should have gone in bows on rather than alongside; and an effort should have been made to destroy the lock gates with point blank gunfire.[34]

Herbert Grant, in an account left with his papers entitled 'The Immortal Folly of Zeebrugge and Ostend,' was much more savage in his views:

> The massacre of Zeebrugge … for no such folly was ever devised by fools as such an operation as that of Zeebrugge. For what were the bravest of the brave massacred? Was it glory? … for sailors to go on shore and attack forts, which Nelson said no sailor but a lunatic would do, is not only silly, but it's murder and it is criminal.

This quotation is attributed by Deborah Lake to Fisher, and certainly its tone and content is entirely consistent with the old admiral's style of correspondence. He was extremely sceptical of the official reports of the attack on Zeebrugge, observing of these on May 3 that 'the champion liar at the Admiralty is on the job again to make the episode rank with the siege of Troy.' To Winston Churchill he wrote three weeks later:

> These recent attacks on Zeebrugge and Ostend are heroic and magnificent, 'mais ce n'est pas la guerre.' We run away. We lose 6 ships more wanted for a vital operation. We lose irreplaceable heroes! It's 'tip and run.' We want: 'J'y suis, j'y reste.'[37]

Grant was disgusted when he reflected on his involvement in the preparations for the operation; he wrote that 'nothing is more distasteful to me than thinking or writing of the Zeebrugge attack and often I wish that I had had nothing to do with the affair. The most consummate folly.'[38] Bitterly observing that Keyes 'believed his own heroics,' he asked for a transfer.

Newbolt, as his readers would expect, had his own take on the way in which the operations should be viewed. If the result was far below expectations, he wrote:

> Are we, on that account, to conclude that the operations were no more than exhibitions of high courage? By no means; for success in war is not always measurable by objectives which have been won, or by purposes which have been achieved in whole or in part. The blocking expeditions were a sort of complement to the measures which Admiral Keyes had been executing with relentless vigour for five whole months, and no estimate of their success or failure would be complete without an accompanying estimate of their contribution to the general war plan.[39]

And, of course, he was much impressed by the public relations value of the exercise, and the way the news had been received. He expressed this in characteristically purple prose:

> The feeling aroused was not merely British pride in a British triumph – it spread like fire, from country to country, from continent to continent, it raised the captive Belgians from their dark oppression, it excited fierce joy in the most distant American training camp. But above all it brought about that prevision of victory which often in great conflicts appears to be the deciding force.[40]

As Marder notes, the publication of the last volume of the German Official History 'once and for all revealed that Zeebrugge, though "the perfect example of a well planned, excellently prepared and bravely executed attempt to eliminate a strongly defended enemy base by approaching from the sea and blocking it," had been a failure.' He quotes a passage summing up why at first the attack might have been thought successful:

> It is understandable that the British at first regarded the attack on Zeebrugge as having achieved complete success. The entrance was blocked at low water, so that the Marine Corps instructed those U-boats which were at sea that when returning they should enter by Ostend. This order, passed by W/T and intercepted by the enemy, strengthened the British impression that Zeebrugge had been successfully blocked. The Germans at first had a similar impression. On the morning after the attack, when the German Flag Officer, Admiral von Schröder, inspected the mole and locks, and saw the block ships lying in the narrow entrance, he naturally felt anything but happy about the situation; it looked as if the enemy had succeeded in delivering a grievous blow to the prosecution of the U-boat war. Yet the true situation very soon proved to be entirely different … Closer examination of the situation very soon showed that the conduct of the war from Zeebrugge had suffered only minor and temporary restrictions.[41]

41

The Last Sortie of the High Seas Fleet

While Keyes and his staff were preparing for the assault on Zeebrugge, Scheer and his staff were planning the next sortie of the High Seas Fleet. It was to be conducted with the greatest possible care in order to avoid the kind of ill luck that had dogged so many previous ventures. Wireless intercepts and reports from U-boats had disclosed that large forces were now being committed to the escort of the Scandinavian convoys, including independent battle squadrons. These were a tempting target for the High Seas Fleet, as Richmond and others had predicted they would be. Scheer explained his objective:

> A successful attack on such a convoy would not only result in the sinking of much tonnage, but would be a great military success, and would bring welcome relief to the U-boats operating in the Channel and round England, for it would force the English to send more warships to the northern waters. The convoys could not be touched by light craft. But the battle cruisers could probably, according to information received, deal with all exigencies likely to arise if they could have the necessary support from the battleship squadrons.[1]

The care with which the operation was planned was exceptional. For a month before the operation was due to take place the German minesweepers were working hard to open channels through all the minefields which lay in the path of a northward movement. The lessons of past operations had been carefully learned for, as Hipper's biographer explained, 'we had something special in view:'

> Accordingly we threw a veil of silence and mystery over our preparations, a veil so thick that even an incautious word would give no hint of what was coming. Sham orders, drafted with great skill, played an important part. The real truth was known to a very small circle of the initiated. Everything went smoothly and our preparations proceeded according to plan.[2]

The likelihood that Scheer would attempt a bold stroke of the kind that he was engaged on planning had been much in Beatty's mind. The requirement for heavy units from the Grand Fleet to cover the Scandinavian convoys amounted to a permanent reduction in its battle strength while offering a target that would be vulnerable to a major High Seas Fleet attack. This, Beatty made plain at a conference at the Admiralty on January 2 and 3 1918, arguing that it was now in Britain's 'interest to adopt measures which would tend to postpone a Fleet action.'[3]

He was asked to bring forward a paper outlining the strategy he advocated and the reasons for it, which he did on January 9. It marked a substantial retreat from the kind of bullish noises which had for so long characterised the attitude of the Grand Fleet. Confidence in the outcome of a major fleet action had drained away; Beatty was not taking any chances that any blame might subsequently fall on him:

> The possibility of an encounter with the High Seas Fleet resulting in an indecisive engagement, or one in which the British losses are greater than those of the enemy, cannot be disregarded, and I am desirous that my views should be on record in case of any subsequent enquiry.[4]

Marder, rightly, considers this report to rank with Jellicoe's memorandum of October 30 1914 'as one of the two most important British naval documents of the war.' In it, Beatty warned that Scheer's interior position gave him the opportunity to mount an attack with superior forces. The covering force of the convoys would almost certainly be unable to join forces with the main fleet if the enemy came out. Nor was Beatty at all happy with the relative quality of the ships that would be engaged. He had, in his earlier paper presented to the Admiralty, frankly described the inadequacy of his own vessels:

> As regards Battleships, though superior in numbers, the British ships are inferior in construction and protection. The latter has to some extent been improved by alterations made since May 31 1916, but these, at best, are a makeshift and do not compensate for radical defects in design, more particularly as regards magazine protection.[5]

In addition, Beatty argued that the enemy could choose his own moment for action, enabling him to prepare submarine traps and minefields which would, it was anticipated, cause casualties even before battle was joined.

He was no more optimistic about the comparative situation in battle cruisers:

> We have nine to the German six: *Mackensen, Seydlitz, Moltke, Hindenburg, Derfflinger, Von der Tann*. A considerable superiority on paper, but of the British vessels only three, viz. *Lion, Princess Royal* and *Tiger* are fit to be in the line against the German five. [sic] The *Renown* class are insufficiently armoured, they cannot stand a hammering. The *New Zealand* and *Invincible* classes are deficient in speed, protection and armament.[6]

The firmly held conviction in the Grand Fleet that *Mackensen* had been completed, and had joined the High Seas Fleet, was of course quite wrong.

Beatty was also anxious about his narrow margin in light cruisers, and his inferiority in submarines, as well as the detachment of so many of his destroyers engaged in anti submarine work. He also reiterated his concerns about the quality of shell with which his ships were supplied, concerns which would not be remedied until the summer. All this led him to advocate an extremely passive strategy – ironically, far more cautions than anything that Jellicoe had put forward:

> The correct strategy of the Grand Fleet is no longer to endeavour to bring the enemy to action at any cost, but rather to contain him in his bases until the general situation becomes

> more favourable to us. This does not mean that action should be avoided if conditions favour us, or that our role should be passive and purely defensive.[7]

One wonders what the *Daily Mail* would have thought of all this.

The Admiralty reviewed Beatty's memorandum on January 17and broadly accepted it. Mindful of the fact that their own paper would have to go to the War Cabinet, the members of the Board were at pains to point out 'that the adoption of this policy is rendered necessary only by the exigencies of the present situation and should be regarded as a purely temporary measure.' This spoonful of sugar evidently helped the medicine to go down. Beatty's paper and that of the Admiralty came before the War Cabinet, who apparently looked 'very glum,' but accepted the new policy. Jellicoe was scornful of the 'somewhat tardy realisation by the War Cabinet of some of the dangers attendant upon a system of convoy for mercantile trade.' He concluded his later book, on the subject of Admiralty policy in 1917, by pointing out the huge change in strategy that the politicians were now prepared to accept:

> The only change in Naval War Policy during 1918 was the decision come to by the War Cabinet that the Grand Fleet was no longer to do its utmost to force an action on the High Sea Fleet. I find it difficult to reconcile the decision thus arrived at with the views expressed to me by Mr Lloyd George in 1917. In that year he pressed for more offensive action on the part of the Navy in general, and the Grand Fleet in particular, pointing out the superior Naval strength possessed by us as compared with the Germans. The proper offensive action for the Grand Fleet was to seek engagement with the High Sea Fleet if an opportunity should arise, or if by any means the High Sea Fleet could be induced to put to sea. The 1918 decision cancelled this.[8]

If Beatty's paper had appeared over the signature of Jellicoe, Lloyd George and Geddes would no doubt have given it short shrift, and his waspish comment was in the circumstances entirely reasonable. Jellicoe was unimpressed by the argument that the Grand Fleet was vulnerable; it was, he pointed out, much stronger than it had been at Jutland, and even if *Mackensen* and *Hindenburg* had been added to Hipper's force, 'the disparity in force was not very serious, nor was it very important in a real fleet action, although no doubt adding somewhat to our scouting difficulties.' In fact, Marder concludes, the new strategy was really the same as Jellicoe's; and Madden thought the same, telling Jellicoe on January 28 that 'when History is written these papers will be a complete vindication of your policy, as Commander-in-Chief and as First Sea Lord.'[9]

Early in 1918 there was one particular change in the personnel of the Grand Fleet, when Sturdee left the 4th Battle Squadron to become Commander-in-Chief at the Nore; he was succeeded by Vice Admiral Sir Montague Browning. Beatty was glad to see the back of him, as he wrote to his wife on February 1:

> Old Sturdee departed yesterday for good. I gave him a farewell banquet and an eulogistic speech which pleased him and did no harm. Between you and me, I am glad he has gone. He was becoming very tiresome and is obsessed with the idea that every man's hand is against him and he has been badly treated, when in reality he is the luckiest man in the service. He has made many mistakes, big ones, and has suffered for them not at all.[10]

During his time as Commander-in-Chief Beatty had a compelling reason for seizing every opportunity to visit the Admiralty, since it gave him a chance to visit his mistress, Eugénie Godfrey-Faussett. After returning from his meeting on January 2-3, he wrote to her: 'It was a joy to see you again, even for so short a time, still I do not grumble, five minutes happiness is not to be sneezed at and I don't believe it was a minute more.'[11] He was back in London again in late February and early March, arguing unsuccessfully with Geddes and Fremantle for an air torpedo attack on the High Seas Fleet; to his great frustration, he was unable to see Eugénie on either occasion.

The idea of an aerial torpedo attack on the High Seas Fleet greatly appealed to Beatty. It would exhibit a willingness to conduct offensive operations without hazarding the capital ships of the Grand Fleet, and would absorb German resources in preparing defensive measures against such attacks. A successful attack, he thought, 'might profoundly influence the whole campaign' and in particular might improve the chances of being able to undertake other offensive measures against the High Seas Fleet. Because of the need to keep up a campaign of continuous attacks, however, and the lack of carriers from which to launch them, the Admiralty turned down Beatty's proposal. Richmond, who had been enthusiastic about the torpedo project, had a conversation with Cecil Malone, one of the great pioneers of naval aviation, in March, which depressed him:

> Malone came over and saw me yesterday. He gives a gloomy account of the Admiralty. Fremantle is now the block to every scheme in the Admiralty: Godfrey Paine and Mark Kerr ... block all proposals concerning the air.[12]

The prospect of a German attack on the convoy escort of a Scandinavian convoy was exercising Wemyss's mind in February, when he wrote to Beatty:

> The routes and dates of sailing of this convoy can, within certain limits, be estimated by the enemy with a fair approach to accuracy. We may also assume the possibility that the enemy has become aware of the fact that the strength of the covering force is pretty uniform, viz. a light cruiser squadron with either a division of the battle fleet or a battle cruiser squadron; and when the escorting force consists of the 12 inch Dreadnoughts, or of the 2nd Battle Cruiser Squadron its strength is insufficient to meet the whole of the enemy's battle cruiser force.[13]

If advance intelligence of a German raid was available, he thought, 'it is easy for us to send out the whole of the Grand Fleet.' If such information was not available, however, the security of the convoy could not be relied on; and he wondered whether the use of a battleship division or battle cruiser squadron was altogether advisable. The prevention of such intelligence reaching the British Admiralty was of course central to the precautions being taken by the High Seas Fleet as they planned their forthcoming operation.

Beatty continued to be extremely reluctant to beef up the covering force any more; he remained very anxious not in that way to reduce the strength of his battle fleet. Two ways of reducing the risks were explored. One was to change the time intervals between convoy sailings. Beatty wished to avoid the necessity for two covering forces to be at sea at any one time, and proposed an increase to a four day interval, from three days. The Admiralty believed that the amount of traffic justified three day sailings, but agreed to a trial of the longer period in March. The other option was to change the route, with the convoys sailing further north; Beatty preferred this, but the Admiralty insisted on the direct route, in order to save time.

The intelligence problem was serious. By now, Room 40 was no longer getting as much information as previously since the Germans were suspicious of what had in fact been the case and were taking precautions to limit wireless traffic, and were changing their signal books. It was certainly true that reconnaissance submarines in the Bight might detect significant movements, while unusual Zeppelin activity was a clear pointer to something being in the wind; but Room 40 was a vital part of British responsiveness. Beatty discussed the issue with Captain Kenneth Dewar, the Assistant Director of Plans Division, on March 7:

> The Commander-in-Chief said that so far as possible he considered that all dispositions would be made on the supposition that Intelligence was not available, and he strongly deprecated the present system of relying on this. He felt that the Scandinavian supporting system was wrong.[14]

He told Dewar that in his opinion the volume and importance of the traffic was not sufficient to justify the risk of the enemy surprising and defeating the covering force.

In March there had begun discussions about bringing Richmond back to the Admiralty. There were many there who opposed this; they included Wemyss, who later told Richmond that he had only consented because he thought it rather small to oppose his coming, since a lot of others wanted him there, and it was ridiculous to be afraid of him. 'If I could not keep you in hand, I should not be worth much,' he told Richmond. The latter's post was to be Director of Training and Staff Duties; he felt ambivalent about it, since he saw it as cutting away all chance of going into Operations. On April 10 Richmond made the rounds of the fleet to say his goodbyes. He found the Commander-in-Chief in pessimistic vein, still foreseeing many possibilities of trouble at sea, and profoundly critical of muddle at the Admiralty:

> He gave me many examples of the lack of coordination, owing, so it appears to me, to absence of definition of duties of the various branches, which, in its turn, is owing to lack of clear reasoning as to the functions of each division, and, largely, he said – and I expect he's right – to jealousy, childish jealousy.[15]

Meanwhile Scheer was completing his plans for the projected sortie of the High Seas Fleet. The information that he had received from U-boats was that the Scandinavian convoys were running only once or twice a week, and were now much larger. This information, as far as it went, was more or less true; but what it did not disclose was that in fact the convoy sailed at regular intervals. As Newbolt points out, Scheer had only to find out the date of one sailing or arrival in order to calculate subsequent dates. The regularity of the sailings was something that the German consuls in Norway could easily have discovered, which would show that the information from U-boats was thoroughly misleading:

> For they must surely have known that the dates of departure were separated by intervals made as regular as the weather would allow, and that the actual days of the week had nothing to do with the dates of sailings or arrivals … If the U-boat commanders were his

> only sources of information, it is truly extraordinary that he or his staff should not have amplified their reports by inquiries from civilian officials.[16]

A reliance on guess work was an uncharacteristic lapse on the part of the usually meticulous German staff; and it was an error that was to cost the High Seas Fleet yet another missed opportunity.

Scheer's plan had to take into account the limited fuel capacity of the destroyer flotillas and some of the light cruisers, which restricted the operation to three days in all. This would enable him to spend one day in the area west of Norway in which he expected to find his prey. Hipper, with the I Scouting Group of battle cruisers, II Scouting Group of light cruisers (under Rear Admiral von Reuter) and II Destroyer Flotilla was to attack the convoy and its covering force. Scheer, with the main body of t he High Seas Fleet, would be in support to the SSW, some sixty miles away. Scheer would take with him the I Squadron, III Squadron (minus *Markgraf)* and IV Squadron of battleships, IV Scouting Group of light cruisers (minus *Stralsund*) and the I, VI, VII and IX Destroyer Flotillas. The fleet was assembled on the evening of April 22 in Schillig Roads; the official reason for its assembly was given out as the carrying out of exercises in the Bight next day. There would be no Zeppelin cover available due to a stiff easterly wind.[17] Coincidentally, the date chosen for the commencement of the operation was that on which the raid on Zeebrugge was taking place. Tyrwhitt was at sea between the Brown Ridge and the Texel, covering Keyes's force; there was particular concern at the Admiralty lest the High Seas Fleet should interfere, but of that there was no indication.

Scheer took careful steps to make certain of a smooth start to his operation:

> To ensure safety of progress through the minefields in preparation for this enterprise, protective barriers had been placed about 70 sea miles west of Horns Reef and this protective barrier was to be the starting point of the expedition. The U-boats that had recently put to sea had received orders to seek opportunities for attack off the Firth of Forth and to report all warships and convoys that were sighted.[18]

Above all, however, Scheer relied on greatly improved signal security. All orders to the fleet, and to such as light ships and minesweepers, were issued in writing, and strict wireless silence was imposed. In several respects Room 40 was less able to decode such transmissions as were picked up, due to changes in German signal codes. Furthermore, the Germans were using where possible 'damped wave' low power transmissions which were difficult to intercept. Finally, U-boats at sea were warned of surface operations by the use of catchwords which, even if intercepted and decoded by Room 40, gave no clue as to what was conveyed. These precautions were so effective that in its daily signals of German activity, Room 40 on April 22 and 23 reported: 'No sign of activity in the Bight.'[19]

The High Seas Fleet sailed at 5.00 am on April 23, with high hopes; opportunities such as this operation might produce to pounce on a detached part of the Grand Fleet were just what the High Seas Fleet had been hoping for since the outbreak of war. There had been a recent change in all call signs, and not all of these had been identified, while a change of key had been made on April 21 which was not broken until April 24. Thus, when the High Seas Fleet was obliged to anchor near Heligoland at about 10.00 am due to extremely heavy fog the consequent exchange between Scheer and Hipper was not at once decoded. In fact, five signals were picked up, though not decoded, which should have alerted Room 40 that something was going on, particularly as there had been a change of W/T control. After the operation was over, Room 40 launched an inquiry into its failure on this occasion:

> The various small craft protecting the route were very nervy, frequently imagining an enemy air raid. Owing to their protection the Fleet was able to proceed without [further] signalling. The outpost craft had been strictly ordered to make no reference to the passing Fleet.[20]

The thick fog soon cleared, and the High Sea Fleet was able to resume its journey northward. As it did so, it crossed the line of four British submarines that had been stationed in the approaches to the Bight along a rough quadrant between the Texel and Lyngvig to give warning of any German operation. One of these, *J6,* sighted Hipper's five battle cruisers but, convinced that these were British, her commander, Lieutenant Commander G Warburton, made no report of the sighting. He had already previously seen a group of light cruisers and destroyers; he had been warned that British cruisers might be operating in his area. Half an hour after sighting Hipper, he saw heavy ships, which were no doubt the battle squadrons of the High Seas Fleet. Again, he made no report, his conviction that all these units were British being quite unshaken by any possible doubt.[21] Beatty observed to Wemyss that Warburton's error was 'incredibly stupid and indeed heart breaking;' but Marder quotes from a lecture given by the then Commander John Creswell in 1931 which showed a more thoughtful consideration of the mistake:

> It is easy enough to see now what a grave neglect of duty this was; but it is not so easy to judge to what extent it was personal fault of the captain of *J6,* and how much may be attributed to the High Command failing to make it quite clear to junior subordinates – junior flag officers and captains of detached ships – what was required of them. One does not know, for instance, whether any officers had recently been rapped over the knuckles for reporting forces which were actually our own.[22]

It was certainly not the first time that such an error had occurred.

Both Hipper and Scheer were accordingly able to continue their journey northwards without any countermeasures having been initiated. Their prey, however, was already about to elude them.

When dawn came up on April 23, the homeward bound convoy of thirty four vessels, which had left Selbjorns Fjord at 1.15pm the previous day, escorted by the *Duke of Cornwall, Lark* and *Llewellyn,* was already far advanced on its journey, being only 140 miles east of the Orkneys. It had been met by a covering force consisting of the 2nd Battle Cruiser Squadron and the 7th Light Cruiser Squadron, which was proceeding to the south of the convoy. This, of course, was Scheer's target; if he had got his intelligence about convoy sailing times right, he would have got exactly the result which he planned. As it was, the convoy and the covering force had by nightfall on April 23 reached the latitude of Buchan Ness, having sailed all day through the fog, which was by now thicker than ever. It was, however, safely out of Scheer's reach, and would enter harbour at Methil on the following day.[23]

By now the Admiralty's suspicions that Scheer was up to something had been aroused; its first response, early on April 24, was to order Tyrwhitt, who had returned to Harwich after the Zeebrugge raid was over, to raise steam. For the moment, the Admiralty allowed the next Norway bound convoy to sail, with its escort of two destroyers; a warning went to Beatty that some operation was pending in the Bight. On receipt of this he put the fleet at two and a half hours for steam.

Scheer's operation had proved abortive, although he was as yet unaware of this. In the meantime, however, it had suffered a serious setback with an accident to the battle cruiser *Moltke.* At 5.10 am she lost her starboard inner propeller, and a gear wheel flew to pieces, smashing an auxiliary condenser. Water entered first her starboard engine and then her midships engine. She signalled the news to Hipper, who ordered *Moltke* to join the battle fleet; he could not afford to conduct the operation at the speed of which *Moltke* was capable. Carrying on, he next learned that *Von der Tann* was limited to 21 knots due to bad coal. Remembering *Blücher's* fate at the Dogger Bank, he resolved to carry on, but in order to keep closer to Scheer, he reduced speed to 15 knots.[24]

Moltke was by now in serious trouble, reporting to Scheer at 6.43 that her speed was down to 4 knots; two hours later, she was reporting that she was out of control. Under the impression that Scheer had not received this signal, Hipper turned towards *Moltke* to give her assistance. When Scheer came up with *Moltke* at 10.00 he ordered *Oldenburg* to take the battle cruiser in tow, and he turned the High Seas Fleet for home. *Moltke* was soon able to get her port engine working and could steam at half speed. Meanwhile Scheer ordered Hipper, who by now had come into sight, to continue the operation and search for the convoy and its covering force:

> Two minutes later, Hipper's squadron was heading north-north-west again. Behind him the waves were rent by the foaming wake of his ships. Ahead swept the light cruisers on their task of reconnaissance. It was a bright, sunny day, and visibility had seldom been better. Hipper's spirits rose again. The worm of disillusionment had gone to earth.[25]

Room 40 had not, thus far, been able to be of much help in elucidating what was occurring. However, the British direction finding stations had picked up *Moltke's* reports to Scheer of her situation; being low power transmissions, an accurate fix was not possible, and the change of call signs confused the issue. At 7.58 am on April 24 the Admiralty sent a signal to Beatty that two call signs, one believed to be *Moltke,* had been located in 58 degrees N and 6 degrees E at 7.00 am. Beesly is severely critical:

> The position given was some twelve miles inland from Bergen, and both the Admiralty and Beatty were stupid in not respectively stating and accepting that it indicated the presence of an important German unit close off the Norwegian coast. Instead, it took nearly two hours before Beatty's query and the Admiralty explanation made this clear.[26]

While Hipper was searching again to the north, Scheer had to decide on the route to be taken homewards by the High Seas Fleet. The route through the Kattegat would certainly avoid any chance of encountering the Grand Fleet; but it was very roundabout, and negotiating the Belt would be difficult for *Moltke.* It was, he considered, undesirable, first because it would offend the Danes, and secondly because it might prompt the British to mine the Kattegat. Accordingly, he set course towards the Bight, at a speed of 11 knots, taking the risk that the Grand Fleet might catch up with him. During the afternoon he received from the Naval Staff information that the convoy had crossed the North Sea on April 23, which 'indicated that we had not been lucky in our choice of day to attack them.'[27]

Hipper's cast northwards produced nothing; profoundly disappointed, he turned his battle cursers for home at 2.00 pm, though sending Reuter to scout for a further 20 miles. Still nothing was sighted, and Reuter rejoined Hipper at 4.30 pm. A signal was picked up from a U-boat to Scheer that it had sighted eleven ships steering southwards; almost certainly, this was Hipper's own force. By dawn on April 25 Hipper had rejoined the High Seas Fleet. *Moltke*, off List, was cast loose from her tow, and preceded under her own steam; by now she was able to work up to 15 knots. She was not yet out of the wood, however; she was sighted by the submarine *E42* about 40 miles north of Heligoland, which hit her with a torpedo; the damage was slight, but the port engine room was flooded, and she was again brought to a halt. After a while, however, she was able to get going again, and reached the Jade under her own steam.

Meanwhile Warburton, at about 4.00 am, had sighted Reuter's force heading south; he submerged, surfacing again about ninety minutes later in time to see Hipper's complete force, now reunited, steaming southwards, It was not until 6.30 am that he reported them to Beatty. The latter had sailed with the whole of the Grand Fleet, less the 2nd Battle Cruiser Squadron, in the afternoon of April 24, proceeding at full speed in spite of thick fog. In the lecture referred to above, Creswell calculated that Warburton's failure to report promptly made no difference; even if action had been taken at once, Scheer was safely out of Beatty's reach.[28]

For the German commander the failure of the operation was deeply disappointing. He took comfort, however, from the achievement of his men in getting *Moltke* back to port:

> The bringing in of the *Moltke* under such unfavourable conditions of sea and weather as arose during the night of the return journey was an eminent military, feat especially the part played by the *Oldenburg* (Captain Lohlen) which towed her, and the work done in stopping the leak by the men on board the *Moltke* deserves great praise.[29]

It was the final sortie of the High Seas Fleet. As Newbolt observes, it had been planned and executed with great skill, and from first to last the British were completely baffled. If Scheer's intelligence had been more accurate 'he would have had an excellent chance of doing enormous damage;' a day earlier or a day later, and Scheer would have had a major victory.[30]

For his part Beatty was naturally also disappointed, although he somewhat overstated the extent of the lost opportunity when he wrote to Keyes about the operation on June 20:

> We ought to have done it but one very little thing slipped. I got the whole pack out of [Firth of Forth] in the shortest time in record thick fog without a W/T signal and missed by 2 hours!! And we ought to have had ten hours in hand. I could have fought him all night and returned in the cool of the morning. Ye Gods it was and is maddening and is a Tragedy.[31]

There was one other potential outcome of the High Seas Fleet's sortie, which Professor Halpern notes. The covering force for the Scandinavian convoys of April 17-19 was the American battleship squadron, under Rear Admiral Rodman, which had accordingly, missed the sortie by less than a week. Had this been the covering force on duty at the date of the sortie, and had the squadron met the whole of the High Seas Fleet, it could have suffered extremely serious losses:

The service of the American battleships with the Grand Fleet has traditionally been treated as a rather ho-hum affair, dull but necessary. One wonders about the effect on American public opinion had those battleships fallen in with the High Seas Fleet with a loss of three or four ships and a few thousand lives.[32]

42

The Development of Naval Aviation

One of the most authoritative historians of naval aviation in the First World War has written that its historiography stands in the way of an approach to its history, commenting that 'for decades the conflict's aero naval aspects have been segregated into compartments labelled 'aero' and 'naval'. Even worse, 'countless naval histories ignore even the existence of aviation, or, if acknowledging it, shove it off into a corner.' Even Professor Marder attracts rebuke: 'his only extended discussion of Royal Navy aviation occupies merely twenty two of the 1866 pages in his five volumes.'[1]

The charge is justified, and the present author is uncomfortably aware that he too must plead guilty to devoting only limited attention to the impact which naval aviation had on the conduct of war in the North Sea. The problem which a historian faces is that in respect of most of the naval operations during the war, aviation played only a peripheral and frequently disappointing part in their outcome. During the First World War at sea, the impact of naval aviation was limited, and its influence was to be seen in its potential rather than its performance. Naval aviation was, however, at the heart of many of the bitter political disputes that racked the British government throughout the war.

Naval aviation in the First World War came from modest beginnings. The Royal Naval Air Service came into existence on July 1 1914, when its functions were officially separated from those of the Royal Flying Corps, which continued as the air branch of the army. The RNAS comprised all naval aircraft and personnel, and was to be administered by the Admiralty. Its resources, on the outbreak of war, were extremely modest, consisting of 2 seaplanes, 39 land planes, and seven airships. Total personnel consisted of about 130 officers and 700 other ranks. Only about half the seaplanes were serviceable, but 16 of them did carry radios.[2] Modest though this force was, it was far superior to the German naval air arm, which consisted of 36 seaplanes, of which only about 12 were fit for operational use, and none of which were equipped with radio; total personnel amounted to about 200, including 30 pilots. As to the much feared fleet of Zeppelins which rumour suggested might be 20 strong, the Naval Airship Division began the war with just one, *L3*. This followed disasters to the first two that had been built, and the facilities for operating airships were in any case not yet available. The Naval Airship Division began the war with 12 officers and 340 men.

Early in August 1914, however, a crash programme of airship construction began, with the construction of the necessary building facilities. Hangars were erected at various points from which the new Zeppelins would operate. New models were designed, while as a stop gap ten based on the *L3* design were completed by February 1915. Chief of the Naval Airship Division was the relatively junior Lieutenant Commander Peter Strasser, who was to prove its driving force; he has been described as 'a man of remarkable organising ability, indomitable energy and great personal charm, who during the succeeding years made his mark as one of the outstanding naval leaders on either side in the First World War.'[3]

In the early months of the war the Zeppelins were largely ineffective; this was in all the circumstances, hardly surprising, as Otto Groos pointed out: 'When giving orders to any of the air units, one had to consider that this weapon was still in its earliest stages of trial and development.'[4] For the German navy, the important aspect of the Zeppelin programme was the development of sea reconnaissance; but in the minds of British planners, the threat was seen as potential bomb carrying raids on the British Isles, and it was not long before suggested raids on the German coasts began to focus on the Zeppelin base at Nordholz, near Cuxhaven, as the target. An attempted raid by the Harwich Force, employing the converted seaplane carriers *Engadine, Riviera* and *Empress*, on October 24/25, turned out to be a fiasco due to very adverse weather conditions. Another attempt, intended for November 24, and due to be supported by the Grand Fleet, was cancelled at the last moment.

A further operation, to become famous as the Cuxhaven Raid, took place on Christmas Day 1914, when nine seaplanes, from the three carriers, were sent into the Bight, escorted by Tyrwhitt's Harwich Force, as described in Chapter 27, with the Grand Fleet in support. The raid was a failure; four seaplanes were lost; two battleships were temporarily disabled when *Conqueror* and *Monarch* collided as they returned to Scapa Flow. Nordholz was not attacked; in fact none of the raiders even found it. But the British claimed a moral victory; the Admiralty issued a statement recording its appreciation of 'the success with which that reconnaissance and attack were carried out.' RD Layman, in his account of the raid, argued that it contributed much to the morale and tradition of the RNAS.[5]

As further Zeppelins came into service, the High Seas Fleet made increasing use of their reconnaissance capability. This, always, was subject to weather conditions; but successive commanders of the fleet strongly argued, successfully, for the expansion of the Naval Airship Division. Pohl, in a submission made to Tirpitz on June 4 1915, wrote that 'the experiences of the last few months have confirmed the great value of airships for naval warfare,' and set out the many ways in which this had been demonstrated. He called for an establishment of 18 Zeppelins which would ensure that 12 would be available at any one time, and this was approved.[6]

Jellicoe and Beatty were also strong proponents of the value of airship reconnaissance. The former had argued before the war that 'one Zeppelin is worth a good many light cruisers on a suitable day.' After the battle of Jutland, and the operations of August 19 1916, he claimed that the Germans owed their escape to their Zeppelins: 'unless we can compete with Germany in this respect on favourable terms our fleet is greatly handicapped in its operations.'[7] Beatty, when he took command, continued to press the Admiralty in similar terms.

Churchill, as First Lord, was an enthusiast for naval air power, but not in favour of airships. British policy towards them was half hearted in the extreme, and even after Balfour succeeded Churchill, and new construction orders were placed. British airship design was far inferior to that of the Zeppelins. By the end of the war, the best that the British airship designs could do was to operate to a maximum altitude of 9500 feet, with a top speed of 65.5 mph and a range of 2,215 miles. The standard Zeppelin type could fly at 20,000 feet, at a similar speed, but with a range of 3000 miles.[8]

The British had been more effective in the development of heavier than air aircraft, both seaplanes and land planes. Churchill himself took flying lessons, although unlike Prince Henry of Prussia, who was also an air enthusiast and qualified as a pilot, he did not complete the course. He continued to support developments in naval aviation throughout his time at the Admiralty. It has been noted that he was particularly intrigued by technical innovations, supporting such as the torpedo plane, the flotation bag and the folding wing, while he claimed to have coined the word 'seaplane' to replace 'hydroaeroplane.'[9] At first, it was seaplanes that were regarded as the most effective aircraft for naval use, since they were able to take off from and land on the sea; and it was, therefore, to carry seaplanes that the first carriers came into existence. None were available at the start of the war; but the three seaplane carriers that took part in the Cuxhaven raid, which were converted cross-Channel steamers, were acquired in August 1914. These had hangars for four seaplanes. As the month went by, they were joined by *Ark Royal* in December 1914, the first vessel to be designed and fitted out as a seaplane carrier, the Cunard liner *Campania* of 20,000 tons in April 1915, and two ex Isle of Man steamers, *Vindex* and *Manxman*. Each of these had a short forward flying off deck, which in practice was little used; it was never used for landing.[10]

Campania and *Engadine* were with the Grand Fleet at the time of Jutland. The former did not receive sailing orders in time, and did not accompany the fleet when it weighed anchor; although she set off after the fleet, Jellicoe, wrongly underestimating her maximum speed and reckoning that on its own *Campania* would be vulnerable to submarine attack, ordered her back to base. *Engadine,* however, which accompanied the Battle Cruiser Fleet, took part in the battle. She was equipped with two Short 184s for reconnaissance and two Sopwith Babies for anti airship work. One of the Shorts was successfully launched; piloted by Flight Commander Frederick Rutland, it was able to spot Boedicker's II Scouting Group of light cruisers and destroyers, and to correctly report the identification by radio to *Engadine*; she, however, was unable to pass on the report to Beatty despite repeated efforts to do so. Layman rejects Marder's criticism of *Engadine* for not fulfilling her reconnaissance role, pointing out that two of her four aircraft were not suitable for reconnaissance, and it made sense to keep one of the Shorts in hand.[11] Of course, it is right to note the limitations of sea reconnaissance at this time; Layman draws attention to the remarks of Admiral Chalmers on the subject. Noting that the two battle fleets were approaching each other in ignorance that the other was at sea in strength, Chalmers wrote:

> It may seem strange that such a situation could arise, but in those days naval air reconnaissance was almost non existent. Scheer had hoped to have Zeppelin cover, but this did not materialise. Beatty had the seaplane carrier *Engadine* with him, but the range of her few seaplanes was very limited, and once they had flown off the water it was problematical if they would ever return. It was not possible to maintain an air reconnaissance patrol for any length of time, so it was the usual practice to conserve the seaplanes until there was some indication that the enemy was in the immediate vicinity.[12]

By early 1916 the competition between the RNAS and the RFC for resources of all kinds had intensified to the point where it was causing serious concern. On February 25 the Cabinet established the Joint War Air Committee of which Lord Derby was Chairman, with representatives of the Admiralty and the War Office, and Lord Montague as 'Independent Advisory Member.' Its function would be 'to collaborate in arranging questions of supplies and design for the matériel of the Naval and Military Air Services.' Intended to achieve harmony between the contending parties the committee would look at anything 'in aerial matters' that it might find of interest and assistance; the members were under a duty to report anything of the kind.[13]

It was not just the questions of matériel that divided the two services; there was a continuing dispute as to which service should be responsible for long distance bombing, which clearly needed to be resolved. If not, as Commodore Lambert, the Fourth Sea Lord pointed out at an Admiralty meeting on March 21, 'constant friction was bound to arise which would lead to a separate Service for the Air, which in his opinion would be fatal to Admiralty interests.[14] For the moment, it was agreed to go on ordering long range bombers for the RNAS.' In a paper, probably written by Admiral Sir Reginald Custance, circulated by Lord Derby to his committee on March 31, it was contended that 'the demand for a Minister of the Air and a separate Air Department would seem to be based on unsound principles and imperfect knowledge of war requirements.' Montague, a supporter of such a demand, circulated his own paper calling for an 'Imperial Air Service' five days later. By then Lord Derby had reached the conclusion that the task of the committee was, as presently constituted, impossible, and he wrote to Asquith to resign.[15] Roskill's view is that in effect the Admiralty wrecked the committee. The disputes, accordingly, rumbled on, and the next attempt to bring order out of chaos was the creation on May 15 of an Air Board under the presidency of Lord Curzon. This, however, also lacked executive powers, being described as 'an advisory Board in relation to its President;' it would be 'free to discuss matters of general policy in relation to the air, and in particular, combined operations of the Naval and Military Air Services.'

One aspect of naval aviation that particularly enthused its supporters was the use of aircraft to drop torpedoes. Experiments had begun in 1913, and the then Captain Murray Sueter became convinced that it was a weapon of huge potential. Practical experience in the Dardanelles, when two Short 184 seaplanes torpedoed and sank three Turkish ships, confirmed Sueter's hopes. However, his proposal that 200 torpedo carrying planes be built was rejected at the end of 1915; in October 1916, though, he was in conjunction with Thomas Sopwith, able to produce a design for a torpedo carrying aircraft of particular promise. This was the Cuckoo, capable of delivering an 18 inch torpedo; it had a range of 160 miles, a top speed of 103 mph and a ceiling of 12000 feet. These aircraft would take some time to come through, and for the moment it was proposed to concentrate on torpedo carrying seaplanes. It was to set up a force of these that Sueter went out to the Adriatic, and the Cuckoo project lapsed until mid 1917; at that time an order for one hundred was placed, followed, at Beatty's urging, by three hundred and fifty more.

In August 1917 Richmond put before Beatty an ambitious plan to make use of the Cuckoos:

> It is recommended that the question of attacking the High Sea Fleet with torpedo planes should be immediately examined. An attack at dawn by torpedo planes on a very large scale, accompanied by aircraft of the larger type carrying 230 lb bombs to attack lesser craft and dockyards, would be most difficult to repel. If by such an attack the heavy ships of the Fleet could be sufficiently damaged to prevent them from taking part in local operations, then the question of blocking would form the next step in the programme.[16]

Beatty passed the plan on to Jellicoe; reporting on his subsequent conversation with the First Sea Lord, he told Richmond that the believed that the Admiralty was only prepared to look at it to prove that the kind of offensive operations being called for were impracticable. When the

Admiralty responded on September 25, it did not absolutely reject the scheme, but did not do a great deal to enable it to be carried into effect. The Admiralty's position was that the time to fit out sufficient ships to carry the force of torpedo planes put forward by Beatty meant that it would not be possible to mount the raid for the best part of a year. The paper that went to Beatty did, however, review the situation with regard to carriers. Four dedicated carriers could carry 16 reconnaissance panes and 12 fighter planes; 3 more fighters could be carried on cruisers. By Spring 1918 a further capability of 21 reconnaissances and 15 fighter planes would be added, while additional facilities could be fitted to the partially converted light battle cruiser *Furious*. *Glorious* and *Courageous* might be similarly converted.

Meanwhile the debate about establishing a separate air force had continued. In August the so called Smuts Committee issued a report strongly favouring the proposal. Jellicoe equally strongly objected; Geddes was cautious. Beatty, when sent a copy of the report, wrote that it was a move in the right direction; he did not think that there would be 'any grave difficulties about the provision of assistance to the Navy by the new service if it is adopted.' This had the effect of undermining the Admiralty's case for opposing the scheme, which the War Cabinet approved on August 24. Beatty's biographer was extremely outspoken about his response:

> Beatty's support for the Smuts Report was perhaps the gravest misjudgement of his whole career; for it contributed, perhaps decisively, to the navy losing virtually all its experienced aviators and technicians. Furthermore because the RNAS was absorbed in the much bigger RFC the combined service was predominantly military in training and outlook.[17]

Marder is equally critical of Beatty:

> His seemingly supine attitude in the summer of 1917 is beyond rational explanation, since he possessed a lively appreciation of the role that air power had come to play in sea warfare.[18]

The Royal Air Force came into existence on April 1 1918. For those on shipboard, there was not a great deal of effect; but the situation was very different for the land based RNAS units. The Dover Command, for instance which had made extremely effective use of the aircraft at its disposal, was particularly affected. Keyes wrote to Wemyss on May 28 to say that his force at Dunkirk had been 'entirely disintegrated,' having lost six of its eight fighter squadrons and five out of six of its bomber squadrons.[19]

The North Sea was, however, to see before the end of the war two operations which portended the future for naval aviation. On July 19 a raid was launched against the Zeppelin sheds at Tondern. Seven bomb carrying Sopwith Camels took off from the deck of *Furious*, and destroyed the Zeppelins *L54* and *L60* in their shed in what has been justly described as 'the most outstandingly successful carrier operation of the war.'[20] Escorted by three destroyers, and by the 1st Light Cruiser Squadron and five more destroyers, with the 1st Battle Squadron, 7th Light Cruiser Squadron and eight destroyers in support, *Furious* launched her aircraft from a position off the Schleswig coast. The Germans made no move to intercept the naval force. Much more was needed, however, before such a raid of this kind in the future might see all the aircraft returning safely; only two got back to the carrier, but were forced to ditch alongside due to the faulty design of the flight deck; another fell in the sea, and the pilot was drowned; the rest were forced by bad weather to land in Denmark.[21]

The second operation was one of Tyrwhitt's sweeps from Harwich. Since June, he had been taking coastal motor boats with his force, with orders to attack all the minesweepers they could find near the mouth of the Ems. On August 10 at 9.00 pm he sailed from Harwich with four light cruisers and thirteen destroyers, five of them with seaplane lighters and six coastal motor boats. As it happened, there was not a breath of wind, and the seaplanes intended to cover the CMBs could not get airborne; and the failure of a flight of aircraft from Yarmouth to receive Tyrwhitt's signal meant that the CMBs had no cover. As they swept past Terschelling, they sighted a group of aircraft; at first they were thought to be friendly, but it was soon seen that they were German. Firing their Lewis guns, the CMB's were able to hold off the aircraft for a while, but when they turned west, so that the Germans, now reinforced by four fighters, were able to attack with the sun behind them, they were riddled with bullets. One of them made it to the Dutch coast; two others were rescued by a Dutch torpedo boat. But the remainder were sunk.[22] It was a striking illustration, on a small scale, of what air power could achieve.

The British navy had, by the end of the war, achieved less in developing a sea going air arm than might have been the case. This, the Official History suggests, was due to the preoccupation with the Zeppelin, the responsibility for home defence and the need for aerial support against the U-boats.[23] These factors diverted attention from building up the fleet's scouting capability, and diverted resources that might have supported it. Layman summarised the situation as it turned out, and its consequences for the war in the North Sea:

> German faith in the airship and British concern over it resulted in the influence of aviation on the North Sea struggle, as expressed in aerial reconnaissance, resting on a paradox – it was exerted not by what it actually accomplished but on what German mentality believed it could accomplish and what British mentality feared it could accomplish. These differing perceptions combined to help prevent what might have been an all out fleet action that would, in one way or another, have profoundly affected the character, duration and perhaps the outcome of the entire war.[24]

43

Convoys and U-boats

As has been seen, the fearful toll of merchant shipping exacted by the U-boats after the commencement of unrestricted U-boat warfare began steadily to fall during 1917, to such an extent that it could be said that it was on Jellicoe's watch that the tide had actually turned, at least in home waters. This was far from obvious at the end of the first year of the campaign; the total of shipping lost was staggering, as the official historian of seaborne trade during the war recorded:

> By January 31 1918, the unrestricted submarine campaign had raged for just twelve months, and during that period the world's shipping had been reduced, through war casualties, by nearly 6,200,000 tons gross, of which 3,750,000 tons was British. In ocean going steamers on the register of the United Kingdom alone, the losses amounted to 3,500,000 tons, or more than 20% of the tonnage available in January 1917. Nor was this all: during the same period about 1,175,000 gross tons of shipping of which 925,000 tons was British had been damaged by enemy action, and the majority of ships so damaged were out of service for a period of from four to six months ... With such losses the programme of new construction was utterly unable to cope; nay, as we have seen, it was unable even to keep up with the current rate of loss, greatly as that rate had been reduced since the summer of 1917.[1]

These terrifying figures, however, were in steady decline; and for this the introduction of a complex general convoy system was responsible. It was, of course, a heavy drain on Britain's naval resources, as Jellicoe had always pointed out would be the case. He described the extent of this in his book *The Submarine Peril* setting out the vast number of vessels engaged in escort work in November 1917:

> The number of destroyers, sloops and P-boats in use for the escort of our Atlantic trade through the submarine zone and English Channel totalled 170 (including 37 US destroyers). In addition we had 32 similar vessels employed in the escort work of the Scandinavian Convoy. For the Mediterranean convoys we required at least 30 such vessels, giving a grand total of 232.[2]

In addition to these there were the destroyers with the Grand Fleet, the Dover Patrol and the Harwich Force, together with others for escorting such as troopships and hospital ships, which he calculated as amounting to a further 217, a complete total of 449.

The convoy system had been particularly effective at reducing losses of merchant shipping by mines, because ships in convoy, unlike those sailing independently, were continuously under naval operational control. Convoys could be prevented by their escorts from steaming into known minefields. In the last eighteen months of the war 160 ships sailing independently were lost to mines, but only 5 out of the approximately 8400 which sailed in convoy.[3]

U-boat successes in 1918, well below the peak figures of the previous year, averaged about 200,000 tons per month of British shipping for the first four months of 1918. Thereafter, they began steadily to decline. Whereas in the first period 270 British merchant vessels were destroyed, in the next four months the total was 186, with a corresponding fall in tonnage lost. Total losses to the enemy, including British, Allied and neutral up to the end of August had nonetheless amounted to 2,328,202 tons, which was a huge amount, and represented a further cumulative reduction in the amount of merchant shipping available. Marder points out:

> It was not until June, and not again until September, that total British mercantile shipping construction surpassed the tonnage destroyed by direct war causes, and not until September that new construction exceeded war losses and marine losses combined.[4]

However, accelerated repair and new construction meant that there was more shipping available at the end of June than at the beginning; and in terms of world construction, it exceeded losses in March and continued to do so for the rest of the war.

Month by month, the convoy system was making it more and more difficult for the U-boats. Karl Doenitz, a relatively junior U-boat commander, destined in the Second World War to lead the U-boat arm and later the German navy, reflected on the U-boat experience in 1917-1918:

> In the First World War the German U-boat arm achieved great successes; but the introduction of the convoy system in 1917 robbed it of its opportunity to become a decisive factor. The oceans at once became bare and empty; for long periods at a time the U-boats, operating individually, would see nothing at all; and then suddenly up would loom a huge concourse of ships, thirty or fifty or more of them, surrounded by a strong escort of all types. The solitary U-boat, which most probably had sighted the convoy purely by chance, would then attack, thrusting again and again and persisting, if the commander had strong nerves, for perhaps several days and nights, until the physical exhaustion of both commander and crew called a halt.[5]

He drew a firm conclusion from his experiences of conducting individual attacks:

> The greater the number of U-boats that could be brought simultaneously into the attack, the more favourable would become the opportunities offered to each individual attacker. In the darkness of the night sudden violent explosions and sinking ships cause such confusion that the escorting destroyers find their liberty of action impeded and are themselves compelled by the accumulation of events to split up. In addition to all these practical considerations,

> however, it was obvious that, on strategic and general tactical grounds, attacks on convoys must be carried out by a number of U-boats acting in unison.[6]

Here again was the rationale for the introduction of the 'wolf packs' of the Second World War; but the doctrine was not generally adopted in 1914-1918, in spite of Bauer's proposal to this effect, although from time to time two or more U-boats were used in cooperation.

One instance of this was an operation conducted in the Western Approaches in May 1918, when up to eight submarines were deployed in the track of incoming convoys. Although some success was achieved – *U55*, skilfully handled, sank two ships of a Gibraltar convoy on May 17 – the results overall were disappointing, as Newbolt records:

> Since May 10 the U-boats had sunk or damaged only five vessels in what, a year before, had been their most productive zone: three of these ships had been in convoy, it is true, but during the same time 183 convoyed vessels had reached harbour safely, and 110 had been escorted outwards towards the danger zone.[7]

Meanwhile U-boat losses had continued to mount. In January 1918 eight were destroyed, four more in February, five in March, seven in April, fourteen in May and three in June, a total of forty one.[8] There had, during the same period, been a steady increase in the delivery of new U-boats, and by the end of June forty seven had been completed. This, of course, barely made good the losses, but it did mean that the number of U-boats at sea during 1918 was as high as ever. In fact, during the war, 344 U-boats were completed, and 226 were building when it ended, and another 212 were projected.[9]

Winton, in his study of the defence of seaborne trade, acknowledges that convoy had not as such defeated the U-boats, in the sense of the number sunk, but contends, obviously rightly, that convoy had defeated the campaign. He goes on to make the challenging statement that 'it could even be argued that the sinking of U-boats did not in the end matter very much. What counted was the safe and timely arrival of the merchant ships.'[10] However, although it is tempting to accept this proposition, it does ignore one major effect of the U-boat losses, and that was in the steady attrition of the boldest and most skilled U-boat commanders previously described. The loss of their expert seamanship and grim determination was not made good as easily as their submarines, and the steadily reducing harvest of merchant vessels sunk testified to this.

The failure of the unrestricted submarine campaign to deliver the promised victory within six months did not completely destroy the hopes at Imperial Headquarters that the situation might be turned around. In any case, for the first few months of 1918 German hopes were pinned on the offensives to be launched on the Western Front. Meanwhile on January 9 Müller received a visit from Trotha to discuss what would be the naval leadership after the war. He proposed that Scheer should head the Admiralty Staff, Vice Admiral Georg Hebbinghaus the Imperial Navy Office, Souchon the High Seas Fleet and he himself the Naval Cabinet. Müller made no comment in his diary about this, although he may already have been considering the question of replacing Holtzendorff. The latter was persona non grata with Prince Henry, as was apparent at a lunch on February 1:

> At midday today Holtzendorff reported from Kreuznach … mainly to give the results of a year's U-boat war (which was supposed to have broken England's will to fight within six

months). He received the Oak Leaves to his Pour le Merité and was allowed to eat with His Majesty and Prince Henry, who rudely ignored him.[11]

The failure of the U-boat campaign would almost certainly have brought Holtzendoff's tenure of office to a close sooner or later; but it now looked as if his health was failing. By May Holtzendoff was asking to be allowed to take a cure in the Taunus, as his heart, liver and kidneys were affected by arteriosclerosis; by the end of the month Müller was discussing with the Kaiser the question of who should replace both Holtzendorff and Capelle.

On July 3 Scheer and Trotha travelled to Berlin for a meeting with Müller for a discussion which the latter recorded as being 'very professional' but at which 'far reaching demands' were made. As had been the case in 1916 when Jellicoe replaced Jackson, it was almost inevitable that the Commander-in-Chief of the fleet should be appointed to succeed Holtzendoff, since he alone had the standing and reputation to be acceptable to the navy. The proposal came as no surprise to Scheer; it gave him the opportunity to do something about the complex, ineffective and illogical command structure that had so hampered the German navy's war effort. In his memoirs he set out something of the 'far reaching demands' which he and Trotha made. Hitherto he had felt inhibited from suggesting the reforms that were needed in the structure of the naval command:

> The system was a failure, was not very popular in the Navy, and our success was less than we had a right to expect. I could not very well recommend myself as head of this department, all the more so as the command of the Fleet involved personal danger, and I did not care to avoid this by getting a position on land. Even the very frank discussions which had taken place between the Chief of the Naval Staff and myself had not resulted in the full satisfaction of the demands of the Fleet.[12]

It seemed to Scheer that Holtzendorff, whom he personally respected, was, in the way his post was structured, too vulnerable to political pressure. What was needed was the Naval Staff to have the powers of a supreme command, and its Chief 'must be included in the number of those commanders who were directly responsible for the conduct of the war.' This of course, was entirely right; it was obvious that the reform of the naval structure in time of peace had been a disastrous mistake, and that it must be reversed.

The new structure required new men:

> A change of Secretary of State (Admiral von Capelle) seemed also very desirable. It was not to be expected that a man who was convinced that he had done all that was humanly possible would pledge himself, without reserve, to carry out new proposals which would bring him into opposition with his previous conduct of affairs.[13]

Scheer had been particularly dismayed at Capelle's failure to press ahead with the construction of new U-boats, apparently in the belief that it would be rendered unnecessary by the promised success of the U-boat campaign within six months. Capelle, therefore must go; Trotha, who was making much of the running on the subject, was uncertain whether it should be Souchon or Behncke who succeeded him. In the end Behncke was selected.

The extent of Scheer's powers as Chief of the Naval Staff was still under debate at the end of July; Müller was amazed on August 7 when Levetzow, arriving at Imperial Headquarters with proposals for sweeping changes in the organisation of the Naval Staff, insisted on Scheer's right to issue orders. Müller said that the Kaiser would always reject this, because he was the Supreme War Lord. On August 9 Scheer put his proposals in writing, which Müller put to his master:

> The Kaiser refused categorically to sign. He has not the slightest intention of making a change in the organisation of the Navy in the middle of a war. He was still the Supreme War Lord etc. I had to pacify him. I begged him to handle Scheer with kid gloves and to allow him an absolutely free hand with his subordinates.[14]

That was then. Two days later Scheer and Holtzendorff had an audience with the Kaiser. Scheer knew that he held the high cards, and was firm in his demands, and in the event the Kaiser backed down without putting up a fight. Scheer noted that 'it was of course understood that the Supreme War Lord should be informed of the general trend of matters, and of important projects, and that his consent should be obtained thereto.'[15] Scheer was, however, in no doubt that so far as was necessary he would in future be able to manage the Kaiser.

Scheer's appointment naturally meant a change in the command of the High Seas Fleet. Just as there had been little doubt that Beatty must be Jellicoe's successor, so now was it plain that it must surely be Hipper who took over:

> His great experience in matters appertaining to the Fleet, his efficiency in all the tactical situations in which he had found himself with his cruisers, seemed to point to him as the most suitable person to whom I could confidently hand over the weapon from which I never thought to be separated in this life.[16]

Probably Behncke, who now took office as State Secretary of the Imperial Naval Office, would have been the only serious alternative. Hipper's biographer suggests that there might have been some doubt as to the succession:

> It was not at first certain that Hipper would be Scheer's successor. Here again conflicting views led to an impasse which had more or less to be cleared up forcibly. Hipper stood on one side while the question was being settled. When a rumour got round that one of his colleagues was to be appointed Commander-in-Chief, he in no way felt hurt by this possibility. On the contrary, he said at once that even in that case he had no objection to remaining commander of the Scouting Group.[17]

Raeder, by now commanding the light cruiser *Köln*, paid a visit to Hipper soon after his appointment, which took effect on August 12; he found him 'happy over the new changes in the command structure.'[18] Trotha would remain, as Hipper's Chief of Staff, while Reuter was to take command of the battle cruisers. Levetzow was to accompany Scheer to act as his Chief of Staff.

The most important problem with which Scheer had to grapple was of course the future conduct of the U-boat campaign. It was soon apparent to him that there were three principal reasons for the decline in sinkings:

> This reduction in successes was due mainly to the stronger and more perfect measures of defence taken by the enemy, and also to the loss of some of the older and more experienced commanders ... Judging by the reports as to building, it was to be feared that within a short time the newly constructed tonnage would be greater than the amount sunk.[19]

Marder gives a remarkable statistic that demonstrates the effect of the loss of experienced commanders, pointing out that out of 400 U-boat captains about 20 were responsible for about 60% of all Allied losses to U-boats; these remarkable figures show how important were the ability and enterprise of the individual commanding officer.[20]

Although it was the introduction of convoy that was the single most important component of the defensive measures referred to by Scheer, there were other factors, as the German Official History described:

> Towards the end of the war the U-boats experienced considerable difficulty in breaking through the North Sea to and from their operation areas west of England. The closure of the Dover Straits had become more or less effective. It was difficult to break through the Pentland Firth, because the patrols forced the U-boats to submerge, where the current made navigation extremely difficult. In the north the Northern Barrage made its presence felt.[21]

The Northern Barrage referred to was one of the most ambitions and large scale projects conceived with the object of beating the U-boas. The scheme was initially propounded by the Americans and accepted in principle by the British Admiralty in September 1917. It involved closing the North Sea exits by laying a mine barrage between the Orkneys and the Norwegian coast. It stretched for 240 miles from the Orkneys to Hardanger Fjord; by the end of the war 15,093 British mines and 56,033 American mines had been laid. It was divided for operational purposes into three areas. Area A, in the centre, 130 miles in length, was laid by the American navy; Area B, to the west, about 50 miles long, and Area C, to the east, were jointly mined.[22] Beatty disliked the scheme from the outset, because he feared it would hamper his movements. He continued to make no secret of his views, telling Balfour when he visited the Grand Fleet on August 21 that the whole scheme was American, and that the Admiralty had allowed themselves to be rushed into it without sufficient experimental knowledge. He went on to explain in considerable detail the reasons for his objections.[23] In particular, Beatty demanded that there be a ten mile passage between the mine barrage and the Orkneys, and it prompted a stern letter from Wemyss on August 23 on the subject, on which he said Sims had strong views. As to this, Beatty noted on the letter: 'So do I and I have to command the sea, not Admiral Sims.' Wemyss, between a rock and hard place, went on:

> The American Government desire to complete the Northern Barrage from land to land, and nothing short of this will satisfy them; their views being that any gate in the barrage, however small, renders it ineffectual. If it is ineffectual, they consider that the whole of their great efforts and large expenditure is thrown away, and Admiral Sims would, under those circumstances, recommend his Government to stop work on the whole business. Now such a state of affairs will have a very much more disastrous effect on our relations with the United States than it would on the actual material position.[24]

Wemyss asked Beatty to reconsider the question of the ten mile passage, saying that it would be a 'calamity' if the Americans gave up on the Northern Barrage.

A week later Wemyss wrote again; Beatty's conversation with Balfour was being seen as an appeal by Beatty to the Foreign Secretary, and there had been an exchange of telegrams on the issue with Geddes. Beatty was irritated; he replied that he was 'at a loss to understand what the fuss is all about.' He had said nothing to Mr Balfour that he had not also said to the Admiralty. He had, he said, acceded to the wishes of the Admiralty in practically every respect:

> But you will allow I have to look at it from the GF point of view and I dread to think what the North Sea will be like after winter gales with mines floating about with fathoms of wire attached which will catch our PVs, and the deep switches failing to operate.[25]

This storm in a teacup soon calmed; Wemyss wrote a placatory letter to Beatty, observing 'how difficult it is to get these Americans into a sane, clear and sound state of thinking.' They had, he remarked,' much to learn.'

Although it was the Americans that insisted on the project being carried through, there were certainly misgivings felt in US naval circles. Secretary of the Navy Daniels wrote in his diary on October 29 1917 that it was

> a stupendous undertaking – perhaps not impossible but to my mind of doubtful practicability. North Sea too rough and will necessitate withdrawing all our ships from other work and then can we destroy the hornets nest or keep the hornets in?[26]

David Trask observes that the United States had a particular motive for giving such high priority to the project:

> One of the reasons for the extensive commitment to the northern barrage was the continuing fear that Germany would sooner or later undertake submarine operations in distant waters, particularly in the mid-Atlantic and in waters adjacent to the American coast. Such an offensive could be undertaken by two types of vessels: fast German cruisers might break out into the Atlantic and undertake a massive raid on merchant shipping, or huge submarine cruisers might come into play in areas where they could not be counteracted by destroyer escorts.[27]

The mine laying went on until the end of the war; in September, the Norwegians were persuaded to close their territorial waters by extending the barrage near Utsire, which was one of things for which Beatty had pressed. He did not get his ten mile passage, however; a gap of only three miles was left at the western end. This leaves only the question which Marder poses: How effective was it? He notes that it was 'a great technical achievement, largely the product of American ingenuity, drive, and resources.' After the war, the Americans certainly claimed it as having been a great success; their commander of the mining operations, Admiral Joseph Strauss, wrote that it 'would have ended the submarine menace.' Marder, however, points out that the evidence showed that from four to six submarines were destroyed in the barrage, with two or three more damaged. It was, he says, 'a meagre result for an enormous expenditure of mines; these might have been employed with better results elsewhere.'[28] Some German views of the project were that it was impracticable. Michelsen, in a passage from his book on the U-boat campaign quoted by Marder, wrote:

> For some unknown reason many of the mines detonated spontaneously. This tendency was well known to our U-boats... Considering the number of mines lost in this way, one will readily appreciate that this barrage was far from being a complete seal to the North Sea's northern exit, and could have no more than a limited effectiveness ... In fact, it might be said that the Barrage was more of a danger to the minelayers and minesweepers (post war) than to the U-boats.[29]

On the other hand, the German Official History considered that the barrage 'made its presence felt,' because it lay too far from German bases to enable minesweeping operations or for U-boats to be escorted. Just how effective the Northern Barrage would have been against the U-boat war in the long term therefore remains an open question.[30]

44

Operation Plan No 19

News of the changes in the upper echelon of the German navy was naturally of great interest to Wemyss and Beatty, and the former wrote on August 6 to give the C-in-C his view of the position:

> It will be as well to presume that the changes of personnel at the German Admiralty will carry with them a change of policy. What that change of policy will be is difficult to foretell. I have always maintained, and I see no reason for altering my opinion, that it is only psychology which will bring the German Fleet out with the idea of engaging our forces, and it is difficult to believe that Von Scheer would ever willingly seek an engagement. On the other hand, he may initiate more activity in surface raids etc, and in combination with this, possibly more activity in mining ... There is, of course, the possibility of their concentrating all their mining efforts in one area to be used in combination with a raid on the Coast.[1]

Beatty, replying on August 10, saw the overall position as largely unaffected:

> Such changes cannot make any alteration to our view of the naval situation. The danger points which existed previously are still the same and can be summarised as being:
>
> 1 Atlantic Convoy
> 2 North Sea Convoy
> (a) While crossing the North Sea and in close proximity to Norwegian coast.
> (b) While voyaging along the coast between the Thames and the Firth, more especially between Humber and Farne Islands.
> 3 Attack on Dover Patrol or raid on Channel Ports
> 4 Raids on East Coast
>
> What may be expected and anticipated is greater activity, and this will require greater vigilance on our part... There is also the possibility that the enemy may display greater enterprise in attempting to bring to action our Light Cruiser Squadrons when on distant sweeps, and also to interfere with our mine laying excursions in the North and their attendant supports. In the past we baited the trap with forces varying from a battle squadron to a light cruiser squadron, the traps being the convoy. We took considerable risks with our

> eyes open in the hope of achieving a great success, and as you know, we all but brought it off on April 25 1918.[2]

This last comment was putting a considerable spin on the circumstances which surrounded Scheer's sortie; but Beatty was always ready to burnish any account of his own activities.

Wemyss agreed with Beatty that the German command changes should make no difference to their views of the position and the naval situation generally. He noted that Scheer, when interviewed in 1917, 'had been made to state that he was a firm believer in the submarine campaign, but was careful not to prophesy when the submarines were likely to achieve definite results.'[3] Meanwhile Hall had been keeping an eye on the situation following the command changes, and their possible relation to German plans for an offensive riposte to the Zeebrugge raid. He wrote to Keyes on September 10:

> What I am looking for is some false information which would make us think of moving our Fleet either North or South. This I think will give us a line as to where the probable attack will come off – i.e. if we hear rumours of a portion of the German Fleet being in the Atlantic to attack American troop transports, we may look for the real attack down south – that is to say, the Thames or the Channel – or vice versa.[4]

There had been rumours of discontent in the German Navy, which it was assumed had prompted a visit by the Kaiser to Kiel on September 24 and 25. William, who in private veered from irrational optimism to extreme pessimism, had in fact agreed at Scheer's request to visit Kiel, not because of the rumoured unrest, but to visit the U-boat school. The Kaiser delivered a bullish speech to 400 U-boat officers. Müller, conscious of the effect that it could have, gave instructions that it was not for publication. Three hours later news came that the Bulgarian army had collapsed and that the King had asked for an armistice, and William relapsed into a state of the profoundest gloom.[5] Elsewhere the news was just as bad; in Palestine, the Turkish armies were in full retreat, and it seemed likely that Turkey would follow Bulgaria out of the war. In a letter to his wife at the end of September Beatty reflected on what the unsettled situation might bring forth, in the light of the Kaiser's visit to Kiel:

> There are two ways of looking at that. If there is real discontent, the best way to kill it is to send them to sea. On the other hand if there is no discontent, the advent of the Kaiser may be the preliminary to an undertaking by the Naval Forces; whichever way you have it, it might be said to portend the advent of the High Seas Fleet... But generally speaking the prospects are poor. It is terrible to think that after all these weary months of waiting we shall not have an opportunity of striking a blow. But events are moving so rapidly just now that anything might happen.[6]

The retreat of the German armies in the west continued. The German Chancellor, Hertling, was replaced by Prince Max of Baden, and he formally asked President Wilson for an armistice on October 5. One of the preconditions of an armistice insisted on by Wilson on behalf of the Allies was that U-boats would immediately cease attacks on passenger ships. By itself, such a condition would be acceptable to the navy; but the effects went much further, as Scheer recorded:

> It was to be expected that the Government would agree to sparing the passenger steamers, for this concession seemed insignificant. But its consequences might be very serious, for, according to former experience, if the U-boats were again reduced to cruiser warfare, their effectiveness was lost, and so far as one could see, it would be impossible, if hostilities continued, for us to resume the unrestricted U-boat campaign.[7]

Scheer's position, therefore, was to give up the U-boat campaign only if an armistice was agreed. On October 17 he believed that the Government had agreed to this; but in case it gave way on the point, and agreed an immediate cessation of unrestricted submarine warfare, he saw the Kaiser next to obtain clearance for his having in those circumstances a free hand:

> The obligations imposed on the Fleet by the necessity for protecting the U-boats would disappear. If hostilities at the Front continued, it would be neither possible nor permissible for the Fleet to look on idly; it would have to try and relieve the Army to the best of its abilities. His Majesty agreed that in this case the Fleet would have freedom of action.[8]

It was no doubt with this freedom in mind that on October 16 Levetzow had asked Trotha if the fleet's personnel could be relied on in the event of a major naval action; Trotha 'answered without reservation in the affirmative.'[9] When discussing the matter with the Kaiser, therefore, Scheer already had a clear idea of what might ensue.

Hipper, meanwhile, was profoundly gloomy about the overall situation, recording in his diary on October 17 that Wilson was, in response to the German diplomatic Note, 'unbelievably adamant.' It seemed that Germany must give up the monarchy, or at least the Kaiser and the Crown Prince: 'What will become of Germany [one] cannot predict with certainly. Surely its honour will founder.[10]

In spite of all Scheer's arguments the reality of the situation obliged the German government to accept the unilateral cessation of unrestricted submarine warfare, and on October 22 Scheer issued orders for the immediate recall of all U-boats. The circumstances discussed with the Kaiser five days earlier had thus arisen, and Scheer sent Levetzow to the High Seas Fleet to give Hipper the order to prepare to attack the British fleet. The attitude of the German naval leaders was dictated not only by a belief that a success at sea would in some way assist the country in the armistice negotiations, but also by an emotional belief that honour demanded that a bold stroke be undertaken. Trotha had declared on October 6:

> Out of an honourable fight by the Fleet, even if it becomes a fight to the death, there will grow up – if our people do not fail nationally – a new Fleet for the future; there is no future for a fleet hampered by a humiliating peace.[11]

Scheer was of the same opinion, as he had already explained to the Kaiser. His position was that it was 'for moral reasons a matter of honour and existence for the navy to have done its utmost in the last fight.'

Hipper and his staff had been expecting the order brought by Levetzow, and had been working on plans for the proposed operation. Hipper had discussed the question with his staff as early as October 7, when he gave instructions for the preparation of the plan. They had agreed that 'in the final analysis the war should not be allowed to end without the employment of the fleet in its role as the trump card of national power working its full influence.'[12] Trotha presented the draft plan on October 10; it had been accepted by the High Seas Fleet that Scheer must approve the plan before the operation commenced, and this he did on October 27.

Levetzow was, after the war, explicit that the order to the High Seas Fleet was Scheer's responsibility, writing in 1924:

> The Naval High Command, whose Chief of Staff I was, was the highest-placed naval command of the Fleet, and their Chief of Staff was Admiral von Trotha. For the attack by the Fleet the Naval High Command gave the order to the Fleet. Admiral Scheer and I as its responsible chief of staff therefore carry the full responsibility.[13]

Beatty had been watching the position closely; on October 4 he had written to Wemyss of the many new features of considerable importance which affected his view:

> I am afraid I cannot agree with you that there is no change in the situation in the North Sea. The fact that three flotillas have been moved from Flanders to the North Sea constitutes, to my mind, a very considerable change. Also, I cannot agree that the Grand Fleet is not concerned with the situation in the southern part of the North Sea. This is not the policy that has been accepted hitherto.[14]

Two weeks later he wrote to Wemyss to express his concern about 'a sudden change of policy (in the use of his submarines) on the part of the enemy.' If the submarines were concentrated against the Grand Fleet, there would be losses to contend with. Next day Wemyss wrote to him in reply:

> I have always considered a possible banking up of them with a view to their being used otherwise as one of the possible indications of further movements of the High Seas Fleet... The situation is perpetually being watched, and so far, at any rate, there is no indication that this occasion is different from others.[15]

Room 40 was picking up indications that something was in the wind. On October 22 Beatty was told of Scheer's order to U-boats to concentrate in the middle of the North Sea and only to attack men of war by day. Beatty asked for an appreciation of what this meant; in reply he was told that a waiting position had been chosen, in order to be ready for an operation against the Grand Fleet. On October 24 the Admiralty reported 'an unusually large number of messages in a most secret cipher on the night of 23-24 October, but purport unknown.'[16]

The possibility of some significant move by the High Seas Fleet led to the transfer of destroyers from Buncrana, Plymouth and Portsmouth to reinforce the Grand Fleet. Fremantle, in regular communication with Beatty, wrote on October 27:

> There is more likelihood of a Fleet movement of some description now than there has been at any time this year... History impresses on us the tendency in the closing period of a war for public and Military opinion, uneducated in naval warfare, to force out an inferior Fleet (Villeneuve, Cervera, Rodjestvensky). The enemy must realise that some, at any rate, of his Fleet will be demanded of him in the armistice and peace terms and may think that they may as well try to inflict some losses on us before they lose the power altogether of doing so.[17]

The decoding of orders to five U-boats on October 28 to take up patrol positions, coupled with an order to III Squadron to coal at Wilhelmshaven, seemed to confirm that action might be imminent, and Fremantle wrote to Beatty on October 29 to update him:

> The plot has thickened appreciably since I wrote on Sunday, and it seems now absolutely clear that the enemy wishes you to come out to the Southward, over a submarine trap... There is no evidence whatever of any intention to send out raiders, nor do I think the political situation makes that likely.... Hall favours the idea of an attack on the defences of Rosyth, possibly by net-breakers with submarines to follow them. Such an operation offers such a small chance of success that I cannot think it probable.[18]

Fremantle thought that it was more likely that the High Seas Fleet would come outside the minefields, make W/T signals for a few hours, and then return.

Hall and Fremantle both now thought it improbable that the enemy would risk a fleet action while the armistice negotiations were continuing. Beesly notes that these messages to Beatty showed a much better use of intelligence by the Admiralty:

> This appreciation erred in underestimating, for once, the boldness of the Germans. Bearing in mind the *Admiralstab's* cautious policy over the past four and a quarter years, Fremantle and Hall may be forgiven. What is noticeable is the change in the Admiralty attitude to promulgating intelligence. Beatty was being taken fully into the Admiralty's confidence, and was being given the Admiralty's best guess and the reasons behind it. The Chief and Deputy Chief of Naval Staff were at last consulting Hall and his experts before coming to conclusions:[19]

Commenting on the Admiralty's view that a fleet action was unlikely while there were armistice negotiations in progress, Newbolt observes:

> Actually, Admirals von Hipper and Scheer were striving with the greatest energy to provoke a fleet action whilst the negotiations were proceeding; they were planning a stroke similar in its objects to the Dutch attack upon the Medway, which so much affected the negotiations at Breda, at the end of the second Dutch war.[20]

The plan drawn up for the operation was indeed extremely daring. It was not communicated to the Kaiser or the Chancellor, but Ludendorff was let into the secret. Prince Max said later that he would in all likelihood have approved of the plan if he had been told of it, and that 'the navy's lack of confidence in me was unjustified.'[21]

Scheer's attitude was that, the U-boat campaign having been abandoned, the free hand he was given entitled him to embark on such an operation without further authority. The operation was to commence on October 30.

The plan provided for sorties by light cruisers and destroyers in the southern part of the North Sea, attacking any enemy warships en route to attacks on shipping in the Thames Estuary and off the Flanders coast. The Thames group, consisting of II Scouting Group of four light cruisers, with five destroyers, would be supported by Reuter with I Scouting Group; the Flanders group, III Scouting Group of three light cruisers, would be supported by the rest of the High Seas

Fleet, which would leave the Heligoland Bight at dawn, steaming out of sight of the Dutch coast. It was expected that this would be sufficient to provoke Beatty into rushing southward without delay. The light cruisers of IV Scouting Group with a flotilla of destroyers would liberally mine the approach route of the Grand Fleet, which would be patrolled by U-boats all the way down the east coast as far as Terschelling. The U-boats were ordered to make the fullest use of their torpedoes, concentrating on enemy battleships and battle cruisers. It was expected that the Grand Fleet would be brought to action at nightfall on the second day; if this did not materialise, the destroyers would made an offensive sweep northwards to the Firth of Forth. They, like the U-boats, were ordered not to economise on torpedoes.[22]

Ernst von Weizsäcker, serving on Scheer's staff at Imperial Headquarters, read the final draft of the plan. In his view there was a '50 per cent chance of no result, 40 per cent of a lucky result, and 10 per cent disastrous result.'[23] It was an opinion which reflected the fact that once battle was joined, unforeseeable circumstances, meant that the outcome would always be hard to predict. However, Hipper's biographer is certainly right in observing that to pursue such an operation in the light of what the Commander-in-Chief already knew of the unrest in the High Seas Fleet was risky in the extreme.

Tactically there was to be no holding back; Reuter was to steam into the Thames Estuary itself, and cover the operation from Black Deep, near the Sunk lightship, eighteen miles north of Margate and twenty miles east of Foulness Point. At the same time the High Seas Fleet would come down southwards to a line between Clacton on Sea and the Öster Scheldt. Reuter would be flying his flag in *Hindenburg,* the newest battle cruiser, at the head of the four survivors of Jutland; Hipper's flag would be in *Baden*, the newest and largest battleship, and sister to *Bayern*. Eighteen battleships would be escorted by forty three destroyers.

The plan was, in the context of the war in the North Sea, astonishingly bold. Although it was a long shot, it was not without some chance of success. A head on encounter by the High Seas Fleet with the Grand Fleet, when it had nothing to lose, might well inflict heavy losses on the enemy; but it was a desperate venture. It is worth noting that, for his part, Beatty expected that an encounter between the two fleets would cost him heavy losses, which he estimated at eight or nine capital ships.[24]

Scheer and Trotha were solidly behind the plan, even if the prospects for success were doubtful. The former wrote to his wife on October 27: 'If our plan succeeds, which begins on your birthday and as we hope has no more interruptions, that will be an auspicious sign. I am awaiting the outcome with great excitement.' Trotha had always been of a similar mind, writing to Levetzow early in October: 'The operation to go down with honour will pay off, for them we would still be able to inflict a serious wound to Britain.'[25]

It was not, however, to be. The High Seas Fleet was ordered to assemble in Schillig roads on the afternoon of October 29. This prompted considerable unrest during that day, especially among the crews of the capital ships. Rumours circulated of a huge enemy fleet off Heligoland. Seaman Richard Stumpf wrote mournfully in his diary:

> We all knew within our hearts – today is the last time we shall ever see many of our ships. My mind contemplated what would happen if we engaged and destroyed the enemy fleet. I toyed with the most grotesque possibilities. In the final analysis this might still result in our victory.[26]

The situation, however, rapidly deteriorated. There had already been an incident on October 27, when about forty five of the engine room crew of *Strassburg* left the ship, and had to be rounded up. On October 29 between two and three hundred men from *Derfflinger* and *Von der Tann* decamped while the ships were passing through the canal; these, too, had to be rounded up, quite peaceably. It was during the afternoon aboard *Markgraf*, anchored in Schillig roads, that events took a fatal turn, when uproar broke out when someone called for three cheers for President Wilson. Similar scenes aboard *König* and *Kronprinz Wilhelm*, like *Markgraf* part of III Squadron, were followed by insubordination in *Thüringen*. At first, Hipper was inclined to ignore these events; but a report from Vice Admiral Kraft, the Commander of III Squadron, caused him to change his mind. By 10.00 pm, with information of other unrest reaching him, he concluded that it would be impossible to launch the operation, and he called it off. There was, in any case, now a good deal of fog developing in the North Sea, which provided ostensible justification for the postponement. Events in the following days, however, soon made it clear that no offensive action of any kind could possibly be contemplated. The battle history of the High Seas Fleet was ended.

45

Vae Victis

Hipper quickly grasped that action must be taken urgently. There were signs of insubordination in the battleships of the III Squadron during the night of October 29/30; at a conference of his senior commanders that night he was told by Boedicker, the commander of the I Squadron, that it was possible that the crews of his ships would not obey orders. At another conference on the following afternoon, Meurer, the commander of the IV Squadron, said much the same. That night there were serious disturbances aboard *Helgoland* and *Thüringen*; Boedicker ordered a company of 250 marines aboard a steamer, with a torpedo boat and a U-boat to deal with the situation. After a tense standoff the mutineers surrendered. Hipper, meanwhile, issued a placatory Order of the Day to be read to all the crews, to deny the rumours that what was planned was in effect a suicide mission. By now, however, official communications of this kind carried little credibility. Next day he dispersed the fleet, sending an officer to Imperial Headquarters to report that he was contemplating a destroyer sortie; when he saw Levetzow, he found the Chief of Staff complaining that the mutinous ships had not at once been sunk.[1] Levetzow appears to have had in mind the British naval mutinies of 1797 and the firm action taken by such as Sir John Jervis.

Hipper wrote sadly in his diary on October 31:

> There was no doubt that despite the greatest secrecy the men had been told about an operation in preparation and in the belief that they were going to be sacrificed for nothing would apparently refuse orders at the decisive moment, i.e. when passing west of Heligoland. As an exercise of inter-squadron movements *(Evolutionieren)* had been scheduled for the 30th in order to disguise the battle operation, under the circumstances and after discussing the matter with my staff officers I considered that if I did not wish to expose the fleet to a grand mutiny I should call off the operation and go ahead with the *Evolutionieren*.[2]

The situation rapidly deteriorated. Mutinous crews took over many of the capital ships. A Workers and Sailors Council had been formed as early as October 30. By November 6 the Wilhelmshaven naval base was in the hands of the revolutionary forces, although Hipper, meeting a sailor's delegation from Baden that day, found their demands mild enough, and he continued to follow a conciliatory policy. Things went from bad to worse, however, and on November 8, the day the Kaiser abdicated, he personally hauled down his flag from *Baden's* mast.[3]

Meanwhile there had been prolonged and contentious debates among the Allies as to the terms of the proposed armistice. From the start of discussions about the naval terms Beatty had been hawkish in the extreme. He wanted the terms to demonstrate that, although baulked of a second Trafalgar, the navy had won a great victory. He set out his views in a paper which he sent to Hankey after the meeting of the War Cabinet on October 21:

> The Military successes have been great and the Military Terms are commensurate with their achievements. The Navy made them possible and therefore shares in them. The Navy also has won a great Passive Victory, has swept the Enemy from the Seas, and rendered secure the vast lines of communications with our Allies, and permitted the trade of this country, necessary for existence, to continue. Because ours is a Passive Victory, it is no reason why the Empire should not reap the fruits of that victory.[4]

This, he argued, required the removal of the High Seas Fleet, which would reduce Germany to the level of a second class naval power.

The problem for Wemyss, who had accompanied Geddes to Versailles to finalise the armistice terms, was that the French in particular did not see the need to impose such severe naval terms that the Germans might refuse to agree. He wrote to Beatty on November 3, saying that if obliged by order of the Supreme War Council to ease the naval terms, his idea was to 'intern the whole lot in some neutral port without their ammunition.'[5] This provoked a violent telegram of protest from Beatty, who believed that Wemyss 'was not too strong' and so might be talked round. In answer to Wemyss's suggestion that the navy's position might be overridden, and that in that case all he could do was enter a protest, Beatty said that he assumed 'the protest would take the form of the resignation of the Board of Admiralty as a whole.'[6] Beatty was now getting much above himself.

On November 5 Wemyss wrote to update him on the position as it then stood:

> If by any chance the terms are accepted, which I doubt, or rather, which I doubted a few hours ago, perhaps you will consider what you think proper to do in the way of escorting the German Fleet to the neutral port, which will probably have to be Vigo or Arosa Bay, and of leaving there a squadron of supervision.[7]

These two ports in Spain were supposed to be the only two neutral ports large enough to accommodate the whole High Seas Fleet; and it was to be neutral ports in which it was to be interned. In view of doubts about whether this could be negotiated, with Spain or any other country, the final armistice terms read (Paragraph XXIII) that the German vessels should be interned in neutral ports, or failing them in Allied ports. This last provision was inserted by the British, who had no sincere intention of finding a suitable neutral port. To the British Ambassador in Spain was left the task of ensuring that any negotiations with the Spanish government should fail. Indeed, it is not even clear that any substantive inquiries were made, apart possibly in Madrid, of any of the governments of Spain, Holland, Sweden, Norway or Denmark. The Norwegian Navy Ministry apparently later told the German government that it had made preparations to receive the German ships and had been surprised to receive no inquiries.[8]

This dishonesty, if that is what it was, reflected, of course, the British Admiralty's concern not to let the control of the German fleet leave their hands. What Beatty would have liked was that the ships be surrendered; but to hold them under the guns of the Grand Fleet was the next best thing. He had rather hoped that the terms might, at the last, be refused by the Germans, so that he might have the chance of a glorious victory. He was bitter that he had not been consulted sufficiently, which was both unfair and unrealistic; and he was angry that the surrender of Heligoland had not been included as a term of the Armistice, arguing that 'it would be deplorable that Peace should find Germany with an advanced fortified naval base in the Bight still in her hands.'[9]

At all events, Wemyss advised the Allied Naval Council that finding a suitable neutral port would create too much difficulty, and it was agreed that the High Seas Fleet should be interned under British surveillance at Scapa Flow. The arrangements for this required a German emissary to come to Britain to settle the details, and Hipper detailed Rear Admiral Hugo Meurer to perform this extremely disagreeable task. Entirely characteristically, Beatty stage managed the meeting in such a way as to make it evident that what was taking place was indeed the surrender of a beaten enemy. Meurer arrived on the evening of November 15 in the light cruiser *Könlgsberg*, which anchored off May Island, and went with his staff of four officers to meet Beatty in his cabin aboard *Queen Elizabeth*. Beatty gleefully described the meeting in a letter to Eugénie:

> It all began with the advent of Admiral Meurer. You would have loved that, it was Dramatic and Tragic to a high degree. He arrived on board at 7.00 pm, pitch dark, aided by a thick fog, in which he could see nothing and had no idea he was surrounded by the Greatest Fleet in the World. I arranged a most beautiful setting, my Dramatic Sense was highly developed at the moment. When he marched up the Gangway he was met by a blaze of light from groups of the strongest electric sunlights which lighted the Gangway and the Path to be trod from there to my hatchway, outside the Path everything was inky black and perfect stillness. Actually on the edge of the Path of Light, half in and half out, was a line of the fattest marine sentries, about 2 paces apart, with fixed bayonets upon which the light gleamed. Wherever he looked he met a bayonet. He was met by Tommy Brand and Chatfield who were frigidity itself.

Beatty read his prepared instructions, refusing to discuss them, saying that they must be thought over and answered next day. Next day Meurer returned; Beatty described the end of the proceedings:

> Generally speaking, they would agree to anything, they raised points here and there which were firmly squashed … When it came to signing the documents, I thought he would collapse, he took two shots at it, putting his pen down twice, but we got him over it and they returned into the Fog in grim silence.[10]

Seymour, Beatty's Signal Officer, thought he had never seen the C-in-C to better advantage; 'during the discussion he was only stern about twice, the intonation of his voice was low and clear, but it was effective in the extreme.' Madden, too, was impressed, writing to Jellicoe on November 29: 'B carried it through very well and with dignity. The Germans were very quiet and tame.'[11] Among those present, though, was a more dispassionate observer; Lieutenant Commander Alastair Denniston, sent up from Room 40 to act as an interpreter, who took a different view:

> Sir David Beatty is a very wilful man, and has no mercy on a man or a nation he despises ... I confess I did feel sorry for the [German] Senior Officers there. They were keen, efficient men, who had learnt their work and made the German Navy their career, and this was the end of it.[12]

There remained the task of sailing those vessels of the High Seas Fleet designated for internment across the North Sea. The Armistice terms required that, apart from all the U-boats, ten battleships, six battle cruisers, seven light cruisers and forty nine torpedo boats should be interned; the sixth battle cruiser, *Mackensen*, was still incomplete, so *Baden*, the fleet flagship, took her place. *König* was not able to sail with the rest, and arrived later. All the vessels had to be disarmed before sailing, a major task that was completed in time, but with extreme difficulty. The fleet was due to arrive in the Firth of Forth by November 21. Since it was uncertain whether Meurer would have returned in time, Hipper appointed Reuter to command the fleet. As it turned out, Meurer was back on November 18; but he was required as a delegate to the Armistice Commission, so Reuter was confirmed. As the fleet sailed, Hipper wrote in his diary on November 19:

> My heart is breaking with this; my time as fleet commander has come to an inglorious end. The remaining questions of demobilisation, disarmament, and the negotiations with the soldiers' councils can be handled by my chief of staff; I have nothing more to do. I shall remain *proforma* in command for a short time, otherwise I am dead tired.[13]

Reuter had accepted appointment with the greatest reluctance, but was ready to do his duty. He had the opportunity of a discussion with Meurer about his negotiations:

> Admiral Meurer explained to me verbally the written arrangements he had come to with the English commander-in-chief and gave me his personal impressions, which induced me to exercise the utmost care and reticence in my dealings with the English fleet commander. Admiral Meurer mentioned that in his opinion the English had not the slightest intention of allowing our ships to go to neutral ports; I learnt for the first time many months later that Admiral Beatty did not appear to have reckoned on the German fleet reaching the Firth of Forth intact.[14]

Beatty managed the arrival of the High Seas Fleet with his customary flair for the dramatic. As it approached the Firth of Forth, at 9.10 am the light cruiser *Cardiff* took up her station at the head of the German vessels, and led them through two lines of British and Allied vessels to their temporary anchorage in the Firth. Later Beatty had the satisfaction of seeing each of his ships defile past *Queen Elizabeth*, cheering as they went. Photographers, of course, were there to record the scene. At 11.00 am, to reinforce the impression of victory, Beatty signalled: 'The German flag will be hauled down at sunset today, Thursday, and will not be hoisted again without permission.' Punctually at 3.57 the German ensigns were hauled down. It was an order which legally he had no authority to give, since the ships were interned and not surrendered; but Beatty was not going to let that make him miss such a trick. It was a great day for the Grand Fleet; Marder notes that it would have been 'gracious and fitting' tor Jellicoe and Fisher to be present, but they wee not invited; apparently the oversight was unintentional. It is unlikely however that Beatty would have wanted to share his moment of triumph.[15]

The German fleet was transferred to Scapa Flow, escorted by the battle cruisers of the 1st Battle Cruiser Squadron, and Beatty went on board *Lion* to address the officers and crew. The battle cruisers were no doubt chosen to reinforce the point that it was they, under Beatty's leadership, that had been at the forefront of the naval victory. Regrettably, he spoke of the Germans with unconcealed contempt, which his biographer regards as unfortunate; it would perhaps have been wiser, Captain Roskill observes, 'to have shown magnanimity towards his late enemies rather than a desire to humiliate them.'[16]

Reuter and his men now settled down to a mournful existence in Scapa Flow, beset by restrictive British regulations and kept very inadequately informed of what was going on in the outside world. Reuter himself was conscious that his sole object was 'henceforward, to preserve this assembled portion of the High Seas Fleet for the German State, whose property it was.'[17] He did not think it likely that his government would do much to resist the seizure of the ships, if this was attempted, so it was on him that their preservation rested. It was his policy to insist, wherever any point arose, on his legal status as the commander of the fleet. His task was not made easier by the efforts of the Soldiers' Council to assert their authority, such as it was, in the uneasy situation that existed between officers and men. Although, with the establishment of a constitutional government, the Soldiers' Councils were removed from power at home, they continued to exist in the interned ships.

Reuter returned home on leave at the end of December, only returning on January 25. After he got back he talked to Captain Oldekop, his Chief of Staff, about the possibility of sinking the fleet; they thought that it would be best to defer consideration of this while 'the waves of revolutionary passion' were still running high. But as the weeks went by, Reuter's fears that the peace talks might lead to the surrender of the fleet, a suggestion that was reinforced by discussion of the possibility in the British and Allied press. Reuter and Oldekop quietly considered the position, suppressing as far as they could the suggestion of scuttling which surfaced from time to time among the officers.[18]

The crews of the destroyers were, generally, more reliable than those of the capital ships and Ruge records how the commander of the destroyers, Commander Hermann Cordes, took them into his confidence. When Reuter heard of this he was alarmed, since he feared that the premature disclosure of this to the rest of the squadron might jeopardise his own plans; Cordes agreed, and managed to keep the secret. In making preparations to scuttle should the need arise, it would have been relatively easy if they had access to explosives but this of course they were denied, so it was on the flood valves that they must depend. Steps were taken to make it easy to remove the condenser covers; this would be the quickest way to admit the sea water.[19]

Reuter, who had transferred his flag from *Friedrich der Grosse* to the light cruiser *Emden* because of the hostility from the more extreme members of the flagship's crew, was following closely the course of the peace negotiations. The terms demanded by the Entente were made known on May 11; they heightened fears that the ships might be seized, or tamely surrendered by the German government. An opportunity to improve the situation aboard the ships by reducing the size of the care and maintenance parties came with the agreement of both the British and German governments that some 2700 men should be sent home. It was the most intractable sailors that were selected. They sailed for home on June 17, and Reuter felt free then to circulate to his commanding officers the preparatory order for scuttling the fleet. Paragraph 11 of the order read:

> It is my intention to sink the ships only if the enemy attempts to seize them without the consent of our government. Should our government agree to the peace conditions in which the ships are to be surrendered, the ships will then be handed over, to the lasting shame of those who put us in this position.

Commanding officers were to keep the order locked up; it must not fall into British hands. The signal for scuttling would be: 'Paragraph 11. Acknowledge.'[20] A rumour that the British were contemplating seizure of the ships on signature of the peace treaty, rather than its ratification, further strengthened Reuter's conviction that he must be ready to act.

The initial rejection of the peace terms by the German government on May 29 had left matters in the air. The resignation of Chancellor Scheidemann, who opposed the terms, and his replacement by Bauer, who did not, left the way for the Reichstag on June 20 to vote in favour of acceptance. Of this Reuter knew nothing; all he knew on that day came from a four day old copy of *The Times* to the effect that the Allies had given Germany an ultimatum to accept the terms or face a resumption of the war. In fact, the Armistice was extended to June 23. Reuter made up his mind; he would scuttle the fleet on the following day, June 21.

Next morning, accordingly, he appeared on the quarter deck of *Emden* to hear from Oldekop the surprising news that Vice Admiral Fremantle, the commander of the First Battle Squadron on guard duty, had taken all his ships to sea. At 10.30 am, Reuter sent by flag the general signal: 'Paragraph 11. Acknowledge.' repeated by semaphore and by Morse code on signal lamps around the fleet. For the next hundred minutes, after the acknowledgements began coming in, nothing much was to be seen; and then, one by one, their imperial battle flags flying, the ships began to sink. First to go was Reuter's former flagship, *Friedrich der Grosse*, which went down at 12.16 pm. At 1.00 pm Fremantle heard the news, and headed back to Scapa Flow at full speed; the first of his ships returned at 2.00 pm, by which time only three capital ships, three light cruisers and a number of. destroyers were still afloat. It was too late to do very much. British destroyers towed *Emden* ashore; *Frankfurt* was beached and *Nürnberg* run aground. Meanwhile those in the small British guard vessels in the Flow panicked, and began firing; nine Germans died as a result. Reuter, watching the fleet go down, asked to be taken to *Revenge,* Fremantle's flagship, where the Vice Admiral accused him of treachery, and told him he was a prisoner of war. Reuter told him that it was he and he alone who had caused the sinking of the fleet, and accepted full responsibility. He was taken to his quarters under guard. After a game of cards with his flag lieutenant, Reuter went off to bed; it was, he observed, a long time since he had spent such a restful night.[21]

Next day Fremantle delivered an angry lecture on his quarterdeck to Reuter and his staff, accusing them of having breached the armistice, having 'recommenced hostilities without notice by hoisting the German flag in the interned ships and proceeding to sink and destroy them.' His fury was no doubt sharpened by the fact that he looked distinctly foolish at having left Scapa Flow at the material time. Fremantle recalled later that Reuter made no response; however, the latter, who thought Fremantle's address in bad taste, and 'uncommonly unpleasant and humbling for the English admiral', gives the answer he made:

> Tell your admiral that I am unable to agree with the purport of his speech and that our comprehension of the subject differs. I alone carry the responsibility. I am convinced that any English naval officer, placed as I was, would have acted in the same way.[22]

News of the event was, naturally, received with widely differing emotions. The British press, or most of it, denounced the scuttling as an outrage, led as usual by the *Daily Mail*, demanding that penalties be imposed, and generally expressing themselves in violent and extravagant language. The *Morning Post* thought that those responsible for the naval terms of the Armistice lacked the elementary quality of commonsense in leaving the ships in German hands. The *Saturday Review* wrote: 'The scuttling … so indignantly denounced, strikes us as the only plucky and justifiable thing the Germans have done in the war. It is exactly what British sailors would have done had their ships been interned in German ports.'[23]

The reaction of the Allied governments was to turn to the lawyers to see what action could be taken over what appeared to be a clear breach of Article XXIII. While in the United States there was a feeling of good riddance, the circumstances of the sinking, and not least Fremantle's departure from Scapa Flow at the material time, led the French and Italian press to suggest that the British had connived at the scuttling for their own reasons. It was not altogether an unreasonable suspicion, but there is little substantive evidence for it.

It is certainly true that Wemyss was glad to receive the news, writing in his diary that the sinking of the German fleet was 'a real blessing.' For him, 'it disposes once for all of the thorny question of the distribution of these ships and eases us of an enormous amount of difficulties.'[24] British naval opinion was generally of the same mind. In Germany, naval opinion was entirely favourable to Reuter's decision, which one historian, Commander FU Busch, described as 'a manly act – the first sign of light on a dark cloud covered horizon.' Scheer rejoiced to hear the news:

> The stain of surrender has been wiped from the escutcheon of the German Fleet. The sinking of these ships has proved that the spirit of the Fleet is not dead. This last act is true of the best traditions of the German Navy.[25]

Tirpitz, in a letter to Ritter von Mann, was of the same opinion: 'That Admiral Reuter and our officers have saved somewhat the honour of our flag has deeply touched all of us here and quietly reawakens our hope for the future.'[26]

Whether the scuttling could have been prevented was the subject of a good deal of debate. Marder, observing that 'Fremantle was a flag officer of no extraordinary abilities upon whom fortune smiled beyond his deserts,' suggests that others might not have chosen to leave harbour when he did. Probably, though, it made little difference; once the scuttling began there was not much that could have been done about it.[27] Richmond, however, was not so forgiving, writing in his diary:

> The Germans have sunk their ships at Scapa, and have made the British Navy ridiculous. We end the war as we began it – unprepared. Three men are principally responsible – Wemyss, Madden and Fremantle. Fremantle has a particular share in the responsibility, as he was Deputy Chief of the Staff until recently and it would have been his particular duty to initiate proposals for safeguarding the ships, foreseeing what the enemy might do; and he was in command at the moment in Scapa, and had been there for several weeks, and therefore was in the best possible position to visualise what might happen and take steps.

Putting himself in the place of an officer whose ship was interned in this way, Richmond wrote that when all hope of being able to take his ship back to his country was gone, 'and the moment was arriving to hand her over to a hated enemy, the first thing I should plan for would be to destroy her.' To call it an act of treachery, he thought, was nonsense.[28]

Reuter, quite expecting to be put on trial, was detained in Britain as a prisoner of war until after the German Government had signed the Protocol on reparations. He was finally repatriated with the last handful of prisoners on January 29 1920, and sailed to Wilhelmshaven where he received a hero's welcome. Greeted on the dockside by Trotha and other officers, he was cheered to the echo by a huge crowd, the only man, as Dan van der Vat put it, in the history of the world who had scuttled a navy.[29]

46

Retrospect

In reviewing the course of the war in the North Sea, it is convenient to begin with the command structure on each side, and its relationship to the political leadership. In neither case was the structure by any means satisfactory or well fitted to get the best out of the resources available. And, for somewhat different reasons, there was in both Britain and Germany a mutual lack of trust and confidence between the government and the naval leadership. Their relationships were progressively soured by the stresses of conducting a war that was like none that had gone before; the admirals despised their political masters for their unreliability and dishonesty and, in their turn, were derided for their incompetence and closed minds.

Spenser Wilkinson, the military historian and commentator, was at the forefront of those who, at the end of the nineteenth century and the beginning of the twentieth, argued for the creation of a naval staff. He was a profound admirer of the Prussian General Staff system and its leader; accepting that it was the British Cabinet that would have the conduct of a war, he wrote in 1895: 'What we have to do is to provide the Cabinet, or make it provide itself, with a naval Moltke.'[1] The staff would be headed by 'the best naval strategist in the service.' Regrettably, neither Britain nor Germany succeeded in achieving this reasonable aim.

The development of a naval staff in Britain was considerably hampered by the overwhelming personality of Sir John Fisher and to a lesser extent his successor, Sir Arthur Wilson. Both believed absolutely that the devising of naval strategy and the preparation of war plans was primarily the responsibility of the First Sea Lord. It was not until after the Agadir crisis of 1911 that the need for a dedicated naval staff was accepted. Finally established under Winston Churchill in the following year, the Admiralty War Staff began work in the face of considerable scepticism throughout the Royal Navy. Arthur Marder wrote that it was, for years, of little value:

> The chief of the Admiralty War Staff had no executive power, the Operations Division had little or nothing to do with the conduct of operations and was confined to routine administrative work, and there was no Naval Staff College where officers could be trained in staff duties.[2]

Marder argues that even after 1917, when Jellicoe as First Sea Lord also became Chief of the Naval Staff and later that year a Plans Division was established, there was no proper naval staff, and nor were there properly trained officers to perform staff duties. In his opinion, apart from a few talented individuals who arrived at the Admiralty late in the war, the staff was 'merely a nondescript collection of officers,' who were not highly respected within the service. A different view has been expressed by a more recent historian of the Naval Staff during the War. Nicholas Black has written that the Staff 'was not the depository of second-rate, retired or maimed officers, unfit for sea, who passed the war in desk jobs.' He went on to observe:

> While it is undeniably the case that mistakes were made, particularly in the early months of the war in 1914, or at Jutland, to use these as the sole criteria of success or failure would be quite incorrect. Operating until 1917 as a body whose principal task was to provide information to the Board of Admiralty, chiefly the First Sea Lord, the Staff was in no position to dictate the conduct of the war. They must, therefore, be judged on the work that they did, and the advice that they gave. In these terms they must be judged to have been largely successful.[3]

Whether this description of the Naval Staff's function, particularly under Oliver, is altogether correct might be a matter for debate.

Commander Kenneth Dewar, one of the brighter and most iconoclastic officers who finally joined the staff, was soon writing to his friend Richmond on the subject of Admiralty procedure:

> The more I see of the present organisation the more certain I am that no good will ever come of it. Round and round go the dockets solemn slow stately and sure and meanwhile the ships are being sent rapidly to the bottom.[4]

It should be noted, however, that Marder, who frequently quoted Richmond, Dewar and other 'Young Turks,' nevertheless added a note of caution about their opinions. Calling them 'professional agitators,' he was at pains not to credit them with 'an importance of which they were quite devoid.' He thought that Richmond and Dewar in particular were their own worst enemies, contriving to put people's backs up by the manner in which they expressed their views.[5] The same observation could of course be made about Churchill, particularly when out of office. It must be said, however, that Richmond's flamboyant and egotistical diary offers a unique insight into the sometimes fevered atmosphere at the top of the British naval hierarchy.

The mutual disrespect between admirals and politicians was somewhat less marked in the early days of the war. Many in the navy were of course hostile to Churchill; but Balfour, with his calm and civilised demeanour, was far more accepting of professional opinion than his predecessor, and the same was true of Carson. Lloyd George, especially after he became Prime Minster, was constantly determined to see more control exercised over the generals and admirals. As to the latter, he had been long convinced that Balfour was ineffective in managing the Admiralty, and replacing him was one of his key objectives when he arrived at 10 Downing Street. His choice of Carson to succeed Balfour proved to be a mistake; he appeared to Lloyd George to have gone native almost at once. Only when he found a suitable hatchet man in Geddes, willing to do his bidding, did he feel that he had to some extent achieved his objective.

In their extensive correspondence with each other the admirals mirrored the suspicions of the politicians. Beatty, who almost invariably described Lloyd George as 'a dirty dog,' was perhaps the most outspoken: 'These politicians are all alike, a disgusting breed without real patriotism.' Wemyss, who damned all politicians to hell, wrote: 'I am under the impression that I have got on fairly good terms with the Prime Minister, but with these slippery gentlemen you never can tell what their real opinions are.' On another occasion he wrote that he hated Lloyd George, but thought that the remainder of the Cabinet were far worse than him. Even the mild mannered Jackson observed on leaving the Admiralty: 'My greatest relief is that I shall be clear of the politicians. If we win the war, it will be in spite of them, not because of them.'[6]

In Germany, the inevitable stresses arising between the naval and the political leadership were enhanced by the creation of a command structure which was quite unfitted to manage the German naval war effort. William II's decision on March 14 1899 to dissolve the Navy High Command and reorganise its functions imposed on the German navy a quite needless handicap under which it laboured until Scheer compelled the introduction of a reform which everyone could see was long overdue. By then it was August 1918 and the war was as good as lost. William's decision had marked a victory for the *Reichsmarineamt* over the *Oberkommando der Marine*, and meant that thereafter the navy would be subject to a fatally fractured command and organisational structure. The triumvirate of the Chief of the *Admiralstab*, the Chief of the Naval Cabinet and the State Secretary of the RMA all had a major role to play in the conduct of the naval war and in the development of naval strategy. This structure was to cause, as Jonathan Steinberg observes, more difficulty for Tirpitz than all the anomalies of German political life.[7]

In one respect the German system had one practical advantage. The Admiralty Staff defined strategical policy; beyond intelligence reports and occasional directives, it did not issue operational orders. This was the responsibility of the fleet commanders. The British Admiralty, on the other hand, and particularly the Chief of Naval Staff, did issue operational orders, keeping a tight control of the deployment of the ships available. The difference can be illustrated by two instances from the battle of Jutland. It was Scheer who took the decision to allow Mauve's II Battle Squadron of predreadnoughts to accompany the High Seas Fleet, not the Admiralty staff. It was Oliver's decision, as Chief of Naval Staff, to forbid Tyrwhitt from taking part in the battle because of the fear that the operations of the High Seas Fleet were intended to cover a lunge into the English Channel. Both decisions, of course, were serious errors of judgment.

The first, and crucial component of German naval strategy, with all the political, industrial and economic consequences that flowed from it, was the decision to build a battle fleet. Jonathan Steinberg has shown that Tirpitz was by no means the first to argue in favour of this concept. General Albrecht von Stosch, one of Helmuth von Moltke's most trusted collaborators, who headed the Admiralty for twelve years, wrote:

> Without the background of armoured battleships, without the security of finding in case of need the support of a collected battle-ready high seas fleet, the effectiveness of ships in political service cannot correspond to the world position of the German Empire nor long be guaranteed.[8]

Stosch was also ahead of Tirpitz in contending that Germany needed a battle fleet if it was to be a realistic alliance partner:

> If in a major war against a power with superior naval strength the German flag cannot maintain itself on its own, Germany can have no value for maritime allies .... The most effective defence of the coasts of the Fatherland is without question a victory in a battle on the high seas.[9]

Thus, equipped with a battle fleet that although inferior in numbers to the Grand Fleet was nevertheless a powerful fighting force, Germany's strategy must address the question of how it was to be used. As has been seen, this was heavily influenced by questions of geography. Tirpitz acknowledged as early as 1894, and again in 1909 and 1914, that the British might well adopt a distant blockade. On one occasion he flatly stated that 'today a close blockade is no longer possible'. In his memoirs he recorded his views, tempered no doubt to some extent by hindsight:

> I did not think we should seek battle in any case, and in any position. I rather desired that the North Sea fleet should create by continual activity a situation that would compel the English to draw nearer to us. If a battle developed in this manner on our initiative, not too far from our home waters, there was a possibility, especially in the earlier part of the war; that the English would not throw the whole of their united forces into the fight. The history of the war ... will show that such opportunities were in fact offered. At the beginning of the war the fact had not emerged so clearly as it did later that the British fleet fulfilled its raison d'être simply by lying quietly at Scapa Flow. Public opinion in the enemy countries might have made it difficult at that time for the British to avoid battle. Even minor successes on our part might have driven them to seek us out. There was further to be considered the, for us, comparatively favourable numerical relation between the two forces in the first year of the war.[10]

Even allowing for a measure of self justification, there was a good deal of truth in this. But it would have taken bolder men than those at the head of the German navy at the start of the war to adopt such an aggressive strategy.

Admiral Duff, writing after the war had ended, pointed out the acute dilemma facing the Germans:

> It has always been a mystery to me how anyone in possession of the full situation could expect the High Sea Fleet to come out and fight. We piled up a Fleet against them that gave them no possible chance even under the command of a Nelson.[11]

It was a judgment that, if a little overstated, was largely correct; a cautious policy on the part of the leaders of the High Seas Fleet was understandable and yet, as Tirpitz pointed out, a bolder strategy might have yielded remarkable results, even without a Nelson. There were a number of occasions when with better luck, the High Seas Fleet might have pulled off a considerable stroke. Of course, it is also true that with worse luck they might have suffered a disaster.

As Jellicoe knew, and Scheer acknowledged, it was not the business of the Grand Fleet to afford the High Seas Fleet easy opportunities to wear down the British numerical advantage. In an interview with an American journalist after the war, Scheer remarked:

> In itself Admiral Jellicoe's slow blockade strategy was correct and accomplished its purpose. No fault can be found with it, provided his confining the Fleet to a blockade can be reconciled with the traditions of the British Navy.[12]

However, he was critical of the failure of the Grand Fleet not to make the most of its advantages by pursuing a more aggressive strategy in the early part of the war. It could choose its field of action far from the bases of the High Seas Fleet, which would be unable to replace the inevitable losses of capital ships in extended conflicts with the Grand Fleet. On the other hand, as he wrote in his memoirs, the High Seas Fleet might have done more:

> After their experiences in action, the English left the southern part of the North Sea for us to deploy in, and contented themselves with warding off the U-boat danger. Throughout they were forced to be on the defensive. We ought to have tried earlier what the result of a victory by our Fleet would be. It was a mistake on the part of naval leaders not to do so.[13]

The passive strategy of the Grand Fleet attracted a great deal of criticism within the British navy. There were many to be found who argued that the traditions or the past demanded that the Grand Fleet should seek out and destroy the High Seas Fleet. A decisive victory on the lines of Trafalgar would, they believed, entirely change the course of the war, and justified the taking of great risks to achieve it. It would have freed the navy to devote far more resources to defeating the U-boats, have exposed the German coasts to invasion, and gravely damaged German civilian morale.

Against these aspirations the British Admiralty had to weigh the consequences of those great risks actually resulting in a significant weakening of the Grand Fleet. That fleet stood between Germany and the raising of the Allied blockade; it protected the routes of the essential military transports and the communications of the allied armies and defended Britain against a starvation blockade. The extent of those risks was impossible to quantify; the power of mines and of submarines to destroy capital ships bulked large in the imagination of sea going admirals. The British objective was, at all times, to use its maritime power to command the sea – to ensure its use by the Allies and to deny its use to Germany. This objective was, ultimately, achievable by the enforcement of the distant blockade, less dramatically but more surely than by the pursuit of spectacular victories at sea.

For those impassioned exponents of the Nelson tradition, disappointed at the lack of decisive action at sea, and to be found especially among the leader writers of the British Press, a sober corrective could be found in the analysis of one of his biographers:

> The more closely Nelson's actions and letters are studied, the more clearly will it be seen that the point on which his thoughts continually dwell was not the mere 'going at 'em,' but the most advantageous way to 'go at'em;' and that, in every instance, the dash and impetuosity which caught the popular fancy were guided by genius, and controlled by prudence and foresight.[14]

The German failure to take their chances, and the British refusal to be drawn into dangerous adventures, led in the end to the adoption of an unrestricted U-boat campaign. It was a huge gamble, bringing with it a near certainty that the United States would enter the war, and the high probability that if the campaign failed, Germany must lose the war. Early results showed that the statistical evidence for Holtzendorff's confident prediction of an early victory was soundly based – if, and always if, the Allies could not find a means to counter the effectiveness of the U-boats. This was equally true of Jellicoe's pessimistic assessment of the situation in the Spring of 1917. The solution, in the introduction of a general convoy system, came in the nick of time. It was so effective that, in retrospect, it seems astonishing that it took so long before the Admiralty's reluctance to adopt it was overcome.

Aside from the overriding strategic questions, the leaders of the Grand Fleet and the High Seas Fleet had to consider the effect of the tactical decisions which must be taken almost instinctively and with little time to reflect. It was essential, therefore, that all concerned should be carefully prepared for every eventuality by the issue of minutely detailed standing orders, and by the study of the tactical principles to be applied. Frequent exercises testing the battle situations that might arise were particularly necessary because the battle fleets were composed of vessels vastly more powerful than had ever before been in combat. On the whole, perhaps the High Seas Fleet was better prepared in this respect. On both sides, there was considerable anxiety about the threat from mines and torpedoes; Jellicoe, with more to lose, was particularly sensitive to the dangers which he faced from these weapons.

One ever present consideration that affected all command decisions in respect of operations in the North Sea was the weather. It could severely limit effective reconnaissance, both in terms of visibility at sea level and, for the Germans, the ability of Zeppelins to take to the air at all. The information gathered and reported to fleet commanders might, as a result, turn out to be extremely inaccurate. And, even more significantly, the weather could, during combat, make accurate gunnery extremely difficult.

Although the Grand Fleet had throughout the war a considerable quantitative superiority over the High Seas Fleet, this was not the case in qualitative terms. Ship for ship, the Germans had the advantage, as the British naval leadership came to accept. Schoultz, the Russian liaison officer with the Grand Fleet, reflected upon this when visiting the battleship *Hercules*. He noticed a line of twelve pictures depicting each of the ships to have borne that name in the British Navy, and this prompted some acute observations on the wars of the past:

> Comparing those wars with the present, I could not help thinking how often the technical side of British ship construction, the armouring and especially the guns had been inferior to those of the enemy. Battles, however, are not won by ships but by men; not by the guns but by the crews, officers and men, who know how to use them. Materiel has never played so decisive a role as the mind, whose share as a factor in a victorious battle Napoleon estimated at 75 per cent.[15]

He was, of course, perfectly right about the quality of ship construction; down the years, Spanish, French and German ship builders all tended to outperform their British counterparts. With the coming of the dreadnoughts, German design superiority was very evident. Nowhere was this so striking as in the quality of the battle cruisers. By 1917 this was so apparent to Jellicoe and Beatty that panic is scarcely too strong a word to describe their state of mind when they compared the relative strength of the Grand Fleet and the High Seas Fleet in battle cruisers. The margin of superiority which they considered that the Germans possessed led to the desperate proposal to attempt to purchase from Japan their two latest battle cruisers. There was no way in which the Japanese would have assented to this; but it was the only option which the Admiralty could think of to plug the gap.[16] *Lützow, Derfflinger* and *Hindenburg* were much superior to *Lion* and her sisters, and the earlier German battle cruisers were equally superior to the first British ships of this type, particularly in the punishment which they could absorb without loss of their fighting effectiveness. And although *Queen Elizabeth* and her sisters were excellent capital ships, *Bayern* and *Baden* were probably superior, although not tested in battle. The same was generally true of all classes of warship; in particular, German designs usually produced vessels of robust construction. It has been suggested that they had a significant advantage in designing vessels to operate in the confined waters of the North Sea, rather than having to provide a capacity to operate at a longer range; while this may be true in terms of crew accommodation and facilities, it is the case that the operating range of German warships was no less than their British counterparts.

The skill of the designers was tested to the full by the development of modern weapons, the destructive power of which condemned the predreadnoughts of Mauve's II Battle Squadron to the derisive term of 'five minute ships;' their counterparts of the 3rd Battle Squadron were known as the 'wobbly eight.' Their vulnerability was soon crushingly demonstrated.

In one respect there was a striking parallel between the British and German navies in the decade before the outbreak of war in 1914. Each had been dominated by so outstanding a personality that the navies that fought the First World War were in effect the creation of Fisher and Tirpitz respectively. Both of them were brilliant men, who attracted strong supporters and strong opposition. They had left their stamp on the navies they had built, but each was doomed to watch with mounting frustration what he regarded as the misuse of his creation. It might have been a very different war had Fisher remained as First Sea Lord and Tirpitz, as he craved, had been entrusted with the command of the High Seas Fleet.

Fisher had long designated Jellicoe as the man to win another Trafalgar. As a commander he was thoughtful and careful; it was unlikely that he was ever going to make the kind of rash decisions for which the Germans hoped. Fisher, in making him his protégé, saw in him the kind of technical man who could make the best use of the weapon he had forged:

> He believed that a man who performed well in the materiel field would inevitably perform well in battle – would show expertise in the Big Thing – a transferability of leadership qualities, as it were. In selecting a man for a major fleet action, Fisher was inevitably making a decision beyond his own experience. He could only rely on his reading of history and he seems to have got that reading wrong. Yet Jellicoe in many respects was not all that dissimilar from Fisher himself, although very dissimilar in his style of life. Jellicoe was cautious, with little tactical and strategic insight and no sense of staff planning. So was Fisher, despite his aggressive style of communication. Jellicoe shared with his patron Fisher an outlook that belittled the importance of staff work.[17]

Thus John Horsfield, in his book, *The Art of Leadership in War*. It is a judgment that perhaps is a little harsh. Jellicoe carried a great responsibility, and was at all times very much aware of it, sometimes crushingly so. In the end Fisher came to the conclusion that Jellicoe was lacking in one quality in particular:

> I told the Dardanelles Commission (why they asked me I don't know) that Jellicoe had all the Nelsonic attributes except one – he is totally wanting in the great gift of insubordination. Nelson's greatest achievements were all solely due to his disobeying orders.[18]

Although quiet and unassuming in his public manner, Jellicoe was extremely popular with the fleet; his men liked and trusted him. He faced technical and operational problems that were entirely novel, and did so with a remarkable intelligence and breadth of judgment. Horsfield, though, when measuring Jellicoe against Nelson, finds that he lacked more than the ability to disobey:

> Nelson had an aggressive and optimistic spirit and a tactical imagination. He had confidence in, and the total confidence of, his subordinates. Nelson had outstanding clarity of perception, the power of decision, and a mastery of the art of communication. Jellicoe in the supreme leadership had none of these qualities. That is the measure of his failing by the highest standards.[19]

But perhaps such a direct comparison is, in all the circumstances, rather unfair. Horsfield acknowledges that 'the German fleet was a far more efficient mechanism than the fast decaying French and Spanish fleets that Nelson had to contend with.'

Horsfield himself perceptively points out what might be considered a more relevant comparison. Writing of Collingwood and his place in British naval history, he observes:

> It was, of course, Nelson rather than Collingwood who dominated the imagination of the nineteenth and early twentieth centuries. But it was Collingwood's standards that the orthodox and the disciplined could more realistically emulate. Without histrionics Collingwood performed everything his government wanted him to do. If ever another Collingwood was produced, it was Jellicoe, who had to suffer in his career far greater professional frustration, although no more stress, than Collingwood.[20]

And when it comes to assessing his powers of decision, it can certainly be argued that Jellicoe showed himself to be an extremely competent commander, as his crucially important deployment on the port column at Jutland demonstrated. But he was not a bold, and not a showy leader, in sharp contrast with his successor.

Beatty was undoubtedly more charismatic, more physically impressive and more conscious of the effect he was creating; but he was also more headstrong, less consistent and less intelligent than Jellicoe. Beatty was also arrogant, conceited, selfish and a remorseless self advertiser. These qualities did not mean he was not a good leader; he was, for instance, successful in maintaining the morale of the Grand Fleet. He was a brave and determined leader, but he was by no means a great commander, and certainly not Jellicoe's equal. He blamed Jellicoe for, as he saw it, passing up a chance on May 31 1916 to inflict a major defeat on the High Seas Fleet; but, ironically, when he took up the command of the Grand Fleet, he pursued a policy that was even more cautious than that of Jellicoe. Deprived of a chance of winning a decisive victory in combat, he was able to crow at the end of the war of what he described as the 'Passive Victory.'

In combat, Beatty did not display the qualities of a great tactician; neither at the Dogger Bank nor at Jutland was his handling of the battle cruisers free from serious error. Horsfield described his performance at Jutland as 'controversial,' in that he 'failed to give the most effective support to Jellicoe. He failed to cooperate effectively when cooperation was essential.'[21] As Horsfield notes, Admiral Harper identified in particular Beatty's failure to provide precise information, his incorrect disposition of his ships and his faulty signalling. As Commander-in-Chief he did display greater confidence in his subordinates than Jellicoe, and he was certainly much better than Jellicoe in delegating; the latter at times was almost completely overwhelmed by paper work.

Beatty's skill at public relations ensured that on the whole he had a much better press than Jellicoe, whose quiet, even dour, manner was not best fitted to captivate those who interviewed him. To journalists, Beatty was the dashing leader who might have won a second Trafalgar had he been given the chance. On the whole, he has been decidedly overrated as a naval commander.

So, perhaps, have Keyes and Tyrwhitt also been accorded more of a reputation than their abilities and achievements justified. Neither could be described as an intellectual giant, but both were energetic and inspiring leaders, the latter particularly so. Indeed, Marder was inclined to think that 'Tyrwhitt was in many ways the outstanding British sea officer of the war, as Hipper was on the German side.'[22] Both Keyes and Tyrwhitt caught the eye of the public, and perhaps were rather good at doing so. Keyes, indeed, made his reputation with the Zeebrugge operation, which was a failure. Among other leaders in the campaign in the North Sea Goodenough stands out as one whose quickness of decision made him the most successful of the commanders of light cruiser squadrons with the Grand Fleet. The commanders of the battle squadrons, however, were on the whole not an inspiring group; Madden, a brother in law of Jellicoe who had served as his Chief of Staff, was probably the ablest. Marder produced a long list of admirals who made mistakes during the war; the only reason Maddens's name did not figure was that he was not given the chance to make any. Evan-Thomas was also capable; his reputation was marred, however, by the blame unfairly cast upon him by Beatty for his own mistakes.

What did characterise the naval leaders on both sides was a willingness to enter into the most vigorous correspondence with each other, in the course of which they inveighed most violently against their erstwhile colleagues. In this tsunami of criticism and contempt Jellicoe was one of the least industrious; Beatty, on the other hand, frequently demonstrated extreme disloyalty to his Commander-in-Chief.

Jellicoe's supporters were still quick to defend his reputation many decades after the end of the First World War. The publication by Professor Marder of Richmond's diaries in *Portrait of an Admiral* opened up all the old wounds within the Royal Navy arising from the controversies of 1914-1918. Foremost among those survivors of the period who were outraged by the public revelation of Richmond's opinions and conduct was Admiral Sir Frederick Dreyer, who, after reading the book, wrote to Admiral Sir Dudley de Chair in 1952:

> How terrible it is to read. I always knew he was *clever*, and *unbalanced* as well as *conceited* – but the book goes further and makes it quite clear that he, with all the advantages of good birth and upbringing in our Noble Service, was a *disloyal cad*... its only redeeming feature is that it is so bad, wicked and untrue that *it does no harm to our noble service* or to the reputation of Jellicoe and *the large majority of Naval officers* who were outside 'R's Ring.'[23]

It is perhaps only fair to set against Dreyer's extremely partisan view of Richmond the judgment of a more recent historian in Daniel Baugh:

> All in all, Richmond is a remarkable figure, not only as a historian but also as an analyst of strategy. His concept of a navy as mainly an instrument which assists and resists military assaults across water, while operating simultaneously to relieve and to apply pressure on national resources, is a concept which defines the objects of sea power. It is as relevant today as when he wrote. And, although he devoted his life to the naval service and naval studies,

> his steady insistence on dealing with war-making as a whole and on the efficient cooperation of all arms testifies to the breadth and integrity of his outlook.[24]

On the other side of the North Sea, the virulent correspondence tended to polarise around the figure of Tirpitz, who both while in office and after he left it had a large number of devoted followers, with whom he remained closely in touch. One of his closest adherents was Trotha, who served as Scheer's Chief of Staff, and who was extremely influential. Not much needs to be said of Scheer's two predecessors as commanders in chief of the High Seas Fleet; both Ingenohl and Pohl were by nature cautious and were the more so in their command of the fleet because of the pressures put upon them.

Scheer, though, was a very different character. The judgments passed on him by historians have generally not been favourable; the most notable exception to this is the opinion of Commander Frost. It can certainly be argued that, of the four principal commanders at the battle of Jutland, Scheer has been the most underrated. His bold, instinctive leadership was just what the High Seas Fleet needed if it was to overcome the crippling numerical inferiority which it faced. Among recent historians, Andrew Gordon has been the most critical, listing the tactical mistakes made by Scheer in the course of the battle. But a similar list could be compiled of the mistakes of all the others; and when it came to it, Scheer displayed the qualities of boldness and determination that brought him what could be accounted a victory, albeit a narrow, tactical victory. He handled his fleet with notable skill during the battle, and safely extricated it from the position into which Jellicoe's deployment had brought it by the cool aggression with which he punched through the rear of the Grand Fleet during the night. Frost sums up his comparison between Jellicoe and Scheer in these terms:

> As between Jellicoe and Scheer, we believe in general that Jellicoe executed a poor conception of war excellently, while Scheer executed an excellent conception of war poorly. Jellicoe had skill, but as the Spartan said, 'Skill that cannot fight is useless.' Scheer had personality, and could fight, but was deficient in skill. Jellicoe was a McClellan; Scheer, a Blücher without his Gneisenau. It would be most interesting to know what, if anything, Captains Adolph von Trotha and Levetzow contributed to the formulation of Scheer's decisions between 6.45 and 7.30 pm.[25]

In *The Age of Nelson* GJ Marcus summarised the characteristic Nelsonic qualities of instant decision, which he listed as 'unfailing resource, unshakeable tenacity of purpose, brilliant tactical insight, swift and audacious action – combined with the all consuming urge towards victory.'[26] It is generally agreed that none of the four principal leaders in the North Sea in 1914-1918 was a Nelson, or anywhere near him. However, at the risk of inviting outrage from admirers of the other three, I suggest that it can be argued that Scheer came nearest of the four in exhibiting in some measure the characteristics described above. He was decisive when he had to be, resourceful in a crisis, tenacious and possessed of clear tactical insight, and capable of swift and audacious action. If he was unable to demonstrate an overwhelming urge towards victory, it was because a grasp of the reality of his situation never left him.

Of the four principal leaders Hipper usually emerges from the pages of the historians as the most successful. Both Marder and Frost in particular take this view. Certainly, he made fewer mistakes; and certainly he was more fortunate in his ships than Beatty. Calm and unruffled throughout the battle of Jutland, he kept his head at all times, even demonstrating Fisher's prime quality of insubordination when ignoring Scheer's order during the run to the north 'to undertake pursuit' of Beatty's retiring force, realising that to do so would subject the I Scouting Group to heavy punishment without gaining any advantage.[27] He was not in command of the High Seas Fleet for long enough to show how far he would have been prepared to take risks with it, at least until he approved Operation Plan No 19 in October 1918. If that operation plan had been carried out, with caution over mines and submarines thrown to the winds, it might have led to the sort of encounter which the admirals on both sides craved and of which they had almost given up hope.

Of the other German admirals, Reuter displayed considerable ability, particularly in his handling of his light cruiser squadron during the action of November 17 1917; and deservedly succeeded Hipper as commander of the I Scouting Group when the latter was made Commander-in-Chief of the High Seas Fleet. Reuter could never have imagined what would be required of him when he himself took command of the fleet as it lay interned in Scapa Flow; but he deserves credit for the difficult decision he made. Boedicker, who deputised for Hipper in command of the I Scouting Group on one occasion, was somewhat less able than Reuter. Schmidt and Behncke, commanding the dreadnought battle squadrons at Jutland, were capable and reliable; the former enhanced his reputation when commanding elements of the High Seas Fleet in the Baltic in 1918.

For those in the Grand Fleet and the High Seas Fleet, and particularly their senior commanders, the course of the war in the North Sea was one of sustained frustration. The strategic deadlock never was broken. The combatants sought throughout the war and in varying ways to achieve this, but without success. Too much was at stake, and too great the risks, to attempt adventurous strokes. In a wider sense, of course, in terms of grand strategy it was never essential to an ultimate British victory that the deadlock should be broken. If, at the end of the war, Britain's strategic position of advantage in the North Sea had been maintained, then the naval war there would be won; and that, in the end, was what happened.

Appendix A

The Grand Fleet at Jutland

BATTLE FLEET

C-in-C; Admiral Sir John Jellicoe
Chief of Staff: Vice Admiral Sir Charles Madden
Fleet Flagship: *Iron Duke* (Captain FC Dreyer)

FIRST BATTLE SQUADRON (Scapa Flow)
Marlborough (Vice Admiral Sir Cecil Burney)
Revenge
Hercules
Agincourt
Colossus (Rear Admiral EFA Grant)
Collingwood
Neptune
St Vincent

SECOND BATTLE SQUADRON (Invergordon)
King George V (Vice Admiral Sir Martyn Jerram)
Ajax
Centurion
Erin
Orion (Rear Admiral AC Leveson)
Monarch
Conqueror
Thunderer

FOURTH BATTLE SQUADRON (Scapa Flow)
Benbow (Vice Admiral Sir Doveton Sturdee)
Bellerophon
Temeraire
Vanguard
Royal Oak

Superb (Rear Admiral AL Duff)
Canada

Attached Light Cruisers
Boadicea
Blanche
Bellona
Active

Attached Destroyer
Oak

Attached Minelayer
Abdiel

THIRD BATTLE CRUISER SQUADRON (Scapa Flow)
Invincible (Rear Admiral LA Hood)
Indomitable
Inflexible

FIRST CRUISER SQUADRON (Invergordon)
Defence (Rear Admiral Sir Robert Arbuthnot
Warrior
Duke of Edinburgh
Black Prince

SECOND CRUISER SQUADRON (Scapa Flow)
Minotaur (Rear Admiral HL Heath)
Hampshire
Cochrane
Shannon

FOURTH LIGHT CRUISER SQUADRON (Scapa Flow)
Calliope (Commodore CE Le Mesurier)
Constance
Comus
Caroline
Royalist

FOURTH FLOTILLA

Flotilla Leaders:	*Tipperary* (Captain CJ Wintour)
	Broke (Commander WL Allen)
Achates	*Sparrowhawk*
Porpoise	*Contest*
Spitfire	*Shark*

Unity *Acasta*
Garland *Christopher*
Ambuscade *Owl*
Ardent *Hardy*
Fortune *Midge*
Ophelia

ELEVENTH FLOTILLA (Scapa Flow)
Light Cruiser: *Castor* (Commander JRP Hawksley)
Marne *Michael*
Manners *Mons*

(Invergordon)
Flotilla Leader: *Kempenfelt* (Commander HE Sulivan)
Ossory *Mandate*
Mystic *Minion*
Morning Star *Martial*
Magic *Milbrook*
Mounsey *Moon*

TWELFTH FLOTILLA (Scapa Flow)
Flotilla Leaders: *Faulknor* (Captain AJB Stirling)
Marksman (Commander NA Sulivan)
Obedient *Narwhal*
Maenad *Mindful*
Opal *Onslaught*
Mary Rose *Munster*
Marvel *Nonsuch*
Menace *Noble*
Nessus *Mischief*

BATTLE CRUISER FLEET (Vice Admiral Sir David Beatty)
(at Rosyth)
Flagship: *Lion* (Captain AEM Chatfield)

FIFTH BATTLE SQQUADRON
Barham (Rear Admiral H Evan-Thomas)
Valiant
Warspite
Malaya

FIRST BATTLE CRUISER SQUADRON
Princess Royal (Rear Admiral O de B Brock)
Queen Mary
Tiger

SECOND BATTLE CRUISER SQUADRON
New Zealand Rear Admiral WC Pakenham)
Indefatigable

FIRST LIGHT CRUISER SQUADRON
Galatea (Commodore ES Alexander-Sinclair)
Phaeton
Inconstant
Cordelia

SECOND LIGHT CRUISER SQUADRON
Southampton (Commodore WE Goodenough)
Birmingham
Nottingham
Dublin

THIRD LIGHT CRUISER SQUADRON
Falmouth (Rear Admiral TDW Napier)
Yarmouth
Birkenhead
Gloucester
Chester

FIRST FLOTILLA
Light Cruiser: *Fearless* (Captain CD Roper)
Acheron *Goshawk*
Ariel *Defender*
Attack *Lizard*
Hydra *Lapwing*
Badger

THIRTEENTH FLOTILLA
Light Cruiser: *Champion* (Captain J U Farie)
Nestor *Pelican*
Nomad *Nerissa*
Narborough *Onslow*
Obdurate *Moresby*
Petard *Nicator*

NINTH FLOTILLA (part)
Liberty
Lydiard
Landrail
Laurel

TENTH FLOTILLA (part)
Moorsom
Morris
Turbulent
Termagant

Seaplane Carrier: *Engadine*

Appendix B

The High Seas Fleet at Jutland

C-in-C Vice Admiral Reinhard Scheer
Chief of Staff : Captain A von Trotha
Fleet Flagship : *Friedrich der Grosse* (Captain T Fuchs)

I BATTLE SQUADRON
Ostfriesland (Vice Admiral E Schmidr)
Thüringen
Helgoland
Oldenburg
Posen (Rear Admiral Engelhardt)
Rheinland
Nassau
Westfalen

III BATTLE SQUADRON
König (Rear Admiral P Behncke)
Grosser Kurfürst
Markgraf
Kronprinz
Kaiser (Rear Admiral Nordmann)
Prinzregent Luitpold
Kaiserin

II BATTLE SQUADRON
Deutschland (Rear Admiral Mauve)
Hessen
Pommern
Hannover (Rear Admiral von Dalwigk zu Lichtenfeld)
Schlesien
Schleswig-Holstein

I SCOUTING GROUP
Lützow (Vice Admiral F Hipper; Chief of Staff: Commander E Raeder)
Seydlitz
Moltke
Derfflinger
Von der Tann

II SCOUTING GROUP
Frankfurt (Rear Admiral Boedicker)
Pillau
Elbing
Wiesbaden
Rostock (Commodore Michelsen, Commanding Destroyers)
Regensburg (Commodore Heinrich, 2-in-C destroyers)

IV SCOUTING GROUP
Stettin (Commodore L von Reuter)
München
Frauenlob
Stuttgart
Hamburg

DESTROYER FLOTILLAS
First Half Flotilla (Lieutenant Commander C Albrecht)
Second Flotilla (Captain Schuur)
Third Flotilla (Commander Hollmann
Fifth Flotilla (Commander Heinecke)
Sixth Flotilla (Commander M Schultz)
Seventh Flotilla (Commander von Koch)
Ninth Flotilla (Commander Goehle)

SUBMARIINES (Captain Bauer) (aboard *Hamburg*)

U-24	*U-43*	*U-19*
U-32	*U-44*	*UB-22*
U-63	*U-52*	*UB21*
U-66	*U-47*	*U-53*
U-70	*U-46*	*U-64*
	U-22	

AIRSHIPS

L-11	*L-16*
L-17	*L-13*
L-14	*L-9*
L-21	*L-22*
L-23	*L-24*

Appendix C

British Casualties

Ship	Killed	Wounded	Prisoners of War
Battleships			
Barham	26	37	
Colossus		5	
Malaya	63	33	
Marlborough	2		
Valiant		1	
Warspite	14	16	
Battle Cruisers			
Indefatigable (sunk)	1017		2
Invincible (sunk)	1026		
Lion	99	44	
Princess Royal	22	78	
Queen Mary (sunk)	1266	7	2
Tiger	24	37	
Cruisers			
Black Prince (sunk)	857		
Defence (sunk)	903		
Warrior (sunk)	71	27	
Light Cruisers			
Calliope	10	9	
Castor	13	23	
Chester	35	42	
Dublin	3	24	
Southampton	35	41	

Ship	Killed	Wounded	Prisoners of War
Flotilla Leaders			
Broke	47	36	
Tipperary (sunk)	185	2	8
Destroyers			
Acasta	6	1	
Ardent (sunk)	78	2	
Defender	1	2	
Fortune	67	1	
Moorsom	1		
Nessus	7	7	80
Nestor (sunk)	6		72
Nomad (sunk)	8		
Onslaught	5	2	
Onslow	2	3	
Petard	9	6	
Porpoise	2	2	
Shark	86	2	
Sparrowhawk (sunk)	6		
Spitfire	6	19	
Turbulent (sunk)	90		13
Total	6,097	510	177

Appendix D

German Casualties

Ship	Killed	Wounded
Battleships		
Grosser Kurfürst	15	11
Kaiser	1	
König	45	27
Markgraf	11	13
Nassau	12	15
Oldenburg	8	14
Ostfriesland	1	10
Pommern (sunk)	840	
Rheinland	10	20
Schlesien	1	1
Schleswig-Holstein	3	8
Westfalen	2	8
Battle Cruisers		
Derfflinger	154	26
Lützow (sunk)	111	54
Moltke	17	22
Seydlitz	98	50
Von der Tann	12	35
Light Cruisers		
Elbing (sunk)	4	10
Frankfurt	3	21
Frauenlob (sunk)	342	
Hamburg	14	25
München	8	19
Pillau	4	23

Ship	Killed	Wounded
Rostock (sunk)	14	6
Stettin	9	27
Wiesbaden (sunk)	570	
Destroyers		
B98	2	11
G40	1	1
S32	3	1
V4 (sunk)	18	4
V43 (sunk)	90	
Sixth Flotilla	3	16
Ninth Flotilla	120	15
Total	2,545	494

Appendix E

Battle of Jutland: Hits on German battleships and battle cruisers (heavy shells)

	12 inch	13.5 inch	15 inch	Total
König	–	9	1	10
Grosser Kurfürst	–	3	5	8
Markgraf	1	1	3	5
Kaiser	2	–	–	2
Helgoland	–	–	1	1
Pommern	1	–	–	1
Schleswig-Holstein	1	–	–	1
Lützow	8	12	4	24
Derfflinger	10	1	10	21
Seydlitz	8	6	8	22
Moltke	–	1	4	5
Von der Tann	–	2	2	4
Total	31	35	38	104

Appendix F

Battle of Jutland: Hits on British battleships and battle cruisers (heavy shells)

	11-inch	12-inch	Total
Barham	1	5	6
Warspite	2	13	15
Malaya	–	7	7
Colossus	2	–	2
Marlborough	–	–	hit by torpedo
Lion	–	13	13
Princess Royal	1	8	9
Queen Mary	4	3 (est)	7 (est)
Tiger	15	–	15
New Zealand	1	–	1
Indefatigable	5 (est)	–	5 (est)
Invincible	–	5	5 (est)
Total	31	54	85

Appendix G

Admiral Scheer's Report to the Kaiser of July 4 1916

The success achieved is due to the eagerness in attack, the efficient leadership through the subordinates, and the admirable deeds of the crews full of an eminently warlike spirit. It was only possible owing to the excellence of our ships and arms, the systematic peace-time training of the units, and the conscientious development on each individual ship. The rich experience gained will be carefully applied. The battle has proved that in the enlargement of our Fleet and the development of the different types of ships we have been guided by the right strategical and tactical ideas, and that we must continue to follow the same system. All arms can claim a share in the success. But, directly or indirectly, the far reaching heavy artillery of the great battleships was the deciding factor, and caused the greater part of the enemy's losses that are so far known, as also it brought the torpedo-boat flotillas to their successful attack on the ships of the Main Fleet. This does not detract from the merits of the flotillas in enabling the battleships to slip away from the enemy by their attack. The big ship – battleship and battle-cruiser – is therefore, and will be, the main strength of naval power. It must be further developed by increasing the gun calibre, by raising the speed, and by perfecting the armour and the protection below the water-line.

Finally, I beg respectfully to report to Your Majesty that by the middle of August the High Sea Fleet, with the exception of the *Derfflinger* and *Seydlitz,* will be ready for fresh action. With a favourable succession of operations the enemy may be made to suffer severely, although there can be no doubt that even the most successful result from a high sea battle will not compel England to made peace. The disadvantages of our geographical situation as compared with that of the Island Empire and the enemy's vast material superiority cannot be coped with to such a degree as to make us masters of the blockade inflicted on us, or even of the Island Empire itself, not even were all the U-boats to be available for military purposes. A victorious end to the war at not too distant a date can only be looked for by the crushing of English economic life through U-boat action against English commerce. Prompted by the convictions of duty, I earnestly advise Your Majesty to abstain from deciding on too lenient a form of procedure on the ground that it is opposed to military views, and that the risk of the boats would be out of all proportion to the expected gain, for, in spite of the greatest conscientiousness on the part of the Chiefs, it would not be possible in English waters, where American interests are so prevalent, to avoid occurrences which might force us to make humiliating concessions if we do not act with the greatest severity.

Appendix H

First British Communiqué, June 2 1916

On the afternoon of Wednesday May 31, a naval engagement took place off the coast of Jutland. The British ships on which the brunt of the fighting fell were the Battle Cruiser Fleet, and some cruisers and light cruisers supported by four fast battleships. Among those the losses were heavy. The German battlefleet, aided by low visibility, avoided prolonged action with our main forces, and soon after these appeared on the scene, the enemy returned to port, though not before receiving severe damage from our battleships. The Battle Cruisers *Queen Mary, Indefatigable, Invincible,* and the Cruisers *Defence* and *Black Prince* were sunk. The *Warrior* was disabled, and after being towed for some time, had to be abandoned by her crew. It is also known that the destroyers *Tipperary, Turbulent, Fortune, Sparrowhawk* and *Ardent* were lost, and six others are not yet accounted for. No British battleships or light cruisers were sunk. The enemy's losses were serious. At least one battle cruiser was destroyed, and one severely damaged; one battleship reported sunk by our destroyers during a night attack, two light cruisers were disabled and probably sunk. The exact number of enemy destroyers disposed of during the action cannot be ascertained with any certainty, but it must have been large.

Appendix I

German Communiqué, June 2 1916

During an enterprise directed northward our High Seas Fleet encountered on May 31 the main part of the English fighting Fleet, which was considerably superior to our own forces. During the afternoon a series of heavy engagements developed between Skagerrak and Horn Reefs, which were successful for us and which also continued during the whole of the night. In these engagements, as far as is known up to the present, were destroyed by us the large battleship *Warspite,* and battle cruisers *Queen Mary* and *Indefatigable*, two armoured cruisers apparently of the *Achilles* type, one small cruiser, the new flagships of the destroyer squadrons, the *Turbulent, Nestor* and *Acasta,* a large number of torpedo boats destroyers and one submarine. By observations, which are free from any objections, it was stated that a large number of English battleships suffered damage from our ships' artillery and from the attacks of our torpedo boat flotillas during the day and night engagements. Among others, the large battleship *Marlborough* was hit by a torpedo, as has been confirmed by prisoners. Several of our ships rescued portions of the crews of the sunk English ships, among whom were only two survivors of the *Indefatigable.* On our side the small cruiser *Wiesbaden* was sunk by hostile artillery fire during the day engagements and the *Pommern* during the night by a torpedo. The fate of the *Frauenlob,* which is missing, and of some torpedo boats which have not yet returned, is unknown. The High Seas Fleet returned to our ports during the day.

Appendix J

Second British Communiqué, June 5 1916

To Press Bureau for publication, 9 pm – Until the C-in-C, has had time to consult the officers engaged, and to write a full despatch, any attempt to give a detailed history of the naval engagement which began on afternoon of May 31 and ended in morning hours of June 1, would evidently be premature. But the results are quite plain. The Grand Fleet came in touch with the German High Seas Fleet at 3.30 on the afternoon of May 31. The leading ships of the two fleets carried on a vigorous fight, in which battle cruisers, fast battleships and subsidiary craft all took an active part. The losses were severe on both sides; but when the main body of the British fleet came into contact with the German High Seas Fleet, a very brief period sufficed to compel the latter, who had been severely punished, to seek refuge in their protected waters. This manoeuvre was rendered possible by low visibility and mist: and although the Grand Fleet were now and then able to get into momentary contact with their opponents, no continuous action was possible. They continued the pursuit until the light had wholly failed; when the British destroyers were able to make a successful attack upon the enemy during the night. Meanwhile, Sir John Jellicoe, having driven the enemy into port, returned to the main scene of action, and scoured the sea in search of disabled vessels. By noon the next day (June 1) it became evident that there was nothing more to be done. He returned, therefore, to his bases, four hundred miles away, re-fuelled his fleet, and in the evening of June 2 was again ready to put to sea. The British losses have already been fully stated, and there is nothing to add to, or subtract from the latest account published by the Admiralty. The enemy losses are less easy to determine. That the accounts they have given to the world are false, is certain and we cannot yet be sure of the exact truth. But from such evidence as has come to our knowledge, the Admiralty entertain no doubt that the German losses are heavier than the British – not merely relatively to the strength of the two fleets, but absolutely. There seems to be the strongest ground for supposing that included in the German losses are: two battleships, two Dreadnought battle cruisers of the most powerful type, two of the latest light cruisers (*Wiesbaden* and *Elbing*), a light cruiser of the *Rostock* type, the light cruiser *Frauenlob,* at least nine destroyers, and a submarine.

Notes

1 British Strategic Planning

1 'War Plans (War with Germany)'July 3 1914; Admiralty MSS; quoted Arthur J Marder, *From the Dreadnought to Scapa Flow* (London 1961) p 382
2 Marder, I p 372
3 'War Plans,' quoted Marder I pp 372-373
4 German Official History, *Der Krieg in der Nordsee* (Berlin 1920-1937) I p 56
5 Quoted Paul M Kennedy, *The Rise and Fall of British Naval Mastery* (London 1983) p 249
6 Alfred T Mahan, *The Influence of Sea Power upon the French Revolution and Empire 1793-1812* (London 1893 II p 118
7 Shawn T Grimes, *Strategy and War Planning in the British Navy 1887-1918* (Woodbridge 2012) p 8
8 Ibid, p 43
9 Ibid, p 37
10 Alfred T Mahan, *The Influence of Sea Power Upon History 1660-1783* (Boston 1894) pp 82, 138
11 Donald M Schurman, 'Julian Corbett's Influence on the Royal Navy's Perception of its Maritime Function' in *Mahan is Not Enough*, ed James Goldrick and John B Hallendorf (Newport RI 19993) p 57
12 Julian Corbett, *Some Principles of Maritime Strategy* (London 1911) p 91
13 P Haggie, ' The Royal Navy and War Planning in the Fisher Era' in *The War Plans of the Great Powers 1880-1914,* ed P Kennedy (London 1979) pp 120-121
14 Ibid, p 124
15 Ibid
16 Marder I p 330
17 Sir Percy Scott, *Fifty Years in the Royal Navy* (London 1919) pp 274-275
18 Quoted Marder, I p 334
19 Nicholas Black, *The British Naval Staff in the First World War* (Woodbridge 2009) pp 55-58
20 J Crossley, *The Hidden Threat*: *The Story of Mines and Minesweeping by the Royal Navy in World War 1* (Barnsley 2007) p 20
21 Marder, I pp 328-329
22 Black, pp 79
23 Quoted Marder, I p 356
24 Marder, I p 386

25 Sir J Corbett, *Naval Operations* (London 1920) I pp 2-3

2 The Development of the High Seas Fleet

1 Jonathan Steinberg, *Yesterday's Deterrent* (London 1965) pp 277-79
2 Ibid, p 79
3 Quoted Steinberg, pp 83-84
4 Holger Herwig, *'Luxury' Fleet: The Imperial German Navy 1888-1918* (London 1980) p 42
5 Ibid
6 Ibid, p 63
7 Fisher to Garvin, February 1909, quoted Peter Padfield, *The Great Naval Race* (London 1974) p 207
8 Michael Epkenhans, *Tirpitz: Architect of the German High Seas Fleet* (Washington DC 2008) p 43
9 Patrick J Kelly, *Tirpitz and the Imperial German Navy* (Bloomington Ind. 2011) p 64
10 Kelly, p 163
11 Terrell D Gottschall, *By Order of the Kaiser* (Annapolis Md. 2003) p 249
12 Gottschall, p 256
13 David Lloyd George, *War Memoirs* (London 1938) ii p 26
14 Quoted Padfield, p 281
15 Herwig, *'Luxury' Fleet*, p 80
16 Jan S Breemer, *The Burden of Trafalgar* (Newport RI 1993) p 33
17 Quoted Wolfgang Wegener, *The Naval Strategy of the World War* (Annapolis Md. 1989) p 13n
18 Epkenhans, p 54
19 Grand Admiral Alfred von Tirpitz, *My Memoirs* (London 1919) I p 239
20 Ibid, p 263
21 Admiral Reinhard Scheer, *Germany's High Sea Fleet in the World War* (London 1920) p 18
22 Mahan, *Influence of Sea Power;* quoted Holger H Herwig,, 'Germany and Mahan' in *The Influence of History on Mahan* (Newport,, RI 1991) p 78
23 Herbert Rosinski, *The Development of Naval Thought,* ed B Mitchell Simpson (Newport RI 1977) p 55
24 Scheer, p 21
25 Herwig, *' Luxury' Fleet*, p 145
26 Marder, I p 427
27 Wegener, pp 14-15
28 Alfred T Mahan, *Retrospect and Prospect* (London 1905) pp 165-167
29 Paul M Kenndy, *Strategy and Diplomacy 1870-1945* (London 1983) pp 154-160

3 Ships

1 HM Le Fleming, *Warships of World War 1: Battleships* (London 1959) p 23
2 Rene Greger, *Battleships of the World* (London 1997) p 99
3 Le Fleming, *Battleships* p 36
4 Greger, p 24

5 Oscar Parkes, *British Battleships* (London 1970) p 562
6 Greger, p 24
7 Ibid, 35
8 Ibid, p 36; L Fleming, *Battleships,* p 53
9 Greger, pp 44 and 98
10 Greger, p 45
11 Greger, p 36
12 Erich Gröner, *German Warships 1815-1945* (London 1990) I pp 25-27pp 28-30; Greger p 47
13 Gröner, 28-30; Greger p 47
14 Gröner, pp 18-21
15 *The Observer*, June 21 1908; quoted Marder, I p 69
16 Le Fleming, *Battleships,* p 45
17 Ibid
18 Ibid, p 46
19 Greger, p 111; Le Fleming, *Battleships,* p 49
20 Greger, p 37
21 Gröner, pp 53-54
22 Le Fleming, *Battleships*, p 22
23 Gröner, pp 56-57
24 Ibid, p 58
25 HM Le Fleming, *Warships of World War 1 Cruisers* (London nd) pp 43-51
26 Ibid, pp 64-69
27 Gröner, pp 107-109
28 Ibid, pp 110-111
29 Ibid, pp 112-113; Le Fleming, *Cruisers,* p 73
30 Gröner, pp 114-115
31 HM Le Fleming, *Warships of World War 1: Destroyers* (London n.d) 20
32 Ibid, pp 56-78

4 Men

1 Brian Lavery, *Able Seamen* (London 2011) p 154
2 Quoted Lavery, p 172
3 Lavery, p 179
4 Quoted Lavery, 179
5 Tirpitz, I p 148
6 Ibid
7 Holger H Herwig, *The German Naval Officer Corps* (Oxford 1973) pp 68-69
8 Quoted Lavery p 180
9 Marder, I p 412
10 Ibid, p 413
11 Richard Stumpf, *The Private War of Seaman Stumpf*, ed Daniel Horn (London 1969) p 418
12 Marder, I p 405
13 Commander Stephen King-Hall, *My Naval Life 1906-1929* (London 1952) pp 97-98
14 B Mc L Ranft, ed *The Beatty Papers*. (London 1989) I p 46 (cited as *Beatty Papers)*

15 Ibid, I p 50
16 Arthur J Marder, *Portrait of an Admiral* (London 1952) p 107 (cited hereafter as Richmond)
17 Ibid, III p 35
18 Winston S Churchill, *The World Crisis* (London 1923) I p 241
19 Arthur J Marder, ed, *Fear God and Dread Nought* (London 1952-1959) III p 100
20 Ibid, II p 20
21 Quoted Marder, II p 10
22 Ibid, I p 410
23 A Temple Patterson ed, *The Jellicoe Papers*, (London 1966) I p 30
24 Robert K Massie, *Castles of Steel* (London 1966) I p 30
25 Admiral Sir William Goodenough, *A Rough Record* (London 1943) p 91
26 Quoted Stephen Roskill, *Admiral of the Fleet Earl Beatty* (New York 1981) p 42
27 Marder II p 12
28 Ibid, II p 13
29 A Temple Patterson, *Tyrwhitt of the Harwich Force* (London 1973) p 34
30 Marder, II pp 14-15
31 Temple Patterson, *Tyrwhitt,* p 43
32 Marder, II p 14
33 Epkenhans, pp xi-xii
34 Ibid, p 60
35 Quoted Herwig, *German Naval Officer Corps*, p 77
36 Quoted Marder, III p 166
37 Admiral Georg von Müller, *The Kaiser and His Court* ed Walter Görlitz (London 1961) pp xviii-xxiv
38 Marder, ii p 166
39 Scheer, pp 39-40
40 Gary Weir, 'Reinhard Scheer' in *The Great Admirals*, ed J Sweetman (Annapolis Md.1997) pp 389-390
41 Quoted Weir, p 392
42 Ernst von Weizsäcker, *Memoirs* (London 1951) p 31
43 Scheer, p 135
44 Quoted Tobias R Philbin, *Admiral von Hipper* (Amsterdam 1982) p 16
45 Ibid, p 18
46 Grand Admiral Erich Raeder, *My Life* (Annapolis Md.1951) p 123
47 Carl-Axel Gemzell, *Organisation, Conflict and Innovation* (Lund 1973) p 123

5 Heligoland Bight

1 Marder, I pp 432-433
2 Ibid, II pp 5-6
3 Ibid, I p 424
4 WS Hewison, *This Great Harbour*: *Scapa Flow* Edinburgh 2005) p1
5 Eric Linklater, 'The First Attack,' quoted Hewison p 6
6 Quoted Hewison, p 26
7 Quoted Malcolm Brown and Patricia Meehan, *Scapa Flow* (London 2002) p 25

8 Ibid
9 Quoted Marder, I p 425
10 Scheer, p 25
11 Ivo Nikolai Lambi, *The Navy and German Power Politics 1862-1914* (Boston Mass. 1984) p 405
12 Quoted Eric W Osborne, *The Battle of Heligoland Bight* (Bloomington in 2008) p 31
13 *Beatty Papers*, 1 p 120
14 Scheer, p 37
15 Admiral of the Fleet Sir Roger Keyes, *Naval Memoirs* (London 1934) I pp 75-76
16 Corbett, I pp 99-100
17 Ibid, I p 100
18 Ibid, I p 101
19 James Goldrick, *The King's Ships were at Sea* (Annapolis) Md. 2004) pp 85-86
20 Osborne, p 46
21 Raeder, pp 46-47
22 Osborne, p 54; Goldrick p 87
23 Hector C Bywater, *Cruisers in Battle* (London 1939) p 50
24 Osborne, p 83
25 Ibid
26 Temple Patterson, *Tyrwhitt,* p 58
27 Osborne, p 87
28 Admiral of the Fleet Lord Chatfield, *The Navy and Defence* (London 1942) pp 124-125
29 Bywater, p 54
30 Stephen King-Hall, *Sea Saga*, ed L King-Hall (London 1935) p 382
31 Brigadier CF Aspinall-Oglander, *Roger Keyes* (London 1951) p 95
32 Bywater, p 59
33 Chatfield, p 125
34 *Beatty Papers* 1 p 121
35 Ibid, p 132
36 Müller, p 25
37 Scheer, p 56
38 Ibid, p 57
39 Paul G Halpern, ed, *The Keyes Papers*, (London 1972) I p 92 (cited as *Keyes Papers)*
40 Richmond, p 102
41 Ibid, pp 105-106

6 Intelligence

1 *Keyes Papers*. I p 76-77
2 Marder, II p 57
3 Goldrick p 127
4 Ibid, pp 127-131; Corbett, I pp 175-176
5 Goldrick, pp 132-133
6 Alan Coles, *Three Before Breakfast* (Havant 1979) p 145
7 Ricnmond, p 110

8 Admiral Viscount Jellicoe, *The Grand Fleet 1914-1916* (London 1919) p 98
9 Jellicoe, *Grand Fleet,* pp 144-145
10 Admiralty, Naval Staff Monograph, xi p 110
11 Paul Schmalenbach, *German Raiders* (Cambridge 19790 p 144; Goldrick, p 139; Corbett I pp 242-426
12 Corbett, I pp 239-249; Goldrick pp 139-140
13 Corbett, I pp 242
14 Goldrick, p 142
15 Jellicoe, *Grand Fleet,* p 153
16 Goldrick, p 141
17 VE Tarrrant, *Jutland: The German Perspective* (London 1995) p26
18 Scheer, p 67
19 Gemzell, p 178
20 Patrick Beesly, *Room 40: British Naval Intelligence 1914-1918* (London 1982) pp 5-6
21 Admiral Sir William James, *A Great Seaman* (London 1956) pp 128-129
22 Quoted Beesly, p 24
23 Ibid, p 24

7 Churchill and Fisher

1 Marder, II pp 88-89
2 *Beatty Papers,* i p 151
3 Richmond, p 125
4 *Beatty Papers,* I p 164
5 Tarrant, p 31
6 Tirpitz, II p 496
7 Scheer, pp 71-72
8 Corbett, II p 45
9 *Beatty Papers,* I pp 186-191
10 Rear Admiral WS Chalmers, *The Life and Letters of David Beatty* (London 1951) p 175
11 Richmond, pp 130-131
12 Corbett, II p 57-59; Mark Potts and Tony Marks, *Before the Bells have Faded* (Eastbourne 2004) pp 40-44
13 Richmond, p 134
14 Quoted Marder, II p 99
15 *Fear God and Dread Nought,* III p 126
16 Ibid, III p 111
17 Ibid, III p 82

8 The Dogger Bank

1 Raeder, pp 53-54
2 Goldrick, p 249
3 Tobias R Philbin, *The Battle of Dogger Bank* (Bloomington Ind. 2014) pp 109-111
4 Philbin, *Dogger Bank,* p115

5 Goldrick, p 249
6 Raeder, p 54
7 Beesly, p 57
8 Churchill, *World Crisis*, II p 129
9 Tarrant, p 54
10 Captain H von Waldeyer-Hartz, *Von Hipper* (London 1933) pp 148-149
11 Tarrant, p 54
12 Goldrick, p 256
13 Chartfield, pp 132-133
14 Waldeyer-Hartz, p 152
15 Tarrant, p 36
16 Goldrick, p 287
17 Hipper's despatch, quoted Waldeyer-Hartz, p 153
18 Filson Young, *With the Battle Cruisers* (London 1921) pp 174-175
19 Admiral Sir Henry Pelly, *300,000 Sea Miles: An Autobiography* (London 1938) pp 148-149
20 Goldrick, p 275
21 Corbett, II p 97
22 Hipper's despatch, quoted Waldeyer-Hartz, p 153
23 Raeder, p 56
24 Temple Patterson, p 107
25 Corbett, II pp 97-98
26 Douglas Robinson, *The Zeppelin in Combat* (Henley on Thames 1971) p 82
27 Beatty to Jellicoe, *Jellicoe Papers*. II p 32
28 Quoted Marder, II p 167
29 Captain Geoffrey Bennett, *Naval Battles of the First World War* (London 1968) p 167
30 Andrew Gordon, *The Rules of the Game* (London 1996) p 95
31 quoted Marder, II p 168
32 Marder, II p 169
33 Keyes, *Naval Memoirs*, I p 163
34 Philbin, *Dogger Bank*, p 93
35 Quoted Marder, II p 169
36 *Beatty Papers*, I p 231
37 Scheer, p 86
38 quoted Philbin, *Dogger Bank*, p 115
39 Gemzell, pp 176-177
40 Tirpitz, III p 471
41 Ibid, III p 473
42 Müller, p 38
43 Quoted Gemzell, p 181
44 Gemzell, p 182
45 Müller, pp 60-61
46 Tirpitz, II pp 502-503
47 Gemzell, p 183
48 Philbin, *Dogger Bank*, pp 113-114
49 *Beatty Papers*. I pp 223-226

9 Balfour and Jackson

1 Marder, *Fear God and Dread Nought*, III p 133
2 Marder, ii p 211
3 Richmond, p 140
4 Quoted Alan Moorehead, *Gallipoli*, (London 1956) p 69
5 Moorehead p 93
6 Quoted Marder, II p 281
7 Ibid, p 288
8 Quoted Ruddock MacKay, *Balfour* (London 1985) p 273
9 Marder, II p 291
10 Ibid, p 290
11 Ibid, p 291
12 Lord Hankey, *The Supreme Command* (London 1961) I p 335
13 Diary entry, February 24 1916, Hamilton Papers, National Maritime Museum
14 Marder, II p 195
15 Scott, p 292
16 Scheer, pp 87-88
17 Müller, p 61
18 Quoted Tirpitz, II pp 378-379
19 Tirpitz, II 382-383
20 Quoted Halpern, p 288
21 Scheer, p 89
22 Waldeyer-Hartz, p 176
23 RH Gibson and Maurice Prendergast, *The German Submarine War 1914-1918* (London 1931) p 23
24 Quoted Marder, I p 363
25 Corbett, II p132
26 Marder, II p343
27 Ibid, p 344
28 Ibid, p 346
29 Wegener, pp 133-134
30 Gemzell, p 196
31 Wegener, p xxiii
32 Ibid, p 185
33 Ibid, p 193
34 Ibid, p 198
35 Gemzell, p 232
36 Wegener, p xxx
37 Tirpitz, II p 413
38 Müller, p 103
39 Gemzell, p 82
40 Ibid, p 123
41 Philbin, *Dogger Bank*, p 123
42 Scheer, p 95

10 Scheer Takes Over

1 Tripitz, II 456
2 Philbin, *Hipper*, pp 73-76
3 Ibid, p 102
4 Ibid, p 124
5 Waldeyer-Hartz, pp 192-193
6 Philbin, *Hipper*, p 103
7 Ibid, pp 69-70
8 Scheer, pp 98-99
9 Ibid, 101
10 Corbett, III pp 274-275
11 Müller, p 138
12 Tarrant, pp 44-45
13 Corbett, III pp 288-289
14 Ibid, p 295
15 *Jellicoe Papers*, 1 p 207
16 Richmond, pp 202-203
17 *Jellicoe Papers*, I p 157; *Beatty Papers*, I pp 286-297
18 *Beatty Papers*, I p 157
19 Black, p 150
20 Ibid, p 151
21 Ibid, p 152
22 C Ernest Fayle, *Seaborne Trade* (London 1923) I p 127
23 Halpern, p 304
24 Ibid
25 Müller pp 142-143
26 Quoted Epkenhans, p 67
27 Müller, p 146
28 Corbett, III pp 298-290
29 Beesly, p 148
30 *Jellicoe Papers*, II p 242
31 Corbett, III p 306
32 Quoted Waldeyer-Hartz, pp 196-197
33 Tarrant, p 48; Corbett, iii pp 308-309; Halpern, p 313
34 Quoted Waldeyer-Hartz, p 197
35 Marder, II pp 425-426
36 *Jellicoe Papers*, I p 240
37 Quoted Marder, II p 432
38 Corbett, II p 316
39 Richmond, pp 208-209
40 Corbett, II p 313
41 Quoted Marder, II p 434
42 Ibid, p 428
43 *Beatty Papers*, I pp 307-308

44 Corbett, II p 317
45 *Jellicoe Papers*, I p 311

11 Eve of Battle

1 Müller, pp 147-148
2 Corbett, II p 286
3 Müller, p 151
4 Ibid, p 160
5 Halpern, p 309
6 Müller, pp 162-164
7 Quoted Marder, II p 429
8 *Der Krieg in der Nordsee*, V pp 189-190; quoted Tarrant, pp 49-50
9 Scheer, p 133
10 Marder, III p 37
11 Ibid, II p 445
12 Quoted Marder, II p 447
13 Admiral Sir R H Bacon, *The Life of John Rushworth, Earl Jellicoe* (London 1936) p 244
14 Beesly, p 152
15 Tarrant, p 273
16 Beesly, pp 152-153
17 Quoted Marder, III p 45
18 James, p 155
19 Marder, III p 39
20 Gordon, p 354
21 *Jellicoe Papers*, pp 241-242
22 John Horsfield, *The Art of Leadership in War* (Westport, Conn. 1980) p 115
23 Quoted Marder, III p 31
24 Bennett, p 65

12 Enemy in Sight

1 Jellicoe, *Grand Fleet*, p 297
2 Ibid, p 298-299
3 Commander H H Frost, *The Battle of Jutland* (Annapolis Md. 1964) p 125
4 Marder, III p 47
5 Frost, pp 125-126
6 Commodore G von Schoultz, *With the British Battle Fleet* (London n.d) p 112
7 Stumpf, p 1916
8 Frost, p 116
9 Hase, p 69
10 Ibid, p 73
11 Weizsäcker, p 31
12 Waldeyer-Hartz, p 203
13 Quoted Gordon, p 72

14 Ibid, p 73
15 Blake, p 162
16 Corbett, III p 326
17 Marder, III p 73
18 Marder, III p 43
19 Gordon, p 415
20 Langhorne Gibson and Vice Admiral JET Harper, *The Riddle of Jutland* (London 1934) p 140
21 Marder, III p 49
22 Gordon, p 68
23 Gordon, p 98
24 Corbett, III p 328
25 Tarrant, p 65
26 HW Fawcett and GWW Hooper, *The Fighting at Jutland* (London 1920) pp 9-10
27 Gordon, p 87
28 Marder, III p 53
29 Roskill, p 155
30 Quoted Admiral Sir FC Dreyer, *The Sea Heritage* (London 1955) pp 164-165
31 Jellicoe, *Grand Fleet*, pp 323-324
32 Dreyer, p 124

13 'Something wrong with our Bloody Ships today'

1 Waldeyer-Hartz, p 204
2 Raeder, p 66
3 Hase, p 80-81
4 *Beatty Papers,* I p 326
5 John Brooks, *Dreadnought Gunnery and the Battle of Jutland* (London 2005) p 238
6 Frost, p 177
7 *Der Krieg in der Nordsee*, V p 235
8 Frost, p 195; Marder, III p 58
9 Chatfield, p 141
10 Hase, pp 83
11 Ibid, pp 83-84
12 Corbett, III p 334
13 Chatfield, p 142
14 Waldeyer-Hartz p 205
15 Ibid
16 Frost, p 201
17 Corbett, III p 335
18 Fawcett and Hooper, pp 28-29
19 Quoted Gordon, p 115
20 *Der Krieg in der Nordsee*, V p 65
21 Hase, pp 90-91
22 Fawcett and Hooper, pp 31-32

23 Chatfield, p 143
24 John Campbell, *Jutland: An Analysis of the Fighting* (London 1986) pp 78-95
25 Captain T Dorling ('Taffrail') *Endless Story* (London 1932) p 155
26 Corbett, III p 339
27 Frost, p 235
28 Ibid, p 251
29 Goodenough, p 95
30 Marder, III p 62
31 Corbett, III p 340
32 Gordon, p 127
33 Ibid, pp 127-128
34 Ibid, p 131
35 Ibid, pp 134-141
36 Weizsäcker, p 31
37 Tarrant, p 288
38 Jellicoe, *Grand Fleet*, p 323
39 Ibid, p 330
40 Schoultz, p 118
41 Frost, p 190

14 The Run to the North

1 Campbell, p 98
2 Correlli Barnett, *The Swordbearers* (London 1963) p 153
3 Marder, III p 62
4 Rear Admiral JET Harper, *The Truth About Jutland* (London 1927) pp 69-70
5 Brooks, p 255
6 Frost, p 253
7 Hase, p 96
8 Ibid
9 *Der Krieg in der Nordsee*, V pp 262-263
10 Corbett, III p 344
11 Frost, p 258
12 *Der Krieg in der Nordsee* V pp 265-266
13 Marder, III p 75
14 Corbett, III p 354
15 Fawcett and Hooper, p 240
16 Frost, p 276
17 Corbett, III pp 355-356
18 Frost, p 292
19 Ibid, pp 295-296
20 *Der Krieg in der Nordsee*, V p 268
21 Ibid, p 280; Marder III p 76
22 Quoted Marder, p 76
23 Jellicoe, *The Admiralty Narrative of the Battle of Jutland*, quoted Marder, p 77

24 Frost, p 303
25 Ibid, pp 303-304
26 Dreyer, p 146
27 Corbett, III p 361
28 Jellicoe, *Grand Fleet*, pp 348-349
29 Quoted Marder, III p 90
30 Frost, p 306
31 Captain Geoffrey Bennett, *The Battle of Jutland* (London 1964) p 106
32 *Der Krieg in der Nordsee,* V pp 283-284
33 Marder. III p 93
34 Harper, pp 82-83
35 David Allen Butler, *Distant Victory* (Westport Conn. 2006) p 163

15 The Fleets Engage

1 Chatfield, p 145
2 Marder, III p 98
3 Chatfield, p 146
4 Hase, p 100
5 Fawcett and Hooper, p 157
6 Goodenough, p 96
7 Fawcett and Hooper, p 166
8 *Der Krieg in der Nordsee*, V p 295
9 Tarrant, p 133
10 Marder, III p 99
11 Hase, p 103
12 Fawcett and Hooper, p 250
13 Gordon, p 455
14 Admiral Sir Geoffrey Blake to Professor Marder, August 15 1963; quoted Marder, III pp 100-101
15 Gordon, p 409
16 Fawcett and Hooper, pp 40-41
17 Scheer, p 151
18 *Der Krieg in der Nordsee*, V p 298
19 Ibid, p 299
20 Ibid, p 300
21 Ibid, p 300n
22 Quoted Frost, p 328
23 Jellicoe, *Grand Fleet*, pp 404-405
24 *Der Krieg in der Nordsee*, V p 301
25 Marder, III p 102
26 Dreyer, p 168
27 Quoted Dreyer, p 132
28 Corbett, III p 372
29 Waldeyer-Hartz, p 215

30 Raeder, pp 69-70
31 Frost, p 335
32 Campbell, p 198
33 Scheer, p155
34 Corbett, III pp 374-375
35 Marder, III p 111
36 Weizsäcker, pp 32-33
37 Gordon, p 458
38 Gary Weir, 'Reinhard Scheer' in *The Great Admirals* ed J Sweetman Annapolis, Md. 1997) p399
39 Frost, pp 312-313
40 Ibid, pp 346-437
41 *Der Krieg in der Nordsee*, V pp 310-312
42 Ibid, p 313

16 The Second Engagement

1 Corbett, III p 376
2 Tarrant, p 153
3 *Der Krieg in der Nordsee*, V p 316
4 Ibid, p317
5 Harper, p 99
6 Roskill, p 176
7 Marder, iii p 131
8 Frost, p 354
9 Ibid, pp 353-354
10 Campbell, pp 218-246
11 Hase, pp 112-113
12 Ibid, p 113
13 Fawcett and Hooper,, p 185
14 *Der Krieg in der Nordsee*, V p 320
15 Frost, p 370
16 Marder, III p 114
17 Chatfield, p 148
18 Roskill, p 173
19 Frost, pp 374-375
20 Ibid, pp 375-376
21 Gordon, pp 464-465
22 *Der Krieg in der Nordsee*, V pp 332-333
23 Marder, III p 138
24 Ibid, p 123; Harper, p105
25 Gordon, pp 467
26 Marder, III p 124
27 Harper, p106
28 Quoted Marder, III p 126

29 Marder, III p 126
30 Raeder, p 71
31 *Der Krieg in der Nordsee*, V p 345
32 Hase, p 119
33 Tarrant, pp 173-174
34 Corbett, III p 388
35 Bennett, p 126
36 Jellicoe, *Grand Fleet*, pp 374
37 *Der Krieg in der Nordsee*, V pp 350-351

17 Night

1 *Der Krieg in der Nordsee*, V p 356
2 Tarrant, p 285
3 Frost, p 419
4 Ibid, p 420
5 Tarrant, pp 184-185
6 *Der Krieg in der Nordsee*, V pp 357-358
7 Corbett, III p 391
8 Marder, III p 136
9 Frost, p 431
10 Commander Stephen King Hall, *A North Sea Diary 1914-1918* (London n.d) pp 150-151
11 Fawcett and Hooper, p 303
12 *Der Krieg in der Nordsee*, V p 366
13 *Official Despatches, Battle of Jutland* (London 1920) p 114
14 Frost, p 435
15 *Official Despatches*, p 93
16 Quoted Tarrant, pp 195-196
17 Schoultz, p 149
18 Frost, p 436
19 Marder, III p 149
20 Beesly, p 161
21 Ibid
22 Marder, III p 152
23 Ibid, p 150
24 James, p 155
25 Gibson and Harper, pp 219-220
26 Corbett, III 395
27 Frost, p 439
28 Ibid, p 443
29 Corbett, III p 394
30 Ibid, p 396
31 Ibid, p 397
32 Frost, p 447
33 Dorling, p 184

34 Ibid, p 206
35 Bacon, p 288
36 Fawett and Hooper, pp 340-341
37 Frost, pp 451-452
38 *Der Krieg in der Nordsee*, V p 377
39 Ibid
40 Fawcett and Hooper, p 342
41 Dorling, pp 196-199
42 Hase, p 121
43 Fawcett and Hooper, pp 381-382
44 Dreyer, 151
45 Bacon, p 291
46 *Official Despatches*, pp 219-220
47 Frost, p 462
48 *Official Despatches*, pp 224-225

18 Dawn

1 Tarrant, pp 212-213
2 Frost, p 474
3 Fawcett and Hooper, p 380
4 Quoted Bennett, p 146
5 Frost, p 474
6 Tarrant, p 218
7 Fawcett and Hooper, pp 387-388
8 Frost, p 491
9 Tarrant, p 222
10 *Official Despatches*, pp 224-225
11 Jellicoe, *Grand Fleet*, pp 383
12 Ibid, pp 384-385
13 *Der Krieg in der Nordsee*, V p 400
14 Ibid, pp 401-402
15 Frost, pp 479-480
16 *Der Krieg in der Nordsee*, V p 403
17 Tarrant, p 226
18 Ibid, p 227
19 *Official Despatches*, p 225
20 *Der Krieg in der Nordsee*, V p 406
21 *Official Despatches*, p 225
22 Fawcett and Hooper, p 398
23 *Der Krieg in der Nordsee*, V p 408
24 *Official Despatches*, p 488
25 *Der Krieg in der Nordsee*, V p 411
26 Corbett, III pp 416
27 *Der Krieg in der Nordsee*, V p 412

28 Ibid, pp 413-414
29 ibid, p 418
30 Corbett, III, p 418
31 Ibid, p 421
32 Ibid, p 424

19 Aftermath

1 Fawcett and Hooper, p 399
2 Ibid, p 400
3 Chalmers, p 262
4 Quoted Max Arthur, *The True Glory: The Royal Navy 1914-1939* (London 1996) p 83
5 Marder, III p 195
6 Quoted Brown and Meehan, p 101
7 *Beatty Papers*, I p 321
8 Sir Douglas Brownrigg, *Indiscretions of the Naval Censor* (London 1920) pp 49-50
9 *Beatty Papers*, I p 340
10 *Jellicoe Papers*, I p 265
11 Ibid, p 271
12 Quoted Gordon, p 498
13 *Jellicoe Papers*. I p 279
14 Ibid, p 272
15 Marder, III pp 196-197
16 *Jellicoe Papers*, I p 267; *Beatty Papers* I p 335
19 *Jellicoe Papers*, I p 268
18 Fawcett and Hooper, p 4
19 Leopold S Amery, *My Political Life* (London 1953-1955, 3 vols) II p 258
20 Rear Admiral Dannreuther, Letter to Professor Marder, November 5 1962, quoted Marder, III p 193
21 *Beatty Papers*, I 369
22 Marder, III p 192
23 Richmond, p 213
24 Ibid, p 352
25 Churchill, III p 112
26 Weizsäcker, p 32
27 Scheer, p 167n
28 *Der Krieg in der Nordsee*, V p 420; Marder, III p 197
29 Quoted Tarrant, pp 247; Robert K Massie, *Castles of Steel* (London 2004) p 659
30 Quoted Philbin, *Hipper*, p 137
31 Quoted Tarrant, p 233
32 King-Hall, p 167
33 Quoted Christopher M Bell, *Churchill and Sea Power* (Oxford 2013) p 77
34 Nicholas Wolz, *From Imperial Splendour to Internment* (Barnsley 2015) p 113
35 Ibid, p 120
36 Jellicoe, *Grand Fleet* pp 434-425

37 Marder, III p 192n
38 Newbolt, IV p 21
39 Quoted Marder, III p 192

20 Who won at Jutland?

1 Frost, p 505
2 Ibid, p 506
3 Ibid, p 509
4 Gordon, p 562
5 Frost, p 511
6 Ibid, pp 512-513
7 Ibid, p 513
8 Corbett, III p 418
9 Newbolt, IV p 1
10 Ibid, p 9
11 Marder, III p 204
12 Ibid, p 205
13 Tarrant, p 249
14 Halpern, p 238
15 Gordon, p 562
16 Bacon, pp 306-307
17 Butler, p 189
18 Massie, p 665
19 Jon Sutherland and Diane Canwell, *The Battle of Jutland* (Barnsley 2007) p 175
20 George Bonney, *The Battle of Jutland* (Stroud 2002) pp 207-208
21 John Costello and Terry Hughes, *Jutland 1916* (London 1976) pp 236-237
22 Hase, p 126
23 Nigel Steel and Peter Hart, *Jutland 1916* (London) p 425
24 Keith Yates, *Flawed Victory* (London 2000) p 223
25 Harper, pp 192-193
26 Gibson and Harper p 249
27 Commander Carlyon Bellairs, *The Battle of Jutland* (London n.d) pp 265-266
28 Schoultz, p 183
29 Ibid, p 186
30 Brooks, pp 284
31 Ibid, pp 297-298
32 Campbell, p 337
33 Nicholas Jellicoe, *Jutland: The Unfinished Battle* (Barnsley 2016) p 338
34 Quoted Jörg Hillman, 'Remembering the Battle of Jutland in Germany' in *Jutland : World War 1's Greatest Naval Battle*, eds Michael Epkenhans, Jörg Hillman and Frank Nägler (Lexington, k Ky 2015) p 333
35 Werner Rahm, 'The Battle of Jutland from the German Perspective' in *Jutland: World War 1's Greatest Naval Battle*, pp 187-192
36 Angus Konstam, *Jutland 1916: Twelve Hours to Win the War* (London 2016) p 321

37 Quoted Gary Staff, *Skagerrak: The Battle of Jutland Through German Eyes* (Barnsley 2016) p 241
38 John Brooks, *The Battle of Jutland* (Cambridge 2016) pp 514-543
39 Barnett, pp 182-183
40 Bennett, ppp 160-161
41 Captain Donald McIntyre, *Jutland* (London 1957) pp 202-203; Marder, III p 186
42 Marder, III p 186
43 Quoted Marder, III p 194

21 Lessons

1 Marder, III p 213
2 Dreyer, p 205
3 Jellicoe, *Grand Fleet*, pp 420-421
4 Chatfield, pp 150-151
5 Dreyer, p 205
6 Jellicoe, *Grand Fleet*, p 419
7 Marder, III p 218
8 Chatfield, pp 151-152
9 Ibid, p 154
10 Ibid, p 157
11 Dreyer, p 234
12 Admiral Sir William James, *The Eyes of the Navy* (London 1955) p 119
13 Jellicoe, *Grand Fleet*, p 428
14 Newbolt, IV p 15
15 Ibid, IV p 16
16 Jellicoe, *Grand Fleet*, p 409
17 Marder, III pp 223-225
18 Ibid, p 227
19 Quoted Marder, III p 227
20 Marder, III p 228
21 Quoted Marder, III p 229
22 *Beatty Papers*, I pp 367-369
23 Scheer, p 169
24 Herwig, *'Luxury' Fleet,* pp 186-189
25 Raeder, p 74

22 The August Sortie

1 Marder, III p 235
2 Scheer, p 180
3 Newbolt, IV p 31
4 Scheer, p 180
5 Schoultz, pp 188-189
6 Keyes, *Naval Memoirs*, II p 73

7 *Jellicoe Papers*, II p 41
8 Ibid, p 43
9 Beesly, p 165
10 Ibid
11 Scheer, p 180
12 Naval Staff Monograph, p 95
13 Dreyer, p 200
14 Naval Staff Monograph pp 95-96
15 Schoultz, p 193
16 Ibid, pp 193-193
17 Temple Patterson, *Tyrwhitt*, p 170
18 Naval Staff Monograph, p 99
19 Marder, III p 239
20 Naval Staff Monograph, p 100
21 Scheer, p 181
22 Marder, III p 241
23 Churchill, *World Crisis*, III p 163
24 Jellicoe, *Grand Fleet*, p 439
25 Dreyer, p 201
26 Newbolt, IV p 36
27 Naval Staff Monograph, p 106
28 Ibid, p 102
29 Scheer, p 182
30 Naval Staff Monograph, p 30
31 Marder, III p 243
32 Scheer, p 182
33 Quoted Marder, III p 243
34 Newbolt, IV p 41
35 Naval Staff Monograph, p 104
36 Jellicoe, *Grand Fleet*, p 442
37 Naval Staff Monograph, p 109
38 Jellicoe, *Grand Fleet*, p 443
39 Newbolt, IV p 47
40 Ibid, p 43
41 Scheer, pp 183-184
42 Marder, III p 243
43 Temple Patterson, *Tyrwhitt*, p 43
44 Frost, pp 522-523
45 *Der Krieg in der Nordsee*, VII p 60
46 Marder, III p 245

23 Strategic Changes

1 Jellicoe, *Grand Fleet*, p 448
2 *Jellicoe Papers*, II p 66

3 Quoted Marder, IIII p 249
4 *Jellicoe Papers*, II p 47
5 Ibid, p 45
6 Ibid, p 36
7 Ibid, p 71
8 Ibid, pp 73-83
9 Quoted Marder, III p 30
10 Ibid, pp 253-254
11 *Jellicoe Papers*, II p 72
12 Newbolt, IV p 47
13 Quoted Marder, III p 251
14 *Jellicoe Papers*, II p 76
15 Richmond, pp 219-220
16 Naval Staff Monograph, pp 93-94
17 Ibid, pp 124-126
18 Scheer, p 186
19 Ibid, p 186-187
20 *Der Krieg in der Nordsee*, VI p 135
21 Jellicoe, *Grand Fleet*, p 454
22 Newbolt, IV p 51
23 Marder, III p 256
24 Scheer, p 192

24 The Submarine Threat

1 Tirpitz, I p 138
2 Quoted Dan van der Vat, *Stealth at Sea* (London 1994) p 59
3 Scheer, pp 223-224
4 Van der Vat, p 59
5 Gibson and Prendergast, p 25
6 Müller, pp 162-164
7 Scheer, p 243
8 Müller, pp 174-175
9 Ibid, p 189
10 Scheer, p 245
11 Müller, p 199
12 John Terraine, *Business in Great Waters* (London 1990) p 12
13 Scheer, p 247
14 Gibson and Prendergast, p 115
15 Ibid, p 114
16 *Jellicoe Papers*, III p 87
17 Ibid, p 89
18 Ibid, p 91
19 Mackay, *Balfour*, p 299
20 Marder, III p 278

21 Quoted Marder, III p 278
22 Black, p 168
23 Quoted Marder, III p 282
24 Quoted Stephen Roskill, *Hankey: Man of Secrets* (London 1970) I p 315
25 Marder, III p 282
26 Quoted Marder, III pp 282-283
27 Roskill, *Hankey*, p 315

25 The Dover Straits

1 Scheer, p 187
2 Mark D Karau, *The Naval Flank of the Western Front* (Barnsley 2014) p 75
3 Newbolt, IV p 53
4 Ibid, pp 54-55
5 Ibid, pp 54-56
6 Ibid, p 60
7 Ibid, pp 60-63
8 Ibid, p 64
9 Admiral Sir RH Bacon, *The Concise Story of the Dover Patrol* (London 1932) p121
10 Marder, III p 259
11 Quoted Marder, III p 260
12 Ibid, pp 260-261
13 Quoted Mackay, *Balfour*, p 302
14 *Jellicoe Papers*, II p 94
15 Marder, III p 286
16 *Jellicoe Papers*, II p 104
17 Ibid, p 105
18 Ibid, pp 107-108
19 Quoted Roskill, *Beatty*, p 201
20 *Beatty Papers*, I pp 384-385
21 Jellicoe, *Grand Fleet*, pp 462-463
22 Lloyd George, I p 597

26 The Northern Patrol

1 Louis Guichard, *The Naval Blockade* 1914-1918 (London 1930) p 13
2 Ibid, p 14
3 Ibid, pp 17-18
4 Ibid, p 21
5 John D Grainger, *The Maritime Blockade of Germany in the Great War: The Northern Patrol*, 1914-1918 (Aldershot 2003) p 27
6 Admiral Sir D de Chair, *The Sea is Strong* (London 1961) p 167
7 Grainger, p 58
8 De Chair, pp 183-184
9 Corbett, II p 51

10 A Cecil Hampshire, *The Blockaders* (London 1980) p 48
11 de Chair, pp 210-121
12 Commander Hon. Barry Bingham, *Falklands, Jutland and the Bight* (London 1919) p 39
13 de Chair, pp 190-191
14 Ibid, p 191
15 Grainger, pp 4-5
16 Ibid, pp 12-13
17 Hampshire, p 66
18 De Chair, pp 203-204
19 Grainger, p 769
20 Ibid, p 380
21 Ibid, p 338
22 Guichard, p 57
23 Ibid, p 61
24 Ibid, p 63
25 Grainger, pp 383-389; Hampshire, pp 67-70
26 Grainger, p 390
27 De Chair, p 218
28 Schmalenbach, pp 137-138;Newbolt, pp 176-191
29 Edwin P Hoyt, *The Elusive Seagull* (London 1970) p 206
30 Grainger, pp 636-636
31 Newbolt, IV p 194
32 Grainger, pp 412-413
33 Ibid, p 413n
34 Ibid, p 438
35 Quoted Marder, IV p 40
36 *Jellicoe Papers,* II pp 141-142
37 Ibid, pp 143-144
38 Grainger, pp 775-783
39 Guichard, pp 311-312
40 Quoted Guichard, p 311
41 Grainger, p 22

27 Tyrwhitt and the Harwich Force

1 Marder II p 14
2 Quoted Patterson, *Tyrwhitt,* p 54
3 Patterson, *Tyrwhitt,* p 142
4 Ibid, p 110
5 Corbett, II p 51
6 Quoted Patterson *Tyrwhitt*, p 98
7 Admiral Sir Barry Domvile, *By and Large* (London 1936) pp 72-73
8 Patterson, *Tyrwhitt,* p 135
9 Dorling, pp 126
10 Newbolt, IV pp 28-19

11 Patterson, *Tyrwhitt*, p 168
12 Dorling, p 125
13 Ibid, p 134
14 Admiral of the Fleet Viscount Jellicoe, *The Crisis of the Naval War* (London 1920) pp 219-220
15 Newbolt, IV pp 74-75
16 Ibid, pp 76-77
17 Patterson, *Tyrwhitt*, p 179
18 Dorling pp 111-112
19 Newbolt, iv p 79
20 Patterson, *Tyrwhitt*, pp 179-180
21 Ibid, p 196
22 Ibid, p 201
23 Ibid, p 207
24 Quoted Patterson, *Tyrwhitt*, p 102
25 Paul Halpern, ed, *The Keyes Papers* (London 1972) I p 145n
26 Keyes Papers, I p 144-145
27 Patterson, p 152
28 Ibid, p 181
29 Ibid, p 182
30 *Keyes Papers*, I p 516

28 New Ships, New Men, New Strategy

1 Winston Churchill, *Great Contemporaries* (London 1941) p 300
2 Marder, II p94
3 John Roberts, *Battle Cruisers* (London 1997) p 46
4 Quoted Roberts, p 47
5 Marder, *Fear God*, III p 110
6 Roberts, p 104
7 *Jellicoe Papers*, II p 22
8 Ibid, III p 187
9 Roberts, p 51
10 Le Fleming, *Battleships*, p 49
11 Keyes, *Memoirs*, I p 130
12 Marder, *Fear God*, III p 66
13 HM Le Fleming, *Submarines* (London n.d) p 28
14 Le Fleming, *Destroyers* pp 28-30
15 Mackay, *Balfour*, p 468
16 Le Fleming, *Submarines*, p 41
17 Marder, IV p 53
18 *Beatty Papers*, I p 397
19 Ibid, II p 451
20 Ibid, I p 512
21 Quoted Roskill, Beatty p 220
22 Madden to Lady Jellicoe, February 17 1918 quoted Marder IV p 29n

23 *Beatty Papers*, I p 433
24 Gordon, p 538
25 Quoted Marder, IV p 59
26 Lloyd George, I pp 607-608
27 Marder, IV p 56
28 *Beatty Papers*, I p 386
29 Richmond, p 227
30 Ibid, p 278
31 Marder, *Fear God*, III p 334
32 Marder, IV p 53
33 Herwig, *'Luxury' Fleet,* p 224
34 Scheer, pp 328-329
35 Gemzell, p 187n
36 Müller, p 148
37 Gemzell, p 240
38 Herwig, *'Luxury' Fleet*, pp 202-203
39 Müller, p 199
40 Scheer, p 247
41 Müller, p 204
42 Scheer, pp 248-252
43 Quoted Newbolt, IV pp 268-269
44 Müller, p 231
45 Scheer, pp 254-255
46 Müller, p 236
47 Marder, IV, pp 51

29 The Convoy Debate

1 John Winton, *Convoy* (London 1983) p 14
2 Marder, IV p 116
3 Alfred T Mahan, *The Influence of Sea Power Upon the French Revolution and Empire 1793-1812* (London 1893) II p 217
4 Winton, pp 16
5 Lloyd George, I p 670
6 Ibid, pp 679
7 Quoted Winton, pp 18-19
8 Ibid, p 20
9 Ibid
10 Ibid, p 21
11 Quoted ibid, p 24
12 Ibid
13 Corbett, *Maritime Strategy*, p 266
14 Ibid
15 Marder, IV pp 117-118
16 Winton, p 31

17 Lloyd George, I p 681
18 Quoted Winton, p 47
19 Roskill, *Hankey* I p 355
20 Newbolt, V pp 27-28
21 Roskill, *Hankey,* I p 357
22 Newbolt, V p 10
23 Ibid, p 15
24 Marder, IV, p 109
25 Marder, *Fear God*, III p 428
26 Ibid, pp 429-431
27 Marder, IV, p 113
28 Newbolt, V p 28
29 Naval Staff Monograph, *Home Waters: December 1916–April 1917*, p 182
30 Marder, IV p 141
31 Lloyd George, I p 690
32 Quoted Marder, IV p 127
33 Newbolt, V p 127
34 Admiral William S Sims, *The Victory at Sea* (London 1920) p 9
35 Lloyd George, I p 691
36 Newbolt, V pp 19-20
37 Lloyd George, p 692
38 Quoted Marder, IV p 162
39 Roskill, *Hankey,* I pp 382
40 Ibid, p 383
41 Newbolt, V p 20
42 Ibid, p 23
43 Winton, p 66
44 Ibid, p 67

30 America enters the War

1 Gerhard Ritter, *The Sword and the Sceptre* (London 1973) III p 315
2 Quoted Ritter, III p 331
3 Sir Arthur Willert, *The Road to Safety* (London 1951) p 55
4 Quoted Lloyd George, I p 991
5 Sims, p 1
6 Ibid, p 4
7 Ibid, p 5
8 Jellicoe, *Crisis,* p 155
9 David F Trask, *Captains and Cabinets* (Columbia, Miss. 1972) p 55
10 Trask, p 63
11 Halpern, p 359
12 Trask, p 83
13 De Chair, p 231
14 Sims, p 10

15 Ibid, p 15
16 Quoted Jerry W Jones, *US Battleship Operations in World War 1* (Annapolis Md. 1998) p 6
17 Sims, p 87
18 Ibid, p 98
19 Quoted Jones, p 7
20 Trask, p 93
21 Ibid
22 Ibid, p 96
23 Ibid, p 100
24 Ibid, p 116
25 Jones, pp 8-9
26 Jellicoe, *The Submarine Peril* p 68
27 Jones p11
28 Ibid, p 14
29 Ibid, p 27
30 Charles E Scurrell, *Battleships of Other Nations* (London 1963) pp 18-22
31 Quoted Jones, p 25
32 Quoted Roskill, Beatty, pp 243-244
33 *Jellicoe Papers*, II p 225-226

31 Admiral Bacon and the Dover Patrol

1 Bacon, *Dover Patrol* p 29
2 Marder, *Fear God*, III p 206
3 Richard Freeman, *The Great Edwardian Naval Feud* (London 2009) p 108
4 Quoted Geoffrey Penn, *Infighting Admirals* (Barnsley 2000) p 220
5 *Keyes Papers*, I p 132
6 Ibid, pp 368
7 HM Le Fleming, *Warships of World War 1; Micellaneous* (London n.d) pp 16-18
8 Roy Humphries, *The Dover Patrol* 1914-1918 (Gloucester 1998 pp 49-51
9 Bacon p 111
10 Halpern, *Naval History*, p 347
11 Quoted Newbolt, IV p 65
12 Ibid, IV pp 65-66
13 Bacon, p 137
14 Halpern, p 346
15 Jellicoe, *Crisis*, p 209
16 Newbolt, IV pp 352-353
17 Ibid, IV p 362
18 Ibid, IV p 365
19 Ibid, IV p 388
20 Halpern, pp 348-349
21 Newbolt, IV pp 372-373
22 Ibid, IV p 377
23 Halpern, p 349

24 Newbolt, IV p 378
25 Jellicoe, *Crisis*, p 203
26 *Keyes Papers*, I p 368
27 Bacon, p 311
28 *Keyes Papers*, I p 376
29 Ibid, pp 396-397

32 Shake up at the Admiralty

1 Lloyd George, I pp 692-693
2 CI Hamilton, *The Making of the Modern Admiralty* (Cambridge, 2011) p 234
3 Marder, IV p 174
4 Sims, pp 219-220
5 *Jellicoe Papers*, II p 164
6 Jellicoe, *Crisis*, p 11
7 Marder, IV p 177
8 Richmond, p 252
9 Ibid, p 250
10 Quoted Marder, IV p 179
11 Marder, IV pp 180
12 Ibid, pp 167-168
13 *Beatty Papers*, I p 425
14 Marder, IV p 168
15 *Beatty Papers*, I p 445
16 Richmond, p 247
17 Ibid, p 251
18 Richmond, p 254
19 Ibid, p 254-255
20 Ibid, pp 259-260
21 Quoted Bacon, *Jellicoe*, pp 389-390
22 *Jellicoe Papers*, III p 167
23 Richmond, p 262
24 Ibid, II p 274
25 *Jellicoe Papers*, II p 167
26 Ibid, II p 167
27 Ibid, II p 173
28 Ibid, II p 174
29 Quoted Roskill, *Beatty*, p 221
30 *Beatty Papers*, I p 425
31 Lloyd George, I p 699
32 Ibid, p 699-700
33 Marder, IV, p 204
34 Ibid, IV p 207
35 Roskill, *Hankey*, II pp 404-405
36 Jellicoe, *Crisis*, p 14

37 Quoted Marder, IV p 209
38 Richmond, p 267
39 Quoted Marder, IV p 214
40 Marder, IV p 217
41 *Jellicoe Papers*, II p 185
42 Lloyd George, I p 700
43 Lady Wester Wemyss,, *The Life and Letters of Lord Wester Wemyss* (London 1935) p 357
44 Lloyd George, I p 700
45 Wemyss, p 362
46 Quoted, Marder, IV pp 221-222
47 Keyes, *Naval Memoirs*, II p 110
48 *Keyes Papers*, I p 408
49 Gemzell, p 206
50 Quoted Gemzell, p 207
51 Quoted Philbin, *Hipper,* p 139
52 Quoted Gemzell, p 190

33 The Problem of the Neutrals

1 Commander P Kemp, ed, *The Papers of Sir John Fisher* (London) II p 363
2 Gemzell, p 145
3 Ibid, p 147
4 Quoted Marder, IV p 246
5 Marder, *Fear God*, III p 351
6 Richmond, p 264
7 Gemzell, p 172
8 Wegener, p 181
9 Ibid, p 184
10 Gemzell, p 173
11 Beatty to Geddes, September 25 1917;quoted Marder, IV p 250

34 *Brummer* and *Bremse*

1 Schoultz, p 28
2 Roskill, *Beatty*, p 225
3 *Beatty Papers*, I p 447
4 Scheer, pp 287-288
5 Ibid, pp 287-288
6 Stumpf, p 346
7 Müller, p 294
8 Scheer, p 292
9 Newbolt, IV p 150
10 Ibid, V pp 150-151
11 Beesly, p 152
12 Newbolt, V p 152

13 National Archives, ADM 137/3723
14 *Der Krieg in der Nordsee,* VII p 47; quoted Marder, V p 294
15 *Politiken*, Gothenburg, October 25; ADM 137/3723
16 Quoted Beesly, pp 277-278
17 Richmond, p 283
18 Marder, V p 295n
19 Newbolt, V p 157
20 Admiralty MSS
21 *Der Krieg in der Nordsee*, VII p 52
22 Ibid, VII pp 48-49
23 Quoted Marder, V pp 298-299
24 Marder, V p 299
25 *Jellicoe Papers*, II pp 222-223

35 The Second Battle of Heligoland Bight

1 Newbolt, V p 165
2 Ibid, V p 163
3 Ibid, V pp 166-167
4 Admiralty MSS
5 Marder, V p 300
6 Scheer, p 304
7 Napier, Report to Pakenham, November 20 1917, Admiralty MSS
8 Ibid
9 Newbolt, V p 171
10 Admiralty MSS, quoted Marder, iv p 30
11 Newbolt, V p 171
12 Napier to Beatty, quoted Marder, IV p 302
13 Newbolt, V p 173
14 Scheer, p 307
15 Marder, IV p 303
16 *Der Krieg in der Nordsee,* VII p 75
17 Admiralty MSS op. cit
18 Scheer, p 307
19 Ibid, p 308
20 Ibid, p 309
21 Pakenham to Beatty, November 26 1917, Admiralty MSS
22 *Jellicoe Papers*, II p 232
23 Admiralty MSS
24 Ibid
25 *Jellicoe Papers*, II pp 233-234
26 Ibid, II pp 235-237
27 Quoted Marder, IV p 308
28 *Der Krieg in der Nordsee*, VII pp 83-85
29 Marder, IV p 306

30 *Jellicoe Papers*, II p 243
31 *Keyes Papers*, I pp 418-419
32 Quoted Marder, IV p 308
33 Newbolt, V p 177

36 The Second Convoy Attack

1 Newbolt, V p 184
2 Scheer, p 311
3 Newbolt, V pp 185-186
4 Ibid, p 188
5 Scheer, p 313
6 Newbolt, V p 189
7 Marder, IV p 312
8 Dorling, pp 323-326
9 Quoted, Marder, IV 314
10 Ibid, IV p 315
11 *Jellicoe Papers*. II pp 241-242
12 Ibid, II p 242
13 Chalmers, p 299
14 Report of the Court of Enquiry, December 18 1917, ADM 3704
15 Ibid
16 Quoted Marder, IV p 313n
17 Scheer, p 314
18 Richmond, p 287
19 Ibid, p 288
20 Ibid, pp 289-290

37 The Submarine Campaign in 1917

1 Halpern, p 335
2 Ibid, pp 338-339
3 Colonel Charles Repington, *The First World War* (London 1920) I p 440
4 Ibid, II p 467
5 Terraine, p 46
6 Gibson and Prendergast, p 162
7 Ibid, p 163
8 Newbolt, IV p 379
9 Gibson and Prendergast, p 172
10 Newbolt, IV p 380
11 Robert M Grant, *U-Boats Destroyed* (London 1964) p 49
12 Newbolt, V p 119
13 Grant, pp 53-54
14 Quoted Terraine, p 62
15 Churchill, *World Crisis*, II pp 1234-1235

16 Fayle, III pp 42-43
17 Ibid, III p 158
18 Gibson and Prendergast, p 178
19 Halpern, p 344
20 *Beatty Papers,* I p 443
21 Richmond Compton-Hall, *Submarines and the War at Sea*, 1914-18 (London 1991) p 295
22 Gibson and Prendergast, p 204
23 Werner Fürbringer, *Fips,* trans Geoffrey Brooks (Barnsley 1999) p 90
24 Terraine, p 120
25 Scheer, p 263
26 Newbolt, V p 137

38 Keyes

1 *Keyes Papers*, I p 416
2 Marder, IV p 316; Keyes, *Naval Memoirs* II p 124
3 Keyes, *Naval Memoirs*, II p 117
4 *Keyes Papers,* I pp 416-417
5 Keyes, *Naval Memoirs*, II p 121
6 Ibid, II p 123
7 *Keyes Papers*, I pp 419-422
8 Bacon, *Dover Patrol*, p 161
9 *Keyes Papers*, I pp 422-423
10 Quoted Marder, IV p 319n
11 Ibid, IV p 319
12 Ibid, IV pp 319-320
13 *Keyes Papers,* II 424-430
14 Ibid, I p 430
15 Bacon, *Dover Patrol*, pp 162-163
16 Keyes, *Naval Memoirs*, II p 143
17 Wemyss, pp 365-366
18 *Keyes Papers,* I pp 432-436

39 Jellicoe's Dismissal

1 Lloyd George, I p 684
2 Roskill, *Hankey,* I p 356; Lloyd George, I p 687
3 Lloyd George, I p 696
4 Ibid, II p 700
5 Quoted Roskill, *Hankey,* I p 406
6 Ibid, II p 409
7 David Woodward, *Lloyd George and the Generals* (East Brunwick, NJ p 181
8 Roskill, *Hankey*, I p 407
9 *Jellicoe Papers*, II p 412
10 Jellicoe, 'Autobiographical Notes', quoted Marder, IV p 328

11 Chalmers, pp 321-322
12 Newbolt, V p 203
13 Marder, IV p 330
14 Quoted Marder, IV p 328
15 *Jellicoe Papers*, II p 240
16 Wemyss, p 366
17 *Jellicoe Papers*, II p 246
18 Ibid, II p 247
19 Ibid, II p 244
20 Ibid, II p 255
21 Bacon, *Jellicoe*, p 380
22 Marder, IV pp 345
23 *Jellicoe Papers*, II p 248-250
24 Ibid, II pp 250-251
25 Quoted Bacon, *Jellicoe,* p 383
26 Marder, IV p 345n
27 *Jellicoe Papers*, II p 256
28 Ibid, II pp 269-270
29 Keyes, *Naval Memoirs*, II pp 151-153
30 Wemyss, p 368
31 Quoted Ann Parry, *The Admirals Fremantle* (London 1971) p 262
32 Admiral Sir E Bradford, *Life of Admiral of the Fleet Sir Arthur Wilson* (London 1923) p 246
33 De Chair, pp 237-238
34 Richmond, p 290
35 *Jellicoe Papers*, II p 252
36 Quoted Marder, II p 342

40 Zeebrugge

1 Richmond, p 293
2 Ibid, p 294
3 Ibid, p 299
4 *Keyes Papers*, I p 440
5 Ibid, I p 443
6 Keyes, *Naval Memoirs*, II p 157
7 Quoted Paul Kendall, *The Zeebrugge Raid 1918* (Brimscombe Port 2009) p 185
8 Marder, V p 41
9 Keyes, *Naval Memoirs*, III p 170
10 Scheer, p 315
11 Keyes, *Naval Memoirs* II p 174
12 Newbolt, V pp 210-211
13 Ibid, V p 212
14 Keyes, *Naval Memoirs*, III p 174
15 Newbolt, V 216
16 Ibid, p 217

17 Scheer, p 317
18 *Keyes Papers*, II p 459
19 Jellicoe, 'Errors in Naval Operations, Vols IV and V,' quoted Marder, V p 44
20 Bacon, *Dover Patrol*, pp 207-230
21 *Keyes Papers*, I p 451
22 Ibid, I p 477
23 Halpern, p 413
24 Keyes, *Naval Memoirs*, II p 278
25 Marder, V p 56
26 *Keyes Papers*, II p 486
27 Ibid, II p 485
28 Keyes, *Naval Memoirs*, II pp 327-328
29 Ibid, II p 331
30 Marder, V p 60
31 Barrie Pitt, *Zeebrugge* (London 1958) p 210
32 Quoted Marder, V p 60
33 *Der Krieg in der Nordsee*, VII p 267
34 Bacon, *Dover Patrol*, pp 221-224
35 Quoted Kendall, p 184
36 Marder, *Fear God*, III p 532
37 Ibid, III p 535
38 Kendall, p 184
39 Newbolt, V pp 275-276
40 Ibid, V p 277
41 *Der Krieg in der Nordsee*, VII pp 265-269; Marder V p 61

41 The Last Sortie of the High Seas Fleet

1 Scheer, p 318
2 Waldeyer-Hartz, p 240
3 Marder, V p 132
4 Ibid
5 Quoted Marder, V p 133n
6 Marder, V p 133
7 Ibid, V pp 134
8 Jellicoe, *The Submarine Peril*, p 185
9 Marder, V pp 137-138
10 Marder, V p 128
11 Quoted Roskill, *Beatty*, p 251
12 Richmond, p 302
13 *Beatty Papers*, I p 516
14 Marder, V p 148
15 Richmond, pp 308-309
16 Newbolt, V p 239
17 Marder, V pp 149-150

18 Scheer, p 320
19 Beesly, pp 284-285
20 Ibid, p 285
21 Newbolt, V p 232
22 Marder, V p 150
23 Newbolt, V p 235
24 Waldeyer-Hartz, pp 242-243
25 Ibid, p 243
26 Beesly, p 287
27 Scheer, p 322
28 Marder, V p 153
29 Scheer, p 323
30 Newbolt, V p 238
31 *Keyes Papers*, I p 503
32 Halpern, p 420

42 The Development of Naval Aviation

1 RD Layman, *Naval Aviation in the First World War; Its Impact and Influence* (London 1996) p 11
2 RD Layman, *To Ascend from a Floating Base* (Cranbury NJ 1979) p 233; Walter Raleigh, *The War in the Air* (Oxford 1922) p 357
3 Douglas Robinson, *The Zeppelin in Combat* (Henley on Thames 1971) p 25
4 *Der Krieg in der Nordsee*, I p 36
5 R D Layman, *The Cuxhaven Raid: The World's First Carrier Air Strike* (London 1985) p 126
6 Robinson, pp 92-93
7 Quoted Marder, IV p 4
8 Marder, IV p 8
9 Layman, *Naval Aviation*, p 37
10 Marder IV p11
11 Layman, *Naval Aviation*, pp 177-178
12 Chalmers, pp 224-225
13 Captain S Roskill, ed, *Documents Relating to the Naval Air Service* (London 1969) I p 308
14 Ibid, I p 335
15 Ibid, I p 328
16 Richmond, p 268
17 Roskill, *Beatty*, p 240
18 Marder, IV p 333n
19 Layman, *Naval Aviation*, p 196
20 Ibid, p 161
21 Robinson, pp 319-320
22 Newbolt, V p 436
23 HA Jones, *The War in the Air* (London 1922-37) II p 378
24 Layman, *Naval Aviation*, p 168

43 Convoys and U-boats

1 Fayle, III p 255
2 Jellicoe, *The Submarine Peril*, p ix
3 Marder, V p 79
4 Ibid, pp 79-80
5 Grand Admiral Karl Doenitz, *Memoirs* (London 1959) p 4
6 Ibid
7 Newbolt, V p 282
8 Grant, pp 155-157
9 Winton, p 115
10 Ibid, p 114
11 Müller, p 328
12 Scheer, p 324
13 Ibid, p 328
14 Müller, p 378
15 Scheer, p 324
16 Ibid, p 328
17 Waldeyer-Hartz, p 248
18 Raeder, p 76
19 Scheer, p 34
20 Marder, V p 83
21 *Der Krieg in der Nordsee*, VII pp 317-318
22 Marder, V p 66
23 *Beatty Papers*, I pp 540-542
24 Ibid, I pp 543-544
25 Ibid, I pp 546-547
26 Trask, p 154
27 Ibid I pp p 218
28 Marder, V p 73
29 Vice Admiral Andreas Michelsen, *Der U-Bootskrieg 1914-1918* (Leipzig 1925) p 85;quoted Marder, V p 74
30 *Der Krieg in der Nordsee* VII pp 317-318

44 Operation Plan No 19

1 Marder, V p 166
2 *Beatty Papers*, I pp 534-535
3 Ibid I p 536
4 *Keyes Papers*, I p 507
5 Müller, p 394
6 Chalmers, pp 326-327
7 Scheer, p 349
8 Ibid, p 350
9 Herwig, *Naval Officer Corps*, p 254

10 Quoted Philbin, *Hipper,* p 157
11 Quoted Gemzell, p 212
12 Quoted Philbin, *Hipper,* p 155
13 Ibid, p 158
14 *Beatty Papers,* I p 555
15 Ibid, I p 557
16 Quoted Beesly, p 294
17 Quoted Marder, V p 172
18 *Beatty Papers* I p 558
19 Beesly, p 295
20 Newbolt, V p 369
21 Philbin, *Hipper,* p 159
22 *Der Krieg in der Nordsee*, VII pp 344-345; Marder, V p 171
23 Quoted Philbin, *Hipper,* p 162
24 Marder, V p 178
25 Stumpf, p 418

45 Vae Victis

1 Philbin, *Hipper,* p 167
2 Ibid, p 172
3 Quoted Marder, V p 170
4 Chalmers, p 337
5 Ibid, p 338
6 *Beatty Papers*, I p 561
7 Vice Admiral Fredrich Ruge, *Scapa Flow 1919* (London 1973) p 48
8 Beatty to Geddes, November 8 1918; Quoted Marder, V p 186
9 Roskill, *Beatty*, pp 277-278
10 Marder, V p 189
11 Beesly, p 300
12 Quoted Philbin, *Hipper,* p 174
13 Vice Admiral Ludwig von Reuter, *Scapa Flow* (Paris 1929) p 18
14 Marder, V p 182
15 Roskill, *Beatty*, p 280
16 Reuter, p 42
17 Ibid, p 84
18 Ibid, pp 101-102
19 Ibid, pp 107-108
20 Ibid, pp 124
21 Ibid, p 126
22 Quoted Marder, V p 287
23 Wemyss, p 432
24 Quoted Woodward p 185
25 Quoted Kelly, p 428
26 Marder V p 284

27 Richmond, pp 347-348
28 Dan van der Vat, *The Grand Scuttle* (London 1982) p 194

46 Retrospect

1 Spenser Wilkinson, *The Brain of the Navy* (London 1895) p 30
2 Marder, V p 314
3 Black, p 238
4 Quoted Marder, V p 315
5 Marder, V p 299n
6 Marder, V p 341
7 Steinberg p 64
8 Quoted Steinberg, p 66
9 Ibid
10 Tirpitz, II p 366
11 Quoted Marder, V p 306
12 Ibid, V p 305
13 Scheer, p 360
14 JK Laughton, *Nelson* (London 1895) pp 123-124
15 Schoultz, p 259
16 *Jellicoe Papers*, III p 185
17 Horsfield, p 123
18 Marder, *Fear God*, III p 408
19 Horsfield, p 124
20 Ibid, p 81
21 Ibid, p 128
22 Marder, V p 322
23 Quoted Barry D Hunt, 'Richmond and the Education of the Royal Navy' in *Mahan is not Enough*, p 67
24 Daniel Baugh, 'Admiral Sir Herbert Richmond and the Objects of Sea Power' in *Mahan is not Enough*, p 38
25 Frost, pp 517-518
26 GJ Marcus, *The Age of Nelson* (New York 1971) pp 62-63
27 Philbin, *Hipper*, p 133

Bibliography

ADMIRALTY, *Narrative of the Battle of Jutland* (London 1924)
ADMIRALTY, *Official Despatches: Battle of Jutland* (London 1920)
ALTHAM, Captain E, *Jellicoe* (London 1938)
AMERY, Leopold S, *My Political Life* (London 1953-1955) 3 vols
ARTHUR, Max, *The True Glory: The Royal Navy 1914-1939* (London 2002)
ASPINALL-OGLANDER, Brigadier CF, *Roger Keyes* (London 1951)
BACHRACH, Harriet, ed,, *Jutland Letters* (Newton Toney 2006)
BACON, Admiral RH, *The Life of Lord Fisher of Kilverstone* (London 1929) 2 vols
BACON, Admiral Sir RH, *The Concise Story of the Dover Patrol* (London 1932)
BACON, Admiral Sir RH, *The Life of John Rushworth, Earl Jellicoe* (London 1936)
BARNETT, Correlli, *The Swordbearers* (London 1963)
BEATTY, Charles, *Our Admiral* (London 1980)
BEESLY, Patrick, *Room 40: British Naval Intelligence 1914-1918* (London 1982)
BELL, Christopher M, *Churchill and Sea Power* (Oxford 2013)
BELLAIRS, Commander Carlyon, *The Battle of Jutland* (London n.d)
BENNETT, Captain Geoffrey, *Charlie B* (London 1988)
BENNETT, Captain Geoffrey, *Naval Battles of the First World War* (London 1968)
BENNETT, Captain Geoffrey, *The Battle of Jutland* (London 1964)
BINGHAM, Commander Hon B, *Falklands, Jutland and the Bight* (London 1919)
BIRD, Keith, *Erich Raeder* (Annapolis MD 2006)
BLACK, Nicholas, *The British Naval Staff in the First World War* (Woodbridge 2009)
BONNEY, George, *The Battle of Jutland* (Stroud 2002)
BRADFORD, Admiral Sir E, *Life of Admiral of the Fleet Sir Arthur Wilson* (London 1923)
BREEMER, Jan S, *The Burden of Trafalgar* (Newport RI 1993)
BRÉZET, F-E *Le Jutland* 1916 (Paris 1992)
BROOKS, John, *Dreadnought Gunnery and the Battle of Jutland* (London 2005)
BROOKS, John, *The Battle of Jutland* (Cambridge 2016)
BROWN, Malcolm and MEEHAN, Patricia, *Scapa Flow* (London 2002)
BROWNRIGG, Sir Douglas, *Indiscretions of the Naval Censor* (London 1920)
BUCHAN, John, *Naval Episodes of the Great War* (London 1938)
BUTLER, David Allen, *Distant Victory* (Westport CT 2006)
BYWATER, Hector C, *Cruisers in Battle* (London 1939)
CAMPBELL, John, *Jutland: An Analysis of the Fighting* (London 1986)
CHALMERS, Rear Admiral WS, *The Life and Letters of David Beatty* (London 1951)

CHATFIELD, Admiral of the Fleet Lord, *The Navy and Defence* (London 1942)
CHURCHILL, Winston S, *Great Contemporaries* (London 1941)
CHURCHILL, Winston S, *The World Crisis* (London 1923-1931) 5 vols
COLES, Alan, *Three Before Breakfast* (Havant 1979)
COMPTON-HALL, Richard, *Submarines and the War at Sea 1914-18* (London 1991)
CORBETT, Julian, *Naval Operations* (London 1920-1923) 3 vols
COSTELLO, John and HUGHES, Terry, *Jutland 1916* (London 1976)
CROSSLEY, Jim, *The Hidden Threat: The Story of Mines and Minesweeping by the Royal Navy in World War 1* (Barnsley 2007)
DE CHAIR, Admiral Sir D, *The Sea is Strong* (London 1961)
DOENITZ, Grand Admiral Karl, *Memoirs* (London 1959)
DOHN, Arno, *Skagerrak* (Berlin 1968)
DOMVILE, Admiral Sir Barry, *By and Large* (London 1936)
DORLING, Captain T ('Taffrail') *Endless Story* (London 1932)
DREYER, Admiral Sir FC, *The Sea Heritage* (London 1955)
DUPUY, TN and HAYES, GP, *Naval Overseas War 1916-1918* (New York 1967)
EPKENHANS, Michael and GROSS, Gerhard P, eds, *The Danish Straits and German Naval Power 1905-1918* (Potsdam 2010)
EPKENHANS, Michael, *Tirpitz: Architect of the German High Seas Fleet* (Washington DC 2008)
EPKENHANS, Michael and HILLMAN, Jorg, eds, *Jutland: World War 1's Greatest Sea Battle* (Lexington KY 2015)
FAWCETT, HW and HOOPER GWW, eds, *The Fighting at Jutland* (London 1920)
FAYLE, C Ernest, *Seaborne Trade* (London 1923) 3 vols
FREEMAN, Richard, *The Great Edwardian Naval Feud* (London 2009)
FREIWALD, Ludwig, *Last Days of the German Fleet* (London 1932)
FRIEDMAN, Norman, *Fighting the Great War at Sea* (Barnsley 2014)
FROST, Commander HH, *The Battle of Jutland* (Annapolis MD 1964)
FÜRBRINGER, *Fips*, trans Geoffrey Brook (Barnsley 1999)
GARDINER, Leslie, *The British Admiralty* (Edinburgh 1968)
GEMZELL, Carl-Axel, *Organisation, Conflict and Innovation* (Lund 1973)
GERMAN OFFICIAL HISTORY, *Der Krieg in der Nordsee* (Berlin 1920-1937) 7 vols
GIBSON, Langhorne and HARPER, Vice Admiral JET, *The Riddle of Jutland* (London 1934)
GIBSON, RH and PRENDERGAST, Maurice, *The German Submarine War 1914-1918* (London 1931)
GIBSON, RH, *Three Years of Naval Warfare* (London 1918)
GILL, Commander CC, *What Happened at Jutland* (New York 1921)
GOLDRICK, James and HATTENDORF, John B, eds, *Mahan is not Enough* (Newport RI 1993)
GOLDRICK, James, *The King's Ships Were at Sea* (Annapolis MD 2004)
GOODENOUGH, Admiral Sir William, *A Rough Record* (London 1943)
GORDON, Andrew, *The Rules of the Game* (London 1996)
GRAINGER, John D, ed, *The Maritime Blockade of Germany in the Great War: The Northern Patrol 1914-1918* (Aldershot 2003)
GRANT, Robert M, *U Boats Destroyed* (London 1964)

GREGER, Rene, *Battleships of the World* (London 1997)
GREGORY, David, *The Lion and the Eagle* (Woodstock 2012)
GRIMES, Shawn T, *Strategy and War Planning in the British Navy, 1887-1918* (Woodbridge 2012)
GRÖNER, Erich, *German Warships 1815-1945* (London1990) 2 vols
GROVE, Eric, *Fleet to Fleet Encounters* (London 1991)
GUICHARD, Louis, *The Naval Blockade 1914-1918* (London 1930)
HALPERN, Paul G, *A Naval History of World War 1* (London 1994)
HALPERN, Paul G, ed, *The Keyes Papers* (London 1972) 2 vols
HAMILTON, CI, *The Making of the Modern Admiralty* (Cambridge 2011)
HAMPSHIRE, A Cecil, *The Blockaders* (London 1980)
HANKEY, Lord, *The Supreme Command* (London 1961) 2 vols
HARKINS, Hugh, *Light Battle Cruisers and the Second Battle of Heligoland Bight* (Glasgow 2015)
HARPER, Rear Admiral JET, *The Truth About Jutland* (London 1927)
HERWIG, Holger H, *'Luxury' Fleet: The Imperial German Navy 1888-1918 (*London 1980)
HERWIG, Holger H, *The German Naval Officer Corps* (Oxford 1973)
HEWISON, WS, *This Great Harbour: Scapa Flow* (Edinburgh 2005)
HOEHLING, AA, *The Great War at Sea* (London 1965)
HORSFIELD, John, *The Art of* Leadership in War (Westport CT 1980)
HOUGH, Richard, *First Sea Lord* (London 1969)
HOUGH, Richard, *The Great War at Sea* (Oxford 1983)
HOYT, Edwin P, *The Elusive Seagull* (London 1970)
HUMPHRIES, ROY, *The Dover Patrol 1914-1918* (Gloucester 1989)
HURD, Archibald and CASTLE, Henry, *German Sea-Power* (London 1913)
JAMES, Admiral Sir William, *A Great Seaman* (London 1956)
JAMES, Admiral Sir William, *The Eyes of the Navy* (London 1955)
JAMESON, William, *The Fleet that Jack Built* (London 1962)
JELLICOE, Admiral of the Fleet Viscount, *The Crisis of the Naval War* (London 1920)
JELLICOE, Admiral of the Fleet Viscount, *The Grand Fleet 1914-1916* (London 1919)
JELLICOE, Admiral of the Fleet Earl, *The Submarine Peril* (London 1934)
JELLICOE, Nicholas, *Jutland: The Unfinished Battle* (Barnsley 2016)
JONES, Jerry W, *US Battleship Operations in World War 1* (Annapolis MD 1998)
KARAU, Mark D, *The Naval Flank of the Western Front* (Barnsley 2014)
KELLY, Patrick J, *Tirpitz and the Imperial German Navy* (Bloomington IND 2011)
KEMP, Commander P, ed, *The Papers of Sir John Fisher* (London) 2 vols
KENDALL, Paul, *The Zeebrugge Raid* (Brimscombe Port 2009)
KENNEDY, Paul M, *The Rise and Fall of British Naval Mastery* (London 1983)
KERR, Admiral Mark, *Prince Louis of Battenberg* (London 1934)
KEYES, Admiral of the Fleet Sir Roger, *Naval Memoirs* (London 1934) 2 vols
KING-HALL, Commander Stephen, *A North Sea Diary 1914-1918* (London nd)
KING-HALL, Commander Stephen, *My Naval Life,* 1906-1929 (London 1952)
KING-HALL, Commander Stephen,, *Sea Saga*, ed L King-Hall (London 1935)
KONSTAM, Angus, *Jutland 1916: Twelve hours to Win the War* (London 2016)
LAMBERT, Nicholas A, ed, *The Submarine Service 1900-1911* (Farnham 2001)
LAMBERT, Nicholas A, *Planning Armageddon* (Cambridge MA, 2011)
LAMBI, Ivo Nikolai, *The Navy and German Power Politics, 1862-1914* (Boston MA 1984)

LAUGHTON, JK, *Nelson* (London 1895)
LAVERY, Brian, *Able Seamen* (London 2011)
LAVERY, Brian, *Shield of Empire* (Edinburgh 2007)
LAYMAN, RD, *Naval Aviation in the First World War: Its impact and influence* (London 1996)
LAYMAN, RD, *The Cuxhaven Raid: The World's First Carrier Air Strike* (London 1985)
LAYMAN, RD, *To Ascend from a Floating Base* (Cranbury NJ 1979)
LE FLEMING, HM *Warships of World War 1: Miscellaneous* (London nd)
LE FLEMING, HM, *Submarines* (London nd)
LE FLEMING, HM, *Warships of World War 1: Battleships* (London 1959)
LE FLEMING, HM, *Warships of World War 1: Cruisers (*London nd)
LE FLEMING, HM, *Warships of World War 1: Destroyers* (London nd)
LEGG, S, ed, *Jutland* (New York 1966)
LLOYD GEORGE, David, *War Memoirs* (London 1938) 2 vols
LONDON, Charles, *Jutland 1916* (Westport CT 2000)
LÜTZOW, Rear Admiral AD, *Der Nordseekrieg* (Oldenburg 1931)
MACKAY, Ruddock, *Fisher of Kilverstone* (Oxford 1973)
MACKAY, Ruddock, *Balfour* (London 1985)
MAHAN, Alfred T, *The Influence of Sea Power upon History 1660-1783* (Boston MA 1894)
MAHAN, Alfred T, *The Influence of Sea power Upon the French Revolution and Empire 1793-1812* (London 1893) 2 vols
MARCUS, GJ, *The Age of Nelson* (New York 1971)
MARDER, Arthur J, ed, *Fear God and Dread Nought* (London 1952-1959) 3 vols
MARDER, Arthur J, *From the Dreadnought to Scapa Flow* (London 1961-1970) 5 vols
MARDER, Arthur J, *Portrait of an Admiral* (London 1952)
MASSIE, Robert K, *Castles of Steel* (London 2004)
MCINTYRE, Captain Donald, *Jutland* (London 1957)
MCINTYRE, Captain Donald, *The Thunder of the Guns* (London 1959)
MICHELSEN, Vice Admiral Andreas, *Der U-Bootskrieg 1914-1918* (Leipzig 1925)
MOOREHEAD, Alan, *Gallipoli* (London 1956)
MORRISON, Elting E, *Admiral Sims and the Modern American Navy* (Boston MA 1942)
MÜLLER, Admiral Georg von, *The Kaiser and his Court*, ed Walter Görlitz (London 1961)
NEWBOLT, Henry, *A Naval History of the War* (London nd)
NEWBOLT, Sir Henry, *Naval Operations* (London 1920-31) 2 vols
O'HARA, Vincent P and others, eds, *To Crown the Waves* (Annapolis MD. 2013)
OAKESHOTT, Ewart, *The Blindfold Game* (Oxford 1969)
OSBORNE, Eric W, *The Battle of Heligoland Bight* (Bloomington, IND. 2006)
PADFIELD, Peter, *Aim Straight* (London 1966)
PADFIELD, Peter, *The Great Naval Race* (London 1974)
PADFIELD. Peter, *The Battleship Era* (London 1972)
PARKES, Oscar, *British Battleships* (London 1970)
PARRY, Ann *The Admirals Fremantle* (London 1971)
PATTERSON, A Temple, ed, The *Jellicoe Papers* (London 1966) 2 vols
PATTERSON, A Temple, *Jellicoe* (London 1969)
PATTERSON, A Temple, *Tyrwhitt of the Harwich Force* (London 1973)
PELLY, Admiral Sir Henry, *300,000 Sea Miles: An Autobiography* (London 1938)

PENN, Geoffrey, *Infighting Admirals* (Barnsley 2000)
PHILBIN, Tobias R, *Admiral von Hipper* (Amsterdam 1982)
PHILBIN, Tobias R, *The Battle of Dogger Bank*, (Bloomington IND 2014)
PITT, Barrie, *Zeebrugge* (London 1958)
POLLEN, AH, *The Navy in Battle* (London 1919)
POLLEN, Anthony, *The Great Gunnery Scandal: The Mystery of Jutland* (London 1980)
POTTS, Mark and MARKS, Tony *Before the Bells Have Faded* (Eastbourne 2004)
RAEDER, Grand Admiral Erich, *My Life* (Annapolis MD 1951)
RALEIGH, Walter, *The War in the Air* (Oxford 1922) 2 vols
RANFT, Brian McL, ed, *The Beatty Papers* (London 1989) 2 vols
REPINGTON, Colonel Charles, *The First World War* (London 1920) 2 vols
REUTER, Vice Admiral Ludwig von, *Scapa Flow* (Paris 1929)
RIDLEY-KITTS, Daniel G, *The Grand Fleet 1914-19* (Stroud 2013)
RITTER, Gerhard, *The Sword and the Sceptre* (London 1973) 4 vols
ROBERTS, John, *Battle Cruisers* (London 1997)
ROSINSKI, Herbert, *The Development of Naval Thought*, ed B Mitchell Simpson III (Newport RI 1977)
ROSKILL, Captain Stephen, *Admiral of the Fleet Earl Beatty* (New York 1981)
ROSKILL, Captain Stephen, *Churchill and the Admirals* (London 1977)
ROSKILL, Captain Stephen, ed, *Documents Relating to the Naval Air Service* (London 1969) 2 vols
ROSKILL, Captain Stephen, *Hankey: Man of Secrets* (London 1970) 2 vols
RUGE, Vice Admiral Friedrich, *Scapa Flow* (London 1973)
SCHEER, Admiral Reinhard, G*ermany's High Sea Fleet in the World War* (London 1920)
SCHMALENBACH, Paul, *German Raiders* (Cambridge 1979)
SCHOULTZ, Commodore G von, *With the British Battle Fleet* (London nd)
SCHUBERT, PAUL and GIBSON, Langhorne, *Death of a Fleet 1917-1919* (London nd)
SCHURMAN, DM, *The Education of a Navy* (London 1965)
SCOTT, Sir Percy, *Fifty years in the Royal Navy* (London 1919)
SCURRELL, Charles E, *Battleships of Other Nations* (London 1963)
SELIGMANN, Matthew S, ed, *Naval Intelligence from Germany* (Farnham 2007)
SELIGMANN, Matthew S, NÄGLER, Frank and EPKENHANS, Michael, ed, *The Naval Route to the Abyss* (Farnham 2015)
SELIGMANN, Matthew S, *The Royal Navy and the German Threat, 1901-1914* Oxford 2012)
SIMS, Admiral William S, *The Victory at Sea* (London 1920)
SONDHAUS, Lawrence, *Preparing for Weltpolitik* (Shrewsbury 1997)
SOUDHAUS, Lawrence, *The Great War at Sea* (Cambridge 2014)
STAFF, Gary, *Battle on the Seven Seas* (Barnsley 2011)
STAFF, Gary, *Skagerrak* (Barnsley 2016)
STEEL, Nigel and HART, Peter, *Jutland 1916* (London 2003)
STEINBERG, Jonathan, *Yesterday's Deterrent* (London 1965)
STUMPF, Richard, *The Private War of Seaman Stumpf*, ed Daniel Horn (London 1969)
SUMIDA, Jon T, *In Defence of Naval Supremacy* (London 1989)
SUTHERLAND, John and CANWELL, Diane, *The Battle of Jutland* (Barnsley 2007)
SWEETMAN, J ed, *The Great Admirals* (Annapolis MD 1997)

TARRANT, VE, *Jutland: The German Perspective* (London 1995)
TERRAINE, John, *Business in Great Waters* (London 1990)
TIRPITZ, Grand Admiral Alfred von, *My Memoirs* (London 1919) 2 vols
TRACY, Nicholas, ed, *Sea Power and the Control of Trade* (Farnham 2005)
TRASK, David F, *Captains and Cabinets* (Columbia MS 1972)
TUPPER, Admiral Sir Reginald, *Reminiscences* (London nd)
VAN DER VAT, Dan, *The Grand Scuttle* (London 1982)
VAN DER VAT, *Stealth at Sea* (London 1994)
WALDEYER-HARTZ, Captain H, *Von Hipper* (London 1933)
WEGENER, Vice Admiral Wolfgang, *The Strategy of the World War* (Annapolis MD 1989)
WEIR, Gary, *Building the Kaiser's Navy* (Annapolis MD 1992)
WEIZSÄCKER, Ernst von, *Memoirs* (London 1951)
WESTER WEMYSS, Lady, *The Life and Letters of Lord Wester Wemyss* (London 1935)
WILKINSON, Spencer, *The Brain of the Navy* (London 1895)
WILLERT, Sir, Arthur, *The Road to Safety* (London 1951)
WILLMOTT, HP, *Battleship* (London 2002)
WILLMOTT, HP, *The Last Century of Sea Power Vol 1: From Port Arthur to Chanak, 1894-1922* (Bloomington IND 2009)
WINTON, John, *Convoy* (London 1983)
WINTON, John, *Jellicoe* (London 1981)
WOODWARD, David, *Lloyd George and the Generals* (East Brunswick NJ 1983)
WOODWARD, David, *The Collapse of Power* (London 1973)
WOODWARD, EL, *Great Britain and the German Navy* (Oxford 1935)
WRAGG, David, *Fisher* (Stroud 2009)
YATES, Keith, *Flawed Victory* (London 2000)
YOUNG, Filson, *With the Battle Cruisers* (London 1921)

Index

GENERAL INDEX

INDEX OF SHIPS